MANAGING YOUR SMALL BUSINESS

Robert T. Justis, DBA
University of Nebraska–Lincoln

Prentice-Hall, Inc., Englewood Cliffs, N.J. 07632

Library of Congress Cataloging in Publication Data

JUSTIS, ROBERT T.
  Managing your small business.

  Bibliography: p.
  Includes index.
  1.—Small business—Management. I.–Title.
HD62.7.J87   658'.022   80-22723
ISBN 0-13-551010-4

Editorial/production supervision
and interior design by Esther S. Koehn
Cover by Miriam Recio
Manufacturing buyer: Gordon Osbourne

© 1981 by Prentice-Hall, Inc., Englewood Cliffs, N.J. 07632

*All rights reserved. No part of this book
may be reproduced in any form or
by any means without permission in writing
from the publisher.*

Printed in the United States of America

10 9 8 7 6 5 4

Prentice-Hall International, Inc., *London*
Prentice-Hall of Australia Pty. Limited, *Sydney*
Prentice-Hall of Canada, Ltd., *Toronto*
Prentice-Hall of India Private Limited, *New Delhi*
Prentice-Hall of Japan, Inc., *Tokyo*
Prentice-Hall of Southeast Asia Pte. Ltd., *Singapore*
Whitehall Books Limited, *Wellington, New Zealand*

Dedicated to my wife Sue

CONTENTS

        Preface   xi

part 1   *the nature of small business*   1

        1   **The Small Business Arena**   3

            Incident / What is a small business? / Operating a small business / Success story: Ray A. Kroc / Business failures / Important problems facing small business today / Case Study: Speedy Pizza / Chapter questions

        2   **The Small Business: Form and Structure**   20

            Incident / Levels of involvement in the small business / Forms of the small business / Success story: Paul J. Meyer / Summary / Case study: Sirloin Platter Restaurant / Chapter questions

3 The Small Business: A Cast of Characters — 36

Incident / Entrepreneur / Success story: Erma Bombeck / Manager / Promoter / Inventor / Partner / Supplier / Employees / Consultant / Spouse and family / Summary / Case study: Ice Cream Parlor / Chapter questions

4 You and Small Business — 56

Incident / Personal appraisal / Requirements for business success / Success story: Charles Barrow / Business profiles / Time management / Case study: Independent retailer / Chapter questions

part 2 entering the small business arena — 73

5 The Feasibility Study — 75

Incident / Introduction, preface, or general overview / Marketing / Success story: Bob and Priscilla Sims / Management / Accounting, finances, and taxes / Legal aspects / Appendix / Summary / Case study: The Record Shop / Chapter questions

6 Researching a Venture — 107

Incident / Four key stages of a business / Industrial groups / Economic environment / Industrial environment / Marketing environment / Success story: DeWitt Wallace / Business environment / External environment / Case study: Telephone answering service / Chapter questions / Appendix: Researching a Venture Checklist

7 Selecting a Business — 123

Incident / Choosing an existing business / Success story: Mary Kay Ash / Franchising / Case study: Kathy's Hamburger Shoppe / Chapter questions / Appendix: Checklist for Evaluating a Franchise

8 Financing the Venture — 139

Incident / Planning financial needs / Basic financial needs / Financial records / Equity financing and debt financing / Success story: Hachirobei Mitsui / Debt financing / Sources of funds / Case study: The Video Shop / Chapter questions / Appendix

9 Organizing the New Business — 162

Incident / Organization / Staffing / Success story: Gerald Flitter / Direction / Control / Case study: Beauty salon / Chapter questions

10 Buying an Existing Business — 179

Incident / Determine the kind of business / Determine the available resources / Find the right opportunities / Evaluate all opportunities / Handle the decision / Price the business / Success story: H.H. (Bill) Roylance / Purchasing a business / Tax-free reorganizations / Case study: Apparel store / Chapter questions

part 3 operating a small business — 197

11 Accounting — 199

Incident / Single-entry bookkeeping system / Double-entry bookkeeping system / Which system should be used? / Financial statements / Success story: Henry J. Kaiser / Accounting uses and purposes / Case study: LaCrepe / Chapter questions

12 Cash Flow, Financial Statements, and Financial Ratios — 215

Incident / Cash flow / Success story: J.C. Penney / Financial statements / Financial ratios / Case study: Pop Corn Shoppes, Inc. / Chapter questions

13 Financial Planning and Cost Control 232

Incident / Financial planning / Cost centers and revenue centers / Success story: Helen Fisher / Credit / Case study: Larry D. / Chapter questions

14 Community, Location, and Layout 246

Incident / Community / Location / Success story: Phil G. Wizer, Jr. / Layout / Case study: Convenient Food Mart, Inc. / Chapter questions

15 Purchasing, Inventory Control, and Computers 264

Incident / Purchasing / Success story: Woody Allen / Inventory control / Computers / Case study: Building contractor / Chapter questions

16 Pricing 281

Incident / Economic factors / Success story: John D. Rockefeller, Sr. / Mathematical factors / Relationships between costs and volume / Marketing factors / Pricing in actual practice / Making the pricing decision / Case study: Tracy's / Chapter questions

17 Marketing and Marketing Research 304

Incident / Success story: John Wanamaker / Marketing / Marketing strategy / Marketing research / Case study: "Travel Around" travel agency / Chapter questions

18 Sales and Sales Forecasting 322

Incident / Selling / Selling process / Sales base / Sales plan / Success story: Rowland Macy / Sales forecasting / Sales force compensations plans / Case study: Everett 3 movie theater / Chapter questions

19 Leadership and Management — 338

Incident / The individual / Success story: Jeno F. Paulucci / Leadership / Goals / Case study: The Inn / Chapter questions

20 Risk and Insurance — 354

Incident / Handling risk / Business risks / Risk management / Types of loss / Success story: W. Clement Stone / Insurance / Types of insurance coverage / Case study: Campbell's / Chapter questions / Appendices: Essential Insurance Coverages / Desirable Insurance Coverages / Employee Benefit Coverages

21 The Law and Taxes — 380

Incident / The law / Success story: Kemmons Wilson / Taxes / Case study: Barb's Clothing / Chapter questions

part 4 managing the future — 401

22 Growth Planning and Assistance — 403

Incident / Success story: William Petersen / Business life cycle / Product life cycle / Industrial growth / Managerial assistance / Case study: Mary's Secretarial Service / Chapter questions

23 Succession of Management — 420

Incident / Plans of succession / Buy/Sell Agreement / Success story: Aristotle Socrates Onassis / Successor profile / Inventory of business and operations / Inventory of managerial development / Inventory of retirement / Case study: Egbert's Home Furnishings / Chapter questions

24 Small Business Consulting — 434

Incident / The consultant / The client / The written report / Success story: Samuel G. Rautbord / Case study: The Racquet Place / Chapter questions

Glossary — 448

Bibliography — 451

Index — 453

PREFACE

This book presents a very human approach to small business management. Practical information blends with true-to-life incidents, biographies of successful business owners, and anecdotes in a life cycle format; this means that topics are presented in the order that they actually occur in the life of a person considering small business as a career. Designed to aid in developing several learning documents (e.g. the feasibility study, checklists for researching a venture, financing a new business, rating communities and locations, and so forth), this book may be used as a guide to organize and operate a small business.

The four stages of the life cycle that all small business owners experience make up the four major sections of the text.

1. The nature of small business. Before the potential small business owner launches his or her career, the nature of small business should be explored. Questions should be posed; answers sought; decisions carefully weighed. What is a small business? What may the owner expect of a small business? What may the business demand of the owner? Chapters 1 through 4 provide answers.

2. Entering the small business arena. Once the decision to become a small business owner has been made, questions about starting the business must be answered. Undoubtedly, the main question is: What kind of business should I start? This section of the text develops a plan—the feasibility study—for starting a new business. Chapters 5 through 10 cover the second stage of the life cycle.

3. Operating a small business. Once the business is opened, questions concerning the running of the business, both on a day-to-day basis and as a long-term commitment, arise. In-depth analyses of the key functional areas of a small business, including finances, cash flow, accounting, marketing, cost control, sales, inventory control, location and layout, pricing, risk management, and legal and tax considerations, are presented in chapters 11 through 21.

4. Managing the future. There will come a time in a person's small business career when the future becomes the key question. Expand? Sell out? Set up for family management? Retire? Various ways of expanding a small business or leaving a small business are discussed in chapters 22 and 23. The last chapter deals with professional business consulting, a growing source of aid to the small business owner.

Case materials and incidents are drawn from actual business experiences; the biographical sketches are of actual small business owners, some of whom have been amazingly successful. Where possible, key qualities of the individual are given to amplify the characteristics of successful entrepreneurs.

Acknowledgements

Ideas and suggestions for this book came from practitioners (small business owners), professors, and consultants to the small business world. I wish to thank each one of them for their help in the completion of this work. Mike Nolan was the author of three of the chapters and most of the Success Stories; he also served as advisor and editor for the entire manuscript.

Those who helped develop and refine this text at the Small Business Administration include Tom Keating, Linc Simon, Curt Olson, Rick Burr, Craig Rice, Jerry Kleber, Dwight Johnson, and Milt Yudelson. Valuable in-depth reviews were provided by Robert J. Kerber, Illinois State University; Kenneth Olms, University of Texas at Austin, and Murray Leavitt, Small Business Institute at DeAnza College, Cupertino, California. My appreciation is also extended to Oliver Galbraith III, San Diego State University, for his encouragement and insights into the development of this text as well as to Dr. Sang M. Lee and Dr. Fred Luthans, University of Nebraska Lincoln.

Special thanks go to Shelley Everett for her typing, coordinating and managing of several aspects of this book; and to Susan McIntosh Siefkes, Ann Rea, Robert Ryman, Kathy Rassull, Larry Deegan, Greg Hanouw, Mary Johnston, Joyce Anderson, and Angela Sullivan for their help in compiling, editing and working on the manuscript.

I would also like to thank Prentice-Hall's Barbara Piercecchi, acquisition editor; Linda Albelli, editorial assistant, and Esther Koehn, production editor, for their help and support.

ROBERT T. JUSTIS

MANAGING YOUR SMALL BUSINESS

1
the nature of small business

Photo courtesy of Irene Springer, Prentice-Hall, Inc.

THE SMALL BUSINESS ARENA

Chapter Objectives:

1. To know what a small business is.
2. To understand some of the advantages and disadvantages of a small business.
3. To learn why small businesses fail.
4. To investigate some of the important problems facing small businesses today.
5. To investigate the distribution of ownership of small businesses.
6. To understand the importance of small businesses in our economic system.

I never did anything worth doing by accident, nor did any of my inventions come by accident. They came by work.

Thomas A. Edison

INCIDENT: Dale is ready to start his own business. He has worked for a Midwestern electronic company for the last nine years; before that he spent six years working with a major accounting firm as a business consultant. He is unhappy in his job, and wants to start out on his own. He has been talking to his wife, Gwen, for the past six months about starting their own business. He has no real concrete ideas about what to do or even how to start; he just wants to run his own business.

Dale is excited about opening a franchised electronics store, such as Radio Shack, or a small hardware store with True Value or Ace Hardware. Gwen is excited about health-food stores, because for the last three years she has been on a health-food diet. They have decided that together they could do just about anything if they could find a concrete idea. They want to operate close to home, and to remain in the community they have lived in for the last fifteen years.

Dale and Gwen have no knowledge of small business practices, legal structures, or tax considerations, but they *know* that they will succeed. They believe that all they need is a desire for success, and to do a lot of hard work. They believe they will be so successful that, within a year's period of time, they will find a month or two to take off each year for their dream vacation.

Each year in the United States more than 400,000 new businesses are started. The owners' hopes are high, their expectations are great, and their desires are enormous. Each person hopes that his or her new business will be the greatest business in the history of the American free enterprise system. A small business can provide honor, thrill, and challenge—it can be the opportunity of a lifetime.

However, the fatality rate for small businesses is quite high. Six out of every ten new businesses fail within five years. Almost all businesses are cyclical and seasonal by nature, with many small businesses depending upon the Thanksgiving and Christmas holiday seasons for 60 percent of their sales.

The small business owner will find that he or she has committed total life savings, time, home, car, and all that he or she has for the establishment of a business that may or may not actually succeed. The business will be placed on a roller coaster, with all its ups and downs, and may be adversely affected by changes in customer demands, changes in economic conditions, and even the rise or fall of the value of money—including the problem of inflation.

THE SMALL BUSINESS ARENA

The businessperson no longer has the opportunity of working a forty-hour week. As owner-manager, he or she is almost assured of working ten to twelve hours a day, five to seven days a week. The owner will find that he or she may no longer be just a salesperson or simply a president of a business, but rather that he or she will be responsible for the accounting, selling, finances, inventory, pricing, advertising, and all the affairs and operations of that business.

Among all the problems and possible difficulties, there always emerges in our enterprise system owners with entrepreneurial spirits who will find small businesses vastly rewarding. Since most of America's largest companies started out as small businesses, this sort of success is not just an idle dream. These people will enjoy working with their employees. They will see and understand the necessity of being "jacks-of-all-trades." They will enjoy working with the suppliers, the customers, the salespeople, and their own staff. They will enjoy the development and evaluation of a very successful business enterprise. These owners will find that their work will require all of their physical as well as mental stamina, creativity, maturity, and capability. They will find their work to be exhilarating and exhausting, but they will be happy and satisfied, because they are now in control—each is his or her own boss.

What Is a Small Business?

A small business firm, as defined by the Small Business Administration (SBA), is independently owned and operated, and is generally not dominant in its field. A small business has receipts not exceeding $8 million (see Table 1-1), except for the wholesale area in which many small businesses with sales up to $22 million are defined as small. Most manufacturing firms are considered to be small if they average fewer than 1,500 employees annually.

Table 1-1. SBA Small Business Size Standards

INDUSTRY	NUMBER OF EMPLOYEES	ANNUAL SALES REVENUES (million dollars)
Wholesaling		5 to 22
Retailing		2 & up
Services		2 to 8
Construction		7.5 to 12
Shopping Centers		assets less than 8
Communications		2 to 3
Farms		1
Transportation & Warehousing	500 to 1,500	1.5 to 10
Research, Development, and Testing	500	
Manufacturing	250 to 1,500	

SOURCE: Adapted from *Title XIII, Business Credit and Assistance,* Chapter 1. Small Business Administration Revision 13, Part 121.

trends of small business

Small businesses are the backbone of the American economic system (see Figure 1–1). While they provide only 5 to 6 percent of the total business receipts in America, they employ approximately 58 percent of the American work force. Approximately only 2 percent of all business firms in America have receipts of $1 million or more. Therefore, approximately 98 percent of all businesses in America are considered small ones.

There is a need for small businesses to continue to flourish (see Figure 1–2). Many will close and many others will start up. Approximately 80 percent of all businesses in America have gross sales of under $100,000 per year (see Table 1–2). There are hundreds of thousands of people who are interested in starting, opening, and running these businesses.

More women are entering the small business world. As they do, they also become entrepreneurs and owners of small businesses (see Table 1-3). More minority owners are also emerging and are becoming a dominant force in many sectors of the country. The majority of firms owned by women are in the areas of retail trade and services. Women are often owners of finance, insurance, real estate, and

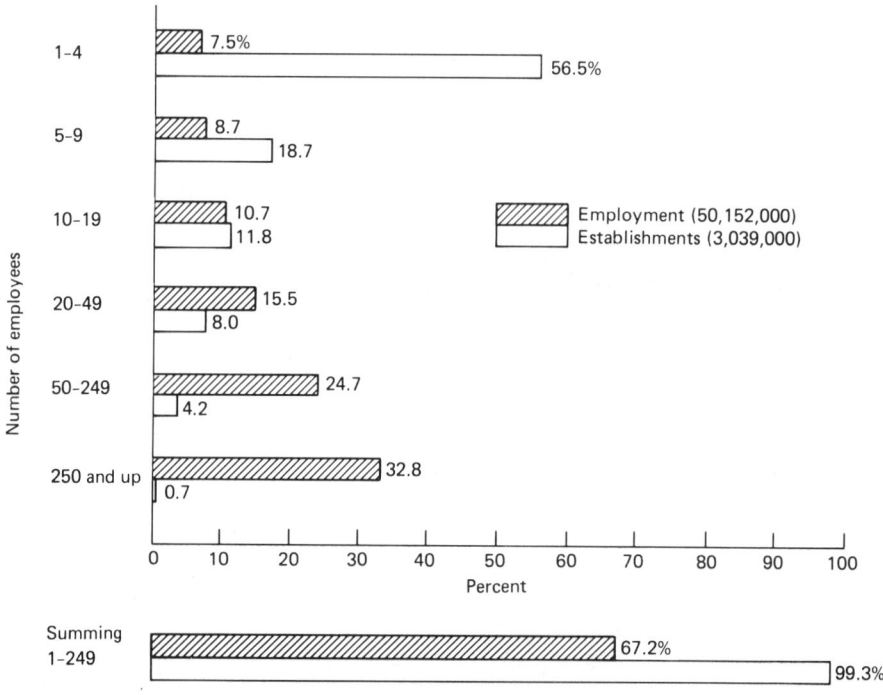

Figure 1–1. *Small business employment of metropolitan areas by size and establishments*

SOURCE: Adapted from U.S. Bureau of the Census: County Business Patterns, 1976 Standard Metropolitan Statistical Areas, U.S. Government Printing Office, Washington, D.C. 1978.

SMALL BUSINESS FACTS

1. The total number of businesses in the U.S. is 13.9 million.
2. The average annual number of new businesses started in the last ten years has been approximately 250,000.
3. Fifty-five per cent of the businesses in the U.S. fail (go bankrupt or are discontinued) within their first 5 years of operation.
4. Small businesses account for nearly 8 of every 10 dollars made by construction firms (excludes farms).
5. Small businesses account for nearly 7 of every 10 dollars in sales made by retailers and wholesalers (excludes farms).
6. Small businesses account for nearly 6 of every 10 dollars in receipts in the service industries (excludes farms).
7. Small business provides 58% of the total U.S. business employment.
8. Small business directly or indirectly provides the livelihood of over 100 million Americans.
9. One third of all small businesses are in the service industries (excludes farms).
10. Nearly ¼ of all small businesses are in the retail trade industry (excludes farms).
11. Approximately 90% of all corporations are small businesses (excludes farms).
12. Nearly 80% of all U.S. businesses employ less than 10 people (excludes farms).

Figure 1-2. *Facts about small business*
SOURCE: "Facts about Small Business and the U.S. Small Business Administration" (Washington, D.C.: Small Business Administration, 1979), 2-6.

construction companies; few become involved in wholesale trade or other manufacturing firms. Minorities are also mostly in the retail trade and selected services areas, followed by finance, insurance, real estate, and the construction industry (see Table 1-4). The majority of these minority-owned firms are from the black and Hispanic populations.

Surprisingly, the number of women-owned businesses is about equal to the total number of minority-owned businesses in the United States. As these two populations become more and more dominant in the free enterprise system, more and more small businesses will open with owners having a desire for expansion and growth. The trend is for more businesses to come into existence. Almost all businesses do start as small businesses before they have a chance to grow into large ones. (See Figure 1-3.)

Table 1-2. Proprietorships, Partnerships, and Corporations—Number and Business Receipts: 1975

	Total		SIZE OF RECEIPTS					
			Number (000)			Receipts (billion dollars)		
	Number (000)	Receipts (billion dollars)	Proprietorships	Partnerships[1]	Corporations[1]	Proprietorships	Partnerships[1]	Corporations[1]
Total	13,979	3,446.9	10,882	1,073	2,024	339.2	146.0	2,961.7
Under $25,000[2]	9,107	54.7	8,088	550	469	48.3	4.0	2.4
$25,000-$49,999[2]	1,519	53.1	1,192	141	186	42.6	5.1	5.4
$50,000-$99,999	1,247	86.3	852	134	261	59.6	9.6	17.1
$100,000-$199,999 }	1,575	330.2	{ 461	114 }	674	{ 63.4	16.2 }	154.7
$200,000-$499,999 }			{ 235	91 }		{ 68.2	27.7 }	
$500,000-$999,999	249	168.7	39	26	184	26.4	17.4	124.9
$1,000,000 or more	284	2,753.9	15	19	250	30.7	66.0	2,657.2
			PERCENT DISTRIBUTION					
Under $25,000[2]	65.1	1.6	74.4	51.2	23.2	14.2	2.7	0.1
$25,000-$49,999	10.9	1.5	11.0	13.1	9.2	12.6	3.5	0.2
$50,000-$99,999	8.9	2.5	7.8	12.5	12.9	17.6	6.6	0.6
$100,000-$199,999 }	11.3	9.6	{ 4.2	10.6 }	33.3	{ 19.0	11.1 }	5.2
$200,000-$499,999 }			{ 2.1	8.4 }		{ 20.1	18.9 }	
$500,000-$999,999	1.8	4.9	0.3	2.4	9.1	7.8	11.9	4.2
$1,000,000 or more	2.0	79.9	0.1	1.7	12.4	9.0	45.4	89.7

[1]Active firms only. [2]Includes firms with no receipts.
SOURCE: *Statistics of Income, Business Income Tax Returns*, and *Statistics of Income, Corporation Income Tax Returns*, U.S. Internal Revenue Service.

Table 1-3. Women-Owned Firms—Number and Receipts, By Industry: 1972

	FIRMS (000)			RECEIPTS (billion dollars)		
		Women-Owned Firms			Women-Owned Firms	
DIVISION BY INDUSTRY	All Firms[1]	Number of Firms	Percent of All Firms	All Receipts	Receipts	Percent of All Firms
All industries, total	8,730	102	4.6	2,381.2	8.1	0.3
Construction	1,020	15	1.5	146.2	0.5	0.3
Manufacturing	437	8	1.8	875.3	0.3	(Z)
Transportation and public utilities	432[2]	7	1.6	159.5	0.1	0.1
Wholesale trade	560	5	0.9	349.4	0.6	0.2
Retail trade	2,381	133	5.6	474.9	4.2	0.9
Finance, insurance, and real estate	1,318	37	2.8	252.8	0.5	0.2
Selected services	2,212[3]	151	6.3	95.5	1.5	1.6
Other industries and industries not classified	370[3]	45	12.2	27.6	0.4	1.4

(Z) Less than .05 percent.
[1]Based on data from U.S. Internal Revenue Service, preliminary report, Statistics of Income, Business Income Tax Returns, 1972. [2]Excludes railroads. [3]Adjusted to exclude legal services and architectural and engineering services out-of-scope of women-owned businesses.
SOURCE: *Women-Owned Businesses, 1972*, U.S. Bureau of the Census.

Table 1-4. Minority-Owned Business Firms—Number and Receipts, By Industry: 1972

(Number and employment in thousands and receipts in billions of dollars, except as indicated. Based on a small canvass, various published and unpublished source listings, and personal contacts with knowledgeable community and governmental representatives, and records of the Internal Revenue Service and the Social Security Administration. "Minority" identified to include the following groups: Black, Chinese, Japanese, Puerto Rican, Mexican or Latin American, American Indian, Filipino, Korean, Hawaiian, etc.)

INDUSTRY	All U.S. Firms (000)	FIRMS OWNED BY—				
		All Minorities	Percent Minorities of All Firms	Black	Spanish Origin	Other
Number of firms, total[1]	8,730	382	4.4	195	120	67
With paid employees	(X)	76	(X)	32	29	15
With no paid employees	(X)	306	(X)	163	91	52
Construction	1,020	40	3.9	20	17	3
Manufacturing	437	9	2.1	4	4	1
Transport and public utility[2]	432	30	6.9	22	6	2
Wholesale trade	560	7	1.3	2	3	2
Retail trade	2,381	121	5.1	57	42	22
Finance, insurance, real estate	1,318	19	1.4	8	6	5
Selected services	2,212	120	5.4	68	32	20
Business receipts, total[1]	2,381.2	16.6	0.7	7.2	5.3	4.1
Firms with paid employees	(X)	12.1	(X)	5.1	3.7	3.3
Firms with no paid employees	(X)	4.5	(X)	2.1	1.6	0.8
Construction	146.2	1.7	1.2	0.8	0.6	0.3
Manufacturing	875.3	1.3	0.1	0.5	0.3	0.3
Transport and public utility[2]	159.5	0.7	0.4	0.4	0.2	0.1
Wholesale trade	349.4	1.8	0.5	0.8	0.5	0.5
Retail trade	474.9	7.5	1.6	2.9	2.5	2.1
Finance, insurance, real estate	252.8	0.9	0.4	0.5	0.2	0.2
Selected services	95.5	2.1	2.2	1.1	0.6	0.4
Employment, total[1]	56,466	456	0.8	197	150	109
Construction	3,398	57	1.7	30	21	6
Manufacturing	18,696	54	0.3	20	21	13
Transport and public utility[2]	3,895	19	0.5	11	5	3
Wholesale trade	4,075	19	0.5	8	6	5
Retail trade	11,648	173	1.5	58	59	56
Finance, insurance, real estate	3,901	28	0.7	18	4	6
Selected services	9,576	98	1.0	49	31	18

(X) Not applicable
[1] Indicates industries not shown separately.
[2] Excludes railroads.
SOURCE: *Statistical Abstract of the United States: 1979*, U.S. Bureau of the Census.

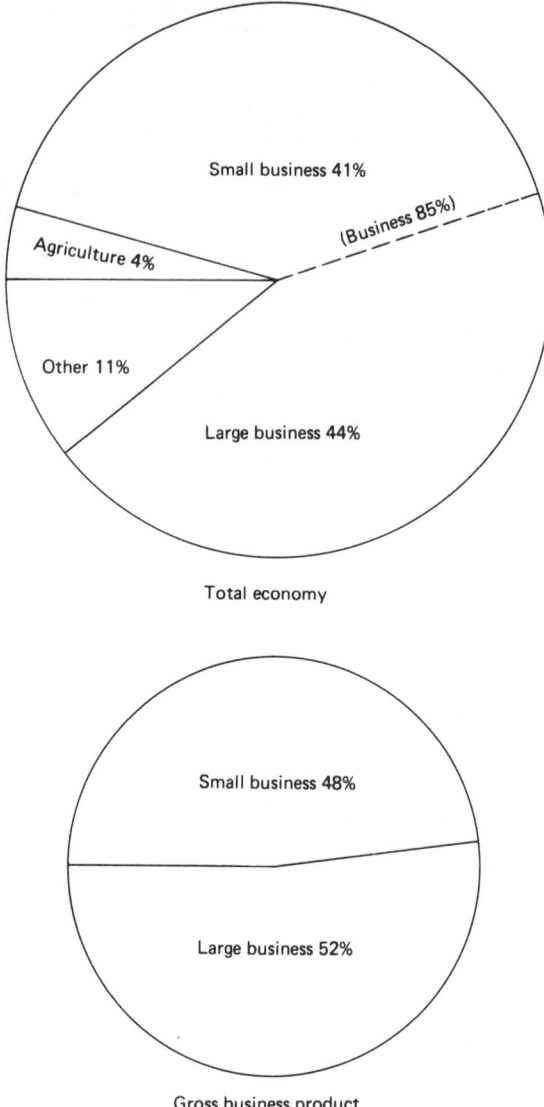

Figure 1-3. *Small business in the U.S. economy*
SOURCE: *Statistical Abstract of the United States: 1979.* Washington, D.C.: U.S. Bureau of the Census, 1979, 435–445 and "Facts about Small Business and the U.S. Small Business Administration" (Washington, D.C.: Small Business Administration, 1979), 2–3.

Operating a Small Business

advantages There are many advantages and desirable outcomes associated with owning and operating one's own business. Each individual has his or her own reasons for operating his or her own business; however, many of these reasons are very common among business owners. Some individuals will state that their reason for

11
THE SMALL BUSINESS ARENA

going into business was "to make money," while others will state that they had a desire to develop a large corporation. Still others had as their primary desire the wish to develop something that they could give to their children as a lifetime's legacy. Regardless of the individual differences, there are several common advantages for going into one's own business, which are: (1) being one's own boss, (2) making money, (3) creating a product or service, (4) helping others, (5) freedom, and (6) self-worth. These factors are characteristic of almost all small business owners.

Being one's own boss. Most people believe that they can manage a small business. The desire to be self-employed and to be in charge has driven several people toward excellence and achievement. The desire to be in control is a need held by corporate executives, government officials, military officials and small business owners. However, it is only in a small business that an individual may properly state, "I am my own boss." The reality of that statement, however, is coupled with the understanding that the customers are often the indirect bosses of the business. The suppliers and salespeople are also seen as bosses who may control inventories and the owner's time. The business owner will realize that time is one of the most valuable assets available, and that many people associated with the business will demand that time.

Making money. The profit motive is present in all small businesses. However, the owner-manager may be required to sacrifice a previous standard of living, as that is above and beyond what the new venture can provide during the first few months or years. Almost all large corporations started as small businesses, including General Motors and Ford Motor Company. However, the opportunities available in a small business are enormous. Through hard work, sacrifice, and devotion (and maybe even a portion of luck) the business can grow to provide a successful income for the owner-manager. Owners of some small businesses, such as ice cream stores, may even find it possible to work twelve to sixteen hours a day during the summer, close down for three or four months during the winter, and yet still make a very handsome profit for the year.

Money is the measure of success for the owner-entrepreneur; it is the method of keeping score. While money may be viewed as providing security, it is also the yardstick by which the owner compares his or her success with others and matches his or her success against the goals previously established.

Creating a product or service. Small businesses are the sources of many technological and mechanical innovations. Many engineers, scientists, or technicians will set up a small business to produce and/or sell some innovative idea. Small businesses are often creative ideas, such as marketing skate boards and setting up fast-food restaurants. Several products, such as solar heating units and useful insecticides, are the results of small business innovation. The smaller firms can develop specialized food products, such as cheeses and sausages. There is often greater flexibility found in small businesses, where the risk factor may be larger for innovative products than among corporate giants (the small businesses cannot afford too many Edsels).

Helping others. Several small business owner-managers created their businesses with friends and relatives. These people have a desire to work together and to help each other. They would like to use their various skills and business experiences in running a new restaurant or developing a new window-washing solvent. They will also seek to create jobs and to expand. Most small business owners realize that one of their greatest assets is good employees, and they are therefore willing to help those good employees who are hardworking and capable in any way possible.

Freedom. Many small business owners feel that they are on their own. They have a sense that their business is dependent upon them; that they can determine how successful that business will be due to their time involvement and workload. Business owners can take their own rest as they see fit, and they can use their time as they desire. They have the freedom of using the business resources as they wish. Whether they will spend their money foolishly or wisely is their own decision.

Self-worth. Small business owners often feel that they have accomplished something. The indivdual is now a success; the owner-manager emerges from a successful business with a sense of pride and a feeling of accomplishment. This person has overcome the odds, and has succeeded where many others have failed. The entrepreneur has a high degree of self-confidence and a sense of self-worth.

disadvantages   There are several disadvantages inherent in a small business, which must be faced by all prospective owner-managers, as well as by entrepreneurs. These disadvantages include: (1) failures, (2) time demands, (3) low income, (4) dislike of work, (5) excessive paperwork and government regulations, (6) undesirables, and (7) economic conditions.

Failures. Probably the most difficult experience an individual can face is to fail in a small business. Because the majority of small businesses do fail, it is important for the owner-manager to realize that the possibility of this occurring is a real one. Such a failure can create problems with one's career, and with one's financial risk (including possible personal bankruptcy), as well as possibly endangering one's family and one's own psyche. Most entrepreneurs are not afraid of failing, and they do realize the severe consequences that may occur. However, many successful owner-managers were previous failures in the same or in related businesses.

Time demands. The involvement in a small business far exceeds the forty-hour workweek. Most small business owners realize that they will now be working ten or more hours a day, five to seven days a week. Very few people are able to run a small business successfully while working short hours. The work conditions are often difficult, and the time demands are excessive.

Low income. It is desirable to make large profits in small businesses. However, few actually "hit it big." Some people will find that they have given up large salaries in corporations to become owner-managers with limited salaries that are below those they previously made. Many small business owners realize that with a limited business inventory (such as not being able to afford 100 TV sets to always be on display) and a limited market share ("We will be lucky to get 10 percent of the restaurant business in our city"), the profit potential and total sales volume are fairly small and restricted.

Dislike of work. Some owner-managers, after they have been working for two or three years, realize that they do not like their chosen business. They do not like the demands the business makes upon them, the people with whom they work, the conditions in which they work, or even the business itself. At this time they have a

13 THE SMALL BUSINESS ARENA

very difficult choice to make—to either stay in that business, or to sell the business and do something else. Before starting one's own business, it is advisable for an individual to work in a related business and, if possible, have some experience as a manager. This will allow the individual to better understand some of his or her own likes and dislikes.

Excessive paperwork and government regulations. One of the major problems facing businesses today is the excessive paperwork and government regulations required of the small business. There is a tremendous amount of paperwork that needs to be maintained and reported on a quarterly, semiannual, or annual basis to several different governmental agencies. The loan officer at the bank also requests monthly statements. The internal paperwork—including inventory records, billing, and receiving—needs to be properly maintained. The owner-manager will find that he or she is the person who is responsible to see that all this paperwork and all the regulations are met.

Undesirables. The owner-manager quickly realizes that he or she is now the subordinate to all the customers: "The customer is always right." Excessive demands will be made by customers, jobbers, promoters, suppliers, and even one's own employees. A small business may require the expense of traveling and being away from one's family. All these undesirables may dictate that a person stay away from the small business environment. The local merchants' association, the city council member, the plumber, and the landlord are all individuals that need to be worked with and dealt with when one is an owner-manager. The local newspaper may provide tremendous support or ridicule, depending upon the owner-manager's activities and support of the community.

Economic conditions. A very real problem for many small business owners is change in economic conditions. Inflation may force them to raise their prices, which in turn discourages customers and causes a drop in sales. The government may extend or develop new rules for a particular business. The interest rate at the bank may go up so high that when a small business owner needs to borrow to purchase his or her Christmas inventory, the interest rate will eat up all profit. The construction industry is traditionally a cyclical industry that is based on the economic condition of the country. During good times people have a tendency to spend freely, but during times of recession they tend to purchase only basic items and necessities. Small businesses engaged in fringe or nonessential items are often forced out of business during these economic downturns. Sufficient capital must be invested or efficiently handled in order to offset economic changes.

SUCCESS STORY: Ray A. Kroc

The Ray Kroc story is not only interesting but it is also truly amazing. In 1955, at the age of 52, Kroc opened his first McDonald's restaurant in Des Plaines, Illinois. In 25 years, McDonald's sales would gross over five billion dollars a year.

Ray Kroc was born in Oak Park, just west of Chicago's city limits, in 1902. He dropped out of high school after his sophomore year. He held various jobs until 1922 when he landed his first steady job selling Lily brand paper cups.

Kroc worked for Lily until 1938, when he went into business with Earl Prince, selling a malt mixer called the Multimixer. The sale of Multimixers declined during the war but picked up shortly after the war ended. Kroc even sold a Multimixer to a guy named Willard Marriott, who was just opening a drive-in called A&W Root Beer.

In 1954, Kroc learned about a small hamburger place in San Bernardino, California, that had not one Multimixer but eight. Ray decided to inspect this phenomenon himself. The operators were Maurice and Dick McDonald. Kroc was amazed by the tremendous business the place was doing. He asked the brothers if they intended to expand their operation by adding new stores. They said they hadn't thought much about it and they wondered aloud who they could get to open restaurants for them. Kroc responded by volunteering himself. The rest is history.

By 1963, McDonald's had grown to 637 stores. By this time a Hamburger University had been established in Elk Grove, Illinois, to train McDonald's managers.

In July, 1966, McDonald's sales topped $200 million. They had sold 2 billion hamburgers. "If laid end to end," they enthused, "two billion hamburgers would circle the earth 5.4 times."[1] Also, in July of 1966, the first store with inside seating was opened in Huntsville, Alabama.

In 1968, the Big Mac was introduced to satisfy demand for a larger sandwich. In 1972, McDonald's entered the breakfast trade by introducing the Egg McMuffin.

Kroc added to his empire by purchasing the San Diego Padres baseball team in 1974. Also in 1976, McDonald's sales exceeded three billion dollars with net earnings after taxes of $100 million.

Today McDonald's consists of some 6,000 restaurants located in the U.S. and 25 other countries. Projects show this figure will grow by about 500 restaurants a year worldwide.

Kroc gave up his chairman of the board position in January, 1977, to become senior chairman of the board, largely a figurehead position. He still remains very active in the organization.

For some people, accomplishments come late in life. For Ray Kroc, it all began at the age of 52.

Business Failures

The chance of failure in a small business firm is ever present—small business failures occur every day. Dun & Bradstreet has reported that business failures are primarily caused by incompetence, mismanagement, and lack of balanced experience on the part of the owner-manager.[2]

The Bank of America has indicated that an additional reason for failure includes the inability of the owner-manager to utilize the financial statements available to provide essential guidelines for control of the business.[3] The Bank of America has claimed that, in many cases of failure, the side most often neglected

---

[1] Ray Kroc, *Grinding It Out* (Chicago: Henry Regnery Company, 1977), 142.
[2] *The Business Failure Record* (New York: Dun & Bradstreet, 1978), 1–13.
[3] *Understanding Financial Statements,* Small Business Reporter Series (San Francisco: Bank of America, 1980), 2.

(as has also been indicated by Dun & Bradstreet) is financial control. The Bank of America has listed the five most common financial causes of business failure as:

1. Not enough sales.
2. High operating costs.
3. Poor credit and collection policy.
4. Too many fixed assets.
5. Too much wrong inventory.

Due to a lack of proper managerial skills, it is difficult for the owner-manager to control all these failure points sufficiently enough to ensure success. Business plans must be developed and forecast in every small business for each year; these plans should be reviewed periodically, and at the end of each financial period they should be compared with the actual sales or costs of running the business.

Business failures may be classified into two different categories: formal fiscal failures and personal failures. Formal fiscal failures include those businesses that are involved in court proceedings or that have resulted in voluntary losses to creditors. There are approximately ten thousand of these failures occurring every year. They provide a larger economic impact on business because of their loss to financial or crediting businesses. The cost of these business failures are primarily due to a lack of managerial competence or lack of experience. (See Figure 1-4.)

Personal failures are more common but generally do not result in loss to creditors. Rather, the loss here is directly sustained by the owner-manager. During a personal failure, all of the owner's equity, as well as many of the assets of the business, will be used to pay off creditors. The owner will agree to pay off all suppliers and creditors on a prearranged basis. The owner becomes the loser and may lose everything he or she has. (In many states, there are homestead laws which prohibit persons from losing their homes due to personal or business bankruptcy.) Although several hundred-thousand businesses are started each year, Dun & Bradstreet has reported that there is "almost an equal number discontinued."

Important Problems Facing Small Businesses Today

There are many problems facing small businesses today. Many of these have remained the same over a great many years. The National Federation of Independent Businesses has reported that the greatest problem facing small businesses today is the economic condition—primarily inflation, closely followed by taxes and government regulations. It is interesting to note that competition and inadequate demand for the product are not major small business problems.

Small businesses do have some common problems, the most common ones being associated with government regulations and taxes. Periods of high inflation

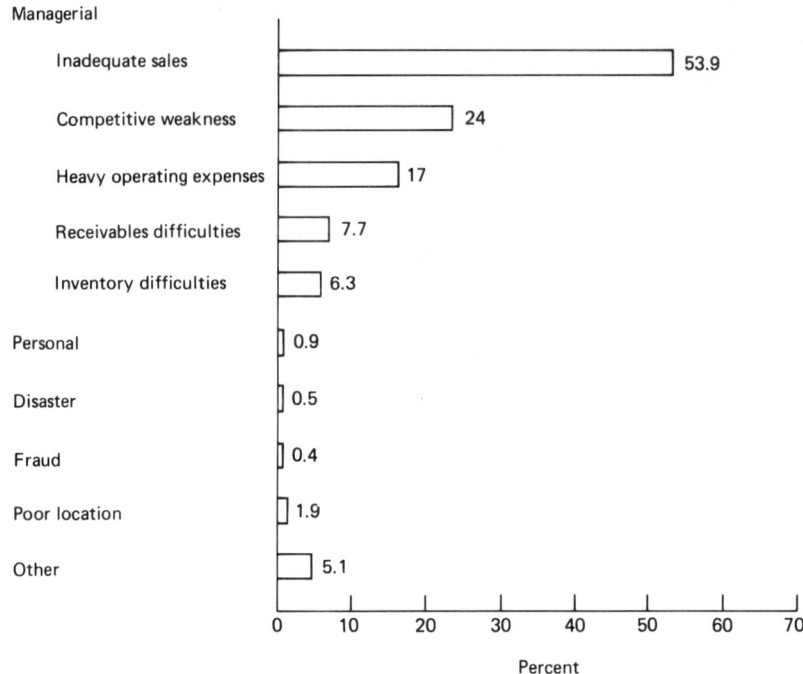

Figure 1-4. *Causes of business failures in 1977*[1]

[1]Some failures are attributed to a combination of causes.

SOURCE: Adapted from *The Business Failure Record* (New York: Dun & Bradstreet, Inc., 1978) 12-13.

also cause a drain on capital reserves, and require excess monies to be spent by the owner-managers for inventory and equipment. Small business owners find it difficult to influence and lobby for favorable legislation. They also find it difficult to work with the many governmental regulatory agencies that require adherence to federal health, safety, and personnel standards.

Double-digit inflation, sky-high interest rates, lack of good employees, energy shortages, and poor production—are all problems of concern for the small business owner-manager. Renewed enthusiasm for the future, based on sound economic and business practices, should help to offset some of these problems. There is reason to hope that incomes will shortly overtake inflation. Business, coupled with technological advances, should flourish in a highly competitive environment.

Businesses will continue to go up and down and have seasonal peaks. No unstoppable, universal business boom is expected, but small businesses have a great future and a promise of opportunity unmatched in past decades. Small businesses will continue to be the heartbeat of our nation. They will continue to provide opportunities for individuals to get rich, to obtain status, and to secure the economic future of countless families and owners.

CASE STUDY: Speedy Pizza

The Speedy Pizza concept developed from study and analysis of similar delivery operations throughout the United States. John, who will be the sole proprietor, learned about this exciting and profitable fast-food delivery business from his brother Syd, a dentist. John is a senior in college, with limited work experience in high school and summer jobs, who has a dream: He wants to build and start his own business.

Speedy Pizza means pizza fast! The recipes will be set up to produce a quality product quickly and efficiently. No sit-down area will be provided, but efforts will be applied to quickly transfer the pizza, hot from the oven, to customers via delivery vehicles equipped with hot portable ovens.

John lives in a city of over 500,000 people; the city has one major state university, and two other colleges sponsored by religious organizations. Only two other pizza businesses deliver within the city, and both of these concentrate on a sit-down business, with delivery as a side-line. John has heard complaints about slow delivery times—one hour or greater on ordered pizzas. He wants to guarantee delivery in less than 45 minutes, with average delivery expected in 25 minutes from the time the order is placed.

John has discovered that the other sixteen pizza restaurants within the city have a carry-out rate of approximately 15 percent of their total business. John wishes to place emphasis on the delivery business and thus realize a greater volume on delivery than anyone else. John believes that the pricing should be competitive with the other pizza establishments. His aim is simply to capture the market that is now going without pizzas, eating frozen ones, or grudgingly picking up something.

John wants to locate his pizza business in a high-density population area, preferably close to the state university. He is thinking about doing his advertising and promotion through the university newspaper, with additional advertising in the form of fliers placed on cars and/or in doors within a mile radius of the business. He believes that his advertising should emphasize product quality and *fast hot delivery.* His theme may be "quality pizza specialists."

John has tried to investigate and learn about the different areas that would be necessary to start up the business. He has developed a start-up cost sheet of $27,155 (see below). This assumes that he will be able to use or lease a store that was previously occupied by some other tenant. He has also developed a projected income statement, with anticipation sales of $215,000 during the first year (see below).

Questions

1. Does John have a good idea?
2. Is he ready to go into the business?
3. Where will he find sufficient funds to open a business?
4. Are his figures and projections realistic?
5. What other information does he need to know before starting a business?
6. What would you recommend John do before starting his business?

SPEEDY PIZZA

START-UP COSTS

1. *Equipment*
   Ovens:
One used Peerless 2-deck	$ 350.00	
One new Baker's Pride Y-600	1,848.00	
Walk-in cooler (Hunts—used 6'x8'—installed)	1,050.00	
Hot-tote warmers: 3 (Wittco—used)	105.00	
Cash register (NCR—used)	427.00	
Coke box (for canned drinks)	263.00	
Outside signs	115.00	
Refrigerated pizza table (Lern Mfg.)	1,100.00	
Misc. pizza/restaurant equipment	600.00	
Three-compartment sink (used)	140.00	
Mixer/cutter (Hobart, Model VCM-40, used)	2,000.00	
Slicer	1,000.00	
Food scales (used)	50.00	
Cutting table (sized to fit, Formica top)	1,250.00	
Glass work (in front counter)	52.00	
	$10,350.00	
		$10,350.00

2. *Leasehold Improvements*
Electrical	$ 1,000.00	
Plumbing	3,000.00	
Carpentry	900.00	
	$ 4,900.00	
		4,900.00

3. *Autos*
AMC Gremlin	$ 3,900.00	
		3,900.00

4. *Miscellaneous*
Permits	$ 68.00	
Food and operational supplies (2 weeks)	2,700.00	
Insurance (1 year)	700.00	
Auto lettering	577.00	
Rent:		
First month	425.00	
Last month	425.00	
Linen (aprons and hand towels)	30.00	
Advertising:		
Newspaper	350.00	
Menus	150.00	
Fliers	80.00	
	$ 5,505.00	
		5,505.00

5. *Owner's Salary During Opening* $ 1,500.00
   1,500.00

6. *Professional Fee* $ 1,000.00
   1,000.00

Grand Total $27,155.00

SPEEDY PIZZA

INCOME STATEMENT

	Dollars	Percent
Net Sales	$215,000	100
Cost of goods sold:		
Food	64,500	30
Supplies	21,000	9.8
Less total cost of goods sold	85,500	39.8
Variable expenses:		
Auto	8,600	4
Advertising	8,600	4
Taxes—payroll	3,219	1.5
Interest	1,687	0.8
Labor	45,000	20.9
	67,106	31.2
Fixed expenses:		
Depreciation	4,048	1.9
Insurance	840	0.4
Rent	5,100	2.4
Utilities	3,000	1.4
Telephone	2,400	1.1
	15,388	7.2
Owner's salary	10,937	5.0
Less total expenses	93,431	43.4
Net Profit	$ 36,069	16.8

Chapter Questions:

1. What is a small business?
2. What is meant by the statement: "Small business is the backbone of the American economic system"?
3. What are some advantages of being a small business owner or manager?
4. What are some of the disadvantages of being a small business owner or manager?
5. Discuss why businesses fail.
6. How is money used to determine the success of a small business?
7. What is the outlook for future businesses?
8. What are some of the major problems facing small businesses today?

2

Photo courtesy of Irene Springer, Prentice-Hall, Inc.

THE SMALL BUSINESS: FORM AND STRUCTURE

Chapter Objectives:

1. To know the different levels of involvement associated with the small business.
2. To know the attitudes often found in the small business toward customers, employees, and the business itself.
3. To learn about the various types of businesses.
4. To understand various forms of small business structures.
5. To be able to distinguish between sole proprietorship, partnership, and corporation.

There are two places to find something: in the Encyclopaedia Brittanica, and at the corner drug store.

Anonymous

The business of America is business.

Calvin Coolidge

INCIDENT: Al and Tony want to open a restaurant. Al is 19 and has just graduated from high school. Tony, Al's oldest brother, is 27; he has worked in several restaurants over the past eight years.

Their family has offered to contribute $5,000 from family savings, and Al and Tony have an additional $5,000 between them. They have also talked to a banker about the possibility of borrowing up to $7,000 for equipment, and have tentative approval from the bank on a note to be secured by the equipment.

Al and Tony intend to buy out Sammie's, a neighborhood hot dog and hamburger shop. Sam and Ruth have run Sammie's for fifteen years, but Ruth's health is failing, and their doctor has ordered her to find a less time-consuming occupation. Sammie's is open six days a week, from 7 A.M. until 6 P.M., and neither Sam nor Ruth has had a vacation for over ten years. Sam and Ruth are asking for $5,000 now, and $3,000 a year for five years for their business. The store is rented, but some furnishings would be included in the purchase.

Al and Tony intend to change Sammie's into a pizza shop, remodeling it to provide more counter space and room for a pizza oven. The majority of the business is a captive lunch crowd from two nearby office buildings. The nearest other restaurant is six blocks away, and a McDonald's is being built about eight blocks away.

One of the concerns that Al and Tony now face is the type of business their new restaurant will be. They have decided to operate as a partnership, with Tony the senior partner, since he has had more experience. They are uncertain as to how they should handle the offer of their family to help finance them. In fact, they feel that they might not even need the additional capital.

Do they want to remain a lunch operation only, or do they want to take on an evening business as well? Should they offer to deliver pizzas, and if so, over how large an area? Tony is thinking about getting married. How is he to include that in his business plans?

If you were asked to list some businesses, what kind of list would you come up with? To many people, business is represented by *big* business, such as General Motors, IBM, Xerox, and the like.

Did you ever stop to think just how many small businesses you deal with each day? The paper boy or girl who brings you your morning newspaper is running a fledgling business. It is interesting to note how many successful big businesspeople started out delivering newspapers.

If you stopped at a filling station to get gas on the way to work, you dealt with another small business. The restaurant where you ate lunch was probably a small business. Your plumber is a small businessperson, as are your doctor and lawyer. Your grocery store and your barber or hairdresser are small businesses.

While many facets of a small business are the same as those of a big business, there are also many characteristics unique to small businesses. Small businesses are more personal—you know the business, the owner, the employees, and you may have dealt with the business for many years more as a friend than as a customer. If you own a small business, it will affect your entire life. We can categorize many of the more intimate feelings associated with small businesses as being related to the attitudes of the business and the levels of involvement of the owner in the business.

Levels of Involvement in the Small Business

As one becomes associated with a small business, one becomes a close part of it. It is this close level of involvement within the business that makes small businesses the dynamic, exciting experience that they are. There are at least four levels of involvement that will be of concern to the small business owner:

1. Personal involvement.
2. Family involvement.
3. Employee involvement.
4. Community involvement.

personal involvement

As the owner of a small business, one must make a personal commitment to be highly involved in the business. In many cases, the owner of a small business can expect to put in twelve- to fourteen-hour days, six- and seven-day workweeks, and vacations that may be difficult to schedule and take. Some small business owners get totally carried away with their involvement in the business, to the detriment of their personal lives. A small business involvement has probably broken up many otherwise happy marriages.

To be sure, there are many cases of small business owners who have retired (so to speak) at an early age, especially once the business is established. However, in reading the biographies of successful businesspeople in this text, you will note that most of them have spent, and continue to spend, many hours each day working with their businesses.

Although long, hard hours may be involved, many small business owners consider those hours to be very pleasant experiences. There is a challenge associated with small business ownership. Any success achieved by the business is a compliment on the skills and energy of the owner. This challenge and the thrill of success may actually be more important to the small business owner than any monetary rewards that are associated with success.

family involvement

Just as the owner of the business is highly involved in the business, the rest of the family must also make that commitment. Many small businesses are family businesses in which both husband and wife work, with children helping out. As the business grows, several generations of the family can have successful business careers working for the family business.

In addition, the small business may often provide some fringe benefits to the family. The owner of a photo processing lab may well take many more pictures of his or her family than the ordinary person. When children need a part-time job after school, the business can often provide one, even if there is very little actual help needed.

employee involvement

There are many people in the labor force who have found that they cannot work for a large company. These people make the best kind of employees for a small business. What they lack is a sense of identification with the large business; after all, they spend eight or more hours a day there—surely they must have *some* feelings about what goes on in the business. Yet in many large businesses, there is no sense of belonging. In a small business, the employees can be nearly as involved as the owner. During the busy season, they may willingly work the extra hours needed to get everything done, because they understand just how important it is for the business to have a successful season this year.

community involvement

A small business is part of an overall business community, and it is expected to participate in civic activities. The owner can decide how to do this. Most owners will probably want to become a member of the Better Business Bureau (BBB), which is an association of local businesses, usually small ones, devoted to improving the image and reliability of the local business community. The BBB is often the problem solver for the consumer, helping to mediate or prevent disagreements between customer and business.

There are usually many other civic organizations that will invite the participation of small business owners. They offer the chance to meet with contemporaries and discuss common problems. Quite often, these organizations represent the major planning groups for community-level plans.

Community involvement will also require the small business owner to support charity and youth organizations. He or she may want to sponsor a softball team. The business owner can provide his or her time and business resources in addition to donating money in support of these organizations. The owner has a stake in his or her community, which provides customers, employees, and the livelihood of the business.

Attitudes in the Small Business

Just as a commitment to a small business will be stronger than to a large company, the attitudes developed within the small business will also differ from those found in larger companies. A small business is more personal than a large one. This personal attitude will reflect itself in the attitudes held by the small business owner toward customers, employees, and the business itself.

attitudes toward customers

"The customer is always right." That statement may sum up the attitude often held by small business owners toward their customers. If one depends on local patronage, as in a retail store, customers will be known personally. They may be friends as well as customers. Christmas cards may be sent out to special customers as a token of friendship.

Even in cases in which the customer is wrong, the attitude that should be taken is to somehow correct the wrong. If the customer is misinformed as to the goals and purposes of the business, the customer must be educated. If service is not provided, the owner should explain why. Perhaps in trying to explain the reasons, the owner will realize that he or she should be doing business differently.

If customers are well known, the owner will be able to change the business to better meet their needs. By meeting the needs of customers, the odds of the business being a successful one are enhanced.

attitudes toward employees

Just as employees may have made a commitment to the small business, the owner must express certain attitudes toward the employees. The employees will be friends, too. Their working environment is controlled, and can be one in which everyone benefits. By having happy employees, one may find that one has an edge over the competition. Certainly you would rather shop in a store in which everyone seems to be friendly and helpful rather than in one in which everyone tries to avoid waiting on you. Attitudes toward employees will carry over in terms of their attitudes toward customers.

Many of the attitudes expressed toward employees will be set forth in the policies and rules placed on them. The owner is able to provide some flexibility that is unavailable in a large company in terms of allowing longer lunch hours for special occasions and scheduling conveniences—even the frequency with which paychecks are issued can be tailored to help satisfy employees. While a small company cannot match General Motors in terms of health and medical benefits, the owner may be able to provide things that bigger companies cannot afford to sponsor. A company bowling team or softball team can be sponsored, picnics and get-togethers can be held, and families of the employees can be involved in the business. The owner may be asked to buy all manner of raffle tickets for various events, and should concede gracefully. The fringe benefits provided for the owner's family can also be extended to employees, at least in a limited sense.

attitudes toward the business itself

What are the goals and the reasons for wanting to own a small business? The answer to that question will help to identify the relationship one will have toward a business. If it is seen merely as a way to earn a living, perhaps one should not seek to become a small business owner.

While money is often a significant factor for becoming a small business owner, the more important one for many people is the sense of control and freedom associated with small business ownership. One is free to define the type of business

25
SMALL BUSINESS: FORM AND STRUCTURE

he or she will own, and the relationships to be maintained with the various types of people one must deal with.

One way that the freedom associated with a small business can be felt is in setting goals. After the business becomes successful, one may be able to devote more of one's time to civic or church activities, and the business can help in those pursuits. Once the business provides a comfortable living, one may not feel the pressure to continue to grow. This is both an advantage and a potential danger, for the business that stops growing completely often begins to stagnate, then to falter, and perhaps to fail.

Types of Small Businesses

The way one will operate a small business is to a great extent determined by the type of business to be started. Before one decides to form a small business, one must have a clear idea of what is intended, what business one is going to be in. Table 2-1 indicates the most popular small businesses.

Table 2-1. Top 20 Small Businesses in 1975[a]

RANK	NATURE OF BUSINESS	TOTAL NUMBER
1	Farming	3,271,436
2	Building lessors and operators	456,465
3	Real estate agent	421,113
4	Direct sales	406,469
5	Trucking and warehousing	298,346
6	Insurance agent	260,806
7	Restaurants and other eating places	172,313
8	General contractors and operative builders	257,842
9	Beauty shops	233,442
10	Food stores	229,050
11	Auto repair	211,524
12	Physicians	210,000
13	Carpenters	204,165
14	Gas stations	192,035
15	Legal services	185,851
16	Taverns and other drinking places	172,313
17	Public relations	161,671
18	Bookkeeping services (not CPA)	125,135
19	Dentists	101,162
20	Car dealers (used and new)	85,842

[a] A small business is defined as one having gross receipts of less than $5 million.
SOURCE: *Statistics of Income—1975,* Internal Revenue Service, Business Income Tax Returns, Corporation Income Tax Returns.

There are six different types of businesses into which most small businesses fall. A given business may be active in more than one type simultaneously, although one type will usually predominate. The six types are:

1. Retail sales.
2. Wholesale sales.
3. Manufacturing.
4. Services.
5. Finance.
6. Agriculture.

retail sales   The retail business is the most visible form of the small business. A retailer is one who buys items from one or more manufacturers (or wholesalers) and sells them to the general public. There are two basic types of retailers: those who do business from a store location, and those who work on a personal basis with their customers. The latter type is called direct sales, and includes such companies as Avon, Tupperware, Fuller Brushes, and all others that sell items on a one-to-one basis, often in the home.

As a retailer, one must attract or search out customers. This is partially done through advertising. When operating from a store, one is dependent on customers to come in, and so one must make one's presence known. There are over 1.7 million retail businesses in the United States, most of which are small businesses. Table 2-2 shows the total amount of business done by some retail business.

Table 2–2. 1977 Sales for Selected Retail Businesses

	(in millions)
Total retail sales	$723,134
Groceries	147,758
New and used cars	121,883
Department stores	76,909
Gas stations	56,468
Eating places	55,581
Women's clothing	26,591
Building materials	24,726
Drugs	23,196
Furniture	20,316
Liquor	12,967
Radios, TVs, music	8,126
Drinking places	7,695
Mail order houses	7,555
Variety stores	7,094
Men's and boys' clothing	6,943
Home furnishings	6,255
Hardware	6,087
Shoes	5,650
Jewelry	5,428
Appliances	4,734
Sporting goods	4,655
Vending machines	3,945
Mobile home dealers	3,857
Bakeries	2,300

SOURCE: *1977 Census of Retail Trade,* Bureau of the Census, U.S. Department of Commerce.

wholesale sales   A wholesaler is an intermediary who buys goods from a manufacturer and then sells them to a retailer. The wholesaler assists in the orderly distribution of products from manufacturer to consumer. A term commonly used, which means about the same thing as wholesaler, is distributor.

The wholesaler does not sell to the general public, and may have a very limited number of customers. Sales are often made through the use of salespeople who travel around a territory to call on customers and encourage them to place orders. Advertising may be less important to the wholesaler, although there will be a need for some type of promotion to make sure that customers know what is available. There are about 500,000 wholesale businesses in the U.S. Table 2-3 illustrates the relative size of some types of wholesale businesses.

Table 2-3. 1972 Sales for Selected Wholesale Businesses

	(in millions)
Total wholesale sales	$695,223
Automotive parts and supplies	19,930
Paper and paper products	17,280
Industrial machinery	17,098
Industrial supplies	16,451
Lumber and plywood	16,151
Electronic appliances, TVs, radios	12,681
Farm and garden machinery	12,599
Office machines and equipment	10,542
Home furnishings	8,424
Plumbing and heating	7,318
Hardware	6,680
Women's, children's, and infants' clothing	6,085
Photographic equipment and supplies	4,823
Men's and boys' clothing	4,538
Sporting goods	4,435
Brick, tile, and cement	4,306
Heating and air conditioning	3,674
Iron and steel scrap	3,507
Jewelry, watches, diamonds	3,291
Surgical, medical, and hospital supplies	2,399
Household and lawn furniture	2,085
Roofing and siding	1,996
Office and business furniture	1,840

SOURCE: *1972 Census of Wholesale Trade,* Bureau of the Census, U.S. Department of Commerce.

manufacturing The manufacturer produces goods, rather than purchases them. There are many different types of manufacturers. Some may produce items intended for general public use, while others may produce items to be sold to other manufacturers to be used as parts of larger items. General Motors, for example, depends on thousands of small businesses to produce the many different parts needed to assemble an automobile.

Manufacturers may use wholesalers to distribute their products, or they may sell them directly to retailers. Products intended for industrial use are generally sold directly to the users, though for smaller items a distributor may be a more efficient means of achieving product delivery.

Manufacturers of consumer items must assume the burden of advertising their products to their end users, even though they do not sell directly to them. This is because the manufacturer has the biggest stake in the sale of the product. The distributor or retailer probably carries the items of many different manufacturers, and may not be as eager to sell any one item.

services   A service business is one in which the business owner performs some skilled task or function for the customer. A plumber or doctor runs a service business. The retailer who sells and repairs appliances has a small service component to his or her business.

Although there are often products or supplies involved in the performance of the service, it is the task itself that constitutes the major function of the service business. The customers of the service business require someone with the skills needed to perform the task, and it is the skill that they primarily buy.

Many service businesses depend upon their customers to realize the necessity for their services; advertising is often a case of declaration of availability. The so-called professional services—medical, legal, and accounting—have considered advertising to be unethical, and so have placed some restrictions on the use of advertising within the profession. In recent years there has been some challenge to this ban, the result being that some members of these professions have now begun a limited form of advertising. Table 2-4 illustrates the broad range of service businesses.

Table 2-4. 1972 Sales for Selected Service Businesses

	(in millions)
Total service business receipts	$112,970
Hotels, motor hotels, and tourist courts	5,293
Consulting and public relations	4,257
Car rental and leasing	3,558
Computer and data processing services	3,440
Auto repair	3,175
Equipment rental and leasing	2,369
Funeral services	2,218
Body repair	1,776
Sports clubs	1,598
Motion picture theaters (not drive-ins)	1,402
Bowling alleys	1,088
Radio and TV repair	1,086
Coin-operated laundries	878
Photo portrait studios	767
Auto parking	725
Dental laboratories	573
Outdoor advertising	414
Drive-in theaters	413
Dance schools	65

SOURCE: *1972 Census of Selected Service Trade,* Bureau of the Census, U.S. Department of Commerce.

finance   Financial businesses are service businesses to some extent, although there is often a product involved. The three types of financial businesses are: (1) financial services (such as banking), (2) real estate, and (3) insurance. All three have a high degree of professional standards associated with them, and all are regulated to some extent. An insurance salesperson is similar to a direct sales agent in many respects, although he or she deals with a much more sophisticated product. Advertising is usually involved, though the degree and type of it will depend upon the exact nature of the financial product.

agriculture Many people probably do not consider a farm a type of business, but it most certainly is one. Furthermore, there are over three million farms in the United States, so in a sense it is the most common type of business in the country. Recent trends in agricultural education have shown that the people involved in agriculture realize the business aspects of their industry. A farm may actually be one of the more risky types of businesses to undertake.

Forms of the Small Business

There are three basic forms of business organization methods: the sole proprietorship, the partnership, and the corporation. With only a few limited exceptions, any type of business venture can use any form of organization. The factors that will affect the business form chosen are:

1. Ease of formation.
2. Exposure to financial risk.
3. Ability to raise capital.
4. Tax treatment of income.
5. Continuity of business upon death of owner.

A comparison of these factors is summarized in Table 2-5.

Table 2-5. A Comparison of the Three Forms of Business Organization

	SOLE PROPRIETORSHIP	PARTNERSHIP	CORPORATION
Ease of Formation	Very easy	Easy to very easy	Moderate to easy
Legal Requirements	None, except for possible declaration of name	Same as sole proprietorship; written contract between partners recommended	Charter must be secured from state
Ability to Borrow Funds	Limited ability of owner to borrow	Improved ability to borrow due to multiple owners	Can borrow funds directly
How Taxes Are Handled	As part of owner's personal tax return	Profits are divided up among owners and are taxed on each partner's tax return	Pays own income taxes
Degree of Financial Risk	Owner is responsible for all debts	Partners share responsibility for debts	Owners have only limited responsibility for debts in name of company
Number of Owners	One	Two or more	One or more
Continuity of Business	Business is terminated at death of owner	Business may be terminated at death of any partner, unless provisions for continuation are made	Business continues after death of any stockholder

the sole proprietorship

The easiest business form to use is the sole proprietorship, which requires little or no effort. One just begins doing business. However, if one chooses to do business under a name other than his or her own, one may be required to register that name with the state, so that it is public record that the owner is legally responsible for the debts of the business.

A sole proprietor is the complete owner of his or her business, and is responsible for all debts incurred by it. If the business fails, the owner remains responsible for the debts until all are repaid. The ability to raise capital is limited to the financial worthiness of the owner, since the owner will have to sign personally for any bank loans. Since there is no stock involved, there is no ability to sell stock to raise additional funds, nor can bonds be sold.

Income earned by sole proprietorship is taxed along with the rest of the income earned by the owner. If the business runs at a loss, that loss may be used to offset any other form of income. The owner will have to file a Schedule C (Profit or [Loss] from Business or Profession), for each sole proprietorship owned, giving details for the year. This is filed along with the owner's Form 1040. If the business is substantially profitable, the owner of a sole proprietorship may be required to make quarterly estimated tax payments.

Since there is no legal separation between the owner and the business in a sole proprietorship, the business dies along with the owner. Some provision for continuity of operations should be made, since a terminated business is worth substantially less than an active, viable one.

The primary advantage of the sole proprietorship form is the simplicity of formation. Many businesses start out as part-time businesses, for which there may be little risk of large losses. Avon and Tupperware are two products that rely exclusively on a large network of part-time dealers, each of them operating as a sole proprietor of their own business. If the business grows into a major, full-time business, it may then become advantageous to switch the form of the business to a partnership or corporation.

the partnership

A partnership is only somewhat more difficult than a sole proprietorship to organize. There must be an agreement between the owners, or partners, as to the nature of contribution (financial and otherwise) to the business, and for a division of profits. Although it is not required, it is highly recommended that this partnership agreement be drawn up in written form and checked by a lawyer before beginning the business. A partnership may also have to register the name under which it chooses to do business.

In the standard form of a partnership, called a general partnership, all owners are equally responsible for the debts of the business in a failure. The creditors may choose which of the partners they pursue for collection. There is no limitation on the extent of liability, just as there was no limit for the sole owner.

A special type of partnership, called a limited partnership, is sometimes used for attracting additional investors. It allows some limitations on the liabilities of certain partners. Limited partnerships are very complex legal forms, and should be thoroughly checked by lawyers trained in this type of agreement. In addition, the Internal Revenue Service (IRS) has recently begun to crack down on certain types of limited partnerships, restricting their use as tax shelters.

A partnership cannot sell stocks or bonds. However, it can add additional partners, or request additional capital contributions from existing partners to raise funds. The partners will usually have to sign personally if any bank loans are taken, although that is a mere formality, since they are already under obligation.

Partnerships are often considered to have been terminated upon the death of any one partner. For this reason, the partnership agreement should contain specific provisions for the sale of the interest in the business, usually to existing partners, upon the death of any partner.

Profits earned by a partnership are taxed with each partner's personal income, as in the sole proprietorship. The partnership agreement will specify the method for dividing the profits for tax purposes. The partnership will file a Form 1065 return (U.S. Partnership Return of Income). This is an information return; no taxes are paid with it. The partners will each file a Schedule K (Partners' Shares of Income, Credits, Deductions, etc.) with their individual tax returns. Partners may also have to make quarterly estimated tax payments.

The advantage that the partnership offers over the sole proprietorship is the ability to have more than one owner in the business. Many partnerships are purely financial devices used to handle investments, such as real estate deals. In other cases, the necessity for larger sums of capital than could be raised by one owner is what prompts the partnership. Another advantage in the partnership form is that it often assures that the business will have the time commitment and involvement from each partner that is necessary for the business. Many lawyers and accountants form partnerships for this reason.

SUCCESS STORY: Paul J. Meyer

"It was a highly paid rut, and every man who placidly accepts being in a rut ignores the fact that a rut is merely a grave with the ends kicked out." This terse criticism of his own life made when he was a 27-year-old millionaire in the life insurance business is typical of Paul J. Meyer, president and founder of Success Motivation Institute, Inc., of Waco, Texas.

At age 12, Paul Meyer won first place in a statewide contest for selling subscriptions to *Liberty Magazine*. Two years later he established a bicycle repair business in his father's garage. Working after school, he repaired and sold more than 300 bicycles. At 16, he set up a fruit stand, selling prunes, apricots, and cherries. He picked the fruit himself in the San Jose area groves that gave a discount to those who picked their own fruit.

Always conscious of maintaining his uniqueness, Meyer decided to be the best prune picker in the world. Calling the local newspaper, he found out that the record for prune picking was 100 fifty-pound boxes of prunes in twenty-four hours. Meyer tied flashlights to the branches of the trees, and was able to begin picking fruit well before sunup. By sundown, he had picked a total of 101 fifty-pound boxes of fruit, establishing a new record which still stands.

At 18, Meyer joined the paratroopers and became a physical fitness instructor. There he set a record for sit-ups—3,500 at one time.

At 20, Meyer had a desire to become a master salesman. The insurance companies with whom he interviewed gave him aptitude tests that indicated he was introverted, shy, quiet, without sales ability or sales aptitude, and would never make an insurance salesman. Seven years later he was a millionaire—in insurance.

Hearing of a small distributing company in Waco, Texas, Meyer was intrigued with the possibility of energizing it. He called long distance, and was hired on straight commission. He bought a 20 percent interest in the company, became the national sales manager, and created a national distribution system of 1,500 men. By applying the sound principles of sales leadership, Meyer boosted sales 1,200 percent.

In 1960, Meyer struck out on his own again. Convinced that he could motivate others as he had motivated himself, he began, at the age of 32, to sell success from headquarters in a refurnished, drafty garage. Meyer applied the principle of daily repetition as a learning tool to develop personal motivation and goal-setting skills. From a single motivational record, SMI's product line has grown to include approximately 150 cassette tapes that present condensations of outstanding books and especially-prepared scripts in the areas of self-help, personal motivation, sales and management training, athletic achievement, and family life. SMI also has a complete line of major cassette tape programs in these areas suitable for use by individuals and companies.

Among SMI's clients are companies such as Pan American World Airways, Heublein, Inc., American Amicable Life Insurance Co., Delmonico Foods, Inc., and a number of National Football League teams, professional golfers, and other professional athletes.

SMI International, Inc. has grown from a company headquartered in a drafty garage to a parent company with eleven wholly-owned subsidiaries for marketing and manufacturing. The city of Waco has felt the effect of the growth of SMI, which today employs 400 people in the home office and has a distributor organization of over 400 distributors in all 50 states and more than 35 foreign countries. SMI programs and cassette tapes are now produced in eleven languages for worldwide distribution. The home office annual payroll now exceeds $5.5 million.

the corporation   A corporation is a legal entity that is chartered by the state and is empowered to engage in business in its own name. The owners of a corporation purchase stock in the company, the stock ownership signifying the relative control each stockholder has in the business. The stockholders elect a board of directors to run the company, and the directors in turn hire the officers, or the actual management of the company. In a small business, there may be only one stockholder, and that stockholder may also be a director and hold the office of president.

While it is not impossible, it is difficult to set up a corporation without some professional help. It is also not free; there will be an incorporation charge necessary to secure the charter from the state. In addition, the state will require some form of annual fee to maintain the corporation, along with some documentation of officers and directors currently serving the corporation. The nature and timing of this will vary from state to state.

The primary advantage of the corporation is the separation of the corporation from its owners. A corporation may sell stock, may sell bonds, and may borrow money from a bank. In the event of failure, the owners are isolated from the debts incurred in the name of the corporation. A corporation, then, is a means of reducing the financial risk associated with business ownership. In a small business, the ability of the corporation to borrow money may be rather limited, and the primary stockholder may be required to guarantee any bank loans personally. This somewhat reduces that advantage of separation from financial risk.

A corporation is set up as a perpetual entity; it does not cease to exist with the death of one or all of the stockholders. In actual practice, there may be problems in continuing a business when the primary owner—the person who actually runs the business—dies. The stock held by a person is considered part of that person's estate, and ownership may be transferred through the person's will.

A corporation must pay taxes on the income it produces. If the primary stockholder is active in the business, the salary paid may be deducted as a business expense, just as any other salaries are deducted. Payments to the stockholders in general are called dividends, and dividends are taxed as personal income. Furthermore, dividends are not currently considered to be deductible expenses, so they are in effect taxed twice: once on the corporate earnings, and a second time on the individual receiving the dividend. Salaries paid to owner and employees may not be excessive, as the IRS may treat an excess amount as a dividend, and tax it accordingly.

Summary

Owning a small business can be very exciting. As one contemplates starting a business, one must decide if the rewards of small business ownership are worth the effort.

A small business will involve a strong commitment on the part of the owner, and from the owner's family as well. One must be willing to devote such effort to the small business, and to make the sacrifices it may entail. Anyone who is not willing to become personally involved with the business is not as likely to be successful with it.

The business will dictate many of the attitudes held by the owner toward the customers, employees, and the business itself. One may find that one's attitudes toward life will change as a result of small business ownership.

One must also have a strong idea as to the type of business he or she wants to own. What is the prospective owner interested in doing? What skills can be provided, or will be learned? The nature of the business one starts will be restricted by his or her abilities and interests.

Having chosen a business, one must decide what form of business organization to use. One may elect to assume all the risks associated with a sole proprietorship, to spread those risks with a partnership, or to reduce them substantially by forming a corporation.

CASE STUDY: The Sirloin Platter Restaurant

Linda Bailey wants to start The Sirloin Platter Restaurant. Her business would offer only quality menu items, unsurpassed by any other national chain or family-priced local steakhouse. All items on the menu would be prepared in the restaurant, the beef being prepared at pit level where it could be viewed by restaurant customers.

The main menu would include the Strip Steak, a succulent eight-ounce steak charbroiled to order (rare, medium-rare, medium, medium-well, and well-done); the Rib-Eye Steak, a six-ounce juicy steak; the Sirloin Platter, a twelve-ounce steak prepared for perfection; the Chopped Sirloin, a six-ounce portion of chopped steak; and the Platter Burger, four ounces of ground beef served with all the trimmings. The above menu items would be served with baked potato, salad, and homemade bread. The Platter would also have a special salad bar, with a tossed salad, six types of dressing, and five other salad varieties.

Linda would be seeking local college students and downtown businesspeople, but the main market would be strictly the family. This is because the choice locations are primarily located close to residential areas. With neighborhoods nearby, one has what is called a "co-residential backup," which indicates that the restaurant would primarily get its major customer traffic from the neighborhoods.

Linda is primarily interested in stressing the quality of the food that she will offer and prepare. She sees that she will be primarily developing the finest products available anywhere, and using brands that may be used at home. She expects the quality to be widely known and expected by her customers. She will be seeking a very high reputation for food quality and high standards. Quality is involved with providing cleanliness. A customer will generally expect high standards of cleanliness. The Sirloin Platter Restaurant must reflect the demands for cleanliness, and be spotless at all times. Only through the efforts of everyone concerned with the business will this goal be reached. This would include neatness in appearance and in work areas. It has often been found that it is easier to clean as one goes to keep things always at their best.

Another area of concern is service. Both quality and cleanliness may be wasted unless the service is courteous and fast. The golden rule should be remembered, and employees should place themselves in the role of customers in order to understand how they should be treated.

Linda's main concern, though, is the form or structure of business she should choose. Is the restaurant area a good place to start a business? Is there profit in running a restaurant?

SMALL BUSINESS: FORM AND STRUCTURE

Linda is wondering whether she should start her own proprietorship, or look into a partnership and/or corporation. She has projected sales goals for the first year of $600,000, with profits of $30,000; for the second year of $650,000, with profits of $36,000; and for the third year of $700,000, with profits of $45,000. Her turnkey costs to start a business would be $250,000. Linda has only $16,000 saved with which to start the business; she figures that she would have to borrow an additional $34,000 to $44,000 before she could even obtain a loan from a bank to reach the rest.

Questions

1. Should Linda start into business?
2. In starting a restaurant business, what would be the advantages and disadvantages of:
   a. sole proprietorship?
   b. partnership?
   c. corporation?
3. What would you do if you were in Linda's position?

Chapter Questions:

1. Discuss the importance of personal and family involvement in a business.
2. Why are the attitudes held by the small business owner important?
3. Which form of small business organization is best suited for you? Why?
4. Does one type of small business make more money than another? Why or why not?

Photo courtesy of Irene Springer, Prentice-Hall, Inc.

3

THE SMALL BUSINESS: A CAST OF CHARACTERS

Chapter Objectives:

1. To understand that it takes a wide variety of persons to make a successful business.
2. To identify the personality characteristics of successful entrepreneurs.
3. To learn about those traits that help to make a successful manager.
4. To understand the importance and usefulness of promoters and suppliers.
5. To distinguish between the different roles of inventors and partners.
6. To realize the usefulness of employees and families.

Real opportunities lie within a person, not outside. What lies behind you and what lies before you are tiny matters compared to what lies within you.

Ralph Waldo Emerson

INCIDENT: Lou has just bought the property to begin construction of his lifetime dream restaurant. The Gridiron Restaurant is going to be a steakhouse specializing in barbecued steaks, mashed potatoes, salads, and a special blueberry muffin. He had originally thought that the $240,000 he had raised would be sufficient to cover the opening costs plus three months operations, but he now wonders if this initial outlay will even allow him to open his business. He wonders if he should get a full-time manager to help run the business in addition to his wife and himself. He knows that he needs to hire an outstanding chef, but nobody within the city is qualified. Lou wonders if he will have to obtain an additional partner to the silent partner he already has in order to raise additional capital. Although he has commitments with different suppliers for his food products, he is not sure of their performance or their reliability to deliver, and he is worried about the small inventory that he can afford or even have space for in his kitchen. He is finding it difficult to find good employees, waiters and waitresses who will work for only their tips.

Lou is caught up in the entrepreneurial dream of starting and running his own business, while also experiencing the entrepreneurial nightmare of not having sufficient capital, equipment, and employees to be able to profitably run the business. His idea for a steakhouse that is centered on a football theme is unique, and is appropriate for a football-crazed town. The theme will be well carried out through the decor. Lou wants to be able to spend a little more money to get the very best, but does not know if he can even afford the moderately priced equipment and furnishings necessary to establish his business.

Lou has realized that, without additional capital, he will be unable to have the basics of his dream. He has used his persuasive abilities to add an additional partner to his business, as well as to raise additional capital from his family. He has convinced his suppliers to extend him credit during the first few months of operations, and he has possibly found a manager, experienced in restaurant operations, in a town 500 miles away.

The quarterback takes the snap from center, steps back into the pocket formed by the offensive linemen, and throws a completed pass to the split end, who is sprinting downfield for a thirty-five-yard touchdown. To accomplish this, the quarterback had to be able to read the defensive alignment, call the offensive play, understand the capabilities of his teammates, and perform to the best of his own ability. The quarterback is interested not only in executing the perfect play, but in avoiding personal injury and winning the game. Extensive training and experience

SMALL BUSINESS: A CAST OF CHARACTERS

are necessary to bring together the various individuals and their respective positions to form a smooth and integrated working team.

It is critical that the owner of a small business be able to accurately identify and understand the individuals who are necessary to maintain the smooth operations of a firm. Just as in sports, the manager must continually evaluate the strengths and weaknesses of the entire organization. Substitutions will be needed. It is necessary to know every character and player on your "team"—and to use them.

There is a cast of characters that is required to develop a successful small business. The entrepreneur is not alone as he or she first creates, then develops, and finally expands a small business. Other individuals are vitally important to any growth and success of the business enterprise.

It is important to analyze those functions that individuals must perform in order for an organization to function properly. Individuals who are important to the complete business team include:

1. The entrepreneur.
2. The manager.
3. The promoter.
4. The inventor.
5. The partner.
6. The supplier.
7. The employees.
8. The consultant.
9. The spouse and the family.

These individuals and others will help make or destroy the business opportunity. (See Table 3-1.)

The Entrepreneur

The small business entrepreneur, like the quarterback calling his own plays, must succeed or be replaced. The quarterback directs his own organization, faces stiff competition, and needs to be innovative and creative in order to overcome horrendous obstacles. The entrepreneur also needs to develop, to watch the company grow and advance, and to overcome pressing crises. They both need to score, and they both need to win.

Many organizations—as well as various individuals such as students and dreamers—will investigate the opportunity and requirements necessary to open and develop a new business. The investigations, however, are simply feasibility studies. The final decision will rest with the businessperson who makes the final decision. This person—with the managerial insight, desire, and superordinate gut feeling to risk perhaps his or her entire life savings, job, or profession in order to assume the risk of starting a new business—is called the "entrepreneur."

The final decision to invest all the resources available to begin a new small

Table 3-1. Perceived Personality and Role Requirements of Cast of Characters

ROLE	PERSONALITY, CHARACTERISTICS	ROLE REQUIREMENTS
Entrepreneur	High gestalt, total feedback, adaptable strong drive, thinking ability, personal responsibility, growth oriented, medium-long time orientation.	Hard work, technical competence, long hours, innovative, creative, doer, controller.
Manager	Direct and motivate others, goal and profit oriented, required skills and expertise, decisive, cautious risk taker, short–medium time orientation.	Organization person, managerial competence, delegator, security oriented, routine work pattern.
Promoter	Super salesman, high risk taker, short time orientation, low ego-involvement, growth or sales increase oriented.	Organizer, short and intense work periods, high risk taker, innovative, creative.
Inventor	Recluse, creative, imaginative, persistent.	Strong imagination, limited team involvement, limited business-management skills.
Partner	High goal or profit orientation, long time orientation, moderate–high drive, builder works well with others.	Pool resources, using specialized skills, ability to work with partner(s).
Suppliers	Aggressive, low ego-involvement, adaptable, enthusiastic, friendly, persistent, knowledgeable about product.	Knowledge of field, able to help manager or entrepreneur, limited risk.
Employees	Loyal, courteous, energetic, some imagination, low risk takers, short–long range time orientation.	Hard working, accepts responsibilities, able to work with time constraints, sacrifice occasionally.
Consultants	Objective, specialized knowledge, experience.	Expert knowledge, available when needed, willing to listen, external viewpoint.
Spouse and Family	Belonging, being appreciated, doing meaningful things, growing, loving, feeling joy, work as a team, goal oriented.	Understanding, limited participation in business, desire to build family unity, maintain harmony, full participation in family.

business venture rests with the entrepreneur. Capable individuals must be hired and trained to be the work force in helping maintain the business. Managers need to be developed, but it is the entrepreneurs who will generally risk the most of their savings and fortunes, mortgage their homes, leave their former jobs, and go off to a new location to start a business for which they may easily be undercapitalized and understaffed.

While the large corporation may expand in fairly small increments, the small business will generally grow through either: (1) the creation of an entire new business, or (2) an expansionary program that may double or triple in sales volume. The small business does not generally follow the same small increments of growth found in large corporate establishments, nor is it feasible for the entrepreneur to develop needed managerial talent over a number of years. The requirement for management skills, talents, and expertise is apparent at the very start—on even the very first day of operation.

Let us focus on the characteristics of the entrepreneur. What are the traits or behavioral backgrounds that have a tendency to make a person into an enterprising person who desires to own or operate his or her own business? It is interesting to study successful entrepreneurs to understand what has enabled those individuals to build a business career. This method of study is often referred to as the "canary principle"—in order to study a canary, one needs to have a canary to study. The origins of the typical successful entrepreneur are varied and come from all walks of life. Successful entrepreneurs have parents whose principal occupations were unskilled, semiskilled, or skilled labor positions. Some parents were rich, some poor. Several successful entrepreneurs had a poor or underprivileged history as a child in their early family lives.

Many businesspeople argue that education provides an advantage for any entrepreneurial venture. Probably the only time when this is true is in the field of engineering or technological advances. Overall, the educational levels of small, successful entrepreneurs is highly varied. Educational background is equally distributed among entrepreneurs: some are without high school degrees, some have high school diplomas, some have had college courses, some are college graduates, and some have Master's or doctoral degrees. This is not to say that a college degree is of no value in determining and developing a successful entrepreneur. It is important, however, to realize that many individuals have become highly successful entrepreneurs regardless of the education or educational development they received in formal school training.

One factor that many researchers believe is related to the successful entrepreneurial experience is the age of an individual. The young claim that older entrepreneurs are taking advantage of their experience and competence developed in other job-related situations, while the old see the youth as inexperienced, unseasoned, and generally unfit to handle crisis situations. The truth of the situation may lie somewhere between these two extreme viewpoints, but the successful entrepreneur is generally not noted for a particular age. Ray Kroc began McDonald's when he was 52 years old, and Colonel Sanders started Kentucky Fried Chicken after he retired at the age of 65, but J. Willard Marriott started the Marriott Corporation when he was just out of school and in his twenties. Generally, the successful entrepreneur is in his or her thirties or forties, and has had some prior experience with the business that he or she is starting. This age may be a result of the difficulty older people find and face with unemployment or changing a work situation, while younger people find it easier to find another job or continue with their education. The capital and savings requirements necessary to start a business may require a more mature individual. Sex is not a category that may be used in determining a successful or unsuccessful entrepreneur. In recent years, women have become an increasingly larger proportion of the total work force. There is an increasingly higher proportion of women and minorities among the successful entrepreneurs today.

SUCCESS STORY: Erma Bombeck

Erma Bombeck, who used to talk to herself a lot, is the author of a thrice-weekly humor column, "At Wit's End" for 900 newspapers throughout the world. It is read by an estimated 31 million people.

Erma's career began in Dayton, Ohio, where she was born, raised, and educated. As a copy girl for the Dayton Journal Herald, she wrote obituaries and the weather forecast (her first bit of fiction). After five years with the women's department, she retired to stay at home and raise three children. In 1965, Glenn Thompson, executive editor, was responsible for putting her column on domesticity into syndication.

A graduate of the University of Dayton, Erma has authored three books for Doubleday: *At Wit's End, Just Wait Till You Have Children Of Your Own* (with Bill Keane), and *I Lost Everything In The Post-Natal Depression*. Her three books for McGraw-Hill have each been on the New York Times best seller list: *The Grass Is Always Greener Over The Septic Tank, If Life Is A Bowl Of Cherries—What Am I Doing In The Pits?* and *Aunt Erma's Cope Book*.

Women In Communications presented her the Headliner Award in 1969. In 1973, she received the Mark Twain Award given to the top humorist in the nation by the International Platform Association. She was named to the list of the twenty-five most Influential Women In America by The World Almanac in 1978 and 1979.

Erma holds four honorary doctorates, is a member of The Society of Professional Journalists, and was appointed by President Carter to serve on the President's Advisory Committee for Women when the committee was formed in 1978.

For the last four years, she has been a regular on ABC's "Good Morning, America."

When she is not making frequent appearances on the Tonight, Donahue, Mike Douglas, and Dinah shows, she makes her home with her husband, two sons, a daughter and a dog ("I have to keep him. He knows too much.") in Paradise Valley, Arizona.

Her hobby is dust.

While most demographic factors—such as sex, age, and geographical location—do not account for entrepreneurial characteristics, there are several indicators that do indicate possible success or failure among entrepreneurs. These characteristics may be easily summarized as the attitudes that individuals carry concerning their own lives. (See Table 3–2.)

Table 3-2. Entrepreneur/Manager Characteristics

CHARACTERISTICS	ENTREPRENEUR	MANAGER
Time Orientation	Medium to long range, will use years for growth projections 3–10 years planning.	Immediate to medium range, uses daily, weekly, monthly or annual reports to measure performance, seeking next performance.
Thinking	Abstract, high tolerance for ambiguity and uncertainty, creative, imaginative.	Concrete, absolute, low tolerance for ambiguity, seeks certainty, organizational.
Others Oriented	Self-oriented, seeks achievement for self.	Works with or manipulates others, desires power over others.
Risk Taking	Moderate risk taker, calculated risks appear low, will chance income and net worth.	Lower risk taker, has developed a conservative nature and will try to ensure a steady organization posture.
Structure	Is developing structure, informal, whatever is best for the situation, not very important.	Dependent upon structure for organization, formal, department lines of control very important to maintain operations.
Communication	Two-way, desirous of positive and negative feedback.	Most often one-way, seeks positive feedback.
Operations	Control figure, all operations and decisions will be made by this person.	A link in total organizations, a component part of the larger plan.
Managerial Skills	Limited, generally skilled in technical areas of business, often without formal management education.	Broad, highly developed, often has received formal management education, developed theoretical and practical base for managing.

Who is an entrepreneur? Are you an entrepreneur? Can anyone be an entrepreneur? To develop a personality profile of the entrepreneur, we will look at these major personality characteristics:

1. Gestalt.
2. Feedback.
3. Adaptability.
4. Drive.
5. Speaking and thinking ability.
6. Personal responsibility.
7. Growth orientation.

Understanding what is meant by these characteristics may help us to better understand the successful profile of businesspeople entering a new and exciting venture.

gestalt

Gestalt is a German expression meaning "to see as a whole." Most successful entrepreneurs have the ability to envision their business and its various components in a total picture. Many times it is difficult for a salesperson to clearly see the other various components of the business (manufacturing, distribution, purchasing, and the like). The successful entrepreneur has the ability to watch the server working with the cook, or the cocktail waiter or waitress working with the bartender, and seeing that they interact properly in order to provide good service to the customer. A high gestalt would allow one to visualize an accounting department working with a sales department, which would in turn work with production and purchasing areas. On the other hand, a low gestalt would only allow one to envision the immediate surroundings (such as bookkeeping only), or the immediate area of business where one sells or functions.

feedback

It is said that everyone likes to receive feedback on his or her performance but experience generally shows that people really only want positive feedback. Most managers are tuned to receiving positive feedback quite well, but because of the lack of negative feedback they receive, it is very difficult for them to not only solicit such feedback but to also adapt and change in response to such negative feedback.

The successful entrepreneur is different. He or she has the desire to hear both positive and negative feedback, and will at times solicit only the negative so as to know what to change and how to change. When many successful businesspeople lose a sale, they will go directly to the phone and call the client company's president and directly ask, "Why did we lose the sale?" The successful individual will investigate and seek direct feedback, which will help to improve his or her position for the future.

The successful entrepreneur appears to be an individual who solicits both positive and negative feedback, and uses that feedback to improve his or her business' position.

adaptability

The successful entrepreneur is very adaptable. The information received through feedback systems is generally utilized to improve the situation: "If this is the way the situation actually is, then I will change this thing and that thing so we will be more competitive and will be able to obtain a larger market share."

The successful entrepreneur can often see crises or problems as opportunities. If the market were to tell the entrepreneur that the business should be selling chicken rather than steaks, then he or she should probably take a drastic turn and change the goal and/or the product in order to obtain a more favorable business position. (Inventors, scholars, and advertising people are often fixated by their products or ideas; it is very difficult for them to be adaptable in a changing situation, and therefore it is quite difficult for them to become successful entrepreneurs.)

drive

The successful entrepreneur has an inordinate amount of drive; he or she works hard. Work is almost the same as play. The needs and wants of such a person are generally so high in regard to being a successful businessperson that it is difficult for him or her to divert energy and desires to other pursuits. The drive function includes vigor, help, desire, and need. The person is generally driven toward success by a desire to accomplish, against all odds, and to be successful regardless of the circumstances. It would be advisable to allow other people to supply feedback to the would-be entrepreneur that is relative to his or her level of drive and desire.

speaking and thinking ability

Speaking and thinking ability is concerned with creative thinking, experimentation, and analytical thinking processes. The successful entrepreneur possesses these traits. The successful entrepreneur is basically neither a high risk taker nor a low risk taker; rather, he or she is a moderate one. If asked about risk taking in relation to the business, he or she would probably say that there is very little, if any at all, because he or she has thought through all possible problems and crises that may arise. This person may be able to easily relate how and why his or her business has become highly successful: He or she has thought through the entire process and has been able to think in a very concise and encompassing fashion, which allows for a complete understanding of the business. After all the work, he or she perceives the risk to be very low.

personal responsibility

The entrepreneur needs to be in control. He or she is quite often driven by power, and has a desire to be able to say, after the work has been accomplished, "I did it," or, "I made that happen." The entrepreneur seeks personal responsibility. He or she wants to be able to control the people, the economy, and other factors that would influence his or her business. The success or failure of that business will be entirely dependent upon himself or herself. If others were involved and the business was highly successful, the choosing and hiring of those others would give the entrepreneur reason to feel proud and successful in having been able to control the situation. If someone feels that what happens to his or her business is entirely up to God, fate, the economy, luck, or government control, then he or she is not taking total responsibility.

growth orientation

The successful entrepreneur tends to be growth oriented rather than profit oriented. Most entrepreneurs dream of the growth curve, and of the continued success that is illustrated by increasing sales. The entrepreneur will often not accept profit as an indication of success, because that is simply an accounting term that can easily be changed through accounting methods. These people do not trust profit alone. The growth or expansion of the business becomes the utmost concern. The business is not successful if it simply maintains its steady sales picture over a number of years. Rather, the entrepreneur is measuring his or her own personal success by watching the growth or expansion of the business that he or she controls.

The qualities just described are found in different successful entrepreneurs at various levels. Not *all* successful entrepreneurs are high in *all* of these characteristics, but *most* successful entrepreneurs possess at least *some* of these characteristics in fairly high quantities.

The Manager

The diver climbs the steps of the platform, watches the crowd, receives the signal from the judges, envisions the dive, and steps forward to execute it. Each step, each motion, has already been arranged and established on the checklist for this particular dive. Long hours have been spent on training and exercise. The diver is about to execute a plan that has been painstakingly prepared over the years. The diver does not want to be hurt, and cannot afford to miss. The diver has limited the risks, and will be the sole manager of the dive.

The manager is responsible for planning, organizing, staffing, directing, controlling, financing, and coordinating the business. While the entrepreneur generally has a strong desire to create and start his or her own business, the manager is primarily responsible for seeing that the business continues along its predetermined path. The manager will be responsible for seeing that his or her division or department maintains the proper level of activity in the business operations.

There are certain personal characteristics that help to define a profile of the manager:

1. Being able to direct and motivate.
2. Being goal oriented.
3. Possessing required skills and expertise.
4. Being decisive.
5. Being a cautious risk taker.

The manager is the individual who is formally in charge of a particular operation of a business: a department, shop, location, or whatever. The manager is distinguished by the formal authority that the position possesses. The manager will generally not make the firm's product nor provide services directly to the customers of the firm, but he or she will take full responsibility to see that all actions associated with these processes are accomplished. The manager's job is to see that the job gets done, and to follow the directions or to accomplish the tasks that the owner has assigned to him or her.

being able to direct and motivate

One of the main functions of any manager is to direct and motivate workers toward the accomplishment of organizational goals or tasks. The manager needs to possess the interpersonal skills necessary to see that others accomplish the organizational objectives. Most good managers have an ability to integrate the needs of the individual employee with the goals and objectives of the organization. They are also able to highly motivate individuals within the organization so that they successfully accomplish their given roles.

being goal oriented

The manager generally works within organizational goals. He or she may have the opportunity to help establish those goals, but the manager's success and/or failure is often measured by the ability of his or her work group to satisfactorily accomplish business goals. The manager is responsible for seeing that the organization serves its basic purpose of efficiently producing its goods or services. Most organizational goals will also include maintaining stability of the organization's operations. The manager needs to be a decision maker, and needs to be able to establish goals that will properly ensure the high performance and standards of the organization for which he or she works.

possessing required skills and expertise

Most managers need certain skills or expertise before they are called into their positions. The supervisor of an assembly line generally needs some knowledge of the proper handling and production of the assembly-line operations. Almost all successful race-car drivers have a high mechanical skill level, and are able to easily recognize problems and make suggestions for corrections in their cars and automotive equipment.

being decisive

Due to the manager's given authority, he or she serves as a figurehead for the organization. The manager is a symbol of the organization, and is responsible for the behavior of the individuals within that organization. Associated with the position and its authority is the requirement that a good manager be decisive; that is, be able to utilize the scarce information he or she has, and make decisions. Although it is almost impossible to obtain perfect information about any business endeavor, it is important that—through training, skill, and experience—the manager become a decision maker for his or her organization. The manager needs to be able to make a decision and to make it quickly—often at times without as much information as he or she would prefer.

being a cautious risk taker

As an organization develops and grows, it becomes more apparent that a rational, decentralized organizational structure is required, and departmentalization will occur. The organizational objectives and goals will become more defined, and the market-oriented products will have clear and limited channels of distribution. In order to fulfill his or her function, the manager now will develop written records and policy, will employ a full staff complement, and will endeavor to create a value structure that is consistent throughout the organization. The entrepreneur and the manager may be the same person. However, the role of risk taker changes greatly as the business grows. The increase in structure, planning, and control of an organization will necessitate a reduction in risk and uncertainty. The manager who will skillfully drive through the environmental traps and limitations enforced upon the organization will almost certainly have to be a cautious risk taker.

The manager is generally using funds from other people, technical capabilities that others have designed, and the goodwill and reputation of the organization that has already been established. This will tend to increase conservatism, and will cause a successful manager to have lower risk-taking potential. Such cautiousness will often tend to require that the firm now expand externally, through acquisition and merger, rather than through creative and experimental products or services. The self-confident manager will try to increase the sales and the marketability of existing products while maintaining a profitable business under existing conditions and controls. Little time will be devoted to creativity or experimentation due to the severe time and business constraints placed upon the manager.

The manager is a unique individual whose functions are to: (1) *plan,* or determine the business goals and objectives of his or her organizational unit or department; (2) *organize,* or set up functions and departments of workers who can easily establish a work group and can produce a satisfactory good or service; (3) *staff,* or be in charge of the recruitment, selection, training, and development of personnel within his or her organizational unit; (4) *direct,* or provide leadership and supervision in the organization or department where he or she is responsible for the operating functions; (5) *control,* or periodically review the performance, as it relates to standards already established, without causing delay or excessive costs; (6) *finance,* or develop unit budgets and allocation of funds within a particular department that are necessary for the production and distribution of goods and services; and (7) *coordinate,* or schedule activities and tasks within the organization, to provide a minimum amount of downtime or loss time while maximizing the sales of goods or services.

The Promoter

The promoter is vital to a growth-oriented business. The promoter's main focus is centered around the increased sales or marketing of his or her goods or services. He or she usually has little to do with managerial or entrepreneurial experience. The promoter is primarily divorced from any day-to-day operations of the business, and spends most of his or her time contacting outside sources and individuals who might be interested in procuring his or her product.

The promoter is generally characterized as a supersalesperson, with an ability to meet with others and leave them with a desire to purchase his or her goods or services. The promoter is generally a high risk taker, and finds it easy to accept temporary failure. He or she often has a low ego involvement with the business, and finds it very easy to dismiss possible failures. Yet, the promoter is quite highly motivated for personal success, and wants to achieve growth through continued effort for both the company and self.

Unlike the entrepreneur or the manager, the promoter is often referred to as a "short-timer." The promoter's time orientation is in the present or the near future. He or she seeks the immediate sales and increased volume. His or her approach is generally a shot-gun one, in which he or she delivers all the advantages and opportunities his or her product has to the potential customer. The promoter places all his or her eggs in one basket, knowing that there may be only one opportunity to sell the product.

The promoter generally sees his or her success in the volume of sales or services. The promoter is not concerned with the organizational structure or with the building of the business entity; he or she is concerned with immediate increases in sales and growth.

The Inventor

Many businesses start as a result of an inventor's new product or patentable idea. The person responsible for this new creation is referred to as the inventor. It is the inventor who is responsible for today's automobiles, radios, stereos, computers, and digital watches. Almost all of these products were originally made in small shops by the inventor and his or her aides. It was not until later that the entrepreneur came along to use these ideas in the creation of new business firms, which would often later grow into large corporate giants.

The inventor is often considered a creative, imaginative individual. This person has had a goal or idea that he or she believes will make life easier or better. Inventors tend to be highly persistent, and they generally have a large amount of confidence in themselves. Inventors are often referred to as loners or recluses, but this is primarily because of the time and long hours they spend working on their projects and inventions.

The inventor, like the promoter, has little time for managerial or entrepreneurial activities. He or she generally has a very limited, short-term perspective, which requires long and devoted hours in the development of his or her ideas. If the inventor's idea is ever completed or developed, he or she will generally turn to others to help promote, develop, manufacture, or manage the enterprise. The inventor of a flexible night light for receiving docks only sold sufficient quantities of the product to ensure a modest annual income. Although the idea was patented, it was not marketed widely until an entrepreneur came along and developed the idea of selling the product on a mass scale. Once the invention has been created and developed and is being mass marketed, the inventor usually goes back to the drawing board to work on new and advanced models, techniques, or products.

The Partner

A partnership has been formulated when two or more individuals pool their capital and skills as co-owners to form a business organization (see Chapter 2, "The Partnership"). The partner provides ideas, money, or a combination of the two.

The general partner is one who shares in the total liability, responsibility, and management of the business. He or she is responsible for all dealings of the business, and is held personally liable for any actions of the business. There is also an arrangement known as a limited partnership, which is regulated by the laws of the state in which one resides and operates his or her business. The limited partner is generally an investor who does not assume unlimited liability. This person's risk is generally limited to his or her original investment, along with any other stipulations that may be made in a partnership or agreement. Such a partner, though, also has very limited, if any, control over the activities of the partnership. The limited partner is usually not permitted to participate in the management of the firm in any way, although they may be employees of the firm.

The partner generally has a high goal or profit orientation. He or she is usually involved in the business to receive substantial outcomes. The partner often realizes the necessity for long-term involvement, and is willing to wait and work for the growth and establishment of the business. Partners tend to have moderate to high drive strengths, and are often able to work well with others and enjoy having others be inputs and resource persons in their decision-making capacities. Most partners are builders, and have a desire to increase the return on their investment. Partners generally rely on one another for the specialized skills each may possess, and they realize the advantages of pooling the resources of more than one individual.

The Supplier

One of the most important, yet often overlooked careers in the business scene is the supplier. The supplier is the one who will provide the raw goods or services necessary as inputs of a business. If one is going to establish a fast-food restaurant, it is important that one be able to obtain the hamburger, tomatoes, napkins, plates, spoons, grease, and soft drinks to be sold in the business establishment. One may deal with only one supplier or with many, depending upon one's situation. One may wish to use competition between suppliers providing the same product in order to reduce costs or increase performance to one's business. The meat supplier may be able to grind the meat into hamburger patties and even freeze them before delivering them to one's establishment. One of the deciding factors in choosing between restaurant suppliers may be the freezing process they use. Many suppliers will offer sample goods or "freebies" to entice a potential client to buy from their particular business.

The supplier is generally characterized by enthusiasm, friendliness, an outgoing personality, and even persistence. He or she tends to be aggressive in nature, and capable of perceiving limited failure. The supplier is often quite knowledgeable about the product's advantages, uses, and limitations, and is capable of using this knowledge in providing advice to customers. Most suppliers will try to adapt their product to the manager's or entrepreneur's needs, and will be able to meet any and every objection either may have. The supplier is often a specialist in his or her field, and may be the most knowledgeable person about the product he or she provides.

Because of the tendency of certain suppliers to reduce their costs in the face of competition, it is important for a businessperson to "shop around," and find the very best suppliers for the raw goods. It would also be valuable to be familiar with two or three suppliers with the same product, in case of any inability of the main supplier to provide the good or service needed for one's business.

The Employees

A successful business is highly dependent upon the employees working in that business. It is important to recruit, select, and retain employees who will add to the assets of a business. Employees should be able to perform those duties and functions that will increase business and profitability.

Ideal employee characteristics are loyalty, courtesy, hard work, imagination, and ability to work with others. Most employees are low risk takers, and their involvement in the business will be as a principal means of income and support for their families. Certain employees will be involved with the business for a very short time, while others will consider the business to be their work for their entire lifetimes.

Employees often do not have a need to develop managerial skills and techniques. They are also not required to have the basic managerial skills such as being able to direct and motivate others, being decisive, and having the required skills and expertise prerequisite for most managers or entrepreneurs. Many employees are not management oriented, and they do not seek responsibility.

The Consultant

Small business owners are typically very highly independent and self-satisfying individuals. Most will claim full responsibility for the success or failure of their businesses. Generally, these owners will greatly rely on their own initiatives, experiences, and enterprise to make a shoestring operation grow into maturity and become a very profitable business. Small business owners will often receive the respect of customers, suppliers, employees, and the community because of their success. However, this characteristic can also be a major detriment when one is faced with the necessity for additional professional advice and direction.

The consultant is a professional outsider who brings along professional expertise and knowledge. The consultant is usually aware of the managerial tools and techniques that large successful business ventures use. The professional consultant thereby provides advice and service to help overcome trouble spots and to improve performance of the business.

The successful consultant is generally characterized by high self-confidence, high objectivity, specialized knowledge, and expertise in the field represented. The professional consultant tends to focus on managerial competence within the organization. He or she often sees similar problems crop up continually in many businesses.

Five major categories of consultants are available to any small business owner, and need to be periodically used by the manager or entrepreneur. (See Table 3–3.) These categories are: (1) the *accountant,* one who is able to establish bookkeeping and tax systems; (2) the *attorney,* who will provide help in choosing business format and in meeting governmental regulations; (3) the *banker,* who can provide loans and financial knowledge; (4) the *insurance agent or broker,* who can evaluate insurance needs and retirement packages; and (5) the *managerial or marketing consultant,* who specializes in helping with managerial or marketing and advertising problems.

The Spouse and the Family

The young couple held their breath as they watched their daughter lunge toward the big chair. She did not make it. She fell, picked herself up, and took two major steps toward reaching that chair. The child looked around toward her parents and smiled,

Table 3-3. Consultants and Their Services

CONSULTANT	SERVICES PROVIDED	WHERE TO FIND
Accountant	Provide financial statements, balance sheets, income statements, cash flow. May help develop inventory control and record-keeping systems. Often aware of financial opportunities and resources. Will develop tax returns and cash-handling systems.	Other businessmen, bankers and attorneys may provide valuable assistance in recommending accountants and accounting systems. Fees vary according to services provided and size of accounting firm. It is best to shop around. Listed in the Yellow Pages.
Management/ Marketing	Helpful in establishing managerial controls and operations. Able to see entire business from outside viewpoint. May develop advertising and marketing plans. Useful in seeing hidden problems. Familiar with competition and industry.	Assistance is available from professional firms, government and universities/colleges. Seek recommendations from friends, business associates and trade organizations. Government and educational institutions often provide free services. Listed in the Yellow Pages.
Attorney	Valuable in establishing corporation and partnerships. Expert in contracts, leases and supplier agreememts. May provide tax and financial advice. Available to handle local, state, and federal regulations.	Fields of expertise vary among attorneys. Ask associates for advice. Local bar associations may arrange for initial consultation. Fees vary according to service: one-half hour consultation $15–$30; incorporation $350–$700. Listed in the Yellow Pages.
Insurance	Will develop insurance portfolio—life, fire, liability, criminal, automotive, fidelity bonds, and "key person"—for specific business. Comprehensive coverage available.	Will be either an independent (working with several insurance companies) agent or a direct writer (employed by one specific company). Talk with several agents about comprehensive and partial insurance plans. Companies and state laws differ. Listed in Yellow Pages.
Bankers	Valuable financial knowledge. Desirous of seeing your business grow and prosper. Generally funds available for conservative loans. Will provide financial services and advice. Recommend other institutions or individuals who may be helpful.	Bankers close to business or handling personal bank account generally have priority. Shop around and seek best advice, service, and rates. Develop a continuing business relationship. Listed in Yellow Pages.

seeking and waiting for the approval that only parents can give.

One of the happiest times that an entrepreneur, manager, or any businessperson has is sharing the goals, ideas, and successes that he or she has achieved with the family. The family should be an intricate part in the decision-making process of the businessperson. There is usually a happier and more harmonious relationship within the family when goals and desires are shared and appreciated.

Any businessperson needs to feel appreciated and important. People seek fulfillment and an awareness that they are doing meaningful things. One of the greatest sources of appreciation and awareness comes from the family. All individuals, including partners and peer group members, may provide appreciation and a sense of achievement, but the family provides additional comfort and support to the businessperson. A happy and successful family may be characterized by individuals pulling together as a team or a partnership. While family members may have their differences of opinion, they need to be able to work them out and refrain from allowing things to develop into a power struggle—a win-or-lose situation. The family can identify and develop conditions in which a businessperson can feel a sense of belonging, being appreciated, accomplishing meaningful things, and growing in the job and in life.

Many businesses are family partnerships. Both wife and husband work together in providing goods or services for customers. This allows the individuals to work closely with one another, to be dependent upon one another, and to grow while helping the others who provide their income. They will often have separate responsibilities. This partnership, like any other, needs to provide and establish successful goals and seek to achieve them. There is a need to set new goals as old ones are accomplished. Once a particular goal is established, it is necessary to reach out and stretch in striving to establish and reach the following goal.

The spouse or family may be the source of the drive or inner inspiration for the businessperson. The spouse and the family are intricate players needed to provide a complete cast to the business play. Without the complete cast of players, it would be impossible to bring about a complete and successful production. The family may take a leading part, or it may be the painter of the background scenery, but it is a vital link to the success or completion of the business play.

Summary

There is a variety of individuals necessary for the proper functioning of a successful small business. This cast of characters, required for the smooth running of a small enterprise, includes: (1) the entrepreneur, (2) the manager, (3) the promoter, (4) the inventor, (5) the partner, (6) the supplier, (7) the employees, (8) the consultant, and (9) the spouse and the family. It is important that one look around and use those individuals who have the characteristics and skills that would benefit one's business.

CASE STUDY: Ice Cream Parlor and Restaurant

Although Emperor Nero, Marco Polo, and Charles I of England helped develop the delicious delicacy known as ice cream, Tracy hopes to bring an ice cream parlor and restaurant (seating over 200 people) to Lubbock, Texas.

business plan

Goods and services provided. The strength of the ice cream parlor and restaurant is to be centered around a family atmosphere and a friendly spirit. The food menu is to be divided into two parts: (a) the ice cream menu, and (b) the kitchen menu (food items). The ice cream items will range from sundaes of all varieties, through a wide assortment of ice cream dishes, to a spectacular mountain of ice cream that serves fifteen or more adults. The kitchen menu will be comprised of an assortment of sandwiches, and will also include special varieties of hamburgers and hot dogs. Food items will be designed to fit a family during the lunch or dinner hours, as well as provide snack and party items throughout the day and the evening.

The service is to be designed around an ice cream parlor motif of the 1890s. The service will provide fun for both young and old, and will allow for the singing of birthday songs and for special party demonstrations.

Market opportunity. The ice cream parlor and restaurant will be located at the South Plains Mall, the most desirable market area in Lubbock, and includes what is basically a county area, with a current average of more than 40 percent of the mall's visitors coming from outside of Lubbock's city area. Additional areas will be developed within Lubbock's metropolitan area.

Promotion. The initial promotional techniques will be provided by inviting the various civic, city, county, and Chamber of Commerce people to a free preopening event. In addition, several children from the surrounding day-care centers will be invited to a special preopening day, during which free ice cream and prizes will be given. The advertising will be aimed at developing a friendly and family atmosphere in the Lubbock area.

Competition. There is no major direct competition within the Lubbock area and surrounding counties. There are other ice cream stores specializing in the sale of ice cream cones and dipped ice cream, but they will probably not adversely affect this operation. However, as a fast-food service, there will be competition within the mall, which will include Chick Fil-A, Orange Julius, and two hamburger stores. Other competition within a mile radius of the South Plains Mall includes various pizza parlors, a McDonald's, a Kentucky Fried Chicken, a Long John Silver's, a Taco Bell, and various hamburger stands. But due to the *family* and friendly atmosphere of the ice cream parlor and restaurant, there should be a tremendous competitive edge. This form of ice cream parlor and restaurant has been successful throughout the western part of the United States; it is moving rapidly, and is opening in areas of the eastern United States. The ice cream parlor and restaurant should appeal to all segments of the market, and should create a demand for its products and services (see Income Statement and Balance Sheet below).

Management and organization. The ice cream parlor and restaurant will provide an additional eighty employment opportunities in the Lubbock area. Tracy is proud of the managerial and marketing expertise of the owners and he will be using outside restaurant consultants. He anticipates fantastic managerial and organizational opportunities in the ice cream parlor and restaurant.

MONTHLY INCOME STATEMENT

	AUGUST
Sales	$60,000
Cost of goods sold (40%)	24,000
Gross margin	36,000
Operating expenses:	
Salaries	2,170
Wages	8,636
Rent	2,813
Mall fees	282
Utilities	500
Telephone	20
Advertising	500
Taxes—income, social security	727
Maintenance	150
Laundry	50
Insurance	277
	16,125
Net income from operations	19,875
Interest and repayment	5,200
Net income	$14,675

BALANCE SHEET

Current assets		
Cash	$ 81,000	
Merchandise inventory	8,000	
Fixed assets		
Fixtures and equipment	65,000	
Remodeling and improvements	96,000	
Total assets		$250,000
Current liabilities		
Notes payable	$210,000	
Owner's equity	40,000	
Total equity		$250,000

Questions

1. Who are the cast of characters that will be necessary to make this business successful?
2. How many different supplies will be required?
3. How would you raise the money necessary for the business?

Chapter Questions:

1. Do you see yourself as more of a manager or an entrepreneur?
2. There are more managers in the world than entrepreneurs. What do you think is the reason for this?
3. Why would a supplier know more about the product than a retail manager? Is the supplier's knowledge of any value to the manager?
4. How would you use the various characters in your business to augment your sales?
5. What are some areas of family life that may support or limit your business opportunities?
6. Of what value are your employees to you as a manager?
7. List some reasons why small business owners are often unable to bring together the total cast necessary for the smooth functioning of a business.

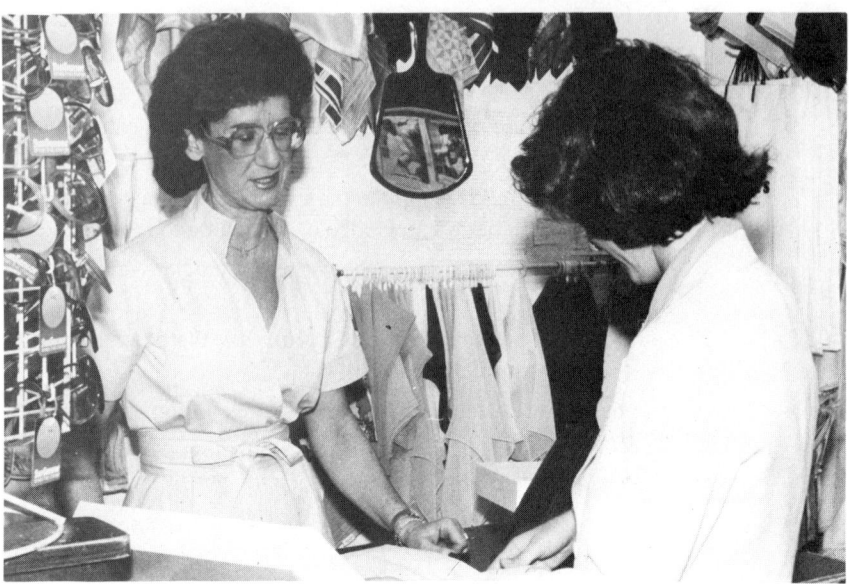

Photo courtesy of Irene Springer, Prentice-Hall, Inc.

4

YOU AND SMALL BUSINESS

Chapter Objectives:

1. To better understand the involvement of the owner and/or manager in the small business.
2. To learn about personal characteristics and objectives of small business owners.
3. To discover and understand the personal commitments required in small business.
4. To learn about employee profiles in business.
5. To review the occupational groupings and educational levels of business owners.

*You have not done enough, you've never done enough,
so long as you have something more to contribute.*

              Dag Hammerskjold

Make the most of yourself, for that is all there is to you.

              Ralph Waldo Emerson

INCIDENT: Jane wants to open a shoe store. Her three children are in seventh, eighth, and tenth grades. Jane has never owned a business, nor has she ever worked in a small business. She is a very successful homemaker. She has some friends who own a shoe store, but they are moving out of the state to relocate their business in a larger population center. They own a shoe store in the downtown area, around the corner from one of the most prosperous banks in the state (where Jane's husband works). This shoe store sells primarily men's and women's casual shoes. Their store lease is $300 a month, or $3,600 a year. After modest salaries, they cleared about $6,000 profit during the last two years.

  Jane thinks she can be an excellent businesswoman. She knows she could be a success. She has talked to her husband and her friends about buying out the business. Her friends want $20,000 for all the inventory, the business name, and the lease rights associated with their business.

  The more Jane thinks about it, the more she wants to buy the business. She is willing to make the sacrifices at home, and she is willing to make the sacrifices at work. She wants to start the business.

  You want to go into business. You want to own your own business. You are not the only one. Every year, hundreds of thousands of Americans try to start and run their own businesses. They feel that they have an idea, a product, or a service that consumers need and want, and they "think" the customer will buy.

  In addition to the hundreds of thousands who start their own businesses, there are a million others who wish to own their own businesses. However, they put it off, and will probably never go into business. People are repeatedly drawn to the idea of starting and managing their own businesses. For many, it becomes an obsession—almost a disease. These people are known as "businessaholics." These individuals believe that in their own businesses they will find freedom of thought and action. They hope to be successful, to acquire more money than they would elsewhere, and to have other people work for them. On the other hand, many individuals are turned off by these desires and thoughts.

Personal Appraisal

Are you ready for business? Is business ready for you? The decision to go into business for yourself is yours and yours alone. The decision to start your own business is one of the most important decisions you will ever make. Once you have committed yourself, it will be very difficult to get out or stop. Most people who do leave their own businesses do so because of failure or bankruptcy. A business failure can wipe you out, not only for the present, but also for many years into the future. You should try to analyze and develop your own conclusion about starting the business.

After you have discussed your business opportunities with friends and relatives and have received their wholehearted encouragement, it is time to stop and think about yourself and small business. Is it true that, just because those closest to you believe you will be a business success, others, including the consumer, will also find your business idea worthwhile? You should be able to tell people what your business will do in the marketplace or for others as well as what your business—your own marketplace—can offer you.

If you see your business career as one with a secure and fixed income, obtained from an eight-hour day from 8 A.M. or 9 A.M. to 4 P.M. or 5 P.M. with little responsibility or chance of failure and a warm blanket of security wrapped around you, then you had better not plan on starting your own business. However, if you think you do have a head for business, a high degree of self-confidence, an ability to achieve and to feel positively about long and hard working hours, and a desire for personal responsibility, then your own small business may be for you.

personal advantages

There are many advantages to owning and managing your own business. These and other advantages should have a strong personal attraction to you before you can enter your business. A list of business advantages should at least include:

1. Being your own boss: being independent, not being subordinate to others, and relying upon your own talents and abilities.
2. The possibility of obtaining wealth: an experience in which your own income level is determined by your own work and productivity and is not dependent upon a fixed salary scale.
3. A feeling of personal worth, achievement, recognition and prestige; a recognition of accomplishment.
4. An opportunity to develop your own idea, product, or service; a chance to work at something you enjoy, a desire to build, doing personally satisfying work.
5. Opportunity to be better: a challenge to be better than the competition and to do that where others have not been successful.
6. A chance to develop security: to establish a business in which your entire family could work and/or later own and operate.
7. Doing something good for humanity: an opportunity to provide a needed good or service and to satisfy the wants and needs of consumers; to do something good for others.

YOU AND SMALL BUSINESS

Business management is both an art and science. It is also logical and emotional, or objective and subjective. Successful business owners start their businesses with a strong combination of logic and emotion. The successful business owner cannot always operate on only one or the other—there is a need for a combination of both.

personal disadvantages

While there are many strong attractions and desires of going into business, it is important to also look at the drawbacks or disadvantages. There are several major drawbacks that you should personally consider and investigate before starting any business. These should at least include:

1. You can fail: you can lose your own investment, and the money of friends or relatives as well.
2. Successful small business owners do not have an eight-hour workday: your workday will dramatically increase to at least ten or twelve hours per day, six days a week. Many people will work fourteen and sixteen hours a day during peak sales periods.
3. Incomes vary: just as most small business sales vary from one month to the next, many business owners are forced to vary their personal draw or income depending upon business success.
4. The responsibility is yours: the weight of running and owning a small business has often crushed many people. The decisions, problems, and responsibilities associated with business dealings often weigh the average person down.
5. You still have a boss: customers, suppliers, and other dealers now become your new bosses. ("The customer is always right.")
6. Lack of time: the business will require nearly all of your time, and will deny you time for friends, family, or other associates.
7. You may not like your business: many small business owners have learned to dislike or even hate their own businesses after three or five years, but they do not sell, move, or change businesses easily.

While several hundreds of thousands of businesses start each year, there is almost an equal number that either fail or discontinue, and many more change that ownership or control. The business owner takes risks. These risks are very similar to those of the gambler who uses his or her time, energy, and money in striving to obtain riches. The business owner, however, generally uses a product or service to obtain his or her success. The gambler, using the same tools as a small business owner, relies on luck, odds, and intuition. Due to greater business know-how and customer needs, the business owner generally has "luck" on his or her side.

Business is a contest, a gamble. The business owner must learn to place his or her skills, talents, and abilities against the environment and the desires of consumers or customers. Most businesses fail because of personal or managerial errors. These errors may be due to lack of experience, poor location, lack of capital, poor merchandise, or simply choosing the wrong business endeavor. A person should study his or her own abilities and desires before going into business.

Requirements for Business Success

There are five essential ingredients for business success. When properly mixed, these ingredients will cause a business to rise and be successful. These ingredients are: (1) the right person, (2) proper business experience, (3) the right business opportunity, (4) a business plan or feasibility study, and (5) sufficient capital.

the right person The most critical ingredient in any business is the right business owner. The business owner is the business. The owner is going to be the motivating force and major worker in the business. Do you want to be that person?

Before deciding to enter the business field, an individual should look closely at himself or herself and ask: Am I willing to commit myself to the time, energy, study, and money necessary to get into business? Am I a self-starter? Am I a good worker? Do I like to organize things? Am I willing to take responsibility? Can I lead others? Is my health good?

Generally people can accurately analyze themselves by determining (a) if they work hard, (b) have prior accomplishments, (c) can think logically and unemotionally, and (d) are able to work well and motivate others.

Personal self-assessment may be made by answering the questions in Figure 4–1. This table helps an individual think about working in a business environment. It provides good insights into the capabilities of individuals especially interested in going into small business.

CHECKLIST FOR GOING INTO BUSINESS

Are you a self-starter?
_____ I do things on my own. Nobody has to tell me to get going.
_____ If someone gets me started, I keep going all right.
_____ Easy does it. I do not put myself out until I must.

How do you feel about other people?
_____ I like people. I can get along with just about anybody.
_____ I have plenty of friends—I do not need anyone else.
_____ Most people irritate me.

Can you lead others?
_____ I can get most people to go along when I start something.
_____ I can give orders if someone tells me what should be done.
_____ I let someone else get things moving. Then I go along if I feel like it.

Can you take responsibility?
_____ I like to take charge of things and see them through.
_____ I will take over if I have to, but I would rather let someone else be responsible.
_____ There is always some "eager beaver" around wanting to show how smart he or she is.

CHECKLIST FOR GOING INTO BUSINESS (continued)

How good an organizer are you?
- _____ I like to have a plan before I start. I am usually the one to get things lined up when the group wants to do something.
- _____ I do all right unless things get too confused. Then I quit.
- _____ You get all set and then something comes along and presents too many problems. So I just take things as they come.

How good a worker are you?
- _____ I can keep going as long as I need to. I do not mind working hard for something I want.
- _____ I will work hard for a while, but when I have had enough, that is it.
- _____ I cannot see that hard work gets you anywhere.

Can you make decisions?
- _____ I can make up my mind in a hurry if I have to. It usually turns out OK too.
- _____ I can if I have plenty of time. If I have to make up my mind fast, I think later that I should have decided the other way.
- _____ I do not like to be the one who has to decide things.

Can people trust what you say?
- _____ You bet they can. I do not say things I do not mean.
- _____ I try to be on the level most of the time, but sometimes I just say what is easiest.
- _____ Why bother if the other fellow does not know the difference?

Can you stick with it?
- _____ If I make up my mind to do something, I do not let anything stop me.
- _____ I usually finish what I start—if it goes well.
- _____ If it does not go right away, I quit. Why beat your brains out?

How good is your health?
- _____ I never run down!
- _____ I have enough energy for most things I want to do.
- _____ I run out of energy sooner than most of my friends seem to.

Now count the checks you made.

How many checks are there beside the first answer to each question?
_____

How many checks are there beside the second answer to each question?
_____

How many checks are there beside the third answer to each question?
_____

If most of your checks are beside the first answer, you probably have what it takes to run a business. If not, you are likely to have more trouble than you can handle by yourself. You had better find a partner who is strong on the points you are weak on. If many checks are beside the third answer, not even a good partner will be able to shore you up.

Figure 4–1. *Rate yourself as an entrepreneur*
SOURCE: *Checklist for Going into Business,* Small Marketers Aids. #71 (Washington, D.C.: Small Business Administration, 1979) pp. 4–5.

proper business experience

The major ingredient for a successful business owner is prior experience in the field. Dino wanted to start his own bakery shop, but had no prior experience in the field. After talking to his wife, he decided he would seek a part-time job with a baker during the early morning hours. After two years of practical experience, working at every conceivable job associated with the bakery business, Dino started his own business. The banker was willing to loan Dino the necessary funds based on his integrity and experience.

Proper business experience cannot be overlooked. The lack of such experience is one of the major causes of failure. The experience provides the business owner with insights in the business that cannot be obtained from any books, schooling, or classes. "Experience is the best teacher."

It may be advisable for a person to work one to five years in a special field before starting a business. This period of experience will provide education as well as an opportunity to make contacts with future customers, suppliers, and bankers. The need for experience cannot be overlooked.

the right business opportunity

Business owners must find the right business opportunities before they can succeed. Good management requires an intelligent investigation of all possible available business opportunities. Few business owners can be inventor, purchasing agent, financial analyst, cost accountant, marketing expert, advertising genius, and effective business owner all at the same time. You need to pick out an area of business that you enjoy and where you will work well. Before entering any business, you should look at your own personal strengths and weaknesses. You should investigate your willingness to sacrifice time and money in creating and building a business. You may want a business where you will only have to work for ten to twelve hours a day. Some people even want to be an absentee owner, and have other people manage their business affairs for them (for example, physicians, dentists, and sometimes lawyers).

Everyone, before entering a business, should analyze their reasons for going into that business—whether those reasons are for growth, fame, wealth, security, shorter workdays, being your own boss, or just wanting to do something different. Many small business owners prefer downtown locations, where they can be open from 10 A.M. to 6 P.M., rather than in a large shopping mall where they will need to be open from 10 A.M. to 10 P.M.

If a business owner lacks experience and capital, then franchising may be the route to follow. Owning a franchise will allow you, as the franchisee, to have the distribution rights for a product (such as McDonald's) or service (such as "Martinizing") in a given geographical area. This is often a convenient way for some poeple to become an owner of a business, satisfying a desire with a minimum of risk coupled with a maximum opportunity for success and profits. One then has the opportunity to learn the business from experts, and may receive such services as location analyses, store design, equipment purchasing, management training, advertising, standardizing procedures and operations, merchandising, purchasing and financial assistance. Franchise businesses account for over $250 billion in annual sales equal to approximately 31 percent of all retail sales. Clearly this is an opportunity that many business beginners should thoroughly investigate.

Business opportunities should provide you with the opportunity of enjoyment, feeling free, and being your own boss. The monetary reward should be sufficient to meet your needs and desires. The opportunity should provide you with growth and a strong possibility for success over a long period of time. Business understanding, coupled with the correct business opportunity, should fill those requirements for business survival.

business plan or feasibility study

Before beginning any business it is important to develop a thorough business plan or feasibility study that outlines the correct managerial, marketing, accounting, financial, and legal requirements you will face in your business.

This plan should thoroughly document the financial requirements and profit picture available in this business. It is advisable that three, four, or even five different sales levels (revenues) be used to determine different profit levels for the business. A complete financial outline should be developed and understood before one ever ventures into a business activity.

A good feasibility study is one that can be used as a guide or outline for the first year of business operation. This study would allow the business owner to know how many employees he or she will need to hire, employee policies, merchandising and advertising, and management requirements that are needed for the first year. The study should outline the potential sales and growth of the business during the first few months and year, and it should indicate a detailed breakdown of cost, mark-ups, and sales of each major product item or service.

The business plan should be complete and reviewed by friends, relatives and other business associates. The plan should also be reviewed by a local banker and/or accountant to ensure feasibility or to review the practicality of the business.

sufficient capital

Business takes money. Very few businesses can open without a sizeable investment by the owner. Few businesses today are capable of starting on a "shoestring," although many people still try to do it.

The amount of money you will need will depend upon the type of business that you enter. Money required to set up or start a business is generally referred to as *initial capital,* and the money required to keep the business going until it pays for itself is called *working capital*. There are always bills to pay.

One of the major problems of new businesses is the lack of sufficient beginning capital. Many business owners run into financial problems during the first three to six months, and then realize they began with insufficient funds. This is one of the major problems of early business failure.

Your feasibility study should determine the financial needs of your business *before* starting. Many people forget, though, that money is needed to cover personal expenses and family responsibilities until the business is able to generate profits. While many people dream of skyrocketing $100 to $1,000 into a vast fortune, there are very few businesses today that can do so. This is rather a gambler's outlook on business. In today's economy, the odds are over 1,000 to 1 that such an opportunity will never occur. Careful planning needs to go into developing and accurately portraying the capital requirements of your new business venture.

SUCCESS STORY: Charles Barrow

In 1932, while the United States of America was in the Great Depression, Charles Barrow was out of work. He was living in the Philadelphia suburb of Germantown and had been without steady employment for over two years. He worked around his community repairing small appliances, mowing lawns, and trying to invent some useful gadgets or products he could sell. He met with failure after failure, and had been unsuccessful in promoting a simplified bridge scoring pad, as well as a combination bat and ball.

Even though he was unemployed and found it difficult to provide for his family, Barrow still continued to search for employment and be creative. Something inspired him to sit down at his kitchen table and to develop a game. Because the table was round, the game board he created was also circular. He decided that he was going to play the game of employment and riches. He named places on his game board after avenues and utilities in the town of Atlantic City. He also included transportation centers or railroads and even a place similar to unemployment—jail. The participants were issued "play money," and they had the option to buy various houses as well as companies and utilities. Players could auction their assets, buy or sell houses, and even mortgage property to raise cash to buy additional properties or assets. The game could go on for hours or even days. It never officially ended until one player was finally able to bring the other players to total financial ruin. He called the game "Monopoly."

As Barrow and his wife played the game nightly along with neighbors and friends, the round board became square and the rules were changed, improved, and fixed. When his neighbors asked Barrow for a copy of the game, he made sets and sold them for $2.50 each. Finally a neighbor offered to paint the sets so that Barrow might be able to sell them to retail stores and toy departments. In 1934, the John Wanamaker Department Store of Philadelphia sold the first store-bought "Monopoly" set.

Barrow wrote to Parker Brothers, and encouraged them to buy and sell the "Monopoly" set. Parker Brothers turned him down because the game violated too many of the established rules and laws of games currently on the market. Parker Brothers felt the game was too complicated and "unplayable."

This did not deter Barrow; now he borrowed and obtained funds from family and relatives in order to make 5,000 sets. These sets he took to Wanamaker's and other stores in New York. The F.A.O. Schwartz toy store in New York finally sold a set to a friend of the daughter of George Parker, founder of Parker Brothers. After receiving rave reviews, the president replayed the game, changed his mind, and Parker Brothers began to sell "Monopoly."

"Monopoly" has become the biggest game sold in America and throughout the world. It has produced over $240 million in sales. Parker Brothers, on the brink of bankruptcy when it bought "Monopoly," is now an international leader in the games field.

Business Profiles

Before taking the final leap into the business world, you should look at business in general. What are the various types of businesses available to you?

Your final decision will be influenced by the money you can invest (from your own pocketbook), potential profit, prior work experience, personality, knowledge and skills, and the nature of the work itself. Our economy is in a capitalistic society, where business is available and open to everyone. Our business community provides one of the highest standards of living in the entire world. Our businesses are privately owned and controlled, and our laws, regulations, and customs require private and not public (government) ownership of business. Our laws are established to help and protect business.

Business owners and economists generally divide our economy into nine major industrial categories under two broad groups: goods producing and service producing (see Figure 4–2). These categories are:

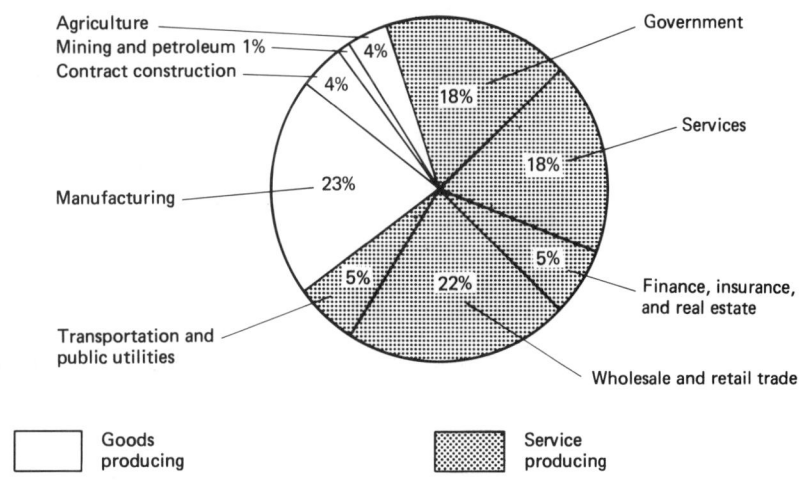

Figure 4-2. *Where people work, 1976*
SOURCE: Bureau of Labor Statistics, *Occupational Outlook Handbook*, 1978-79 Edition, U.S. Department of Labor (Washington, D.C.: U.S. Government Printing Office, 1978.) p. 20.

1. Agriculture.
2. Mining and petroleum.
3. Contract construction.
4. Manufacturing.
5. Transportation and public utilities.
6. Wholesale and retail trade.
7. Finance, insurance, and real estate.
8. Services.
9. Government.

66
YOU AND SMALL BUSINESS

Government is growing, but it still only accounts for 18 percent of the total work force in America. Small businesses are the primary source of new jobs. Most new businesses, though, come under the heading of four major business categories, which are: (1) manufacturing, (2) wholesaling, (3) retailing, and (4) service businesses.

Most of the nation's workers are employed by the service-producing industries in America, such as health care, transportation, banking, finance, insurance, education, and repair and maintenance. The goods-producing side of our economic environment produces only about 13 percent of the country's work force. This would include farming, mining and petroleum, construction, and manufacturing.

occupations

Occupations are also generally divided into different major classifications. White-collar workers are generally considered to be those who are in professional, technical, clerical, sales, and managerial jobs. Blue-collar workers are those who are generally found in labor, craft, and operations work. Service and farm workers are generally considered as separate classifications. Figure 4–3 illustrates the occupational profile recently found in America.

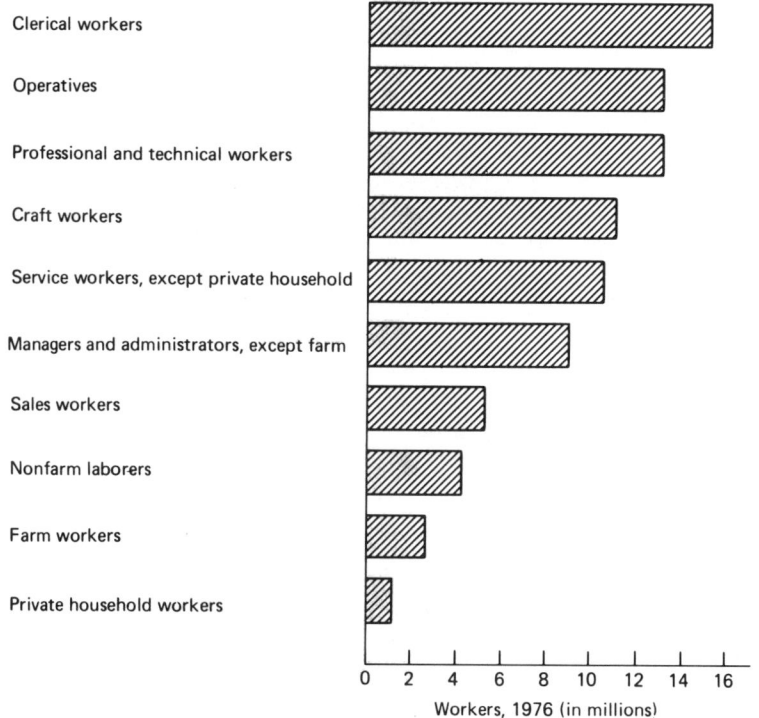

Figure 4–3. *Employment in major occupational groups*
SOURCE: Bureau of Labor Statistics, *Occupational Outlook Handbook*, 1978–79 Edition, U.S. Department of Labor (Washington, D.C.: U.S. Government Printing Office, 1978.) p. 22.

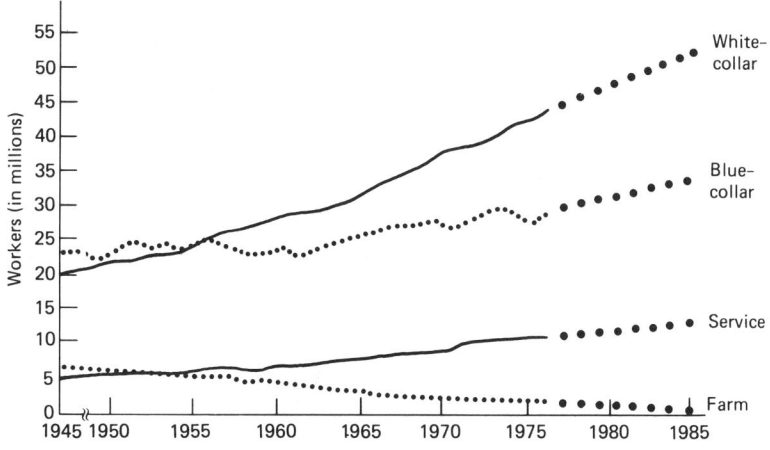

Figure 4–4. Occupational projections. The shift toward white collar occupations will continue through 1985.

Note: Fourteen- and fifteen-year olds are included prior to 1958 only.

Major increases have been found in both the white-collar and service areas (see Figure 4–4). White-collar workers today account for almost one-half of the entire work force. Service workers have also risen rapidly, due to the influx of new small businesses. Blue-collar workers have risen gradually, while farm workers have shown a steady decline since the 1940s.

Changes are found in occupational groupings due to different growth rates of businesses (see Figure 4–5). Different industries have different growth rates,

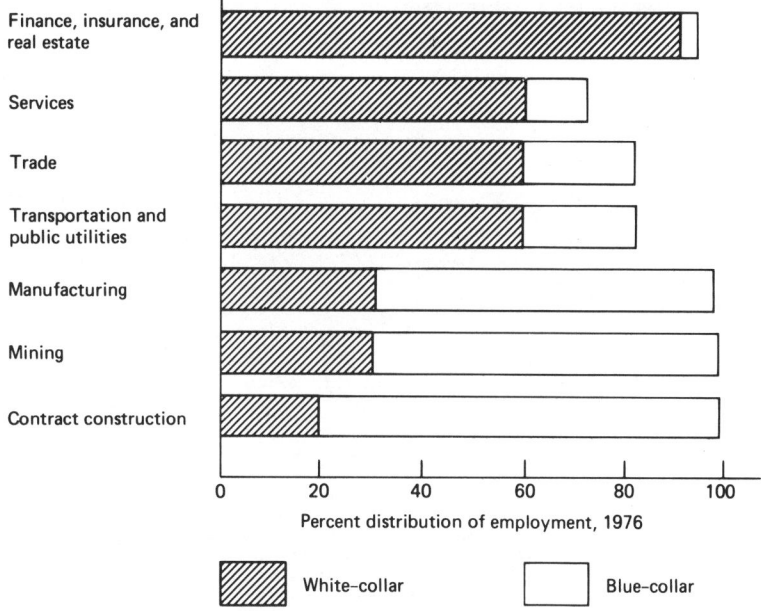

Figure 4–5. Industries differ in the kinds of workers they employ

SOURCE: For Figures 4–4 and 4–5. Bureau of Labor Statistics. *Occupational Outlook Handbook*, 1978–79 Edition. U.S. Department of Labor (Washington, D.C.: U.S. Government Printing Office, 1978.) p. 23.

which require changes in the number of white-collar, blue-collar, service, and farm workers. For example, growth in the finance, banking, insurance, and real estate areas would require a large increase in white-collar workers, while growth in construction, mining, or manufacturing would result in a large blue-collar worker increase.

Another indication of future growth in business economy is expected future job openings. Total new job openings result from new business openings, employment growth, retirements, and even transfers to other businesses. Replacements in the next ten years are expected to count for nearly two-thirds of all new job openings (see Figure 4–6). The greatest number of job openings will occur in the service-oriented businesses. For example, service workers are predicted to have the second largest increase during the next decade.

education and income

Many individuals will make a decision at the end of high school whether to go and pursue a college or some other postsecondary education. For those individuals who have graduated from high school, the unemployment rate drops steadily as the

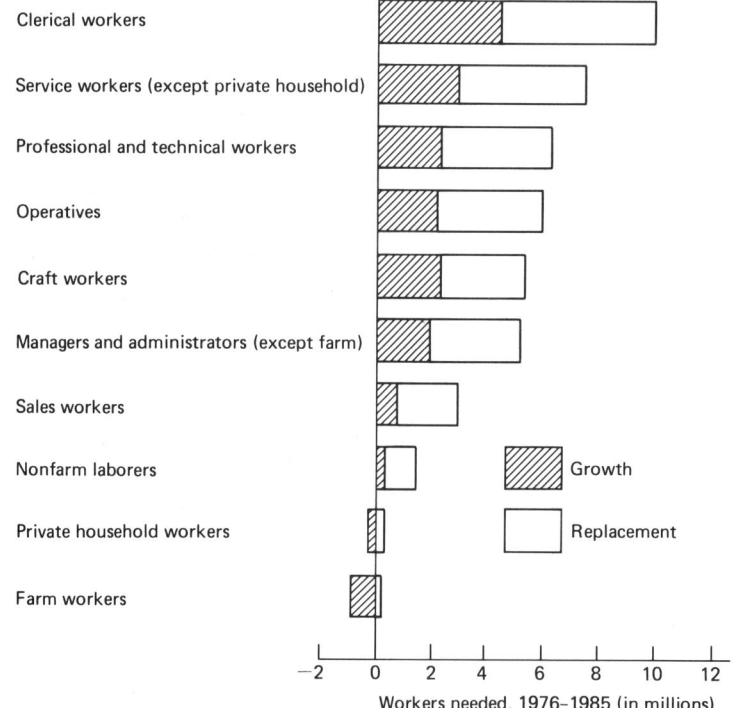

Figure 4–6. *Future job openings are determined by replacement plus growth*

SOURCE: Bureau of Labor Statistics, *Occupational Outlook Handbook,* 1978–79 Edition, U.S. Department of Labor (Washington, D.C.: U.S. Government Printing Office, 1978.) p. 25.

amount of education completed increases. (Figure 4–7 indicates that the average yearly income rises for the amount of education completed.) In 1975, college graduates averaged one-third more income than high school graduates. Persons who have started graduate college programs, or who have five years or more of education, earned one-fifth more than those who only completed four years of college.

There are many well-paying jobs that do not require a college education. The construction, manufacturing, mechanical, and repair occupations are generally designed for high school graduates. Many of these employees earned more than workers with college degrees who are employed in other businesses. The size of the work force with college degrees has risen dramatically in the last twenty-five years. The labor force with college degrees has risen from 7.9 percent to 16.5 percent between 1952 and 1976. College graduates should reach an expected level of 20 percent of the total labor force by 1985.

Business opportunities are not dependent upon college or high school educations. Business success is usually determined by the character, drive, and personality of each individual owner. Education does indicate that the skills and knowledge obtained will generally enhance the possibilities for success. However, through conscious effort, most people may obtain that knowledge and develop the skills that are essential for complete business success.

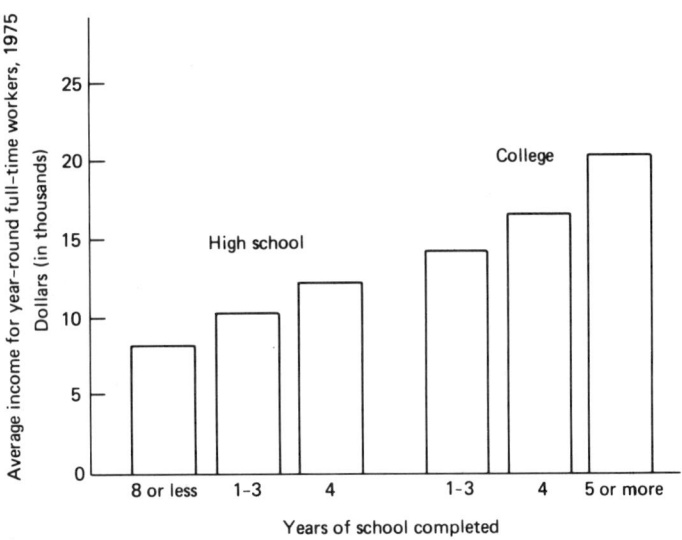

Figure 4-7. *Income increases as the number of years of schooling increases*

SOURCE: Bureau of Labor Statistics, *Occupational Outlook Handbook*, 1978–79 Edition, U.S. Department of Labor (Washington, D.C.: U.S. Government Printing Office, 1978.) p. 26.

Time Management

One of the major problems you will face when you enter the business world is the proper use of time. Many business owners have found that they will spend most of their time on trivial matters and never accomplish the major tasks that need to be finished. Valuable time is often wasted. The objective of the business owner must be to work *smarter* not *harder*.

Time is life. Once a minute is wasted, it is gone forever. A person needs to be able to budget his or her time efficiently and effectively. This requires a tremendous amount of discipline, and the realization of making better use of your time. Good managers "put first things first." Work is assigned a priority according to its importance and need.

Alan Lakein, in his book, *How to Get Control of Time and Your Life,* defined six major points that are essential to effective time management:

1. List goals, set priorities.
2. Make a daily "To Do" list.
3. Start with *A*s... not with *C*s.
4. What is the best use of my time right now?
5. After sorting, handle each piece of paper only once.
6. Do it now![1]

After listing your own personal goals, it is important to set priorities on those actions you plan to take to accomplish the goals. Those actions with the highest priorities should be given an *A,* those with the next highest priority a *B,* and those with the least priority (those you may never get to) a *C.* After the priorities have been established, it is important to accomplish those with an *A* rating.

To help accomplish the priorities established, it is important to make a daily "To Do" list. This list should contain those *A*s that are necessary to do during that day. You should start with the *A*s and not with the *C*s, although the *C*s tend to be smaller and less time consuming. The *A*s may never get done if they are never started.

A question that is always important to ask is, "What is the best use of my time right now?" It may be to simply gather information about an *A* item. This may only take ten minutes and may be done between meetings or phone calls. But action should be taken on *A* items, and the best use of your time will be to accomplish those *A* items.

A managerial technique that most successful managers have learned is to never handle a piece of paper more than once. Many people are placed on reader lists, mailing lists, and "junk mail" lists. Before putting that piece of paper down, you may wish to accomplish the task required, or to send it on to another individual for clarification or opinion.

Most of us are great procrastinators. We can all put off until tomorrow what

---

[1]Alan Lakein, *How to Get Control of Time and Your Life* (New York: Signet Books, 1973).

we should be doing today. However, this is a very large waste of time. We should follow the rule: we should "do it now!"

delegation   To be an effective manager of time, you need to be able to delegate activities, work, and responsibility. You need to learn how to delegate work and tasks so that you may be free to accomplish more important items. You will probably also find that, through effective delegating, an effective subordinate can probably do the job as well (if not better) than you can yourself.

Delegation also builds responsibility in others. Most workers are happy to receive delegated tasks if they can see some reward or accomplishment in fulfilling the assignment. Failure to delegate is failure to manage.

Before delegating, it is important that the other person be: (1) capable of performing the assignment, (2) willing to accept the assignment, (3) sure he or she understands and is responsible for the assignment, and (4) able to review and evaluate the final accomplishment.

Business owners often fall into the problem of working on their favorite or "easy" task. For example, one business manager bought out his owner, and continued to spend an hour each day after work recording the sales figures for the business. This required some extensive bookkeeping, which both his wife as well as one of his other employees had volunteered to take over. But rather than work on purchasing, store layout, or sales promotion, he decided to continue with the task at which he had been successful during the prior three years of time. This was a waste of managerial and owner effort.

You need to spend some time each day developing a daily "To Do" list and analyzing your own time management. It *takes* time to *manage* time. However, those people who have developed this technique have found that they save valuable time in the long run. They are more successful, more happy, and have found time to spend with their friends and family that they would have wasted otherwise. Time may be your most important possession. Use it wisely.

CASE STUDY: Independent Retailer

Dot Masters has been a representative of a large cosmetic manufacturer for over three years. She thoroughly loves and enjoys her occupation. She is able to arrange her own working hours, and sell as much product as she wishes. She enjoys calling on customers and has developed a strong clientele.

When she first sought employment, Dot preferred flexible hours. She had a large family that she wanted to raise, and a husband who was working hard in his own occupation. Dot preferred something that would allow her to work 15 to 40 hours a week. The cosmetic company offered her a job that required only the use of a personal car, a telephone, and no other full-time job. She is a success due to her very pleasing personality and her ability to work easily with others.

The profit margin on all items sold for the independent retailer is about 40% of the list price. The company publishes a sales catalog every two weeks. Only on "daily items" (soaps and certain colognes) is the profit at 25 percent. They have twenty-six sales campaigns during the year, which provide ample incentives and opportunities for profit in the business.

Dot attends a regular monthly sales meeting, and sends in orders twice a month at the end of each sales campaign.

There are different achievement plateaus that the independent retailer can reach. The retailer may also purchase demonstration models. Special gifts are provided the independent retailers for different sales volumes during each sales period, as well as total sales at the end of the year. Membership in the Presidential Club is limited to those independent salespeople selling over $6,500 worth of merchandise each year. Dot firmly believes that this is the right job for her. She is excited about being a member of the Presidential Club this year.

Questions

1. Independent retailers represent one of the largest occupations in the United States. Might this be the business for you?
2. What kind of person may choose to go into business as an independent retailer?
3. Could everyone be successful as an independent retailer? Why or why not?

Chapter Questions:

1. What are some factors that may affect your success in business?
2. What are some personal characteristics that may cause one to be successful in business?
3. Why is experience necessary before starting your own business?
4. Explain the "ingredients" that will increase your likelihood for success in a business.
5. Which business areas are growing the fastest? Why? Why is there an increase in white-collar workers?
6. Discuss the steps that are important to effective time management.
7. Why is delegation a key ingredient for effective time management?

2
entering the small business arena

Photo courtesy of Irene Springer, Prentice-Hall, Inc.

5 THE FEASIBILITY STUDY

Chapter Objectives:

1. To be able to develop a feasibility study for a small business.
2. To know the basic accounting statements used in a feasibility study.
3. To understand the management requirements important to a small business.
4. To learn how to develop a marketing profile.
5. To investigate the financial requirements of a proposed business.
6. To understand the legal requirements of businesses.

*The tree that never had to fight
For sun and sky and air and light,
But stood out in the open plain
And always got its share of rain,
Never became a forest king,
But lived and died a scrubby thing.*

*The man who never had to fight
To win his share of sun and sky and air and light
Never became a manly man,
But lived and died as he began.*

*Good timber does not grow in ease—
The stronger the wind, the tougher the trees.*

Anonymous

INCIDENT: Jim and Judy are excited. They have a tremendous idea about starting a new business. They have talked to several of their friends and have decided above all they want to go into business themselves so they can be their own boss, determine their own hours, and create their own profit.

They have decided that, after looking around in their midwestern community of 180,000 people, they want to develop a retail record store selling popular music records primarily. After the initial discussion with friends and relatives, they seek the advice of a neighbor who is a banker. The banker asks them how many other record stores there are in town. Jim and Judy respond that there is one major record store in town and that their competition would be very low. They have neglected to include several other record stores that are located in discount and department stores throughout the city. They have also neglected a major record store that is opening in a new mall far out on the east side of town. But Jim and Judy are excited about the future and the possibilities of developing and running their own business.

Jim and Judy were raised in the same city; both attended the same university. Jim is now working with an electronics firm in town, and Judy is the mother of two young sons. Additional questions are raised about distributors and the initial cost of records to Jim and Judy. They do not have the answers nor have they really thought it out. They do not know what the cost of leasing or buying the property would be nor do they understand the idea of cost plus or mark-up pricing. They really do not understand that the major record store in town is a discount store and that unless they go into a very low cost rent district, it will be very difficult for them to compete at the same price level as the major competition.

Jim and Judy do not understand what their market is or the age group that they will be trying to sell their records to. They really have not yet developed the concept of market strategy nor do they know whether they are going to be a specialty store or a regular retail business selling at suggested retail prices. They do not know if there are licensing requirements, legal requirements, or taxes that they will have to pay. But they are excited. They want to start a business. They are going to start a business. They are asking a banker if he would supply them with the needed capital which will be necessary to open and run the business that they have dreamed of. Jim and Judy have not yet decided what form of accounting records they will keep or what use of financial records they will have. They do not understand the importance of record keeping for tax purposes or the necessity of obtaining an employer identification number from the Internal Revenue Service.

Are Jim and Judy ready to start their own business? Why? What additional information do they need? Would a feasibility study help them? How?

A feasibility study is similar to a personal financial plan. Individuals need to assess their total incomes and to allocate their expenses to keep within them. Many people will spend a considerable amount of time developing a personal or family budget. The budgetary process allows one to see if his or her proposed income will be able to satisfy needs and wants in buying various products for his or her family. The checkbook is a good sample of a budgeting system used by a family or individual. One can establish credit and receive periodic loans in order to buy appliances, cars, or other accessories in order to make his or her life more pleasant.

The successful business owner should make the same effort in analyzing the economic conditions, possible sales, and required expenses in determining the possible degree of success that his or her business should be able to attain. The business owner is interested in being able to predict sales and expenditures, and to develop a positive net revenue.

Questions that often arise are, "How does a person develop a feasibility study?" and "How does someone assess his or her income against the expenditures for his or her business during a time of economic uncertainty?" The feasibility study is designed to help a prospective business owner ascertain the probable success of a new business, a new venture, an expansion, or a new product line. The feasibility study, when properly prepared, is designed to measure revenues against expenses in an uncertain economic environment, while illustrating possible projections for future income and/or losses.

A well prepared feasibility study contains at least six major sections:

1. Introduction, preface, or general overview.
2. Marketing.
3. Management.
4. Accounting, finances and taxes.
5. Legal aspects.
6. Appendix.

A preliminary analysis of a business situation should contain all of these factors. (See Figure 5–1.) While no one factor is more important than another, it is important that all be well developed and to the point. After appraising these six areas, you should know whether your business proposal and its related ideas have the potential to be successful in the business world. To facilitate the preparation of your

FEASIBILITY STUDY CHECKLIST

I. *Introduction, Preface, or General Overview*
   - _____ Objective of feasibility study
   - _____ History (if you are purchasing an ongoing concern)
   - _____ Overview of the industry

II. *Marketing*
   - _____ Objective and supporting strategies
   - _____ Product description: goods and/or service explained in detail
   - _____ Identify target market: who, where and how many
   - _____ Place: location, size, traffic counts, channels of distribution
   - _____ Price determination: competition's prices, price list with profit margin
   - _____ Promotion: specific detail plan (how, when, where, and cost); personal selling, mass selling, sales promotion

III. *Management*
   - _____ Personal expertise
   - _____ Organizational structure
   - _____ Personnel management (wage and salary administration)
   - _____ Policies (general and departmental)
   - _____ Inventory control

IV. *Accounting, Finance and Taxes*
   - _____ Start-up or turnkey cost (itemized)
   - _____ Equity, or unencumbered cash
   - _____ Collateral
   - _____ Credit references
   - _____ Loans: amounts, types, and conditions
   - _____ Proforma income statement (profit and loss statement)
   - _____ Proforma balance sheet
   - _____ Projected cash flow
   - _____ Working capital
   - _____ Break-even analysis (units and/or dollars)
   - _____ Ratio analysis
   - _____ Provisions for taxation

V. *Legal Aspects*
   - _____ Contracts, licenses, and other legal documents
   - _____ Business structure
   - _____ Type: sole proprietorship, partnership, corporation, etc.
   - _____ Conditions and terms: responsibilities, liabilities and compensation of principals.
   - _____ Insurance: types and costs
   - _____ Provisions for business termination

```
            FEASIBILITY STUDY CHECKLIST (continued)
   VI. Appendix
       _____ Working papers
       _____ Charts
       _____ Graphs
       _____ Diagrams
       _____ Layouts
       _____ Résumés
       _____ Other
```

Figure 5–1. *Feasibility study checklist*

SOURCE: Robert T. Justis and Barbara Kreigsmann, "The Feasibility Study as a Tool for Venture Analysis," *Journal of Small Business Management* 17, no. 1 (January, 1979), 35–36.

feasibility plan, it is important to develop each of these six major parts. A brief explanation of each area follows, with appropriate suggestions in order to successfully complete the feasibility study.

Introduction, Preface, or General Overview

Explain what you intend to do. The introduction, preface, or general overview should contain the name of the basic product or service you are going to provide or sell. This introduction should be able to clearly explain to another person the ingredients that the business will use to be successful.

You need to clearly and precisely state what you are going to be doing, to whom you are going to be selling, what product(s) you will be using, and what the basic prospects for success are.

It is important that you precisely explain the historical background of a product or service you are going to sell. If you are selling color television sets, then state which brands, what kinds of service (delivery and repair), and what kinds of accessories you will offer. You should include information about the history of the industry as well as the history of your own business. It is also appropriate at this time to include reference to the Robert Morris Associates' *Annual Statement Study,* to the National Cash Register (NCR) *Expense Statement,* or to Dun & Bradstreet's *Business Ratios,* all of which contain information concerning the historical and financial information relative to the industry which you are in.

It is also necessary to include information about the economy and the economic projections for the future and how your business would fare in and benefit from a changing economic situation. This information may be obtained from various state organizations (including the State Department of Economic Development), as well as from many Bureaus of Business Research associated with the major colleges of business in the various fifty states. You will need to be as accurate as possible in developing the historical background in order to facilitate the proper appraisal by a banker, venture capitalist or any outside funding agent.

You will need to be well informed about the product or service that you are going to sell. You should be able to answer the questions:

1. Is my product ready to sell?
2. Has the product already been marketed?
3. Am I still in the process of planning the product?
4. Do I have an accurate estimate of the cost of production?
5. Is my product a dream or a reality?

Be honest in the appraisal of each question, and explain in complete detail the current status of the product or service and how you are going to provide it. You will need to explain if the product will be sold in a retail store or wholesale outlet. You should also be able to precisely describe the services you will provide. For example, if you are to be in the appliance business, selling small appliances such as electric mixers, electric coffee makers, refrigerators, televisions, and various appliances, will you also be providing a service of installation and repair? You will need to be very specific, and list the goods and services you plan to sell. You may find it appropriate to rent various appliances to customers. Do not forget any good or service that you may be providing in your shop.

You should also be able to discuss the various strengths and weaknesses of your business. You should know the competitive advantages you have for the product that you are selling, as well as any apparent weaknesses of your product, and how you plan on compensating for those weaknesses. It is very rare for one product to have a complete advantage over other products in the line in all details. Although one television brand may provide a sharper and clearer picture, another one might provide a longer warranty or greater service reliability.

Marketing

It is believed that cave dwellers marketed their goods or services to their own best advantage. Marketing has been used by humans ever since one had what another needed or wanted.

You are marketing yourself when you seek a new job position. You try to put your best foot forward when presenting a proposal or suggestion to your boss. In a dating relationship, both partners try to market themselves to the other in order to make an impression of their own worth and value.

Marketing is concerned with the distribution of business products or services to a satisfied customer. Many companies have failed due to a lack of marketing research, a lack of a marketing strategy, heavy competition, and poorly planned sales and marketing policies. It is therefore important that, in the development of a feasibility study, time and effort be expended to develop a marketing profile that would include:

1. The objective and the supporting strategies.
2. A product description.

3. An identification of the target market.
4. The place: location, size, traffic counts, channels, and distribution.
5. Price determination.
6. Promotion.

The satisfactory completion of this list will enable you to market your product in a successful fashion.

the objective and the supporting strategies

The logical beginning for any marketing program is to establish the marketing objective and supporting strategies. The establishment of a marketing objective is very similar to preparing a personal résumé for a job interview:

1. The needs of the customer or future employer must be determined.
2. How you will be able to satisfy those particular needs must be decided.
3. The area of market you believe you can satisfy, fulfill, or serve must be selected.
4. The strengths you can use to either obtain the new job or to sell or provide a competitive edge must be established.

The marketing approach should particularly satisfy the needs of customers. It is important that all salespeople, as well as management, distributors, and service workers, realize the importance of developing satisfied and happy customers. The strategies for determining the target market to which you will be selling, the packaging of your product or services, the location and size of your store, the prices at which you will sell your particular goods, and the promotional items you will use should all be aimed at providing high quality and worthwhile service to the customers. It is necessary to remember that most satisfied customers will return.

a product description

If you were going on a vacation, you would probably describe in great detail the activities you will undertake, the places at which you will stay, and perhaps even your limitations of spending. The marketing product description should be just as detailed. It should describe the basic goods and services that you will be selling in your particular business. For most businesses, it would be important to provide an itemized listing of all the products you plan to sell. For example, in a men's clothing store you would need to list such items as suits, sport coats, sweaters, rain coats, rain jackets, shoes, shirts, pullovers, socks, and so forth. It may be important to list the size ranges you will be offering for each of these products. You might also list the services you will provide, such as alterations or tailoring. Due to the expertise of your tailor, you may find that you can provide a high-quality alteration service that will give you a competitive advantage at your location.

It should be as easy for you to describe the products or services of your business as it is to describe the interior of your home. You should be as familiar with your products as you are with your car, your clothes, or even your toothbrush. Once you are able to describe your business products, you are ready to proceed in developing your marketing program.

an identification of the target market

It is necessary for you to define your product's total market. For example, if you are going to sell records, you should know the age group to which you will be selling. You should arrange to have the appropriate variety of records for that market segment, and you should also realize which age groups will probably be excluded from your business. Most record stores near high schools do not try to sell classical music as their main record type.

In the development of a feasibility study, you should stipulate your target market. You could, for example, examine your target market according to:

1. Sex: male/female.
2. Age: 0–11, 12–17, 18–24, 25–34, 35–44, 45–64, and 65 and over.
3. Income: Under $7,000; $7,000–$14,999; $15,000–$24,999; and $25,000 and over.
4. Geographical area of the city: northeast, southeast, southwest, and northwest.
5. Number of children living at home: 1, 2, 3, 4, 5, 6 or more.

This information will provide the basic demographic information necessary for you to understand the target market to which you will sell your goods or services. This information will also help provide information as to where the target market lives, and as to how many of them who live in close proximity to your store you may anticipate having as customers. In a town of 30,000, it is probably not advisable to have a business that will require a population base of 60,000 for success.

The city and state government—including the county clerk's office and other governmental agencies—may be vital resources in providing information on population and census reports. This information is vital in determination of possible market and market segmentations. From the demographic and statistical data, you will determine your sales forecast in both dollars and units for your business. Check as many sources of market data as possible, including trade journals and associations.

SUCCESS STORY: Bob and Priscilla Sims

After working fifteen years as an oil company representative, Bob Sims came to the conclusion that what he really wanted to do was open his own business. He and his wife, Priscilla, decided that during his vacation from the oil company he should work for a small business just to find out what it would be like.

In the outskirts of the Texas town where they lived Sims found a small restaurant owner who agreed to hire him for a two-week period for food only, no pay. Sims's two weeks of research went quickly. He found fourteen- to sixteen-hour days were not uncommon for small business owners; he learned how to wash dishes and how to prepare food. He learned what a grease pit was and how to handle fire hazards. He learned the importance of pleasing customers and how to deal with fellow employees. Most important of all, Sims learned that he wanted a small restaurant of his own.

Sims and his wife, who left her bank job, spent the next six months getting ready for the opening of their first restaurant which they called "Fish & Chips." Their success was phenomenal. Their seating capacity was filled at lunch time and dinner time; their drive-through window accounted for nearly half of their business. Customers kept coming back.

The couple decided to build a second restaurant in the same town. But when the landlord required a percentage on all business done under the "Fish & Chips" name because he felt he had rights to the title of the company, the Sims changed the name of their second restaurant and sold their first restaurant. Sims's clientele followed them to the new location, and the success of the first enterprise was repeated.

Four years after the opening of their second restaurant, Bob Sims was elected president of the local restaurant association. He and his wife are expanding their business into other areas in their hometown and into other towns in Texas. The dream Bob Sims and his wife worked so hard to make come true is being fulfilled.

the place: location, size, traffic counts, channels, and distribution

One of the most important aspects of starting or running a business is determining its location and place of business. You should try to determine two or three possible locations for your particular type of business. Before fixing upon a final location, it is strongly recommended that you locate the competition already existing in the city where you plan to establish your business. It is also important to find out what other types of stores are located in the area and their attitudes toward the shopping area, the customers, and the landlord. Although the rent or lease may be a determining factor in location site, it should not be the sole determinant of a location site.

One particular store owner decided to relocate because the landlord was increasing the rent, choosing to move into a vacated shopping center in a nice neighborhood. However, only half the stores in the shopping center had established businesses. After relocation, the business owner realized that there was very little foot or automotive traffic past the business, and very few people saw any advertisements or signs stating that the business was there and open. Although the price was right and the size was larger than the previous location, the owner soon realized the terrible mistake made in not properly determining traffic counts or other factors relating to the new location.

A proper channel of distribution should be established for the business, especially if it is in a new manufacturing or wholesale enterprise. These channels of distribution may be through mail, jobbers, or discount stores, or direct to the consumer. Transportation may be a major factor, in which case it would be prudent to locate close to an airline, rail, or trucking center.

price determination

There are various ways to determine the price for a particular product. Before any price decision has been made, however, it is appropriate to determine the price of competitive goods and their relation to your own pricing structure. Almost all major businesses will seek to learn how competitive goods are being priced in the same city. It would be very difficult for a new fast-food restaurant to open in a town if it was offering basic hamburger or chicken at 25¢ higher than the competition. Most people would not frequent the higher-priced establishment. Prices may also be determined by the suggested prices of wholesalers or distributors. One of the easiest and most common methods for price determination is to set a basic mark-up price to charge on most items being sold in the store. Most apparel stores offer a basic 50 percent mark-up on all clothes sold within the shop; that is, if you buy a suit for $50 you would sell it for $100—the base cost is 50 percent of the selling price.

promotion

How you advertise and promote your goods and services will reflect the image of your business. Advertising and promotional expenses generally range from zero percent to 7 percent of gross sales for most retail and wholesale establishments. Cosmetic and soap products are traditionally priced higher but primarily due to industrial advertising efforts rather than the local store. (Tide and Cheer mainly advertise on an industrial basis, and promote their products nationwide rather than to promote the shopping centers or supermarkets in which they may be purchased.)

A feasibility study should contain information about how much will be spent on promotional items, in what media the advertisements will be made, when the promotional items will be presented to the public (seasonal or Christmas items should be advertised during their particular season), and the overall costs of all promotional or advertisement of the business. Efforts should also be made to explain how personal selling will take place, and how the manager will promote sales through bonuses, commissions, or fringe benefits within the organization.

Management

Management has been properly defined as "getting things done through people." Management is not a new idea: there are recorded transactions between tribes going back to 5000 B.C. One of the earliest and most significant contributions to management was developed by the Babylonians. During the Babylonian Empire, Hammurabi developed a code containing 285 laws that covered the matters of his empire. This code provided very significant advances in management thought, due to its established guidelines for administering a kingdom. The great code contained laws pertaining to business as well as to real estate, personal property, trade, and family affairs. Hammurabi worked closely with the clergy, and allowed the priests a great deal of freedom in his empire. As a result of working with the clergy and providing direction for the people, Hammurabi demanded and received immense respect and obedience from his people. He was one of the first great managers—he was able to coalesce the activities of government, religion, and business into a unified whole.

Think about your experiences as a manager. You have had to manage your time, money, school, and work in order to be able to accomplish what you have. You have been required to plan, organize, direct, and control your life so as to maximize the possible returns you may get for your efforts. You have been required

THE FEASIBILITY STUDY

to act as a manager of your family in providing for their needs and desires. Everyone at some time has had worthwhile management experiences, and we have all been required to coordinate the affairs of our government, religion, business, and social affairs into a worthwhile life style.

The managerial function is one of the more important aspects of business success and failure. The manager needs to strive to ensure that the organization or business will serve its basic purpose of providing good and efficient services or products at a reasonable profit. The manager must also be able to design and maintain an efficient organization that will ensure the smooth running of the business. The manager also needs to be able to cope with the environmental changes, and to allow the business to grow through changing economic conditions. The small business manager must also make certain that the business serves those people who work with it and control it.

To help ensure these basic actions of a manager in a small business, it is important to include the six basic steps in a feasibility study for that business:

1. Personal expertise.
2. Organizational structure.
3. Personnel management.
4. Policies and procedures.
5. Inventory control.
6. Production and operations.

personal expertise

It is important to be able to list the characteristics and expertise requisite to the manager's position in a small business. Be precise. Be exact. If you are starting a new restaurant, it is doubtful that you would wish to employ a manager who has not had any restaurant- or business-related experience. Just as likely, you would not employ a cook who has never cooked for anyone before.

If Jim and Judy, whom we met in the chapter opening incident, are going to start a record shop, it would probably be important for them to have some understanding of the recording industry. It would also be of help if they have had some prior experience in a music or a record store, and if they have had prior experience in the retail trade business or in selling products. It is important for people to have experience in the field in which they wish to work.

organizational structure

It is important that you include in your management section a diagram of the structure of your managerial organization. This may include a fairly lengthy organizational chart that includes a Board of Directors with a president, a vice president, and sales personnel. This chart may also be very simple, including just yourself as president, along with two or three associates who would serve as vice presidents or as sales personnel.

This information is of vital importance to anyone reviewing your feasibility study because it allows them to understand your organizational and delegation capabilities. It would be important for you to also include specific duties for each individual within the organization within or along with the organizational chart.

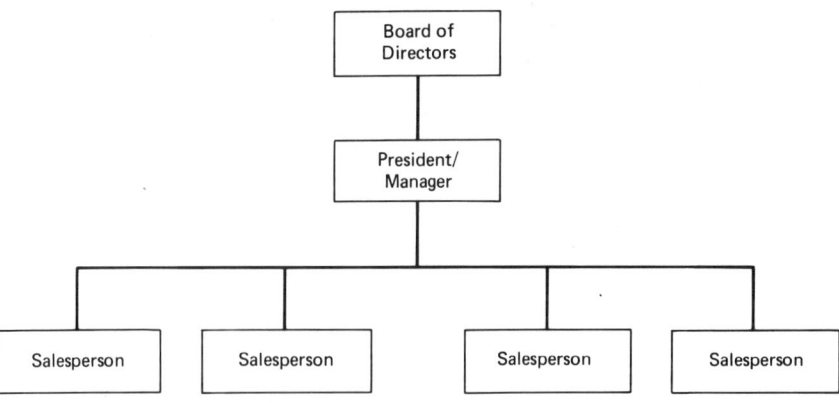

personnel management

Every organization must be able to define its personnel practices. It is important for the small business manager to be able to specify wage and salary programs for his or her personnel, which might include base wage rates on an hourly basis for most of the employees. It may also become involved with bonuses and commissions for salespeople. Also of importance is the manager's ability to explain the company's policies with respect to tipping or gratuities in a restaurant or food establishment.

In a feasibility study, the policies to which personnel need to adhere in a business should be explained. For instance, some clothing stores use commissions based upon sales as incentives for their personnel. Other clothing stores have found that this increases competition and reduces the friendliness between employees, and also reduces the positive feelings between salespeople and the customer. Due to competition initiated by commissions, several managers have discontinued them based on individual sales, but have developed bonus programs for all individuals within the organization based upon personnel evaluation for that year. This allows the profits to be distributed somewhat more equitably among employees for the work they have all done together as well as individually during the year.

policies and procedures

Will you allow employee discounts on merchandise within your store? Will you allow employees working within your restaurant to take home excess food after hours? Will you also allow these employees the opportunity of eating at the restaurant free of charge, or will you provide them with a certain discount? What policies will you have for fringe benefits, and for time off and holidays? What policies will you establish for working overtime, and for time-and-a-half or double-time wage payments?

These are indications of just several of the policies which need to be developed by management before a business begins. The establishment of policies in a general sense will allow the employees to understand their limitations and freedoms within the business. Some of these policies may be departmental and be specific only to a certain type of employee. For example, someone working as a bar-hop may receive a different percentage of tips from the person serving tables. A salesperson may be paid on commission; a delivery person may be restricted and unable to take tips. It is important to point out that all monies may be required to be sent directly to the business, and that no representatives of the company may accept personal checks or cash paid directly to them.

Who will have access to the cash register? Who will be able to conduct and transact the financial affairs of the business? Who will be responsible for all the checking and payment of bills and for receiving payments?

inventory control

Inventory is cash. The money tied up in purchasing inventory is unavailable to the business. It is important to realize that all monies associated with inventory are unavailable for the business to use for purchasing or buying additional goods or services. Therefore, it is extremely important to be able to control the business inventory. It is unwise to have too much inventory because of the money required to develop and maintain that inventory. On the other hand, if you have too little inventory you will not be able to supply or sell your product. Therefore, middle ground must be found that will assure your customers of a large enough inventory that is small enough to not tie up too much of the business capital.

There are several different methods of showing inventory. Some of these may be known as economic order quantity or the ABC analysis. Whatever inventory control method is used should be well thought out beforehand, and should be simply noted in the feasibility study to ensure the proper conduct and control of the inventory of the business. This is very similar to your going to your checkbook and discovering that there is no cash left in the checking account—your inventory has been depleted. On the other hand, if all the cash available to you is tied up in your checkbook and you do not use it, then your inventory (checkbook) is too large (the money could be drawing interest in a savings account).

production and operations

If you are going to be involved in the manufacturing process, you need to clearly and simply state the production and operation system you will use to develop and manufacture the item. You will also need to list, in detail, the supplies to be used, the available labor market, the quantity and quality of materials needed, the discount prices available, and the money and time required for the production and sale of the goods.

Many manufactured products now require government approval; several also require state or federal licensing. The feasibility study should contain such information, as well as data concerning the license required and the licenser. Does the product have a patent? What is the stage of development of the production process? How long will it take for the product or service to be developed and ready for sale? It is also necessary to list the strengths and weaknesses of the product including: (1) the advantageous design features of your product, (2) the life expectancy of your product, (3) the technical or competitive advantages and disadvantages of your product, and (4) any possible expansion of the product line. The list of disadvantages should include any negative features of the product.

Accounting, Finances, and Taxes

accounting

In the Sumerian civilization in Mesopotamia around 3200 B.C., the priests of Ur kept records to keep track of the transactions between the priests and laypersons. The accounting profession has developed greatly since the Babylonian and Egyptian Empires, and since the double-entry bookkeeping system of Genoese merchants of 1340.

The feasibility study should include the three major accounting records that are usually required:

1. The balance sheet.
2. The profit and loss statement (income statement).
3. The cash flow statement.

The various branches of the Medici Bank were required to submit annual balance sheets to the main office and the Medici family in Florence, Italy, during the fifteenth century; businesspeople today are also required to report their financial picture to their bankers, loan officers, and the Internal Revenue Service.

Accounting, on a large scale, has been associated with governmental activities for centuries (primarily for tax collection), but the Industrial Revolution created a need for additional accounting methods. This revolution created a dual ownership entry of two distinct groups: (1) investors, and (2) managers who are generally personified as one individual in a small business; that is, the owner.

The balance sheet. The balance sheet, formally called a "Statement of Financial Position," is designed to give a "snapshot" of the business financial picture at a particular point in time. This snapshot is of interest because it (1) shows how the business has used the resources available to it for financing receivables, inventory, long-life assets, and other items that should provide cash in the future, and (2) shows the source of money to finance the business or how much of the finances came (a) from creditors and (b) from the owners (capital and retained earnings). (See Figure 5-2.)

The balance statement allows one to differentiate between money used to benefit the business over a short period of time (current assets) and money used to provide longer-run benefits for the business (fixed assets). The balance sheet also indicates how the firm receives the money invested in it, such as creditors' funds (liabilities or debts) and the funds of the owner (initial investment plus retained earnings).

The profit and loss statement (income statement). The profit in the business is simply the excess of the prices of goods sold (revenues) over the resources expended (expenses) in selling or servicing the goods and services of the business. It is easy to see why the income statement may then be regarded as a "Profit and Loss Statement," or a P & L. The income statement illustrates the measures of earnings (revenues minus expenses) performance of the business for a particular time period—generally for one year. The net income or profits of a business, in accounting terminology, is equal to the revenues minus the expenses (see Figure 5-3). The revenue is described as a measure of inflow of net resources from the selling of goods or providing services to others. The expenses are usually considered to be the outflow of net resources that are used or consumed while in a process of developing revenues. It may be simply stated that the revenues reflect the value of the goods or services rendered by the firm, while the expenses illustrate the expended efforts required of the business.

Many small businesses prepare an annual report using the calendar year for the accounting period. However, there are a growing number of firms (many small

BALANCE SHEET

	Last Year	This Year
Current Assets:		
Cash	_____	_____
Accounts receivable	_____	_____
Less bad debt allowance	_____ _____	_____ _____
Inventory	_____	_____
Fixed Assets:		
Land	_____	_____
Building	_____	_____
Vehicles	_____	_____
Furniture and fixtures	_____	_____
Less depreciation allowance	_____ _____	_____ _____
Leasehold improvements	_____	_____
Other Assets:		
Licenses	_____	_____
Good will	_____	_____
Total Assets	_____	_____
Current Liabilities:		
Accounts payable	_____	_____
Notes payable (due within one year)	_____	_____
Payroll and withheld taxes	_____	_____
Sales taxes	_____	_____
Accrued expenses	_____	_____
Long-Term Liabilities		
Notes payable (due after one year)	_____	_____
Other	_____	_____
Total Liabilities	_____	_____
Net Worth (Assets–Liabilities)	_____	_____
Total Liabilities plus Net Worth	_____	_____

Figure 5–2. *The statement of financial position*

businesses included) that use the natural business year for accounting purposes. This is acceptable and is in compliance with regulations of the IRS. The idea of using the natural business year is to provide the accounting period for when most business transactions have been concluded for that year. This ending period will differ from one business to another. For example, a bookstore near a university may use the end of June as its ending period, after the major university semesters or quarters have concluded. Sears uses the natural business year ending January 31, which allows for all the Christmas and holiday business to have been finished. A. C. Nielsen, the providers of television and radio ratings, uses August 31 as an ending and reporting date, as it is just prior to the beginning of the new television season.

INCOME STATEMENT

	Last Year	% of Sales	Jan.	Feb.	Mar.	Apr.	May	June	July	Aug.	Sept.	Oct.	Nov.	Dec.	Year's Total	% of Sales
Net Sales:																
Cost of goods sold																
Gross profit																
Salaries (owners/mgrs.)																
Wages (office, other)																
Payroll taxes																
Total Salaries and Taxes																
Nonfixed Expenses:																
Advertising																
Automobile																
Dues and donations																
Delivery																
Legal and professional																
Office supplies																
Telephone																
Utilities																
Miscellaneous																
Total Nonfixed Expenses																
Fixed Expenses:																
Depreciation																
Insurance																
Loan payments																
Rent																
Taxes and licenses																
Total Fixed Expenses																
Total Expenses																
Net Profit (Loss) (before taxes)																

Figure 5–3. *The profit and loss statement*

The cash flow statement. While the income statement may be the financial statement that is most interesting to many small business owners, the cash flow statement is an accounting document that is as important, if not more so, to managers and creditors. The cash flow statement basically shows where the firm has obtained its cash, and how it was spent. Many individuals use their own checkbook as a simple cash flow statement. The checkbook, when properly recorded, categorizes the cash deposits ("sources") and details and purposes for the expenses ("uses"), or why the checks were written.

Cash flow statements are especially beneficial for projecting future cash needs; actually, you are looking ahead to see if the business will have sufficient sources of cash available when necessary. Where the uses would exceed the sources, the small business owner or manager must arrange in advance to borrow or obtain funding to cover these "emergency" periods, paying off the loan during months when the cash inflows exceed the expenses. (See Figure 5-4.) This is very similar to using one's checkbook and personal budget to ascertain if there is a sufficient checkbook balance to meet future rent or food payments. The overdrawn checkbook is a sample of a cash flow in the red.

A one-to-three year projected cash flow statement may easily indicate the "short falls" that a small business will experience. The cash flow statement should sound an alarm to indicate when the funds are short, as well as to show when funds are available in excess. This flow statement should allow a manager to offset the high periods against the low periods, and to allow for maximum utilization of income resources in properly handling business and seasonal affairs.

The feasibility study should show a projected balance sheet, income statement, and cash flow statement for a three-to-five year period. This will enable others to evaluate and to properly analyze the business condition of the firm.

finances

One of the major purposes for this section is to provide information that will be useful to the small business owner in making his or her investment and start-up decisions. The financial analysis should embrace those methods used in assessing and developing information based on results of past performance, current financial position, and projected figures for that particular business.

Most people do this periodically, at the beginning or end of each month, when they pay all their bills, analyze their checkbooks, and project the possibilities for surviving the next month. A business owner uses the financial analysis to determine the expected return to be realized from his or her business, including the risk of uncertainty associated with business practice. The statements necessary for accurate financial analysis include the basic accounting records: the balance sheet, the profit and loss statement, and the cash flow statement.

However, a feasibility study should clearly outline:

1. The start-up or turnkey costs.
2. The break-even analysis.
3. The ratio analysis.
4. The provisions for taxation, collateral, credit references, and loan requests and terms.

CASH FLOW FORECAST

	Jan.	Feb.	Mar.	Apr.	May	June	July	Aug.	Sept.	Oct.	Nov.	Dec.	Total
Cash Receipts:													
Cash sales													
Payments on account													
Other cash received													
Total Cash Receipts													
Cash Payments:													
Inventory purchases													
Salaries and wages													
Rent													
Taxes and licenses													
Utilities													
Other cash payments													
Total Cash Payments													
Cash Flow from Operations:													
Cash balance (beginning of month)													
Cash received from loans													
Cash payments on loans													
Cash Balance at End of Month													

Figure 5–4. *The cash flow statement*

The start-up or turnkey costs. One of the most important and exciting parts of the feasibility study is the creation and explanation of the start-up or turnkey costs that are required to open the business. This part of the study should include all expenses that will be required before the first customer comes in and buys the first product. In establishing a small restaurant, this would include such costs as buildings, rent, advertising, supply, delivery expenses, utilities, telephone and telegraph, insurance, taxes, interest payments, maintenance, legal and professional fees, decorating and remodeling, fixtures and equipment, starting inventory, deposits for public utilities, licenses, permits, installation of equipment, advertising and promotions, plus such speciality items as counters, storage areas, cabinets, display stands, shelves, cash registers, sale window display fixtures, tables, chairs, special lighting, outside and inside signs, delivery equipment, and, if appropriate, plumbing and restroom facilities. These costs should be itemized, and they should provide a complete picture of the total expenses necessary to start and run a business. (See Figure 5–5.)

STARTING COSTS

Money needed for owner or manager	$_____	Until opening
Living Expenses:		
Moving expenses	_____	Once
Salary for owner or manager	_____	1–3 months
Land (buy or lease)	_____	1–3 months
Building	_____	Once
Building Expenses		
Equipment	_____	Once
Fixtures	_____	Once
Decorating and remodeling	_____	Once
Salaries and wages	_____	1–3 months
Inventory	_____	1–3 months
Advertising	_____	3 months
Telephone	_____	1–3 months
Business Expenses:		
Utilities	_____	1–3 months
Insurance	_____	As required
Legal and professional fees	_____	1–3 months
Vehicles	_____	Once
Supplies	_____	1–3 months
Starting inventory	_____	Once
Utility deposits	_____	Once
Licenses	_____	Once
Advertisng and promotion for opening	_____	Once
Cash Reserve (Petty Cash; Credit Accounts)	_____	1–3 months
Total Cash Required to Start a Business	$_____	

Figure 5–5. *"Turnkey" costs necessary to open a business*

The establishment of a turnkey cost is very similar to buying a car. It is necessary to find out how much the car will cost with all the accessory items. One must find out what the license and tax will cost. Before you can drive a new car off the lot, you will be required to provide financial backing for that car, which will include insurance as well as providing personal and financial information to the bank or car leasing agency. Before you actually buy the car, you will look for every hidden cost that may be associated with it, including certain maintenance costs and projected gasoline costs.

Starting a business is a big risk at best, but the listing of sound start-up costs will help you to better understand the problems and to work out as many of them as possible. It is important to discuss start-up costs with others in the industry, or with personal friends who may question and find other costs of which you are unaware as yet.

Break-even analysis. How can we determine if we are making a profit or losing money? How long will it take for revenues to offset costs? It is estimated that on May 4 of each year the average American will break even with federal taxes. That is, his or her revenues will just equal the cost of taxes. The term *break even* signifies when the revenues just exactly equal the cost of business.

Break-even analysis may be performed by using mathematical equations. It may also be done by superimposing on a graph lines representing the costs and revenues lines of the firm. The intersection of these two lines will determine the break-even volume and revenue stipulating where revenue and costs are exactly equal. Such a chart will illustrate the level of sales and productivity needed to cover all costs. A sales level that covers all costs is known as the break-even sales volume for the business.

The *break-even analysis* in the feasibility study will illustrate the required volume of business before any profit may be assumed by the owners. Such an analysis may also determine the month or days required before the business will show the capability of paying back outstanding loans and credit.

Your checkbook is an illustration of break-even analysis. When the balance in the checkbook approaches zero, you are approaching the break-even point; that is, your revenue versus your expenses are approaching a break-even point. As long as the balance in the checkbook is positive, you are maintaining some profitability for yourself—but when the checkbook does equal zero, your costs equal your revenues, and any increases in expenses will result in a net loss.

Ratio analysis. The major purpose for the preparation of a ratio analysis is for purposes of comparison. At times it is difficult to interpret the importance of financial figures found in accounting or financial data. For example, the profitability of a firm is very difficult to ascertain by just looking at the business itself. While the profitability may look bright in comparison with other firms within the same industry, it may be very low and marginal at best. It is helpful to compare the earnings of one business with another in the same industry, but because of varying sizes of businesses within an industry, it is difficult to directly compare revenues or profits. It is easier to compare ratios across industries and even with direct competitors. Ratios are useful financial analysis tools—they conveniently summarize the financial picture of a business and make it more easily understood, comparable, and valuable to the business owner.

Ratios are of very little value by themselves. They should primarily be used to compare your own business with its projected budgets or with other businesses in your competing industry. The uses of ratio analysis are extensive in financial institutions. Any bank loan officer or large loaning organization will perform a ratio analysis before extending you a loan. Some of the major uses of ratio analyses are:

1. Comparision with your own planned budget for the current accounting period.
2. Comparison with the same ratio for prior planning or accounting period.
3. Comparison with a similar firm in the same industry.
4. Comparison with larger or smaller firms in the same industry.
5. Comparison with other firms outside your own industry.

Many people use financial ratios in planning and developing their own life styles. For example, a general guideline is that one should not purchase a new home for a price greater than two and one-half times one's annual salary. The average family will spend approximately 20 percent for food and beverage, 24.9 percent for rent or housing, 8.6 percent for clothing and shoes, and approximately 3 percent for transportation. Family financial counselors warn families not to deviate too much from the standards of other families in the United States. Bankers or loan officers will also tell business owners that they should not radically vary from other successful firms in the same industry.

Provisions for taxation, collateral, credit references, and loan requests and terms. In any feasibility study, it is valuable to include some brief statement concerning the taxes that you will be paying, the collateral that you will be putting up in order to obtain a loan, and any credit references you have that would significantly alter or improve the chances for a favorable loan application. It is also necessary to include any special request for loan provisions that would be important to your business. For example, if you are starting a new business, it may be important for you to receive immediate funds in order to buy the land, build the property, and purchase the equipment and supplies necessary to begin the business. These statements should be short, concise, and to the point so that the loan officer need not spend excessive time to read your loan application.

taxes

One of the most complex problems faced by a new business is the various taxes and the tax structure which must be met. Taxes generally are collected on the federal, state, or local government levels. There are four major general types of taxes that business is subject to or is responsible for collecting and holding:

1. Taxes on the business itself.
2. Taxes on sales.
3. Taxes on property.
4. Employee-related taxes.

Business is subjected to some if not all of these taxes plus additional taxes depending on the type or size of the business. To help further understand the federal tax program, the Internal Revenue Service furnishes a "Mr. Businessman's Kit" upon request that specifies the various taxes and tax schedules which businesses should adhere to. This tax kit also includes an application for a federal employer identification number from the Internal Revenue Service that is necessary for most tax transactions.

Federal taxes. Income from proprietorships, partnerships, and other incorporated businesses are subject to individual income taxes and require a standard individual income tax form. Business corporations including sub-chapter S and 1244 stock are subject to U.S. corporate laws. Their tax provisions will vary depending upon the size of profit of the firm. The small business corporation may, however, elect to have its current taxable income taxed to its stockholder according to sub-chapter S and other Internal Revenue Service regulations. Additional taxes would include excise tax, occupational tax, stamp tax, manufacturer's excise tax, federal use tax, retailers excise tax, and federal unemployment tax. Tax situations and how they apply directly to one's business need to be accounted for in your feasibility study for they will influence your profitability profile.

State taxes. Proprietorships, partnerships, and other incorporated businesses are subject to many state individual income tax provisions. Several states also require state property tax. However, in many locales, the real estate and personal property taxes are levied by county and municipal sub-divisions, including school districts. Most states today have a sales tax, which is levied against business receipts for:

1. Retail sales and rentals of tangible personal property.
2. Utilities, with certain exceptions.
3. Admissions to places of entertainment.
4. Production, fabrication, processing, printing, and imprinting.
5. Rentals of lodging for periods of less than thirty days.

The use tax basically relates to changeable personal property purchased, leased, or rented to sources outside the state. Sales taxes and use taxes vary from state to state.

Local taxes. The major taxes levied by city, county, or municipal governments pertain to real estate and personal property taxes; there are also sales and municipal taxes. Most property taxes are required by state or city laws to be assessed at a minimum of 30 percent to 65 percent of actual value. Due to the wide variation in cities and towns, it is important for you to ascertain your tax structure within your own municipality.

Legal Aspects

Now that you have made your introduction, and have established the major marketing, managerial, accounting, and financial strategies of your firm, you are about ready to start business. Before you go any further, however, it is necessary for you to establish the legal requirements for your venture. Before you purchase a home or buy a new car, you would surely investigate to make sure that the title and the property will legally be yours upon purchase. You will be responsible for signing several documents, and for filing with your local government. You need to learn if there are licensing requirements or insurance prerequisites that are necessary before you can purchase a home or car. The business world requires the same amount of caution and legal insight.

Your feasibility study should cover the following legal areas:

1. Contracts, licenses, and other legal documents.
2. Business structure, such as:
   a. Type: sole proprietorship, partnership, corporation; or holding company.
   b. Conditions and terms: responsibility, liability, and compensation of principals.
3. Insurance: types and costs.
4. Provisions for business termination or succession.

This section will help you immensely in understanding complex legal systems in which your business will operate. Laws have been established to guide and protect individuals within our society. It is necessary to know and to adhere to these legal conditions. They are intended to help and benefit the honest business owner in his or her dealings with customers and other business people.

contracts, licenses, and other legal documents

Your business or occupation may require certain licensing from your state or local government. To determine which licenses are required, check with the city or county in which you plan to establish the business and register the name of your company. The place to register the trade name of your business usually is the county clerk's office. An assumed name certificate or name of business permit are the more common names of the registration forms. If you are going to be doing extensive work regarding legal contracts, it is best that you investigate the use of legal counsel.

In most states businesses are regulated by specific state agencies or departments. The list of state licensing boards and professions is extensive in each state, but some of the more common ones are:

- For accountants, the State Board of Public Accountancy.
- For architects and engineers, the State Board of Examiners for Professional Engineers and Architects.
- For barbers, the Board of Barber Examiners.
- For cosmetologists, the State Department of Health.
- For real estate agents, State Real Estate Commission.
- For pharmacists, the State Department of Health.
- For surveyors, the State Board of Examiners for Land Surveyors.

business structure

There appears to be a very large gap in the knowledge of business owners about the various advantages and disadvantages of the different forms of business ownership. Before starting your business you should determine whether the legal form of your business should be: (1) a sole proprietorship, (2) a partnership; (3) a corporation—subchapter S (section 1244 stock), or (4) a holding company.

As well as determining the legal type of business that you plan to conduct, you should also determine the conditions and terms of your business. Responsibilities and liabilities need to be specifically outlined and written down in order to ensure the continuity of your business. If you have silent partners, it is important for them to have limited or restricted responsibilities and liabilities for the success or failure of that business. A major provision of all businesses is the compensation of principals or owners of that business. For example, one owner in a two-person partnership put up most of the initial capital and expenses for the start of the business. This partner did not plan to do any of the work to maintain or keep the business going. In spite of this, this person received a salary equal to that of the other partner, who had started with almost no capital expenditure but who acted as manager and operator of the business itself. This was agreeable to both partners and was the condition for compensation of their business. You will need to decide what sort of arrangement will be most appropriate for your business.

insurance: types and costs

Most loan officers or bankers require certain insurance policies before a loan is made. When large sums of monies are being transferred, it is wise to arrange for life insurance coverage on the lives of the principal owners that names the lending agency as benefactor. In addition, other insurance policies should be contemplated and investigated.

The small business owner creates a risk by placing himself or herself in a situation with an uncertain outcome. Although personal desires are usually for profit, statistics indicate that business failure is a very real possibility. Because of the strenuous situation, the business manager creates both speculative and real risk. The speculative risk involves three possibilities (1) profit, (2) status quo, and (3) loss. Pure risk exists when only two outcomes are possible: loss or no loss.

Insurance is a social action taken to "transfer" pure risk to other institutions. Speculative risks generally are not insurable. The three major classes of pure risk are (1) property risk, (2) liability risk, and (3) personal risk.

Property risk occurs when there is damage to or loss of tangible property due to fire, windstorm, flood, hail, lightning, or other natural disasters.

Liability risk occurs when the loss of existing assets or future income becomes apparent due to legally liable actions resulting from bodily injury or property damage to others. Business owners have been held legally liable for defective products, for sharp corners on toys, for snow or ice on sidewalks in front of their businesses, or for general conditions unsafe to the public.

Personal risk occurs when the business owner's ability to produce income is altered through death, sickness, retirement, accident, or disability. Most employers make certain that their insurance does cover pure risk situations.

The basic methods of handling risk are (1) risk avoidance, (2) risk assumption, (3) risk reduction, (4) risk shifting, and (5) risk transfer.

Risk avoidance generally is considered to be the most difficult of the methods of handling risk because often risk may not be avoided simply. For example, owners may assume that their business will never be harmed by fire or hail but this assumption does not negate the reality of the risk.

Risk assumption is a second possibility, but a very difficult one for a business person. Most small business owners rarely have the opportunity to become self-insured, which would require the setting aside of a certain sum of money every month for possible perils or hazards in the future.

Risk reduction is when the owner takes part in those business practices that will reduce the frequency and severity of probable loss. Good housekeeping and the implementation of safety standards are beneficial in reducing the chances of loss.

Shifting risk to others is most commonly accomplished by contract, usually by subcontracting, establishing surety bonds, or hedging against the fluctuations in future market prices.

Risk transfer, the most common method of handling risk, is accomplished through the purchase of insurance. Insurance is not a substitute means of handling risk if other methods are more appropriate, although it does transfer risk to second parties.

Property. Fire insurance is one of the most common and needful insurance coverages for any business. Other perils may be added to this basic insurance—windstorm, vandalism, smoke, explosion, hail, and malicious mischief, say—for a relatively small additional cost. This is referred to as an extended coverage endorsement. Burglary and robbery insurance are also available and will compensate the business owner for stolen property in cases of forced entry and pay for losses of property if violence or the threat of force are involved. You may also desire the additional business interruption insurance that provides coverage for your business activities in the event of business closure following fire or other insured peril.

Liability. Liability insurance may be classified in three categories (1) general liability insurance, (2) product liability insurance, and (3) automobile liability insurance. The general liability insurance covers costs and judgments brought against the business because of personal injury and/or damages to property of another. Product liability insurance covers judgments and defenses against the business due to harm caused by the product. It is advisable to have automobile liability insurance. This provides coverage for accidents or damages caused by traffic accidents.

Personal. Personal insurance coverage should include: employee benefit coverages, worker's compensation, and bonding. Insurance coverages that benefit employees include group life insurance, group health insurance, disability insurance, retirement income, and key-man insurance. Such insurance policies help ensure the smooth operations and functions of a business. They also provide income and continuity to the employees of the business. The key-man insurance would further protect the company against financial loss caused by the death of a partner, proprietor, or valuable employee.

Most states require worker's compensation programs. This insurance provides benefits to employees injured during their work regardless of the legal liability of the business. Benefits from worker's compensation are established by state law and vary from one state to another. Premiums generally range from 1 to 10 percent of the salary and are based upon both the employees' wage level and the type of work required.

Another form of personal coverage is bonding. The act of bonding is simply the shifting of risk or financial responsibility for the employee or job to a third party. This third party is referred to as the surety, and generally is a licensed bonding company or a private insurance company. An employer who has a fidelity bond on an employee will receive compensation from a surety for any losses in a business due to that employee. Employers who permit employees access to any sizable portion of company funds need to have these employees bonded. A surety bond also will guarantee the performance of the job. For example, a general contractor may be reimbursed if a subcontractor fails to complete a job according to the terms of the agreement or standards established for that job.

An insurance contract is a complex document. It often is difficult to fully understand. It generally is advisable to use professional insurance agents to more fully understand the needs and conditions of the particular business. It should be remembered that insurance is a last resort and that the transfer of risk through insurance should be undertaken only when absolutely necessary.

The employer usually contacts an insurance company to "buy" a group insurance plan for his business. The employer may pay the whole cost of the insurance or pay part of the cost and have the employee pay part of the cost.

When choosing an insurance plan you should contact more than one insurance company to get the best plan. Shop for an insurance plan that covers the most common needs such as accidental injury, or most causes for hospitalization. (Maternity insurance tends to be expensive, especially for small companies—a self-insurance format may be preferable.) Life insurance should have survivor benefits, disability benefits, and accidental death benefits.

provisions for business termination and/or succession

What would happen to your business if one of the owners died? How would you go about replacing a key executive in the business? What would happen if personal interests conflict with the objectives of the venture? These are questions that need to be determined and satisfied as a business develops and grows. It is important to address these problems early in the life of a business because all too often a sudden heart attack or cancer may take the life of one of the principal owners. The proprietor or partner may easily and swiftly be forced out of business. While legal provisions have been established to handle such emergencies, court tie-ups may make it impossible for the firm to progress and grow as it should.

Appendix

The appendix may be one of the most important visual aids that you can have in your feasibility study. This appendix should contain such items as charts, graphs, diagrams, layouts, résumés, and working papers associated with the establishment of your business. You should include a personal budget record (see Figure 5–6) and a personal financial statement (see Figure 5–7) in the appendix, as bankers and loan officers will request this information. You may find it appropriate to develop a detailed list of all the competitors you anticipate having in the city, locating them on a reduced city map included in your appendix. In addition, a store layout and diagram of parking facilities are important to those who will be reviewing the feasibility study, as well as to yourself, as you plan and develop the business. Both internal and external diagrams of your business operation should be drawn.

Architectural, technical, and professional drawings may also be included in the appendix. A restaurant may place its complete menu in the appendix, and sample advertising and promotional material may also be included there.

```
                        PERSONAL BUDGET RECORD

    Home and Shelter Maintenance:       Personal Expenses:
        Rent                _____           Clothing            _____
        Car expense         _____           Recreation          _____
        Utilities           _____           Vacation            _____
        Telephone           _____           Medical & dental    _____
        Supplies            _____           Education           _____
        Repairs             _____           Dues                _____
        Other               _____           Contributions       _____
                                             Books, etc.         _____
                  Total     _____           Spending, allowance _____
    Food:                                    Other               _____
        Grocery             _____
        Away (outside meals) _____                    Total     _____
        Other               _____      Tax Expenses:
                                             Federal             _____
                  Total     _____           State               _____
                                             Personal property   _____
    Insurance:                               Other               _____
        Health              _____
        Car                 _____                    Total      _____
        Life                _____
        Other               _____      Monthly Income:
                                             Salaries and wages  _____
                  Total     _____           Other               _____

                                         Monthly Expense         _____

                                         Net Monthly Income (Loss) _____
```

Figure 5–6. *Personal budget format*

PERSONAL FINANCIAL STATEMENT

IMPORTANT: Read these directions before completing this Statement.

☐ If you are applying for individual credit in your own name and are relying on your own income or assets and not the income or assets of another person as the basis for repayment of the credit requested, complete only Sections 1 and 3

☐ If you are applying for joint credit with another person, complete all Sections providing information in Section 2 about the joint applicant

☐ If you are applying for individual credit, but are relying on income from alimony, child support, or separate maintenance or on the income or assets of another person as a basis for repayment of the credit requested, complete all Sections, providing information in Section 2 about the person whose alimony, support, or maintenance payments or income or assets you are relying

☐ If this statement relates to your guaranty of the indebtedness of other person(s), firm(s) or corporation(s), complete Sections 1 and 3

TO:

SECTION 1 - INDIVIDUAL INFORMATION (Type or Print)	SECTION 2 - OTHER PARTY INFORMATION (Type or Print)
Name	Name
Residence Address	Residence Address
City, State & Zip	City, State & Zip
Position or Occupation	Position or Occupation
Business Name	Business Name
Business Address	Business Address
City, State & Zip	City, State & Zip
Res. Phone Bus. Phone	Res. Phone Bus. Phone

SECTION 3 - STATEMENT OF FINANCIAL CONDITION AS OF _____ 19, ____

ASSETS (Do not include Assets of doubtful value)	In Dollars (Omit cents)	LIABILITIES	In Dollars (Omit cents)
Cash on hand and in banks		Notes payable to banks - secured	
U.S. Gov't & Marketable Securities - see Schedule A		Notes payable to banks - unsecured	
Non-Marketable Securities - See Schedule B		Due to brokers	
Securities held by broker in margin accounts		Amounts payable to others - secured	
Restricted or control stocks		Amounts payable to others - unsecured	
Partial interest in Real Estate Equities see Schedule C		Accounts and bills due	
		Unpaid income tax	
Real Estate Owned - see Schedule D		Other unpaid taxes and interest	
Loans Receivable		Real estate mortgages payable see Schedule D	
Automobiles and other personal property			
Cash value-life insurance-see Schedule E		Other debts - itemize	
Other assets - itemize			
		TOTAL LIABILITIES	
		NET WORTH	
TOTAL ASSETS		TOTAL LIAB. AND NET WORTH	

SOURCES OF INCOME FOR YEAR ENDED _____, 19 ___	PERSONAL INFORMATION
Salary, bonuses & commissions $	Do you have a will? _____ If so, name of executor
Dividends	
Real estate income	Are you a partner or officer in any other venture? If so, describe
Other income (**Alimony, child support, or separate maintenance income need not be revealed if you do not wish to have it considered as a basis for repaying this obligation**)	Are you obligated to pay alimony, child support or separate maintenance payments? If so, describe
	Are any assets pledged other than as described on schedules? If so, describe
TOTAL $	

CONTINGENT LIABILITIES	
Do you have any contingent liabilities? If so, describe	Income tax settled through (date) _____
	Are you a defendant in any suits or legal actions?
As endorser, co-maker or guarantor? $	Personal bank accounts carried at
On leases or contracts? $	
Legal claims $	
Other special debt $	Have you ever been declared bankrupt? If so, describe
Amount of contested income tax liens $	

(COMPLETE SCHEDULES AND SIGN ON REVERSE SIDE)

Figure 5-7. *Personal financial statement format provided by local bank*

Summary

Every business begins with an idea. The evolution of that idea into an actual business is time consuming and difficult. Whatever the business, the owner needs to develop a feasibility study or a comprehensive plan to bring the dream to reality. This detailed plan should describe, in writing, the proposed business with its related revenues, costs, plans and policies.

The feasibility study should include: introduction, marketing information, management ideas, accounting, financial and tax data legal requirements, and appropriate appendices. The feasibility study is a managerial aid and a valuable resource in soliciting investment funds.

CASE STUDY: The Record Shop

Overview of the industry. The record business supplies a popular product that has been experiencing a growing and diversifying demand. The industry began years ago with bulky 78-RPM records and has grown and become refined into an industry supplying everything from 45-RPM singles to 33⅓-RPM albums, to cassette and eight-track tapes. As disposable income and leisure time have grown, along with the rise in popularity of pop, rock, and country music among our youth, we have seen a demand growing for the method of reproducing this music.

Marketing objective. Our company's marketing objective is to obtain, in the first year, 70 percent of the record and tape business of the youth market for southeast Lincoln, within a one or two mile radius of our store. This translates into sales of approximately $250,000.

According to a recent Gallup Survey (included for reference in the appendix), 62 percent of young people spend a median of $12 per month purchasing records and/or tapes. This being a national average, and given that the target market segment has an average annual income well above the national average family income, it would be reasonable to assume that, to use Gallup's figures, we would have a fairly conservative yet reasonable first year sales goal of $250,000, because there is a student population of 4,069 in the one- to two-mile radius of the store. The sales goal was obtained by the following means:

4,069 students × 0.62 × $12 per month × 12 months = $363,280.32

$363,280.32, discounted 30% for the first year   = $254,296.23

The wholesale price on records and tapes (direct from the manufacturer) runs somewhere around $4.25 each. Therefore, we can calculate the following information:

	COST	PRICE	MARKUP	PROFIT MARGIN
Albums	$4.25	$6.89	62%	38%
45s	0.50	1.00	100%	50%
Tapes	4.50	6.98	55%	35%

THE RECORD SHOP
Turnkey Costs

ITEMS		COSTS
Fixtures and equipment:		
Record and tape player		$ 500.00
Display racks	(5 @ $200)	1,000.00
Display cases		800.00
Cash register		500.00
Calculator		170.00
Check-out counter		500.00
File cabinet		100.00
Total fixtures and equipment		$ 3,570.00
Starting inventory:		
Tapes		6,000.00
Records		24,000.00
Total starting inventory		30,000.00
Decorating and remodeling:		
2000 sq. ft. @ $9/ft.		18,000.00
Advertising sign		500.00
Total decorating and remodeling		18,500.00
Legal and professional fees		500.00
Licenses and permits		0.00
Advertising for opening		1,000.00
Beginning operating cash		10,000.00
Grand Total		$63,570.00

THE RECORD SHOP
First Year Income Statement

Net Sales		$250,000
Cost of goods sold		153,750
Gross margin		96,250
Salary Expenses:		
Manager	15,000	
Salespersons	17,920	
Total salaries		32,920
Other Expenses:		
Rent expenses	13,000	
Telephone expense	360	
Advertising expense	10,008	
Store supplies	2,500	
Office supplies & postage	1,000	
Repairs to store	5,000	
Credit card sales expenses	3,125	
Depreciation expense	7,365	
Interest expense	4,584	
Insurance expense	891	
Property tax expense	998	
Total Expenses		81,751
Net Profit (Loss) before tax		14,499
Estimated Income tax		4,640
Net Profit (Loss)		$ 9,859

THE RECORD SHOP
Two-Week Grand Opening Advertising Blitz

Week preceding the opening:		AMOUNT
Radio—17 thirty-second spots @ $10.10. A time slots (In addition to regular ads)		$ 171.70
Sun Newspaper—¼ page ad	$112.56	
(Credit for ad previously budgeted for week)	(59.64)	52.92
Week of the opening:		
Radio—24 thirty-second spots @ $16.80. AAA time slots (In addition to regular ads)		403.20
Sun Newspaper—¼ page ad	112.56	
(Credit for ad previously budgeted for week)	(59.64)	52.92
Opening week prizes		99.98
Handbills (printing and distribution)		219.28
Total		$1,000.00

THE RECORD SHOP
Ratio Analysis 198X

	ROBERT MORRIS	SOUND MACHINES
Net sales	100 %	100 %
Cost of sales	61.5	61.5
Gross profit	38.5	38.5
All other expenses net	33.9	32.7
Profit before tax	4.6	5.8
Ratios:		
Quick	0.5	0.9
Current	1.9	2.1
Debt/worth	1.1	0.7
% Profit before taxes/total assets	9.2	6.7
Sales/working capital	5.4	6.5

SOURCE: *Annual Statement Studies* (Philadelphia: Robert Morris Associates, 1980).

Questions

1. Develop a feasibility study for The Record Shop.
2. What are the major problems?
3. Is The Record Shop feasible? *Why?*

Chapter Questions

1. What is the purpose and the value of a feasibility study?
2. How would you use a feasibility study in seeking financial support for your prospective business?

3. Which areas of the feasibility study are more important for your business? for a wholesale business? for a retail business? for a manufacturing business?
4. What are some of the limitations of a feasibility study?
5. List the steps involved in developing a feasibility study.
6. How would you use a feasibility study as a guide to establish a business? to run a business?
7. Discuss the importance of balance sheets, income statements, and cash flow statements.

Photo courtesy of Irene Springer, Prentice-Hall, Inc.

6 RESEARCHING A VENTURE

Chapter Objectives:

1. To learn how to research (investigate) a small business.
2. To understand the steps to be taken before deciding to start a business.
3. To know the processes required during a business opening.
4. To understand the growth stages of a business.
5. To improve understanding of the economic and industrial environments.
6. To learn about the marketing and business environments and how they help or limit a business.

> *I know of no more encouraging fact than the unquestionable ability of man to elevate his life by conscious endeavor.*
>
> *Henry David Thoreau*

INCIDENT: Matt wants to learn about men's clothing stores. He has had some experience working with friends and relatives in their clothing stores. He has one year of studies left before he will graduate from the state university with a bachelor's degree in business administration.

A shopping center will be opening on the outskirts of town, and many people are wondering if the town of 160,000 can support its first major shopping mall. Matt does not know where to begin. He wants to open a men's clothing store, and has started to study a business in the downtown area. He has even called upon a couple of men's clothing stores. The owners of these stores discouraged him, telling him that it is very difficult—almost impossible, in fact—to obtain the financing and the merchandising skills necessary to be successful in the men's clothing business.

Matt does not know what the economic environment is, nor does he understand what the market demand may be or his market share. He is not sure how to study the business or the industry, or where he can obtain the accurate and valuable information that may allow him to open his store.

Matt does have some connections, and an understanding of where to buy the various garments he would be selling. He has been able to arrange for three buying trips with friends and relatives to New York, Chicago, and Dallas. Where will he go? What will he do? Should he start his business?

(Two years later, Matt did open his clothing store in that large shopping mall. He had successfully analyzed and researched his business venture, and is one of the most prominent, if not the most successful, men's clothier in the western part of his state.)

Jill is planning to buy a car. She has taken the time to determine what the size and the cost of the car should be. She has estimated the finance figures, and has come to the conclusion that she can probably afford a compact or subcompact car.

Just as you make decisions about purchases for yourself, family, or friends, so the small business owner must evaluate the business opportunities that surround him or her. Researching and evaluating a business is primarily composed of guesswork and must be described as an uncertain art, in the most favorable of circumstances.

To study a business, the owner or manager should investigate the economic environment, the industry, the market and the market share, and the business itself. This process may be simplified by looking at the different time constraints—that is, the key stages—in all related business activity.

The Four Key Stages of a Business

Businesses generally go through four key stages:

1. *The pre-business stage,* in which an idea is thought about and is developed.
2. *The business stage,* in which the idea is launched into a successful business endeavor.
3. *The growth stage,* in which the entrepreneurial spirit emerges and the business shoots forward through expansion, new production, acquisition, or merger.
4. *The termination stage,* in which the owner's or manager's business is sold, is liquidated, is acquired by others, or is given to friends or relatives.

the pre-business stage

The pre-business stage is composed of five major areas of concern, shown in Figure 6-1. First, the basic business idea is conceived and one reviews the possible dangers, outcomes, and profitabilities associated with the endeavor. Then, the business idea is closely followed by an entrepreneurial decision—that is, the decision of someone to risk time, talents, and fortunes in the establishment and running of his or her own business. One needs to determine if he or she properly fits the entrepreneurial role and characteristics. The owner needs to provide a self-assessment and analyze his or her own personal characteristics and desires for starting a business venture.

Third, the coupling of a capable and realistic entrepreneur with a sound business idea requires an identification with an entrepreneurial team. The entrepreneurial team should be comprised of individuals who can add to the potential success and profitability of the business. An entrepreneurial team is not only composed of friends or relatives, but includes the soundest and most qualified people and materials available. In buying a car, you are not just seeking a vehicle that looks good but also one that will provide long-lasting and reliable transportation. The entrepreneurial team is comprised of individuals who can provide technological, financial, managerial, and economic success to the business.

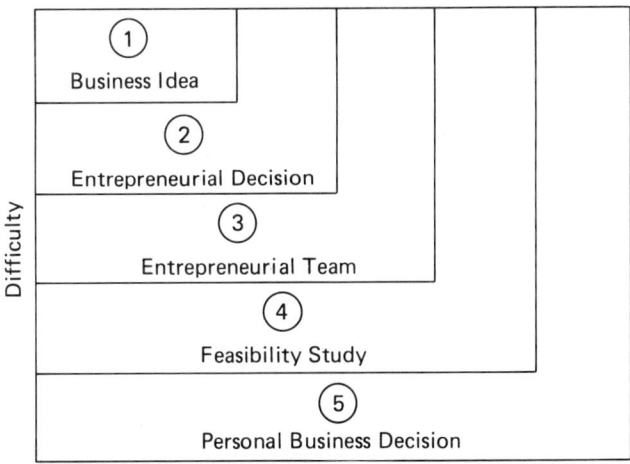

Figure 6-1. *The pre-business stage*

A fourth and vital component to the pre-test stage is the development of a strong feasibility study (see chapter 5). The feasibility study should be a supporting document that outlines in detail the steps, facts, and figures necessary for a successful business. It will emerge as the initial business plan for the first year's operation. This study must comprise all the essential financial, managerial, marketing, legal, and operational information that is required by any successful business, which will allow the owner to seek and obtain financing for his or her business. All required capital may be raised by the entrepreneurial team, through personal loans, or through preferred banking arrangements, or even through insurance companies or venture capital companies. Based on the successful development of these key factors, it is possible to obtain all the data and financing required to start a new business.

Fifth, the entrepreneur or new owner will have to make one of the greatest decisions of his or her life: to make a personal commitment to start a business. The entrepreneur will put his or her life's fortune, time, energies, and all personal resources into that new venture. Usually the entrepreneur will quit his or her former job and will commence a journey on one of the most uncertain paths anyone may ever undertake. That path will often lead to failure, but in many instances it will lead to success—possibly to a vast fortune.

the business stage

The actual opening and operating of a small business requires that a lot of activities take place at the same time. It is necessary for the owner to build the entrepreneurial team. All team members must be able to work together. The owner must understand the strengths and weaknesses of each member of the entrepreneurial team, and how they relate to the business.

The development of a product or service is of major importance to the success of the business. If the business is selling stereo equipment, the owner needs to be knowledgeable about the complexities and variances of the various components, such as the different specifications of amplifiers, recorders, receivers, and turntables. The owner must understand the services to be provided, which may include the initial set-up and installation. If the business will be involved in repair service, it will be necessary for the owner to know how to repair the

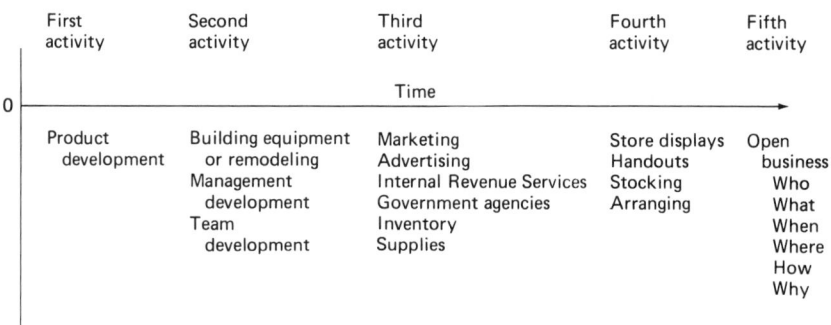

Figure 6–2. *The business stage*

amplifiers or speakers of complex stereo systems, or to have a reputable repair person on hand.

While the owner (or the owners) and the employees are busy working with each other and developing the product, the business is in the process of being launched. The building is being built or remodeled, and arrangements are being made with the bank, the IRS, and the other governmental agencies with which the business will be dealing (see Figure 6-2). Inventory, equipment, and supplies are being ordered. Delays, shortages, and poor workmanship may become problems at this time.

While dealing with these problems, the owner will need to develop marketing and advertising systems. Advertising sketches will be analyzed and critiqued, leaflets and handouts will be developed, arrangements will be made for in-store advertising slogans and store displays, and allocations will be made for space for different suppliers. The owner will be involved with the business. Decisions will be made that will make the business a success or a failure.

The owner must know the time and energies that will be involved in the development of the business stage. The time requirements and the fiscal responsibilities need to be evaluated together. The managerial expertise that will be expected of the owner to perform these various functions must be evaluated. In evaluating a business, it is important to be able to allocate operations and functions to various owners and managers. There must be a plan indicating who is going to do what, when, where, how, and why.

the growth stage

One of the major problems that any entrepreneur or owner must face is the opportunity for growth. Contrary to the opinions of many people outside of the small business world, most owners and managers do not wish their businesses to have tremendous growth. Most small businesses will reach a happy plateau, with an adequate profit for the owner or manager, leaving enough free time for hobbies, family, or activities. The small business owner does not necessarily seek to maximize profits; rather, he or she seeks to be able to control his or her own situation, to enjoy a reasonable success, and to be able to allocate time as he or she sees fit. For this reason, the owner must often make a vital decision of growth or no-growth for his or her particular business. If the decision is for no-growth (and in most cases it will be), the entrepreneur or owner will usually remain at a plateau, and will conduct his or her business to the best of his or her ability.

Two major ways that a business may grow are (1) through expansion of current products or services and (2) through the development of new products or services. The latter is the most common form of growth, even for large corporations, and it is mainly carried out by repeating the pre-business and business stage for a new product or service.

Another alternative available to the business owner is to grow through acquisition or merger with other businesses. One businessperson had such a tremendous success with a T-shirt shop in a shopping mall that he used the profits from it to open a sporting goods store. He started the sporting goods store with the idea of spending most of his time in building and developing the sporting goods shop into a successful business. He had always enjoyed sports, and really saw this as a business hobby.

As a business goes through a growth period, the owner will generally experience what is often referred to as "an entrepreneurial experience." That is, he or she will be creating and building something newer, more effective, and more useful than ever before. The entrepreneurial owner will be creating and developing. He or she will be using the immediately present resources, and will control his or her environment to create a newer and bigger organization and/or business. The entrepreneur is an agent of change, whether it be financial, business, social, political, or economic.

Unique to the entrepreneurial experience is that when the entrepreneur has been successful, he or she will quite often bring about the termination of his or her own position. Due to the growth of the business and the success it encounters, the owner will often be forced to seek professional managers. The creative genius of the entrepreneur will no longer be required to develop innovative ideas, designs, and concepts. Rather, professional managers will come in and take over the operation, developing the accounting and the specific managerial guidelines required for all situations. The organization becomes so large that a managerial overload forces the entrepreneur to seek help elsewhere or else lose business through poor organization and control techniques.

Many entrepreneurs are quite happy to leave the successful growing company into the hands of the professional managers. They often seek new ventures, new ideas, and new opportunities. They may stay with their own company and try to develop new products and ideas, or they may completely sell out and go elsewhere to once again try to establish and develop a successful business.

The complete analysis and evaluation of a business requires that an individual investigate the opportunities for growth and analyze the personnel and financial requirements for a growth process. The owners of a business may easily decide that they do not want their annual sales to exceed $500,000, because this would require the addition of vice presidents for personnel, production, or new technological engineers. The owners may decide that they would prefer to keep the business small, and work toward developing a positive image and reputation in their own community.

the termination stage

While most business owners hope they will never need to end their business careers, it is an area that should be investigated and analyzed before one even starts a business. There are several reasons why businesses are terminated—the death of an owner, mismanagement, lack of sales, and even economic changes, for example. The three most common forms of terminating a business are: (1) to sell—to friends, relatives, or other business persons, (2) to be acquired—to allow another business to acquire one's own business through merger or acquisition (the owner may opt to stay on with the business as a chief operator or even a president of that division of the larger company), and (3) to close the business—to terminate the actual and future operations of that business by locking the doors and closing the business for good. When the latter termination form is accomplished, it is most common to have going-out-of-business sales or other such endeavors, in order to sell off all inventory, equipment, and even fixtures to obtain sufficient capital to pay off all creditors and suppliers. It would also be nice to obtain sufficient funds from the sale of the land and building to provide a profit for the owners, and to allow them to start another business.

The owner often needs to be able to explain to bankers, loan officers, or other fiscal lending agencies how they would successfully terminate the business before it is even started. Many fiscal officers are desirous of being able to regain all the monies they have loaned to the business, and they make sure there would be no loss to their own businesses. Bankers and others will generally require the owner to name land and building as collateral, and to list any other inventories, fixtures, or furnishings that may be sold to pay off any mortgages or loans.

The termination of a business can be a very satisfying and positive experience. The owner may have started the business so that he or she may sell out at early retirement age, and live on the proceeds for the remainder of his or her life. The owner may also be able to help someone else start in the business at a reasonable rate, having them pay monthly installments of the debt incurred when the business was first acquired or bought.

summary: the four key stages

Analyzing these four key stages of a business will provide the owner with the key ingredients necessary to start his or her own business. The owner will have successfully investigated and analyzed almost all the important relevant information related to the business venture. The owner should be able to determine his or her own relative fitness or suitability with the future business, and should be able to handle most of the economic conditions as well as general crises that will occur to his or her business. In essence, these four stages are a guide to the owner as to understanding how to analyze, investigate, and evaluate business opportunities that may be made available to him or her. By following and developing these different stages, the owner should be protected against fraud, harm, and basic mismanagement of his or her business opportunities.

Industrial Groups

Entrepreneurs are present in almost every industry, although they do have a tendency to be more prevalent in the retail and service industries. This is primarily because of the opportunities and requirements that are available in these areas. There are four basic industrial groups that should be examined here:

1. Manufacturing.
2. Wholesaling.
3. Retailing.
4. Services.

manufacturing

The manufacturing business area mainly involves the conversion of raw materials into products, which are then sold to wholesaling or retailing establishments, who will then sell the products directly to the customers.

wholesaling   The wholesaling business area's people are often described as "middlemen"—they operate between the manufacturers and the retailers. Wholesalers generally buy manufacturers' products, store them in warehouses, and then sell them to retail outlets. Wholesale produce companies buy produce from farmers or from other produce companies, inspect and package the produce, then sell it to stores or retail outlets.

retailing   People in the retailing business areas, retailers, buy products from manufacturers or wholesalers, and sell directly to the end consumer, or customer. Automotive dealers buy their products from the parent company, and then sell them directly to you. The hamburger restaurant does the same.

services   The service business area's firms do not deal in products, but in services or personal skills. They provide their abilities to manufacturers, wholesalers, retailers, or customers. Automotive repair servicers sell their skills directly to the customers, either as an independent or as part of a retail operation. Plumbers sell certain skills to customers.

The Economic Environment

Before beginning a new business venture, it is important to analyze the economic environment. The economic environment would include information about: (1) the national economic picture, (2) the local economy, (3) available financing, and (4) future economic projections. It is harder and more hazardous to start any business during a recession, a depression, or when future projections show a downturn in the national economic picture.

The National Economic Forecast may be easily obtained by consulting with the United States Department of Commerce or with any of the Bureaus of Business Research that are located in every state of the union, generally at the major state university. The local economic picture is also very important. Information about the local economy may be obtained from the Chamber of Commerce, banks, or the Bureau of Business Research. Most states also have a Department of Economic Development which will provide information about economic conditions throughout the state.

It is difficult to obtain financing for a new business during periods of recession or anticipated downturn in the economy. Finance charges can go as high as 15 percent to 16 percent, which causes undue pressures on someone seeking to obtain a loan for the creation or expansion of a business. Inflation or recession will also cause people to cut down on their spending habits, causing a decline in the sales volumes of most businesses.

A major problem of any business during its creation or expansion is the obtaining of funds for debt capital. Banks and lending institutions prefer to loan money for short periods of time (short-term liabilities—one year or less—most preferable; long-term liabilities—payable beyond one year and generally not more than five—least preferable) during times of economic growth and prosperity. Lending institutions usually have large sums of money to loan at fairly reduced rates. This is often when many people have other sources of funds available, or need not borrow from a bank. However, during the downturns or falls in the economy, money becomes tighter (less money is available), and interest rates soar. During a poor agricultural crop year in the the Midwest, money becomes scarce and it is difficult to obtain funding for another expansion or growth period. The banks will save their available funds and will allocate them on a priority basis to their existing businesses and preferred customers.

It is very important to discover future objectives for the economy. One business owner decided to start a beauty store just prior to an economic recession. Since beauty aids are generally considered an impulse item, customers did not frequent the store, and it did not stay open long enough for the economy to turn and provide customers with funds to buy the items. The business went broke. It may be necessary to wait a year or two, but it is desirable to start a new business at the end of a recession or economic downturn, and to ride the upswing as a successful business develops.

The Industrial Environment

It is important that one investigate the industry—a collection of businesses engaged in similar activities—before creating a new business. The industrial environment should include: (1) the historical background, (2) the growth potential, (3) trade information and professional news, and (4) market and obsolescence factors.

Any industrial study should analyze the history of the business. The history may show limitations and sales potential of the business. The industrial background should also provide information about the growth potential of the particular business. If the industry is growing at an average rate of 10 percent, then it is fairly reasonable to predict that the business will grow at an annual rate approaching 10 percent.

A study of the industry should also include trade journals and other professional services that are available to businesses within the industry. Certain trade journals will supply information about start-up costs, and will develop partial feasibility studies for a business in the trade. For example, food trade journals provide lists of foods most commonly bought and a rank order of the convenience foods sold in stores.

A review of the industry will also provide information about market obsolescence factors and market potential. The industry may indicate future trends in the business and new products that are developing for that industry.

The Marketing Environment

An ideal new business would find a market that is large, is growing, and would allow it a fair market share resulting in significant sales volume. The competition should be strong, but not too strong—that is, not monopolistic or overwhelming.

The marketing environment, although initially small, should be sufficient to allow adequate profits and returns on investment. Finally, it is important to determine which marketing tactics may be allowed within the marketing environments.

An analysis of the marketing environment should allow for determination of the size and potential growth market for a particular product or service. This analysis should be complete, and should provide actual dollars and units of the total market size available. The total market area and the market data relevant to that geographical area should be determined.

It is also important to ascertain the level of competition—its strengths and weaknesses. Be specific and determine who the leading competitive sales leaders are, as well as the quality leader, the image leader, the price leader, the most aggressive competitor, and the one with the most potential growth. Information on specific competitors may be obtained from Dun & Bradstreet.

Information about competition will lead a potential owner to determine the total market and market segment that may be specifically expected. After determining the total market within the geographical area, the initial market share and the projected future estimated sales (with respective market shares for the coming three to five years) should be estimated. If a large market share is required to obtain sufficient returns or profits, the owner should probably rethink about opening the business, and should either go elsewhere or consider a different industry.

It is important to analyze the business tactics or methods of marketing sales that are allowed within the business area. Is it appropriate to use direct sales, distributors, or sales representatives? Should a guarantee or service warranty be provided in order to make each sale? Will it be necessary to provide a money-back guarantee? Is it ethical to advertise your goods or services? Can the proposed product or service be priced to sell for a profit in the geographical area? Will a new business be able to enter the market without undergoing price wars with the competition and being forced out of business?

The Business Environment

Before being able to develop a preliminary analysis of the industry or market, one must be able to explain and describe a specific business and the impact it will have upon the environment. (Can snowmobiles and related service successfully be sold in the South, around Atlanta or Houston?) Describe the new business and explain exactly what the product or service is that will be sold. Develop strengths and weaknesses you, the owner, will have, and finally, examine a time schedule that will make it feasible or not feasible to begin business operations.

business description

It is important for a new business to be accurately described and defined very clearly. What business will be started, and how will it interact with the business community and its customers? One must determine if the goods to be sold are: (1) impulse items, (2) convenience items, (3) utility items, (4) necessities or staples, or (5) luxury or durable items (see Table 6-1). The analysis should accurately describe the kind and type of business that will be started.

Table 6-1. Merchandise Classifications for Small Retail Stores

IMPULSE ITEMS	CONVENIENCE ITEMS	UTILITY ITEMS	NECESSITIES OR STAPLES	LUXURY OR DURABLE ITEMS
Displayed near checkout	Displayed near front or on main aisles	Displayed anywhere	Displayed anywhere	Displayed anywhere (luxury items often locked)
Candy Drinks Notions Health aids Costume jewelry	Magazines Tobacco products Paperback books Greeting cards Certain medicines	Brooms Garden tools Hand tools Wastebaskets Soaps	Men's clothing Shoes Prescription drugs Women's clothing Food	Jewelry Furniture TV sets Stereo sets Refrigerators
Bought on the spur of the moment; conveniently located on attractive displays	Bought frequently in small quantities. Easy access.	Bought for use in home or business. Easy access not required.	Bought to satisfy need. Located centrally or on sides of store.	Bought after planning, expected to last. Located where they may be supervised.

It is also important to explain what product and/or services will be sold. Many small business owners sell appliances and claim that to be their total business; however, they also provide repair services, installation, and replacement parts.

A business will also have specific strengths and weaknesses. What are the key benefits or advantages, and who will have a competitive edge in the market? Be very specific, and avoid such possible generalizations as lower prices and greater advertising. Analyze why a 5 percent price advantage in a fast-food hamburger shop will have a competitive advantage—it probably will not.

Finally, develop a time schedule that will allow the examination of time and cost required to achieve a business start-up and a market segment. If an owner starts with zero information and just an idea, can a business be started within six months, one year, or two years? How much lead time will be required to develop manufacturing processes or obtain inventory? Be specific.

External Information

Information about the creation and start-up of new businesses is becoming more readily available. The Bank of America provides different consulting guides with their small business reporter series. *Entrepreneur* magazine provides feasibility studies and business plans for approximately 170 different business ideas. Trade associations provide additional information concerning their industry and business. Most trade associations publish information concerning the sales, operating expenses, net profits, and projected financial performances for stores in different geographical regions. Such information is often available for new store outlets, as are historical figures for three to five years or longer. Personnel and compensation records are also available from many trade associations regarding relevant salaries and wages.

SUCCESS STORY: DeWitt Wallace

DeWitt Wallace was born in St. Paul, Minnesota, in 1889.[1] He attended Macalester College, where his father was president, for two years, then went on to the University of California for an additional two years. After leaving college, he took a job as an advertising salesman.

A voracious reader, Wallace was annoyed that he had to wade through so many magazines to "keep abreast of world thoughts." He felt that a new type of magazine was needed, one that would cull the best articles from other publications and reprint them, condensing them somewhat. World War I prevented him from doing anything about his idea immediately. After the war, however, he began to practice condensing articles. He did this in his spare time while working in the publicity department at Westinghouse.

In 1921, during the postwar business panic, DeWitt Wallace was fired. He moved to New York, got married, and borrowed $3,000. With that, he began to publish his magazine, which he called *The Reader's Digest*.

The first issue of *The Reader's Digest* appeared in February, 1922. Only 5,000 copies were printed. Despite the predictions of early bankruptcy by other editors, some $5,000 of subscriptions came in, and Wallace was able to continue.

The Reader's Digest defied publishing norms. It concentrated exclusively on nonfiction when most magazines published fiction. Wallace and his wife, who was also co-editor, were told that such a serious magazine would never have a circulation over 250,000. Circulation was 290,000 by 1929, and 1,500,000 by 1939. For 33 years, *The Reader's Digest* appeared without advertising.

Although the Wallaces, who continue to own 100 percent voting stock of *The Reader's Digest,* are wealthy, they are not interested in accumulating money, feeling that "there are more satisfying uses for it." Wallace has given $36,000,000 to Macalester College, while his wife has supported such far-flung causes as the Metropolitan Museum, art, the restoration of the house and gardens of Claude Monet, and the University of Oregon.

CASE STUDY: A Telephone Answering Service

Susan and Sydney have been married for about two years. They have been wanting to find something that they could do together. They have looked at different business ideas, but have never found something satisfactory. They have saved

---

[1]Donald Robinson, *The 100 Most Important People in the World Today* (New York: G. P. Putnam's Sons, 1970).

approximately $4,000 in cash, and a friend has recently advised them about starting a telephone answering service.

They started to do research on the industry, and found that telephones were being used more and more by businesses. They also discovered that telephone companies were advertising long-distance business calls as an option to travel. Phone use was up, and the future looked bright and promising.

Their initial research showed that a typical one-office operation, once established, is able to have an income of $125,000 to $200,000 annually, depending on the number of switchboards and workers taking calls. The overall net profit averaged 15 percent to 18 percent, and may reach 35 percent to 40 percent in large, well-run shops.

Susan and Sydney found that it would be possible to establish the business at their home, using their garage and a spare room. They anticipated to have sales of approximately $100,000 for the first year. This would be done by using a ten-position call director phone system with four attached switchboards. They estimated some start-up expenses and a profit and loss figure for the first year.

The market. The market is composed of any and all people or businesses who need to use a telephone. Many professional businesspeople—such as doctors, salespeople, plumbers, electricians, and professors—are often out of their offices and need phone answering services. A major focus would be on people requiring twenty-four-hour service or "on call" status, such as the many service agencies (repair services, dishwashers, clothing dryers, blood banks, and ambulances). Several smaller businesses also require phone services.

Sydney and Susan also found that a basic charge of $35.00 per month was the average for a specific number of calls, with an additional 25¢ extra for calls over that number. The general rate was sixty calls per month.

They were surprised to find that it was important to be close to the main telephone company station. They would only be able to handle the phone exchanges that the centralized phone station handled. In other words, they would be limited to serving customers within the exchange group of that telephone system, unless special equipment was installed at a greater cost.

The telephone company indicated to them that they rented phone lines in groups of twenty for approximately $35.00 per month. The traditional switchboard generally handles 100 incoming phone lines with fifteen major office trunk lines. If they had only thirty-two customers initially, it would probably be best to order only forty lines and have the additional lines installed as customers come on board.

TELEPHONE ANSWERING SERVICE
Start-Up Expenses

Rent (3 months)	$ 900
Switchboard installations	5,000
Cable installations	3,000
Building preparation	1,000
Utility deposits	100
Furniture and equipment	2,000
Accounting	200
Legal	500
Advertising	1,500
Salaries	2,000
Insurance (3 months)	600
Licenses	100
Total	$16,900

TELEPHONE ANSWERING SERVICE

Income:		
Gross Sales	$112,000	$112,000
Expenses:		
Salary (owners)	21,600	
Telephone expense (Rental and charges)	17,520	
Payroll	40,400	
Rent	3,600	
Utilities	1,500	
Insurance	2,220	
Supplies	1,000	
Accounting	600	
Advertising	1,680	
Other	500	
Total		$ 90,620
Net Profit Before Taxes		$ 21,380
Percent of Sales		approx. 19%

Questions

1. Susan and Sydney think they are ready to start their business. Are they?
2. Are there any other things they should check first?
3. Have they analyzed the proper things thoroughly enough?
4. Would you like to start this type of business? Why or why not?

Chapter Questions:

1. What are the four key stages through which most businesses go?
2. What are the advantages of the pre-business stage and what is it primarily concerned with?
3. Why are businesses usually broken down into four major industrial classifications? What are they?
4. Why is it important to study the economic environment?
5. Why is there a need to study the industrial environment?
6. What external information is generally available to research a venture idea?
7. Why is it important to research a venture before actually starting a business?
8. Why is it important to analyze the market environment, and why might such research significantly alter or affect your decision about going into business?

APPENDIX

Researching a Venture Checklist

PRE-BUSINESS STAGE

Business idea	( ) excellent	( ) good	( ) fair	( ) poor
Entrepreneurial decision	( ) strong	( ) good	( ) mild	( ) weak
Entrepreneurial team	( ) strong	( ) good	( ) mild	( ) weak
Feasibility study	( ) excellent	( ) good	( ) fair	( ) poor
Personal business decision	( ) strong	( ) good	( ) mild	( ) weak

BUSINESS STAGE

Product development	( ) excellent	( ) good	( ) fair	( ) poor
Building (remodeling) plans	( ) excellent	( ) good	( ) fair	( ) poor
Equipment	( ) excellent	( ) good	( ) fair	( ) poor
Marketing	( ) excellent	( ) good	( ) fair	( ) poor
Advertising	( ) excellent	( ) good	( ) fair	( ) poor
Internal Revenue Service	( ) excellent	( ) good	( ) fair	( ) poor
Government agencies	( ) excellent	( ) good	( ) fair	( ) poor
Inventory	( ) excellent	( ) good	( ) fair	( ) poor
Supplies	( ) excellent	( ) good	( ) fair	( ) poor
Store displays	( ) excellent	( ) good	( ) fair	( ) poor
Handouts	( ) excellent	( ) good	( ) fair	( ) poor
Personnel training	( ) excellent	( ) good	( ) fair	( ) poor
Management development	( ) excellent	( ) good	( ) fair	( ) poor
Team development	( ) excellent	( ) good	( ) fair	( ) poor
Open business	( ) excellent	( ) good	( ) fair	( ) poor

GROWTH STAGE

Expansion opportunities	( ) excellent	( ) good	( ) fair	( ) poor
Develop: New products	( ) excellent	( ) good	( ) fair	( ) poor
New services	( ) excellent	( ) good	( ) fair	( ) poor
Acquisition	( ) excellent	( ) good	( ) fair	( ) poor
Merger	( ) excellent	( ) good	( ) fair	( ) poor
Available finances	( ) excellent	( ) good	( ) fair	( ) poor
Available manpower	( ) excellent	( ) good	( ) fair	( ) poor

TERMINATION STAGE

Opportunity to sell	( ) excellent	( ) good	( ) fair	( ) poor
Opportunity to be acquired	( ) excellent	( ) good	( ) fair	( ) poor
Need to close business	( ) excellent	( ) good	( ) fair	( ) poor

Researching a Venture Checklist (continued)

ECONOMIC ENVIRONMENT

National economy	( ) excellent	( ) good	( ) fair	( ) poor
Local economy	( ) excellent	( ) good	( ) fair	( ) poor
Available financing	( ) excellent	( ) good	( ) fair	( ) poor
Future economic picture	( ) excellent	( ) good	( ) fair	( ) poor

INDUSTRIAL ENVIRONMENT

Historical background	( ) excellent	( ) good	( ) fair	( ) poor
Growth potential	( ) excellent	( ) good	( ) fair	( ) poor
Trade information	( ) excellent	( ) good	( ) fair	( ) poor
Market factors	( ) excellent	( ) good	( ) fair	( ) poor

MARKETING ENVIRONMENT

Large size	( ) excellent	( ) good	( ) fair	( ) poor
Competition	( ) excellent	( ) good	( ) fair	( ) poor
The market	( ) excellent	( ) good	( ) fair	( ) poor

BUSINESS ENVIRONMENT

Description	( ) excellent	( ) good	( ) fair	( ) poor
Strengths	( ) excellent	( ) good	( ) fair	( ) poor
Weaknesses	( ) excellent	( ) good	( ) fair	( ) poor
Future	( ) excellent	( ) good	( ) fair	( ) poor

7

Photo courtesy of Irene Springer, Prentice-Hall, Inc.

SELECTING A BUSINESS

Chapter Objectives:

1. To become familiar with the processes necessary to choose a business.
2. To understand how to choose a business.
3. To understand the methods of evaluating business property.
4. To know the different ways of receiving income from a business.
5. To learn about franchising.
6. To know what to look for in a franchise agreement.

You see things; and you say, "Why?" But I dream things that never were; and I say, "Why not?"

George Bernard Shaw

Great men are said to have four things in common: They speak softly, have a capacity for hard work, a deep conviction for their cause, and a consuming belief in their ability to do it.

John D. Hass

INCIDENT: Hal is sick and tired of his current job. He has been working as a professor of mathematics for eight years; he spent five years before that doing graduate studies beyond a bachelor's degree in order to obtain his Ph.D. in mathematics. He is well respected in his community and by his colleagues. However, he wants to leave that profession to start a small business.

Hal has somehow managed to save $12,000. He also owns two homes in Wyoming that are within two blocks of a growing university campus. These homes could be sold, with a net profit exceeding $16,000 for each home.

Hal does not know what kind of business he really wants to go into. He is somewhat interested in the food business—restaurants, fast-food hamburger places, pizza shops, Orange Julius shops, and Pop Shoppes. He has thought about opening a Dairy Queen or a Baskin-Robbins ice cream store. Someone has also interested him in starting a bicycle shop, and he is also considering that.

How should Hal get started? Where should he go for information? What should be his area of concern and what should he do during the next six months or year? How soon could he start? If he does start the new business, should he resign or should he continue to teach mathematics?

Choosing a small business is very similar to purchasing a car: There are certain steps that need to be followed. First, you need to determine what kind of car you are interested in purchasing. Do not limit yourself to a particular kind of car, such as a Maserati or a Porsche, but investigate the entire industry. Determine what type of Ford, General Motors, Chrysler, Toyota, or American Motors car you would be interested in buying. You may want a car that requires a lot of handling, with a stick shift with dual carburetors. You may want a sporty car that will require a lot of your time to wash, polish, and keep up in general. You may want a car that is small, to be primarily used for transportation from home to work or to the grocery store.

SELECTING A BUSINESS

You also need to determine what size car that you would like to buy, the basic costs of repair and upkeep, and if you "like" the car. The latter is often most strongly influenced by the cost, or by the funds you would have available with which to purchase the car. Instead of buying a large Ford LTD, you may decide that you had best buy a used Plymouth Champ.

You need to be sure that you like the car. You must realize that you will probably be spending a lot of time with it, because you will probably have it for three or more years.

In starting a new business, you need to determine (1) what kind of business you will become involved with, (2) the size of the business, (3) whether or not the business is a "good" one, (4) the operational costs of that business and its associated profitability (are the profits sufficient for your total commitment?) and (5) whether or not you will be willing to spend your lifetime with that business. These decisions must be investigated before any final decision is made about choosing a small business.

Choosing an Existing Business

Many of the factors involved in choosing a business are personal ones. The desirability for any one business is particular to any given individual. The type and size of the business are personal factors, as well as being limited by available financing. In choosing a business, either as an existing business or as a franchisee, it is important to properly evaluate the business opportunity.

The evaluation of any business is the crucial stage prior to the actual opening of that business. The prospective owner faces the dilemma of determining fair costs associated with reasonable profitability for a particular business. Such an evaluation should cover the following points:

1. The reason for the sale.
2. Earnings or profit evaluation.
3. Assets.
4. Book value.
5. Liquidation value.
6. Replacement value.
7. Liabilities.
8. Image and other areas.

reason for selling

In the case of the small business owner going out of business, the reason to sell may easily be for ill health, a death in the family, a desire to relocate, or even to pay off tax debts. Causes that should be of major concern to you would be declining business, poor location, declining industrial strength, obsolete products, new competition, loss of lease, or simply poor management. Changing economic conditions, inflation, or recession may also make it difficult to collect accounts receivable and to stay in business. There may also be problems with suppliers or creditors that are forcing an owner to sell.

earnings or profit evaluation

One of the most important factors in evaluating a business is the earnings or the profit potential of that business. It is expected that if earnings, the rate of growth of earnings, and the long-run stability of the earnings picture have a positive trend, then it should follow that the business will continue to progress and should have increased earnings and profits in the future. Predictions of all future earnings, however, are suspect, as they are always dependent upon economic conditions and market desires. To properly estimate the potential earning or profit power of the business, one must obtain reliable records of: (1) the business income for the past three to five years, (2) a breakdown of sales and expense figures for the same historical period, (3) the future earning potential under current owner, and (4) the earning potential of the business under your (new) ownership. It is impossible to objectively figure all of these four categories; however, it is important that you endeavor to obtain as much information as possible. Be alert for the seller who will fail or will refuse to provide adequate historical figures; this is a sign that there is something wrong with the business, if only sloppy bookkeeping.

It is difficult, if not impossible, to properly evaluate a business without some historical information about the business. Forms that are generally available from a seller include (1) federal and state income tax returns, (2) income statements showing sales and operating expenses, (3) bank statements showing deposits and reconciliations, (4) sales records, (5) inventory records, and (6) purchase records.

In addition, it is important to obtain proper financial statements from the current owner. The three statements that would be the most useful are (1) the income statement, (2) the cash flow analysis, and (3) the balance sheet. The income statement and balance sheet may be used to compare with other businesses in the same industry. It is easy to compare sales figures for comparable size stores and more important, you can compare percent figures of the cost of goods sold, assets, and liabilities between companies. Such comparative figures are published by Robert Morris Associates, Dun & Bradstreet, and National Cash Register. This analysis should include the potential business of the current owner as well as any future profitability under new ownership. If the business is highly unprofitable in this projection, you should stop looking for further transactions. If the current owner cannot improve earnings, this should be a warning to you that you could have some trouble handling the business, as the chances for improvement are slight, and—unless you have sufficient expertise to at least duplicate the current owner's position and management skills—you might soon lose the business.

assets

The potential assets of any new business need to be closely investigated and evaluated. These assets include (1) inventory, (2) accounts receivable, (3) equipment and real estate holdings, (4) furniture and fixtures, (5) the lease, (6) business good will, including customer lists in any business or credit records, and (7) other good will, trademarks, copyrights, business names, reputation, clientele and credit relations.

There are three major forms of evaluating assets (1) book value, (2) liquidation value, and (3) replacement value.

Book value. The easiest and simplest form of evaluation of assets is the *current* book value. (However, if a business is more than three years old, this is probably one of the worst evaluation procedures available.) The book value is a starting point, and it provides a tangible, known dollar quantity. A book value follows generally accepted accounting principles and procedures, and lists all fixtures, inventory, equipment, and buildings at cost. All assets of a business are recorded, when obtained, at their cost. For example, if you started a shoe store four years ago and paid $100,000 for your building and the internal fixtures and equipment, the value of that building, fixtures, and equipment today would be $100,000. However, because of inflation, it is known that the value is probably at least $140,000, even though the books would only show a value of $100,000. The book value does not state the actual market value of tangible assets such as building and equipment. (See Table 7–1.) Over time, the equipment of a business would probably be depreciated to zero, while the tangible assets (such as the building and the land) may appreciate in value far beyond the original cost. It would be easy for a businessperson who started a fancy restaurant in the mid-1960s at a cost of $200,000 to have a current book value of $200,000, but a market value of close to $400,000 today.

Liquidation value. A second method of asset evaluation is to determine the net cash amount realized if assets were sold; that is, the liquidation value of a business; which is the sale of all assets minus the paying off of all liabilities. If you sell your car for $600 but you still owe $350 on it, the liquidation value is $250. This value takes into account all the current market values of the business and provides a real cash value of the business. The liquidation value, however, does not reflect an inherent value of staying open and continuing as a going business, nor does it include the reputation or the ability to retain customers for future business. The liquidation value does show a cost below which the seller would generally be unwilling to sell, because he or she could obtain at least that price through liquidating the entire business.

Replacement value. The replacement value of a business is determined by

**Table 7–1. Asset Evaluation
Super Sandwich Restaurant**

	BOOK VALUE	LIQUIDATION VALUE	REPLACEMENT VALUE
Current Assets:			
Cash	$ 6,525	$ 6,525	$ 6,525
Merchandise inventory	3,000	600	3,900
Investments	38,500	21,000	41,000
Fixed Assets:			
Fixtures and equipment	32,000	12,000	39,000
Remodeling and improvements	18,000	0	26,000
Land	18,000	24,000	24,000
Building	82,000	102,000	121,000
Total Assets:	$198,025	$166,125	$261,425

figuring the cost of duplicating that business as it exists today. How much would it cost to buy your car today? This would be the cost you would incur if you hired someone to build the same building, and to obtain the same equipment, fixtures, furniture, and inventory that the business currently possesses. This is generally the highest value of the three, due to the high cost of the building, land, and purchasing of new inventory and equipment. This evaluation is primarily used as a reference point rather than in serious consideration. In almost all cases, it is cheaper to open a new business than to provide the replacement value of an existing one.

liabilities

Before buying any business, it is important to obtain a true picture of all current and future liabilities. The hidden liabilities of a business may be quite expensive. Liabilities may be placed into four categories: (1) notes payable (IOUs to bank suppliers or creditors), (2) accounts payable (IOUs to trade organizations), (3) income taxes (IOUs to the government, federal and state), and (4) long-term liabilities to banks, to savings and loan organizations, or to other financial institutions for plant or equipment mortgages. Any sales contract between buyer and seller of a business should contain, in writing, all liabilities that would be assumed by the new owner. Such a contract should also include a statement that all claims not shown on the contract or the balance sheet as of the date of acquisition are to be assumed by the seller. Such a legal formality will protect the buyer against any past or future liabilities incurred by the previous owner.

image and other areas

There are several additional economic and business areas that need evaluation before one buys a business. Just as you would seek all possible information about the other person before going on a date, you should seek all available information before taking on a new business. The economy of the community, history of the location, licensing requirements, sales forecasts, and capital requirements are all important in buying a business. (See Figure 7–1.)

There are five major ways for an owner or manager to take out personal income from a business:

1. Salary and interest, where both are personal income and are taxed at the personal level. In a sole proprietorship or a partnership, there is no corporate tax levied.

2. Dividends received from a corporation are the least desirable of all methods for an individual to receive a return from his or her business. Dividends are first taxed at the corporate level before they are distributed to the share owners. If a dividend received the maximum corporate tax rate of 48 percent (sliding scale of 22 percent to 48 percent current tax rate) and a maximum personal income of 70 percent, the resulting double taxation (corporate and personal) would reduce one dollar of pre-tax corporate profit to 15¢, which the individual may keep after all taxes.

3. Fringe benefits are not really cash items at all but are considered by the IRS as well as by businesses as being equivalent to cash items or direct benefits. These include company cars, expense accounts, country club

NONFINANCIAL AREAS OF EVALUATION

	Excellent	Good	Adequate	Poor	Disastrous
1. The neighborhood and community	[ ]	[ ]	[ ]	[ ]	[ ]
2. Competitors in similar firms	[ ]	[ ]	[ ]	[ ]	[ ]
3. History of the location	[ ]	[ ]	[ ]	[ ]	[ ]
4. Condition of the building and equipment	[ ]	[ ]	[ ]	[ ]	[ ]
5. Meeting local building and health code laws	[ ]	[ ]	[ ]	[ ]	[ ]
6. License requirements	[ ]	[ ]	[ ]	[ ]	[ ]
7. Licensing eligibility	[ ]	[ ]	[ ]	[ ]	[ ]
8. Ability to pay loan repayments	[ ]	[ ]	[ ]	[ ]	[ ]
9. Low total capital needed	[ ]	[ ]	[ ]	[ ]	[ ]
10. Low working capital required	[ ]	[ ]	[ ]	[ ]	[ ]
11. Projected sales and profits for the next twelve months and three to five years	[ ]	[ ]	[ ]	[ ]	[ ]
12. Economic conditions	[ ]	[ ]	[ ]	[ ]	[ ]
13. General health and welfare of the community	[ ]	[ ]	[ ]	[ ]	[ ]

Figure 7–1. *Evaluation rating scale*

memberships, and so forth. Although the law is continually changing, these benefits are primarily received by an individual without taxation at either the corporate or personal level. These benefits must also meet certain limitations and regulations of the government and the IRS.

4. Debt repayment has a special advantage of being tax free at both the personal and the corporate levels. This may occur while allowing the entrepreneur to maintain a continuous equity interest with the business.

5. Capital return from the sale of the business; upon selling the business, the owner or manager receives all of the money up to the original cost input at a tax free level. Any capital gain obtained from the sale of the business would be taxed at a rate lower than regular income.

SUCCESS STORY: Mary Kay Ash

Mary Kay Ash exemplifies the fact that all successful middle-aged entrepreneurs are not men—some are women.

Mary Kay started at the bottom of the economic ladder. She grew up in Houston, Texas, keeping house for an invalid father while her mother worked fourteen hours a day. Although she got straight A's in school, there was no money to send her to college, so she directed her energy toward another important activity: marriage. This, however, ended when her husband filed for divorce upon returning from World War II. With her hopes and her dreams shattered, she still had to continue as there were three children to provide for.

Mary Ash then entered the career of direct sales through home shows. The direct sales organizations she worked for included Stanley Home Products and the World Gift Company. Her first home show netted her $2.01. After a subsequent trip to a regional sales convention in Dallas, she vowed to be next year's queen of sales. Ash coupled her determination with what she had learned at the convention and did become queen the following year. After working for the World Gift Company for a period of time and reaching the position of national training director, she resigned to open a small business of her own. She wrote down everything she knew about direct sales, and ended up with a formula for a successful company. The product she chose for her company was a skin cream produced by a local tanner's granddaughter. She was eager to sell her formula and so Mary Kay Cosmetics was started on September 13, 1963, in a rented storefront with a life savings of $5,000. By the end of 1963, sales reached $34,000 and a profit was shown. The first full year's sales were $198,000; the next year they rose to $800,000. Mary Kay Cosmetics was well on its way, and is still continuing its success with a market value of almost $50 million and retail sales in 1979 of $175 million.

So Mary Kay Ash has built her small venture into a multimillion dollar business. But what policies has Ash used and continued to use to attain this success? She, more than almost anyone else, is clued in to female psychology—women need praise. So Mary Kay follows the philosophy of praising. Incentives Mary Kay uses are pink Cadillacs, mink coats, diamond rings, gold pins, silver coffee services, diamond-studded bumblebees, and—most important of all—approximately 2,000 personally hand-signed letters per week. She also brings innovations to the direct sales field including very high commissions, no fixed assigned territories, a new system of incentives for recruiting, and beauty shows: a two-hour beauty-care program plus personalized make-up lessons in a hostess's home. All of these have contributed to the success of Mary Kay Cosmetics. Not only are Mary Kay Cosmetics and Mary Kay Ash successful but so are the thousands of independent saleswomen that work for her.

Franchising

A very common and growing form of business that offers a means for any individual to become an owner or manager with limited business experience is franchising. Franchising may be described as a form of licensing by the owner (franchisor) to use affiliated dealerships (franchisees) for wholesale or retail distribution. The franchisee generally becomes the owner or operator of that business in a particular geographical location, or for a particular number of units within a location.

The goods, service, or method being marketed by the franchisor is generally identified by a brand name (such as McDonald's) and the franchisor maintains control over the marketing methods employed by the business. This is similar to a large grocery chain store (Safeway, for example) or a department store (like Montgomery Ward) with their trademarks, equipment, symbols, uniforms, and standardized services or practices.

franchisor

The franchisor will generally maintain control over the operation of the franchisees, and will require them to meet particular standards of performance and quality. The success of the business is often dependent upon the name, reputation, operating, and managerial skills of the franchisor. The extent of the franchisor's control will vary. In many cases, the franchisees are required to conduct every step and operation according to a specific guidebook or handbook of instructions. This may be desirable in that the franchisee may have little or no experience in the business. The franchisor is also responsible for maintaining leadership in the quality of goods, marketing, customer appeal, and innovative management techniques used throughout the chain. The parent company is responsible for the future of the business and for the expansion of the business into new and different localities.

franchisee

The franchisee becomes the local owner or manager of the new business. He or she is responsible for all the activities and profitability of that business. He or she will need to operate within the standards and guidelines established by the parent company. The franchisee will find it easier and less expensive to go the franchise route rather than trying it alone. The franchisee can expect and demand expertise in marketing, management, product control, and customer relations from the franchisor.

The franchisee can also expect the following from the parent company:

1. Product, product design, and marketing.
2. Store layout, design, and equipment purchasing.
3. Financial assistance in the start-up of the business.
4. Location analysis.
5. Building development and space allocation.
6. Management and employee training.

7. Advertising and marketing assistance.
8. Standardization of procedures and operations.
9. Centralization of purchasing with volume discounts.

franchise agreement

Any franchise agreement is a long and involved legal document involving checks and balances for both franchisor and franchisee. It will develop, in great detail, the regulations and limitations that a franchisee must meet in order to continue the agreement while explaining what the franchisor will provide in the form of business assistance and services during the continuation of the franchise agreement. A good basic franchise agreement will stipulate the conditions for both parties, and will contain information on:

1. Initial cost.
2. Product service method stipulations.
3. Royalties.
4. Location and territorial rights.
5. Training.
6. Controls.
7. Termination.

The franchisee should check to make sure that all these areas are satisfactorily covered before signing any franchise agreement. (See checklist in Appendix.)

initial cost

Franchises vary in initial fees from a few hundred dollars to several hundred-thousand dollars, depending on the form of business and agreement. The franchisee must be able to determine the total start-up or turnkey cost required by the franchisor. This may be a total lump sum amount, or—for a larger restaurant or other expensive franchise—only a down payment. The initial cost should include:

1. The franchise fee or the cost associated with the right to use trade names, procedures, goods, or services of the parent company. Generally, this also includes initial training and assistance.
2. Land and building costs or lease deposits.
3. The location or site evaluation fee, which may include parent company marketing studies.
4. Equipment costs, including new or used equipment or leases.
5. Enough working capital to cover operating expenses or to ensure success for the first few months of business operation.

product service method

An important aspect of a franchise agreement is the explanation and description of the product service or method of operation to be employed by the franchisee. For example, a service station may be limited to the Texaco trade name and use of inventory that must be purchased from the franchisor. Accounting or tax services, employment agencies, and other business service firms might establish a franchise that would use simply their name, forms, or different operating methods. More elaborate franchises will require total conformity as to products, services, and even the operating methods imposed by the franchisee. This would include the location, erection of the building, store front, even the tables, chairs, and wallpaper used within a business. Most "Wendy's," "Burger King," or "Pizza Hut" restaurants are identical. Many of these more expensive and elaborate franchise stores will require specific uniforms and quality control checks on products and their usage.

royalties

In addition to the initial franchise fee, many franchisors will require a royalty in return for the use of their name, goods, or services. The royalty is generally figured as a percent of gross sales of the business, and it typically ranges from 1 percent to 14 percent of the total revenue of the business. Many fast-food restaurants charge from 2 percent to 4 percent of gross sales for the franchise rights. Additionally, the franchisor may be required to pay for national advertising, local advertising, management services, product research, and even inventory control records. The franchisor may also obtain additional funding from inventory sold to the franchise, interest on available financing, lease arrangements, and even markup on equipment or supplies.

location and territorial rights

Most parent companies and some small franchisors will provide plant or site location studies to provide the best overall location for profitability or usage. The location study is conducted to ensure large market areas and geographical exclusivity. Included in this part of the agreement should be clarification as to: (1) who will own or purchase the site, (2) territorial restrictions, (3) franchise exclusivity (where the franchisor will not open a business itself nor provide a direct franchise to another), and (4) any requirements for growth within the geographical territory for the duration of the franchise agreement. (For example, the Pizza Hut may require that you build an additional four stores within your geographical area during the next ten years, or lose your franchise agreement.)

training

Almost all reputable and large franchises provide managerial and employee training for the franchisee. This will last for a period of one week to four months and may require the franchisee to travel to the home base for such training. A "Hamburger University" has been established by one company, McDonald's, to train its franchisees and provide up-to-date training for owners and managers. Training costs may or may not be included in the initial franchise cost, and should be investigated. Many programs will provide the franchisee with experience in the actual operations of a going franchise elsewhere in the nation. This on-the-job training includes working in an operating franchise unit for a small period of time. Additionally, many franchisors provide managerial assistance during pre-operation and operation of the business. Company newsletters, magazines, tapes, advertisements, journals, and brochures are often provided from the parent company to the affiliated businesses.

controls   Most franchise agreements involve the controls and operating agreements established between the franchisor and the franchisee. The controls are primarily established to ensure the proper use of names, figures, symbols, equipment, furnishings, building design and layout, and product usage and quality. An operations manual is also included, which will specify how the business should be run and include company policies and practices that often cover: hours of the business, recipes, food storage, recordkeeping methods and procedures, hiring of employees, business forms, and fixtures. These operating guidelines are often one of the major causes of dissatisfaction with the franchise business.

duration and termination   Most franchise agreements run for a long duration—ten, twenty, or possibly thirty years. The service station or automotive agencies generally offer franchise grants for shorter periods, while others such as sporting good stores or soft drink companies may allow franchises for perpetuity. The duration of a franchise agreement is very important, and it is often coupled with a termination clause. The termination portion will stipulate what conditions have to be met by the franchisees to ensure the duration of the business. Franchisees will often find themselves at a disadvantage, because franchisors will have specific rights to cancel or even refuse to renew the contract, often for very minor or insignificant reasons. As the duration clause comes to an end, the franchisee may suffer greatly from the insecurity of possible nonrenewal or loss of the franchise.

The franchisee should be certain that it states in the contract that he or she has the right to renew the contract upon its expiration and also has the opportunity to transfer (if possible) or sell the business to the highest bidder.

The franchisee may also request that the franchisor promise to buy back the franchise should it fail or go out of business. It is very rare, if ever, that the franchisor will share in a financial loss associated with a franchise.

government restrictions and the future   Many states are now requiring franchisors to provide full disclosure operating statements, allowing franchise purchasers to make more informed and knowledgeable decisions. Government regulations are also trying to eliminate price fixing and to stipulate that franchisors cannot set, but can only suggest, a price at which the franchisee may sell his or her goods or services.

While many states argue that all types of territorial registrations need to be eliminated, franchisors generally limit the use of trademarks, signs, and other franchisees from entering a specific geographical location. However, the franchisor may not prohibit the franchisee from selling to any customer not operating outside of a specific geographical area. Legislation has also been established to ensure that a franchisor cannot force franchisees to buy general merchandise and equipment from the company or specific suppliers. The franchisor may only require equipment that ensures the quality or standardization of the final product or service.

summary of franchise system   The future of the franchise system is bright. The food and drink industry will provide the primary growth, while the automotive and truck dealers, service stations, and even soft drink bottlers—the traditional franchisee companies—will probably have a limited extension or a drop in the number of operations. Although people criticize the franchise system, it does allow the independent businessperson or small entrepreneur to compete against the corporate giants.

CASE STUDY: Kathy's Hamburger Shoppe

The hamburger has become the major fast-food item in America. The ground beef patty sandwiched between two halves of a bun is as popular in America as pasta in Italy and rice in China. However, this popular food for all ages has been preshaped, frozen, shrunken, and mistreated to the extent that it may be no longer worthy of its position.

Then in 1970, Kathy Collins decided to develop an original old-fashioned hamburger. Her offspring became the custom-built, cook-to-order feature of Kathy's Hamburger Shoppe. Assembling all of her personal assets and with resources from friends, Collins set out to market the "quality first" concept. This involved her knowledge of merchandising and quality food commitment. Kathy's menu consists of a single (quarter-pound) hamburger; a double (half-pound) hamburger; a triple (three-quarter pound) hamburger; French fries, Kathy's own secret-recipe vanilla freeze (a thick shake you can eat with a spoon), and various drinks. A unique feature of Kathy's is the rustic style interior decorations and the drive-thru window, an innovation in the hamburger industry. Dressed in the esthetic charm of the Tiffany shades, cane-back chairs, rich red and brown carpeting, glistening colored beads and flocked wallpaper, Kathy's dining room is charming and attractive. With 46 successful units now in operation, Kathy's operation has proven to be mechanically and fiscally sound through the past decade. Quick service, high quality food, and quality standards have undergirded Kathy's start in the fast-food market.

The popularity of franchises in the United States has grown tremendously in the last several years. Investors like franchises because the firms have proven their market acceptance, and customers identify with the nationally known product.

Scott has been saving for over six years to start a Kathy's Hamburger Shoppe in a southern California city of approximately 250,000. There are no other Kathy's restaurants within the city limits; the closest one is approximately 47 miles away in a neighboring town. Scott likes Kathy's limited menu centering around the fresh-cooked one-quarter, one-half, three-quarter pound hamburgers, the rustic dining room and the unique "pick-up" window.

Scott has learned Kathy's International, Inc. does not require prior fast-food business experience. They do require a minimum capital outlay, a good business knowledge, and the desire to work hard to make the investment successful. The parent company expects a $200,000 equity capital base with a total investment of $400,000 plus. The parent company will provide no financial assistance.

Kathy's International, Inc. will provide two eleven-week training sessions for the manager or operator in the classroom and on-the-job at Kathy's Hamburger School in Salt Lake City, Utah, prior to the opening of the restaurant. The parent company will also provide manuals and services to cover cost controls, develop personnel management, control quality, plus field consultations and helps in purchasing and operations. The franchise fee is approximately $25,000 per unit. The franchise is an exclusive performance contract that runs for approximately 30 years. Although Kathy's International, Inc. does have national contracts with processors throughout the country, which may save money, buying is not restricted to these particular companies; the franchisee may purchase supplies and equipment from any source he or she likes.

Scott sees his start-up costs as:

Franchise fee	$ 25,000
Land	125,000
Building	145,000
Site work	25,000
Sign package	15,000
Opening inventory	3,000
Equipment package, including:	75,000
Cash registers	
Patty machines	
Permits	
Executone equipment	
	$413,000

Questions

1. What additional information would be necessary to protect the franchisee?
2. If you were Scott, would you be able and willing to start a Kathy's Hamburger Shoppe?
3. What else should Scott do before starting his Kathy's restaurant?

Chapter Questions:

1. In what ways is choosing a small business like buying a car?
2. What factors should be considered before buying a new business?
3. What are the three major forms of evaluating assets?
4. Which evaluation technique would be considered to be a reference point rather than a serious consideration? Which evaluation technique is the most practical?
5. What are the major ways in which an individual may obtain profits from a business?
6. Why is franchising becoming increasingly popular?
7. What would you look for in obtaining a franchise?
8. What points would be important to include in a franchise agreement?
9. Why are government restrictions important to any small business?

APPENDIX

Checklist for Evaluating a Franchise[1]

The Franchise:

1. Did your lawyer approve the franchise contract you are considering after studying it paragraph by paragraph?
2. Does the franchise call upon you to take any steps that are, according to your lawyer, unwise or illegal in your state, county, or city?
3. Does the franchise give you an exclusive territory for the length of the franchise, or can the franchisor sell a second or third franchise in your territory?
4. Is the franchisor in any way connected with any other franchise company handling similar merchandise or services?
5. If the answer to the last question is yes, what is your protection against this second franchisor organization?
6. Under what circumstances can you terminate the franchise contract, and at what cost to you, if you decide for any reason at all that you wish to cancel it?
7. If you sell your franchise, will you be compensated for your good will, or will the good will you have built into the business be lost by you?

The Franchisor:

1. For how many years has the firm offering you a franchise been in operation?
2. Has it a reputation for honesty and fair dealing among the local firms holding its franchise?
3. Has the franchisor shown you any certified figures indicating exact net profits of one or more going firms that you personally checked with the franchise?
4. Will the firm assist you with:
    (a) a management training program?
    (b) an employee training program?
    (c) a public relations program?
    (d) capital?
    (e) credit?
    (f) merchandising ideas?
5. Will the firm assist you in finding a good location for your new business?
6. Is the franchising firm adequately financed so that it can carry out its stated plan of financial assistance and expansion?
7. Is the franchisor a one-person company, or is it a corporation with an experienced management trained in depth (so that there will always be an experienced person at its head)?
8. Exactly what can the franchisor do for you that you cannot do for yourself?
9. Has the franchisor investigated you carefully enough to assure itself that you can successfully operate one of their franchises at a profit to them *and* to you?
10. Does your state have any laws regulating the sale of these franchises, and has the franchisor complied with these laws?

[1]U.S. Department of Commerce *Franchise Opportunities Handbook,* (Washington, D.C.: U.S. Government Printing Office).

The Franchisee:

1. How much equity capital will you have to have to purchase the franchise and operate it until your income equals your expenses? Where are you going to get it?
2. Are you prepared to give up some independence of action in order to secure the advantages offered by the franchise?
3. Do you really believe you have the innate ability, training, and experience to work smoothly and profitably with the franchisor, your employees, and your customers?
4. Are you ready to spend much or all of the remainder of your business life with this franchisor, offering its product or service to your public?

The Market:

1. Have you made any study to determine whether the product or service which you propose to sell under franchise has a market in your territory at the prices you will have to charge?
2. Will the population in the territory given you increase, remain static, or decrease over the next five years?
3. Will the product or service you are considering be in greater, about the same, or less demand five years from now?
4. What competition already exists in your territory for the product or service you contemplate selling?
    (a) nonfranchise firms?
    (b) franchise firms?

8

Photo courtesy of Irene Springer, Prentice-Hall, Inc.

FINANCING THE VENTURE

Chapter Objectives:

1. To understand different ways of financing a venture.
2. To learn about the importance of planning financial needs.
3. To know about those financial records required in financing a business.
4. To understand the differences between equity financing and debt financing (working capital and capital expenditures).
5. To learn the four Cs of credit.
6. To learn about the major sources of funds available for a small business.

Never spend your money before you have it.

Thomas Jefferson

Expenditure always rises to meet income.

Cyril Northcote Parkinson

INCIDENT: Dennis will be leaving the military in the next two months, after five years of active duty. He is a pilot in the United States Air Force, is a graduate of a local state university, and is married to his college sweetheart.

Dennis wants to open a hardware store in his hometown. He is fairly certain that he has received sufficient training as a leader and manager in the military, and that he is very capable of running his own small business. He has always been handy with tools, and is quite adept at working on machinery. He thinks that he and his wife could manage the business and take care of all the ordering, inventory, and bookkeeping functions. Dennis has already written to his local banker as well as to a few friends back home, asking for advice and suggestions for starting his new business.

Dennis is quite excited because, during his five-year period in the military, he has been able to save a little over $14,000. He is hoping that this will be sufficient capital to allow him to obtain a sizable loan with which to start his business. His dream is to have a large hardware, paint, and lumber company all combined in one large store operation. His major concern is financing. How will he be able to finance this business? He hopes that his father might be able to advance him $4,000 to $5,000. He also hopes that his in-laws might provide a similar amount to help get the business started.

Most people make some kind of financial transaction for themselves or for their businesses everyday. Most individuals have very limited resources for finances, as do most small businesses. Small business companies are generally at the bottom of the totem pole as far as ability necessary to obtain loans or financing to improve business. In addition to these frustrations, most small business owners do not have the time or the financial expertise to be able to understand or know about all of the financial resources available to them. It is very difficult for a small business owner to get a foot in the right door at the right time and to have any power or negotiating rights that would allow favorable treatment in obtaining loans or finding investors.

Insufficient capital and a lack of understanding financial management is one of the major causes of small business failure. Many small business owners find that they have an inadequate cash flow or insufficient funds available to pay their

141
FINANCING
THE VENTURE

expenses after the first three months of operation. Many small businesses will fail or will go bankrupt simply because of a lack of appropriate financing and financial management.

Planning Financial Needs

Before an individual leaves on a date or takes the family out to a local restaurant, he or she will usually check his or her financial resources to make sure that he or she can pay for the evening. Planning the financial needs of a business is very important. The owner or manager needs to be able to ask the following questions:

1. **Why do I need the money?** Expansion is the answer one individual will give. Another will give remodeling as an answer. A third person will state that they need the money to start a new business. There are many reasons why money and capital are needed in a small business. However, it is important to be very specific about the amounts and the kinds of money that are necessary. The general areas of need for money are: (a) starting a new business, (b) inventory, (c) expansion, (d) remodeling, and (e) improving cash flow or working capital.

2. **When will I be able to repay the money?** A major criterion for any financial position is an understanding of repaymentability. Friends, bankers, and business associates are always interested in knowing when and how you anticipate repaying loans. The majority of loan repayments come from sales of merchandise and inventory.

In today's changing economy, it is also important to consider the cost of money borrowed. With interest rates varying from 10 percent to 20 percent, it is difficult for many small business owners to repay sizable loans. When interest rates are high, it may be necessary for the business owner to wait for interest rates to go down or to curtail plans for expansion or remodeling.

3. **How much money will I need?** It is important to be able to specify how much money you will need. It is advisable when doing any financing to be able to stipulate the amount of dollars that you will be using and to specify if it is to be used to buy a new car, purchase inventory, pay salaries or wages, or even to be used to purchase new equipment.

4. **Where will I obtain the money?** Most small business owners will obtain additional monies from banks, friends, or relatives. There are many times when it is preferable to use banks. However, it is often advisable to use your own personal savings or to encourage friends or relatives to invest in your business.

type and size of business

When planning financial needs for a business, it is important to consider the type of business for which the funds will be used. Probably the business with the highest start-up costs is a manufacturing business using high technology and complex production systems. Quite often, expensive equipment, tools, and machinery are

FINANCING THE VENTURE

necessary to establish the business. The money needed to start a manufacturing plant is usually greater than those funds required to establish an average retail store.

Retail stores often use their funds in acquiring land, constructing buildings, purchasing fixtures and equipment, buying inventory, and paying wages and salaries. The cost of retail stores is often dependent upon the size of the establishment.

A service business (such as a barber shop, plumber, electrician, real estate office, employment agency, and so on) will often require less funds to operate than retail stores. Service businesses may also have less expenses for land acquisition, constructing buildings (less floor space is often required in a service store than in a retail outlet), buying small inventories, and paying wages and salaries.

The size of a business will also determine the financial need for that business. It is often true that many business owners will "bite off more than they can chew." It is wise to start off small, and to use the profits from the business for growth and expansion. Several service operators are able to use their own homes for their business address, driving to their customers. It is generally true that the smaller the business is, the less will be the financial needs of that business. Financial needs tend to directly decrease as the size of a business operation decreases, and will increase as the size of the business increases.

Basic Financial Needs

inventory

Businesses that have seasonal sales peaks often need to purchase inventory and other supplies on short-term credit. They need to borrow money ahead of time in order to purchase sufficient large quantities of materials to sell during their peak periods. Many small retail establishments will sell up to 60 percent of their annual gross sales during the Christmas holiday season.

The risk with short-term inventory loans is centered around whether the inventory will sell as predicted. Generally, most inventories will sell. However, one may find oneself buying something in July, before an economic downturn that will discourage Christmas or seasonal buying. This may leave a business with an inventory that is unsold and insufficient funds to repay debt.

A proper cash flow statement will indicate to the owner when it is necessary to borrow or when it is necessary to save in order to purchase inventory and supplies. The owner should plan for seasonal peaks, and adjust his or her cash flow if at all possible to pay for seasonal upswings.

expansion

When businesses need to expand, to purchase new equipment, or to increase facilities, they are primarily involved with long-term debt financing. They will attempt to borrow sufficient monies to build or expand, which will be paid back over a number of years. The repayment will come through increased sales and profits.

Income statements (profit and loss statements) and cash flow statements should be developed for the next three to five years to illustrate how the increased sales would allow for the repayment of the debt. Money borrowed for expansion will generally have to be repaid within a period of one to five years.

remodeling

Remodeling is one of the major occasions of financial borrowing. One of the important aspects of remodeling any business is to make sure that it will also improve the business or make it more presentable to ensure increased sales.

improving cash flow (working capital)

At the end of April, Wilson's Cleaners finds it difficult to pay all its bills. Wilson realizes that he needs to pay his employees but he is not sure how to handle his suppliers. Wilson overextended when his cash flow was good and his sales were high. Now that the sales have declined, he still needs to pay for his fixed expenses and finds it difficult to handle all his bills.

The banker may find it necessary to loan him the money to meet his payroll but will probably discourage him from borrowing money to pay for supplies or equipment. This short-term loan is becoming more and more frequent during times of inflation and unrecognized cyclical periods of prosperity and droughts during the business year.

Most successful businesses can ward off this financial borrowing need by better managing their money or cash flow. During times of prosperity they need to save their money to meet the expenses of when business is slower. Cash flow projections would probably have uncovered the necessity of hoarding money previously and expending that money during slack periods of sales. Banks and other financial lenders generally encourage business owners to improve their cash management and to develop projected cash flow statements to ensure that repayment will be possible and also to help prevent a similar situation from occurring in the future.

The income statement (profit and loss statement) and cash flow statements will indicate the need for financial borrowing for most businesses. These statements will illustrate the need to borrow funds for short-term as well as for long-term lending. A quick look at the balance sheet will also indicate the net worth of the business, and its soundness at any given period of time.

Financial Records

There are three major financial records necessary to properly run any small business: (1) the income statement (profit and loss statement), (2) the balance sheet, and (3) the cash flow statement. These three financial records may easily be kept by the business owner or by an accountant.

When applying for a loan it is important for these three statements to be prepared and included in a loan request. When starting a business, these figures should be projected for the coming year and a balance sheet should be prepared for the day the business will open. Income projections may be requested for the upcoming five years, but generally anything beyond that is speculation.

If applying for a loan with an existing business, then the past three to five year's statements should be included in the loan package. This would indicate to the financial lender the strength and success of the business. An income statement and a cash flow statement should be projected for the coming year or for years during which the loan will be outstanding. If the loan request is to be paid within a year's period of time, then only a one-year projection should be developed. However, if the loan is to be a long-term loan for a period of three to five years, then income projections and the ability to repay need to be shown for the three- to five-year period.

personal financial statement

It is necessary to include in the loan package prepared for the bank or other financial institution a personal financial statement, which indicates the personal net worth of an individual. It shows the assets and liabilities the individual currently has, and indicates his or her source of income and debt currently held. The financial statement will also include such things as insurance, accounts and notes receivable, stocks, bonds, and real estate holdings. It will also indicate the personal financial worth, and indicate to the bank the risk factor that would be taken in personally loaning you the money. Most small business loans of any size will require this statement, and all Small Business Administration loans will require it. A sample SBA personal financial statement is shown in Figure 8–1.

The personal financial statement is simply a personal balance sheet. This statement will list what the individual owner owns, minus what that individual owes, resulting in a personal net worth at any particular given moment. This personal balance sheet can be utilized to indicate strengths or weaknesses of the individual owner and his or her ability to repay personally any loan.

collateral

Of equal importance to the lender is the collateral that the borrower will put up to secure the loan that he or she will receive. Collateral refers to the personal or business possessions an owner is willing to assign to the lender as a contract for debt repayment. If the borrower does not repay the debt, all collateral remits to the lender to repay the loan.

Most lenders will require a collateral statement in writing to ensure the loan and to reduce the liability of the lender in case the loan is not to be repaid. (See Figure 8–2.)

Financial institutions that lend money look at the financial records as a major consideration before making a loan. It is important to consider the debt-to-equity ratio, or the mixture of the loan dollars to the owner's own dollars, which is what would be required to fuel the firm. Generally, the greater the ownership dollars involved in a business, the more stable is the business. Companies with heavy ownership dollars will find it easier to borrow funds than businesses with low ownership dollars.

Firms that already have a high debt-to-ownership (equity) ratio seeking loans are already highly leveraged, and would probably be advised to obtain additional

PERSONAL FINANCIAL STATEMENT	Return to:	For SBA Use Only
As of _____, 19 ___	Small Business Administration	SBA Loan No.

Complete this form if 1) a sole proprietorship by the proprietor; 2) a partnership by each partner; 3) a corporation by each officer and each stockholder with 20% or more ownership; 4) any other person or entity providing a guaranty on the loan.

Name and Address, Including ZIP Code *(of person and spouse submitting Statement)*

This statement is submitted in connection with S.B.A. loan requested or granted to the individual or firm, whose name appears below:

Name and Address of Applicant or Borrower, Including ZIP Code

SOCIAL SECURITY NO. _____
Business *(of person submitting Statement)*

Please answer all questions using "No" or "None" where necessary

ASSETS		LIABILITIES	
Cash on Hand & In Banks	$ _____	Accounts Payable	$ _____
Savings Account in Banks	_____	Notes Payable to Banks	_____
U. S. Government Bonds	_____	*(Describe below - Section 2)*	
Accounts & Notes Receivable	_____	Notes Payable to Others	_____
Life Insurance-Cash Surrender Value Only	_____	*(Describe below - Section 2)*	
Other Stocks and Bonds	_____	Installment Account (Auto)	_____
(Describe - reverse side - Section 3)		Monthly Payments $ _____	
Real Estate	_____	Installment Accounts (Other)	_____
(Describe - reverse side - Section 4)		Monthly Payments $ _____	
Automobile - Present Value	_____	Loans on Life Insurance	_____
Other Personal Property	_____	Mortgages on Real Estate	_____
(Describe - reverse side - Section 5)		*(Describe - reverse side - Section 4)*	
Other Assets	_____	Unpaid Taxes	_____
(Describe - reverse side - Section 6)		*(Describe - reverse side - Section 7)*	
		Other Liabilities	_____
		(Describe - reverse side - Section 8)	
		Total Liabilities	_____
		Net Worth	_____
Total	$ _____	Total	$ _____

Section 1. Source of Income		CONTINGENT LIABILITIES	
(Describe below all items listed in this Section)			
Salary	$ _____	As Endorser or Co-Maker	$ _____
Net Investment Income	_____	Legal Claims and Judgments	_____
Real Estate Income	_____	Provision for Federal Income Tax	_____
Other Income (Describe)*	_____	Other Special Debt	_____

Description of items listed in Section 1 _____

*Not necessary to disclose alimony or child support payments in "Other Income" unless it is desired to have such payments counted toward total income.

Life Insurance Held *(Give face amount of policies - name of company and beneficiaries)* _____

SUPPLEMENTARY SCHEDULES

Section 2. Notes Payable to Banks and Others

Name and Address of Holder of Note	Amount of Loan		Terms of Repayments	Maturity of Loan	How Endorsed, Guaranteed, or Secured
	Original Bal.	Present Bal.			
	$	$	$		

Figure 8-1. *Suggested format for a personal financial record*

> Section V. Summary of collateral: if your collateral consists of (A) Land and Building, (B) Inventory, and/or (C) Accounts Receivable, fill in the appropriate blanks. If you are using (D) Machinery and Equipment, (E) Furniture and Fixtures, and/or (F) Other, please provide an itemized list (labeled Exhibit B) that contains serial and identification numbers for all articles that had an original value greater than $500.

V. Summary of Collateral	Present Market Value	Present Mortage Balance	Cost Less Depreciation
A. Land and Building			
B. Inventory			
C. Accounts Receivable			
D. Machinery and Equipment			
E. Furniture and Fixtures			
F. Other			
Total Collateral $			

SBA Form 4 (9-78) Previous Editions Are Obsolete

Figure 8-2. *Summary of Collateral*

private or personal funding rather than seek additional debt from financial lenders. Any additional loans to an already highly leveraged firm would drastically increase its debt and would reduce the stability and chances of success for the business.

There is no ideal debt-to-equity ratio for a business. This varies widely from one business to another. However, most bankers and financial lenders do read the *Annual Statement Studies* published by Robert Morris Associates to obtain debt-to-equity ratios and other financial ratios recorded on an industrywide basis. The median debt-to-equity ratio varies greatly from one industry to another. However, most bankers generally use as a rule of thumb a debt-to-equity ratio of 1:2.

The financial records of a business should indicate the stability of the business, how any funds borrowed will be used, and how their repayment will be rescheduled. The historical financial statements will indicate the stability of the business while the projected financial records will indicate how the borrowed funds will be used, and how and when they will be repaid.

Equity Financing and Debt Financing

There are two major forms of financing any business: equity financing and debt financing. Equity financing involves giving up ownership of the business to the investors. It also involves the dividing of the business ownership among the various investors. That is, instead of repaying an investor or one who is giving money to the business, the investor now becomes an owner and receives money from the business primarily through dividends or other profit-sharing systems. (See Table 8-1.)

Table 8-1 Equity versus Debt Financing

EQUITY FINANCING	DEBT FINANCING
Money invested	Money borrowed
Ownership	Debt
Dividends and profits	Repayment
Sources:	Sources:
Self	Friends and relatives
Friends and relatives	Banks
Investment companies	Other financial institutions

If there is only one person who has put up all the money or capital required to open that business, the firm is legally designated as a sole proprietorship. There is only one owner (one equity investor), and that person is responsible entirely for all business debts.

If more than one investor is involved in the establishment of a business, a partnership may be developed. These investors (equity owners) add additional money or capital to the business, and they may or may not be sharing the responsibilities and liabilities of that business. Generally partners give both money and time to the business, and are responsible for all business transactions and liabilities. Limited partners contribute money or capital only, and they are only liable to the limit of their investments. A limited partner, therefore, may be allowed to contribute capital to the business and receive a proportionate share of the profit of a business without being liable for the actions of that business, but he or she does not have the right to manage or direct the affairs of that business.

The most efficient method of handling equity investment is through the use of a corporation. A privately held corporation is one that may have an unlimited number of stockholders. However, it is generally not traded through stock or "over-the-counter" exchanges, but is principally held by the major stockholders. A small business may incorporate in any state of the union, and it may be privately held and controlled by family, friends, and business associates.

A publicly held corporation is often viewed as the ultimate investment opportunity in that its stock is offered to the public at large through the national stock exchanges (the New York Stock Exchange and the American Stock Exchange are the most common) or "over-the-counter" exchanges. Stockholders in a corporation have very limited liabilities and are not generally held liable for any business debts.

Most small business owners are desirous of maintaining ownership and control over their businesses and are therefore reluctant to obtain additional money or capital through equity financing. This method of financing brings new owners into the business and may even require the business to change its structure from a sole proprietorship to a partnership and/or a corporation.

The professional investors or "venture capitalists" often seek to invest in those small businesses with large growth potential in technical areas. These professional investors prefer to invest their money in equity to obtain ownership of the business for its growth and potential in the future.

Any business owner would be advised to consult legal experts before assuming equity investors. These investors may desire a greater share of ownership than their money should buy. A legal document should be developed that would specify ownership, investment amounts, terms, risk, and withdrawal from a business experience.

The four most common forms of equity financing in a business corporation are:

1. **Common Stock.** This is the most widely used form of equity financing, and provides the greatest potential return on investment for the investor. It is important to remember though that if the firm does fail, all of the creditors and investors would be repaid before the common stockholders are repaid.

2. **Preferred Stock.** Preferred stock provides a preference for stockholders during failure or bankruptcy. Preferred stockholders must be repaid in full before other common stockholders are repaid. Because of this preferential treatment, the preferred stockholders receive smaller dividends or returns on their investments than do common stockholders; therefore, convertible preferred stock may be used, allowing the investors to convert their preferred stock to common stock at any time in the company's future.

3. **Convertible Debentures.** This is a long-term debt that would be paid off by an investor, with the option of the investor to convert the debt to common stock before being repaid.

4. **Debt Warranties** are similar to convertible debentures but would allow the investor or creditor the option to purchase a specified number of stock at a specific set price. This option to purchase is available to the investor or creditor, even after the debt has been repaid but before the warranty has expired. This generally provides a longer time period for investment (ownership) for one providing debt financing to a corporation. That is, the debt warranty would allow someone loaning money to a business the opportunity to own part of the business even after the debt has been repaid until the time when the warranty expires.

Both debentures and debt warranties are debts and, therefore, must be repaid before either common stockholders or preferred stockholders are repaid in case the business fails. All four of these opportunities are good opportunities to invest in businesses and provide potential ownership to investors who are interested in that specific business.

internal revenue service

The IRS currently provides certain tax benefits in order to encourage investment in small businesses. These encouraging provisions include:

1. A subchapter S stock, which, according to the IRS code, allows corporations with fifteen or fewer stockholders the opportunity of electing income to be taxed as a partnership or sole proprietorship.

2. Section 12.44 of the IRS code, which allows investors in a small business meeting certain IRS standards to claim $25,000 on a single tax return, or $50,000 on a joint return, as ordinary loss rather than being taxed as a capital loss. This allows a greater deduction for individuals from losses in small business, more than would be allowed on a loss with a public corporation. This section also allows for capital gains from investments to be taxed at a preferential capital gains rate rather

than at the personal income tax rate. This realization allows for a 25 percent to 65 percent reduction below the normal personal income tax rate.

3. Many individuals may prefer to be a limited partner and such an investor is allowed to deduct partnership losses as personal income loss.

professional venture capitalist

Professional venture capital firms are in the business of lending money to make money. These firms primarily invest their money in technological firms promising growth, so that later on their funds may be returned several times over through investment and ownership. Venture capitalists are looking for businesses that may provide growth and/or expansion, thereby yielding a substantial return on investment.

Most venture capital firms are owned by banks, financial institutions, insurance companies, or a conglomeration of large corporations. The smaller venture capital firms may invest as little as $5,000 to $10,000 in a business, while the larger venture capital firms invest from $0.5 million to several million dollars in a business at one time. The most preferred form of ownership by venture capital firms is convertible preferred stock, although common stock is a very common source of ownership. The venture capital firms are interested in those firms which may grow into regional or national prominence with sales in the millions of dollars.

federal and state investment companies

Most private investment firms find it difficult to spend the time and energy required in building small businesses. In an effort to help the small business community, the federal government authorized the Small Business Investment Companies (SBICs) in 1958. The SBICs are privately-owned venture capital firms that are eligible for federal support and financing to augment or increase the funds available to be loaned to potential small businesses. In addition to the SBICs, the government developed the Minority Enterprise Small Business Investment Companies (MESBICs), or 301 (d) licensees, in 1969 to serve the small businesses that are strictly owned or operated by minority group members of the economically or socially disadvantaged American.

These investment companies are licensed, regulated, and controlled by the federal government. They have a minimum private capitalization requirement of $150,000, and are then eligible for matching amounts of $3 to $4 in federal funds for every $1 in private funds for investment purposes. The federal government then supports local private enterprise in developing the small business community through the allocation of federal funds that would match the local funds available for loans to small businesses.

The SBICs and MESBICs may spend 20 percent to 30 percent respectively of their private capital funds per client. They are restricted by federal regulations to supply loans only to the small businesses who meet the size requirements developed by the Small Business Administration (SBA)—assets less than $9 million, net worth less than $4 million, and net income after taxes less than $450,000.

Most states have now passed legislation creating one or more State Businesses and Industrial Development Corporations (SBIDCs). These are created at a local level to increase statewide development of small businesses and to increase employment rates. Although SBIDCs are encouraged in most states, they are not owned, managed, or directed by the states. Generally, the utilities, oil companies, insurance, and major retail chains are the stockholders in the SBIDCs, and they provide the equity funds for investments. Additional funds are also received from banks and from savings and loan companies to allow for long-term debt financing.

Usually the federal and state investment companies are more conservative than many of the private venture capital firms. They all, however, tend to prefer businesses with great growth potential, and they look for a three to five times return on investment over a two to five year period.

The professional venture capital firms prefer common or preferred stock; the federal and state development corporations prefer debentures or debts with warrants as a preference to equity investments.

SUCCESS STORY: Hachirobei Mitsui

At the age of fourteen, Hachirobei Mitsui was sent to Tokyo to learn the dry goods trade, but when he returned to his hometown fourteen years later he set himself up as a moneylender. He did open his own dry goods store at the age of 52 in Kyoto, however, and by so doing founded one of Japan's great mercantile families, for the store Mitsui established in Kyoto was opened in 1673.[1]

Hachirobei Mitsui must have been an exceptional businessman. He brought many innovations to the Japanese business scene. In 1673 he hung out a (now-famous) sign that read "Cash Payments and a Single Price." He established a central warehouse and set up a profit-sharing plan for his employees. He used double-entry bookkeeping. He even used advertising. On rainy days his Tokyo store—he founded six stores before his death—would lend customers umbrellas with the name of Mitsui boldly printed on them. He put up billboards with his name on them. He paid artists and playwrights to work the name of Mitsui into dramas—in effect, anticipating radio by 250 years.

His success is even more impressive when contrasted with Japanese society in his day. Japan was a feudal society then, isolated from the rest of the world. Hachirobei Mitsui's business practices were developed independently from the commercial world of Europe, though they bear a striking resemblance to modern western practices. His cash-and-carry, one-price store must have been a curiosity in the bickering, bargaining trade world of seventeenth-century Japan. He founded a family corporation, giving one of his stores to each of his six sons to prevent the fortune he had amassed from being dissipated. His code of family ethics is still followed by his descendants. The Mitsui family became one of the three wealthiest families in Japan. The Tokyo store he opened in 1686 is still in operation today as the largest department store in Japan, although the Mitsui family sold it in 1904.

Debt Financing

Debt financing is like going into a large department store. You can find and obtain almost anything you like if you are willing to pay for it. There is a vast variety of items available for any individual in a department store, and there are any number

[1] John T. Flynn, *Men of Wealth*, (New York: Simon & Schuster, 1941).

of different lenders who are willing to loan money at various interest rates and repayment schedules.

Basically, there are two different forms of debt financing: (1) working capital and (2) capital expenditures. *Working capital* is generally provided through short-term debt financing to provide inventories, payroll, or accounts receivable as needed. It is often needed to increase inventories and payrolls which are necessary before higher levels of profit are obtained for the business. Working capital is generally financed through short-term bank loans, credit unions or trade credit.

Capital expenditures is the second form of debt financing; it is almost always long-term debts. Long-term debt is generally provided for the expansion or remodeling of a business. It is also used to start a business or to provide additional fixtures or equipment. The major sources of capital financing are commercial banks, venture capitalists, the SBA, life insurance companies, vendors, and mortgage lenders.

banks

The center of the money lending market is the commercial banks, which are by far the most viable commercial lenders. They have become most actively involved in loaning money to business enterprises. They generally establish the overall rate of interest for loans to businesses. Other financial institutions generally vary their lending policies around those established by the banking community.

Banks are conservative lenders; and are primarily involved in granting short-term loans (loans to be repaid within a year's period). They will accept either a personal signature loan for small loans, or collateral for larger loan amounts. The collateral offered is simply "secondary support"—the loan itself will rest upon the ability to repay, the managerial skill, and the character of the business owner. Of course, a financial statement is required of the loan applicant. A sample of the statement form suggested by the Federal Reserve Bank of New York is shown in Figure 8-3.

The short-term loan is the "bread-and-butter" of the banking industry. All types and sizes of businesses use this loan form to help handle suppliers, discounts, seasonal sales, inventory, and production rush periods. These loans are self-liquidating—that is, they are repaid when the goods or services purchased have been turned into cash. For example, when the skis that were bought in fall were sold in winter, the loan is repaid.

If the loan exceeds a specific amount or if the business has not already established a sufficient line of credit, bankers may often stipulate that a compensating balance be required of the owner or business. The compensating balance is generally a requirement to maintain a specific balance in your checking account. For example, if you borrowed $25,000, the bank may require that you keep your checking account above $5,000 at all times. Because you only have the use of $20,000 of the $25,000 stipulated in the loan ($5,000 remaining in the compensating checking account) at an interest rate of 10 percent on the $25,000, the business owner ends up paying an interest rate of 12.5 percent on $25,000. This reserve requirement of cash in a bank account is referred to as the compensating balance, and it will not generally exceed 20 percent of the loan amount.

The banking community has established general guidelines on commercial loans. These include:

Form CR 9
Statement Form Suggested By
FEDERAL RESERVE BANK OF NEW YORK

FINANCIAL STATEMENT
As of .... 19 ......

PARTNERSHIP
(SHORT FORM)

NAME ....
BUSINESS .... **DATE ESTABLISHED** ....
ADDRESS ....

We make the following statement of all the assets and liabilities of this partnership at the close of business on the date indicated above
to ....
(Name and Location of Financial Institution)
and give other material information for the purpose of obtaining advances on notes and bills bearing our signature, endorsement, or guaranty, and for obtaining credit generally upon present and future applications.

BALANCE SHEET

ASSETS		LIABILITIES and NET WORTH	
Cash on Hand	$	Notes Payable to Banks — Unsecured Direct borrowings only	$
Cash in Banks		Notes Payable to Banks — Secured Direct borrowings only	
Notes Receivable — Current & Collectible From customers, excluding affiliates		Notes Payable to Trade Suppliers Excluding affiliates	
Accounts Receivable — Current & Collectible From customers, excluding affiliates		Notes Payable for Machinery & Equipment Due within one year	
Due from Affiliates — Current & Collectible For sale of goods on regular terms		Accounts Payable to Trade Suppliers Excluding affiliates	
Inventory		Advances & Deposits from Customers	
Life Insurance — Cash Surrender Value (Do not deduct loans)		Loans against Life Insurance	
Securities — Readily Marketable U. S. Government & listed on Stock Exchanges		Due to Affiliates	
		Due to Partners	
Total Current Assets	$	Due to Relatives & Friends For loans, advances & other payables	
Securities — Not Readily Marketable Unlisted stocks & bonds		Real Estate Mortgages Payable Mortgages & installments due within one year	
Investments in Affiliates		Accrued Liabilities For taxes, wages, interest, etc.	
Due from Affiliates Loans, advances & other receivables			
Mortgages Owned		**Total Current Liabilities**	$
Land & Buildings (Do not deduct mortgages or depreciation reserve)		Notes Payable for Machinery & Equipment Due after one year	
Leasehold Improvements (Do not deduct amortization reserve)		Real Estate Mortgages Payable Due after one year	
Machinery, Equipment, Furniture & Fixtures (Do not deduct mortgages or depreciation reserve)		Other Deferred Liabilities Due after one year	
Notes & Accounts Receivable Past due, slow or doubtful of collection			
Due from Partners Loans, advances & other receivables		**Total Liabilities**	$
Due from Employees, Relatives & Friends Loans, advances & other receivables		Depreciation & Amortization Reserves	
Prepaid Expenses Taxes, insurance, interest, rent, etc.		Other Reserves	
Goodwill, Patents, Trademarks, etc.			
		Net Worth — General Partners' Account	
		— Special Partners' Account	
TOTAL ASSETS	$	**TOTAL LIABILITIES & NET WORTH**	$

OPERATING STATEMENT — For the .... month period ended .... 19 ......

Gross Sales	$	Administrative, General & Selling Expenses (Incl. depreciation & amortization $ _____)	
Less Discounts, Returns & Allowances		Net Operating Profit	$
Net Sales	$	Other Income	
Cost of Sales (Including depreciation & amortization $ _____)		Other Expense (Incl. bad debts $ _____)	
Gross Profit	$	Net Profit for the Period	$

Opening Inventory $ .... ; Closing Inventory $ .... ; Basis of Inventory Valuation: ....

RECONCILIATION OF NET WORTH — For the .... month period ended .... 19 ......

Net Worth — Beginning of Period	$	Carried Forward	$
Additions to Net Worth:		**Deductions from Net Worth:**	
Net Profit for the Period	$	Partners' Salaries and Other Withdrawals	$
Partners' Capital Contributions			
Forward	$	Net Worth — End of Period	$

(Continued on Reverse Side)
NOTE: The use of Form CR 109 is suggested for a more detailed presentation of the financial condition of a partnership.

Figure 8–3. *Financial statement for a partnership suggested by the Federal Reserve Bank of New York*

1. Inventories: loan amounts advanced for up to 50 percent of value.
2. Start-up: 50 percent to 60 percent of a new business cost.
3. Equipment loans: 60 percent to 80 percent of the equipment value.
4. Real estate loans: up to 75 percent of the property value, amortized over a period of ten to twenty years.
5. Equipment leasing: up to 80 percent of equipment's useful life with a minimum of a three year lease.

trade credit

One of the most excellent sources of short-term credit can be from your supplier. This will allow you to use the supplier's goods or services for a particular period of time at zero or low interest rates. It is probably the most widely used source of short-term funds for small businesses.

Trade credit needs to be established over a period of time. Most businesses are hesitant to establish trade credit with new businesses without some demonstration of solidarity and success.

Once trade credit has been established with a supplier, it is a valuable source for inventories and other goods or services you wish to sell. For example, suppose you buy one hundred radios, which cost you $1,000. The invoice reads: $1,000 at 2/10, net/30. This states that if you pay for the goods ($1,000) within ten days, you can deduct 2 percent or $20 from the purchase price and pay only $980. You have now received a ten-day extension of credit and a nice ($20) discount is included. However if you do not take the discount and pay within ten days, it is necessary that you pay the full amount of the invoice, or $1,000, within the thirty-day period. This means that you really have a thirty-day extension of credit (you do not have to pay for goods for thirty days) from your supplier. Ideally, you may talk your supplier into granting you a credit line that reads: 2/10, net/60 or 90. Given ninety days to repay the invoice amount would allow you to order the merchandise and receive it in October and not have to repay until the end of the Christmas season or the end of December. This is an excellent way and opportunity for you to finance your inventory. The difficulty with this method is finding those suppliers that will grant you thirty-, sixty-, or ninety-day extensions.

On the other hand, you may realize that, if you do not take the discount period, you are in essence paying 2 percent to borrow money for a twenty-day period on a net/30 invoice. This means that by paying $1,000 at the end of the thirty-day period, instead of the $980 within ten days you are effectively paying 36 percent a year on that money you have used for the past month.

borrowing money

Borrowing money is both an art and a science. A business owner's ability to borrow money is going to be based upon the history of the individual, prior business success and failure, credit history, purpose of the loan, track record, and many other factors. The lender is basically going to be looking for the four Cs of credit:

1. The *character* of the borrower.
2. The *collateral* pledged to secure the loan.
3. The *capital* provided by the borrower.
4. The *capacity* of the borrower to repay the loan.

character   Most bankers stipulate that the character worthiness of an individual will account for approximately 30 percent to 50 percent of the final decision to make or not make the loan. The character of any individual is always uncertain. It is an imponderable factor that is very important in determining whether a person will be granted a loan. Is the entrepreneur honest, reliable, trustworthy, and good-intentioned? Does the owner or manager have a strong, positive reputation of being hard working and responsible? A loan officer will have a very limited amount of time in which to evaluate the character of the applicant. Some of areas of concern will be if the business owner considers the job a full- or part-time occupation. Will the person be able to use the money wisely and for the correct reasons? Is the person committed to success, or does he or she limit himself or herself to an eight-hour work day? Affirmative answers to these questions will help improve the character reputation and opportunities to acquire a loan.

collateral   Most business loans are made with collateral or with the assets you promise to secure a loan. Many small (under $5,000 to $10,000) loans may be granted on a signature basis but larger loans generally require some type of security or collateral to obtain the wanted loan. The better and more collateral provided, the more secure the loan is to the bank or financial institution.

When businesses have grown to a point of security and stableness, it is usually then possible to develop and obtain a loan on an unsecured basis. Once the credit worthiness of the business and the owner has been determined, the demand for collateral is lessened. Most long-term debt needs to be secured by collateral. It may be interesting also to know that not all collateral put up is accepted at face value. Most inventories placed as collateral is valued at only 50 percent, while real estate and building is generally valued at about 75 percent of property value. The equipment of the business, if placed as collateral, may only be valued at 50 percent to 80 percent or even less, depending upon its condition. Generally, only cash and marketable securities are evaluated at current or face value.

capital   Capital refers to the amount of money you are putting into the business or your own personal net worth. A large capital investment shows a strong personal interest in the business. The amount of capital also acts as a backup in case the business does not succeed and the loan must be paid back. Most banks or financial lenders will not loan money without 30 percent to 50 percent capital investment by the owner.

capacity   Capacity refers to one's ability to repay a loan. One of the major factors in investigating any loan application is capacity. A loan officer will try to decide whether you have the character and capacity necessary to make good on the loan, regardless of any other business conditions.

Capacity also refers to one's ability as a manager and to work with the business conditions surrounding the enterprise. Part of your capacity is judged on the presentation you make for the loan application. Another part of your capacity is determined by the financial records that indicate the success or failure of your business.

If the four Cs of credit are strongly positive, then you may be assured of working with a financial lender and securing a loan. The stronger these Cs are, the greater your possibility of obtaining financing for your venture. However, it is also important to realize that the money market may also regulate your chances for obtaining financing. For example, during times of inflation and high interest rates, many lenders or bank officers are hesitant to loan to small businesses over long periods of time. They are not sure that the business can afford high interest rates.

It is important to understand, as a borrower, that a bank is a business; it has a product like any other business. The loan institution has to buy its raw materials and then resell those materials at a higher price to obtain a profit. A bank must allow a large enough margin to cover their "cost of goods," operating expenses, business risk, and still provide a profit for the owners or stockholders.

The interest rate that you would receive on a bank loan application would be comprised of those three factors: cost of goods, operating expenses, and business risks. If your business is new or struggling, the risks are higher, operating costs may be higher, and you would probably have to pay a higher rate of interest than other larger borrowers.

The prime interest rate is that rate of interest a bank charges its major or principal borrowers. The prime rate is generally only given to those individuals or businesses who can assure over 100 percent that they will always guarantee the loan. Only major corporations or the very wealthy will ever qualify for a prime interest rate.

It is not strange to find a small business being charged 2 percent, 3 percent, or even possibly 4 percent points higher than the prime interest rate. Therefore, if the prime rate is 15 percent on all money borrowed, a small business person may expect to be charged 18 percent on a short- or long-term loan.

Sources of Funds

Many small business owners often forget the position of eminence our capitalistic society has in the world. We are a nation built upon a free enterprise system, built on a capitalistic method of economics. Public, private, and institutional sources provide capital to industry in exchange for equity or interest. This exchange is the system whereby our business environment has been able to thrive and grow. Historically, bartering was the means of securing goods and services from others. The blacksmith would provide services to the tailor in exchange for clothes. The farmer would provide food in exchange for goods and services. Therefore, every individual was both a seller and a buyer, since he or she offered goods or services (selling) and received in exchange (buying) the goods or services desired. Gradually, as people became more specialized and moved into the trades, it was important that a different mode of exchange be developed. The form of exchange that came about is known as money. The bartering system continues, but it is now an economic system of exchanging goods or services for a medium of exchange: money.

People are involved in lending money with one major objective—to make lots of money in return. Many venture capitalists are looking for a 20 percent to 25 percent compounded rate of return on invested money. Some business operators are excited about investing in firms wherein they could obtain four times their investment in three years, five times their investment in four years, six times their investment in five years, and so forth. However, it is important to note that these projections of earnings are based on the banks' or financial lenders' projections, not on those of the owners or entrepreneurs.

Following is a list of thirty financial resources that are used by small businesses:

1. Commercial banks.
2. Commercial finance companies.
3. Venture capitalists.
4. Credit unions.
5. Customers.
6. Employees.
7. Equipment manufacturers.
8. Factoring companies.
9. Family investment firms.
10. Financial consultants, finders, advisors.
11. Founders and industrial banks.
12. Insurance companies.
13. Investment bankers.
14. Investment clubs.
15. Leasing companies.
16. Mutual funds.
17. Mutual savings banks.
18. Pension funds.
19. Private individual investors.
20. Private investment partnerships.
21. Relatives and friends.
22. Savings and loan associations.
23. Small Business Administration (SBA).
24. Small Business Investment Companies (SBIC) and (MESBICs).
25. State Business & Industrial Development Commissions (SBIDCs).
26. Tax exempt foundations.
27. Charitable foundations.
28. Suppliers.
29. Trust companies (bank trust departments).
30. Veterans Administration (VA).

CASE STUDY: The Video Shop

Joyce and Wes Constant have been married for fourteen years, and now Joyce is interested in going into business for herself. Wes is encouraging her to do so, and he is willing to offer her any assistance that she may need.

Wes has been working with a utility firm for the last fifteen years. He has worked in the engineering field and is currently in management. He is a professional electrician. They have three children, aged 12, 10, and 9.

Joyce is excited about the possibilities of opening a video shop. She has always been interested in audio-visual equipment. She graduated with a degree in education from a large state university. She is particularly interested in opening a store to sell video cassette recorders, video disc recorders, wide-screen televisions, regular televisions, and tape libraries.

Joyce has recently found a location just outside the downtown area on a major business street, which could supply ample off-the-street parking in the back, and little foot traffic. She could get the 14,000-square-foot store for a rental price of $8 a square foot.

157
FINANCING THE VENTURE

She has been doing a lot of research, and has found that she will probably be able to obtain the rights to sell the Sony, Toshiba, Zenith, RCA, Sanyo, and Magnavox video cassette recorders: she has already made arrangements to sell their TV sets. The prices on the video cassette recorders would be from about $695 to over $2,000. She has also found that she can do about 10 percent to 15 percent of her business by selling accessories, which would include film cassette libraries, video cameras, tripods, electrical cords, and the like. She investigated wide-screen television and found that there is a large variety. However, the manufacturers do not substantially differentiate the actual products, which would sell for somewhere between $695 to over $5,000.

She has planned a store layout that would allow a seating area for viewing a wide-screen television, plus an opportunity to sit and watch different TVs, video tapes, or video disc recorders.

Joyce is interested in starting this business and is interested in learning how to obtain financing for this venture. She has developed a set of start-up costs, which she expects to be fairly close to the actual expenditures. She does not know if it would be best to try to arrange the $35,000 financing through debt or equity. She is uncertain about where to begin, although she believes she ought to talk to her husband first. She is also wondering if it would be possible to obtain this money

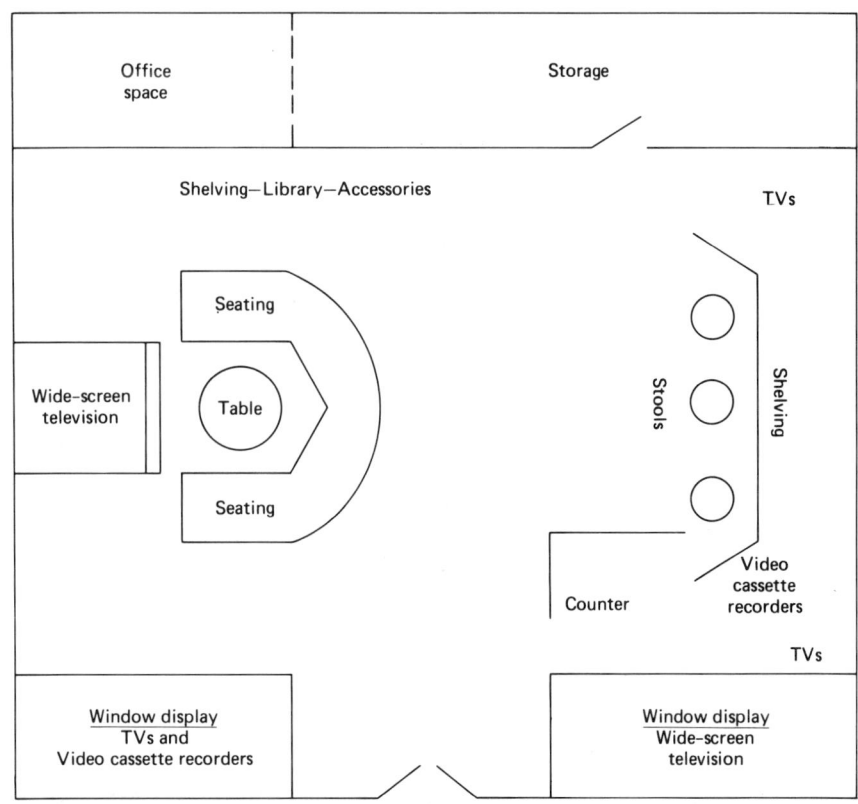

from a bank, and she is not certain what the bank would expect her to put up as her part of the loan.

She has figured out a profit and loss statement on a monthly basis. She feels that this would be an average for the next twelve months of her business, and that it would show a monthly profit of approximately $2,750. This is over and above her own salary, which she would be drawing out of the business. This illustrates that the gross profit margin in the video cassette industry runs about 25 percent to 30 percent. (Therefore, if a dealer was to sell a unit at $1,000 dollars it would probably cost somewhere between $700 and $750.)

START-UP COSTS

Items:

Merchandise inventory	$18,000
Fixtures and remodeling	8,000
Rent (2 months)	1,800
Signs	2,000
Utilities deposit	100
Phone deposit	50
Advertising and promotion	1,500
Legal and accounting	1,000
Other	1,000
Owner's salary (pre-opening)	1,250
Total	$34,700

PROFIT AND LOSS STATEMENT (MONTHLY)

Gross sales:		$22,000
Cost of goods sold		16,000
Gross profit from sales		6,000
Rentals		500
Gross profit		6,500
Expenses:		
Rent	$ 900	
Utilities	180	
Payroll (salesperson)	1,000	
Advertising and promotion	200	
Insurance	70	
Supplies	50	
Others	100	
Owner's salary	1,250	
Total expenses		$ 3,750
Net profit before taxes and loan payment		$ 2,750
Percent of sales		12.5%

Questions

1. What type of financing should Joyce anticipate?
2. Will she be able to use trade credit?
3. Should Joyce seek a bank loan?
4. Does she need to handle debt or equity financing?

Chapter Questions

1. Does the type or size of business have anything to do with the financial needs of that business? Please explain your answer.
2. What are some of the different financial needs of a small business?
3. How and when is it important to borrow money?
4. What financial statements are generally required when obtaining a business loan? Why?
5. Discuss the advantages and disadvantages of equity financing.
6. Discuss the advantages and disadvantages of debt financing.
7. Discuss the importance of the four Cs of credit when obtaining a loan.

APPENDIX

There is a common practice used by bankers to determine whether the equity base and financial position of a business are sufficient. Industry-composite financial data is used for financial projections. A common source for such data is Robert Morris Associates' (RMA) *Annual Statements Studies*. To illustrate the procedure, we will use the example of a borrower who has $50,000 in ownership money with which to capitalize a new hardware business.

From RMA *Statement Studies* (Figure 8A–1), we find that hardware stores with assets of less than $250,000 have a net worth of 46.3 percent of total assets. Thus:

$$\text{where } x = \text{Total assets}$$
$$\text{Capital} = 46.3\% \text{ of Total assets}$$
$$\$50,000 = 0.463\,x$$
$$\frac{50,000}{0.463} = x$$
$$\$107,991 = x \text{ or Total assets}$$

RMA also provides us with all asset categories as a percentage of total assets. Thus, a balance sheet can be constructed assuming $107,991 in total assets, and using the RMA percentage figures. For example, we know from Figure 8A–1 that:

$$\text{Cash} = 5.8\% \text{ of Total assets}$$
$$= 0.058 \times \$107,991$$
$$= \$6,263$$

Cash (5.8%)	$ 6,263	Notes Payable (9.1%)	$ 9,827
Accounts Receivable (14.4%)	15,551	Accounts Payable (14.9%)	16,091
Inventory (57.2%)	61,771	Other liabilities (11.8%)	12,743
Fixed assets (14.3%)	15,443	Long-term notes payable (15.7%)	16,955
Other assets (8.3%)	8,963	Other liabilities (2.2%)	2,375
Total assets (100%)	$107,991	Total liabilities (53.7%)	$ 57,991
		New worth (46.3%)	50,000
		Total liabilities and net worth (100%)	$107,991

The projected balance sheet has limitations because it reflects businesses of an ongoing nature, not the new businesses that we have assumed. Nonetheless, it does provide the basis for determining what size hardware business could be supported with a $50,000 capital base.

An income statement can also be projected with a bit more accuracy and usefulness.

We will assume the business plans to operate on a $61,771 inventory level. From the RMA statistics, we find a medium inventory turnover ratio of 2.6 to 1. Thus:

Cost of goods sold = $61,771 × 2.6 = $160,605
Cost of goods sold = 65.7% of Sales

where x = Sales
$160,605 = 0.657 \, x$
$\frac{160{,}605}{0.657} = x$
$244,451 = x$, or Sales

Sales	$244,451
Cost of sales	160,605
Gross profit	83,846
Operating expenses (28.2%)	68,935
Operating profit	14,911
Other income (expenses) new (1.5%)	(3,667)
Profit before taxes (4.6%)	$ 11,244

Net income must cover debt service, capital investment expenditures, and working capital requirements, as well as taxes. It is clear that our prospective borrower's income before taxes will not meet these needs. Once this fact is established, the entrepreneur has little opportunity to present a logical defense of the feasibility or profitability of the venture. A financial plan has little relevance in the face of the statements based on industry data. Given the conservative nature of bank lending, there is a low probability attached to individuals superseding these averages.

Knowing the assessment method, however, could have helped this individual to make the best possible presentation available to the banker or loan committee. Going through this procedure prior to requesting the loan would have yielded valuable information about the total financial situation of the business. Before proceeding with any other work on the request presentation, further possibilities for equity capital should be explored. Sometimes personal assets are overlooked, such as borrowing against the cash value of life insurance, taking a second mortgage on a home, or using savings and investments. Private investors—such as doctors, dentists, and other professionals with high incomes—may be able to provide necessary cash. Whatever the possibilities, the point is that banks are only willing to accept a certain portion of the risks in any case. Using this method of analysis will reveal deficiencies that are very important.

RETAILERS	HARDWARE				
	SIC# 5251				
	57(6/30-9/30/76)		149(10/1/76-3/31/77)		
ASSET SIZE	0-250M	250M-1MM	1-10MM	10-50MM	ALL
NUMBER OF STATEMENTS	84	83	34	5	206
ASSETS	%	%	%	%	%
Cash & Equivalents	5.8	5.4	5.7		6.2
Accts. & Notes Rec. - Trade(net)	14.4	21.9	19.8		14.2
Inventory	57.2	50.1	53.0		50.7
All Other Current	1.5	1.3	1.9		1.0
Total Current	78.9	78.7	80.6		72.2
Fixed Assets (net)	14.3	14.9	13.8		22.3
Intangibles (net)	1.8	.3	.5		1.4
All Other Non-Current	4.9	6.1	5.1		4.2
Total	100.0	100.0	100.0		100.0
LIABILITIES					
Notes Payable-Short Term	9.1	9.7	7.8		6.6
Cur. Mat.-L/T/D	3.2	2.8	.9		4.2
Accts. & Notes Payable - Trade	14.9	17.2	17.3		16.2
Accrued Expenses	4.0	4.6	6.6		6.8
All Other Current	4.6	3.9	2.4		2.1
Total Current	35.8	38.2	35.1		35.9
Long Term Debt	15.7	12.6	10.4		11.6
All Other Non-Current	2.2	1.1	4.8		2.2
Net Worth	46.3	48.2	49.7		50.3
Total Liabilities & Net Worth	100.0	100.0	100.0		100.0
INCOME DATA					
Net Sales	100.0	100.0	100.0		100.0
Cost Of Sales	65.7	67.2	70.7		69.1
Gross Profit	34.3	32.8	29.3		30.9
Operating Expenses	28.2	28.5	24.9		24.9
Operating Profit	6.1	4.3	4.4		6.0
All Other Expenses (net)	1.5	−.3	.0		1.2
Profit Before Taxes	4.6	4.5	4.4		4.8
RATIOS					
Current	3.7	3.0	2.8		3.2
	2.4	2.3	2.1		2.2
	1.7	1.7	1.8		1.7
Quick	1.0	1.2	.9		1.0
	(83) .5	.7	.6	(205)	.6
	.2	.4	.4		.3
Sales/Receivables	9 39.4	17 21.2	12 29.7	11	32.0
	15 24.1	33 11.1	29 12.6	24	15.5
	27 13.5	47 7.7	47 7.8	39	9.4
Cost of Sales/Inventory	111 3.3	91 4.0	91 4.0	94	3.9
	140 2.6	130 2.8	107 3.4	130	2.8
	203 1.8	174 2.1	159 2.3	183	2.0
Sales/Working Capital	3.7	3.5	4.2		3.7
	5.2	5.2	6.0		5.4
	9.3	8.1	7.8		8.5
EBIT/Interest	12.0	15.2	10.5		12.0
	(59) 3.7	(74) 5.1	(30) 4.8	(168)	4.7
	2.0	2.7	2.4		2.4
Cash Flow/Cur. Mat. L/T/D	3.4	4.2	13.2		5.6
	(13) 2.0	(27) 1.5	(17) 5.7	(60)	2.1
	.4	.9	2.1		.9
Fixed/Worth	.1	.1	.1		.1
	.3	.2	.2		.2
	.8	.5	.4		.5
Debt/Worth	.5	.6	.8		.5
	1.3	1.1	1.0		1.1
	2.9	2.0	1.9		2.2
% Profit Before Taxes/Tangible Net Worth	46.2	30.2	25.0		32.1
	(78) 19.7	(33) 19.6	15.0	(199)	19.2
	5.7	10.8	9.0		9.3
% Profit Before Taxes/Total Assets	16.4	13.7	12.6		14.7
	9.2	8.2	7.2		8.5
	2.8	4.3	3.4		3.5
Sales/Net Fixed Assets	56.6	53.5	53.7		54.3
	27.1	25.0	29.7		26.5
	11.0	7.3	11.1		10.3
Sales/Total Assets	2.7	2.5	2.9		2.6
	2.2	2.2	2.2		2.2
	1.8	1.6	1.9		1.7
% Depr., Dep., Amort./Sales	.6	.6	.3		.5
	(73) .9	(76) .8	(32) .6	(185)	.8
	1.4	1.2	.8		1.3
% Lease & Rental Exp/Sales	1.6	.8	.2		1.0
	(64) 3.1	(59) 1.8	(28) 1.1	(151)	2.2
	4.4	2.9	2.2		3.7
% Officers' Comp/Sales	5.1	3.1	1.7		3.4
	(51) 7.7	(52) 4.2	(13) 3.3	(116)	5.1
	11.2	6.5	4.3		8.6
Net Sales ($)	26769M	90095M	222847M	369181M	708892M
Total Assets ($)	11830M	41750M	90789M	142878M	287247M

M = $thousand MM = $million

Figure 8A–1. Data for determining debt-to-equity ratios

SOURCE: Robert Morris Associates, *Annual Statements Studies*. Used with permission.

Photo courtesy of Irene Springer, Prentice-Hall, Inc.

9

ORGANIZING THE NEW BUSINESS

Chapter Objectives:

1. To understand the major functions of management.
2. To understand the importance and uses of planning.
3. To be able to develop an organizational structure and framework for a business.
4. To be able to staff a small business.
5. To learn about managing and directing the affairs of a small business.
6. To understand better the control procedures in running a small business.

Without labor nothing prospers.

Sophocles

Perhaps any of us could get along with perfect people.
But our task is to get along with imperfect people.

Richard L. Evans

INCIDENT: Daryl Henderson has just graduated from a major college of dentistry. He has moved his wife and family down to the Texas Panhandle. They had visited relatives there during one holiday season, and had enjoyed the high plains with their surrounding open spaces and wonderful climate.

While he was a senior in dental college, Daryl had purchased his dental equipment from a local manufacturing representative. He is now ready to open his new one-chair dental office. He has looked around and found a suitable location. The bank is willing to grant him a loan to start his business. He is happy with his progress and success; he is proud of his diploma and is grateful to be a dentist. Now all he has to do is to start his practice and be a success.

As he looked around he realized, as most people do, that he was not sure how he should organize his practice. He has already hired a receptionist and a dental assistant, but he is not sure what kind of plans he should use for the next year, or even if his staffing is complete. He knows that he has to keep business and dental records, but he is not clear how they will fit together or help him control the financial affairs of his business. Furthermore, he is asking himself, how does one motivate people in a dental practice?

Two young men sailed from Europe in the early 1880s. Debt, hardship, and the opportunity to reach for a new life had encouraged them and their families to journey to America. They both traveled to Cincinnati, and there established their homes. William Procter became an apprentice soap maker, and James Gamble became an apprentice candle maker. In 1842, they combined their efforts and started a soap and candle manufacturing business. Today, that company is known as Procter and Gamble.

In the process of developing any small business, it is important to start at the beginning. If you are going to have a party, take a trip to Hawaii, or go out to a movie it is important to plan and organize your activities. Planning is the main ingredient that will bring about success. Planning is valuable in our daily lives, as it allows us to organize our actions and help us to achieve our goals.

When organizing a small business, it is important to develop all of the functions of management. These functions include: (1) planning, (2) organization, (3) staffing, (4) direction, and (5) control.[1]

Most small businesses fail because the owners do not develop these management functions. Owners often feel that they are in total control, and that they know everything about everything and need not rely upon managerial techniques or skills. This becomes the major cause for business failure.

Most business owners have some skills in one, if not in all, of these areas. However, it is difficult to fully develop the skills necessary to satisfy each and every area. Individuals need to practice and develop managerial skills sufficiently in order to promote all managerial functions. Without proper planning, business organizations will fail. Firms that are unable to properly staff or control their organizations are almost certain to fail. Business owners cannot do everything; it is not possible to wear twenty hats at one time.

As business owners recognize that they do not know everything and that it is important to utilize their personnel, plan their actions, and organize their resources, then and only then do they have the chance to succeed. It is usually true that only the well managed business will succeed in the long run.

planning

As a business becomes more complex, it becomes more necessary to plan the business activities. You usually would not go to a play or to a football game without planning to buy the tickets, arrange for transportation, and pick up everyone who would need a ride. A business owner must plan in order to ensure the success of the firm. Planning is the process of determining what should be done to achieve the company's objective; it is a very important managerial function. Goals are often viewed as the *why* of planning, which is also concerned with the *who*, the *what*, the *when*, the *where*, and the *how*. Therefore, to plan is to determine who should do what, when, where, and how it should be done in order to accomplish a specific objective. (See Figure 9–1.)

Planning is often viewed as a four-step approach:

Step 1: the establishment or the setting of goals or objectives for the organization.

Step 2: the development of a needs assessment for the business, which explains what the business must do.

Step 3: understanding the resources and alternatives open to obtaining the set objectives; the resources will often explain who and where the action should take place to accomplish these objectives.

Step 4: the development of the action steps, which are necessary to accomplish the objectives.

For example, Bob wants to increase the profits of his fast-food hamburger restaurant. His goal is to obtain a 20 percent increase over last year's profits. To do this, which is step one, Bob realized that he needs to increase the volume of sales as well as draw more customers to his business (step two). One alternative available is to start a new line of sandwiches, which could be made and sold at the shop by his employees (step three). His final plan of action will be to introduce the new

---

[1]Harold Kootz and Cyril O'Donnell, *Principles of Management: An Analysis of Management Functions,* 5th ed. (New York: McGraw-Hill Book Company, 1972).

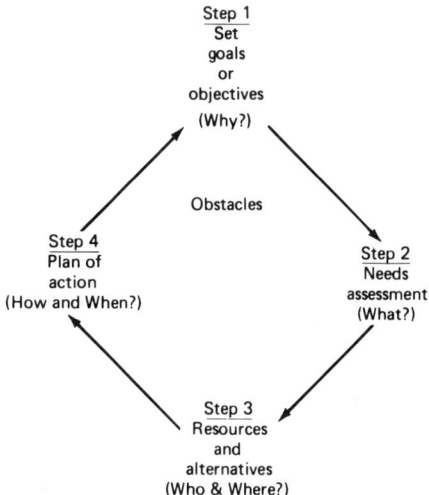

Figure 9-1. *Planning*

sandwiches right before the summer vacation which starts next month (step four). The sandwiches would sell for $1.29, with a cost to Bob of 65¢.

Planning will often involve budgeting, which is the allocation of one's resources; forecasting, which is the prediction of future activities or profits; and flexibility, which is the ability to change plans in order to meet and overcome obstacles.

Planning requires time. Many large corporate executives may spend a third or more of their time in planning, but it is difficult for a small business owner or manager to spend that much time in the planning process. Interestingly, if you investigate the different levels of management typically found in organizational structures—that is top-level management, middle-level management, and supervisory management—you would see that the small business owner spends most of his or her time in a fashion similar to that of a supervisory manager. (See Figure 9-2.) The small business owner or manager is often in a crisis situation, spending his or her time in solving and handling the problems that are immediately confronting him or her. This is similar to the task of the supervisory manager, who spends most of his or her time directing, motivating, and controlling the workers in a business. It is difficult for a small business owner to take or spend the time to plan or organize the activities of that business.

Organization

Organization refers to the institution, as well as to the process of organizing or the way that a business uses its resources to accomplish its plans. Business firms, government agencies, schools, churches, and even hospitals are often referred to as organizations.

The process of organizing is very important. It should allow for the smooth operation and functioning of the business. A successful organization generally has

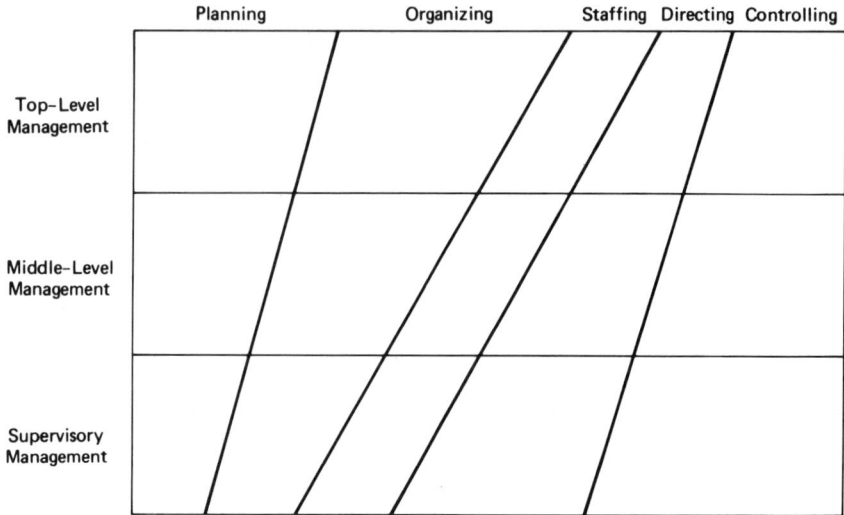

Figure 9-2. *Management functions*

a division of work, a scalar chain (the authority chain from top to bottom), and a coordination of all work activities.

A properly organized business usually uses an organizational chart, which is a diagram of the functions, divisions, departments, and positions of people within the organization. The organizational chart will often describe: (1) the type of work being performed by the different people in the organization, (2) the relationship between the owner and the subordinate and between the managers and the subordinates, and (3) the relationship between workers in an organization.

Regardless of the size of the business or the number of employees, the owner should develop an organizational chart that breaks down the different functions and business processes, and organizes them into a working coordinated business. A good complete organizational chart should indicate who is doing what to accomplish the organizational goals and plans. Even if an activity is accomplished by someone outside of the business, such as an accountant doing bookkeeping, it should still be part of the organizational structure and its chart. As a business grows, the organization structure of that business will need to grow.

The organizational structure is generally divided either by function (as seen in the organizational chart in Figure 9-3) or by product, personnel, geography, or time. Small businesses that wish to divide their managerial structure by function

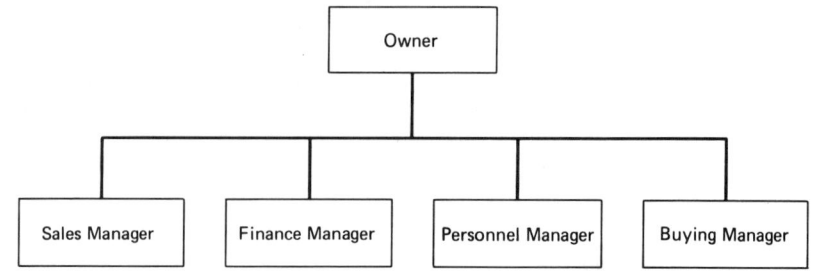

Figure 9-3. *Organizational chart*

will generally use the primary functions of sales (or marketing), finance, personnel, and production (or buying). Many entrepreneurs or owners will maintain control of all these functions, and will become managers of the sales, finance, personnel, and production areas. However, it is difficult to properly manage these functions as the business grows and sales increase.

Small businesses are also organized by product. Ms. B's Clothing Boutique has its women's apparel shop divided into three different lines: dresses, shoes and accessories. At Ms. B's, there is a supervisor over each of those areas who is responsible for that area's buying, inventory, sales, and advertising. This is one of the most common forms of organizing for small business firms. A shoe store will have one manager in charge of men's shoes, a second manager in charge of women's shoes, and a third manager in charge of children's shoes. This sort of division of labor promotes a good spirit within a business and allows each individual manager an area of responsibility and accountability.

A division by personnel occurs when a manager is responsible for a business or production group that is entirely responsible for the good or service. For example, a small manufacturer of mobile homes can divide the working staff into different production groups. Each group can have one manager who is responsible for the success and/or failure of that group of employees. The different personnel groups can then compete against each other as to the quantity and quality of mobile homes produced by that plant. At the end of the year the personnel group having the highest productivity record can be rewarded with a substantial bonus.

Another method of formal organization structure is division by geography. The owner of a warehouse or wholesaler will often distribute the work within the business firm by geographical areas, with the state or city divided into different sectors. Most suppliers, independent sales people, or even newspaper boys are generally divided along geographical lines.

Another organizational procedure may be to group managers according to time divisions. The fast-food restaurant operator may have a manager over the lunches, a second manager over the dinners, and a third manager over the nighttime activities. Many manufacturing companies have a hierarchy structured around time periods. For example, a small watch manufacturer may have a managerial team for employees who work between 8:00 A.M. and 4:00 P.M., another set from 4:00 P.M. to 12:00 midnight, and a third set from 12:00 midnight to 8:00 A.M. (known as the graveyard shift).

The organizational structure also provides for efficient communication and interaction between employees, and for the satisfaction and possible fulfillment of the personnel. Opportunities for job enrichment by increasing job knowledge need also be provided. A strong small business organization will be able to define the job, its scope (the number or range of work assignments required), specialization, and depth (individual control or determining how a job is to be done).

Staffing

Probably the most crucial resource of any small business is its human element; its members. Staffing is a critical function of organizing and managing a successful business. All companies, whether large or small, are involved in the staffing process. All businesses run the same risk every time they hire a new employee. The staffing function is generally divided into four major categories: (1) staffing needs, (2) acquisition, (3) motivation, and (4) retention.

staffing needs

Picking a staff is similar to choosing friends. A staff person should have a certain skill, personality, and ability to work with other individuals. You will generally choose as friends people with whom you like to be associated. Friends quite often have similar insights, attitudes, abilities, skills, interests, hobbies, athletics, and activities.

The first step in defining the needs of your business is to describe the skills and requirements that are necessary to fill a position in your business. Before filling a staff position you need to describe it.

It is necessary to develop a job description—that is, a detailed outline of work assignment—for most employees. This description should be specific enough to be understood by future employees. The secret of a good job description is that a new employee will be able to describe the job and to perform it the same way it was written.

It is also important for you to define the skills and abilities that a person should have in order to fulfill that job. If you are hiring a salesperson, does he or she need to have a pleasing personality? Should the person be attractive? Is it necessary for the salesperson to have a technical background? Does the person need to be a licensed contractor or a licensed beautician?

It is important for that new employee to be able to work with the owner or manager and with the other employees of the business. One of the top criteria in recruiting is that the recruiter hire someone with whom he or she would be willing to work and would feel at ease when talking to him or her.

acquisition

After the needs of the business have been developed and the skills required have been identified, one must contact applicants. The acquisition process can be broken down into three areas: (1) hiring, (2) interviewing, and (3) training.

Hiring. The recruiting of new employees is an exciting opportunity. If you are seeking a person to fill a managerial or administrative position, it is quite often possible to hire from within. This allows the owner to consider his or her present employees for new job openings before going outside of the business to hire new employees. When hiring from the outside, there are several places employers can go. Most communities have private employment agencies, which help in the recruitment process and require the employer (and sometimes the employee) to pay a fee for each employee hired. Also, each state has some form of employment service (employment service agency, public employment, or unemployment bureau). All state agencies are affiliated with the United States Employment Service, which screens applicants by using aptitude tests.

Newspaper advertisements are a major tool for acquiring new employees. In addition, a help-wanted sign in the store window often provides several applicants. Local high schools, colleges, and universities are yet another source of readily available employees. Most community colleges have students who are trained in certain technological, mechanical, or electrical skills. Many part-time students will have a desire to stay with the business after finishing school.

Friends, business associates, service clubs, and local organizations may also supply names of individuals seeking employment. To a large extent, the success of the business will be due to the employees. It is necessary to find and hire the "perfect" employee. The employment application (Figure 9–4) is an excellent tool for screening prospective employees.

Application for Employment

Name: _____ Date:_____
     Last   First   Middle

Present Address: _____ Social Security No._____

Telephone Number:_____ Driver's License No.:_____

Indicate Dates You Attended School:

    Elementary From _____ to _____ High School From _____ to _____ College From _____ to _____.

    Other (Specify Type and Dates) _____

Can You Be Bonded? _____ If Yes, In What Job? _____

Do You Have Any Physical Defects Which Preclude You From Performing Certain Kinds of Work? _____ If Yes, Describe Each and Specify Work Limitations: _____

List Below All Present and Past Employment, Beginning with Most Recent (include military service, if relevant):

Name & Address of Company	From Mo/Yr	To Mo/Yr	Name of Supervisor	Reason for Leaving	Weekly Salary	Describe the Work you did

May we contact the employers listed above? _____ If not, indicate which ones you do not wish us to contact _____

Remarks: _____

Figure 9–4. *Application for employment*

SOURCE: Walter E. Greene, *Staffing Your Store,* Small Marketers Aids No. 162 (Washington, D.C.: Small Business Administration, 1977), p. 6.

The Civil Rights Act of 1964 prohibits discrimination in employment practices based on race, religion, sex, or national origin. Title VII of this Act covers and restricts discrimination in employment. The Civil Rights Act of 1964 further prohibits the use of psychological or personality tests for discriminatory practices in hiring employees. The Equal Employment Opportunity Commission (EEOC) is a federal commission established to regulate discriminatory employment practice and increase job opportunities for minorities and women. Public Law 90-202 further prohibits discrimination on the basis of age for those individuals who are at least forty years of age and less than sixty-five years of age. The Equal Pay Act of 1963, the Age Discrimination in Employment Act of 1967, and the Equal Employment Opportunity Act of 1972 further prohibit discrimination in employment and rule against discrimination based on physical handicaps.

Interviewing. The first contact a small business owner may have with an applicant is in the actual interviewing process. The personal interview is a face-to-face meeting between the employer and the prospective employee, and it helps the employer determine whether or not that applicant can fill the job description and can work well with other employees in the business. It is important to remember not to discriminate against applicants during the interviewing process, as this can lead to legal action against the business.

The interview provides an opportunity for a business owner or manager to subjectively evaluate the applicant. Would this applicant be easy to work with? Does he or she have the necessary skills? What is the work experience of the applicant? Does the applicant reply in a direct and forthright fashion? Does he or she put forth a positive and pleasing personality?

When the interview is over, it is appropriate for the owner to ask the applicant to check back after the rest of the applicants have been interviewed. It is wise not to commit yourself during the initial interview. At times this may even be against the law. You need to check all applicants and make sure that you have selected the right individual.

After an employee has been hired, and before that person is given the opportunity to work, it is important for that individual to understand the personnel policies of the business. In addition to formal training procedures, it is advisable to develop a personnel policy and some procedure guidelines. These should at least consider the following areas:

1. Hours.
2. Compensation.
3. Vacations.
4. Time off with pay.
5. Time off without pay.
6. Fringe benefits:
    a. Employee discount.
    b. Life insurance.
    c. Health insurance.
    d. Pension plans.
    e. Automobiles.
7. Retirement.

8. Grievance procedures.
9. Termination.
10. Promotion.
11. Evaluation.
12. Sick leave.
13. Maternity benefits.

Specific, written policies and procedures will help the owner and the employees to better understand the conditions of employment. They will guard the employer from embarrassment or legal action. They will also allow employees to review the policies and procedures at a later date and become familiar with them at their own leisure.

Training. A second major function of employment acquisition is training. Once an employee has been hired, that employee must be oriented to his or her job responsibility, work, and fellow employees. The orientation may include a medical examination. The actual training will continue throughout that employee's stay with the business. The two major types of employee training are: on-the-job training and classroom training.

Most small business owners find it convenient and easy to train new employees on the job. This kind of training is basic for any new employee, but it should include the rules, regulations, and policies of the business organization. On-the-job training is usually supervised by an experienced employee or by the owner.

Several service firms require new employees to go through apprenticeship training, which is a form of on-the-job training. Most plumbers, electricians, and construction workers are required to have had some form of apprenticeship training, which may last from two months to several years. Employers often work closely with unions and trade union programs to ensure that the proper training and skill requirements are developed.

Several jobs will also require that classroom training be offered to employees. Classroom training or seminars may range from teaching technical skills to fostering an understanding of correct checking, cash handling, and business procedures. Many businesses will require employees to take classroom training before they are licensed, such as beauticians, mechanics, and barbers. Classroom training can provide valuable insights into basic business practices as well as refining and developing new skills. Classroom training is now the basis for most management-development programs. These programs allow managers and executives to refine their managerial skills and increase their supervisory capacities.

A practice of job rotation will allow managers and other employees an opportunity of working at the various stations or operations of the business, which will provide additional skill and insights for the employee.

motivation

An important aspect of staffing the small business is motivating the employees. Performance standards should be established for each individual. These standards should describe the work that has to be done and how much of that work should be accomplished over a period of time. Employees often expect managers to tell them exactly what should be done and how.

The employee should feel part of the business team. Ideally, the employee would be the perfect person to fill the function required. The job standard, qualification, and expectation should be similar to a contract for the employee. The employee should understand why he or she is being hired, what he or she is expected to do, and how he or she fits into the business.

Motivation processes are concerned with exciting and directing behavior of an employee toward a specific goal. The employer should do whatever possible to increase the likelihood that an employee would desire to work for the business and would put forth his or her best efforts. A motivated employee will generally increase his or her performance level; and will have a desire to do well and work well for the business.

retention

The major problem associated with staff acquisition is to keep good employees after they have been hired. It costs money to train employees, as well as to hire new employees. Therefore, it is very important, once a good employee has been hired and trained, for the employer to do everything possible to keep that employee working for the business.

One of the most important factors in employer retention is employee compensation. A fair and equitable pay system should be developed. Employee and labor costs are a major portion of small business expenses. Wages that are too high make it difficult for the small business owner to stay in business and to be competitive; inadequate wages lead to high turnover rates, discipline problems, or ineffective workers. A well thought-out and competitive compensation plan should attract, motivate, and keep employees.

Associated with compensation programs is a job evaluation system. Job evaluation is a method of evaluating the performance of employees against set performance standards. Job evaluation is used to determine merit pay increases. Job evaluation attempts to develop a wage scale for each job, and to eliminate wage differences or inequities between jobs. For example, when Matt developed a job evaluation program for his clothing store, he found a big difference in wages between the salesperson in the shoe department and the one in the shirt-and-accessory department. Each employee was bringing in about the same dollar amount of volume sales, with relatively the same profits, but their wages were significantly different. The job evaluation program showed Matt the need to adjust the wages so that they were fair for both employees.

Retention rates may be increased by providing incentive wages or bonuses for exceptionally good work. Profit sharing is another incentive wage program, in which a percentage of company profits are given to employees who are most responsible for the profits. In addition, most businesses offer fringe benefits to employees, including pension plans, sick-leave pay, health and life insurance, and vacation time. These benefits help retain good employees for the business.

Employees need to feel wanted. Many employees want to participate in the decision-making processes of the business. Employees often have good suggestions. Many of them can suggest new products, better ways of selling, and how to improve business. A general rule is that the employees who are involved and needed in a business will stay longer.

SUCCESS STORY: Gerald Flitter

Sometimes the secret to a successful business venture is not to be a big cheese, but a little one. For Gerald Flitter and the other members of his Minnesota Farmstead Products Cooperative, the secret was in part not to make big cheeses, but to make little ones.[2]

Flitter is president of his cooperative, which was formed in 1976 as a result of a pilot program at the University of Minnesota. It was felt that if these dairymen could produce Gouda cheese from part of their milk rather than sell it all in liquid form, they could increase their incomes. Gouda cheese is a soft, mild cheese imported from Holland. At first the cooperative sold its cheese in their own shops and in local stores, but it was felt that this market was too limited.

Little success was had initially in soliciting sales to the larger supermarket and chain markets. One problem was that the cooperative was producing only ten-pound wheels, which were not very consumer-oriented. The stores were interested in a product that didn't have to be cut up before selling. So the cooperative began to make some two-pound and five-pound wheels, although not very many because of the higher costs involved.

Following Dutch tradition, the farmers coated their cheese with yellow wax. But Americans expect Gouda cheese to be coated with red wax. The dairymen changed colors after a test they conducted showed that red-coated cheese outsold the yellow-coated by four to one.

The "Minnesota Farmstead Gouda" label was changed on the advice of a marketing consultant. The consultant reasoned that the original label emphasized Minnesota and that to most consumers good cheese comes from Wisconsin, not from Minnesota.

The biggest mistake made by the cooperative, however, was in trying to bypass the middleman and deal directly with the retailer. Most stores prefer to deal with a distributor who can offer all kinds of cheese. The cooperative was only producing one kind, and for that matter still is. Since 12 percent of the cheese plants account for 57 percent of US cheese production, the cooperative was at a disadvantage. After trying two cheese brokers, the cooperative finally located one who could move their cheese. However, although their cheese retails for between $3 and $4 a pound, and though they were able to get $2.25 a pound at their own shops, they only get $1.60 a pound from their broker. In fact, one family chose to restrict production to the local market capacity rather than accept the lower return.

While Flitter and the other members of the cooperative have had some success, they aren't making nearly as much money as had been hoped. The University of Minnesota originally estimated that each farmer could increase his income by $17,000 each year by making cheese. Now the estimate is around $9,700. However, sales are still growing and the cheese has received plaudits from several sources. It was recently praised by food critic Roy Andries de Groot in *Esquire* magazine.

[2]*The Wall Street Journal,* December 18, 1979.

Direction

One of the most important functions of any owner or manager is the direction or leading of individuals toward the accomplishment of organizational goals or objectives. Many managers often consider the managerial function to be a directing function only, often eliminating the other functions of planning, organizing, staffing, and controlling.

The direction function is very important in small business management. Managers "get things done" when they are properly directing their employees or subordinates. Directing is the "human" or "people" function of management.

Direction is concerned with sparking the motivation that is required for the job to be accomplished. Motivation is the quality or factor within an individual that may arouse, channel, or cause behavior toward a specific goal. Motivation can be thought as a "kick in the pants" or as a desire to fulfill a need. There are basically four different approaches to motivation: (1) drive, (2) incentives and expectations, (3) cognition, consistency, and clarity, and (4) reinforcement.

drive

Ever since the beginning of time, people have had drives to satisfy needs. Needs, basically, are things that are useful and/or required for living. Motivation is simply an inner factor or state that causes someone to satisfy a need or to accomplish a goal. Drives originate from biological need—such as the need for food and water—and are an internal process.

$$\text{Needs} \longrightarrow \text{Drive} \longrightarrow \text{Goal}$$

A manager may increase the drive strength or motivation of an employee by increasing the employee's goals and making them more reachable. Bonuses and incentive pay are examples of goals that have a tendency to increase drive and motivation. People are often driven to increase their performances for goals such as grades, profits, success, or fame.

incentives and expectations

People have a tendency to work for incentives and/or expectations. An incentive is the reward or reinforcer that a person receives for accomplishing a goal. An incentive will heighten the activity of that person toward reaching that goal if it is something he or she needs or desires. For example, a salesperson may see a free trip to Hawaii as a strong incentive when it is attached to a sales goal that he or she may reasonably expect to gain by a lot of hard work and effort.

A person's expectations will also directly affect his or her performance. An expectation is a probability or the chance that, by accomplishing a goal, a certain outcome will occur. For example, if a student studies hard in class and works to develop a good term paper, his or her expectation for a grade of A may be very high. Similarly, an employee of a shoe store may reasonably expect a bonus at the end of the year or month if he or she works hard and increases sales during that month period.

People tend to work toward things that will satisfy their needs or desires.

Most people expect that after a hard month's work, they will be paid for that work. This is a high expectation level, and if they are not paid, they will quit. Most people do not like to work without being paid for that work in some way.

Not all employees seek the same incentives or desire the same outcomes. It is necessary for an employer to investigate all possible incentives for the employees. For example, one dentist found it appropriate to offer the receptionist and dental assistants plane tickets to Hawaii. One of the staff members preferred to travel to Texas to visit relatives. The dentist then changed the incentive for that employee, and the final outcome was beyond the expectations of the dentist. Work and revenues increased beyond the dentist's expectations, and each staff member received a plane ticket to a place of his or her choice.

cognition, consistency, and clarity

People act to maintain their own self-esteem and self-worth. They also tend to behave in a self-consistent manner; for example, people who consider themselves to be hard workers will generally work hard.

Most managers have learned that if they respect their employees, their employees will respond by honoring that respect and working to maintain it. Many people who believe that they *can* succeed *will* succeed. Those who believe they *will* be failures *are* failures. Most people who say that they *can* perform a task *will* perform it if they are given an opportunity to do so.

People usually try to make their behavior consistent with their thoughts. Those who think of themselves as being honest and truthful will generally be just that. A small business manager, by setting high standards and expectations for employees, will often find those employees reaching those standards and expectations. Many employees who doubt that they can do a job will go forth and do it excellently when their employer tells them they can do it and shows confidence in them. Employers can motivate employees by making them live up to their own high personal standards of conduct and work expectations.

reinforcement

People provide reinforcement to others as a support to good behavior because they believe that actions or behaviors that are reinforced (rewarded) will be continued or repeated. Actions or activities that lead to pleasant outcomes will generally be repeated, while actions or activities that lead to unpleasant outcomes will generally be discontinued. Additionally, most people have learned to obey the law and authority at work and at home, because they have found by so doing they will receive pleasant outcomes and that if they disobey the law or authority, they will often receive negative or punishing outcomes.

Direction is also concerned with providing leadership for the organization. A leader is one who can direct the activities of others within an organization toward objectives or goals. The owner must be able to inspire and praise his or her employees for work well done. The leader should apply objectives and be a catalyst toward reaching the goals of the organization. The leader may also provide suggestions and directions for the employees, to help them establish proper work patterns and procedures. The owner must lead his or her employees toward the final goals and accomplishments of the business.

Proper management and direction of a business requires an ability to influence others to behave in certain directions. The manager needs to study his or her organization and staff to be able to properly direct the overall effectivensss of the business. If management is properly planned, organized, and staffed in the small business, the manager should be able to direct, motivate, and lead the employees within that business toward great heights of profitability. A manager must be able to direct others toward achieving the goals of the organization.

Control

The organization of a business will be complete when the control function has been accomplished. The control function is concerned with seeing that what *did* happen was what was *supposed* to happen. It is concerned with comparing the plans with what actually occurs in the business.

Planning is a prerequisite for control; control cannot happen without a plan. The plan needs to be developed so that the work will be done. Control is the follow-up to see that the work was done properly.

Accounting is the major method of organizing data about the finances of a business. Accounting statements are tools that business owners may use when controlling the budgets and expenses of the business. For example, sales budgets are plans that indicate the volume of sales expected for the coming year. Accountants collect the data to see if the sales expectations were reached. The manager uses accounting statements to (1) see if the budgets were reached, (2) find out why they were not reached, if appropriate, and (3) determine any weak spots or differences that should be changed. Action is taken generally after the follow-up or control has been started.

A football game is an easy illustration of the management's control function. Films of the game are used by the owners and coaches of the football team to determine if the players have performed to the best of their ability. Most college and professional teams use films to rank each player's performance. A manager uses plans, budgets, and financial statements to review each employee's performance.

The control function is needed when individual objectives differ from organizational objectives, when an individual performance differs from actual performance, or when time delays occur between when goals are developed and when they are accomplished. (See Figure 9–5.)

Effective control systems should be understandable, economical, and useful. Most managerial controls are established to help improve performance and are used for decision-making centers. Controls must provide some flexibility, to allow for contingencies or for environmental variables that may cause changes to occur.

forms of control

There are many different forms of control—most are quite simple. Some require only the observation of employees. Others require an investigation of financial statements. Still others require extensive accounting or mathematical development. Some of the most common forms of control are:

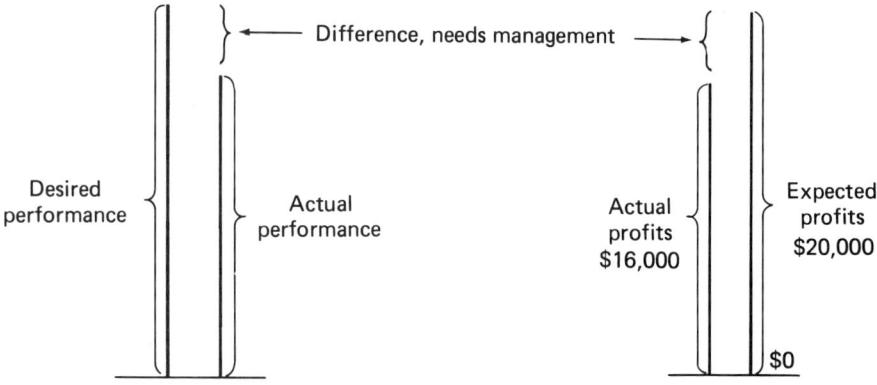

Figure 9-5. *Control function*

1. Breakeven chart.
2. Financial statements:
   a. Income statement.
   b. Balance sheet.
   c. Cash flow statement.
3. Ratio analysis.
4. Budgets.
5. Job evaluations.

Control compares what has actually happened with a plan, and allows for necessary corrections when events differ from the plan. The process of control allows a manager to compare what *did* happen with what was *supposed* to happen. This function is vitally important in making necessary adjustments, thus ensuring the success and profitability of a business. Control is an essential part of business success.

CASE STUDY: Beauty Salon

Joni wants to start her own beauty salon business. She has recently read that sales climbed to a record of $5 billion dollars in the last year, and that there are expectations of even higher sales in the future. Joni has found that new beauty shops are now considered to be "hair design salons" or "hair studios" rather than traditional beauty shops. The increase in the demand for beauty has required greater technical expertise in hair cutting, which has resulted in higher prices and profits. The former weekly appointment has been changed to a once-a-month or once-every-six-weeks appointment period. Customers are not limited to women; many men are referred by relatives or friends.

Customers are now concerned about the condition of their hair as well as its style. They have heard about protein, pH balance, and various conditioners, which help treat such hair problems as split-ends or "the frizzies." The salon customer is interested in personal care service, and there is a need for the salon owner to develop a personal relationship with the customer. The owner should be aware of current trends and future fads. Customers will often ask for advice about hair care and styling.

Location is one of the key elements of a successful salon business. Many salon owners have realized that a salon in the high-fashion district may be able to gross $200,000 a year, while its suburban counterpart may be able to gross only half that amount. Joni is concerned about finding the right location, and realizes that she must investigate many factors:

1. Family income levels in the surrounding area.
2. Lease requirements.
3. Size of the store.
4. Parking facilities.
5. Nearness of other shops or services.
6. Attractiveness of the area.
7. Accessibility for customers.

Joni thinks that she may have to incorporate, but is still hesitant. She does not see any need for that expense, and would rather limit herself to a sole proprietorship. She is currently going to school to obtain her cosmetologist's license, which is required to perform beauty services. She has already contacted her county courthouse and has obtained a business license, and she has gotten a seller's permit from her state board of equalization. The IRS has sent her an employer's identification number, and she thinks she is about ready to start business.

Joni wants to start a four-chair salon. She is unsure about the proper layout and about how to handle the other staff members. She is considering offering a commission along with a guaranteed minimum wage. She has found that commissions generally average between 45 percent to 55 percent of sales price after costs are deducted. However, if she wants an expert stylist, she may have to pay up to 60 percent of her gross sales as a wage.

Questions

1. How should Joni organize her business? Justify your answer.
2. What kind of layout would be most useful and attractive?
3. How should Joni organize her personnel?

Chapter Questions:

1. Discuss the major functions of management.
2. Describe the four steps of planning. Why are they important?
3. With which managerial function do small business owners spend most of their time? Why?
4. What problems should small business owners look for in organizing their businesses?
5. What are the proper steps in staffing a business?
6. Discuss motivation of employees.

10

Photo courtesy of Irene Springer, Prentice-Hall, Inc.

BUYING AN EXISTING BUSINESS

Chapter Objectives:

1. To understand the kind of business you should buy.
2. To learn how to evaluate business opportunities.
3. To learn the methods of pricing a business.
4. To learn how to purchase a business.
5. To become familiar with tax-free reorganizations.

"Forward, the Light Brigade!"
Was there a man dismayed?
Not though the soldiers knew
Someone had blundered.
Theirs not to make reply,
Theirs not to reason why,
Theirs but to do and die:
Into the valley of Death
Rode the six hundred.

Alfred, Lord Tennyson

INCIDENT: George is in his early thirties. He is married, and he and his wife have two small children. He has been working at a service station for twelve years, and has become the chief mechanic. He is second in charge to the owner, Mr. Tracy. The service station has done quite well over the past several years; it is in an older and more well-to-do section of town.

Mr. Tracy started the service station over thirty years ago and has watched it grow into a prosperous and worthwhile business. He is now in his late sixties, and wants to retire. He has approached George about buying the business from him. The price that Mr. Tracy is asking is $250,000. He is willing to finance $100,000 of that with George over the next twenty years, at 10 percent interest. The business has been all paid for, and new pumps were added only three years ago. The station consists of a main office area and two fully-equipped service bays. There is an additional car-wash unit, which was attached over six years ago and is completely automated and functional. Mr. Tracy is the sole proprietor, and he has shown profits of $34,000 a year, before deducting his own salary.

George was very excited when he was approached by Mr. Tracy. He sees this as his future, and knows that he can make a big success of the business. He has had experience in all phases of the business, and knows that the location and clientele are excellent. George is now making $18,000 a year at the station, and he has saved about $5,000 over the past three years.

George wants to know (1) whether or not he should buy, (2) how he can buy, (3) what the risks are, and (4) how many years it will take before he can completely own the business.

Every day, thousands of people start their own businesses. Buying a business is quite similar to getting married. Before buying a business or getting married, people must review their actions and analyze what they are about to undertake. It is important to realize the limitations, financial as well as physical, that must be faced

BUYING AN EXISTING BUSINESS

before getting married or starting a business. The decision to begin is critical, and is one that will affect each person for the rest of his or her life. However, a surprisingly large number of people enter into such adventures without adequate information or preparation. The final decision is often made by emotions and feelings rather than by planning and reason.

In buying a new business, the buyer must plan ahead. There are five major steps that should be reviewed and developed before starting a business:

1. Determine the kind of business to be undertaken.
2. Determine the available resources that can be drawn on to buy or purchase the business.
3. Find the right opportunities.
4. Evaluate all opportunities.
5. Handle the decision.

Determine the Kind of Business

The kind or type of business one chooses to undertake is primarily a personal decision. Most business principles are interchangeable and operate across all kinds of different businesses, but it is important for a person to go into a business that is compatible with his or her goals and ideals.

One should investigate the working hours and requirements of any business before buying it. It is important to know if the business stays open seven days a week and requires an owner's constant attention, or if it has an absentee ownership that requires minimal attention by the owner. Can the buyer handle all the managerial tasks with his or her own family, or will these require people with additional managerial experience—the hiring of additional managers?

Determine the Available Resources

The buyer must evaluate and determine all available resources. The type and size of the business are determined by the finances available for the business. It is cheaper to open a T-shirt shop in a shopping mall than to open a large, high-priced restaurant on the outskirts of town. The available financing may also determine the quality of merchandise sold or the elaborateness of the fixtures and furnishings of the business.

Sources of financing include personal savings, family banks, suppliers, trade associations, and government agencies. (See Chapter 8.) Regardless of outside financial support, it is generally necessary for at least 10 percent to 20 percent of the total financing to come from your personal or family resources. No banker or other lending officer (including government agencies) will finance a business without any private or personal financial backing. All will require 10 percent, 20 percent, or more backing by the owner(s).

Knowing one's own financial limitations will allow the buyer to limit his or her search to a realistic business opportunity. The buyer should now know the financial range within which he or she will keep when evaluating business opportunities.

Find the Right Opportunities

There are several major sources of information about business opportunities within a community, which include:

1. The local Chamber of Commerce deals with most businesses in the community and often knows of business owners who are interested in selling their businesses. The Chamber of Commerce may also be able to supply you with leads for other locations throughout the country by working with other Chambers of Commerce.

2. Newspaper and magazine advertisements are another major source of business opportunities. Ads may be listed in the classified ads or in the business section of local newspapers. Talking to business editors of newspapers may also provide additional insights.

3. Trade sources are an excellent information source of business sellers. These trade sources would include:
   a. Suppliers.
   b. Manufacturers.
   c. Distributors.
   d. Trade associations.
   e. Trade publications.
   f. Jobbers.

4. Realtors or business brokers often know of businesses for sale. Both realtors and business brokers receive a commission from the seller, causing the price to the buyer, therefore, to be increased. Their commission is generally based upon a percentage of the final selling price. They often require a specific period of time in which to work, and have exclusive rights to sell during that time period. (This means that, regardless of who sells the business, whether the seller or another agent or relative, the broker will receive a commission on the final sale.)

5. The business owner is a surprising source for a sale. A buyer may determine a business that he or she would like to purchase, and can directly approach the business owner. The buyer may be able to talk the owner into selling the business. Businesses are often sold by this very direct method of contact.

Evaluate All Opportunities

A buyer should evaluate all opportunities that are available. The old adage still applies: "Let the buyer beware." It is assumed that the buyer has evaluated and

BUYING AN EXISTING BUSINESS investigated all the activities of the available opportunity. The final decision has supposedly been made after careful consideration and analysis of all actions and activities of that opportunity. The following may be used as a checklist in evaluating a business opportunity:

1. History of the business and its related industry.
2. Business profit, sales, and expense figures: past and projected (five or more years back; one to three years in the future).
3. The reason for the sale:
    a. Owner's health and age.
    b. Owner's interest.
    c. Owner's family.
    d. Profitability.
    e. Bankruptcy.
    f. Moving.
    g. Location.
    h. Obsolete merchandise or inventory.
    i. Poor management.
4. Determine what is being bought:
    a. Assets.
    b. Liabilities.
    c. Employees.
    d. Good will.
5. Other areas of concern:
    a. Location.
    b. Parking.
    c. Licenses.
    d. Merchandise line.

This checklist should be used as a guideline to determine and evaluate any business opportunity. The successful completion and analysis of these guidelines will require time and effort, but such an investment will highlight the dangers and obstacles to becoming successful as a business owner. Such an approach affords one an opportunity to analyze and evaluate the business instead of just jumping off either to sink or swim. The buyer should fully realize the burdens of ownership, the time and effort that will be required to own and operate the business, and the sacrifices and limitations that the business demands.

the history of the business and its related industry

It is very important to ascertain a proper and accurate history of any business venture. The buyer should realize that any business that was successful during the past few years may have seen a strong downturn due to the economy or market conditions. An understanding of the history of the industry, whatever it may be, will provide additional insights into the possible profit or loss of the business. The markets for slide rules, black leather jackets, and Studebaker cars are not as strong as they used to be. However, the future of the electronics and repair businesses looks very bright. An historical analysis of the business and its related industry should reflect the growth potential and market potential of the business itself.

business profit, sales, and expense figures

Buying a successful business is no guarantee of continued success. Therefore, it is important to determine the profitability of the business. A business is bought because the buyer perceives adequate profitability in the future. It is the *potential* of the business for growth and profitability that attracts buyers.

To assess the potential earning power of a business concern, it is important to look at the historical profits, sales, and expense figures in addition to projecting them for the next one to three years. These figures may be obtained from the current owner and from the business records—the balance sheet and income statements—as well as from the owner's personal income or tax statement. The audited or unaudited business records from the past five years will provide sufficient information to ascertain the profitability as well as the sales and expense figures for the past. These figures and any associated operating ratios may be compared with industrial averages or the projections of the buyer.

The future potential earning power of the business should also be determined by projecting the sales, expenses, and profitability for the next one to three years. This may be done by using a simple trend analysis or by increasing sales on a percent equal to that over the past one or two years. These projections should be in line with the historical trends of the business as well as with those of other businesses in the trade.

Buyers often tend to overestimate the sales potential of the business they are buying, or to underestimate the costs or expenses associated with it. It is therefore wise and appropriate to always compare, on a percentage basis, the expenses, cost of goods sold, and other items to the going business or the industrial averages.

One restaurant owner went bankrupt only six months after buying a successful restaurant, one that had been profitable for over sixteen years. He thought that he could increase his price and at the same time reduce the cost. What he did not know or realize was that people had come to the business because of the high quality of food for the price being offered. He reduced the percent of his cost-of-goods-sold items from 45 percent to 33 percent, which was far below the prior business averages as well as the national average.

Buying a business without investigating these areas is like marrying someone before even asking his or her name. Additional information is easily obtained from friends, from neighboring business owners, and from bankers as to the future potential of the specific business.

the reason for the sale

It is often overlooked or forgotten, but it is important to remember that all sellers have a reason for selling. The seller may be old or in ill health. The owner may have become disinterested or may have found that his or her family wanted to move to a different location. However, the reason is often a lack of profitability, the loss of a lease, poor business, or a bad location. The reason may also be that the product is becoming obsolete, the competition is becoming better or even too strong, there has been a change in traffic patterns, the facilities are antiquated, or even that the owner has been unable to collect accounts receivable.

The prospective buyer should conduct a thorough investigation of the location and market conditions of the business. Contact should be made with the local Chamber of Commerce, the Better Business Bureau, zoning offices, and municipal government agencies to ascertain the conditions of the existing business. Will new and improved management increase the profitability of the business? Will a new approach bring success to the business?

determine what is being bought

Before buying any business, it is extremely important to determine exactly what is being bought. The major area of interest will be concerned with the assets, the liabilities, the management, the employees, and the good will of the business.

When investigating the assets of the business, one should review the tangible and the intangible assets that are associated with the business. Included in these assets should be an understanding of the inventory and a realistic price reflecting its true value, the furniture and fixtures, the equipment, and the building, with an appropriate price that reflects both the historical and the current value as well as the accounts receivable. Are any of the accounts receivable current enough to be collectable? What is the current credit standing or the general quality of the customers? The older the accounts, the less likely they are to be collectable and the less value they will have. All these assets should reflect a relevant value and an association with their age and condition. Steps need to be taken to see that the exact inventory, fixtures, furniture, building, and accounts receivable are accurately recorded.

Other assets of major concern include good will (the worth of the business name), the customer list, the mailing list, the business or credit records, and usage of the former owner's name with the business. Is the lease transferrable or renewable, or must it be renegotiated? If the latter, is it possible to renegotiate or will it be a sublease? Is the franchise an exclusive franchise, or is there a right to transfer? Does the franchiser need to be contacted? What are the duration, cost, and terms of the franchisee, trademarks, business names, and so forth?

Liabilities of the business may be extensive and expensive. It is easy to get married and then find that your spouse has an outstanding education loan of $7,200, with credit card bills of over $2,600 and car payments of $3,200 yet to be paid. These would be just a few of some fairly expensive liabilities associated with a marriage contract.

Liabilities associated with buying a business may be unpaid bills, contractual obligations, mortgage contracts, employee obligations, chattel mortgages, back taxes, pending or potential legal suits, liens against assets, creditors' claims, and accounts payable. It is crucial to be sure that the liabilities associated with buying a business will be listed in writing and will be a part of the written agreement. It is best to simply state that all claims not shown on the balance sheet at the time of sale (date of transaction) are to be assumed by the seller. By carefully following this legal procedure, the buyer will be helped, and will be assured of not being responsible for prior claims against the business.

Key personnel are vital to a business. It is extremely difficult to hire and retain new personnel. Before buying a business, it would be advisable to understand how many employees will remain with the business. Would the business be able to continue if key personnel were lost or moved from the business? The buyer should determine what staff changes would be necessary, the cost of training new employees, and key personnel for the continuation of the business.

The buyer should also be aware of the good will and/or reputation of the existing business. Is the clientele satisfied? Will the customers stay with the new management, or will the seller reenter the business in a different or better location? Will the buyer have access to all the customer lists and mailing lists associated with the business? Will the new buyer be able to retain all the clientele now using the business? A good figure for a buyer to estimate is the percentage of business held by the existing business due to the owner's personality. What percent of sales are made because of a personal attachment between the seller and his or her current customers?

Are there good relations between the business and the suppliers or creditors today? Will the new buyer be able to maintain the current suppliers, or will he or she have to seek other credit sources or suppliers?

other areas of concern

Before a buyer makes a final determination, he or she should investigate other areas, such as the location (his or her market and economy), available parking, license requirements, and the merchandise line. The buyer should try to ascertain the market strength of the current location. Is the market location strong? Is it in an area for growth and expansion? Or is the market deteriorating—are customers leaving that particular location to shop elsewhere?

Parking may be a very major problem, especially in a downtown area or in a small shopping center. On-the-street parking is often insufficient, and certain locations do not provide sufficient parking for zoning or licensing requirements.

Are the licenses transferable to a new owner? In buying a liquor or restaurant business, it is often difficult to transfer liquor or beer licenses to new owners without prior business experience. Does the new owner have the technical expertise required to obtain a license for a barber or a hair-grooming salon? The buyer should check into all licensing requirements by the city and state, to be sure that he or she will be able to properly conduct the business after purchasing it.

The buyer should also be able to maintain the same merchandise line or sell the same products. The new buyer may not be able to obtain the same high-quality line of merchandise that the prior owner carried, and this would affect his or her profits. These areas need to be thoroughly investigated before any final decision is reached by the potential buyer.

The information in Figure 10–1 should be useful for the business being bought. The three-month figures should help overcome any weak or slack period, and should enable the buyer to have an accurate understanding of all costs associated with buying a business. These figures should provide sufficient flexibility for the buyer to accurately estimate his or her initial costs in buying a business.

Handle the Decision

After one has determined the kind of business that will be entered into, ascertained the available resources, and evaluated the various business opportunities available, it is crucial that the buying of the business be properly handled. This will become a very important legal matter, and no final action should be taken without

FINANCING A NEW BUSINESS

1. *Personal Living Expenses:*
   Salary (three months) _____

2. *Family Living Expenses:*
   Moving expenses _____
   Living expenses _____

3. *Price of Business:*
   Total amount _____
   Monthly payment (three months) _____
   Down payment _____

4. *Legal and Other Professional Fees* _____

5. *Estimated Monthly Expenses:*
   Salaries and wages of employees (three months) _____
   Rent (three months) _____
   Utilities (three months) _____
   Taxes (three months) _____
   Other (three months) _____

6. *Licenses, Deposits, and Prepayments:*
   Utility deposits _____
   Sales deposits _____
   Business licenses _____
   Insurance _____

7. *Start-Up Costs (one-time expenditures):*
   New fixtures and equipment _____
   Decorating and remodeling _____
   New inventory _____
   Advertising and promotion of opening _____
   Accounts receivable _____

8. *Cash:*
   Petty cash _____
   Change _____
   Miscellaneous _____

Total _____

Figure 10-1. *Factors to be reckoned with when buying a new business*

consulting a lawyer to protect the buyer and to fulfill all legal requirements of the state.

Included in the final legal documents should be the conditions, clearly written, which explain the transfer of the business and the property to the buyer. The contract should also clearly indicate which assets and liabilities are specifically being purchased by the buyer and which the seller will retain. All agreements should be in writing and properly notarized. The sales document should also contain information about insurance and real estate taxes and about how they are to be prorated between the seller and buyer. When the business is actually transferred from the seller to the buyer, it should be stated who will pay what legal fees and who will be responsible for the accounts receivable and accounts payable after a specific date.

If there is any time between the signing of the sales contract and the actual transference of the business, it is advisable to use an escrow company or the escrow department of the bank to handle all business transactions. The escrow agent, once knowledgeable of all the instructions and conditions related to the business, may see that the suppliers and creditors are properly reimbursed and handle all bills for the business during this transfer period. The escrow agent is merely a referee in business; it is important to close the deal as soon as possible so that the seller cannot deplete the inventory and so the buyer may take over the managerial process as quickly as possible.

Price the Business

Many businesses have very definite and established rules of thumb for establishing the selling price; however, most do not. For example, florists will often sell for the fair-market value of their equipment and inventory, with an additional 25 percent of the annual sales for the best of any of the previous five years. Drug store owners, on the other hand, will establish a price based on fair market value for the building fixtures and equipment; accounts receivable at 90 percent of face value and inventory at cost, plus an additional 75 percent of the average annual profit for the last three years (good will).

When there are no general guidelines established, it is important to provide a realistic approach in establishing a price that is based on the current earning power and on the potential profitability of the business. A major block in determining the price of the business is the value of the intangibles often referred to as "good will." Good will should be based on the current condition and earning power of the business, not on past investments of money or time. A buyer should not be forced to pay for a seller's mistakes or desires for increased income.

The common formula for developing a price is approached from a buyer's point of view. Although all businesses are different, this pricing formula may be used as a guide in determining a fair market value of the business. This approach should generally fall within 20 percent of the seller's asking price. If the price is appropriate, the buyer may begin negotiations to purchase the business. The formula is derived by obtaining the value of the tangibles or the adjusted value of the tangible net worth (assets minus liabilities) and subtracting the intangibles from the adjusted value of the business. The easy formula is then:

$$\text{price} = \text{adjusted value} + 3 \times (\text{profit} - \text{personal value})$$

$$\text{personal value} = \text{salary} + \text{alternative earning power or alternative investment} + \text{risk}$$

so that

$$\text{price} = \text{adjusted value} + 3 \times (\text{profit} - \text{salary} - \text{alternative earning power} - \text{risk}).$$

Therefore, if the adjusted value is $50,000, the profit is $30,000, your salary $16,000; alternative earning power 10%, and risk 10%:

$$\text{Price} = \$50{,}000 + 3 \times [\$30{,}000 - \$16{,}000 - (0.1 \times \$50{,}000) - (0.1 \times \$50{,}000)]$$
$$= \$50{,}000 + 3 \times (\$4{,}000) = \$62{,}000$$

This formula is a rough guideline for determining a basic price for an ongoing business. If the business has been quite successful during the past three to five years, it would then be appropriate to multiply the intangible portion by four or even five, instead of by three.

A step-by-step approach to determining the selling price of a business progresses through eight levels:

Step 1: Determine the adjusted value of the tangible net worth. (Total assets minus liabilities.)

Step 2: Take into account the current salary of the buyer or the normal salary for the owner or manager of a similar business.

Step 3: Determine the alternative earning power (10 percent—an arbitrary, changeable figure that depends upon interest rates and alternatives available). Consider if money to be spent in purchasing a business were invested elsewhere, such as in savings and loan, securities, or other businesses.

Step 4: Figure out the risk, which is a very arbitrary figure that is generally 5 percent to 10 percent of the adjusted value. This may be greater if the business previously failed or was unsuccessful.

Step 5: Determine the business profit or earning power of the business by using the average annual net earnings (the net profit prior to subtracting the owner's salary) based on the immediate past few years. It is important to see if the earnings have been increasing or decreasing during the past several years.

Step 6: Obtain the earning power of the business by subtracting the buyer's salary, alternative earning power, and risk from the average business profit or earnings of the business (step 5 − steps 2, 3, 4).

Step 7: Calculate the value of intangibles by multiplying the earning power of the business by the "strength of business" multiplier. This multiplier would be 3 for a moderately successful business and may be increased to 5 or 6 for a very successful and valuable business with a favorable location. A new, younger and growing business may have a multiplier of only 1.

Step 8: Obtain the final price by adding the adjustable value tangible net worth plus the value of the intangibles (steps 1 + 7).

Example A in Table 10-1 illustrates the seller obtaining the substantial value for intangibles (good will) of $12,000 when the business has been moderately

Table 10-1. Pricing a Business

	A	B
Tangibles:		
1 Adjusted value	50,000	50,000
Intangibles:		
2 Salary	16,000	16,000
3 Alternative earning power 10 percent	5,000	5,000
4 Risk 0.05 to 0.10 or greater	5,000	5,000
5 Business profit	30,000	20,000
6 Earning power of business (line 5 − [2 + 3 + 4])	4,000	−6,000
7 Intangibles, value (3 × line 6)	12,000	-0-
8 Final price (lines 1 + 7)	62,000	less than $50,000

successful and of worth to the prospective buyer. Within three years the buyer should regain the $12,000 paid for good will in the price of this business. In example B, the seller has zero value of intangibles, suggesting a price equal to or lower than the adjusted value of the tangible net worth. The buyer in example B may feel that the business would not be worth the adjusted value of tangible net worth because the earning power (negative) of the business is not sufficient to sustain a profitable level of business.

negotiate the selling price

There are generally five areas of concern in the negotiation process, of which the buyer should be aware: (1) the seller's personality, (2) the price, (3) the interest rate, (4) the down payment, and (5) the transference of systems.

After a fair price for the business has been determined, the buyer may start negotiations with the seller. The buyer should understand the seller's reasons, motivation, and desires to sell. It would be advantageous to know the seller's background. Does the seller need cash? Is he or she willing to finance part of the agreement? What terms is the seller seeking?

After analyzing the seller, next consider the price. If it has been previously determined that the business is worth $62,000 and the seller wants $65,000, the buyer should offer him or her $54,000 or less. If the seller has only asked for $60,000 and indications are the business is worth more than that, the buyer might still offer him or her $55,000 to begin. There is the possibility that the seller will accept the lower figure; if so, this is money that may be retained and used to make a profit in a very short time period. Allow the seller time in negotiating. Do not press the seller for a quick decision.

Encourage the seller to let you buy on terms, such as to pay the $62,000 agreed price over a period of ten years at a particular interest rate. It is advisable to start with a minimum down payment and suggest a low interest rate. Interest rates may vary from 6 percent to 15 percent, and the years of the loan of payment may vary from two to twenty years. The negotiations will evolve around the major financial areas of: (1) low price, (2) low interest rate, and (3) low down payment.

Once the seller has begun to talk, he or she has shown interest and has begun negotiations.

Another area of concern that may be important to the buyer is transfer assistance. The buyer may desire the former owner's assistance during the transition period. Negotiate with the seller to work at the business for about eight hours during each of the initial five days, plus about four hours a day for three weeks after that. This will allow the new buyer and the seller to develop and transfer the business as successfully as possible.

SUCCESS STORY: H. H. (Bill) Roylance

In October, 1970, H. H. (Bill) Roylance and a partner bought the *River Queen,* a floating restaurant, located in Portland, Oregon. The ship, originally christened the *Shasta* in 1922, had served 40 years as a ferry in the San Francisco-Oakland Bay area and the Puget Sound. In 1962, she was remodeled extensively and started her career as a restaurant. By 1970, she was tired looking and run-down, yet she was still a good operation. The two partners cleaned, painted and fixed up the ship and with their wives as cashiers-hostesses embarked on the restaurant business.

After a while the partnership dissolved and Roylance and his family decided to go it alone. Despite having to pay off a hefty financial settlement on the dissolution of the partnership and sustaining large current operating losses, the Roylance family decided to go deeper into debt and refurbish the River Queen. Air conditioning, a football-field worth of new carpeting, rich red velveteen drapes, handsome railings, partitions, and nautical decor were installed. Two Roylance sons, Doug and Chuck (not yet 21), painted the exterior of the 231-foot, four-deck ship. With their home and life savings on the line, and nearly $750,000 in debt, the Roylance family began again.

This time Roylance approached the business operation from the customers' point of view. He found out what customers wanted and then provided it at a price that was appealing. He selected purveyors with excellent reputations and purchased the finest meat, produce, poultry, and staples. He employed skilled chefs and cooks. He set firm standards of quality, cleanliness, and service. He created a warm, comfortable, relaxed atmosphere where customers are served by a friendly, helpful staff. How was this accomplished? Through the implementation of literally hundreds of policies and rules, such as:

1. A manager is to be on duty, every minute of operating hours.
2. Lunch and dinner menus are built around the steak and seafood house concept with additional items to round out the customers' choices.
3. Uniformity of preparation of established recipe is stressed. Fifteen cooks prepare fish and chips in identical fashion from a recipe that has not been altered in more than nine years.
4. Quality and quantity control are rigidly enforced. For instance, the bar is equipped with automatic dispensers set at one and one-quarter ounces to ensure the customer will receive a full measure of liquor in each drink. The wells are stocked with recognized quality name brands.
5. A balance of good inexpensive and selected fine wines is maintained; the customer can select from 80 wines priced at a fair value.

6. Special inexpensive banquet menus are available for group parties.

As Roylance says, "The list is endless and most policies, if mentioned individually, appear insignificant and of little consequence; but added together they are the ballgame."

Purchasing a Business

The buyer is primarily interested in the future earning power of the business. He or she should logically attempt to deduct a reasonable salary while obtaining a fair return on personal investment. If terms and arrangements have been agreed upon by the buyer and the seller, the actual purchase can take place.

Purchase of the business for cash is the simplest means by far of changing ownership of a business. When the buyer gives up a large sum of cash, he or she receives all the rights, privileges, and obligations of the business in exchange. The seller will often prefer this method of transfer because it frees him or her of all obligations and responsibilities, and also provides a valuable commodity—cash.

A problem arises when the buyer is unable to raise sufficient cash for the outright purchase of the business. It can be difficult to arrange sufficient capital from a financial institution—from banks, savings and loans offices, insurance companies, for examples. The buyer must now seek help from the seller to finance the purchase—the seller may agree to receive payments in the future based upon the success and profitability of the business. Such an installment purchase helps the buyer finance the purchase and allows the seller to have a set income for a number of years in the future. It will also delay payment of taxes on the sale of the business. Tax laws generally permit that the profit received from the sale of the business be reported during the year when the payments are actually made, as long as the initial payment in the first year does not exceed 30 percent of the total selling price.

Personal tax problems will arise when a buyer purchases the entire business directly from the seller. The buyer will have to pay personal income tax on all money obtained from the corporation or business, including those monies obtained from the business to pay back the seller's note or the installment purchase agreement. This personal tax problem may be substantially reduced by (1) purchase through the creation of a new corporation, or (2) use of a "seed purchase."

A buyer may establish a new corporation by depositing cash and receiving stocks in return. The buyer's company then buys the seller's company for some cash and installment notes. If more than 80 percent of the stock of the seller's company is then owned by the buyer's company, dividends may pass tax free from the seller's company to the buyer's company. The buyer's company can then pay off the seller without using any personal income of the buyer.

A "seed purchase" is accomplished by the buyer purchasing a small percentage of the business from the seller, then having the company sign the payoff of the remainder of the money owed. This is done through notes and an immediate cash settlement. The buyer then owns all outstanding shares of the business, while the company itself holds the remainder of the stock and will pay off the seller over a specific period for the full value of the business.

Both of these methods allow for the reduction of personal income taxes upon the buyer. They also allow the seller to look forward to a given income for a number of years. These methods also provide for the company itself to pay for the acquisition of the business through its profits.

Tax-Free Reorganizations

The reorganizations provisions of the Internal Revenue Code allow for the acquisition or merger of businesses that are nontaxable to the seller and to the buyer. Legislatures and the IRS have often felt that it is unfair to require a taxpayer to recognize income or gain when selling a business and receiving stock or another business in return. The taxpayer is merely changing the form of his or her investment. However, in certain circumstances, cash and debt securities (referred to as "boot") that the seller receives in exchange for his or her business may be taxable. There are three types of acquisition reorganization, generally referred to as "A," "B," and "C" reorganizations.

Probably the most common form of reorganization is "A," and it is referred to as "a statutory merger or consolidation" (consolidation being a bringing together of two corporations into a third new corporation; and statutory merger being when one corporation merges into and is a part of the surviving corporation). The entrepreneur or business owner has greater freedom in selecting payment in this type of reorganization than in any other type. The "A" reorganization, in order to maintain its tax-free status, must continue to operate the business of the acquired corporation in some form for a period of time.

The "B" reorganization allows a "stock-for-stock" exchange. The acquiring company must acquire "solely-for-voting" stock, which is a controlling interest of the acquired corporation at the time of the acquisition. The IRS has defined control of ownership as possessing at least 80 percent of all classes of stock. If any consideration other than voting stock is given for the acquisition, the entire exchange becomes taxable with few exceptions.

The "C" reorganization provides for a "stock-for-assets" exchange. The buyer company must acquire substantially all the properties of the seller corporation solely for the voting stock of the buyer's company. This form of free reorganization allows a buyer to purchase or acquire a business. In the "C" reorganization, it is possible that the buyer's company will not assume the selling company's liabilities. The seller's company may then have to sell some of the buyer's stock or have the shareholders assume responsibility to pay the seller's liabilities.

In an "A" reorganization, the seller's corporation goes out of existence. In a "B" reorganization, the seller's company will remain active and open for business and the buyer's company will take over. In a "C" reorganization, the seller will remain in existence and continue to conduct business unless the buying company liquidates the other company as part of the transaction. These are simple general guidelines for "A," "B," or "C" reorganizations, mergers, or acquisitions. Due to the legal and tax considerations involved in these forms of reorganizations, it is imperative that legal counsel be obtained in conducting such mergers or acquisitions.

CASE STUDY: An Apparel Store

The proverb states, "clothes make the man," and Andrew and Janet Long believe it. They both graduated from college four and one-half years ago, and Andrew had gone to work in the computer section of a large telephone company. Janet, meanwhile, had gone to work for a large department store and had rotated assignments throughout the store. Between them, they have saved a little over $20,000, and they are excited about the prospects of going into a small business.

In discussing their dreams with a neighbor who is a banker, they were informed of two business owners who are thinking of selling their businesses. One has a medium-to-high priced men's and women's clothing store, located in one of the new shopping malls on the outskirts of town. The second business that may be for sale is located in the downtown area. The Longs are excited about both opportunities.

The Longs have spent some time studying the apparel business, and have found that more than $75 billion is spent annually by Americans on their dress. After food, shelter, and transportation, the family spends approximately 7 percent of the total budget in clothing for the family. There are approximately 130,000 apparel stores in America, all trying to keep abreast of consumer needs and desires. The Longs have learned the "five rights" of apparel merchandising: (1) the right time, (2) the right place, (3) the right quantity, (4) the right merchandise, and (5) the right price.

The business in the mall is a combined women's and men's clothing store, which carries women's merchandise that includes dresses (short and long), skirts, sweaters, coats, pants, lingerie, swim suits, and sportswear. It also stocks most menswear: suits, shirts, pants, coats, sweaters, ties, underwear, belts, and men's sportswear. The price range is aimed at the moderate-to-high income levels. The shopping mall has been doing well since its opening ten years ago. It has an occupancy rate of 96 percent, and is in the process of raising rents. The owner of the mall clothing store wants to sell, retire, and move to a more southern and warmer climate. The owner of the mall store is interested in selling the entire business, having the new owner buy it out, including all accounts payable, accounts receivable, inventory, assets, and furnishings and equipment. The store is in excellent condition; it has 2,000 square feet and a new-lease option of $15 per square foot per annum and/or 5 percent of gross sales.

The downtown store is being offered for sale for $150,000. This store contains 2,200 square feet, and it has an outstanding reputation. It is a family clothing store, providing merchandise for all ages but no shoes are sold. An inventory of $20,000 is included in the selling price. The owner of the downtown store plans to leave the business and go to work with her husband at his business. She may be open to the idea of renting or leasing the building rather than a total, direct buy-out.

THE APPAREL STORE

	DOWNTOWN STORE	MALL STORE
Sales:	$196,000	$226,000
Cost of goods sold	113,680	140,120
Gross profits	$ 82,320	$ 85,880
Expenses:		
Wages (including owner's)	$ 35,280	$ 38,200
Rent	9,800	12,820
Insurance	1,570	2,260
Advertising	4,900	5,780
Utilities and telephone	2,940	3,840
Supplies	1,960	2,710
Licenses	1,760	2,200
Professional services	1,900	2,310
Depreciation	1,400	1,290
Travel	1,180	1,530
Miscellaneous	980	1,080
Total expenses	$ 63,670	$ 74,020
Net income (before taxes)	$ 18,650	$ 11,860

Questions

1. If you were the Longs, which business would you buy?
2. What additional information do they need before they make their decision?
3. What are the different options available in buying each store?
4. What are the advantages of buying the downtown store?
5. What are the advantages of buying the store in the mall?
6. What additional experience or expertise should the Longs have before they enter business?
7. Are the Longs ready to start business? Why or why not?

Chapter Questions:

1. What factors should be considered when buying a business? Why?
2. What financial resources should be considered when buying a business? Why?
3. Why is a legal contract important when buying a business?
4. Explain the required costs normally associated with financing a new business.
5. Discuss the selling price of a business.
6. Discuss tax-free reorganizations.

3
operating a small business

11

Photo courtesy of Irene Springer, Prentice-Hall, Inc.

ACCOUNTING

Chapter Objectives:

1. To learn what accounting is about.
2. To understand single-entry bookkeeping.
3. To determine what is necessary in, and how to keep, a single-entry bookkeeping system.
4. To understand what an income statement is.
5. To understand what a balance sheet is.
6. To understand why accounting is important.

If it is not right, do not do it;
If it is not true, do not say it.

Marcus Aurelius

INCIDENT:

George has just opened his new pizza restaurant one block off campus. His dream is finally coming true. He had been working for seven years since his college graduation to save money to establish a pizza and fast-food restaurant near campus to serve the students.

The Pizza Palace has a twenty-foot front and inside there is seating for eighty-four people. The main floor has seating for sixty people, set around fifteen different tables that are all movable. There is a second floor at the Pizzeria, which contains seating for twenty-four at one end. In the middle are located two billiard tables and two electronic football games, and at the other end are six pinball machines in a row. George has a liquor license that is limited to serving beer; the primary menu consists of pizza, sandwiches, and cold drinks.

George has just invited his best friend Don into the business. Don asked him how he was doing and George told him to come back to the cash register. He told Don, "I want you to see my books," and he punched up a "no sale" on the cash register. Don looked and realized that George was using his cash register as his books. George added, "Oh, hold it" and he pulled out the till where the coins were kept and underneath were three bills that had not yet been paid. George said, "See, I'm doing really well. I have enough money left in the till to pay the only outstanding bills I have. I am able to pay my wife her allowance and have some money to take home for myself. I have more than ample money in my till to pay off all my debts right now and I have only been open for two weeks. We are going to be a huge success!"

George is convinced that this is all that is necessary to handle all his records and to control his money. He is happy and excited about the future and the coming year of business.

Accounting is like handling your own checkbook. With your check stubs you list all income and deduct all expenses. Accounting is simply an information system designed to convey knowledge about specific financial activities. The information is primarily in financial terms and is restricted to those activities which may be measured and are reasonably precise. Accounting is primarily designed to make sure that at the end of the month, as well as at the beginning of the month, there is sufficient money in the checkbook to make ends meet.

Accounting is the language of business. It records, classifies and communicates sales, expenses, and other financial information important to owners or managers. The accounting function provides management the financial information and control system that helps to operate a business. Accounting answers the questions: Are there sufficient funds available to meet all expenditures? Will our paycheck be sufficient to pay for all of our wants, needs and extravagances?

The Single-Entry Bookkeeping System

Each of us must decide how accurate and up to date we will keep our own checkbook. A business owner has the right to make a decision between using a single-entry bookkeeping system or a double-entry bookkeeping system. This is very similar to the choice most of us have in keeping track of our finances through the use of a checkbook or a more elaborate set of records generally including journals (books where transactions are recorded as they occur) and ledgers (books where transactions are recorded in separate, specific accounts) sheets.

Although generally not taught in colleges or universities, the most common form of bookkeeping system available today is the *single-entry bookkeeping system*. It is the easiest system to maintain and is sufficient to satisfy the Internal Revenue Service. The single-entry system, though, may not be satisfactory for all taxpayers. It does not have a record of checks or balances against income and expenditures; rather, it is a partially complete system of accounts that concentrates on the profit and loss aspect of a business rather than on its overall picture.

The single-entry system is a simplified system of accounts that portrays the income and expenditures of a business. It does not require a balance sheet (as does a double-entry bookkeeping system). This system is limited but may be used effectively by an individual starting or running a small business. (See Figure 11–1.) The single-entry system generally consists of three records: (1) a daily summary of cash receipts, (2) a monthly summary of receipts, and (3) a record of monthly disbursements.

The *daily summary of cash receipts* (or the daily activity report) is a necessity in all small businesses. This record allows the business owner to determine what is selling, what is not selling, inventory levels, and which employees are selling the most or least. Some cash registers may record most of this information. Preprinted sales slips are also readily available to record this information.

The *monthly summary of receipts* is the monthly total of the daily summary of cash receipts plus any other income received. This informs the business owner of all money received for the month. The *record of monthly disbursements* reports all of the expenses paid out by the firm for a month.

The most common form of single-entry bookkeeping is the checkbook. If you (1) add all income (receipts) on a daily basis, (2) record all expenses (dis-

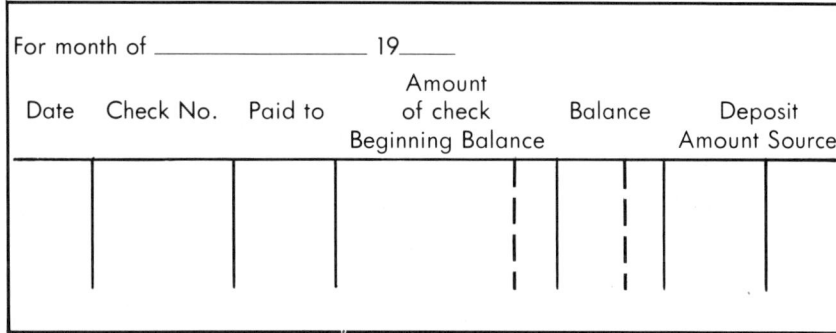

Figure 11–1. *Single-entry bookkeeping system*

```
          Tenth National Bank              Date and Balance this statement
          10th and Main Street             01-03-81    3725.02
          Encino, California

          Eco-Enterprises                  Average Balance   4863.62
          2840 Grand Ave.                  Min. Bal. 12-30-80   3737.02
          Encino, California

              Date     Transaction    Deposits      Balance
              12-07       15.60                     4829.70
              12-11       24.00                     4805.70
              12-12       13.38                     4792.32
              12-13                    1676.23      6468.55
              12-15     2400.00                     4068.55
              12-17        5.90         20.70
                         159.97                     3923.38
              12-20     1068.00        3272.68      6128.06
              12-22      868.00                     5260.06
              12-24     1200.00        2360.73      6420.79
              12-27      283.77                     6137.02
              12-30     2400.00                     3737.02
              01-03       12.00SC                   3725.02

SYMBOLS:   CM—Credit Memo                 OC—Overdraft Charge
           DM—Bank Charges (Debit Memo)   CH—Check Handling Charge
           LP—Loan Payment                PC—Payroll Credit
           LA—Loan Advance                DA—Debit Accumulation
           SV—Savings Transfer            SC—Service Charge
           PA—Pre-Authorize
```

Figure 11–2. *Bank statement*

bursements), and (3) use your monthly bank statement to balance all transactions, then you use a single-entry bookkeeping system. (See Figures 11–2 and 11–3.) Most of us employ this method in our daily lives. It is also permissible to use this system to record business activities for income taxes.

Single-entry bookkeeping is a partially complete system of accounts in that it usually concentrates only on the profit and loss statement and not the balance sheet. While this system has its limitations, it may be used effectively by one starting out in a small business. A single-entry system can be a relatively simple one which records the flow of income and expense. Through the use of a daily summary of cash receipts, a monthly summary of receipts and a monthly disbursements journal, this system can be used to record income and expenses adequately for tax purposes.[1]

The Double-Entry Bookkeeping System

The form of bookkeeping that is most commonly used and recommended by accounting agencies and universities is the *double-entry bookkeeping system*. This system uses the income statement employed by the single-entry bookkeeping

---

[1] "Recordkeeping for a Small Business," Publication 583, Department of the Treasury.

```
HELPS TO BALANCE YOUR CHECKING ACCOUNT
STEP 1  Compare and mark (✓) the amount of each check received on
        your statement.
STEP 2  Arrange your checks in the order they were written.
STEP 3  Verify the amount of each canceled check with the amount on
        your check register and mark (✓) each entry for a paid check on
        your record.
STEP 4  If a check is not marked off of your record, enter the check on the
        form.
STEP 5  Complete the form.

Fill in the amounts from your bank statement and checkbook.

Bank Statement

Balance shown on              Last balance shown in
bank statement    _____    your checkbook        _____

Add deposits made             Add any deposits not
since last date on            entered in checkbook  _____
statement         _____    Total                 _____

Subtract checks written
by you but not on state-
ment:             _____

Subtract checks written by you but   Subtract all checks and charges
not on statement:                    not entered in checkbook:

   Date or                              Date or
   number      Amount                   number       Amount
   _____    _____                   _____     _____
   _____    _____                   _____     _____
   _____    _____                   _____     _____
   _____    _____
                                     New balance for
              _____                your checkbook  _____
```

Figure 11–3. *Balancing a checkbook*

system, as well as a balance sheet that indicates the assets, liabilities, and net worth that a company maintains. This system also uses journals and ledgers. The transactions are first entered into journals, then summary totals are posted or shown in ledger accounts (generally monthly) to indicate the income, expenses, assets, liabilities, and net worth of that particular business. Both the income and expense accounts are closed at the end of each accounting period while the assets, liabilities, and net worth accounts are kept open and maintained on a permanent basis.

The double-entry system provides additional benefits over the single-entry system in that it is self-balancing. It also has built-in checks and balances, which assure the accuracy and control that the single-entry system is unable to provide. Because all business transactions consist of an exchange of one item for another, the double-entry system is used to show this two-fold effect, and it records each transaction—as a debit entry in one account and as a credit entry in another.

Double-entry bookkeeping systems are preferred by the Financial Accounting Standards Board, and by all accounting societies in general. In using this system, the journal entries are posted to the ledger accounts, and the total of the amounts that are entered as debits must equal the total of the amounts entered as credits. Errors occur in the system when the debits and the credits do not balance, and corrective steps will need to be taken to bring the accounts into balance. At the end of each accounting period, usually monthly or annually, the financial statements will be prepared from these balanced accounts. The two major financial statements used are the income (or profit and loss) statement and the balance sheet. The income statement reflects the current operations for the year or month, and the balance sheet shows the financial picture or position of the business in terms of assets, liabilities, and net worth at an exact point in time. The balance sheet is primarily developed at the end of the fiscal year, and reflects the state of the business at that particular time.

Which System Should Be Used?

The choice of using either a single-entry or double-entry bookkeeping system belongs to the business owner. The single-entry system is probably the most commonly used system in small businesses. The business owner simply uses his or her own checkbook to record the transactions of the business for either a monthly or a yearly schedule. If the business owner deposits his or her daily summary of cash receipts in the bank, and records them in a checkbook, and if he or she totals them on a monthly basis from the monthly bank statement, he or she has, in effect, a single-entry bookkeeping system. That checkbook will also record all expenditures for the business, and the bank statement may serve as both a monthly summary of receipts and a monthly disbursement statement. Almost all of us use a single-entry bookkeeping system to prepare personal income tax returns.

Financial Statements

Financial statements are simply summarized reports of the financial conditions of a business. The two primary financial statements that illustrate the fiscal condition of a firm are the income statement and the balance sheet.

income statement

The *income statement* shows the performance of a business by matching its activities (sales, customer receipts) and its expenses (costs associated with the business, costs of goods sold and other related expenses). (The income statement is also referred to as the statement of earnings, or the profit and loss [P&L] statement.) The income statement is generally in terms of current dollars and is a straightforward account of receipts minus expenditures. The revenue (sales) is shown first: This represents the total sales volume accomplished by the business for that income period. (See Figure 11–4.) Expenses are then listed—they show the funds needed to operate the business during that same time period. Once the operating expenses are deducted, an operating income results from which interest and tax expenses are deducted, showing the net income for the business for that time period.

The statement is shown in either a single-step or a multiple-step format. The single-step statement will list all revenues and expenses without listing any subtotals, while the multiple-step statement will contain one or more subtotals for either the revenue or expense portion, as is illustrated in Figure 11–4.

Single Step Income Statement		Multiple Step Income Statement	
Sales	$	Sales	$
Cost of goods sold		Drinks	
Gross Profit		French fries	
Expenses		Hamburgers	
Net Profit (before interest and taxes)		Other	
Interest		Cost of Goods Sold	
Taxes		Drinks	
Taxes		French fries	
Net Profit (after interest and taxes)		Hamburgers	
		Other	
		Gross Profit	
		Expenses	
		Wages	
		Supplies	
		Repairs & maintenance	
		Advertising	
		Car & delivery	
		Rent	
		Utilities	
		Insurance	
		Taxes	
		Other	
		Depreciation	
		Net Profit (before interest and taxes)	
		Interest	
		Taxes	
		Net Profit (after interest and taxes)	

Figure 11–4 *Types of income statement.* Also called statement of income and expenses; profit and loss statement (P+L).

Subtotals are developed to help the manager in the decision-making process. They are designed to highlight relationships and common expenses. Three common subgroups are: (1) revenues, (2) cost of goods sold, and (3) cost of operating expenses. The revenues subgroups may be helpful in picturing the revenue from different parts of a business (for example, sales and service in a car dealership, or drinks, French fries, hamburgers, and sandwiches in a fast-food restaurant). When the cost of goods sold is deducted from the gross revenue, we have the gross profit or gross margin. This shows the manager the size of his or her margin above merchandise cost, which is very important for comparative reasons and decision making. Operating expenses may be summarized from adding the selling expenses, administrative expenses, and depreciation expenses. Deducting the operating expenses from the gross profit margin gives the operating income for operating profit.

Interest expense is more a financial matter than an operating decision; therefore, it appears as a separate item on an income statement, following operating expenses. This is important to many business owners for comparison purposes over different years. Because some businesses require heavy debt, it is important for them to keep track of their interest expense and do not allow it to become a heavy burden on profits.

Income taxes are a very significant part of any income statement. They are deducted separately, after all other expenses, in the income statement. The final result on the income statement is the net income, which shows the business owner his or her final profit or loss.

This is similar to a person receiving a bank statement and realizing that he or she is overdrawn. In such a case, the person shows a net loss for that particular accounting period. However, if the person has a positive balance shown in the bank statement, then he or she shows a net income or profit for that particular period.

The income statement measures the performance of the business over a period in time, usually compiled yearly, monthly, or quarterly. The income statement, therefore, becomes the major link between the balance sheets. Like the bank statement, it shows how much you have saved or overspent for the last month.

balance sheet   The *balance sheet* (or statement of financial position, or statement of financial condition) is a "photograph" of the financial position of a business at an instant of time. The balance sheet is in two counterbalancing sections (each section must equal the other): the assets and the equities (as shown in Figure 11–5). Assets are economic properties that are expected to provide future benefits or resources for the business. Equities, on the other hand, are claimed against the assets of or interest in the business. The balance sheet is simply an equation:

$$\text{Assets} = \text{Equities}$$

Suppose you purchased a used car for $1,600 by paying $300 in cash and borrowing $1,300 from a bank. The asset side of your balance sheet would show the car (valued at $1,600). The equity side would show in the liability portion the

```
                            BALANCE SHEET

         Assets                              Liabilities

What the business owes itself      What the business owes others (claims
                                   by creditors against assets—the
Current assets: items being converted  debt of the business)
   into cash within 12 months
      Cash                         Current Liabilities: debts owed to be
      Accounts receivable          paid within next 12 months
      Inventory                       Notes payable: I.O.U. to banks
                                      Accounts payable: I.O.U. to
Fixed Assets: items used to operate                       trade and
   business—not for resale                                creditors
      Real estate (land and buildings)  Income taxes payable: I.O.U.
      Leasehold improvements                              to
      Equipment                                           government
      Vehicles
      Machinery                    Long-Term Liabilities: debts owed to
      Accumulative depreciation    be paid beyond next 12 months
                                      Accounts payable: I.O.U. to trade
Total Assets                                              and creditors
                                      Mortgage payable: I.O.U. for real
                                                          estate
                                      Notes payable: I.O.U. to banks

                                   Total Liabilities
                                   Net Worth

                                   Owner's share of the business (invest-
                                   ment; owner's equity; stockholder's
                                   claim)
```

Figure 11–5. *Total Assets = Total Liabilities + Net Worth*

amount the bank is willing to finance ($1,300), and your own contribution (of $300). Therefore, while you "own" the car, the bank has a claim against that car of $1,300 and you have a claim of $300.

```
Asset                  Liability
   Car        $1,600      Note Payable              $1,300
                             (to bank)
                          Owner's Equity           $  300
   Total Asset $1,600     Total Liability and Owner's Equity  $1,600
```

This illustrates the fundamental equation of the accounting balance sheet:

$$\text{Assets} = \text{Liabilities} + \text{Owner's Equity}$$

The liabilities of the business are the debts of the firm. Owner's equity represents the excess value of the assets over the claims on those assets; in other words, the assets minus the liabilities.

The balance sheet is usually developed on a quarterly or annual basis. The balance sheet may be divided into five different sections. There are two asset sections, current assets and fixed assets; there are two liability sections, current liabilities and long-term liabilities; and there is also a section on net worth. Also, working capital is a financial figure that you may find valuable to include.

Current assets. Current assets are defined as being properties, belonging to a business, that will be converted into cash and spent within the next twelve months. This includes three major items: (1) cash, (2) accounts receivable, and (3) inventory. Cash includes the money you have on hand and that in the bank. Accounts receivable is the amount that customers owe the business for goods or services they have purchased. Inventory is the goods that you have on hand which may be ready to be sold, in some stage of production or manufacturing, or basic raw materials prior to handling or production.

Fixed assets. Fixed assets are properties, belonging to a business, that are not intended for resale and are used to operate the business. The fixed asset portion of the balance sheet may be divided into four major areas: (1) real estate (land and buildings), (2) leasehold improvements, (3) equipment, vehicles, and machinery, and (4) accumulative depreciation on buildings and equipment. Real estate is listed on a balance sheet at cost, as it is used by the business for its proper operation. Leasehold improvements are permanent installations that are installed in a leased building to prepare it for business. Equipment, machinery, and vehicles are items, listed at cost, that are used by the business to conduct its operation.

Finally, because all the fixed assets are assumed to be "used up" by a firm during its conduct of business, this diminishing value is referred to as depreciation. The business claims this loss of value as an expense of conducting business affairs. For example, the business car may have cost $7,500 and have a useful life expectancy of five years. Straight-line depreciation allows a $1,500 per year expense deduction over each of five years, or a total of $7,500. A running total of this value loss is referred to as *accumulative depreciation*.

Current liabilities. Current liabilities are debts that will be paid by the business within the next twelve months of operation. These may be easily divided into three major areas: (1) notes payable, (2) accounts payable, and (3) income taxes. *Notes payable* are debts incurred by the business that are owed to banks or trade creditors. *Accounts payable* are debts owed by the business to other commercial establishments or suppliers. Both notes payable and accounts payable may include interest payments and charges in association with their usage. *Income taxes* are debts that are owed by the business to the government; they include such things as sales tax, use tax, employer's withholding tax, and—in certain states—different franchise taxes.

Long-term liabilities. Long-term liabilities may be defined as debts owed by the business that will be paid *beyond* the next twelve-month period. The two major items in this area are (1) bank loans and (2) mortgage loans. *Bank loans* are given for extended periods of time, and they are primarily obtained to pay for such fixed assets as cars, fixtures, and equipment. Mortgage loans are long-term liabilities that are generally obtained from savings-and-loan institutions or from other financial institutions to pay for land and buildings used to conduct business.

Net worth. Net worth may be defined as the owner's claim on the assets of the business or as ownership of the business (that is, equity in the business). Net worth is generally explained in terms of: (1) equity, (2) capital stock, or (3) retained earnings. *Equity* is the owner's original investment, plus any profit reinvested by the owner in the same business. *Capital stock* is the value that was originally assigned to the stock by the directors of the corporation, if stock was issued to raise funds to open or to successfully operate the business. *Retained earnings* are profits that have been reinvested in the business after the payment of dividends to the stockholders. When there are no stockholders in a business, and when neither the capital stock nor the retained earnings will be stipulated in the business, the net worth statement will show the owner's claims on the business.

Working capital. Another valuable financial figure is working capital. *Working capital* is the difference between current assets and current liabilities. This is the money the owner will have to work with to pay off his or her payroll and immediate expenses during the coming year in the business. For example, if the cash on hand is less than the bills and expenses, the owner has a negative working capital and will find it difficult to pay his or her payroll and bills. Working capital is only an estimate of operating capital for the coming period. It is a figure that will provide an indication of the "ballpark" area within which the business can expect to operate. The working capital figure will help the owner to understand what monies are available to the business, to establish budget forecasts, and to plan for possible expansion of the business in the immediate future.

SUCCESS STORY: Henry J. Kaiser

Henry J. Kaiser was born on May 9, 1882, in a white frame farmhouse at Sprout Brook, New York, one of four children of Francis J. Kaiser, a shoemaker and Mary Yops Kaiser, a practical nurse, both immigrants from Germany.

Young Henry Kaiser traveled as a photographic salesman in upper New York state. At Lake Placid, New York, he offered to work for the owner of a photographic shop for nothing on condition that if he doubled the business in a year, he would receive a half interest. He trebled the business, became a junior partner at 22, bought out the business a year later and added new stores at Daytona Beach and Miami, Florida, and Nassau, the Bahamas. Outside his first store he placed a prophetic sign: "Meet the Man With a Smile."

He established his first company—Henry J. Kaiser Company, Ltd.—at Vancouver, B.C., in 1914, and the first job was to pave a road two miles long in that Canadian city.

During the next seven years, he continued road paving work in Washington, Idaho and British Columbia and created a new way of doing the job by replacing mules with machinery. Doing jobs better and faster with new ways became a Kaiser trademark. He saved his men many back-breaking hours by putting pneumatic tires on wheelbarrows and diesel engines in bulldozers.

He moved into the sand and gravel business in 1923 while he was paving a road between Livermore and Pleasanton in California. The aggregate plant developed into Kaiser Sand & Gravel, now one of the largest producers of aggregate in northern California. It was also Henry Kaiser's start in the business of mining and processing raw materials, a basic strength of the Kaiser companies today.

The year 1927 was a turning point in Henry Kaiser's career; he went to Cuba to build a 200-mile, 500-bridge highway. The principle of teamwork learned on this huge project guided Kaiser's future work. He conceived the joint venture concept that led to partnerships and associations of contractors for cooperative construction of projects too large for a single builder.

While the dams were being built in the 1930s, Kaiser's men were building piers for the world's longest bridge—the San Francisco-Oakland Bay Bridge, levees on the Mississippi River and pipelines in Kansas, Texas, Oklahoma, Arizona and Montana. Up to the start of World War II, Kaiser and associated firms built some 1,000 projects worth a total of $383 million.

Today, Kaiser Cement & Gypsum Corporation is the largest cement company in the West, with 43 plants and facilities, annual sales of $99 million, and assets of $150 million. Kaiser Aluminum & Chemical Corporation has assets in excess of $1.1 billion and annual sales exceeding $781 million. The fourth largest aluminum producer in the world, it has 88 plants and 27,500 employees.

Accounting Uses and Purposes

Accounting may easily be used as an effective means of: (1) internally reporting to the owners and managers as they develop their controlling and planning activities; (2) comparing one business with another, and the operations of one business with the average of the other business in the industry; and (3) externally reporting to agencies, trade associations, the government, and stockholders. The accounting records should help owners or managers to fulfill their organizational objectives for the business, and help them to realize where they may be strong and where weak with regard to their business operations.

Financial statements should be utilized in the managerial process of planning and control, as they show business owners if there is a profit. The owner or manager needs to use income statements both to determine historical sales and profits as well as to analyze future projections and growth trends. The owner or manager can ascertain from the profit and loss statement the areas that were too costly or the factors that moved too slowly to successfully run the business. The planning and control functions are augmented by the development of budget systems. The planning of how we are going to spend our money is called budgeting. The budget is designed to allocate our resources over a period of time.

One of the most useful processes associated with financial statements is comparison. Through the use of percentage figures, one may compare the administrative expenses between businesses and the various costs associated with doing business. For example, a highly successful hamburger restaurant has a cost of goods sold at 44.8 percent, while a planned fast-food restaurant's cost of goods sold is estimated to be 33.7 percent. The planned fast-food restaurant's cost are so far below those of a successful restaurant that the owner of the planned restaurant should realize his or her estimated costs are lower than average and too low to be realistic.

Dun & Bradstreet and Robert Morris Associates provide composite financial information that may be used in comparing businesses with specific industries. The Robert Morris Associates' *Annual Statement Studies* is probably the most widely used set of financial data in the United States. Most banks subscribe to this service and use the *Annual Statement Studies* in evaluating prospective loans and businesses. These statements provide comparative information in the form of a balance sheet, income statement, and various analyses of ratios. They vary across a wide range of items from ladies' clothing stores to hardware stores and construction businesses. Most business owners can easily find some similar business within these reports with which to compare their own.

A major and important function of the financial statement is to provide information to external parties. Stockholders, the government, and other parties are all interested in knowing the financial condition of business. The increase in business competition, the price/cost squeeze, rapidly developing technology, and increasing government involvement all demand an increase in this external reporting function.

preparation of financial statements

The preparation of financial statements may be done by yourself, by hiring other individuals to serve as financial consultants, or by hiring an accounting firm. If you plan to use a single-entry bookkeeping system, you will probably find it easiest to keep the records yourself and to develop an accounting system of your own that will be accurate and efficient for your time and business demands.

If you plan to use a double-entry bookkeeping system, you will probably find it more advantageous to use accounting firms, bookkeeping firms, or private accounting consultants to handle your business affairs. This may be done on a monthly, a quarterly, or an annual basis. You should make sure that the accountants prepare a balance sheet and an income statement, and that they provide you with a ratio analysis that you may use to compare your business with others and your current business position with historical data. If you use an accounting firm, you will also find it extremely advantageous to ask them to prepare a cash flow statement—or you may do this yourself.

CASE STUDY: La Crepe

Business overview. La Crepe is a restaurant franchise business with its headquarters in Miami, Florida, that is currently in an expansionary program—it is allocating franchises throughout the United States. The business usually has an inside seating capacity of fifty to seventy people. Its restaurants may be located in a mall, or they can be private restaurants or drive-in organizations.

The crepe itself is a simple item. Basically, it is a deep-fat fried bread. The variations come by slitting the crepe and inserting various stuffings, such as ham, fish, chili, pork, refried beans, crab, shrimp, beef, or barbecued foods. It also can be stuffed with various jams, jellies, or honey for a dessert item. The menu is centered around the crepe, except for the drinks, which include soft drinks, shakes, milk, tea, and coffee and the side items, such as potato chips and French fries.

Business plan: goods and services provided. La Crepe will provide a friendly atmosphere, wholesome fast-food, and a delivery service. The basic food items will include main dishes, and desserts, all with a crepe basis, plus drinks. Friendly service will be provided by the employees, who will work at a main counter area and who will also clean the tables and the restaurant area.

Market opportunity. The newest La Crepe location will be at the Pacific Plaza Mall, 5000 Mexicali, LaJolla, California. The market area for the Pacific Plaza Mall is the most desirable in LaJolla. Additional areas will be developed within the LaJolla metropolitan area. La Crepe, Inc. anticipates being able to expand into sixty units throughout California.

LA CREPE MENU

Breakfast Crepe: Eggs and Bacon

Burger Crepe	Ham Crepe
Beef Crepe	BBQ Crepe
Senor Crepe	Fish Crepe
Crepe Puppy	Crepe Fries
Crepe Cone	Crepe Ship

Justa Crepe

Crepe Sundae

Sweet Crepe

Crepe Pie: Apple, Cherry

Crepe Shake   Crepe Blast

Coffee   Tea   Milk   Hot Chocolate

7-Up   Pepsi-Cola   Root Beer   Cherry Soda

SPECIAL OF THE WEEK

Promotion. Promotional techniques will be provided by La Crepe, Inc. In addition La Crepe will supplement this promotional package by providing particular promotional techniques related to Southern California and LaJolla community.
Management and organization. La Crepe, Inc. provides a vigorous managerial, merchandising, and marketing training program for all of their franchises developed over a period of years. In addition to this professional training, immediate support may provide an additional expertise and training to the local organization. La Crepe will provide twenty additional employment opportunities to the LaJolla labor pool.

La Crepe
Balance Sheet

Notes payable	$ 15,525.00
Cash	6,525.00
Remodeling and improvements	18,000.00
Rent	14,400.00
Legal and accounting fees	1,800.00
Sales	180,000.00
Owner's equity	6,000.00
Merchandise inventory	3,000.00
Laundry	900.00
Advertising	3,600.00
Food	57,600.00
Franchise mgt. fee	7,200.00
Paper	9,000.00
Taxes and licenses	1,800.00
Fixtures and equipment	32,500.00
Investments	38,500.00
GROSS PROFIT	123,400.00
Payroll	43,200.00
Insurance	1,800.00
Utilities	3,600.00
Total operating expenses	87,300.00
Debt service	4,200.00

Questions

1. Develop an income statement for La Crepe.
2. Develop a balance sheet for La Crepe.
3. How should you evaluate this business?
4. What kind of additional information would an accountant provide if he or she worked for La Crepe?

Chapter Questions:

1. What are the three important records in a single-entry bookkeeping system?
2. What are the advantages and disadvantages of a single-entry bookkeeping system?
3. What financial statements are found in a double-entry bookkeeping system?

4. Why do most large businesses or corporations use the double-entry bookkeeping system?
5. What financial statements are primarily concerned with sales and expenses?
6. What are the uses of an income statement for planning and control?
7. How would you use a balance sheet to determine owner's equity and working capital?
8. List the uses of a balance sheet.
9. What are the major components of a balance sheet?
10. Who might best prepare your financial statements?
11. Problem:

The following information is taken from Gordon's Restaurant for the year ending December 31, 198X. There was no beginning or ending inventories.

Wages	$ 54,000	Sales: Drinks	$ 24,000
		French fries	18,000
Rent	14,000	Hamburgers	106,000
		Other	11,000
Fixtures and equipment	100,000	Accounts receivable	8,800
Owner's salary	?	Bank note payable (12 mo.)	60,000
Building	70,000	Bank note payable (3 mo.)	4,000
Cash	4,500	Accounts payable	2,600
Inventory	4,000	Advertising	4,000
Income tax payable	6,000	Insurance	3,600
Owner's equity	?	Repair	2,200
Cost of goods sold	65,000	Supplies	6,000
Utilities	4,800		

a. Prepare an income statement.
b. Prepare a balance sheet.
c. Determine the value of working capital.
d. Discuss what additional information is needed (what other records should have been kept).

12

Photo courtesy of Irene Springer, Prentice-Hall, Inc.

CASH FLOW, FINANCIAL STATEMENTS, AND FINANCIAL RATIOS

Chapter Objectives:

1. To understand the importance of cash flow.
2. To learn how to develop a cash flow statement.
3. To improve an understanding of financial statements.
4. To be able to compare financial statements.
5. To know about financial ratios.
6. To be able to analyze better the financial strength of a business.

When prosperity comes, do not use all of it.

Confucius

INCIDENT: "Business is great," Jack Riley exclaimed. "Our sales this past season were 10 percent over last year at the same period of time."

Riley, aged 52, is the owner of a small sporting goods and rifle store on the west side of town. The pheasant season opened two weeks ago, and deer season will open next Saturday morning. Business was brisk. Riley has recently seen an increase in sales of shotguns and rifles. He is looking forward to the next holiday season, and is wondering about advertising his hunting equipment.

Riley is a very proud owner and manager, but does his growth truly reflect an increase in business? Is his sales increase meeting inflationary demands? Will the profits he receives be sufficient to buy new inventory at increased prices?

Many successful businesses should look very carefully at their successes, before they are forced to "go out of business." Will Jack have enough cash to meet his future needs? Will he be able to pay his bills and meet his payroll? Does his increase in sales reflect an increase in profits? Does Jack have sufficient cash to run his business?

Cash—the money on hand or in a bank account—is the heartbeat of a business. How an owner or manager handles and manages the cash situation is critical. Cash is needed to buy inventory, pay salaries and wages, buy equipment, pay expenses, and have a profit. Just as gasoline is needed to run a car, cash is needed by a business to keep it operating. Gas supplies fuel to the engine, causing the engine to operate and go forward; it is important to keep the engine operating properly to obtain the best possible mileage of each gas dollar. Likewise, it is important to keep the business running efficiently and to make sure it is operating smoothly, so that it might get the best possible use of each business dollar.

Managing the finances of a business is one of the most important and most difficult managerial functions. Do not depend on banks or lending institutions for financial help for your business—they do not see themselves as mechanics responsible for "fixing up" small businesses. They only provide assistance for growth and expansion; they provide short-term lending for inventory or other necessary expenses.

Cash Flow

Many business owners are hesitant about keeping track of their financial position. They are worried about the paper work, hours, and drudgery of compiling the information necessary to understanding cash flow in a business. Cash flow is the movement of cash through a business. If there is sufficient money on hand to handle all expenses, to meet necessary payrolls, and to buy required inventory supplies, a "positive" cash flow exists. However, if it is not possible to pay necessary expenses or to cover the monthly payroll, a "negative" cash flow exists. If a positive cash flow situation occurs, then a business is generally successful and a profit is being made. If a negative cash flow exists, there is need for additional money in order to save the business, otherwise it may be necessary to go out of business.

cash flow cycle   The cash flow cycle is a simplified method of keeping track of the increases or decreases in the amount of cash in the business. Cash is decreased by purchasing equipment or supplies, or by paying off mortgages for a building or land. Money is also paid out to suppliers and creditors (accounts payable). Purchases allow for inventory, which is then sold to customers who generate sales and/or accounts receivable. The sales will generate either cash or accounts receivable. (The latter comes about when customers use credit cards to purchase inventory or services.) As these accounts are paid, cash flows into the business and the accounts receivable are reduced. Cash flow refers to the inflow and outflow of money (see Figure 12–1). Cash flow is important not only to the owner or manager, but also to creditors, stockholders, and even investors, because it reflects the ability of the business to meet expenses and liabilities (debts), to pay dividends, or to expand.

cash flow statement   The cash flow statement covers a specific period of time (generally, a month or a year), and it reflects increases or decreases in the cash position of the business. The cash flow statement is like the gas gauge in an automobile, in that it reflects the amount of fuel (cash or gas) left to cause that business or car to move forward or be stopped. The cash flow statement monitors the flow of cash in a business by showing the sources and uses of cash in that business.

The cash flow statement should show a firm what its sources are for a given period; it should also show how that cash was used during that period. This information is very helpful in planning business operations and cash needs, and in maintaining control over business activities.

The main purpose of developing a cash flow statement is to determine the excesses or losses in cash that are necessary to operate a business for a particular time period. If the cash flow results in a minus figure, plans must be made to alter business activities to develop more cash. For example, a storewide sale may be necessary to receive sufficient cash to pay salaries and inventories. It may also be

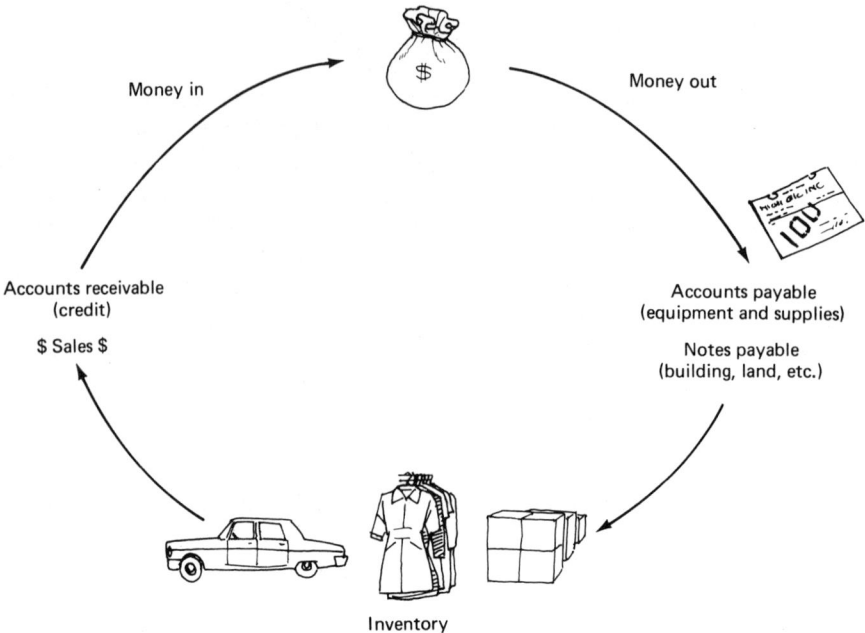

Figure 12-1. *Cash flow cycle*

necessary for the owners to put more money (owner's equity) into the business to meet necessary expenses. If the cash flow reveals excesses, it may be necessary to use that money for expansion, increased inventory, or other growth objectives. The successful cash flow statement will develop a well managed cash flow throughout the business, which can be used to obtain maximum profits, or a return on investments to the business.

The form of the cash flow statement. The form of the cash flow statement shows the cash revenues and expenditures and the flow of cash through the business. (See Figure 12-2.)

The cash flow statement is divided into four major areas: (1) cash on hand, (2) cash receipts (3) cash out, and (4) new cash position. The cash on hand is simply the cash position from the previous month (Figure 12-2, number 7). The cash in position is concerned with cash receipts, the cash sales, collections from credit accounts, and any loan or other cash injections received during the past month. Once all the cash coming in for the month has been added, the total cash receipts may be added together, and finally the total cash available for that month may be calculated (Figure 12-2, number 1 plus number 3). There are four major sources of cash to a business: (1) sales or profitable operations, (2) sale of owner's equity, (3) decrease of any asset, and (4) increase of any liability.

One of the most valuable tools of the cash flow statement is the cash out section, where all expenses to the business are calculated, added together, and

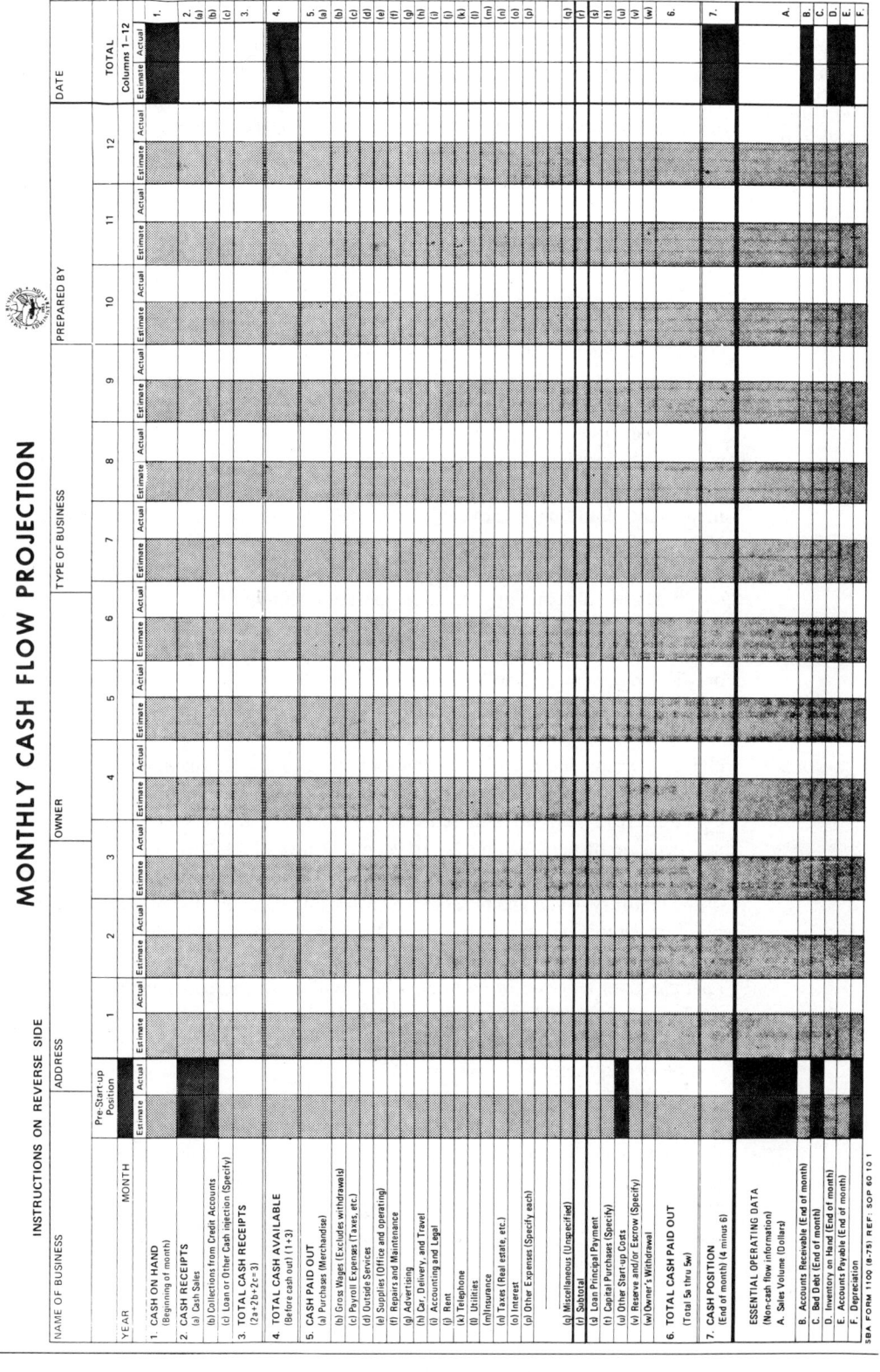

Figure 12–2. *Monthly cash flow statement*

deducted from the total cash available. The salary of the owner or the manager is included in the last item, which is owner's withdrawal. The owner's withdrawal section should include payment for salary, social security, health insurance, income tax, and executive fringe benefits. There are also four major uses of cash in a business: (1) lack of sales or unprofitable operations, (2) buying back ownership (retiring stock) or dividend payment, (3) increase in assets, and (4) decrease in liabilities.

Once the total cash out has been added, a new cash position may be developed by subtracting the total cash paid out (Figure 12–2 number 4 minus number 6), total cash available and obtaining the new cash position. This end-of-the-month cash position will provide the owner or manager with information concerning his or her current cash level, ability to pay for inventory, payroll, growth, or expansion. The profitability of the business or the losses the owner or manager is currently undergoing should be indicated by the cash position.

Cash flows into a business through the sales of goods or services. Money may also be received through equity financing, the selling of ownership to investors, or through corporate stock. Decreases in assets occur when inventory, equipment, land, buildings, or even accounts receivable are sold and cash is received. This would reduce the asset account and increase the cash situation. Also, any increase in liabilities may result in an increase of cash to the business's account.

Lack of sales and unprofitable operations tie up money and reduce its availability. Buying out a partner or paying dividends will also reduce available cash. Increasing assets require payment for inventory, equipment, land, building, and so on. The payment of liabilities is also a use of cash. (For example, paying off a mortgage or a creditor will reduce cash availability.)

Small business owners often fail to understand that the use of cash to purchase inventory or to allow accounts receivable to increase is just as major a decision as is expansion or the purchase of new equipment. For example, an expenditure of $12,000 to increase an inventory of sweaters and suits that will not sell because of poor styling is just as real a loss of cash as the purchase of new equipment or an expansion. In fact, there may be a greater loss in this case, because of the inability to sell and redeem the cash value from the inventories, whereas the plant or equipment might provide additional income in the future.

The cash flow statement will provide a picture of the cash balance of the business over a period of months, which will show increases and decreases from one month to another with high and low seasonal sales. The statement will also show low cash periods when it is necessary to borrow funds to meet business and inventory requirements.

The cash flow statement may be the most important financial tool available to a small business owner, and it should provide guidance in every step or business decision made by the manager. Watched closely, the cash flow statement may provide insights into growth, trends, or sales declines from month to month and from year to year. This may help to point out strengths or weaknesses of the business.

SUCCESS STORY: J. C. Penney

James Cash Penney, the Merchant Prince, was born into the family of James C. Penney, a farmer–preacher. Young Penney was raised to take care of himself. His father always told him to live by the Golden Rule, to be honest, and to never profit at another person's expense. When he was only eight years old, Penney's father informed him that he must begin buying his own clothes. Terror struck the little boy as he set out thinking of ways to earn money. He started by raising pigs and prospered, but this was put to a halt when neighbors began to complain about the smell. Penney went through numerous jobs, and with each job he learned a lesson that he would remember all through his life.

Penney had his first big chance in January, 1895, when his father, then a very sick man, took him into town (Hamilton, Missouri) and helped him get a job at J. M. Hale and Brother's dry goods store. Here, after going through a hazing by the elder clerks, Penney asserted himself and no longer backed down when the clerks would try to steal his customers. In one year, Penney became the second best clerk at J. M. Hale. He had started at a pay of $2.27 a month and after the first year received a raise of $18.00 a month.

Bad health forced Penney to move to Longmont, Colorado, where he opened a butcher shop and there learned another lesson. He was forced to bribe the owner of the biggest motel in Longmont in order to stay in business. He decided that he would not bribe people to get customers, a decision that meant losing his job again.

Penney next worked for another dry goods store in Longmont; after proving himself there, he was offered a job with the same store in Evanston, where he became a partner in the new expanding store. Penney continued to work his way up in this store, becoming a manager of one of the stores. He married and had two sons.

Penney changed the name of his stores from THE GOLDEN RULE to JC PENNEY's and on January 17, 1913, PENNEY's was incorporated.

PENNEY's had been founded on the principle of partnerships. The manager would hire someone, teach them everything and then help them establish a new store. This principle was maintained even after the incorporation.

The next big step was centralized buying. Members of JC PENNEY's were at first reluctant, but when Earl Sams, then vice-president, voiced his approval, everyone agreed and the main office was set up in New York City. J. C. Penney then resigned as president; Sams was unanimously elected to replace him.

Growth and expansion continued through the years. Good employees and the constant belief in the golden rule and honesty helped bring JC PENNEY's from a small business to an organization that in 1961 was grossing well over $1 billion.

Financial Statements

Financial statements may be very meaningful and helpful tools in the managerial decision-making process. However, they are all basically historical statements, concerned with what *has* happened during a given time period. The value of these financial statements is in determining what *will* happen in the future period of the business. The use of financial analysis is to predict the future by direct evaluation, comparison, statistical, or trend analysis.

The business owner will find it interesting to compare his or her own financial statements from one period to another. The business owner will also develop trend analyses over a number of years, which will show instances of increases or decreases. Such comparisons will tell the business owner about seasonal peaks and general increases or decreases in the cash position over a period of time.

There are few figures on a financial statement that are meaningful by themselves. They obtain most of their importance when compared with the other figures on the financial statement. For example, the expenses on an income statement are of little significance unless they are compared with the sales and revenues of that business. To understand financial statements, it is important to compare the figures that are found on these statements: (1) comparative size forms, and (2) ratio analysis.

An easy way to begin the analysis of financial statements is to place the statements in a comparative form by developing a common-sized statement that places the items in a percentage form rather than in a dollar form. Each separate item is then a percentage of the total, of which that item is an important part. This development of percentage statements is referred to as vertical analysis.

One important application of percentage forms is to state the balance sheet as common-sized percentages.

As illustrated in Table 12–1, it is easy to understand the relative importance in different sizes of assets. It is also very valuable to notice the changes from one year to the next. This can easily pinpoint different trends to show different successes or failures the business might face. A decline in accounts receivable might indicate that it is more difficult to collect from customers.

It is also very important to investigate the liabilities and net worth of the business. An increase in accounts payable or liabilities will indicate a greater increase in debt, and it may sound a warning to the business owner. The net worth position shows either an increasing strength or a decreasing value of the business. A decrease in net worth over a long period of time would probably force the closure of the business. The percentage of net worth for a highly successful business should be on the increase.

Another use of percentage comparisons is to look at income statements as a percentage form of total sales. This comparative common-sized income statement is illustrated in Table 12–2. It will indicate the changes in cost in gross margin in prorating expenses that occur, relative to other years. It is now easily possible to determine if the cost of goods sold are going up as a percentage of sales over the last

Table 12-1. Comparative Common-Sized Balance Sheet

Jones Company
Common-Sized Comparative Balance Sheet
For December 31, 19X8 and December 31, 19X7

ASSETS	19X8	19X7	19X8	19X7
			Common-Sized Percentages	
Current Assets:				
Cash	$ 5,000	$ 4,000	3.4	3.0
Accounts receivable	15,000	12,000	10.1	9.0
Inventory	36,000	30,000	24.3	22.3
Total current assets	$ 56,000	$ 46,000	37.8	34.3
Fixed Assets:				
Land	$ 30,000	$ 30,000	20.3	22.4
Building and equipment, net	62,000	58,000	41.9	43.3
Total fixed assets	$ 92,000	$ 88,000	62.2	65.7
Total Assets	$148,000	$134,000	100.0	100.0
LIABILITIES AND NET WORTH				
Liabilities:				
Accounts payable	$ 34,000	$ 30,000	23.0	22.4
Long-term notes payable	80,000	84,000	54.1	62.7
Total liabilities	$114,000	$114,000	77.1	85.1
Net Worth:	$ 34,000	$ 20,000	22.9	14.9
Total liabilities and net worth	$148,000	$134,000	100.0	100.0

Table 12-2. Comparative Common-Sized Income Statement

Jones Company
Common-Sized Comparative Income Statement
For Years Ending December 31, 19X8 and December 31, 19X7

	19X8	19X7	19X8	19X7
			Common-Sized Percentages	
Sales	$240,000	$210,000	100.0	100.0
Cost of goods sold	120,000	110,000	50.0	50.0
Gross margin	$120,000	$100,000	50.0	50.0
Operating Expenses:				
Selling expenses	$ 50,000	$ 34,000	20.8	16.2
Administrative expenses	40,000	40,000	16.7	19.0
Total operating expenses	$ 90,000	$ 74,000	37.5	35.2
Net operating income	$ 30,000	$ 26,000	12.5	12.4
Taxes (25%)	7,500	6,500	3.1	3.1
Net Income	$ 22,500	$ 19,500	9.4	9.3

year. It is equally easy to find out if expenses are increasing or decreasing, relative to the sales level.

The common-sized comparative statements show changes in proportions by use of percentages. There are three important factors to remember when setting up the common-sized balance sheet: (1) the total assets are assigned a value of 100 percent (2) the liabilities total and the owner's equity combined are assigned a value of 100 percent and (3) each asset (such as cash, accounts receivable, fixtures, land, and buildings), liability (such as notes payable and mortgages) and owner's equity items are shown as a fraction of a 100 percent total. These percentages may then be used to compare the same asset liability or owner's equity with previous years or with other businesses in the same industry.

The common-sized income statement is developed similarly to the balance sheet. Net sales are assigned a value of 100 percent, and then each other item appears as a percentage of net sales. This common-sized (percentage) income statement is then very useful as a managerial tool, and is extremely helpful in making pricing decisions. When the common size of 100 percent sales amount is used to represent one sales dollar, the rest of the expenses show the percentage cost of every item bought and received in that business. For example, the restaurant owner may find that, for every dollar worth of sales made, the cost of goods sold is 44¢, and wages and salary account for 26¢. This may also illustrate that the owner receives only 3¢ profit for every sales dollar made.

The comparative common-sized (percentage) format for financial statements greatly enhances the ability of an owner or manager to analyze his or her financial statements. This also allows comparison with other businesses within the same industry, or even in different industries. Current information relative to different businesses and industries are compiled annually by Robert Morris Associates, *Annual Statement Studies,* Credit Division, National Bank Building, Philadelphia, PA 19107; *Almanac of Business and Industrial Financial Ratios,* Prentice-Hall, Inc., Englewood Cliffs, NJ 07632; *Key Business Ratios,* Dun & Bradstreet, Inc., 99 Church Street, New York, NY 10017; *Expenses of Retail Businesses,* National Cash Register Corp., Marketing Services, Dayton, OH 45409. Both the *Annual Statement Studies* and the *Expenses of Retail Business* contain information in a comparative common-sized format for many retail, wholesale, and service businesses in the United States.

Financial Ratios

In business, the study of financial ratios is very similar to the study of gear ratios on automobile engines or mix masters. Ratios are studied to develop the most efficient method of operation. Ratios will explain what strengths, weaknesses, pressures, and forces are currently at work in your business operation.

Almost all financial analysts—such as bankers, commercial loan oficers, investors—will use ratio analyses. After developing a set of ratios for a particular firm, they will compare them against industrial averages, using the previously mentioned books.

225
CASH FLOW, FINANCIAL STATEMENTS, AND RATIOS

The income statements, balance sheets, and cash flow statements help explain what you have done and how your business stands. These financial statements have often been done by accountants or by business owners; they explain the financial records or facts of the business. They are a summation of business activities, and they are bookkeeping records of the financial activity of your business. Financial statements help put together different important areas of business finance. For instance, current assets generally refer to the cash accounts receivable, inventory, and prepaid expenses which a business has recorded. Relationships then begin to fall into place. Ratios such as debt to net worth have a definite meaning and help explain the level of debt which your business has in comparison also with other businesses.

Once you have developed the ratios for your own business, you may easily compare them with others, using the Robert Morris Associate's *Annual Statement Studies;* Dun & Bradstreet, Inc.'s *Key Business Ratios;* Prentice-Hall's *Almanac of Business and Industrial Financial Ratios,* or the National Cash Register Corp.'s *Expenses of Retail Businesses.* Ratio comparisons will help you to better understand and analyze your business in relation to other successful or similar businesses in the industry. They will help the business owner to better understand the strengths and weaknesses and the financial position of his or her business in relation to others.

There are five major categories of financial ratios: (1) profitability ratios, (2) liquidity ratios, (3) coverage ratios, (4) leverage ratios, and (5) operating ratios.

profitability ratios

Profitability ratios are developed from the income statement data, and are designed to indicate how profitable or successful the business is. The easiest of these ratios to determine is the net profit margin; the other is the return on equity.

Net profit margin. The net profit margin ratio is determined by dividing the net profit for the year or the month by the sales for the year or the month.

$$\text{Net profit margin} = \frac{\text{Net profit}}{\text{Sales}}$$

This profitability ratio illustrates the profitability of a business. Most businesses will maintain a net profit margin of between 3 percent to 7 percent. Margins above 12 percent are welcome signs for competitors who see a strong and profitable market.

Return on equity. The return on equity is determined by dividing the net profit by the owner's equity (investment).

$$\text{Return on equity} = \frac{\text{Net profit}}{\text{Owner's equity}}$$

This profitability ratio shows the profit on investment. Most private investors and individuals look for 15 percent plus return on equity. Investment firms require a 20 percent to 40 percent projected return on investment before putting money into a business.

liquidity ratios   Liquidity means the ability to pay the obligations or debts a business faces with current assets. A person is in a good liquidity position if, after eating a steak dinner, he or she is able to pay for it. There are five major ratios used to determine the ability of a business to pay its debts or liabilities: the (1) current ratio, (2) quick ratio, (3) sales-to-receivables ratio, (4) cost of sales inventory ratio, and (5) sales-to-working capital ratio.

Current ratio.   The current ratio is determined by dividing the total current assets by the total current liabilities.

$$\text{Current ratio} = \frac{\text{Total current assets}}{\text{Total current liabilities}}$$

The current ratio is calculated to indicate the ability of the business to pay its current debt or obligations. The higher this ratio, the greater the ability for the assets or cash to pay off the liabilities or debts. Successful liquor stores may have a current ratio of 1.5, while printing manufacturers may have a current ratio of 1.9. Generally speaking, the higher the value, the greater liquidity position. (See Figure 12–3.)

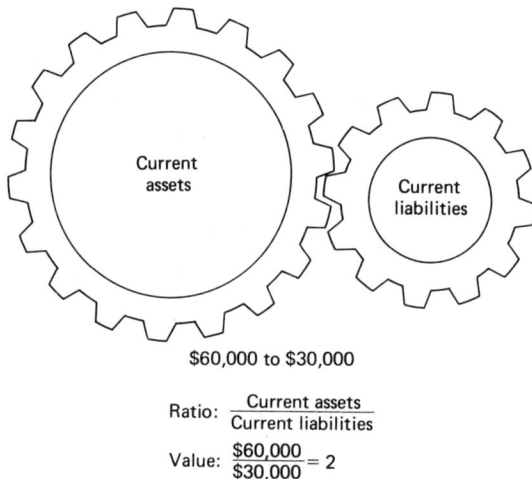

Figure 12-3. *Current ratio*

Quick ratio.   The quick ratio is determined by adding cash and accounts receivable, then dividing this amount by total current liabilities.

$$\text{Quick ratio} = \frac{\text{Cash + accounts receivable}}{\text{Total current liabilities}}$$

The quick ratio (also known as the "acid test") is a more conservative ratio of the liquidity position of a business. The quick ratio is primarily concerned with how quickly a company can pay off all current debts (liabilities) by using cash or close equivalents. Generally, if the value of the quick ratio is less than 1, it shows a "dependency" on inventory or other current assets to help finance current debt (liability). Typically, a liquor store may have a quick ratio of 0.2, while a hardware store may have a quick ratio of 0.7.

Sales-to-receivables ratio. This ratio is determined by dividing net sales by accounts receivable plus notes receivable.

$$\text{Sales-to-receivables} = \frac{\text{Net sales}}{\text{Accounts receivable + notes receivable}}$$

The sales-to-receivables ratio is important to many businesses because it determines or shows the time between sale and actual cash collections. This ratio measures the number of times the accounts receivable and notes receivable actually turn over during a given time period. For example, a jewelry store with sales of $750,000 and receivables of $75,000 would have a sales-to-receivables ratio of ten; that is receivables would turn over ten times a year. This is very different from grocery stores, which would have a sales-to-receivables ratio of 320; that is, receivables would turn over 320 times a year. When comparing your own business, with others, it is important to determine if your business is turning slower than other businesses in the industry. If so, this should cause some alarm, and point management in the right direction.

Day's receivables may be determined from the sales-to-receivable ratio. To do so, divide the number of days in one year, or 365, by the sales-to-receivable ratio.

$$\text{Day's receivables} = \frac{365}{\text{Sales-to-receivable ratio}}$$

This information shows the number of days it takes to receive an outstanding account. For example, with the jewelry store in the sample above, we have 365 divided by 10, which is equal to 36.5 days; therefore, the average receivable is collected in 36 to 37 days. This might allow you then to think about taking out a 60-day short term loan for the purchase of inventory. That is, you would have 60 days to pay back the loan amount and generally all your sales collections would be within a period of 36.5 days. If the average number of days receivables are outstanding was 92.6 days, it would not be very wise to obtain a 60-day short-term loan for any sales or inventory promotions.

Cost of sales-to-inventory ratio. This ratio is determined by dividing the cost of sales by inventory.

$$\text{Cost of sales-to-inventory ratio} = \frac{\text{Cost of sales}}{\text{Inventory}}$$

This is a very important and simple measure of the number of times inventory is turned over during the year. A high ratio average indicates a stronger liquidity position or superior merchandising methods. It may, however, simply show a shortage of inventory required for sales. A dairy product retailer may have a cost of sales-to-inventory ratio of 17.1, while a carpet manufacturer would have one of 6.7.

Day's inventory ratio may be calculated by simply dividing the number of days in a year, 365 by the cost of sales-to-inventory ratio or:

$$\text{Day's inventory ratio} = \frac{365}{\text{Cost of sales-to-inventory ratio}}$$

This provides you with the average number of days a unit is in the store's inventory.

Sales-to-working capital ratios. This ratio is determined by dividing the net sales by the net working capital (the difference between current assets and current liabilities).

$$\text{Sales-to-working capital} = \frac{\text{Net sales}}{\text{Net working capital}}$$

This is a primary indicator of how efficiently money is used by the owner or manager. This ratio is also a measure of the protection creditors may have for a business. This ratio indicates the ability of business to finance current operations.

coverage ratios

These ratios are designed to determine a firm's ability to handle and service debt. The main coverage ratio is the earnings before interest and taxes (EBIT-to-interest ratio.

Earnings before interest and taxes-to-interest ratio. This ratio is determined by dividing the earnings before interest and taxes (EBIT) by annual interest expense.

$$\text{EBIT-to-Interest Ratio} = \frac{\text{EBIT}}{\text{Annual interest expense}}$$

This ratio is designed to tell creditors and those holding IOU's on the business if the firm has a strong ability to meet interest payments. The higher the ratio, the greater the likelihood that the business borrower would be able to pay interest obligations on a loan. This equation is also used to help indicate the ability of a business to take on additional loans or debts.

leverage ratios

Leverage ratios are developed to help one understand the financial position a business would have during economic downturns or loss of business. Businesses with high leveraged accounts (high debt amounts in relation to net worth amount) are more vulnerable to business changes and downturns.

Fixed-to-worth ratio. The fixed-to-worth ratio is determined by dividing net fixed assets by tangible net worth as shown in Figure 12–4.

$$\text{Fixed-to-worth ratio} = \frac{\text{Net fixed assets}}{\text{Tangible net worth}}$$

This ratio illustrates the extent of loaner's equity (capital) in equipment and fixtures (fixed assets). A lower ratio indicates a better position or value that the

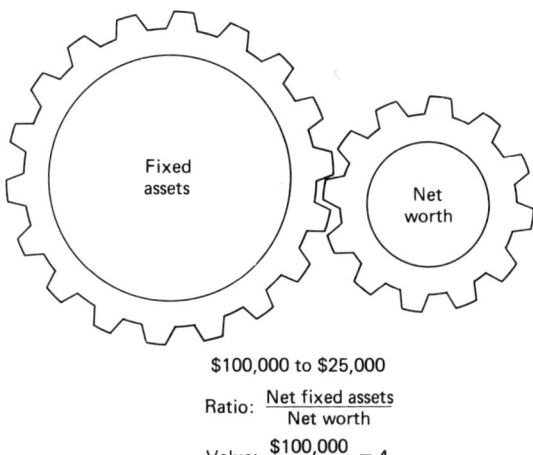

Figure 12–4. *Fixed-to-worth ratio*

owner has in the business. This is a good sign to creditors, because it indicates that the owner is strongly invested in the business and owns a high degree of the assets in the business. A soft-drink bottler may have a fixed-to-worth ratio of 1:1, while a heating and plumbing retailer would have a fixed-to-worth ratio of 0:2. The value of this ratio varies widely according to industry and business.

Debt-to-worth ratio. The debt-to-worth ratio is determined by dividing total liabilities by tangible net worth.

$$\text{Debt-to-worth ratio} = \frac{\text{Total liabilities}}{\text{Tangible net worth}}$$

This is a ratio that illustrates the amount of money that creditors and owners have in a business. Total liabilities are accounts owed to creditors; this is the debt of the business. The net worth is a description of the owner's equity or level of ownership of the business. A low ratio indicates a strong financial position of the owner, and allows the owner or manager greater flexibility in future borrowing. Firms with high debt-to-worth ratios are already heavily in debt and are not usually considered to be good potential borrowers. A typical motel or hotel business may have a debt-to-worth ratio of 4:2, while a sporting goods manufacturer would have a debt-to-worth ratio of 1:2.

operating ratios These ratios are generally designed to help evaluate managerial performance. The two ratios here described are primarily concerned with evaluating the success and influence of management upon a business.

Percent of profits before taxes-to-tangible net worth ratio. This ratio is determined by dividing profit before taxes by tangible net worth and then multiplying by 100.

$$\text{Percent of profits before taxes-to-tangible net worth ratio} = \frac{\text{Profit before taxes}}{\text{Tangible net worth}} \times 100$$

This ratio is one of the major ratios that indicate successful or nonsuccessful managerial performance. It should be used with all other ratios to help correctly determine the status and position of a business firm. It illustrates a rate of return on money used. The higher the ratio, the more effective management would be considered. A low ratio indicates unsuccessful or inefficient managerial performance. A successful furniture wholesaler may have a ratio of 22:4, while a data-processing service center may have one of 40:4.

Sales-to-total assets ratio. The sales-to-total assets ratio is determined by dividing net sales by total assets.

$$\text{Sales-to-total assets ratio} = \frac{\text{Net sales}}{\text{Total assets}}$$

This ratio is also used to determine managerial effectiveness. It shows the firm's ability to generate sales for the assets used. This ratio should only be used in comparison with similar businesses in the same industry. This ratio would also be of help in determining if you are obtaining more or less sales per asset in the business. A successful household appliance dealer may have a sales-to-total assets ratio of 2:5, while a sporting club may have a ratio of only 0:6.

CASE STUDY: Pop Corn Shoppes, Inc.

The Pop Corn Shoppes are in the business of making and selling popcorn. They also supply popcorn confections, a variety of different kitchen candies, and seasonal or related snack food items. Most new Pop Corn Shoppes are located in major shopping centers, with a floor space of 400 to 640 square feet.

The business hours kept by these businesses are the same as the malls in which they are located. In most of the shoppes, the company will accept the primary lease liability from the shopping center and will sublet the lease to the owner operator. There are approximately 216 shoppes in 39 states within the United States. The business has been in operation since 1930, and it has a strong success record.

Sam owns a Pop Corn Shoppe located in South Mall. The initial equity capital that was required was $35,000; the total cost for his business was $70,000 in turnkey costs. Most of the expenses went to increasing construction costs. The company assisted Sam in arranging a convenient bank loan, although they will also help obtain Small Business Administration loans and will allow the franchises to arrange their own financing.

Sam received intensive training in his own Shoppe, which lasted for almost two weeks. He has also received a bookkeeping system and a complete operations manual from the head office. These provided an invaluable service and have been of tremendous help to Sam.

Sam's Pop Corn Shoppe

	JAN	FEB	MAR	APRIL	MAY	JUNE	JULY	AUG	SEPT	OCT	NOV	DEC
Sales ($ thousands)	12	10	10	12	16	22	30	30	20	14	16	24
Cost of goods sold	40%											
Gross profit	60%											

Expenses
- Wages $ 5,000/mo
- Rent $ 400/mo
- Utilities $ 200/mo
- Other $ 1,000/mo
- Owner's draw (salary) $ 1,000/mo

Questions

1. Would a cash flow statement be useful to Sam? Why? Why not?
2. What kind of profitability ratios should Sam use to show if he is doing well in his business?

Chapter Questions:

1. Discuss the advantages and uses of a cash flow statement.
2. Explain why it is important to develop comparative common-sized financial statements.
3. Suppose that you have been turned down on your application for a short-term loan from the bank. You had indicated that your company has a 2-to-1 current ratio, which the bank said was inadequate. Please explain the bank's position.
4. Why would you use a quick ratio?
5. Explain how you can use a ratio analysis to evaluate managerial performance.
6. Suppose that your company started the year with an accounts receivable of $60,000, and that at the end of the year it was only $40,000. Is this decrease in accounts receivable a source or a use of funds for your company? Please explain your answer.
7. Of what value is the cash flow statement in determining money needs for the year? Explain your answer.

13

Photo courtesy of Irene Springer, Prentice-Hall, Inc.

FINANCIAL PLANNING AND COST CONTROL

Chapter Objectives:

1. To understand financial planning.
2. To be able to develop budgets for management.
3. To understand the difference between cost centers and revenue centers.
4. To learn about different credit policies and procedures.
5. To understand the need for financial planning and control.
6. To be able to use financial planning tools.

The way to be nothing is to do nothing.

Nathaniel Howe

INCIDENT: Jane has been experiencing some difficulty understanding how she should spend her funds in her clothing store. She has found, through analyzing sales, that a good portion of her business is done in the jeans and slacks division. However, she is hesitant about putting more money into that particular area; she would prefer to increase sales in dresses, pant suits, sweaters and tops.

Jane has found that sales are about equal between the men's and the women's departments. However, she has noticed that approximately 85 percent of all purchases are made by women. She has also found out that it is easier for women than for men to sell men's and women's clothing. Of the eleven people who work in Jane's store, only two of them are men—they primarily handle stocking and selling of equipment in the outdoor and ski shop of the store. She has found that even men buying men's clothing (they do not stock men's suits) have a preference for women sales clerks.

Jane is wondering if she should increase different lines. She is also questioning her advertising budgets. She is wondering about how much money is tied up in inventory. Should she take trips to New York, Chicago, California, or Dallas to buy her clothing lines? How should she allocate her sales dollars? What tools might help Jane to improve her managerial effectiveness?

Management is increasingly becoming aware of the need to plan what the business will do to obtain profits. This profit planning has recently become one of the most crucial and important managerial tools that an owner or manager uses. However, it is one area of management that is often overlooked or forgotten. Profit planning is generally developed through the use of budgets.

Most people have learned, through simple practical experience, the need to keep budgets. The budget is a plan of future action. It shows how individual or business resources will be spent over a given period of time. It is a plan of action for the future expressed in formal quantitative and monetary terms. The act of making a budget is referred to as budgeting. The use of budgets to control an individual or business expenditures is called "budgetary control."

Janis works in a downtown department store and she has learned that the only way she can make ends meet is to budget her money for the month. Although she is paid every two weeks, she needs to take out a certain amount of money at the beginning of the month for rent, car payment, gas, food, and a certain amount for fun activities. This act of keeping track of her finances and spending her income on given activities is referred to as keeping a budget. Most people keep some type of budget to restrict spending to a certain limit; that is, using the budget system to help control expenses and to manage money. Some budgets may exist only in the mind, but even these are real budgets.

Financial Planning

The budget is a road plan that will allow you to set a goal and to develop routes necessary to reach that goal. Budgets are generally developed from either forecasting sales of the business and working down, or by developing a forecast of profits, and working up. Financial planning should be looked at in terms of (1) budget objectives, (2) budgeting periods, and (3) budget preparation.

budget objectives

The two major purposes of developing budgets for a business are (1) to plan and (2) to control. Planning is the development of future actions through study and evaluations. A business owner plans for the future by developing the best conceivable ideas and actions that can reach the objectives of the business. Controlling is the means by which management assures itself that the business is operating properly and is moving toward the objectives of the plans. The budgeting system provides for both planning and control. The development of the budget allows for the planning process. Making sure that income is expended only for budgetary items assures control of the business. Nearly everyone plans and controls their income by using some form of budget.

One of the great advantages of the budgeting process is that it forces the owner or manager to plan business activities. It also provides a vehicle for coordinating, motivating, and communicating the business plans to other employees or partners. It requires thinking ahead. It provides certain standards to achieve a business.

Consider the following example of problems met when one does not budget. Company A is a business that makes, sells, and puts stained glass in place. It was profitable for many years, and was in existence during both world wars. However, the company fell on hard times. It became difficult for anyone in the company to make bids on new stained-glass projects for churches, schools, businesses, or government offices. No one fully understood the costs necessary to obtain a profit. The company was finally bought out by a new group, which required it to establish and keep budgets. This required reshuffling of personnel, with different people being made project managers for particular contracts. Employees now know what everyone else is doing and they know the costs associated with given types of work. Employees can now develop accurate bids for new contracts and now no projects are completed at a loss to the company. At the end of the first year, one employee remarked; "It is more interesting to work here now, because we know what is expected of us and what everything costs."

budgeting periods

Budgeting periods vary considerably, according to the needs of a business. Normally, budgets often coincide with the accounting year. However, many businesses develop long-range budgets for acquisition or capital equipment budgets that may extend for five to twenty years into the future. It is the practice of many businesses to develop budgets for five years, with anything longer than that being indecisive or primarily used to explain capital (that is, land, buildings, and equipment) improvements. The more common operating budgets are generally prepared on an annual basis. The one-year period is often broken down into quarterly or monthly

235
FINANCIAL PLANNING AND COST CONTROL

budget periods. These short-term figures are established with great accuracy, and they help provide both planning and control systems for the business. Monthly budgets require constant review and planning on the part of the owner.

Continuous budgets are becoming more and more popular. These are twelve-month budgets that are developed on a continuous or perpetual basis, in which a new month is added as the current month is completed. Continuous budgets are desirable because they require management to continuously plan ahead and to supervise the financial affairs of the business.

budget preparation

The proper preparation of a budget for a business should involve everyone within that business. Budgets are generally not made at the top then handed down as the "rule," rather, they are a collection of figures and estimates developed from the different departments of a business. The final budgets should reflect the input from all the areas of the business. The owner or manager should provide the guidelines and directions for budget preparation. Employees should report the goals, desires, and costs associated with their future plans and activities to the manager.

There are generally four main budgets that should be developed for every business:

1. The sales budget, including expected cash receipts.
2. The selling and administrative budget.
3. The cash budget.
4. The budgeted income statement.

In addition to these four main budgets, there are a few other ones that may be used.

the sales budget

When preparing a comprehensive budgeting system, it is important to start with the sales budget. Most other budgets are somehow related to this budget. The estimate of sales for the coming year is necessary because most other activities of the business are related to the sales budget.

The sales budget is commonly prepared from last year's sales, forecasted business conditions, expected increases in sales, and estimates submitted by sales-people, managers, and owners. Combined, these people will develop a sales budget that will usually include an expected cash receipt statement to indicate the future cash projections of the business to the owner. An illustration of a sales budget is found in Table 13–1.

the selling and administrative budget

Once a tentative sales budget has been developed, it is important to create the selling and administrative budget. This budget will contain a list of expenses for selling and administration, which should provide for the sales level of the coming year. Expense figures should be developed at the same time that sales figures are being estimated for the coming year. It would be very difficult to have a sales figure increase of 10 percent over the last year if the expenses increased by 50 percent. This would probably lead to a decrease in profits and would probably even force the business to go into bankruptcy. Expense budgets are often based on previous

Table 13-1. The Sales Budget

Shelley's Appliance Store
Sales Budget
for the Year Ending December 31, 19X2

	YEAR'S TOTAL	1ST QUARTER	2ND QUARTER	3RD QUARTER	4TH QUARTER
Sales					
Appliances	$160,000	$30,000	$30,000	$40,000	$60,000
Service	40,000	5,000	10,000	10,000	15,000
Total Sales	$200,000	$35,000	$40,000	$50,000	$75,000
Expected Cash Receipts:					
Accounts Receivable 12/31/X1	$ 35,000	$35,000			
1st Quarter Sales ($35,000)	35,000	21,000	$14,000		
2nd Quarter Sales ($40,000)	40,000		24,000	$16,000	
3rd Quarter Sales ($50,000)	50,000			30,000	$20,000
4th Quarter Sales ($75,000)	45,000				45,000
Total Cash Collections	$205,000	$56,000	$38,000	$46,000	$65,000

Note: 60 percent of the quarter's sales are cash, with 40 percent collected the following quarter.

experience, adjustments for wage and salary increases, changes in other expenses such as rent, advertising, telephone, utilities, and so forth, and any other expected changes. Table 13–2 illustrates a selling and administrative budget.

the cash budget After the sales budget and the selling and administrative budget have been developed, the cash budget is prepared. This budget is very important to management. The company will need sufficient cash on hand to meet the needs of the business. As shown in Table 13–3 the cash budget generally consists of four parts: (1) the cash receipts section, (2) the cash payments section, (3) the cash excess or deficiency section, and (4) the financing and ending balance section.

The *cash receipts section* is concerned with the opening cash balance, brought forward from last year or month and added to the cash collections during

Table 13-2. The Selling and Administrative Budget

Shelley's Appliance Store
Selling and Administrative Budget
for the Year Ending December 31, 19X2

	YEAR'S TOTAL	1ST QUARTER	2ND QUARTER	3RD QUARTER	4TH QUARTER
Commissions	$20,000	$ 3,750	$ 3,750	$ 5,000	$ 7,500
Salaries	30,000	7,500	7,500	7,500	7,500
Rent	5,000	1,250	1,250	1,250	1,250
Advertising	5,000	1,000	1,000	1,000	2,000
Telephone	3,000	600	600	600	1,200
Insurance	1,000	250	250	250	250
Supplies	1,000	250	250	250	250
Bad debt expenses	2,000	500	500	500	500
Other	3,000	700	700	700	900
Total cash needed	$70,000	$15,800	$15,800	$17,050	$21,350

Table 13-3. The Cash Budget

Shelley's Appliance Store
Cash Budget
for the Year Ending December 31, 19X2

	BUDGET SCHEDULES	YEAR'S TOTAL	1ST QUARTER	2ND QUARTER	3RD QUARTER	4TH QUARTER
Beginning cash balance		$ 2,000	$ 2,000	$21,700	$20,900	$ 10,000
Cash collections	1	205,000	56,000	38,000	46,000	65,000
Total cash available		$207,000	$58,000	$59,700	$66,900	$ 75,000
Purchases (cost of goods sold)		$100,000	$17,500	$20,000	$50,000	$ 12,500
Cash payments (selling and administrative expenses)	2	70,000	15,800	15,800	17,050	21,350
Taxes		12,000	3,000	3,000	3,000	3,000
Total payments		$182,000	$36,300	$38,800	$70,050	$ 36,850
Cash excess (deficiency) cash available—payments		$ 25,000	$21,700	$20,900	$(3,150)	$ 38,150
Financing:						
Notes payable*		$ 13,150	—	—	$13,150	—
Repayments		(13,150)	—	—	—	$(13,150)
Interest (at 15% per annum)		(490)	—	—	—	(490)
Total financing		$ (490)	$ 0	$ 0	$13,150	$(13,640)
Ending cash balance*		$ 24,510	$21,700	$20,900	$10,000	$ 24,510

*Minimum cash balance of $10,000 suggested.

the year (or month). This provides a total of cash on hand. The major source of cash revenues will come from sales.

The *cash payments section* will consist of the selling and administrative expenses, plus any other purchases, labor, manufacturing overhead, dividends, or interest statements. This section should include all expenses the business may incur during the year or a given time period.

The *cash excess or deficiency section* shows the difference between cash receipts and cash payments. When positive, this provides the cash excess for the business, which leads to profits. (A cash excess for a given period does not mean that there are profits for that particular month or quarter. However, if at the end of the year there is a cash excess, this generally provides profits for the business.) When a cash deficiency exists, it will require the business to acquire some type of outside financing or a bank loan to cover the costs of operations for that quarter or given time period. Any excess should be used to repay any previous loans or to invest in growth or short-term investments.

The *financing and ending cash balance section* illustrates in detail the loans and repayments that a business carries. This section will generally include the interest payments for any loan. Banks and financial agencies are looking more and more for cash budgets to ensure one's ability to repay loans. The conclusion of this section provides for an ending cash balance, which shows the amount of cash available at the end of that time period to be used as the beginning cash balance of the next time period or to be used for profits and/or investments. There are few things more harmful than running into a problem or crisis with a cash budget.

The cash budget is very important to a business and to its management as a control tool. It is broken down into quarters; sometimes into months. This provides additional goals that may be achieved to ensure profitability for the firm.

the budgeted income statement

After compiling the sales budget, the selling and administrative budget, and the cost budget, it is necessary to develop the budgeted income statement. This is one of the key elements in managerial planning and control. The budgeted income statement will explain how profitable or unprofitable the business will be for the upcoming time periods. It may be used as a bench mark or goal that the business should achieve for the year. (See Table 13–4.)

additional budgets

There are several additional types of budgets that may be used by firms to improve the picture of their business finances. These budgets would include: (1) the cost of goods budget, (2) the production budget, (3) the direct labor budget, and (4) the budgeted balance sheet.

The cost of goods budget. Once a sales budget has been developed, many manufacturing, wholesale, and retail businesses will also establish a cost of goods sold budget. This budget is used to handle the merchandise that must be purchased before being resold to customers. This budget will generally include the direct material or merchandise purchased plus for manufacturers any direct labor or manufacturing overhead expenses involved in making the final product before being resold.

The production budget. This budget is prepared basically in the same way as the merchandising budget is for a retailer. However, the production budget is primarily concerned with beginning and ending inventory requirements, the difference between these being the production requirements of the business. The production budget will illustrate the numbers and the dollar amounts required by the manufacturer to produce the necessary inventory.

The direct labor budget. Many small manufacturers find it valuable to develop

Table 13–4. The Budgeted Income Statement

Shelley's Appliance Store
Budgeted Income Statement
for the Year Ending December 31, 19X2

	BUDGET SCHEDULES	YEAR'S TOTAL	1ST QUARTER	2ND QUARTER	3RD QUARTER	4TH QUARTER
Sales	1	$200,000	$35,000	$40,000	$ 50,000	$75,000
Cost of Goods Sold	3	100,000	17,500	20,000	50,000	12,500
Gross Margin		$100,000	$17,500	$20,000	$ 0	$62,500
Expenses (Selling and Administrative)	2	$ 70,000	$15,800	$15,800	$ 17,050	$21,350
Taxes (City, State, Federal)	3	12,000	3,000	3,000	3,000	3,000
Interest Expense	3	490				490
Total		$ 82,490	$18,800	$18,800	$ 20,050	$24,840
Net Income		$ 17,510	$ (1,300)	$ 1,200	$(20,050)	$37,660

a direct labor budget. This budget is generally developed to allow the owner or manager to understand the labor costs involved in producing given items or products. This budget may also be included with a manufacturing overhead budget, which accounts for the utilities, supplies, taxes, depreciation, and rent involved in the manufacturing process. These budgets are important to a manufacturer before he or she determines prices and profitability for the manufacturing business.

The budgeted balance sheet. Some businesses prefer to also develop a budgeted balance sheet. This is developed by taking the previous balance sheet and adjusting it for data contained in the budget schedules.

This should provide a very important introductory overview of the budgeting process. Budgets are dependent upon the revenue and expenditures of a business. Just as you do not spend all your money on food without allowing some of it to go for rent and clothing, so a business will not allocate all of its funds for salaries without providing some cash to buy materials, merchandise, and pay for salaries and wages. Budgets help the owner or manager plan how to distribute the resources (cash) of a business.

These budgets may be used as tools for managerial control, or to even help evaluate managerial performance. They provide information to management about expected sales and expenditures for the coming time period.

Cost Centers and Revenue Centers

cost centers

Cost centers are areas of business that have a higher expenditures than revenues. That is, if a parts department is not selling enough parts at a high enough price to cover the expenses of the employees who work there, it would be considered a cost center. One of the easiest ways to determine cost centers in any business is to divide the income statement into the various departments or areas of the business. The divided income statement in Table 13–5 illustrates how a business may be losing money in one part of the organization while creating profits in another area of the business.

Table 13-5. Dividend Income Statement

Shelley's Appliance Store
Segmented Income Statement
for the Year Ending December 31, 19X2

	TOTAL	TOTAL APPLIANCES	TOTAL SERVICES
Sales	$200,000	$160,000	$40,000
Cost of goods sold	100,000	75,000	25,000
Gross margin	100,000	85,000	15,000
Selling and administrative expenses	$ 70,000	$ 50,000	$20,000
Taxes	12,000	10,000	2,000
Interest expense	490	490	
Total	$ 82,490	$ 60,490	$22,000
Net Income (Loss)	$ 17,510	$ 24,510	$ (7,000)

revenue centers Revenue centers are areas of a business that provide more income than expense to the business. Revenue centers may be easily detected by looking at the divided income statement as shown. This indicates which part of the business is supporting not only its own area but other areas within the firm as well. During times of success, many business owners fail to investigate their cost and revenue centers. This often misleads business owners into thinking they are making profits and are excellent managers, when in fact parts of their businesses may be suffering, even causing them to move toward failure.

Revenue centers are the backbone of any business. The correct use of budgets and income statements will readily illustrate the cost and revenue centers of any business. A beauty salon operator refused to raise the cost of her services until she realized that only her merchandise (from cosmetics and perfumes) was providing the profit for the business. After this, she raised her prices to become more competitive with other beauty salons and by doing so, she also increased her profit picture.

The determination of a cost center or revenue center is made by adding the fixed expenses and the variable expenses of that center and subtracting the sum from any sales or revenues created by that center. Fixed expenses (such as rent, property taxes, insurance, salaries for employees, and building maintenance costs) occur regardless of sales. The variable expenses occur directly because of sales. For example, sales commissions, direct labor, advertising, and delivery expenses are all dependent upon the sales level of a business.

The income (loss) of a business is the difference between the sale and the sum of fixed and variable expenses required to produce those sales. If this difference is positive, a revenue center is being profitable for your business. However, if the difference is negative, you have a cost center that is draining funds from your business and may easily cause it to fail.

SUCCESS STORY: Helen Fisher

Without training and experience in cosmetology and business management, Helen Fisher suddenly found herself operating two B. F. Goodhair salons—one in Omaha and one in Lincoln. Slowly but surely, Fisher is on her way to becoming a successful and competent business person—after being thrust into the business world by the death of her husband, Bill.

Since taking over the management of B. F. Goodhair, Fisher has paid one of her large creditors in full. In addition, she has managed to pay within 30 days all bills that she has incurred. However, Fisher is the first to admit that all of this was not easy. During her husband's month-long illness, business concerns went unattended. When she finally began to organize these concerns, she found all kinds of bills, even IRS penalties which had to be paid.

Fisher resisted offers to sell the Omaha and Lincoln shops. Instead, accompanied by her attorney, she informed her late husband's banker that she would operate the salons. Companies who were her suppliers lent a helping hand providing her with, among other things, individual briefings.

One of her first acts as owner was to staff the Omaha salon with employees who would be loyal to her. She has little problem with her Lincoln salon; in fact, the Lincoln salon tends to be self-sufficient.

A credit card company informed her that they could not issue her a card because her husband had not requested it; instead, he had requested that she be permitted to use his card. Other frustrations related to collateral demands; Fisher felt that they were unnecessarily stringent. Both of these frustrations of the once-married-now-single woman have been resolved.

Despite the above, Fisher states with pride that she has gained the respect of her attorney, banker, and accountant. More importantly, she has finally found her identity as a business person. She has gained confidence in her judgment as evidenced by her action to appeal the IRS fine of $130. Fisher has several marketing ideas which she believes will bring the Omaha salon to full capacity. Asked if she had any regrets, Helen replied only that she had not involved herself in the salons prior to her husband's death.

Who is Helen Fisher? A businesswoman of today!

Credit

The majority of goods and services that move through our economic system do so on credit. Credit is one of the most powerful forces in business today. It can easily increase sales—the denial of credit will usually decrease sales. It is important that credit be managed.

Almost all businesses grant some kind of credit to their customers in order to improve sales and revenue. There are a few large or small businesses today that can operate without the use of credit. The major problem with credit sales is in transferring credit sales into cash.

The use of credit varies strongly from industry to industry. It is estimated that manufacturers and wholesalers may use credit in as much as 85 percent to 90 percent of their sales. This is compared to retail businesses, that account for almost 60 percent of their total sales as cash. The small fast-food restaurant may rely entirely upon cash sales, while the appliance dealer will use installment or credit buying. Competition, location, industry, and income level of customers are major determinates of granting credit.

Credit systems are generally handled either in-house or outside of the business. The in-house credit systems may be informal, or they may be very formal systems that require extensive bookkeeping and billing systems. In-house systems will increase expenses, due to an employee and bookkeeping costs.

The majority of businesses use credit systems outside of their own business. The largest credit systems employed by business owners are the credit card system established by banks and financial institutions, such as: (1) VISA, (2) Master Card, and (3) Diners Club. VISA and Master Card are credit card systems that may be very expensive to the business owner. They generally charge 2 percent to 9 percent of any sale as a service charge to the business owner. These charges offset any bad debts or other losses to the bank. However, these systems are lower than any other in-house credit systems. The Fair Credit Billing Act of 1975 allows discounts of up to 5 percent for cash purchases—a practice that most retailers have refused to practice.

credit policy Most credit policies of small businesses are determined during the beginning stages of business. Many factors will go into deciding whether or not to originate a credit policy. These policies are generally determined by: (1) business conditions, (2) industrial credit policies, (3) nature of the business, (4) general policy of the business, (5) income level of customers, (6) price of product to customer, (7) influence of competition, (8) customer preferences, (9) cash flow needs of business, and (10) product or service line.

Credit policies may range from the extremes of an easy extension with liberal conditions, to zero credit or to a strict extension of credit with very narrow and limiting collection policies. During periods of rapid business growth and prosperous economic conditions it is easier to grant credit; however, when business is in a downturn and when economic conditions are tight a more strict control of credit is generally needed.

A liberal extension of credit may allow greater sales to a car garage. However, it may also provide greater exposure to collection risks, and may even force the garage out of business if its owner or manager is unable to collect on past credit. A strict credit policy restricts possible losses due to bad debts and also losses for collection. However, too strict a policy may curtail sales and not allow for growth of the business.

The primary reason for bad debt losses is the easy extension of credit to someone who is unable to repay. Before granting credit to any customer, it is important that a thorough investigation be made as to that customer's credit worthiness. Most business owners have learned, through sad experience, that the easiest customer to sell is generally the least credit worthy. An investigation into any customer's worthiness should include consideration of: (1) the results of a check with local credit bureaus, (2) the size and the dollar value of the order, (3) the income level of the customer, (4) the length of time business has been done with the customer, (5) the amount of time for which the credit is to be extended, (6) the importance of the customer to the business, (7) the type and cost of the product or service, (8) whether or not the credit risk falls within the credit policy of the business.

credit collections The collection of credit payments is a very real part of business. It is important to keep accounts receivable as small as possible, thereby allowing cash to operate in the business. Time is very important when handling credit and collections. Regardless of the kind of business, a slow-paying customer will cost it money. The money that is tied up in credit cannot be used to buy additional inventory or to pay salaries or wages. Therefore, it is very important to collect all sales made on credit, and to do so as quickly as possible.

An efficient collection system must be developed that will provide for timely and accurate collections. Certain methods may be used to improve collection procedures, such as: (1) billing promptly, (2) following up within a reasonable period of time, (3) maintaining tight credit terms (adhering to federal and state credit laws), and (4) developing an effective collection procedure.

Most customers, whether they are individual people or other businesses, will not pay before receiving a bill. Usually, you will not pay your rent or house payment before the first of the month, nor will you pay your phone bill before you receive it. The longer you hold a bill within the business, the greater will be the delay in receiving payment. If a customer purchases a new television on the second of the month and you do not bill that customer till the end of the month, you have lost the use of that money for an entire month. Some banks and several computerized billing services will provide services to help reduce this problem. The cost for this service varies according to the sales volume and number of transactions, but it will generally cost between $100 and $4,000.

It is important to seek payment as soon as possible after the collection due date has occurred. Customers who are past due on their accounts should be contacted immediately. It is not true that you will increase good will by extending credit terms. This just tends to lead to an increase in bad debts. Businesses that are overextended in credit generally find their losses increasing due to bad debts. Contact should be made to customers immediately when accounts become overdue.

A mathematical tool available to the small business owner is the day's sales outstanding or the accounts receivable turnover. This is computed as follows: the average accounts receivable balance for the last three month's-end periods, times 90, divided by sales for last month—this equals the day's sales outstanding.

$$\frac{\text{Accounts receivable (3 months)} \times 90}{\text{Last month's sales}} = \text{Day's sales outstanding}$$

Another formula used more often is the days receivable figure, which expresses the average time, in days, that accounts receivables are outstanding. This figure is computed as follows:

$$\text{Day's receivable} = \frac{365}{\text{Sales-to-receivable ratio}}$$

For example, if Shelley's Appliance Store has sales of $200,000 a year, with receivables of $40,000, she would have a sales-to-receivable ratio of 5:1, or receivable turnovers of 5 times a year. But when developing a day's receivables from this example, we would find that $365 \div 5 = 73$. This means that the average bill is collected in 73 days. Therefore, for over two months the money may not be used by Shelley to pay her expenses or buy new machinery or inventory.

CASE STUDY: Larry D.

Early in 198x, Larry D., production manager for a large sporting goods store, began to explore the possibility of developing a new method to manufacture softballs. He believed that he could find a cheaper way to produce softballs for the mass market. By spring, Larry had applied for a patent and was in the process of starting his own manufacturing business. His new production method would allow for a sizable cost reduction in manufacturing and would permit entry into a softball market that has annual sales estimated at 6.2-million units.

Originally Larry thought that the product would sell at retail for about five dollars. The wholesale margin would be 25 percent; the retail margin, 100 percent—both at cost. But now he is uncertain. He is thinking that he ought to offer a variety of softball lines that would differ primarily because of the covering and the stitching on the ball. A synthetic fabric-covered ball could sell at $4.25 retail; a genuine cowhide leather-covered ball, the top of the product line, would retail between ten and twelve dollars. He could probably distribute a wide line of softballs through various sporting goods and department stores.

Larry's main concern is with the pricing of the products and the profit margin for the business. He is quite worried about what budgets he should maintain.

Unit Costs

Manufacturing price per unit	$0.46			
Cost of inside materials	0.18			
Cost of covers				
Synthetic fabric	0.14			
Strong fabric		$0.36		
Imitation cowhide			$0.96	
Cowhide				$1.64
Additional cost (packing, delivery)	0.08			
Profit contribution (at least 10¢ per unit)	0.10			
Total	$0.96	$1.18	$1.78	$2.46

Proforma Profit and Loss Statement

Sales, estimated		$962,000
Cost of goods sold		(481,000)
Gross margin		481,000
Expenses		
Wages and salaries	$162,000	
Rent	40,000	
Utilities	6,000	
Other	22,000	
Interest payment	84,000	
Total expenses		$314,000
Loan payment, annual		$100,000
Profit		$ 67,000

Questions

1. How can using proper budgeting techniques help Larry as a manager?
2. What financial planning suggestions would you make to Larry?
3. What form of credit should Larry use with his customers?
4. What financial planning steps should be taken?
5. Explain why a cash flow statement would be useful.

Chapter Questions:

1. Why are budgets important?
2. Discuss the advantages and disadvantages of using a sales budget.
3. Discuss the advantages and disadvantages of using a cash budget.
4. Why is a budgeted income statement important to a business person?
5. Why is it important to determine cost and revenue centers in a business?
6. Discuss credit policies.

14

Photo courtesy of Irene Springer, Prentice-Hall, Inc.

COMMUNITY, LOCATION, AND LAYOUT

Chapter Objectives:

1. To learn community evaluation.
2. To be able to properly evaluate community and site selection.
3. To understand the vital importance of a proper location.
4. To know the steps involved in choosing a correct location.
5. To understand the importance of a proper layout.
6. To properly evaluate the store layout and design.

Make the most of yourself, for that is all there is to you.

Ralph Waldo Emerson

INCIDENT:

Greg and Mary want to start a popcorn, cheesecorn, and caramelcorn shop. They live in a city with a population of 500,000 in the southeastern part of the state. They have looked all over the city and have only found one competitor, who is located in one of the city's two large malls.

They figure that if they can lease a location, they can start their business for approximately $15,000. This amount does not include any renovation or redecorating. They have approximately $12,000 between them, and plan to obtain a signature loan from a local bank to help start their business.

One of Greg's closest friends owns a shoe store in one of the malls. Greg and Mary have been asking him what factors they should consider in choosing the location of their store. Greg and Mary think they would like to stay in the community, but do realize that they may have to go to another town in order to find a place ideally suited for them. They have always been told that location is very important to business success, but they are not sure whether this is just "lip service" or if it really is very important.

What should the shoe store owner have told Greg and Mary when they came to him about how to choose a community and a location?

Selection of the right community and location for his or her business is one of the most important decisions a business owner will ever make. The location of a store may be the most crucial factor to the final success of the business. This is important whether one is opening a new store, expanding into additional store locations, or even renewing a lease.

The game of volleyball is played by a team of six individuals, strategically placed on the playing area. They have set positions or locations, which they are to take in the beginning of play as well as during the action. The spiker must be in a given position at a given time for the best possible results. If the spiker is not, the play will probably fail. Choosing the right location is also necessary for success of a business.

A careful study of all possible community and site locations is important. Each trading area and geographical location must be evaluated, information should be gathered concerning each possible location, and all data should be analyzed and developed to provide the best possible situation.

Community

Every type of business has a trading area. For manufacturers, this may be an entire country or countries. Wholesalers may restrict themselves to states or cities; most

248
COMMUNITY, LOCATION, LAYOUT

retailers have a trading area within a specific community. For each of these types of businesses, it is important to choose a community that will support and sustain them.

The study of a community and its value to a business may be viewed through three major factors: (1) business considerations, (2) family and individual considerations, and (3) economic considerations.

business considerations

Regardless of the kind of business you are entering, the community will be a tremendous help or hindrance to your business. Cities and towns vary considerably according to their ability to support and provide profits for businesses.

Most large companies have store location departments that specialize in investigating and analyzing new store locations. They will investigate the size (population), average age, and income levels of a particular community. They will look at the traffic count surrounding a business. The small business owner should also study and evaluate the town of his or her preference in these ways.

Most small business owners will choose the community in which they live as the place to start their businesses. Also, they will probably expand into new store fronts in the same community or in neighboring towns. However, to properly evaluate a community, it is important to consider its business conditions. Consider whether the product or service is needed by that community. Does the community really need another shoe store or popcorn stand? What is the population or size of that community? Is the market large enough to support another business of that kind? Is your particular business the first of its kind in the community?

What kind of competition is available in the community? Is there a building space available, and are the locations favorable to this kind of business? Is there professional help or business consultants available? Are supplies and materials readily available? Will transportation be an excessive expense in this community? Will it be easy to obtain necessary licenses and zoning permits? Is a good and strong work force available to help you in your business? These questions are of vital importance to you and the success of your business. (See Table 14–1.)

The Bureau of Census of the United States Department of Commerce provides readily available publications to help evaluate the business conditions of most communities. Census tracts are developed for each Standard Metropolitan Statistical Area (SMSA). SMSAs are geographical areas that contain a central city of at least 50,000 persons plus other outside cities or towns. The census tract is a subdivision of the SMSA and shows population and area characteristics of about 4,000 to 5,000 residents. The tract contains information for a geographical unit of a community small enough for a retail store location analysis. These tracts will list:

1. General characteristics of the population:
    a. Race.
    b. Age (by sex).
    c. Male/female, all ages.
2. Social characteristics of the population:
    a. Parentage and country of origin.
    b. Years of school completed.

3. Labor force characteristics of the population.
4. Income characteristics of the population.
5. Housing values.
    a. Value.
    b. Automobiles available.

The Bureau of Census also develops a census of business for each SMSA or for cities over 2,500 population. The census of business is developed every five years and is published in the years ending in 2 and 7 (for example, 1977 and 1982). These census reports contain nationwide statistics on wholesale, retail, and selected service trade establishments. They relate information about the total consumer purchases (wholesale, retail, or service) in that particular city or community (see Table 14–2). Additionally, *Sales and Marketing Management* magazine publishes a "survey of buying power" in one of their summer issues showing the purchasing and buying power of individuals in various communities, counties, and states. The use of this information should provide a strong relative measurement for different communities and trading areas. Although these reports are of inestimable value, they should be supplemented with your own personal evaluations and on-the-spot analysis.

Table 14–1. Business Considerations

Provide community ratings from 1 (very poor) to 10 (excellent) for each category.

	COMMUNITY A	COMMUNITY B	COMMUNITY C	COMMUNITY D
1. Needed product or service				
2. Market (population)				
3. Building space available				
4. Lack of competition				
5. Available help or consultants				
6. Good locations available				
7. Community support for type of business				
8. Available supplies and materials				
9. Good working force available				
10. Ease in obtaining licenses, parking, and zoning				

Table 14-2. Summary Statistics for the State: 1977.

KIND OF BUSINESS	ALL ESTABLISHMENTS		Unincorporated businesses		ESTABLISHMENTS WITH PAYROLL				
	Number	Sales ($1,000)	Sole proprietor-ships (number)	Partner-ships (number)	Number	Sales ($1,000)	Payroll entire year ($1,000)	Payroll first quarter ($1,000)	Paid employees for week including March 12 (number)
Eating and drinking places	**40,050**	**8,051,883**	**22,256**	**6,522**	**33,875**	**7,832,136**	**2,072,080**	**493,383**	**443,162**
Eating places	31,733	7,294,900	16,933	5,070	26,958	7,120,373	1,904,400	451,056	408,025
Restaurants and lunchrooms	**	**	**	**	13,926	4,277,705	1,216,435	290,222	248,022
Cafeterias	**	**	**	**	757	169,967	44,551	11,031	8,744
Refreshment places	**	**	**	**	10,700	2,318,985	542,559	125,572	130,319
Other eating places	**	**	**	**	1,575	353,716	100,855	24,231	20,940
Drinking places (alcoholic beverages)	8,277	756,983	5,323	1,452	6,917	711,763	167,680	42,327	35,137
Drug and proprietary stores	**4,311**	**3,039,579**	**1,362**	**360**	**4,107**	**3,029,218**	**411,842**	**109,172**	**48,796**
Drug stores	**	**	**	**	3,983	3,004,940	407,892	108,126	48,168
Proprietary stores	**	**	**	**	124	24,278	3,950	1,046	628
Miscellaneous retail stores[1]	**53,102**	**7,745,249**	**37,806**	**5,555**	**25,262**	**6,879,001**	**963,518**	**229,350**	**141,845**
Liquor stores	5,673	1,790,399	2,931	1,304	5,015	1,715,533	139,467	33,673	23,959
Used merchandise stores	5,648	487,369	4,331	474	2,028	410,184	77,294	18,460	11,463
Miscellaneous shopping goods stores	19,697	2,896,388	13,012	2,164	10,371	2,629,995	371,558	89,464	57,324
Sporting goods stores and bicycle shops	3,571	631,527	2,290	468	2,154	574,880	71,849	18,235	10,921
General line sporting goods stores	**	**	**	**	795	289,893	34,124	9,134	4,971
Specialty line sporting goods stores	**	**	**	**	1,359	284,987	37,725	9,101	5,950
Book stores	1,714	266,269	1,099	179	912	246,158	33,184	8,148	6,484
Stationery stores	895	185,046	484	122	673	177,206	29,382	6,811	4,181
Jewelry stores	4,871	700,466	3,269	409	2,234	623,740	106,604	25,205	11,830
Hobby, toy, and game shops	1,801	257,298	1,303	193	758	231,303	25,663	5,897	4,631
Camera and photographic supply stores	784	219,197	455	72	532	209,004	23,515	5,522	2,756
Gift, novelty, and souvenir shops	3,916	333,493	2,804	491	1,894	286,095	40,380	9,634	8,039
Luggage and leather goods stores	410	60,798	259	37	230	56,117	8,280	1,890	1,107
Sewing, needlework, and piece goods stores	1,735	242,294	1,049	193	984	225,492	32,701	8,122	7,375

[1]Excludes nonemployer direct sellers; see appendix A for more information.
SOURCE: Adapted from the 1977 Census of Retail Trade, Geographic Area Series–California, Bureau of the Census.

family and individual considerations

Any decision to locate a business should take into account the personal characteristics and desires of the owner or manager. Business owners will usually start their businesses in their own communities. Familiarity is often the major reason for choosing a location. There are many other important considerations of family and individual nature which should be investigated before choosing a location.

Some additional characteristics that are important in choosing a business location would include what kinds of housing are good or available. Are the schools good for children? Would the community be a good place to raise a family? Are good shopping centers available? Is there favorable employment? Is there an overall high property value? Are taxes reasonable? Some people will prefer a strong and active social life; others will prefer religious and community service opportunities. In choosing a community, some people will look for good recreational facilities or a lot of cultural events. (See Table 14–3.)

These are all important considerations in choosing a location for your business. Personal preference will probably be the number one reason for choosing a community for starting a business. However, it is important to also consider both the business and economic conditions of the community.

economic considerations

An investigation of a community's economic strength is necessary before finally choosing a community. One would not like to start a beauty shop in a small town

Table 14-3. Family and Individual Considerations

Provide community ratings from 1 (very poor) to 10 (excellent) for each category.

	COMMUNITY A	COMMUNITY B	COMMUNITY C	COMMUNITY D
1. Good place to raise a family				
2. Good schools				
3. Good and available housing				
4. Good shopping centers				
5. Property values				
6. Reasonable taxes				
7. Favorable climate				
8. Good recreational facilities				
9. Religious and community service opportunities available				
10. Social life and cultural events available				

that everyone is leaving because the coal mines have been closed for the last three years. The business owner must look at the strengths and weaknesses of the economic conditions of the community.

Some questions that are important to investigate as far as the economic potential community is concerned are: (1) Is the community growing? (2) Is business activity growing in the community? (3) Is transportation readily available and reasonably priced? (4) Are the income and wage levels above average? (5) Is the banking and consumer credit community strong and active? (6) Is there new business coming into town? (7) Are retail or service sales growing in the community? (See Table 14–4.)

For capital buying, income figures will also indicate growth potentials for businesses in the community. These figures may be obtained through the Bureau of Census and in *Sales and Marketing Management* magazine's "Survey of Buying Power." As mentioned previously, this marketing information guide provides data about the economic strengths of communities across the nation.

Chambers of Commerce will usually mail kits of information on local areas (cities and states) to prospective business owners. Many states also have Departments of Economic Development (or of Industrial Development) that will also provide up-to-the-minute information about economic considerations in cities and states. These sources of information will prove to be invaluable as you compile and develop community and business evaluations.

Table 14–4. Economic Considerations

Provide community ratings from 1 (very poor) to 10 (excellent) for each category.

	COMMUNITY A	COMMUNITY B	COMMUNITY C	COMMUNITY D
1. Growing community				
2. Readily available transportation				
3. High income levels				
4. Growing business activity				
5. Average wage levels				
6. Good, high consumer credit				
7. Strong and active bank loans				
8. New business coming into town				
9. Strong economic base in the community				
10. Retail (service) sales growing				

Location

When considering a location, it is important to determine what kind of business will be using that location. There are three different types of businesses to take into account when considering locations: (1) the unique business, (2) the competitive business, and (3) the comparative business.

The unique business, such as a picture-framing store or a shoe-repair business, require people come to that business. There is no real reason for a high-rent or high-traffic location. This type of business will draw customers from throughout the community to their location, wherever that may be.

The competitive business will offer the same kinds of goods or services that other businesses offer. For example, grocery stores, record shops, and the like would prefer to not have competitors nearby. This type of business is very interested in traffic flow and traffic count. It is desirable for foot traffic as well as car traffic to be close by.

The comparative business will offer such things as clothing, shoes, or fast food. This type of business is usually helped, rather than hindered, by having competition nearby. Comparative businesses are present in shopping centers, malls, or downtown locations, as many customers will prefer to compare different products before making a final decision.

Whether you are in a unique business, a competitive business, or a comparative business, you will require different types of locations to ensure success. The site location is generally determined by first choosing a town, then selecting an area in the town, and finally determining an actual site, basing each selection on location analysis.

The selection of the retail location is generally determined by analyzing the population, accessibility of location to customers, appearance, neighborhood, competition, cost, and site value. (See Table 14–5.)

information gathering

One of the first areas of concern in location analysis is the determination of the accessibility that customers have to the business. How far are people willing to travel to buy at a fast-food restaurant? Are people willing to go across town to attend a movie theater? Are they willing to travel a few miles or as many as 20 miles? Answers to these types of questions can be found in information compiled by trade associations.

In most fields of business today there are trade associations which publish a lot of useful information. Trade associations can provide facts and figures about trade businesses and trading areas based upon national averages. A trading area is a territory in which people live, trade, or shop within a given distance (a community). Any national figure provided by a trade association can be adjusted to local conditions.

Census tracts also tell how many people live in a given shopping area. Census tracts break down populations on the basis of sex, age, and income level. Most libraries and universities have copies of census tracts; they may also be obtained from local and county governments.

Table 14-5. Location Selection

Provide location rating from 1 (very poor) to 10 (excellent) for each location.

	SITE A	SITE B	SITE C	SITE D
1. Accessibility to customers (including distance)				
2. General appearance				
3. Drawing power				
4. Floor space				
5. Available parking				
6. Neighborhood				
7. Competition				
8. Growth potential				
9. Costs (including taxes and utilities)				
10. Site value in ten years				

There are other sources of information that will help to determine the buying power of individuals within a shopping area. *The Census of Retail Trade,* published by the Bureau of Census, U.S. Department of Commerce, and "Survey of Buying Power," put out by the publisher of *Sales and Marketing Management* magazine, contain information about the buying power of individuals within specific cities, towns, or communities.

Barbara is interested in opening a women's clothing store in the southeast part of town. She wrote to the national trade association for information concerning women's apparel shops and consulted the census tract to learn how many women between the ages of 18 and 65 live in the southeast trading area. Barbara got clues as to the quality and price of merchandise she should stock when she learned that the average family income in the southeast trading area is $14,000. But Barbara also needs to know how much of the total market she might expect. Most small business people guess, but there are ways to estimate the market share of a specific product line at a given location.

market share   One way to estimate market share is to determine the number of families in the trading area (from census tracts or Chamber of Commerce data) and multiply this figure by the estimated annual purchasing power of families in that area for the product. Using this information, one can then figure out how many competitors are in the trading area and estimate their drawing power. For example, Barbara would find that the average family spends about $250 a year on women's clothing. Multiplying this figure by the number of families in the trade area, say 25,000, Barbara would conclude total possible sales may reach $6,250,000 for women's clothing.

$$\begin{array}{ccccc} \text{Family purchases of} & & \text{Number of} & & \text{Trade area's} \\ \text{women's apparel} & \times & \text{families} & = & \text{annual sales} \\ \$250 & \times & 25{,}000 & = & \$6{,}250{,}000 \end{array}$$

Because she estimates her competitors to be strong whereas her business is new and struggling, she may estimate sales for the first year of only $200,000. This is probably the most common form of market share analysis.

A second way of determining the market share is to determine, from trade associations or census information, the average dollar amount spent per year for a product. For example, Barbara found that the average woman spends approximately $250 per year on women's clothing. With 25,000 women in the store trading area, total sales for that shopping area would amount to $6,250,000. However, there may be 20 women's apparel stores in the shopping area; thus, Barbara's estimated sales could reach $312,500 a year. That is:

$$\begin{array}{ccccc} & & \text{Individual} & \text{Number} & \text{Sales} \\ \text{Population} & \times & \text{annual purchases} \div & \text{of stores} = & \text{(Market share)} \\ 25{,}000 & \times & \$250 & \div\quad 20\quad = & \$312{,}500 \end{array}$$

This does not mean necessarily that Barbara's share of the market will be $312,000—rather, it indicates what a fair share of the market may be. Since Barbara's business is new, her annual sales would probably range between $200,000 to $300,000.

A third method of determining market share is to obtain information from the Bureau of Census or the buying power survey, mentioned previously, for the total volume of dollar sales for a product line in a given community or area. For example, our hypothetical merchant could now learn that in the total community, sales for women's clothes were equal to almost $6 million. With this information, Barbara can look through the Yellow Pages of the telephone directory and determine the number of competitors (say, 20) within that community and divide the $6 million by that number. That is:

$$\begin{array}{ccc} \text{Community buying power} & \text{Number} & \text{Sales} \\ \text{for a specific product} \div & \text{of stores} = & \text{(Market share)} \\ \$6 \text{ million} \quad\div & 20 \quad = & \$300{,}000 \end{array}$$

Again, this would be only a rough estimate of the market share; it would have to be adjusted for the strength or weakness of the merchant's business.

It is important to remember that it takes time to build regular and steady customers, however business people state there are three major factors on which this depends: (1) location, (2) location and (3) location.

Other concerns should involve the general appearance of the particular store site. Is there sufficient floor space and ample parking space? Is there room for expansion? Can delivery be made in the rear as well as in the front? Is the outside of the store attractive? Are there other stores nearby that will draw customers to the area? Is the store easy to get to? Are there bus stops or other mass transit stops close by? Is the neighborhood attractive? Is there growth potential for the site selected and for the neighborhood?

One of the most important and often overlooked aspects of site selection is analysis of competitors. A telephone book and a map can indicate who competitors are and where they are located. One needs to consider the nearness or distance of competitors. A part of town where there is no competition may be an ideal site for a business.

Local and state laws and regulations must be investigated. It is important to talk to the local zoning commission to determine if your business would be in a properly zoned area. In addition, you may find that there are laws requiring a certain number of parking spaces for your type of business. There are probably also licenses and certificates that you need in order to open or run your business in a given area of town.

For wholesale or manufacturing plants, the major considerations for local site selection would primarily be concerned with transportation, parking facilities, industrial parks, and lease arrangements. Many new industrial parks are being developed that are close to main highways, providing ready access to many parts of the city. These are ideally suited for new manufacturing or wholesaling businesses.

shopping centers

Different businesses have different needs for site locations. Shopping centers are distinctly different from other business locations. A shopping center is a set of planned buildings that allows for interaction between businesses or tenants. Shopping centers are designed to attract customers to the location, and to allow for plenty of parking space and foot traffic among the stores.

Most customers like the idea of shopping centers because they find it easy to drive in, park, and walk to the various stores with relative ease and safety. Many centers (malls) also provide protection from the weather and an atmosphere of shopping comfort with a wide variety of stores available.

The developers or owners of shopping centers look for traditional and successful retailers. They are concerned with filling all the available spaces in their centers as quickly as possible. New businesses are generally discouraged from going into new centers because of their lack of credit and standing within the community. However, if it becomes difficult to fill a center, developers may relax their standards and solicit new businesses.

Each shopping center is usually centered around one or several large major tenants. Therefore, shopping centers are classified according to their leading tenants. There are three major types of shopping centers: (1) neighborhood, (2) community, and (3) regional.

Neighborhood shopping centers. Neighborhood shopping centers usually have a supermarket, drug store, or hardware store as the leading tenant. This is the smallest but most common kind of shopping center found in the United States. This type of shopping center generally draws from a neighborhood, and its primary customers are located in near surroundings. Neighborhood shopping centers will draw from populations of 5,000 to 40,000, with typical site areas of four acres and leasable spaces of 40,000 to 60,000 square feet.

Community shopping centers. Community shopping centers are usually centered around a department or variety store that has a large number of specialty stores attached to it. Occasionally, there will be a major movie theater as the major tenant, with restaurants and other specialty stores associated with it as a community center. Community shopping centers draw from neighboring communities and provide for a wide price range, greater style selections, and more impulse buying items. Community shopping centers generally draw from populations of 30,000 to 100,000 with typical site areas of eight to twelve acres and leasable spaces of 100,000 to 200,000 square feet.

Regional shopping centers. Regional shopping centers or malls rely on one or more department stores as the major tenant(s). This is the largest type of shopping center and has become widely spread throughout all major cities in the United States. There are often two, three, four, or even five large department stores all located within one shopping center with connecting walkways or approaches between those department stores.

Most regional shopping centers place the department stores on the outer edges and provide wide walkways between the department stores with smaller speciality shops located off the walkways. The enclosed mall is designed to shut out the weather and to allow customers a complete and wide variety and choice of goods. Customers have access to the open store fronts, easy entrances, and all-weather shopping. The entire mall becomes a display area, with stores using the full width as display cases. Sliding or overhead doors may be used to lock the stores at night.

Regional shopping centers generally draw from populations of 100,000 or more with typical site areas of twenty to fifty acres or more and leasable spaces of 300,000 to 1 million square feet. Some mall owners will even hold back building funds during the original construction of the mall to help offset costs for tenants who will be building their stores in the mall.

For example, mall owners may build a new mall costing $20 million. However, they may only use $15 million in the construction of the basic building, ceiling, walls, parking lot, and utilities. The remaining $5 million will be used for construction costs by the first tenants. The owners figure that these costs would be approximately $5 per square foot for tenants building their businesses in the mall for the first time. (Subsequent businesses in the same mall location would have fixed floors, bathrooms, and ceilings already installed.) With that $5 per square foot, a new tenant could use that money to help put up walls, bathrooms, and ceilings; it could also cover whatever other expenses would be involved in establishing a shop in the mall area. With a lease with the mall owners for 1,000 square feet, the new tenant will have $5,000 to use in completing the interior of the business. This is a common practice used by many mall owners to help improve the chances of success for new businesses in their malls.

SUCCESS STORY: Phil G. Wizer, Jr.

Phil G. Wizer, Jr., a native Kansan, was transferred to Lincoln, Nebraska, in 1964 as controller and systems manager by a wholesale grocery company. Four years later he moved to Omaha where he worked as manager of systems and training procedures for a computer supply company. In 1971, Wizer purchased his first Thrifty Rent-A-Car franchise in Omaha. Today he owns and operates five Thrifty franchises: one in Nebraska, one in Iowa, two in Arizona, and one in California. In addition, Wizer serves on the national advertising committee for Thrifty Rent-A-Car.

The commercial traveler accounts for a large portion of all the car rentals. But as more and more individuals enjoy more and more leisure time, the pleasure traveler's segment of the rental car business will expand, Wizer feels. A 50 percent increase is projected for the rental car business in the 1980s. With this in mind, Wizer expects his franchise to generate more than $2 million in 1981 alone.

Wizer attributes much of his success to his management team and his personnel. Each manager is trained to utilize a profit and loss statement, including the balance sheet, to control expenses through objectives. Wizer's employees undergo an extensive training program that includes study of the competition. This allows Wizer's staff to observe the shortcomings of Thrifty's competition so that the staff members can do a better job themselves. All employees are trained to provide friendly, courteous customer service. To Wizer, this is the key to success.

As to the future of the industry, Wizer sees a definite place for solar-powered and electric-powered cars to combat high gasoline prices. As for himself, Wizer aims to expand his managerial base so that he can explore attractive new locations, particularly in the Sun Belt areas. With a strong management team and a good customer service policy, the future for Phil Wizer appears unlimited.

Layout

After a location in a given community has been determined, it is important to plan the layout of that building and/or business. Small businesses in the U.S. are growing, diversifying, and spreading out. All too often, one of the problems in this growth is the lack of planning and design associated with the store layout. Very little, if any, consideration is given to the store layout or to the movement of merchandise or materials through the building.

Small manufacturers and small retailers alike must look at the flow of traffic, goods, material, and personnel in trying to facilitate and improve the operation of a business. Making a new layout is a major undertaking for any business owner. It is an activity that should be well thought out and investigated before completing. Much time and many changes will be required before the final layout is used. Before constructing a new building, a small business owner will have to obtain an architect or contractor. However, he or she will generally purchase the goods and equipment without even thinking of how they will fit in the store layout or design.

The layout and design of a store is a very complex and often expensive experience. Such a project may range from a new store front that must prove to be interesting and attractive, to a complete store renovation that will cause extensive changes and renovation. A store that is well laid out will provide easy movement for the customer throughout a store or easy flow of materials throughout a plant to allow for maximum efficiency. A new and proper layout for a retail store would include a needs statement of business, customer profile, merchandise, market, staff requirements, atmosphere, costs, growth potential, and operational characteristics of the business. The layout should facilitate and augment sales. It should provide the most attractive atmosphere and should draw customers to the store.

manufacturers and warehouses

Manufacturing plans and wholesale warehouses have several business characteristics in common. Most require easy access for deliveries, places for storage of materials, space for office activities, and easy access for shipping completed orders. The manufacturing plant also needs areas laid out for production facilities and equipment. The most common factory or warehouse design consists of a long building with receiving at one end, storage and production in the middle, and shipping at the other end of the building. This often allows for the shipping out to be handled by trucks at one end while receiving from boxcars is being handled at the other end of the building.

Another layout design used by manufacturers or warehouses is the traditional "U-Shaped operation," which allows the receiving and shipping of goods to take place at the same end of the building, and the flow of equipment or warehousing to occur along the curve of the "U" inside the building. Many manufacturers using this design will place any office activity in the middle of the U-shape.

retail stores

The most difficult layout designs are those for retail stores. These layouts are concerned with the basic functions of the store, and should result in a positive impact on sales. Major considerations for an effective retail store layout include: (1) adequate entrance space, (2) appropriate aisle space, (3) comfortable and free-flowing traffic patterns, (4) displays developed for maximum attraction to customers, (5) appropriate atmosphere, (6) good lighting, (7) control of cash registers and goods within the store, and (8) an overall attractive appearance. (See Figure 14–1.)

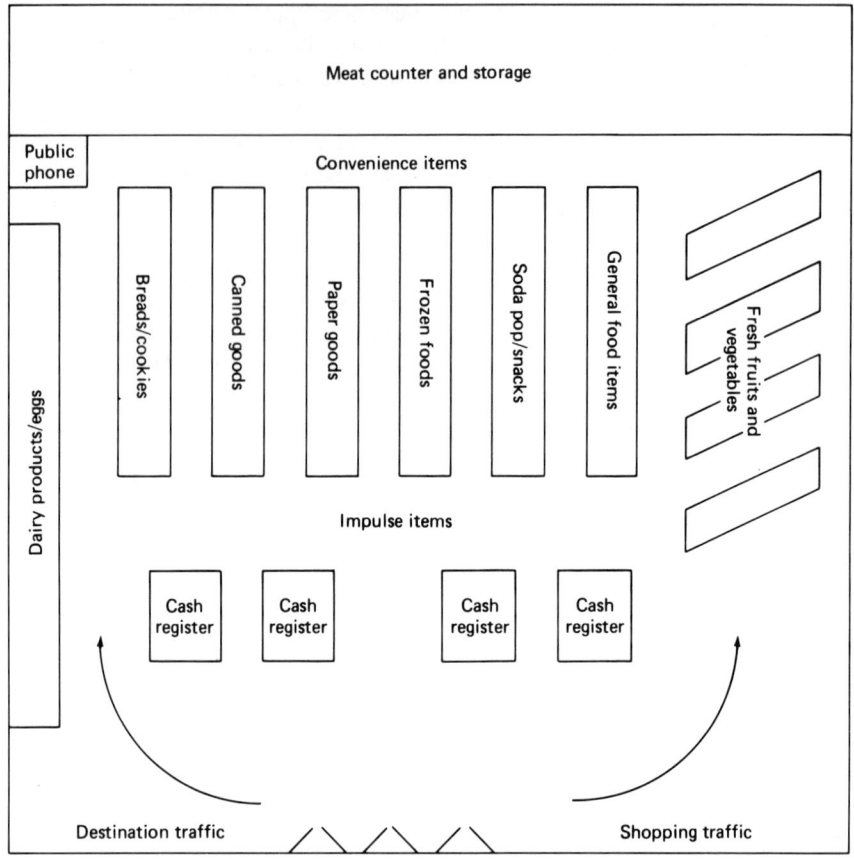

Figure 14–1. *Floor traffic and merchandise location for a small grocery store*

customers   Customers are people. They usually behave the same within a store as they do outside a store. There are two basic types of customer traffic through a store: destination traffic and shopping traffic. Destination traffic customers have already made up their minds about what they are going to purchase, and upon entering the store, they will usually try to move directly toward that merchandise to pick it up. They have a tendency to turn left upon entering a store. Shopping traffic is the larger group of customers. These customers tend to turn right when entering a store. They are in the store without a specific buying objective; for example, in a grocery store they will travel from one end of the store to the other, looking at as much of the merchandise as possible in order to decide what to buy. Shopping traffic generally moves counterclockwise around the store, while the destination traffic moves clockwise.

Due to standard customer traffic through a store, many convenience items and services are located in the rear of the store. For example, the meat counter of a grocery store is generally located in the back. On the other hand, impulse items are located in the front of the store close to high customer traffic areas or checkout stands. For example, bubble gum and cigarettes are often sold around checkout stands. Different locations in the store have different values (see Figure 14–2). Locations closest to entrances tend to have the greatest value, due to greater customer exposure; that is, these areas have the greatest sales potential and have an assigned value of 1 in Figure 14–2. Therefore, it is advisable to locate the highest profit merchandise somewhere close to entrance areas. If more than one entrance is available, traffic flow counts should be taken. Locations in the back of the store generally sell less and are less profitable to the store owner. These back locations are assigned values 5 and 6 in Figure 14–2.

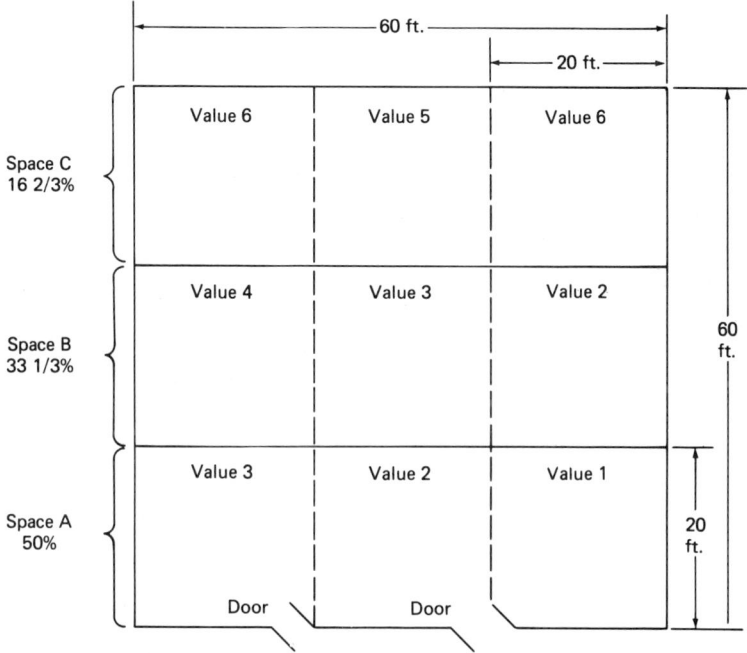

Figure 14–2. *The 3-2-1 rule*

When allocating space values, some retailers will use the 3-2-1 Rule. Figure 14–2 illustrates the 3-2-1 Rule, which states that the front third of the store layout, Space A, should account for 50 percent of the sale items. The second third, Space B, should account for 33⅓ percent, and the back area should account for 16⅔ percent. This may also be allocated to rent cost. For example, if a store had a rental cost of $3,000 per year, one-half (50 percent) of it would be $1,500. This would be the typical rental cost, therefore, of the front third of the store. The middle third rental cost would be one-third (33⅓ percent), or $1,000, and the final or back space should account for one-sixth (16⅔ percent), or $500, of the rent.

These general guidelines can provide additional information, and can also help to provide effective retail store layouts. Each kind of business is different; therefore, it is important to analyze and lay out your store according to the best knowledge available. It may also be helpful to have someone act as a lookout and diagram the flow of customer traffic through the store. One owner of a very successful clothing outlet has a twelve-foot ladder, upon which an employee sits for a period of two hours and draws a line along a map of the store layout where a customer has walked. At the end of the two-hour period, if all the foot traffic has moved to the right front part of the store, then this owner relocates his merchandise to draw customers to the other parts of the store. If on the other hand, the owner notices that the foot traffic flows equally in all areas throughout the store, then his general rule is not to change or disrupt the layout of that store.

Many store managers have also found it very important to locate cashiers near the exit ways of businesses. This allows for greater control and a reduction of shoplifting. This is especially important in large regional shopping centers or in malls, where large amounts of traffic are found.

The layout of the store should be attractive. It should also provide a proper atmosphere as well as convenience and service to the customers. Low display cases and wide aisles provide a sense of spaciousness, convenience to the customer, and control by the owner or manager.

CASE STUDY: Convenient Food Mart, Inc.

Dick is about ready to open his Convenient Food Mart, Inc. franchise. Before he can do so, however, he needs to find the right location. He has been able to raise the $25,000 equity capital needed, and believes that he can obtain financing up to $45,000 for six years of equipment, signs and interest at the available rates. He has recently received his franchising agreement from Convenient Food Mart, Inc. and is excited about opening a grocery store of approximately 2,600 square feet with ample parking.

His store will be open 365 days a year, from 7:00 A.M. to midnight. The store will stock a complete line of the top-name, national-brand merchandise that is normally stocked in the chain supermarkets, with the exception of fresh red meat. Dick is working with the regional franchiser to select a location. The franchiser will take a long-term lease, and will then sublease it to Dick, who will be the owner and operator. Dick's will be one of 800 Convenient Food Marts throughout the United States. The business has been in operation since 1958.

Dick's most important decision will be where to locate his business. The successful Convenient Food Marts are most often located in densely populated residential areas, close to large consumer traffic.

He thinks that he should find a location that can be seen from two or three major directions. Because rush hour traffic will also be one of the busiest business times, he will try to locate easy access, easy entrance, and easy exit for his business location. A speed limit of 35 mph or less on the adjacent thoroughfare is preferable. Dick is also questioning what kind of signs he should have outside.

The layout should be uncluttered, so that goods are easily available to customers who are in a hurry. Dick has discovered that the checkout counters or registers should be located closest to the entrance to allow maximum visibility and convenience. This checkout counter will also reduce theft and shoplifting. Everything in the store should be able to be seen from the checkout counter.

COMMUNITY, LOCATION, LAYOUT

Questions

1. Dick knows that he needs to get an overall picture of the prospective communities. How and where can he get the information he needs?
2. Dick's store will be selling cold items, (such as frozen foods, deli products, produce, soft drinks, beer, and dairy products) plus other food items, magazines, comics, candies, sandwiches, coffee and tea, cleaners, and other assorted food items. What would be the best layout design for his store?
3. Draw a store layout or a floor plan for a business that is 60 feet wide and 40 feet deep.

Chapter Questions:

1. What factors are important in determining a proper community for a business?
2. Why is location analysis so important?
3. What factors are important when reviewing or analyzing locations?
4. Why is it necessary to weigh location factors?
5. Why is a store's layout so important in doing business or increasing a sale?
6. What is the difference between destination traffic and shopping traffic?
7. What area is usually the most valuable in a retail store?
8. What is the 3-2-1 Rule?
9. How would you determine the best community and location for a business of your choice? (Choose a hardware store, a fast-food restaurant, or the like, and specify which factors are important as to community and location.)
10. Where would you go to get information about populations, purchasing power, age, and income characteristics of the population?

15

Photo courtesy of Irene Springer, Prentice-Hall, Inc.

PURCHASING, INVENTORY CONTROL, AND COMPUTERS

Chapter Objectives:

1. To identify the stages in the purchasing process.
2. To identify several controls on the purchasing process.
3. To understand the ABC method of inventory control.
4. To identify some of the visual inventory control systems.
5. To name the basic components of a computer system.
6. To identify some of the problems and benefits of using a computer in a small business.

20 percent of your merchandise will account for 80 percent of your sales.

Pareto's Law

If anything can go wrong, it will.

Murphy's Law

Murphy was an optimist.

Mrs. Murphy's Law

INCIDENT: The salesperson had taken Jim out to lunch and had convinced him to place an order for 25,000 units of a commonly used item, rather than the normal order of 10,000 units. Jim agreed to the larger order because he liked and trusted the salesperson, and because there was a 10-percent price reduction on the larger quantity. Delivery was to be in five weeks, rather than the standard three weeks on prior orders, but Jim did not consider that to be a serious problem. He had two months' supply on hand, and the company had supplied this item before, always promptly and of a high quality.

Five weeks later, the salesperson informed Jim that there would be a slight delay in delivery, as some problems had occurred in the order. Jim okayed the delay, but indicated that he only had about four weeks' supply left.

Two weeks passed, and Jim heard nothing about his order. He called the salesperson, who informed him that the order was in final inspection, and would be shipped out in a day or two. Demand was a little higher than usual, and Jim was getting nervous, as he had less than two weeks' supply on hand.

The following Monday, Jim called the factory, and after being shuffled around somewhat, he found that the order was on the loading docks awaiting a truck to pick it up. Jim had two days' supply left, and the factory was over 500 miles away. He called in the salesperson, and instructed that a portion of the order be sent immediately by air express. The salesperson met the plane at the airport and delivered two boxes of the items personally. The cost of the special shipment to Jim was $150, or about half of what Jim had saved by placing the larger order. The remainder of the order arrived the next week, and lasted over seven months.

As Jim reviewed the experience afterwards, he began to ask himself some questions about his inventory and purchasing habits. When should he place orders, and for how much at a time? How should he decide what supplier to order from? What was the proper amount of inventory he should carry? Was he spending too much on inventory, or too little?

266 PURCHASING, INVENTORY CONTROL, AND COMPUTERS

Successful small business owners know their products. This is not limited to retail businesses. Just as butchers must know meat, wholesalers must know what goods will sell, and manufacturers must know not only about the products being produced, but also about the raw materials from which those products are derived. Even in service businesses, there are usually some supplies that must be carried.

Since one cannot sell what one does not have, it is important for a small business owner to maintain the correct items in stock. Items must be ordered, received, and kept track of. Ordering and receiving of goods is part of the purchasing function in a business, while keeping track of the goods is called inventory control. These two activities are closely related, especially in the smaller businesses, where both activities are likely to be the responsibility of the business owner or manager.

In the analysis of business failures, it is often possible to list improper purchasing and inventory management as two of the factors leading to the downfall of the business. Failure to select the right merchandise to carry will result in poor sales volume. Running out of an item is doubly costly; not only is the sale lost, but the potential customer may lose respect for the business and go elsewhere for future business. It is foolish, however, to carry too much merchandise, for this can tie up a great deal of money in inventory. It is not only expensive, it is risky, for the inventory can be broken, stolen, or become obsolete.

In recent years, the cost of computers has dropped dramatically, and the potential uses made of computers have grown. Small businesses are now turning to the computer to aid in such areas as purchasing and inventory control. In fact, many computer makers have set up special marketing forces that are especially targeted towards small businesses. The computer is rapidly becoming just another tool to aid small business owners in managing their companies effectively.

Purchasing

Purchasing is not just talking to salespeople and placing orders. It is the first step in realizing a profit. To illustrate the potential value of purchasing properly, suppose that a typical small business with sales of $500,000 per year can save 1 percent on purchasing by proper management.

This seemingly insignificant 1 percent savings translates to a 16⅔ percent increase in net profits. To achieve that much additional profit by increasing sales, over $83,000 in additional sales would have to be generated. The effort required to generate that much additional sales surely has to be more than the amount of effort devoted to effective purchasing. (See Table 15–1.)

the stages of purchasing

The purchasing process can effectively be divided into three stages. First, specifications must be stated as to what order will be made, what items will be involved in the order, and of what quality. Second, selection of a supplier must take place, and the order given. Third, follow-up on the order must be continued until it has been received and accepted.

Table 15-1. The Effect of a 1% Savings in Purchasing on Profit for a Typical Business

	WITHOUT 1% SAVINGS	WITH 1% SAVINGS	
Net sales	$500,000	$500,000	
Cost of goods sold	250,000	245,000	
Other expenses	220,000	220,000	
Net profit	$ 30,000	$ 35,000	
Improvement in profit			$ 5,000
Percentage improvement			16⅔%

Specifications. Unless items are being custom manufactured, specifications often are drawn from supplier catalogs. Before that can be done, however, it is important to have a clear idea of what is needed. Options and frills can add to the cost of an item. These options can both enhance and detract from the salability of an item. Choice of color or colors cannot be left to chance. In Nebraska, Oklahoma, Texas, and in many states where "Big Red" football teams have enthusiastic followings, almost anything will sell in the proper shades of red. In fact, East coast garment makers occasionally question orders from these regions because they request so many red items, and red is not usually a popular color.

In retail businesses, it is especially important to keep the target market in mind when preparing specifications. A store with an exclusive image must be especially careful to order high-quality merchandise.

Selection of a supplier. Only after a clear idea of what is wanted is reached is it proper to call the salesperson or open the catalogs. Even then it is possible to waste a great deal of time matching the specifications to what is being offered.

Quite often when standard or stock items are being ordered, none of the offered items will meet the specifications exactly, but many different items will be quite close. The best rule of thumb is to spend only as much time as the total value of the item being ordered is worth. It would be silly to spend hours deciding on a replacement for the office coffeemaker that probably costs less than $50. On the other hand, a rash decision on a $50,000 computer system or a new kind of machine for a factory could have disastrous results.

Meeting with salespeople can be a pain or a great deal of fun. A pushy salesperson can ruin one's attitude toward the product being ordered. The truly great salesperson will be well informed on his or her product, and can be helpful in making sure that the specifications are correct. It is best, however, not to become too dependent upon salespeople for product information. After all, they must sell their merchandise to make a living.

Wherever possible, orders should only be placed in writing; otherwise, written confirmations of orders placed by phone should be sent at once. This is most important for larger orders, although few suppliers will accept large orders by phone.

The small business owner is often at a disadvantage in dealing with suppliers. Without any substantial buying power, he or she cannot get the price breaks or other concessions that many companies will give to their larger customers. In some types of businesses (notably, grocery stores), buying groups have been formed to create the strength in numbers needed to reach a stronger point of negotiation. Local and national trade associations have occasionally also set up buying plans. One method that can sometimes be used to get a better deal is to guarantee business for a certain period of time, such as a year, in return for a price break. Since this reduces the supplier's sales effort for additional business, it is reasonable for the supplier to pass some of that savings along to the customer. If the item under consideration has stable usage, it may be possible to place a standing order, where a set quantity is received each day, week, or month. This standing order can be reviewed periodically to make sure that it is still reasonable.

Follow-up. The purchasing process cannot stop once the order is placed. As circumstances change, it may become necessary to modify the order before it is received, or to change the scheduled delivery date. Sometimes, when the order fails to arrive, it is necessary to chase it down, a task that is seldom enjoyable.

When the order arrives, it is important for it to be inspected and counted. Shortages and overages should be detected and reported to the supplier. Quality control tests are often performed when standards have been specified to make sure that the proper quality has been achieved. Damage incurred in transit should be noted and reported to the shipper for adjustment.

Part of the follow-up process is making sure that the invoice is proper and then paying it promptly. Unless a price change is noted, the invoice total should be compared to the expected total of the order. Spot-check orders on occasion to make sure that they add up properly, and that any tax is appropriate and accurate. If possible, get an estimate on shipping charges as part of the order, then compare it to the actual total.

using the purchase discount

Many suppliers offer terms such as 1–10/Net 30, which translates to a 1 percent discount if the invoice is paid within ten days. Otherwise, the invoice is due in thirty days. These terms can sometimes be negotiated with the supplier. Terms within individual industries are usually standardized, with all suppliers offering similar terms.

Proper use of the purchase discount is one easy way to save money on purchasing. If the cash is available, by all means take advantage of the purchase discount. Even if cash is tight, it might pay to borrow the money to pay the bill. For example, in a 1–10/Net 30 invoice, you are in essence paying 1 percent to hold onto your money an additional twenty days, since you could take the discount anytime in the first ten days. This is an annual rate of 18.25-percent interest. If you can borrow funds at a rate less than 18.25 percent, you save money by borrowing the money to pay the bill in ten days, rather than waiting the full thirty.

the purchasing agent and purchasing control

In the very small business, the business owner will do all the purchasing. As a business grows, however, proper delegation of authority dictates that some or all of the purchasing task be given over to employees. Where the company is large enough, a purchasing agent will be employed to handle the purchasing function.

The purchasing agent can assume the tasks of dealing with suppliers and following up on orders. By doing so, other managers and employees can be relieved of that task, freeing them to concentrate on their own jobs.

In actual practice, however, the purchasing agent often becomes a middleman in the purchasing transaction. Large orders will often require top-level management approval. Very small orders may often be best handled by the user department, rather than to consume the time of the purchasing agent or purchasing department. Controls must be established to make sure that the purchasing agent has the responsibility and authority to perform his or her function. Dollar limits (or usage period limits) can be set beyond which orders must be approved by the purchasing agent. For example, a department may be allowed to order up to $100 worth of office supplies without approval during a six-month period. Such controls can become ridiculous, however. In one case, a public relations department was not permitted to order a $50 electronic flash for a camera, because it was a capital equipment order. The department was permitted, however, to order flashbulbs, and proceeded to spend over $200 on flash bulbs each year.

The purchasing agent for a retail store is often called a buyer; he or she may specialize in a particular type of merchandise. Larger businesses, such as department stores, often have many buyers. In smaller businesses, department managers may be given buying authority for their areas. Buying budgets for each department can be established, and deviations from these budgets should require explanation to make sure that they are reasonable.

purchasing in a manufacturing environment

Retailers and wholesalers must buy all of their merchandise, but manufacturers may choose to make themselves or to buy from secondary manufacturers the components needed. This make-or-buy decision may have to be made on an item-by-item basis. The decision should rest upon the feasibility of making the item, and on its appropriateness. If the item can be bought for a lower price than the manufacturer can make it, it is more sensible to buy it. The cost to make the item must include the capital costs for any necessary equipment. Furthermore, it does not make sense to make a product that does not fit into the general nature of the business. For example, a maker of custom trailers would not want to get into the sheet metal rolling business merely to supply the metal needed for siding.

purchasing ethics

Part of the purchasing control process should be the setting of some ethical standards for purchasing. For example, it is unfair to invite a company to bid on an order if there is little or no chance of that company receiving the order, regardless of the price. The exception that may be made to this rule is for new suppliers, who may be asked to submit a trial bid. The purchasing agent may control a great deal of money when all the transactions are considered, and the possibility for fraud or collusion certainly exists. A business that is large enough should have some separation of purchasing functions to reduce this possibility.

Several practices in purchasing are somewhat shifty, and may result in higher purchasing costs in the long run. If several suppliers are bidding on a particular order, it is important to give the order to the lowest bidder. Otherwise, word may spread that there is no benefit in being the lowest bidder, and subsequent bids may end up being higher as a result. It is also considered a poor practice to drive a price down by promising additional business that does not develop, or by taking advantage of a dominant position in the supplier's overall business. Business owners who persist in "nickel and diming" suppliers over each order and invoice may find themselves without willing suppliers at some point, or the suppliers may decide to return the favor.

One persistent problem in purchasing is the gift problem. Salespeople delight in taking their customers out to lunch, and many big orders have been closed at the dinner table. While this is an accepted sales practice, it may be a problem when experienced from the other side of the coin. The Christmas season is a tempting one for gift giving by suppliers. While there is no real danger in accepting calendars and other harmless doodads, there is a question about where the line should be drawn. The business owner must consider the gift-giving problem from both sides—in accepting them from suppliers and in presenting them to customers.

SUCCESS STORY: Woody Allen

Woody Allen, a distinguished actor-film-maker, started his career as a stand-up comedian early in the 1960s. He presented himself as a self-apologetic, meek person from Brooklyn, and carried this over to the screen.

Woody Allen was born Allen Stewart Konigsberg in Brooklyn, New York, on December 1, 1935. Throughout his schooling, the only class that was of interest to him was English composition. Comical sketches about his parents were frequently used early in his career.

When Woody was fifteen, he was writing quips under the name of Woody Allen, and sending them to newspaper gossip columns for publication. After graduation from high school, he began working on the staff of Sid Caesar's television show. In 1961, Allen entered into the unstable world of performers, giving up an excellent writing job for the Garry Moore show that paid $1700 a week.

A night in 1964 when motion picture producer Charles K. Feldman and actress Shirley MacLaine watched Allen's act was the turning point in his career. After that he wrote the screen play and played a supporting role in the movie, *What's New, Pussycat?* The film grossed over $17 million but Allen hated it because he was restricted, so he became a director.

Allen began making movies on his own in 1969 with *Take the Money and Run*. Allen lets his producer-manager, Charles Joffe, handle most of the business affairs. Woody spends a good deal of his time creatively controlling his pictures. All of Allen's movies have been termed successful with the more famous ones considered to be *Take the Money and Run, Love and Death, Annie Hall,* and *Manhattan*. The film, *Annie Hall,* received Academy Awards for best picture, best director (Allen), best screenplay (Allen and Marshall Brickman) and best actress (Diane Keaton).

Allen insists he is "not reclusive"—just "not gregarious." Allen's work, especially writing, is very enjoyable to him and can be done anywhere, but he prefers writing in his bedroom.

Inventory Control

It is not difficult, especially in a retail business, for well over half of the capital of the business to be tied up in inventory. Walk through the average store, and you will find bare spots on shelves where items have sold out, and you will also find items that have sat on shelves long enough to accumulate a layer of dust. The out-of-stock items represent lost sales (and hence lost profits) to the business. The items gathering dust were purchased and paid for some time ago—there is money invested in inventory, and unless the item sells, the money is not making any profit for the business.

Most business owners recognize this fact, and often hold periodic inventory-reduction sales. During the waning days of 1977, when merchants were trying to dump their supplies of 23-channel CB radios, the price of a unit fell from over $100 to under $20 for the same model unit. At least one CB maker went bankrupt during this period due to the obsolete inventory created by the changeover to 40-channel CB radios.

inventory holding costs

Not only does it cost money to purchase inventory in the first place, it costs *more* money to keep it around. Some of the additional costs associated with the holding of inventory are:

   1. **Financing costs.** If money must be borrowed to purchase additional inventory, part of that cost should be attributed to items already in inventory. If they were sold, the additional cash might allow the immediate payment of new invoices without bank borrowing.

   2. **Insurance costs.** Fire insurance costs are directly related to the amount of inventory being insured.

   3. **Storage costs.** Inventory takes up space, and that space must be leased or purchased.

   4. **Obsolescence costs.** When the 40-channel CB radio was introduced, many merchants learned a painful lesson in obsolescence.

   5. **Breakage and damage costs.** The longer an item sits on the shelf, the more likely it is to be accidently damaged.

   6. **Shelf-life costs.** Many items, such as film and batteries, have a limited shelf life, after which they must be discarded. Perishable items, such as produce and dairy products, also have very limited shelf lives.

   7. **Fashion costs.** Women's clothing, in particular, is very sensitive to fashion and the right season; styles can change very rapidly.

   8. **Opportunity costs.** The money invested in an item on the shelf could be invested in some other item instead. If that other item is out of stock, a sale is lost.

Experts generally assume that the cost of holding inventory is about 20 percent of the value each year. (In a period of high interest rates, that number may be somewhat understated.) What this means is that if a business can reduce its inventory by $100, it should reduce its out-of-pocket costs by about $20 to $25 a year.

the abc method of inventory control

In any inventory mix, there will be important items and unimportant ones. It is ridiculous to spend the same amount of effort controlling each item in inventory. One easy method of determining which items need tight control is the ABC method. The ABC method recognizes the key fact that a large percentage of inventory value will be taken up by a few items. This fact is the 20/80 rule: 20 percent of the items should take up 80 percent of the time spent on inventory control. The remaining 80 percent should only take up 20 percent of that time.

Many times in a small business, collecting essential data and calculating an inventory policy on a particular item in stock can be exceptionally difficult and expensive. Frequently, the cost of developing this policy is greater than the cost savings it can provide. Therefore, businesses seldom create a policy for each item carried in stock. Most companies have items that contribute very little to the profits and growth of the business, while others constitute a tremendous portion of the income. It is for this reason that the ABC Method of Inventory Control was developed and is used. The ABC Inventory Model divides all items into three basic divisions. Class A represents the large income items, Class B represents the middle income items, and Class C represents the low profit items.

Class A contains only 25 percent of the inventory items but contributes 78 percent of the total dollar value. Class B contains another 25 percent of the items, but constitutes only about 15 percent of the total dollar value. Class C, which contains 50 percent of the entire inventory, constitutes only 7 percent of the total dollar value. (See Figure 15–1.) Therefore, Class A should be viewed as having the most potential profits and should be handled much more in detail and concern. Tight inventory control is also used in this class. The Class B items are of

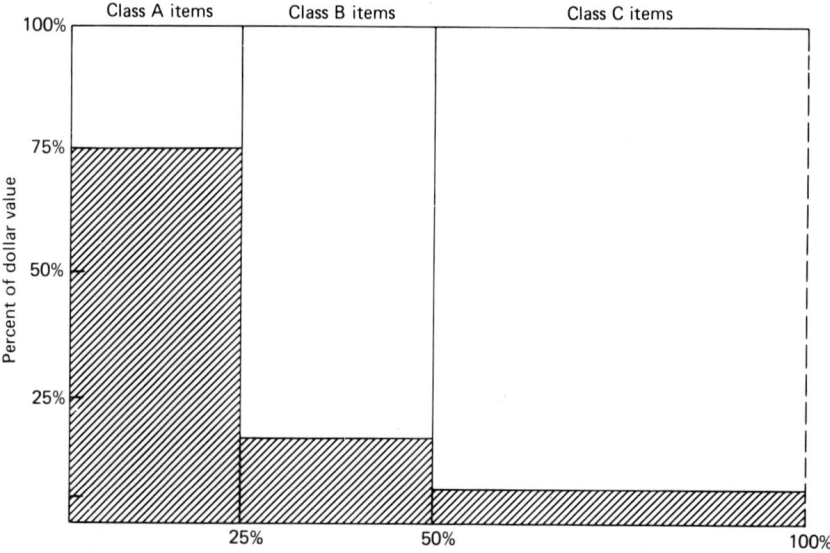

Figure 15–1.

Table 15-2. ABC Method Illustrated

ITEM	ANNUAL SALES (UNITS)	COST	ANNUAL USAGE VOLUME	ABC CLASS
AAA	50	$ 2.50	$ 125	C
ABC	6,000	0.05	300	C
DEF	800	60.00	48,000	A
GHI	10,000	3.00	30,000	A
ZZZ	100	0.50	50	C
DDD	400	8.00	3,200	B
RRR	25,000	0.10	2,500	B

less concern but they are reviewed every three to six months. Class C items do not require close control and inventory checks should be used only once or twice a year.

To use the ABC method, prepare a list giving the annual sales (in units) of each item and its cost. Multiply this out to determine the annual usage volume. (See Table 15-2.) Now rank those items. The largest usage volume items are Class A items, and deserve careful attention. The smallest usage volume items are Class C items, and need very little attention. Those in the middle are Class B items, and should receive moderate attention.

Class A items represent the majority of inventory value, and reductions in average units carried will produce substantial effects on total inventory value. Thus it is typical to order less items at a time when they are "A" units, and to order more often. Where there are price breaks based on quantity, this may still be possible.

For Class C items, an increase in average inventory will not affect the total inventory figure much, so they can be ordered in large quantities on an infrequent basis. For example, an annual order of paper clips could be placed.

Exceptions to the ABC Method of Inventory Control as developed here can always be made. It might be desirable to treat all items in one class of product (for example, machine screws in a hardware store) as if they were just one item. It is also reasonable to group items together if they are very closely related in use, such as all the chemicals required for a particular batch of photo developing. If there is an extremely large setup cost associated with a particular item, it would be prudent to take steps to order it less often and in greater quantity per order.

economic order quantity

The ABC method produces an ordering for inventory monitoring, but it does not suggest actual order quantities. A more powerful tool for inventory control is the Economic Order Quantity (EOQ). The formula for EOQ is:

$$EOQ = \sqrt{\frac{2SD}{I}}$$

S = Setup or order cost per order
D = Annual demand (equal to annual usage value in ABC method) in dollars
I = Inventory holding factor (typically around 0.20)

Applying this formula to the items in Table 15–2 produces Table 15–3. Note that the items coded as "C" are ordered a maximum of 3 times a year, while the "A" items are ordered more than 25 times each year. This implies that much closer attention is being paid to the Class A items, and that much less of them is being carried relative to annual demand. The Class B items fall in between the Class A and Class C items, which is what would be expected.

There are many variations on the basic EOQ model to account for stock-out costs, safety stocks, variable price structures, seasonal demand, and so on. These can be found in any standard text on operations management. What is important to remember about the EOQ method is that it is just a tool for analysis, not a hard-and-fast rule. It would be dangerous to rely on EOQ data without doing any additional checking on inventory levels.

Table 15–3. Economic Order Quantities for Items in Table 15–2*

ITEM	ANNUAL USAGE VOLUME	EOQ	ORDERS/YEAR
AAA	$ 125	$ 79	2
ABC	300	122	3
DEF	48,000	1,549	31
GHI	30,000	1,225	25
ZZZ	50	50	1
DDD	3,200	400	8
RRR	2,500	354	7

*These calculations assume an order cost of $5.00 per order, and an inventory holding factor of 20 percent per year (0.20). The values given in the EOQ column have been rounded off to the nearest whole number.

visual inventory control systems

There are three basic inventory control systems that can be readily adapted to small business use: the perpetual inventory method, the periodic inventory method, and the two-bin method.

1. The perpetual inventory method. The perpetual inventory method is the most accurate method because it provides the most data. In a perpetual inventory system every transaction affecting an item is logged. Cards may be purchased that will facilitate this record-keeping. Perpetual inventory requires a great deal of paper work, especially for very active items. It is often placed in a computer.

2. The periodic inventory method. The periodic inventory system is just what the name implies; it is the taking of inventory on a periodic basis—for example, monthly. It is only accurate at the point at which the inventory is taken, and is not recommended for highly volatile items. It requires that inventory transactions be halted during the inventory-taking period, or that they be taken into account. A periodic inventory, or physical inventory, should be taken once a year or more regardless of the inventory control system used.

A variation on the periodic inventory is the flagging of individual items in inventory, by placing a tag on every twentieth or so item. By monitoring these tags, a reasonable approximation to actual inventory usage can be gotten, at considerably less effort. This system requires that items be used in order, however, or its purpose is defeated.

3. The two-bin method. The two-bin method is one well suited for class C items, In it, two bins of the items are maintained. When the first one empties and the second is begun, it is time to reorder. Since the two-bin method usually requires a larger average inventory, it is well suited for low usage value items. The second bin is often much smaller than the first one, to hold enough of the item to last until the next order arrives. One problem with the two-bin method is making sure that the empty first bin is reported properly, so that the replacement order can be placed.

the out-of-stock problem

The other side of having too much inventory is having too little, and running out of items. This can be an annoyance to customers. With an ABC system, close monitoring of Class A items can help prevent stock-outs on high dollar volume items. The infrequent stock-out of a low dollar volume item is of less concern. There is a middle ground, between too much and too little inventory, that is the level most desired. Unfortunately, there are no formulas to predict this level. It must be arrived at by conscious decision-making on the part of the small business owner. There may be items that are, as a matter of policy, never allowed to be out of stock, because of their importance to customers, or to maintain a certain standard of performance.

Computers

A computer may be thought of as a cross between an adding machine and a filing cabinet. It is able to perform calculations at speeds in the millions of instructions per second. It is also capable of storing large amounts of information, with memory capacity of 100 million or more characters within easy reach.

The first business applications placed in computers were financial ones, accounting, payroll, billing, and so on. Compared with the ones of today, these computers were relatively slow and very expensive. One byproduct of the space age has been the modern high-speed electronic computer. It is possible to purchase a complete computer system for a small business for less than $30,000. A widely known electronics store is selling a computer system for under $500.

computer system components

There are two separate items to consider in a computer system. The first is the actual machinery being purchased, called hardware. The other is the set of instructions for the hardware and the directions as to what is to be done and how, called software, or programming.

hardware   Most computer makers aiming at the small business market have prepared package systems of computer hardware, sized to meet several levels of needs. These are generally referred to as Small Business Computer Systems (SBCS). Many have been packaged into desk-like configurations, with built-in keyboards for entering data into the computer. A typical Small Business Computer System would have the following items (see Figure 15–2):

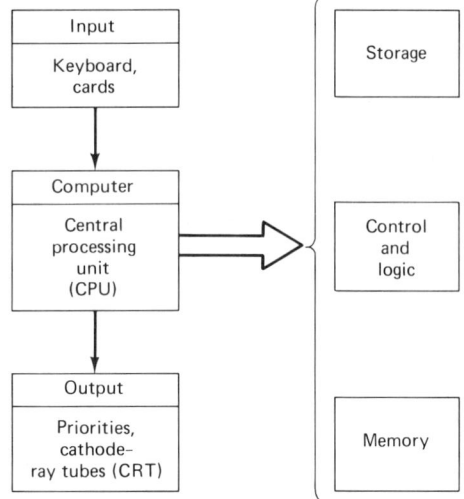

Figure 15–2. *The computer structure.*

    1. The computer itself. The computer is often referred to as the processor, or CPU (Central Processing Unit). It is composed of the high-speed electronic circuitry needed to perform the various instructions to be given.

    2. Memory. There are two kinds of memory present in most computer systems. One is called primary storage, and it consists of very fast electronic circuits that will hold a certain amount of information, usually limited to the actual instructions being performed in a program. The other type of memory is called secondary storage, and it consists of a larger quantity of somewhat slower (and hence cheaper) memory, often stored on a device called a magnetic disc, which is rather like a combination of a tape recorder and a record player.

    3. An input device. It is necessary that there be some way of entering the data into the computer. The typical SBCS uses a keyboard like a typewriter's. Many also have a ten-key numeric keyboard, similar to one found on an adding machine, to allow the operator to put in data more comfortably.

    4. An output device. Most SBCSs actually have two output devices. One of them is a television screen, which can display a limited amount of data. It is possible to call up information about a particular customer or item and display it on this screen. In addition, since some form of printed output is usually desirable, most computer systems have a printer attached to them, capable of printing at speeds ranging from 50 lines per minute to 300 lines per minute or more.

5. A removable storage device. One necessary feature in a computer is the ability to remove data from the machine and store it for safekeeping. This is usually called keeping a backup copy, and it is a prime requirement of a successful computer system. The computer system may use a type of magnetic tape, similar to a cassette or eight-track tape deck for this backup device. On some systems it is possible to remove one or more of the magnetic disc units. A spare disc can be placed into the computer to have information copied onto it, then it can be removed and placed in a safe location. It is desirable for this information to be kept in a different location from the computer, in case there is a fire or other disaster.

software

The computer is not useful until it is told what to do. Along with the hardware, it is necessary to buy or write a series of programs instructing the computer to perform each of the applications to be placed on the computer system. Many small business owners are dismayed at the high cost of these programs, which can possibly exceed the cost of the computer hardware. It is not unreasonable for each application (such as payroll, general ledger, accounts receivable, and so on) to cost several thousand dollars.

There are several sources for these application packages. The maker of the SBCS will generally have many of these applications programmed and ready to go. Other companies (called software houses) also prepare packages for some of these computer systems. Of course, it is possible to hire programming experts to write these programs directly for the company, but a good computer programmer can demand a $20,000 salary. In many cases, the computer maker or software house will be willing to write the application specifically designed to meet the exact needs of a particular business. These custom software packages are generally more expensive than those already written, but may generate the precise information needed, whereas the pre-written ones may either leave out needed items or include unwanted ones.

There is also an item called an operating system, which is usually billed separately from the hardware and applications programs. It is almost invariably written by the computer maker, and acts as a go-between. It is, in fact, a special type of software, and can usually be expected to add a few thousand dollars to the overall price tag.

taking on a new computer

When a small business owner decides to buy a computer, it does not just arrive the next day. Manufacturers generally quote lead times of 60 to 180 days from the time the order is placed until the equipment arrives. If custom programs are to be developed, it may take an additional couple of weeks or months until they are ready.

There will have to be a place prepared for the new computer. It will have special power requirements, and may need an air filter and air conditioner. Computers are somewhat sensitive to temperature extremes and dirty air. Large computers are often put in specially prepared rooms with controlled environments.

A decision will have to be made as to who is to run the computer. Although most SBCSs are advertised as being usable by any employee, in general there will be some training needed before the computer can be used intelligently and correctly. All the people who will use the computer will require some of that training, in various degrees. Many companies find that it is easier to hire someone to enter data into the computer and run it than to train an existing employee to fill that job.

One problem that may surface is resistance to the computer. People fear computers, although such fear is usually unjustified. Computers seldom cause a reduction in employees. regardless of common opinion. The more common case in the small business is that the computer allows the business to continue growing without increasing the number of employees as much as would have been required without the computer. This savings in payroll can pay for the computer in a matter of a couple of years. The key to preventing computer resistance is understanding and participation. Employees should be told what the computer is to do, and why. Where possible, they should be involved in the design of the computer programs, especially where the employees are the primary users of the information that the computer is to supply. A minor modification in input or report format can change the computer from a feared object to a highly useful tool. This is especially true when part of the computer's task is to rapidly prepare information that has been very time consuming to gather. In one example, the saving grace to the computer was its ability to prepare the monthly account statements in a couple of hours, whereas before the computer, several secretaries had spent the first week of each month typing statements. Not only was this dull task eliminated, but the statements were available several days earlier.

The actual task of converting to the computer system may take several weeks or more. Customer files of names and addresses, along with account history data, must be entered into the computer when it first arrives. This data must then be checked for accuracy. It is desirable to run the computer for a period while maintaining the old manual system to check that both sets of data are the same. Computers are sometimes brought into use in several stages, computerizing one operation or part of one operation at a time. The actual conversion period can last as long as several years.

living with the computer

There are two trains of thought usually found in dealing with computerized information. The first is the notion that "the computer could not have made a mistake." The second is the notion that the computer will really mess things up.

Neither of these is completely true. Most "computer mistakes" can be attributed to someone putting the wrong data into the computer in the first place. Computers are not very smart—they cannot detect errors that are obvious to humans. If a name is spelled wrong when fed into the computer, the computer may never find it when searching for it. When the computer actually does make a mistake, it is usually caused by an equipment failure, and it causes more than inaccurate bills—it generally causes the computer to stop working altogether.

The occasional hardware failure is the most aggravating part of living with the computer. If the computer is completely down—that is, totally inoperable—there is nothing that can be done until the repairperson arrives. Information that would normally go into the computer must wait for it to be fixed, and information that would normally be retrieved from the computer is temporarily unavailable.

The value of making backup copies of vital data is proved the first time it becomes necessary to access the backup data. This can be caused by a hardware failure, or by the entry of wrong data into the computer of such a nature that the best remedy is to go back and try it again.

Service is an important part of a computer system, and a service contract is a necessity. The annual cost of this service contract will depend on the size of the system, but can easily be $3,000 or more per year. The hours of service are usually flexible; the more hours of service availability one wants, the more one must pay. In larger cities, it is sometimes possible to contract a firm specializing in computer maintenance, but the usual course is to purchase maintenance from the computer maker.

what can a computer do for a small business?

To understand what a computer can do for a small business, it is also important to understand what it cannot do. Computers can only do what they are told (programmed) to do. If they are given rules, they will follow them blindly, and to the letter. Computers can be used to enforce policy decisions (such as credit limits). They can be used to handle accounting records, billings, inventory, and expenses. They can be used to keep track of complex situations, and to analyze enormous amounts of data. They are usually much more accurate than human calculators, and much more patient. Computers can be used to eliminate the boring and time-consuming tasks in a business, or to lessen their intensity. They can provide nearly immediate access to voluminous amounts of data, locate data that would be impossible to find in a conventional storage file, and provide answers to questions that would otherwise be unanswerable.

Once a computer is set up, however, it is difficult to go back and change the way it works, or at least very expensive to do so. A great deal of foresight is required in setting up the computer and in anticipating the future of the business and its information requirements.

The best use of the computer, however, is usually in eliminating the unnecessary information while finding the vital information. This is called management by exception, and allows managers and employees to concentrate on the exceptional cases. The computer, for example, could easily provide the ordered list for the ABC Method of Inventory Control. Moreover, it is usually possible to select these exception criteria as desired. A manager could request a list of all customers with outstanding balances over sixty days or in excess of $5,000 and receive the information from the computer in a matter of minutes. This flexibility to choose what information is important and what is trivial is the most important part of a computer. The days of the 100-page daily status report are over, or at least they should be. With a computer, small business owners can select the items they wish to study further, and in so doing they can choose the way they want to manage their businesses.

CASE STUDY: Building Contractor

Brent started his building contractor company about fifteen years ago, after six years of service as an apprentice carpenter, a supervisor, and then a general contractor. When he started his own company, he was able to do everything by himself. He was able to establish his own bids and perform the work to accomplish or satisfy the contract. Today, due to the specialization and complexity of the building industry, there is a need for extensive record keeping and subcontracting work. Automation has caused several problems for Brent. Several of his competitors have moved to computerized bidding procedures, and he was recently unable to obtain several bids.

Brent's construction firm has been involved in several builder–developer projects, including a 104-apartment building complex, during the last year. These projects required an extensive use of subcontracts and work with other small businesses.

Brent has recently found it extremely difficult to develop accurate calculations for big bids, which must include the cost of materials, labor, overhead, bond agreements, subcontracts (from twelve to twenty subcontractors, electricians, roofing, plumbing, heating, and so on), plus an additional cost for profit.

Several of his competitors now use extensive computer packages to develop bar charts for effective scheduling procedures and to develop critical path networks to show a plan or diagram that may be used to illustrate which construction steps come first and the time required to complete each step and their interrelationships. The computers are also used for financial control, accounting, purchasing, cash flow, and bid development.

Question

How might Brent best utilize advanced technology and computers to help improve his business dealings, control his inventory, and compete with his fellow building contractors?

Chapter Questions:

1. Discuss the different stages of the purchasing process and the importance of each stage.
2. Why are purchasing discounts important?
3. Discuss the use of the ABC Method of Inventory Control.
4. What is the 80/20 rule?
5. Discuss the basic operations of a computer system.
6. When would a computer system be of value in a small business?

16

Photo courtesy of Irene Springer, Prentice-Hall, Inc.

PRICING

Chapter Objectives:

1. To be able to distinguish between elastic and inelastic goods.
2. To learn how to calculate markups and markdowns, as either a percentage of cost or a percentage of retail price.
3. To learn how to construct a break-even chart.
4. To be able to explain the strategies of skimming or penetration pricing.
5. To identify other concerns that may influence pricing decisions.

> *The real price of everything, what everything really costs to the man who wants to acquire it, is the toil and trouble of acquiring it.*
>
> *Adam Smith*

INCIDENT: Ray's plans for his new business are coming along just fine. He has been offered the exclusive rights to distribute a new type of insect killer in North America. He assisted in the testing of the product and in the certification process required to clear it for sale in the United States. He knows that the product is a very good one.

Ray has great plans for his new company. He feels that he will need at least five or six full-time salespeople and a real crackerjack sales manager. He feels he ought to be able to sell at least one million cans of the product in the first year alone—possibly even more!

The main problem bothering Ray is what price to charge his customers and what price to suggest for retail sales. He knows the chemical costs from the manufacturer, and thinks it ought to sell on the retail market at about $10 for a quart can. The real question is one of markup; how much of a markup should he retain for his company, and how much of a markup should he allow the retailers? If he sets the suggested retail price too high, will that affect the sales of the new product? How can he allocate his costs for office help and warehouse space? Can he charge different prices to different customers? At what price should he sell it outside of North America?

Before any merchant places goods on a shelf, someone has made a decision as to what prices to charge. Many manufacturers provide suggested retail prices as a guideline to merchants in setting prices. A doctor must decide the value of his or her services to patients. *Every* business manager, whether the business is large or small, must at some time face the issue of deciding prices.

For some small merchants, the decision may be easy—just accept the suggested retail prices provided by the manufacturer. However, this option leaves the business owner at the mercy of the manufacturer. If the price is insufficient to generate a profit, the business could fail. If it is much higher than the competition, no one will buy. There could be local factors, such as store rental, that might not have been considered by the manufacturer when suggesting the prices.

The small manufacturer faces a more difficult task. In addition to establishing the prices to be charged to retailers, the suggested retail price will have to be developed. Thus, the pricing decision must be considered from two different viewpoints; that of the manufacturer and that of the retailer.

In the service industry, there is no suggested price on which to fall back. Each individual business is left on its own in setting prices. Competition may prove to be an overriding factor here.

Economic Factors

Regardless of the nature of the business, a sensible approach to pricing decisions can be used. There are at least two factors—demand and elasticity—that can be used to establish a rough estimate of price, after which it can be refined into a final price. With these factors to work with, some, although certainly not all, of the entrepreneurial risk associated with pricing can be eliminated.

demand

The quantity of a product that will be bought is closely related to the price that will be paid for it. This is easy to demonstrate. Suppose you need to buy a pair of socks. If you are desperate, you might pay ten dollars for a pair, if that is all you can find. Under more normal conditions, you might go into a store that sells socks for $3 a pair, and buy two pairs. If you had found them in a different store at $2 a pair, you might have bought four pairs. At $1.50 a pair, you might have purchased six pairs of socks. The quantity you purchase depends on the price you must pay. More importantly, the lower the price, the more money you are willing to spend overall!

In theory, one could look for this relationship between price and quantity for each customer and set prices accordingly. However, in actual practice it would be an impossible task to develop all these relationships, which are called demand curves. It is also unnecessary.

elasticity

From demand curves, economists derive a factor that relates the change in quantity purchased to the price charged. This factor is called the price elasticity of demand. If there is a strong reaction to a price change, the item is called price elastic. When prices are increased for an elastic item, the sales will decrease dramatically. Similarly, if the price is decreased, the sales will increase substantially.

The opposite of a price elastic item is an inelastic item. In this case, the reaction to a price change is less dramatic. A price increase still results in a sales decrease, but the impact of the sales decrease will be offset by the increased revenue from each item sold. This gives a rule of thumb that may be useful to the small business owner: To increase sales revenue, increase prices for inelastic items and decrease them for elastic ones (see Figure 16–1).

If the price of an inelastic item is increased sufficiently, it will begin to behave in an elastic fashion. In other words, whether an item can be considered elastic or inelastic depends on the price range under consideration. In actual practice, many goods can be considered elastic or inelastic only. When making a pricing decision, one thing which must be considered is whether the item is primarily elastic or inelastic, as this will suggest a general direction for pricing. In many cases, essential goods and services are elastic, while luxuries are inelastic. One can probably survive without a two-dollar eclair, but when one needs a plumber, one *needs* a plumber!

It could also be said that expensive items are more inelastic than inexpensive items. While you might not notice any difference if a 19¢ pen is increased to 29¢, you would be very sensitive if a $6,000 car was repriced at $9,000.

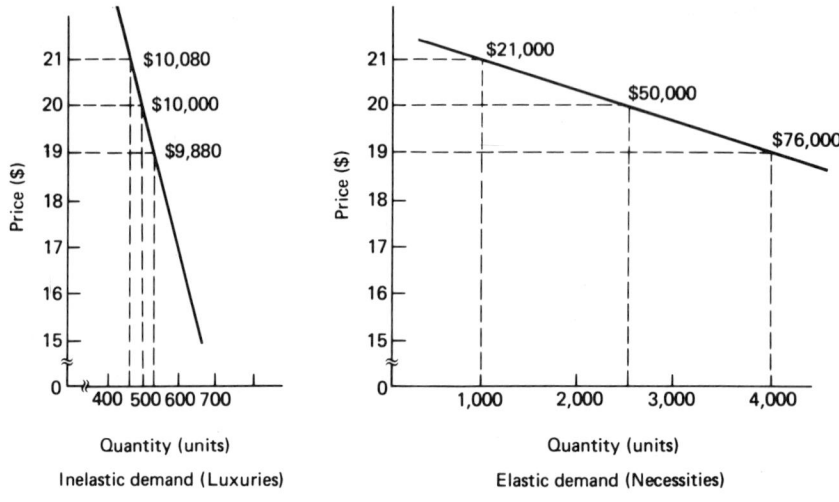

Figure 16-1. *Consumer demand—inelastic and elastic*

SUCCESS STORY: John D. Rockefeller, Sr.

John Davison Rockefeller, Sr., was born on a farm at Richford, in Tioga County, New York, on July 8, 1839, the second of the six children of William A. and Eliza (Davison) Rockefeller. The family lived in modest circumstances.

When he was a boy, the family moved to Moravia and later to Owego, New York, before going west to Ohio in 1853. The Rockefellers bought a house in Strongsville, near Cleveland, and young John entered Central High School in Cleveland. He left high school in 1855 to take a short business course at Folsom Mercantile College. He completed the six-month course in three months and, after looking for a job for six weeks, was employed as assistant bookkeeper by Hewitt & Tuttle, a small firm of commission merchants and produce shippers. Young Rockefeller was not paid until after he had worked there three months, when Mr. Hewitt gave him $50 (which figured out to $3.57 a week) and told him that his salary was being increased to $25 a month. A few months later he became cashier and bookkeeper.

In 1859, with $1,000 he had saved and another $1,000 borrowed from his father, Rockefeller formed a partnership in the commission business with another young man, Maurice B. Clark. In that same year the petroleum industry was born, with the drilling of the first oil well at Titusville in western Pennsylvania.

John Rockefeller and Maurice Clark went into the oil business as refiners in 1863. Together with a new partner, Samuel Andrews, who had some refining experience, they built and operated an oil refinery under the company name of Andrews, Clark & Co. The refineries of that day were small and simple operations, nothing like the huge complex plants of today. The firm also continued in the commission business. In 1865 the partners, now five in number, decided to sell the refinery to whichever of them bid the highest. Rockefeller bought it for $72,500, sold out his other interests and, with Andrews, formed Rockefeller & Andrews.

Rockefeller's stake in the oil industry increased as the industry itself expanded, spurred by the rapidly spreading use of kerosene for lighting. In 1870 he organized The Standard Oil Company, with his brother William, Samuel Andrews, Henry M. Flagler, S.V. Harkness and others. By 1872 Standard Oil had purchased and thus controlled nearly all the refining firms in Cleveland, plus two refineries in the New York City area.

It was estimated that Standard Oil owned three-fourths of the petroleum business in the United States in the 1890s. In addition to being the head of Standard, Rockefeller was the owner of iron mines and timberlands and had investments in various manufacturing, transportation and other companies.

Rockefeller's philanthropic gifts amounted to $531 million. The organizations which received them were many and varied, with the principal items being The Rockefeller Foundation, $182,851,000; General Education Board, $129,209,000; Laura Spelman Rockefeller Memorial, $73,985,000; Rockefeller Institute for Medical Research (now The Rockefeller University), $59,931,000.

Rockefeller died on the morning of May 23, 1937, at The Casements, his home in Ormond Beach. He was 97 years old. He was buried in Lakeview Cemetery, Cleveland.

Mathematical Factors

markups

A markup is the difference between the cost of a product to the business and its selling price. If a pair of shoes costs the shoe store $30 (wholesale price) and sells for $50 (retail price), the markup on that pair of shoes is $20 ($50 − $30 = $20). That markup helps to pay the rent for the shoe store, the salaries of the salespeople, the electric bill, the phone bill, and so on. It also represents a certain amount of profit to the shoe store. If there is no profit, the price of the shoes is too low and the shoe store is unable to stay in business.

Markups are most commonly expressed in terms of a percentage figure, as a percentage of the cost, called a markup on cost, or more often as a percentage of the retail price, called a markup on retail. The pair of shoes with the $20 markup has the following markup percentages:

$$\text{Markup on retail} = \frac{\$20}{\$50} \times 100 = 40\%$$

$$\text{Markup on cost} = \frac{\$20}{\$30} \times 100 = 66\tfrac{2}{3}\%$$

Many pocket calculators now offer keys that can perform markup calculations on cost or retail. Although these devices take the drudgery out of these calculations, it is important for the student of small business to know the relationship between markup on cost and markup on retail and how these markups are calculated. This is illustrated in Table 16–1.

The important thing to remember about markup on cost versus markup on retail is that the markup on cost, as a percentage, is always greater than the corresponding markup on retail. Clothing is commonly marked up 100 percent on cost, which is equivalent to a 50 percent markup on the retail price.

markdowns

A markdown is a reduction of a retail price, usually done in order to improve the sales of the product. It is common for clothing stores to mark down items in order to clear them out, especially at the end of the season or when only a few items of a particular style remain. Markdowns are usually expressed as a percent of the retail price. A 20 percent markdown on an $8 blouse is $1.60, giving a sale price of $6.40 (20% of $8 = $1.60; $8 − $1.60 = $6.40). If a further 10 percent markdown is

Table 16–1. The Relationship between Markup on Cost and Markup on Retail.

% MARKUP ON COST	% MARKUP ON RETAIL
10.00	9.09
11.11	10.00
20.00	16.67
25.00	20.00
30.00	23.08
33.33	25.00
40.00	28.57
42.86	30.00
50.00	33.33
60.00	37.50
66.67	40.00
70.00	41.18
75.00	42.86
80.00	44.44
90.00	47.37
100.00	50.00
125.00	55.56
150.00	60.00
175.00	63.64
200.00	66.67
233.33	70.00
300.00	75.00
400.00	80.00
500.00	83.33
900.00	90.00

*The relationship between markup on retail and markup on cost can be found by the following two equations:

$$\% \text{ Markup on cost} = \frac{\% \text{ Markup on retail}}{100\% - \% \text{ Markup on retail}}$$

$$\% \text{ Markup on retail} = \frac{\% \text{ Markup on cost}}{100\% + \% \text{ Markup on cost}}$$

needed, the resulting price will be $5.76, since 10 percent of the reduced price of the item is the amount of the second markdown (10% of $6.40 = $.64; $6.40 − $.64 = $5.76).

cost-plus analysis

Cost-plus analysis is one of the most commonly used methods of determining price. This method adds a profit margin, and any other necessary expense to the basic cost of the item to obtain a specific price (see Table 16–2).

If the price is to be set by a standard markup, some analysis is required to determine the percentage to be used. (See Table 16–2.) There are three techniques that can be used to arrive at the markup margin: the traditional approach, the contribution approach, and the absorption approach.

Table 16–2. Cost-Plus Analysis

COST	+	MARKUP	=	PRICE
Of products Of materials		Percentage of cost Percentage of price Profits Expenses		

The traditional approach. The traditional approach uses a fixed percentage applied to the cost of the product. It is most often used in a retail environment. Many clothing stores mark up 100 percent from their cost; grocery stores mark up 25 percent to 35 percent from their costs. The danger in the traditional approach is that there is always a risk that the markup will be insufficient for a given merchant, even though it may be the industry norm.

The contribution approach. The contribution approach is to gather all the costs directly associated with the sale. The key to identifying contributing costs is to ask the question, "If the sale is not made, does this particular cost go away?" If the answer is yes, then that item is a contributing cost. For example, if a shoe salesperson is paid a percentage commission on his or her sales, the commission is a contributing cost to the sale. However, store rental continues regardless of the sale of one particular pair of shoes, so it is not a contributing cost. The sum of all the contributing costs is called the *base cost*.

All other costs are considered indirect, and are to be covered through the markup. The assumption made is that overall volume will be large enough so that the markups on all the items sold will add up to equal the sum of all the indirect costs, as well as providing some profit.

The absorption approach. In the absorption approach, the variable selling and administrative costs are deliberately excluded from the base cost, since there will be a percentage markup on each item that will cover those items. Instead, the indirect costs are absorbed into the base cost. In order to do this, one must determine an approximate sales volume. For example, if the annual rent for the shoe store is $15,000, and if approximately ten thousand pairs of shoes will be sold during the year, then under the absorption approach, a cost of $1.50 for store rental should be absorbed into the base cost for each pair of shoes:

$$\frac{\text{Rent (expense)}}{\text{Units sold}} = \text{Additional absorption cost}$$

$$\frac{\$15,000}{10,000} = 1.50$$

A conservative estimate of sales volume is better than an optimistic one, since if volume fails to reach the goal, the indirect costs will not be fully met for the year. If the goal is exceeded, profit will be somewhat higher than forecast—hardly an unpleasant experience.

The contribution approach is more suitable for a manufacturing environment, while the absorption approach is more often adapted for retail purposes. In both cases, however, serious thought as to the isolation and determination of all costs—fixed or variable, direct or indirect—must be made. Since this is not an easy task, many business owners opt for the traditional approach and hope for the best.

Suppose a clothing manufacturer can make a pair of jeans for $4 worth of materials and labor. In other words, that $4 represents the variable costs for each pair of jeans. The factory and machines cost $50,000 a year to rent and maintain; there are also electricity and phone costs, plus a small office staff (one secretary). The manufacturer has a contract with Sears to sell them all the jeans he can make at $8 a pair. How many pairs of jeans must be made a year in order to break-even? How many pairs must be made in order to realize a $10,000 profit? If 10,000 pairs are made, will the manufacturer make or lose money?

break-even analysis

These are questions that can be answered with break-even analysis. Break-even analysis can be very useful in making pricing decisions because it illustrates the approximate profit or loss that arises from various sales levels. By finding the desired profit total, the necessary sales goal can be calculated.

There are two ways to use break-even analysis: a graphical approach, or an algebraic (mathematical) one. The graphical approach is illustrated in Figure 16–2, in which a line has been drawn at the $50,000 mark to show the amount of fixed costs in the clothing manufacturing example. The variable costs are illustrated by a line beginning at the origin on the graph; for each additional unit made, the costs increase by $4. If we add these two costs together to produce the total costs, we get a line that starts at the $50,000 point. This line is marked as the total costs curve. A line starting from the origin represents the sales revenue curve; for each additional unit sold, the revenue increases by $8. We can use the resulting graph as follows: to find the profit from any sales level, go to that sales level on the horizontal axis of the graph, and follow it up the graph to the levels of the cost and sales revenue curves. The distance between these two points is the profit or loss arising from that

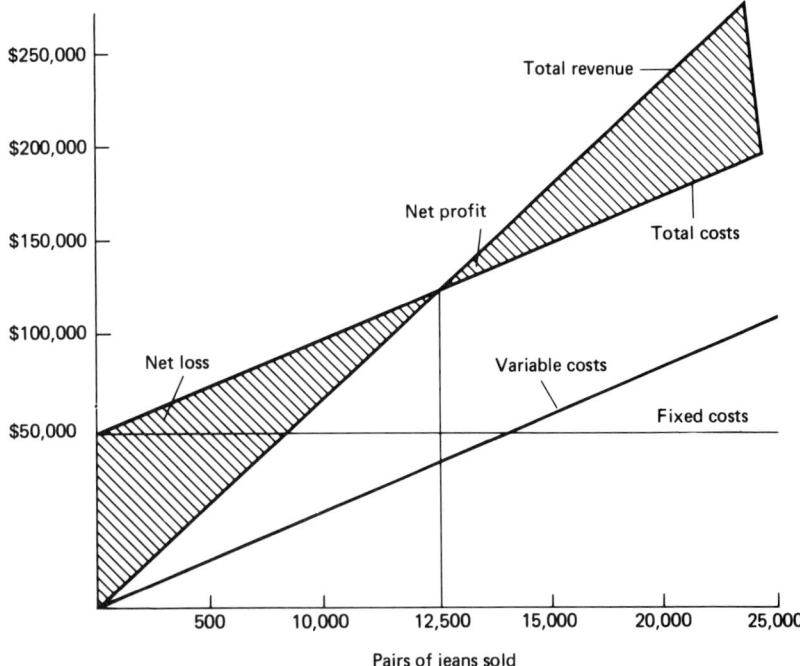

Figure 16-2. *A break-even chart*

sales volume. This graph is called a break-even chart, and is a very useful tool for small business owners.

It is not necessary to draw a break-even chart in order to use the information it presents. A little high-school algebra can be used to find out the break-even point. Suppose that P equals the sales price, N equals the number of units sold (sales volume), F equals the fixed costs, and V equals the variable costs (per unit). The break-even formula is as follows:

$$F + V \times N = P \times N$$

To find the break-even point, substitute the appropriate figures and solve for N. In our example:

$$50{,}000 + 4N = 8N$$
$$50{,}000 = 8N - 4N = 4N$$
$$N = 50{,}000 \div 4 = 12{,}500$$

If we add profits to the formula, the sales volume to produce any desired profit level can be calculated.

$$\text{Profit} + F + V \times N = P \times N$$

To produce $10,000 in profit, use the equation above:

$$\$10{,}000 + 50{,}000 + 4N = 8N$$
$$60{,}000 = 8N - 4N = 4N$$
$$N = 60{,}000 \div 4 = 15{,}000$$

So 15,000 pairs of jeans must be made in order to realize a $10,000 profit.

To find the profit for a particular sales volume, simply substitute the known information into the formula:

$$\text{Profit} + 50{,}000 + 4 \times 10{,}000 = 8 \times 10{,}000$$
$$\text{Profit} + 90{,}000 = 80{,}000$$
$$\text{Profit} = 80{,}000 - 90{,}000 = 10{,}000$$

or, Profit = $-10,000 at 10,000 units (a loss!)

Relationships Between Costs and Volume

Another way to look at the break-even formula is to consider the relationship between price and variable costs. In the case of the jeans maker, this is $8 − $4, or $4 per pair. This is called the "contribution margin," since it represents the covering of fixed costs, just as the contribution costs did in the cost-plus analysis earlier.

This has an additional use. Suppose the jeans maker loses the contract with Sears but K-Mart offers a contract on a one-time basis to produce 10,000 pairs of jeans at $6 each. Should the jeans maker accept it? The answer is "yes." If this is the only business available this year, the jeans maker will take a loss of $30,000. If the jeans maker does not accept the contract, and has *no* business during the year, a loss of $50,000 will be taken. Thus, the losses can be reduced by $20,000 by taking the contract offered by K-Mart. This will enable the jeans maker to keep busy while searching for a newer, more profitable contract elsewhere. The contribution margin on the K-Mart contract is $6 − $4, or $2 per pair. Thus, each pair of jeans made under this deal will contribute $2 towards the covering of fixed costs. These fixed costs will occur *whether or not any jeans are made at all!*

The contribution margin can also be used to calculate the break-even point. Since each unit produced will contribute equally towards the covering of fixed costs, the break-even point equals the fixed costs divided by the contribution margin:

$$\frac{\text{Fixed costs}}{\text{Contribution Margin}} = \text{Break-even point}$$

or,

$$\frac{\$50{,}000}{4} = 12{,}500 \text{ pairs for the jeans maker}$$

One limitation to break-even analysis is the assumption of linearity. Doubling of sales volume may not, in fact, produce a doubling of revenue, because a reduction in unit price might have been necessary to achieve the volume increase. However, for the limited range surrounding the break-even point, it will be accurate enough to serve a useful purpose. Beyond that range, assumptions of non-linearity in revenue and cost curves will have to be made.

Marketing Factors

Under the marketing approach to pricing, there are two things to consider: (1) what the consumer is willing to pay, and (2) what the consumer is likely to expect for his or her money.

Consumer willingness to pay is closely related to the concepts of demand curves and elasticity. In the marketing approach, however, this can be reduced to one simple question: Are the goods and services being provided consistent with the prices that customers expect and are willing to pay? To answer this question, small business owners or managers must examine the type of customer they wish to attract, the competition they will face, and the type of products they wish to sell.

market segments

It is important for a business owner to understand what his or her target market is: Are the customers young or old? Are they affluent or poor? What are they seeking when they enter the store? The portion of the population that the owner wants to reach is the target market or market segment.

There are five market segments that can be used to describe the target market in terms of the goods and associated services that attract customers:

1. The exclusive outlet.
2. The specialty outlet.
3. The regular (or standard) outlet.
4. The discount outlet.
5. The combined outlet.

Each of these types of outlets (or stores) will attract a different kind of customer who will expect different levels of service and who will tolerate different price levels.

The exclusive outlet. The exclusive outlet is exactly that—exclusive. It may be the sole dealer for a particular type of merchandise or service, at least within a large area. Prices will be very high, because the customers have no alternative source for that particular item. To compensate for the high prices, the customers will expect a great number of services, which can range from delivery and installation (at a stated price, or "free," with the cost built into the sales price) to special arrangements for showing merchandise to potential buyers. Repair and maintenance service is usually provided. High-fashion merchandise is often sold through exclusive outlets. Some stereo equipment is sold only through special dealers. Foreign sports cars are especially good examples of products sold through exclusive outlets.

The specialty outlet. A specialty outlet sells only one particular type of merchandise: only stereo equipment, records, jeans, or shoes, for example. The specialty store will be equipped to handle problems that may accompany the particular product. The sales staff may be trained in fitting or demonstrating the product. It would be very reasonable, for example, to expect a salesperson in a gun shop to be very familiar with different types of guns and ammunition. Furthermore, the staff of the gun shop may include specialists in particular types of guns, or experts in solving problems with guns. This additional knowledge and service is expected by the customers. Indeed, it may be the reason for the customers' presence in the first place. If a customer wants to examine a large selection of children's shoes, for example, then a children's shoe store would be the best place to go. Certain factors—selection, service, and expertise—will be strong motivating forces for attracting customers. A certain amount of value can be attached to these forces, so it will be reasonable for the specialty store to price accordingly.

The regular outlet. Most stores are regular outlets carrying a fairly broad line of merchandise. Some limitations, such as to clothing only, may be found. Department stores, hardware stores, and restaurants are all regular outlets. Traditionally, the bulk of stores were regular outlets, and the majority of all merchandise was sold by them. Pricing in a regular outlet is often based on manufacturers' suggested prices, or on competition. The services that may be offered would be fewer than in an exclusive outlet, and they would probably be priced separately from the merchandise. The trend toward shopping centers has probably caused a reduction in the number of regular outlets in recent years, especially as small businesses.

The discount outlet. The discount outlet represents the lowest-priced segment. The theory behind discounting is that the ancillary services, clerks, wide selections, deliveries, installations, repairs, and the like are eliminated in favor of a very low price. The volume generated by the lower prices is supposed to make up the difference in sales margin. Discounting is a huge business! Most discount stores carry a large range of products, from televisions to toasters, from toys to laundry supplies; clothes, appliances, records, and paints.

The combined outlet. One advantage of the combined outlet concept is that it can be applied separately to different products. A store can be a regular outlet in some products, an exclusive outlet in others, and a discount outlet in still others. Specialty stores can be exclusive dealers for particular types or brands of merchandise. Discount stores are sometimes arranged as a collection of specialty stores, loosely connected.

competition

As indicated earlier, the prices charged by competition for their goods and services is very important in making the pricing decision. Competition can be measured in terms of spatial relationships: nearby competitors and distant competitors. Competition can also be measured in terms of the nature of the competing goods: substitute (replacement) goods or alternative goods.

Nearby competitors. Nearby competitors are neighbors—stores within a certain geographical region around your business. For a lunch counter in a downtown metropolitan area, this might be only a few blocks. For a distributor, this could be several hundred square miles. The nearest competitors are the ones that must be matched in terms of price. Otherwise, customers may very well go across the street. Small differences in price will probably not be significant, since the customer's perception of the advantages and disadvantages of one business over the competition can override some small price variances.

Distant competitors. Distant competitors are those outside of the immediate region, however it is defined. The price differences between a business and its distant competitors is of less importance, although it is still worth knowing. If the price difference is significant, customers may travel the extra distance to take advantage of the price breaks available. This phenomenon is often noticeable near college campuses, where the stores that rely on the campus traffic charge significantly more for the same products compared to stores farther from campus. These stores depend on the convenience they offer to students, and take advantage of the number of students who lack automobiles.

Substitute goods. If one is selling hot dogs, then the competitors, in terms of substitute lunch vendors, are the hamburger, taco, pizza, and sandwich shops nearby. They provide a similar product—a fast lunch—probably at a comparable price. A fifty-cent taco may be considered an acceptable alternative to a seventy-five cent hot dog. Thus, the price that is charged may be held against a merchant when it is compared to direct competitors. Unfortunately, there is no simple measure of comparing the relative advantages of tacos and hot dogs, even at the same price. Furthermore, since in many instances the competition will be constantly changing, new stores opening and older ones closing, the advantages held this month could disappear next month.

Alternative goods. Someone looking for a quick lunch would not consider a five-course dinner to be a direct substitute, which would represent a totally different alternative for satisfying the basic need—hunger. In a sense, *all* of the stores nearby are competition, although a clothing store may not seem like a competitor for hot dogs. Since customers have limited resources, one is competing against all other goods and services for these resources. For this reason, it is important that a sense of fairness about prices be perceived by customers.

pricing and product's life cycle

Many products go through a life-and-death cycle. At any point in time, the small business owner (especially the merchant) may have thousands of different products available for sale. Some of these products will be new, some will be just gaining acceptance by consumers, and some will be fully accepted products. A few will be products whose usefulness has declined, and that may soon no longer be manufactured. Pricing under the marketing philosophy requires that one know the stage in the life cycle of the product, since this may affect consumer willingness to pay.

New products. When a product is first introduced, there may be reluctance on the part of the average consumer to purchase it. It is important that new products be introduced in an organized manner. There are two pricing strategies that have been used successfully to introduce new products. These strategies, penetration pricing and skimming the cream, will be discussed later. For the moment, it is sufficient to realize that new products do require additional thought in determining the prices at which they will be introduced.

Maturing products. After the initial introduction, consumer awareness of the product should increase, assuming the product is successful and gains the acceptance of consumers. This acceptance may alter the price that the consumer will be willing to pay for the product. The strategy used to introduce the product may carry over into this second phase of the product's life cycle.

Matured products. As the product gains even more consumer acceptance, it reaches a stage of maturity. The fully matured product is most subject to the effects of competition, as the consumer is well aware of the product, its availability, and its price. Most products are fully matured products. Many will remain there indefinitely, such as pencils and pens. Pricing of fully matured products must conform to the market segment at which the business is aiming.

Declining products. The introduction of hand-held electronic calculators in the late 1960s spelled the death of the slide rule. The Model-T Ford caused the demise of the buggy industry. Technology is probably the chief cause behind declining products. A newer product is developed that completely replaces existing ones, as calculators have done to slide rules. Recognize that declining products, with their diminished usefulness, may have to be lowered in price. In the case of drastic reductions in usefulness, they may have to be sold at a loss, or even sold for scrap! Painful as this may be, it may become necessary if for no other reason than to remove the items from inventory so that they can be replaced by their successors.

Pricing in Actual Practice

In addition to the three methods of pricing analysis just discussed—economics, mathematics, and marketing—there are a large number of special practices that have evolved regarding pricing. Some of these are intended to cover special situations, such as the introduction of a new product. Others, such as odd pricing and price lining, deal with perceived consumer reactions to prices. Others are just useful tools or practices that have become commonplace in the business world.

introduction of a new product

The introduction of a new product is always surrounded by a great deal of apprehension regarding pricing. If the initial price is too high, it could cause the product to fail. If it is too low, the resulting profits could be too few to justify the expense of introducing the product. The wrong price could cause the product to fail to attract its intended target market segment.

Two separate strategies have been defined for marketing of new products, which take into account the fundamental costs of producing and marketing the product, especially any cost reductions due to large scale production. In addition, the absence or presence of direct competition is considered. These strategies are called *penetration pricing* and *skimming the cream.*

Penetration pricing. If a product is introduced into a highly competitive market, in which a large number of products are all essentially similar and are competing for consumer acceptance, a new product must penetrate the market in order to achieve success. Penetration pricing is an attempt to accomplish just that.

The new product is introduced with a price as low as can be safely allowed.

This introduction is often accompanied by a significant amount of marketing effort: advertising, special sales, and discounts. Newspaper coupons allowing a few cents off are often distributed. The overall intent is to induce potential customers to try the product once, probably because of the price incentives. If the product is acceptable, it may be adopted by the customers, which will cause additional sales. Furthermore, if the product is competing for valuable shelf space, such as in a grocery store, a high initial volume may cause the merchant to set aside, on a more permanent basis, prime shelf space for that product.

Penetration pricing is a long-range strategy. Until consumer acceptance is sufficiently large, the profits may be small—a loss may even exist. As the product matures and gains a following, it will achieve a respectable market share. At this point, the price must allow the satisfactory profit margin designated by the maker. When all this happens, the penetration strategy has been successful.

Skimming the cream. Many new products have no direct competitors, at least initially. The start-up costs for these products may be immense. This is exactly what happened in the case of the hand-held electronic calculator. The technology to produce these products was expensive. Furthermore, there was no direct substitute—the new calculators were completely different from their closest competitors, slide rules and adding machines.

Most of the calculators introduced in the past few years used the strategy called "skimming the cream." They were introduced at a high initial price, with the price quickly cascading downward. The first four-function calculators cost over $200; essentially identical ones now sell for less than $10. Fancy calculators with many functions cost over $150 in 1975, but by 1978 they were selling for under $30.

The high initial price almost definitely assured a quick return to the makers of pocket calculators. As acceptance grew and competition emerged, the increased production efficiency and strong competition forced the price down rapidly. In some cases, the prices dropped so far and so fast that some of the early calculator companies had to take a substantial loss. At least one of them went bankrupt from failure to predict and adjust to the competition prices.

Skimming the cream assumes the competition *will* emerge. If it does not, prices may have to be dropped anyway, in order to attract a larger segment of the population. It is a short-range strategy. Many of the products introduced with skimming strategies, such as the hand-held calculators, have relatively short life spans. New products are introduced that make older ones obsolete. In a successful skimming strategy, the initial manufacturer makes the most profit, skimming the cream off the market.

odd pricing

There is a theory in the study of consumer behavior that some prices are considered more acceptable than others. Marketeers have called this the theory of odd pricing, or "magic pricing." If prices of 50¢ and 53¢ are considered equally acceptable by the consumer, then the price of 53¢ should be charged, since it will improve revenue and profits.

Many products are priced with the last digit of the price equal to 9, such as 59¢, 99¢, $1.59, and so forth. Eight is also a popular last digit, such as $1.98,

$19.98, and so on. This practice is also seen per-pound prices; meat will be $1.89 or $2.09 per pound.

Although research to prove that this practice is reasonable has been sketchy, it may have reached the point where it is considered "customary" by the consumer. Odd pricing would appear to conflict with the concept of demand curves and elasticity. There is one notable area that has escaped odd pricing—that of canned goods. These are usually so competitively priced that the odd prices may not be reachable. However, when these products go on sale, odd prices are usually used for the sale price.

price lining

If you have ever bought a record album, you know what a price line is. Each record in the store is usually coded with letters from A to EE, indicating the price of the album. All albums of a certain code sell at the same price. This is a good example of price lining, although the traditional example is men's clothing.

In price lining there are certain brackets into which items fall. All the shirts under $10 may be similar in quality. A $25 dress shirt will have features available only at that price. Many stores carry two or three distinct lines of products. Men's suits may sell at the $40 to $60 range (low quality), the $100 to $120 range (medium quality), and the $220 to $250 range (high quality). The gaps between these ranges are seldom filled—if you want a better suit than the $120 suit, you must go to the $200 suit.

Price lining assumes that people have a perception of the range of quality they feel they can best afford and want. Many producers cater directly to this image by marketing three grades of product: good, better, and best. There will be a small price gap between the better product and the best one. Since there is a difficulty in describing something between good and better, there is no product in that mid-range. Most price lined products appear in these sets of threes. Occasionally, another manufacturer may produce a fourth line: the budget line. This is below the good product, with rock-bottom prices and minimal features.

pre-defined prices

Many products are already priced before they reach the merchant. The price has been printed on the package, or "suggested" by the manufacturer. This practice severely limits the options open to the merchant on that product; the merchant can either sell it at that price, accepting the profit that it allows, or reprice the item to the desired price.

In the second instance, the new price cannot be more than the old price. Thus, the pre-defined price limits the amount which can be charged. In addition, the merchant cannot reduce the price indiscriminately. The image being projected must be maintained. If the regular merchant marks down a pre-priced product, this may impart a feeling of discounting. If the discounter *fails* to mark down a pre-priced item, this may destroy the feeling of discounting.

price controls

Price controls have been instituted several times during the past decade, in various forms. They are hinted at continuously, and may emerge again. Since the nature of future price controls is not known, the small business owner (who was most affected by earlier price controls) must be constantly aware of the potential dangers in price controls.

Most recent price-control techniques have revolved around a rollback to a previous price level. This level may be that of a particular date in time, or the average of a period in time. Obviously, detailed accurate records must be maintained of prices charged and price changes in order to comply with this requirement.

Some merchants have attempted to counteract this practice by raising their overall margins on products, to forestall the effects of any future price controls. The success of this practice is yet to be determined.

discriminatory prices

The Robinson-Patman Act, passed in 1936, forbids the pricing of products at different prices to competing customers unless the differences are due to "the differences in the cost of manufacture, sale of delivery resulting from the differing methods or quantities in which commodities are to such purchasers sold or delivered." The courts have interpreted this as referring to the total costs associated with the product, not just the incremental costs. Charging different prices on the basis of covering variable costs is disallowed.

The Robinson-Patman Act is concerned with identical goods and competing customers. Two merchants are allowed to charge different prices for the same product, but one merchant may not charge two different prices to competing customers for that product. In addition, many states have passed legislation dealing with prices. It is important for the merchant to be aware of these regulations and to what extent they influence his ability to set prices. Since these regulations change frequently and some, such as "fair-trade laws," have all but disappeared recently, this information must be monitored continuously.

price tags

Once the prices are set, they must be communicated to the customer. This can be done by posting signs or distributing menus, as in restaurants. In retail stores, however, many states require that most goods be individually priced. (This legislation was enacted to forestall the installation of automated checkout systems in supermarkets.)

Individual pricing requires price tags. A price tag can be a sticker with only the price, or it can contain a wealth of other information. Information that can be given on the tag includes:

1. Item's name and manufacturer.
2. Size.
3. Color.
4. Style.
5. Other identifying information.
6. Date of purchase (by the store).
7. Cost to merchant.

Many stores detach and retain part or all of the price tag to serve as an inventory control ticket. Others, most notably Sears, have installed devices that can scan the ticket and read the stock number and price, retaining this information as well as computing the bill. By including the date of purchase, the small business owner can determine which products are moving quickly, and which are poor sellers. This information can help the owner improve efficiency.

To hide information such as date of purchase and cost, the merchant will need to resort to a coding technique, burying the secret information among a forest of numbers, scrambling it in some manner to make it unrecognizable. One technique used to accomplish this is to use a sequence of letters to represent numbers. The letters usually are some easily remembered sequence. For example, consider the following sequence: RALPH JONES.

1	2	3	4	5	6	7	8	9	0
R	A	L	P	H	J	O	N	E	S

To indicate a date of May 15, 1979 the sequence SHRHOE could be used, or just HRH. Obviously, many different codes can be concocted, and there can be many ways to mix up the information. For example, if the cost of the item was $1.27, this could be indicated by OAR, reversing the digits of the price. Dummy letters can be included to prevent recognition: instead of OAR, TOXAMYRQ.

pricing in foreign markets

If the product is being exported, the price charged in other countries may be different from that charged domestically. There are several factors which must be considered in setting foreign prices: risk, discrimination, time lags, and market characteristics.

Risk. Risk is a considerable problem in selling a product locally, and it is more of one when foreign markets are considered. If the good is priced using local currency, there is the risk that the exchange rate on that currency may be unfavorable. Competition may be different in other countries, and regulations stricter. The government or economy in that nation may be less stable.

Discrimination. If a product being imported into a country competes with local products, regulations or tariffs may be enacted to favor the local products. This discrimination may raise the prices that must be charged and may alter the desirability of the imported good.

Time lags. If you are exporting a product, competitors in the importing country may be better informed about the state of the market. They can react to situations faster than you can, and it will take time for your decisions and products to reach the foreign marketplace.

Market characteristics. If one is only familiar with the local market and intended customers, that market or customer may not exist in a foreign country. Methods of selling may conflict with local customs. The ordinary business practices one is accustomed to may not exist in another country. If the target market is in an underdeveloped nation, prices may have to be lowered to avoid charges of exploitation.

geographical prices and freight charges

If you are selling or delivering a product on a national scale, the distance between you and your customers will enter the pricing decision. Many manufactured products are sold at a price that is "slightly higher west of the Rockies." Alaska and Hawaii typically have higher prices for products than do the other forty-eight states. If there is a distance factor in the market, this must be considered to be part of the pricing function.

The most common method of dealing with this problem is to charge for freight separately. Many companies use the postal service zone system to determine prices for freight. This system based on the number of miles from the buyer to the seller, and charts with concentric circles are available to illustrate this. Many mail order companies use this system, although some eliminate the freight charges on large orders. Some use a flat charge (such as $1 for postage and handling) on orders below a certain minimum amount (such as $25).

One common method for freight charges is the (FOB) charge. "Free on board" means that any freight charges up to the point designated are absorbed by the seller. The buyer is responsible for any remaining freight charges. In addition, the buyer often takes title to the goods at the point designated. FOB can be from the seller's plant, from the nearest warehouse, or at the customer's site (FOB Delivered—no freight charges). Imported goods are often billed FOB Point of Entry—the place at which they reach the country.

pricing and inflation

If the current inflationary patterns continue, anticipate a 6 percent to a 12 percent inflation in any given year. This will affect the pricing decision in several ways. As costs from suppliers increase, it will be necessary to tack these additional costs onto the prices being charged. Price controls in some types of business have made this an extremely difficult process—gas stations, for example.

One possible effect of the continued inflation over the past several years has been the desensitization to price changes on the part of the consumer. Customers have come to expect price changes each month, and so may not react to them in the traditional economic fashion.

The most certain thing that can be said about inflation is that it tends to occur in chunks, rather than smoothly. A supplier may increase all prices 5 percent, the minimum wage seems to be rising at about 10 percent per year, and rent increases generally come once a year. As a result, the small business owner must constantly be aware of the impact of inflation on prices, and must perhaps raise prices as a defensive reaction. If a markup is used, it will have to be periodically adjusted to account for changes in the relative costs of the business.

Making the Pricing Decision

All the tools and techniques given thus far in this chapter will not set prices by themselves. When faced with the need to make the pricing decision, there are four steps that can be followed:

1. Identify the pricing characteristics of the product.
2. Choose a reasonable range of prices.

3. Select a final price.
4. Monitor the results.

identify pricing characteristics   Each product has unique characteristics that determine the reasonableness of the chosen price. The economic factors can be considered: Is the item a luxury? If so, the price will probably tend to be elastic and relatively high. What target market is the business trying to attract? If it is a specialty market, the customers will expect a slightly higher price.

choose a reasonable range of prices   The economic and marketing factors will, at best, indicate a broad range of price levels. At this point, break-even analysis can be used to produce a more precise picture of the revenue needed to produce a satisfactory profit. With that information in hand, a markup margin can be determined, perhaps for application to a broad class of products. Although the best course of action for a business owner would be to make a complete analysis for each item being priced, there is seldom time to do so. Instead, he or she may have to be satisfied with dividing products into several classes and pricing each class according to a particular policy. If a skimming or penetration scheme is to be used, this must be established initially, so that the proper starting points can be determined.

select a final price   Once all the groundwork has been done, a final price must be chosen, by means of mathematical analysis or by rote application of a cost-plus analysis. At this point, competition *must* be considered. It will be next to impossible to sell products if the price is significantly higher than the competition for similar or substitutable items. However, if the price decided on is much less than the competition, perhaps something has been overlooked.

monitor the results   Many business owners probably think that the pricing decision is complete once the price tag is attached and the item is on the rack. This is not the case. If items are selling poorly, it may become necessary to take a markdown in order to get rid of the merchandise. If the costs of doing business change (and they will), it may be necessary to reprice the item in order to stay in business. If volume targets were set and the absorption approach was used to set the margin, is volume meeting the targeted level? If not, the price may have to be increased to make up the difference in absorbed overhead costs.

CASE STUDY: Tracy's

Bob Tracy wants to establish a fast-food sandwich shop in a midwestern city, and he is interested in determining the feasibility of success in that business. The business would handle a special sandwich, along with drinks and French-fried potatoes. Research has predicted that fast-food restaurants will see a high volume of sales in the 1980s. Customers may be eating at least half of their meals away from home. The market is deemed to be large and profitable.

Product description:

1. **Sandwich:** The large and small sandwiches will be made of the same ingredients, unless some ingredients are asked to be deleted by the customer. The small sandwich's bun will be four ounces plus one-half fluid ounce of the special garlic butter spread (secret recipe). For the large sandwich the sandwich bun will be eight ounces plus 1 fluid ounce of the garlic butter spread (secret recipe). The ingredients are listed as follows:

INGREDIENT LIST		AMOUNT OF INGREDIENT AND SANDWICH SIZE	
		Small	Large
Mayonnaise		1 fl. oz.	1½ fl. oz
Swiss cheese		1 oz.	2 oz.
American cheese		1 oz.	2 oz.
Cheddar cheese		1 oz.	2 oz.
Ham		2 oz.	3 oz.
Pastrami		2 oz.	3 oz.
Salami		2 oz.	3 oz.
Lettuce		2 oz.	3 oz.
Tomatoes		2 oz.	3 oz.
Black olives		¾ oz.	2 oz.
	Total weight (including bun and spread)	19.25 oz. or 1 lb. 3¼ oz.	33.5 oz. or 2 lb. 1½ oz.

2. **French-fried Potatoes:** The French-fried potatoes will be made from a commercial brand. They are frozen, Grade-A potatoes, blanched in animal fat with table salt added for cooking. These French-fried potatoes are similar in shape and size to the French-fried potatoes served in large hamburger restaurants. The portion and size will consist of four ounces for the regular order and eight ounces for the large order. The regular order of French fries will cost Bob $.088 per order and the larger order of French fries will cost Bob $.176.

>Potatoes: Frozen Grade-A potatoes
>$9.65 per 27-pound package = 432 ounces
>Serving sizes 4 ounces and 8 ounces
>Cost is $.022 per ounce
>4 ounces = $.088
>8 ounces = $.176
>Shortening: Liquid
>$32.25 per 6 quart case
>1 quart cooks 35 pounds potatoes

3. **Fountain Drinks:** The restaurant will serve four kinds of soft drinks in three different sizes—10 ounces, 14 ounces and 16 ounces.

	MATERIAL COST PER DRINK SIZE		
	10 oz. (serve 9 oz.)	14 oz. (serve 12 oz.)	16 oz. (serve 14 oz.)
Cup	$ .013	$ .017	$ .024
Drink and ice	.081	.108	.126
Cost per drink	$ .094	$ .125	$ .150

Questions

1. Determine the consumer price for the various size sandwiches, French fries, and fountain drinks.
2. Explain which pricing strategy you used in ascertaining the prices.
3. Explain what cost you will assume in determining price structures.
4. Explain which costs of business operations you would desire before determining further price structures.
5. Explain what profit picture you anticipate from this particular business.

Chapter Questions:

1. What is meant by a demand curve? By elasticity? How would these be determined? What use are they to the small business owner?
2. The text implies that the point of profit maximization is not necessarily the same as the point of revenue maximization. Why?
3. Using the information below, complete the following:

COST	MARKUP	RETAIL PRICE	MARKUP ON COST	MARKUP ON RETAIL
1.00	1.00	___	___	___
1.00	___	1.50	___	___
___	1.00	4.00	___	___
___	___	5.00	400%	___
___	.75	___	25%	___
2.50	___	___	20%	___
___	___	3.00	___	50%
___	1.25	___	___	10%
6.00	___	___	___	37.5%
1.35	0.45	___	___	___
1.25	___	2.00	___	___
___	.70	2.10	___	___
.65	___	___	60%	___
___	.47	___	___	16.67%
___	___	1.45	66.67%	___
.51	___	___	___	25%
___	.54	___	___	40%
___	___	.50	42.86%	___

4. What information can be gained from a break-even chart?
5. What is the value of knowing your competitor's prices?

6. Suppose that you have been selling a product for many years, but a new product has just been introduced that will make your product obsolete within six months. What pricing strategy might you use?

7. Suppose that you reduce the price on some products that come pre-priced. Is this a violation of the Robinson-Patman Act?

8. Suppose that your uncle sells air conditioners. He carries an economy model that sells for around $140, a medium-quality model that sells for around $250, and a top-of-the-line model that sells for around $500. He has just been offered a new model that sells for around $350. What advice would you offer him?

9. Odd pricing is not used in pricing many grocery items. Why is this so? Can you come up with other products that are not priced using odd pricing?

10. Which of the following costs would be included in the base cost under the absorption and contribution approaches?
    a. Raw cost of materials for the product.
    b. The president of the company's salary.
    c. The commission paid to the salesperson (4 percent of sales).
    d. The cost of heating the factory during the winter.
    e. Sales tax.
    f. The grease used to lubricate the machines in the factory.
    g. The cost of the packaging material used to box the product.
    h. The salaries of the clerical staff who prepare the invoices.
    i. Fire insurance for the warehouse.

11. Suppose that you run a small camera store. Define a coding technique for placing the following information on the price tag:
    a. Retail price.
    b. Manufacturer's name and model number.
    c. The date placed on the shelf in your store.
    d. The cost you paid for the item.

    If you are willing to let some of your employees know how long the item has been in stock, but not others, how could you do this?

17

Photo courtesy of Irene Springer, Prentice-Hall, Inc.

MARKETING AND MARKETING RESEARCH

Chapter Objectives:

1. To understand what marketing is and why managers are involved in it.
2. To learn how to develop a marketing strategy.
3. To know about marketing segmentation and the importance of the marketing mix.
4. To improve understanding of promotion and advertising.
5. To understand the importance of marketing research.
6. To be able to develop and perform marketing research for a small business.

He who works with his hands is a laborer;
He who works with his hands and his head
is an artisan; He who works with his hands
and his head and his heart is an artist.

P. E. Smith

INCIDENT: Tom and Jill were married only recently and have decided to start their own lawn mower sales and service business. They live in a town of 60,000 people and they are actively engaged in their church and community work. They have no children but would like to have a large family.

They have researched their business extensively and have received support from the local university and from different suppliers in the industry. Tom has experience in this line of business—he works for a major department store's service repair shop. He is a skilled repairman. Jill has selling experience; she worked in a ladies' ready-to-wear store. There is only one other repair service in town and that person works out of a local service station, repairing lawn mowers and small appliances throughout the year.

Their big uncertainty concerns the market, their possible penetration, and the marketing strategy they should develop. They do not know the market demand in the area, but they assume it to be great. They think that their share would be at least 50 percent of the market. They need to know if they should advertise or how they can determine their market.

The field of marketing covers a great many varied, though related, topics. It is a functional area of any business, in the same way that accounting and production are functional areas. As such, marketing is vital to the survival of a business. In this chapter three main aspects of marketing will be covered. The first section develops the history of the marketing concept and defines what a market is. The second section outlines the steps necessary for the development of the firm's marketing strategy. Finally, the third section of the chapter describes marketing research, a tool that should be understood and used by all dynamic small business owners.

Marketing

Bob grabbed the phone and nervously began to dial. He wanted to ask Sue for a date to see a new movie. Sue answered the phone with a sharp, "Yes?" Bob could no longer remember his carefully rehearsed speech. He finally got himself together enough to introduce himself and ask Sue how she was feeling. She said she was not too well. The phone fell silent for a minute. Then Bob continued with his speech and finally, asked Sue to go with him to the movie. To Bob's surprise, the answer was yes, if he would pick her up after work. Bob and Sue have both just experienced a phenomenon called marketing.

Millions of marketing transactions occur around the world every day. Marketing is probably one of the oldest business activities. Basically, *marketing* may be described as a human exchange process that is aimed at satisfying the needs and wants of individuals. Marketing exists because of the desires of individuals to exchange some good for others.

development of the marketing concept

The practice and study of marketing is becoming more important, and it is attracting increased attention. The original marketing concept was developed on a barter system, which is the exchange of one item for another. This was greatly altered by the Industrial Revolution, when the production of goods from individual craftsmakers moved to the assembly line and mass production. With this change, hundreds and thousands of identical high-quality products could be produced for mass consumption. The assembly line ushered in the production era of marketing, with its *production concept* of marketing, which assumed that customers would respond favorably to quality goods reasonably priced and that little, if any, sales, marketing, or promotional efforts were required. The production era was dominant during the last quarter of the nineteenth century and the first quarter of the twentieth century. The production concept is best exemplified by Henry Ford, who exclaimed that one could buy any color Ford one wanted, as long as it was black. The producer–manufacturer was king, and created his own market merely by producing his good for resale.

In the second quarter of the twentieth century, a surplus of goods began to be developed. The supply was then larger than the demand. The *selling concept* of marketing emerged in the 1930s and 1940s. The selling concept assumed that customers would not buy all of a company's product unless major emphasis was placed on selling, advertising, and promotional efforts. Marketing, sales, and distribution divisions were created within organizations to handle the goods produced. The sales force was to sell what the firm produced, and little or no effort was extended by the business to determine the wants and needs of customers. The marketing functions (sales, advertising, market demand, production planning, promotions, and so on) were not coordinated, but were spread throughout the business organization.

The *marketing concept* emerged in the 1950s, in the third quarter of the twentieth century, when new companies began to assume the task of determining the consumers' wants and needs, and developing the company operations to satisfy the customer. Customers became the focal point of the business, and the marketing activities of the business were centralized to help them.

Few businesses today use the barter system, but there are many businesses that still utilize the production or selling concepts rather than the complex marketing concept required today to optimize success. The marketing manager may be the owner or manager of the business, or the vice-president of the organization. The marketing manager must conscientiously strive to achieve favorable exchanges with specific markets. McCarthy has defined the marketing concept from

307
MARKETING AND MARKETING RESEARCH

the perspective of the manager in this way: "Marketing is the performance of business activities which direct the flow of goods and services from producer to consumer or user in order to satisfy customers and to accomplish the company's objectives."[1]

definition of markets

Businesses must be concerned with their markets. What are the markets? Where are they? The term *market* is primarily defined in terms of people, money, and the desire to exchange. The market is generally limited to a particular area, whether this be an entire country (such as the United States) or a small town (such as Eldorado Springs, Colorado). The extent of the market may be limited by geographical area, customers' preferences, competition, or substitute goods.

SUCCESS STORY: John Wanamaker

John Wanamaker opened his first store in 1861, four days before the start of the Civil War. The first day's receipts were $24.67, and all but the change was spent on advertising. The store was only 30 feet by 80 feet. Total sales for the first year were under $25,000. Thus began the business career of a man who is generally considered to have been a marketing genius.

John Wanamaker had left school at 14 to become an errand boy for a publishing house at $1.25 per week. Four years later, he began his career in retailing as a $2.50-per-week clerk. At 23 he opened that first small store and used outdoor advertising posters during the summer. In 1866, he offered a refund if the merchandise was not satisfactory. He began a one-price system in 1871. By then, his store had doubled in size. At the age of 38, he opened what was then the largest retail men's store in the nation. By 1892, his store covered 16 acres of floor space.

Wanamaker served as Postmaster General for President Harrison. As Postmaster General, he was credited with establishing rural delivery, and supported free parcel post, although that system was not instituted for an additional twenty years.

John Wanamaker was also involved in community service, serving as the first salaried secretary of the Philadelphia YMCA and later for eight years as national president of YMCA. During the Civil War, he organized the Christian Commission, which aided sick and wounded soldiers for both sides.

[1] E. J. McCarthy, *Business Marketing: A Managerial Approach.* (Homewood, Ill.: Richard D. Irwin, Inc., 1975), p. 19.

In 1873, Wanamaker gave five reasons for his business success:
1. We advertise what we have for sale.
2. We have for sale what we advertise.
3. The people come to see that it is so.
4. The people buy our cloth because they are pleased with the guarantee we make.
5. The people are satisfied that they get full value for the money they leave with us and they come again and send their friends.[2]

Marketing Strategy

The process of managing the marketing side of business is often referred to as *marketing strategy*. The marketing strategy process generally consists of: (1) defining objectives, (2) analyzing opportunities and alternatives, (3) developing marketing strategy for implementation, (4) carrying out the implementation, and (5) feedback and control. In the following sections each of these facets of strategy will be discussed in detail.

defining objectives

Development of the company's objectives is a major responsibility, often overlooked by most small business owners but necessary to the success of the business. These objectives should specify the company purpose and mission. In other words, each company should begin with a mission or purpose (goal) that should be both definable and measurable, and should be able to meet an environmental or consumer need. Furthermore, the mission statement should describe the nature of the business as well as what the business should be. For example, a fast-food hamburger restaurant's mission should not be to sell hamburgers, but rather the restaurant should provide good, quick, and nutritious food to the customers.

After a statement of mission and purpose has been developed for the company, it is appropriate to develop the objectives necessary to accomplish this organizational goal. The objectives should be realistic, quantitative, and easily defined. They should provide a basis for control, planning, and innovation, and they should provide a specific sense of duty and obligation. Once the primary company objectives have been developed, secondary objectives should be developed for each of the functional areas of the organization, including the marketing and sales area. The purpose of secondary objectives is to give to every person in the organization a set of objectives that will guide and direct their work. The accomplishment of individual objectives should add up to the accomplishment of the overall organizational objectives, thus ensuring the success and prosperity of the business.

analyzing opportunities and alternatives

Once the objectives have been established, it is appropriate to analyze the opportunities and alternatives available to the business. A business opportunity exists when there is an advantage present for a particular business. For example, a hand

[2]Phillip J. Reilly, *Old Masters of Retailing*, (New York: Fairchild Publications, Inc., 1966).

calculator is easier to use than a slide ruler, and the latter may be becoming obsolete, so one would do better to start a calculator business rather than a slide rule business. This advantage should ensure growth, or at least the continuation of customers for the business. The opportunities and alternatives should be a reflection of the objectives of the business. The sources of opportunities can be either external market growth or internal growth.

External market growth opportunities exist when a business is able to increase its: (1) market penetration, (2) market development, or (3) product development. *Market penetration* is concerned with increasing the percentage of sales of current products in a current location or an existing market. The increase in market penetration is generally a result of an increase in sales and marketing efforts. *Market development* occurs when the owner or operator of a business wishes to increase sales by using its present products in new markets or areas. He or she may wish to accomplish this by expanding into additional stores within the same geographical area, or by moving into other towns or states. *Product development* occurs when the owner or operator of a business desires to increase sales through the establishment of new products or services within its current markets. These new products may be modifications of existing product lines or entirely new products or services may be created.

Internal growth may occur as a result of integration or diversification. Integration may occur when a business seeks ownership or control of its supplies (which is known as backward integration). The integration process also takes place when a company seeks ownership or control of its channels of distribution (which is known as forward integration). Finally, integration occurs when a business seeks ownership or control of direct competitors (which is called horizontal integration).

developing marketing strategy for implementation

Before one can begin to develop marketing strategy, the objectives and opportunities must be thoroughly researched and evaluated. The objective defines what a company wants to be; the strategy is the design or plan developed for getting there. The strategy must include all phases of business: the accounting, financial, production, managerial, and marketing. However, the strategy should stress those marketing areas necessary to coordinate the functions of the business. The proper development of these strategies and plans will necessitate an understanding of the following four areas: (1) market segmentation, (2) market entry, (3) marketing mix, and (4) market timing.

Market segmentation. Market segmentation is the division of any market into two or more distinguishable segments, such that significant differences occur between segments in (1) needs, (2) buying styles, and (3) marketing approaches. For example, a fancy, high-priced steakhouse is more likely to be successful if it is located near a well-established residential community than if it is across the street from a college. However, a low-priced, fast-food restaurant would do well near a college. No large market is homogeneous (having one characteristic); markets do consist of a variety of buyers who can be segmented according to their different responses to various marketing programs.

Market segmentation generally requires: (1) a clear differentiation between markets, (2) that each segment be approachable (easy to advertise to), and (3) that segments must be large in size. "College students" or "young marrieds" are market segments often used by furniture and clothing stores, or by restaurants. They represent a market that is clearly differentiable, approachable, and large in size (often over 5,000 people). There are three major approaches to segmentation: (1) analysis of consumer personality or psychological makeup, (2) analysis of consumer traits or characteristics, and (3) analysis of consumer behavior or buying patterns.

Final market segmentation will be focused around (1) demographic characteristics, (2) socioeconomic characteristics, (3) geographic characteristics, and (4) consumer characteristics. This segmentation will allow for target market identification, or identification of that segment's processing characteristics, which make its consumers most likely to buy your product or service. Segmentation enhances marketing strategy; promotions directed at the target segment (market) can be used to increase business and sales.

Market entry. The second phase of market strategy and planning is the determination of how to approach a target market or market entry (the group to which you specifically want to sell your product). It is important to select a specific target market that will allow for maximum opportunity and for optimizing the probability of the business. Businesses cannot do everything for everyone, nor can they be every place at the same time. One cannot sell every style and size of running shoes made in the world. Therefore, it is important to determine the right place in the market, and enter there. Market entry is generally determined through (1) business development, (2) cooperation with other companies, or (3) acquisition. The first method of entering a market, through business development or expanding one's business into a new market area, is generally the result of marketing research, and the development of goods and services for a particular target market. The second method, cooperation with other companies, may also provide an opportunity for market entry. Several stores may get together to develop a new shopping center in a growing residential community. By the third method, acquisition, a business may acquire entry into a new market. One business may buy an existing product or company, and become part of a new market.

Marketing mix. A third major area of concern in developing marketing strategy for implementation is to determine the marketing mix for a particular market segment. The marketing mix refers to the proper adjustment of factors that influence a buyer's response to a product or a service. Several variables may be included in developing a proper market mix, however, McCarthy has popularized the "Four Ps": (1) product, (2) place, (3) price, and (4) promotion. By properly aligning and adjusting these factors, it should be easy to influence the buyer to purchase a particular product or service.

Some areas that would strongly influence the *product* factor of the marketing mix are the quality, quantity, and style of the product, the product's features, the packaging, brand name, warranty, product line, and the services available.

Some areas affecting the *place* factor are availability of the product, location, distribution channel, inventory level, transportation carrier, and sales territory. Research indicates that the quality of the hamburger is the most important aspect of a fast-food hamburger restaurant. The location and nearness of the hamburger franchise, although not nearly as important, can be a decision factor. In a large city, it would be better to have four or five McDonald's restaurants than to have only one for the entire city.

The *price* factor must be developed to allow the product or service to be both profitable and competitive. (See Chapter 16.) This factor is often influenced by the quantity of goods purchased, credit and payment terms, discounts, allowances, and the socioeconomic classification of consumers in the target market.

Promotion is one of the major elements of the marketing mix of the business. Promotion is a form of persuasive communication, and its function is that of informing consumers about a product or service and influencing them to buy that product or service. There are many different promotional tools that are used by businesses to enhance the image of their product, such as mailings, speeches, presentations, contests, packaging, films, catalogs, coupons, posters, and even endorsements. The elements of this list may be classified in the *promotional mix,* which is comprised of four major areas: (1) *advertising*—any paid form of promotion by an identified payer, (2) *personal selling*—an oral conversation involving one or more prospective purchasers for acquiring sales, (3) *publicity*—the development of commercially significant news that results in stimulating demand for a product or a service through a published medium, such as radio, television, or newspapers, and (4) *sales promotion*—any other activities stimulating consumer purchases, such as exhibits, demonstrations, and displays or other extraordinary selling efforts. The promotional mix is an important part of a business's strategy; therefore, each element will be described in greater detail in the paragraphs that follow.

Why do we buy the television we watch, the cars we drive, and even the toothpaste we use? We buy them primarily as a result of *advertising*. Advertising is a part of our daily existence. The clothes we choose to wear and the food we choose to eat are almost entirely the result of advertising. More money is spent on advertising each year than any other promotional activity. In 1978, American advertisers expended more than $30 billion. The nation's largest single advertiser, Procter and Gamble, spends more than $300 million a year on advertising.

The bulk of advertising results from local businesses. Of all the mass media forms, only television receives more national than local advertising. One-sixth of daily newspaper advertising comes from national ads. Approximately three-fourths of all radio advertising is based on local ads.

The use of any advertising medium should be based upon the market to be covered, the size and type of audience, the advertising costs, the time or space available, and the suitability of that medium to the consumers. The advertising message does need to be repeated several times, and must be run at least six times in order to be effective in most mass media presentations. An advertisement placed only once on the radio or television is almost always highly ineffective. Different media provide different advantages to different types of businesses.

    1. The *newspaper* has probably been the favorite advertising medium of retailers for as long as both have existed. Newspapers account for approx-

imately 30 percent of all advertising dollars and are first in advertising media. Newspapers provide the flexibility, longevity, and graphic presentation necessary and appropriate for many retailers. Grocery stores, department stores, and large clothing stores will often run weekly advertisements in their local newspapers.

Newspaper ad-space rates are based on circulation. The larger the circulation, the higher the cost. The space is usually sold in terms of lines and columns, or inches and columns. An example would be a four-column by 50-line ad (four columns wide and 50 lines long); the advertiser would be charged at the rate of 200 lines. Fly rates are also available for large and repetitive advertisers. Weekly newspapers, shoppers, and school papers are less expensive and provide the owner with a specialty newspaper in which a business may promote to a particular target market in specific geographic, academic, or income levels.

2. The *radio* is more common today than ever before. There are over 400 million radios in use in the United States today. Radios reach a wide array of customers and provide great flexibility with a short-lead time requirement. It is important that any message advertised over the radio be repeated a number of times.

Radio advertising is generally sold in amounts of 10-, 15-, 30-, and 60-second spots. The 30- and 60-second spots are the more popular. Costs will vary according to the time of day, the size of the listening audience, and the radio stations that one is specifically advertising on. It is important to remember, as an advertiser, that different radio stations attract different target markets.

3. *Television* is both a "vast wasteland" and one of the most amazing advertising media yet developed. The average person watches over six hours of television per day, and over 97 percent of all homes in the United States have television sets. Television ranks second to local newspapers in terms of advertising dollars. It allows both a visual as well as an audible advertising message. Television advertising is sold in time units of 10, 20, 30 and 60 seconds. The 30-second television advertisement is the most common. Rates will vary according to stations as well as to the time of day.

4. *Magazines* provide a very specific audience. They are generally limited to specific topics or geographical areas. However, there are many nationally-distributed magazines that have wide appeal for the advertising dollar. Unlike radio, television, or even newspapers, magazines last for long periods of time and are often read by more than one reader. The advertisement will last as long as the magazine. However, magazines are usually not very useful for small businesses.

5. *Direct mail* has grown enormously since its beginning in the late 1800s. Direct mail reaches a specific target market and may even be used in the form of catalogs, letters, postcards, coupons, circulars, price lists, or business cards. The rate of return in a national direct mail campaign averages from 2 to 3 percent. For example, if you were to mail an advertisement for a local restaurant to 30,000 residents in the community, you would have

approximately 600 respondents, or 2 percent, who would come to the restaurant for the advertised special.

Directories also provide a specific target market. The most common form of directory is the Yellow Pages of the local telephone book. The directory provides a long-lasting advertisement, usually published annually; often its life expectancy is the longest of any advertising message—a year or more, or as long as the directory lasts.

6. An area that is often underused, but still successful, is that of *outdoor advertising*. Billboards, posters, and even transit advertising may be developed and effectively used.

7. An important advertising idea is *point-of-purchase displays*. Point-of-purchase displays act as a sales representative in the store, and have the capacity to capture impulse shoppers. The vast majority of impulse purchases, up to 80 percent, are made because the shopper sees a display. Displays are especially well suited for new product lines and special promotion areas.

8. *Specialty advertising* is very important, and is growing in size. Specialty advertising involves items often given to customers (such as pencils, pens, calendars, key chains, and T-shirts) on which the name, trademark, address, or slogan of the product or company is listed. Lumberyards and hardware stores often provide free yardsticks on which their name and address is imprinted. This will help establish good will and provide identification for future purchases.

9. Participation in *trade shows* is of value primarily to manufacturers and distributors rather than retailers. Trade show costs will vary according to the locale, the type, and the size of the show. These shows are conducted in local, regional, and national centers.

The preparation of the ad message is very important. Manufacturers, distributors, and suppliers will often help in developing the advertisement message. Most media (such as newspaper, radio, television) will also help in the development of an effective ad campaign. Special advertising agencies are located in most large cities, and they receive their income from commissions for developing an ad campaign. They will generally receive 15 to 20 percent of the total cost as a commission from the medium where the ad was placed. Direct mail agencies also receive either a fixed, flat fee, or a commission of over 20 percent of the cost involved.

To develop an advertising program, it is important to establish an advertising budget. Regardless of the size of the business, every business should contain some form of advertising expense. Different methods of establishing an advertising budget should be considered. Some businesses use the "all-we-can-afford method," which is probably the poorest of all possible conditions. Another method is that of "matching competition," but this prohibits an aggressive or leadership role for a business. A third method is the use of the "objective task method." The precise business owner will establish the objectives and products that will be specifically advertised in the immediate future. The budget is then determined based on the needs and demands of the business. This budget must often be reevaluated, in a downward direction, in order to be realistic for a small business owner. The fourth major method, and the one most commonly used, is the "percent of sales method." The advertising budget is established by taking a percent of sales that will be used for advertising for that year. Although this varies from industry to industry, the most common figure in many businesses is approximately 3 percent of the total annual sales.

A good rule of thumb for analyzing immediate costs is that 80 percent of the advertising dollar should be allocated for space (newspaper or magazine) or time (radio or television), and 20 percent should be used in the development and production of the advertising message. The most successful form of advertising follows the seasonal or cyclical nature of the business. Expenditures for advertising will usually be high during peak sales periods. Advertisements should be limited during periods of low sale potential, so that the budget will not be wasted. For example, toys are generally advertised before Christmas, not during March or July. Advertisers need to remember, though, to always seek their full share of the market.

Personal selling (the second element of the promotional mix) is generally a one-on-one situation in which a representative from a business endeavors to explain and communicate the advantages of a product or service to a buyer. Personal selling may take many different forms, including field representatives (field selling), sales clerks (retail selling), demonstration of the product to an assembled group of individuals (demonstration selling), or even an executive luncheon (executive selling). Personal selling is used for many reasons, and encouraged by all businesspeople to enhance on-the-spot sales.

The most common form of personal selling occurs in small retail stores, where the salesperson meets the prospective customer. This interaction will include a personal confrontation and will result in some definitive response (yes or no) from the customer.

Personal selling is the primary, and often the only, means of selling for manufacturers, insurance companies, and financial institutions. Personal selling requires a high amount of training and close supervision, especially within the small business.

A form of promotion often sought by most businesses, because it is generally free, is *publicity*. The results of free publicity may be truly fantastic. The publicity given to jogging has greatly increased the sales of running and tennis shoes and other related sports equipment. Publicity also has several advantages, including the appearance of truth and authenticity. News stories about a local business probably have a higher degree of veracity than if they were sponsored or advertised by the business itself.

Sales promotion, the last element of the promotional mix, includes all the other promotional tools that are not formally classified under advertising, personal selling, or publicity. These techniques may be classified as consumer promotions, trade promotions, and sales-force promotion items. The consumer promotion area includes coupons, discounts, contests, trading stamps, samples, demonstrations, and the like. Trade promotion often includes free goods, buying allowances, merchandise allowances, or even cooperative advertising. Sales-force promotion involves all the areas that are seen as benefits (contests, bonuses, extra commissions, sales rallies, and so forth) to encourage the sales force to work harder, and receive special gifts for their extra effort.

Market timing. The fourth major concern in developing the marketing strategy for implementation is developing market timing. It is important to determine the proper time to enter a market. Many businesses are seasonal in nature; therefore, it would be important to enter the market on the upswing before it approaches its height of activity. A new clothing store would do best not to open in late January or February, choosing instead to open before the fall and Christmas high-volume seasons.

A contractor for new homes moved North to the Chicago area in September, but found that the market sagged over the winter months during the snow and cold seasons. He returned to the South in the month of May, and wondered why he was not more successful. A businessperson sold a profitable T-shirt shop to a graduating senior of the local university during the month of May. The new owner did not understand why her profits were down or why business slumped during the summer months. She did not fully realize that the university students comprised 80 percent of the business, and were only in classes from September until May. These two examples serve to illustrate the fact that properly timing the businesses entry into the market is important.

carrying out the implementation

The development of company objectives, the analysis of business opportunities and alternatives, and the preparation of business strategies and plans are of little value unless the plans are implemented. A business plan is designed for implementation. "If you fail to plan, you plan to fail." Success can be no greater than the plan provides.

The implementation of the marketing program must be supervised by the owner-manager, the entrepreneur, or the marketing manager. The marketing program should be fully implemented to ensure its proper utilization and reward. Without the implementation no results will occur, and a business may suffer due to a lack of promotion and development.

feedback and control

One of the major areas in any business is the establishment of control mechanisms to ensure the proper function of individuals within an organization. Budgets are established to maintain control over the expenditures of funds within a business. Plans are developed as control mechanisms to ensure that people will follow them. Marketing strategy is developed to increase business, and by periodic follow-throughs and checkups, one may ensure that it is being properly implemented. Periodic reports should be submitted by those who implement the marketing program to ensure that it is being performed, and also to ensure compliance against the master plan.

The business owner should also exercise control by examining the profitability of all the various products or services that are being sold in the business. Control must be spread throughout any business to ensure compliance to the standards established and the plans implemented.

Marketing Research

When making marketing decisions—whether about pricing policies, promotion, location analysis, the channels of distribution, new product design or changes in existing products—they should be based on facts. Experience is a valuable source, but it also may be misleading. With the rapid changes in the environment and economic conditions, most businesses want to use marketing research techniques before they arrive at final decisions.

Marketing research is one of the most overlooked and neglected functions of small business management. As consumers, we rarely do enough marketing research before we buy a new car or purchase clothes. We often purchase the products that appeal to us at the moment and that are close at hand. Marketing research need not be a complex activity, full of statistics and tricky psychological questions. It may be a simple straightforward process used to determine attitudes towards a firm's own products or those of a competitors. Marketing research is often easily determined by interviews and questionnaires.

Marketing research is intended to provide information in the development of a marketing strategy for the small business. Such information may provide valuable insights and understanding about the needs and desires of customers. Thus, marketing research should (1) help provide knowledge about customers' needs, and (2) help to form the guidelines for the business and its employees.

Marketing research may be easily designed and developed by any small business owner to adequately research the following:

1. Consumer attitudes.
2. Consumer behavior.
3. Sales analysis.
4. Channels of distribution.
5. Competitive products and brands.
6. Pricing.
7. Promotion.
8. New products.
9. Packaging.
10. Product planning.
11. Geographical preferences.

four essentials

Marketing research may help determine what style and kind of clothes people will be wearing in 1984, or what size and design of car people would desire in 1988. Marketing research can also help us to understand if home computers are just a fad, if video cassettes will last, and if the CB radio will continue to grow and become a major market. The well-designed marketing research instrument contains four essential parts: (1) questionnaire development, (2) sample design, (3) collection and tabulation of data, and (4) analysis and forecast.

Completion of this marketing research design will allow the owner of a company to understand its own market share, will provide empirical data for a growth-oriented market, and will reveal strengths and weaknesses of that business as well as those of competitors. Market research gives your business an advantage: a knowledge that will allow better marketing plans and increased understanding of the needs and desires of consumers.

questionnaire development

A strong marketing research questionnaire is not as difficult to develop as many people believe. The questionnaire should be designed to provide valuable information about the products of the business and the attitudes of its customers. Six major areas should be covered:

1. Where do shoppers go to make purchases?
2. Why do they go there?
3. What is the market potential for this business?
4. How does this firm compare with its competitors?
5. How effective is advertising at present, and how can it be made more productive?
6. What services should the business provide?[3]

The development of questions related to this questionnaire format will provide the business owner with information that can greatly help his or her business. Coaches are always looking for competitive advantages that they can provide their team members and help them to win. A soccer coach will often send out scouts to view the opposing players and report back on their strengths and weaknesses. Marketing research questionnaires are designed to help the business owner-manager to understand how he or she might best play the game. Examples of questions related to this questionnaire format are found in Figure 17–1 below and on the next page.

SAMPLE QUESTIONS

Where:
1. When considering a fast-food restaurant, where do you go most often?
2. What do you consider to be your primary department store—the store at which you shop most often?
3. Which bank do you use most often or consider to be "your bank"?

Why:
1. Why that particular grocery store? or restaurant?
2. Please tell me what attracts you to that particular brand or piece of furniture?
3. Why do you drink _____ ?

	Very Important	Important	Not Important	Definitely Not Important
a. Taste	_____	_____	_____	_____
b. Brand loyalty	_____	_____	_____	_____
c. Calories	_____	_____	_____	_____
d. Availability	_____	_____	_____	_____
e. Price	_____	_____	_____	_____

---

[3]Justis, Robert T. and William C. Jackson, "Marketing Research For Dynamic Small Businesses," *Journal of Small Business Management,* October, 1978.

> **SAMPLE QUESTIONS** (continued)
>
> *What:*
> 1. How many times in the last month have you purchased shoes?
> 2. What time of day do you usually make a purchase at a fast-food restaurant?
> 3. Within the last month, how many times did you eat food from a fast-food restaurant?
>
> *How:*
> 1. How did you compare pizza restaurant A with the other pizza restaurants in the city?
> 2. How would you compare Restaurant A and Restaurant B concerning the following factors?
>
> | | Restaurant A | Restaurant B | Both Even | Do Not Know |
> |---|---|---|---|---|
> | a. Quality of food | _____ | _____ | _____ | _____ |
> | b. Cleanliness of restaurant | _____ | _____ | _____ | _____ |
> | c. Best price | _____ | _____ | _____ | _____ |
> | d. Lowest price | _____ | _____ | _____ | _____ |
> | e. Friendliness of employees | _____ | _____ | _____ | _____ |
> | f. Presence of manager | _____ | _____ | _____ | _____ |
>
> 3. How would you compare a McDonald's Ronald McDonald television commercial with a Burger King Magic King television commercial?
>
> | | Better | Much Better | Worse | Much Worse |
> |---|---|---|---|---|
> | a. McDonald | _____ | _____ | _____ | _____ |
> | b. Burger King | _____ | _____ | _____ | _____ |
>
> *Advertising:*
> 1. Have you read, seen, or heard any advertising for Store A?
> 2. Can you tell me the slogan for Bank A?
> 3. What would be the best way to reach you with an advertisement about a sale at Store C?
>
> *Services:*
> 1. Do you prefer bank-by-mail or banking boxes located around town?
> 2. Do you prefer a drive-through window at your restaurant?
> 3. What would you suggest to clothing store A's manager if he asked how to improve his store's operations?

Figure 17–1. *Factors to be considered*

Questions are the focal point of any research design. These questions should provide the information that is necessary and important to improve the competitive position of a business. Just as the coach seeks to improve competitive advantage in a sporting event, so the business owner can improve his or her position in the business world by increasing the knowledge and marketing skills that can better serve customers.

sample design

In most cases, it is impossible to survey the entire population of a market with a questionnaire. Therefore, a smaller segment of that market must be sampled. There are three main steps necessary to adequately design the sample. (1) *Describe* the population for which you wish the information. For example, a local record store may want to have information about the 12- to 24-year-old group more so than about the 55-and-older age group. (2) *Explain* sample selection procedures. Will the sample be selected from telephone books, the Yellow Pages, or customer lists? If the tenth name down on every other page in the middle of the telephone book is to be used, then it is important to always be consistent and to always choose names in that manner. (3) *Specify* the procedures for contacting the respondents. How many times should you contact someone to get a valid response? Will only those people who can be conveniently reached on a one-time basis be enough?

While the sample size itself is very important, in most marketing research within limited geographical areas one may find that a hundred individuals are adequate. Professional market research organizations generally consider a sample size of three hundred to be the most cost efficient. Generally, a three-hundred-person sample size will provide a small enough error range to have adequate accuracy in determining responses. There is a maximum error range of about 5 percent for a sample size of three hundred persons, with 95 percent confidence.

collection and tabulation of data

Data collection can often be performed by the business owner or employees before or after working hours. Data collection can be a fun experience, if sufficient questionnaires have been prepared, and if the interviewers have been trained to only ask these specific questions on the questionnaire.

Three different ways that information is generally collected are: (1) mail questionnaires, (2) phone-call interviews, and (3) in-person interviews. The person-to-person contact is by far the best method; the phone-call interview is generally considered the least expensive of the two person-to-person types of contact.

analysis and forecast

A simple graph of the final percentage or number of responses is often sufficient for illustrating the results. It is important to tabulate all of the final answers and to calculate their totals with respect to the total number of persons responding. A summary of your report may then be developed that will highlight the main results of marketing research and will provide insights for the manager and owner. Marketing research, repeated over a period of time, will also provide trends and interesting information that may be of help to the owner.

Marketing research should be a valuable tool to any owner-manager. It is a tool that provides a competitive advantage to anyone who uses it. With an increased understanding of the wants and needs of customers, the owner may be better able to supply the goods or services that will increase his or her profitability. The owner-manager may also have a better understanding how to use the marketing mix, to advertise, price, and promote his or her product as a result of the marketing research.

CASE STUDY: The "Travel Around" Travel Agency

"Travel Around" is a new travel agency located in a Southern city of over 50,000 population. The agency just opened for business last January, and its owner is finding it very difficult to survive.

Owning a travel agency should be considered from the viewpoint of a long-term investment and as a profession in which one would have an opportunity to perform a needed and valuable service to the traveling public. It should not be thought of as a means of participating in free junkets and reduced-rate transportation. A travel agency is a totally service-oriented business. Some of the services provided to the public are:

1. Quotation of fares and/or schedules.
2. Securing of reservations (travel, hotels, motels, and car rentals).
3. Expediting payment for travel.
4. Arrangement for delivery of tickets or other transportation documents.
5. Assistance to clients with other travel arrangements.
6. Development and implementation of tours.

A travel agency makes its income totally from commissions on ticket sales and tours. The commission for each ticket sale is approximately 7 percent, and tours vary from 7 to 30 percent in commission fees. Most new travel agencies are not expected to break even until the third year, according to industrial averages. The most dramatic reduction in costs, up to 50 percent of coach or tourist fares, are made possible by airline charters of regular and supplemental carriers. Charters are generally allowed for youth/student groups, companies sponsoring sales incentive contests, and almost any special group.

The lifeblood of any travel agency is its ability to market its goods and services. The agency is concerned with establishing cruises, escorted tours, package tours, sightseeing tours, private tours, special-interest tours, foreign independent travel, charters, steamship travel, railroad travel, and even bus travel.

The major activity of most travel agencies is the selling of domestic and international airline tickets. This is also the major revenue source for the travel agency.

Hotel and motel business, especially in resort areas, can bring considerable revenue to the agency. The client should be provided complete and accurate information about the hotel. Many clients also like the opportunity to drive themselves around, once they reach their destination. Many package tours now include the use of a car as one of the principle parts of the package.

Unlike most other businesses, a travel agency cannot add a service charge. Customers who come to a travel agency pay no more for their tickets than if they had bought them directly from the airline or other suppliers. Below is a schedule that illustrates the basic commissions paid to travel agents by airlines and other suppliers.

Types of Travel	Commissions (%)	
Domestic Air Travel:		
Point-to-point	7	
Family travel	8	
Tour	11–12	
International Air Travel:		
Point-to-point	8	
Tour	11	
Other:		
Charter air travel	7–30	(variable)
Transatlantic steamship	7	
Transpacific steamship	7.5	(one way)
	10	(round trip or cruise)
Caribbean and short cruises	10	
Major cruises	10	
Sea or air tours	10	
Domestic rail travel	10	
European rail travel	7.5	
Car rentals	10	
Hotels and motels	10	
Escorted package tours	10–15	

The travel agency is concerned with their marketing strategy and their marketing mix. They are uncertain as to which direction to go and how to get there.

Questions

1. What marketing strategy should the travel agency employ?
2. What marketing mix should the agency use?
3. Which area of travel should the agency promote the strongest?
4. What areas of service should the travel agency provide or not provide?
5. What promotional project should the agency employ?
6. Should the agency use college students as part-time employees?

Chapter Questions:

1. Discuss the difference between promotion and advertising.
2. Discuss the importance of personal selling.
3. Discuss the advantages and disadvantages of radio, television, newspapers, and magazines.
4. Develop a market segmentation profile for your community.
5. Outline a market strategy for a new fast-food hamburger restaurant in your community.

Photo courtesy of Irene Springer, Prentice-Hall, Inc.

18

SALES AND SALES FORECASTING

Chapter Objectives:

1. To understand the importance of the selling function.
2. To learn about different selling classifications.
3. To understand the selling process.
4. To describe the different stages of a sales plan.
5. To analyze different methods of sales forecasting.
6. To investigate sales force compensation plans.

Nothing happens until somebody sells something.

Arthur H. Motley

INCIDENT:

Larry is in his early fifties and lives in a large metropolitan city. Five years ago he opened a small convenience grocery store, specializing in items that are most commonly used in the American household—milk, bread, toilet articles, and the like.

Larry is somewhat successful. He, his wife, and their three children are a middle-class family; they enjoy community outings and taking part in religious activities. He has four part-time salespeople who worked for him on alternating shifts. He remains open for business seven days a week, with the exception of holidays, and has found that he must depend a great deal on the integrity and abilities of his four part-time salespeople.

Larry does not know the size of the market, nor his actual share of it. He does not know if he should advertise or change his product line. He does not know the function of selling or how to increase sales.

One of the major problems that Larry has had with his business is the constant flow into his store of salespeople who try to talk him into selling their brands of items—milk salespeople, magazine salespeople, bread salespeople, and so on. When one of Larry's staff told him that they were out of a couple of magazines, his response was, "The magazine distributor will be here in two or three days and I'll restock them then." Another one of his staff asked if he was going to have more milk in soon and Larry smiled and replied, "Yes, the milk truck is coming in tomorrow morning." Someone else asked for a ballpoint pen and Larry responded that the office supply representative was coming in that day. All this has made Larry take note of the sales function and of the sales people who call on him. Although he is a salesperson himself, he is only beginning to realize the importance of selling to other people.

Giant Boeing jets can carry 286 passengers thousands of miles in a few hours. To bring this flight to life, hundreds of small businesses had to sell the plane components to Boeing. Boeing had to sell the giant jets to the various airlines. The airlines, along with many travel agencies, had to sell each passenger a ticket.

Selling

Every new product or idea has to be sold. Although the invention of the wheel was phenomenal and fantastic, its use still had to be sold to the general public. People were afraid of the early automobiles and airplanes. The ideas had to be sold.

Selling is encouraging the transfer of products or services from one individual to another. Today, selling is one of the most important dimensions of any business. Salespeople represent their companies just as you represent your business, school, or family. To many people, the sales representative *is* the company, and their judgment of the company and the company's products are highly influenced by the salesperson. Compared with other occupations, such as bank tellers or factory workers, the salespeople have had a tremendous amount of freedom. It is difficult to closely watch and supervise the daily activity of salespeople. The salesperson needs to be highly motivated and innovative in handling his or her job.

There are several different kinds of selling. Sales activities may be divided into four major classifications: (1) industrial, (2) manufacturing, (3) distribution and wholesale, and (4) retail.

industrial

Industrial sales deal with raw materials that will be used in the manufacturing process to make a finished good. Many small businesses are developed to provide raw materials (such as springs, coal, chemicals, and so on) to other organizations for further production. General Motors purchases parts from literally thousands of small businesses.

Industrial salespeople will often have large geographical sales territories and will have to travel extensively throughout their own territories. Sales representatives generally travel throughout the United States four or five times a year, placing and taking orders with manufacturers.

manufacturing

Manufacturing sales concern the selling of finished manufactured goods to retail or wholesale outlets. Manufacturing salespeople also have large territories and travel extensively. Some small businesses are developed to act solely as manufacturers' representatives; that is, they independently sell the products of one or more manufacturers. Small manufacturers may only have one to fifteen manufacturing representatives, depending upon the size and capabilities of the company. Territories are often assigned to representatives according to geographical areas, ranging from a section of a large city to a large section of the United States.

distribution and wholesale

Distribution and wholesale sales deal with the selling and delivering of all types of products, from ashtrays and candy to office supplies, food, and chemicals. Many small businesses act as distribution warehouses for particular types of products such as furniture, food, or chemicals. Sales representatives often call on their accounts regularly—weekly, twice a week, or possibly once a month. Most cities have several distribution center outlets for different industries. These vary from wholesalers to warehouses stocked with television sets, radios, pliers, cleaning supplies, office equipment, and the like.

retail

The most common form of sales is found at the retail level. Retail sales involve the final sale to a consumer. Selling is a profession that is both a science and an art; nowhere is this more true than at the retail level. The grocery store clerk needs to know a great deal about the prices and differences between goods. The photographer sells more than just a picture; he or she sells an image and a sense of beauty and action.

Retailing is not always done in stores. Retail selling includes door-to-door selling (brushes, magazines), selling in the buyer's home or office (insurance, cosmetics), selling the seller's house (real estate), and selling at especially arranged "parties" (household plastic goods, costume jewelry, women's apparel). All these approaches require well-trained and motivated professional salespeople. These salespeople must know their products, realize the value and importance of their products to their customers, and appreciate the service they are making to society through their sales efforts.

The Selling Process

The selling process is comprised of a sales base and a sales plan. See Table 18–1. A sales base involves the properties—both tangible and intangible—of the product; a sales plan involves the skill and timing of the salesperson. Salespeople should be aware of the selling process and be trained to develop an effective sales procedure.

Table 18-1. The Selling Process

Sales Base

1. Product
2. Product Knowledge
3. Image
4. Need Fulfillment
5. Display

Sales Plan

1. Pre-approach
2. Approach
3. Presentation
4. Meeting Objections
5. Closing

The Sales Base

the product

The product or service itself is the most important aspect of the sales base, as it is the thing that the small business will sell. This product or service will satisfy some needs or desires of the customers; it is often marketed through a particular type of store within a given price range. Athletic shoe stores generally sell only a certain kind of shoe within a limited price range. The product should be useful, desirable, attractive in appearance, and almost certain to satisfy each individual consumer.

product knowledge

An area of primary concern to small business owners and managers is the knowledge that their salespeople have about the product. The sales force should be properly and extensively trained in the use and value of the product. The salespeople should know the strengths and weaknesses associated with the product or service. How does it compare with similar products? What are several of the product's uses? What are its primary advantages? Does the popcorn popper use oil or hot air to pop the corn? Does it contain a unit to melt butter? How many minutes does it take to pop a batch of popcorn? What size motor does this unit have? How much popcorn will it pop at a time?

As a salesperson acquires knowledge about the product, the product itself will become more interesting to him or her, and selling it will be much more fun. The salesperson's confidence will increase, and—because everyone enjoys talking about things they are familiar with—it will be easier for him or her to discuss the product with customers. Creativity and imagination is also enhanced by product knowledge, and inventive ways of selling may be encouraged. Using product knowledge should allow a salesperson to convert that knowledge into customer benefits, which can help sell the item. The knowledge that an automobile provides thirty-six miles per gallon can be transferred into benefits such as that it will allow longer trips, will save money, will save time, will save gas (fewer refills), and will cause less inconvenience.

image

The foundation of the sales base is the image of the product, service, or business. Is the product a high-quality, high-priced item, or does it have a low-quality, low-priced discount appearance? A restaurant offering poor food at very high prices often closes within a period of weeks, while a fast-food restaurant offering a limited quantity of food at reasonable prices will generally be a huge success in the business community. You do not want to sell high-priced clothing in a discount store. You should match the product with its image and price in any business.

need fulfillment

A product or a service must be able to satisfy the basic wants and needs of its customers. A person will not buy a new car unless he or she *wants* to own one. A person will not buy a new-fangled hairbrush unless it satisfies a particular need. A person will not buy clothing unless it satisfies some desire to be fashionable or a need to be kept warm. You do not want to try to sell a freezer to a person who only needed a refrigerator, because he or she may not be back. Seek to sell the product that will satisfy some want or need. Sell the gas mileage, not just the car.

display

The product must be properly displayed. This may just involve the placement of the goods neatly upon the shelves in the store, or it may require the proper dressing of a mannequin in a window display area. The display of the product may also include packaging or wrapping the product so that it will be attractive to the user. The display should highlight the advantages, features, benefits, and easy usage of the product.

The Sales Plan

The sales plan is the heart of selling. It consists of: (1) the pre-approach stage, (2) the approach stage, (3) the presentation stage, (4) the meeting-objections stage, and (5) the closing stage. It is important for all salespeople to become familiar with and to develop skill in these various sales stages. These stages comprise the actual face-to-face interaction of a salesperson with a customer, and they will either increase or decrease the total sales of a business.

the pre-approach stage

The pre-approach stage is often divided into two subcategories: prospecting and pre-approach. The prospecting stage deals with finding people (the prospects) who might become customers. There, is a constant need for new customers and a variety of ways in which new prospects may be discovered. For example, new customers may be found through: referrals, by advertising, from direct mailings, by mailing lists, in telephone books, through other salespeople, through service personnel, by personal observation, in one's sphere of influence, by cold-turkey canvassing, via associations, at meetings and conventions, in directories, and through friends and relatives. There is no one and only way of prospecting, and all ways must be considered.

The pre-approach stage is when the salesperson does everything possible to prepare for the sale before face-to-face contact or communication with the prospect. The purpose of the pre-approach stage is to gain information about prospective customers and to make certain that all steps have been taken to properly display and advertise the product or service. The pre-approach stage should include gathering information (personal and business) about prospects, checking the neatness of store's interior and exterior display and layout, displaying the merchandise within store, advertising, and promotional items available to be given out.

the approach stage

The approach stage is concerned with the appearance, personality, and character of the salesperson. The object is to ensure that the salesperson makes a positive and cordial approach to the customer. The customer will form a positive or a negative impression of the salesperson within the first two minutes of contact. Specific objectives of the approach stage are:

- to gain attention and make sure that the customer is aware
- to awaken a need
- to evaluate the prospect and his or her needs, and
- to prepare the prospect for the presentation.

The approach should alert the prospect to his or her needs and also prepare him or her for the demonstration or presentation of the product or service. There are about as many approaches to selling as there are people. Some of the more common sales approaches include: the introductory approach—introduce yourself and the product you represent ("This pesticide kills all crawling insects that come in contact with the product and it is made by the most successful pesticide manufacturer."); the customer benefit approach—may be the strongest approach ("This double threading insures a longer lasting suit which will withstand use and wear over the years."); the shock approach; the survey approach; the flattery approach; the bonus approach; the question approach; the curiosity approach, and the help-the-salesman approach—probably the least effective ("My boss pays me $5.00 for each sales presentation I make, will you please listen to me?")

the presentation stage

The presentation stage introduces the product or service to the customer. The salesperson's major objectives for the presentation and/or demonstration are:

- to sell the merchandise
- to sell himself or herself
- to sell the company he or she represents
- to sell the demonstration or presentation.

It would be helpful to a salesperson making a presentation or demonstration to remember to show respect for the customer; to be excited about the demonstration (show enthusiasm and good taste); to keep statements and claims conservative; to be factual; to explain warranties and guarantees; to provide any appropriate testimonials; to sell the image and reputation of company, and to explain any personal experiences with and uses of the product.

the meeting-objections stage

The meeting-objections stage is the time when the salesperson must eliminate or overcome any reasons the prospect may have for not buying a particular product or service. The salesperson should often try to align himself or herself with the customer in searching for answers and solutions. Different methods may be used in meeting the objections. Some of the more common techniques are: (1) direct denial (most often used but often ineffective), (2) indirect denial (explaining how someone else overcame the problem), (3) compensation (admitting the objection to be valid but offering features or benefits that will overcome any deficiency), (4) questions (asking questions to further understand the objection or to allow the customer to answer his or her own question), and (5) passing by or forgetting the objection (it may be appropriate to just forget or not be concerned with an objection that seems unimportant or trivial to the sale). (See Table 18–2.)

Table 18–2. Overcoming Objections

Benefit Approach: Restate the problem and list solutions.
    Example: "Your son has too many cavities. Crest reduces cavities, and tastes good, too."

Reinforcer Approach: Show support, reinforce, and expand.
    Example: "This watch shows the time, the date, and continuous seconds. It also lights in the dark and looks very good on you."

Objection Approach: Restate the objection and minimize its seriousness.
    Example: "Costs too much. Let me show you how it will pay for itself."

Proof Approach: Restate benefits and add additional support or testimonials.
    Example: "This detergent is the largest selling detergent in the United States and is used by more homemakers than any other kind."

Probe Approach: Question problem; let them find their own solution.
    Examples: 1. Indirect Probe—"Oh?" or "Any reason?"
              2. Direct Probe—"Why do you feel that way?"

Closing Approach: Review points of agreement and propose course of action.
    Example: "This shoe fits very well, looks extremely nice on your foot, and will feel like a cushion when you walk. Shall I wrap it for you?"

the closing stage

Closing the sale is a result of the salesperson's efforts. The major objectives of closing the sale are: (1) to get the order and (2) to prepare for continuous service and future orders. The order is the salesperson's final payoff, after having prepared for the customer; attracted his or her attention; presented himself or herself, the company, and the product; demonstrated the product; overcome the objections and misunderstandings of the customer and made the sale. It is important to encourage the customer so that he or she will return and provide you with more business. This may involve services to be presented after the sale or installation of the product. It may also involve recording the sale so that the customer can be notified about future sales opportunities. (See Table 18–3.)

Table 18–3. Closing Signals

Closing means getting your customer to decide "Yes."

SIGNAL		
Color	Does this can opener come in yellow?	Yes. May I get you one from our stock room?
Delivery	Can you deliver this to my home?	Yes. Would delivery on Wednesday or Friday be best?
Style	Do you have the new sporting vest?	Yes. Would you also like the reversible vest?
Feature	Does this drill go through metal?	Yes. Do you want both the metal and wood bit or just metal?
Looks	This dress does match my shoes.	Yes. Would you like me to charge that or would you like to pay cash?

SUCCESS STORY: Rowland Macy

Rowland Macy was born on Nantucket Island, Massachusetts, in 1822. When he was fifteen he ventured off on a four-year whaling voyage. On his return from sea, he went from job to job, and finally settled down to retailing at 22.

His first three attempts—in Boston and Haverville, Massachusetts, and Marysville, California—ended in failure. In 1858, Macy founded another dry goods store; this time in New York City and this time a little fancier than the three earlier stores. During the next twenty years, the business grew rapidly and the shop near the corner of 14th Street and Sixth Avenue developed into one of the first department stores in the world.

Macy's sales philosophy can be summed up: buy and sell for cash; charge everyone the same price; sell at the cheapest price possible, advertise and promote goods aggressively.

After Rowland Macy died in 1877, the business went through many owners, but eventually two brothers, Nathan and Isidor Straus, acquired ownership. Even after Macy's was converted into a publicly held corporation, the Strauses stayed in the hierarchy.

The rapid growth at the original location resulted in the store's expansion into a maze of levels and elevations that made shopping complicated. So the Strauses built a new Macy's at 34th Street and Broadway that opened in 1902. In the mid-1920s another store, erected at the same location, filled the whole block and created the biggest department store in the world.

Macy's selling philosophy went through a change, too. "Cash only" sales were abandoned as the clientele widened from strictly middle class. Style and quality that appeals to all income groups made Macy's the store it is today. Interesting merchandise from all over the world found its way to 34th and Broadway as Macy's management worked closely with many overseas producers. Aggressive promotion and advertising are still a hallmark at Macy's; the annual Thanksgiving Day Parade, begun in 1924, is only one example.

Sales Forecasting

There is no easy method of developing a sales forecast. A company's forecast of expected sales is the expected total sales for a given product or service using a specific marketing plan. This means that sales will fluctuate according to the marketing and promotion that is used by the business in selling its goods or services. Factors that influence the sales forecast include: (1) long-range goals, (2) recent or current sales goals, (3) the current business outlook, and (4) outside influences. The long-range goals of a company would consist of the projected sales growth, return on investment, and the expected growth plans of the business. These factors may be large or small, depending on the desires of the owner, the manager, or the executives responsible for marketing.

The current sales level will also highly influence the sales forecast. Factors involved with current or recent sales results include: (1) recent or historical expansion, or (2) growth trends. Many small business owners will utilize the second factor as the only one influencing a projected sales forecast. Some business owners wish to maintain current sales levels and will not even include a projected increase for inflation. This will often result in a decrease in profits, due to an increase in costs when sales remain the same.

The current business outlook may also highly influence the sales forecast, due to (1) the economic outlook for the community, state, and nation, (2) the competitive outlook, (3) industrial growth factors or declines, and (4) public concern for products and safety. The establishment of a new mall in a town may tend to decrease the sales of downtown stores. Public awareness of faults in automobiles may cause a decrease in car sales.

Outside factors that will definitely influence a sales forecast include employees (their attitudes and drives), bankers or lending organizations (available money), suppliers, and other managerial influences or partners. An increase in wage rates may necessitate an increase in the sales level. To pay off equipment or mortgages for the banks may necessitate increasing sales. Limitation by suppliers or their increasing costs may alter a sales forecast.

The sales forecast will provide a total dollar estimate as well as a unit sales estimate for a specific period of time for the business. It will be tied in closely with the marketing plan being used by the business. The sales forecast will be dependent upon the sales potential that a business has. The *sales potential* is the market share of the total market that the company desires to achieve. Basically, the market may be viewed as the expected sales of a product, service or entire industry in a specific geographical area over a stated period of time. The sales forecast may be based on the assumption of an equal share of the total market potential. For example, if $400,000 is the total market potential for a business in a particular city, with one other competing store, the sales potential for that business would be $400,000 divided by 2, or $200,000.

a simplified sales forecasting method

An easy way to start or prepare a sales forecast for a new or existing business would be to determine what the total market is (how much was spent in sales in your city or county for your products during the past year) for your business. This information is often available from (1) trade associations, (2) the Bureau of Census, and (3) the Bureau of Business Research. The State Department of Economic Development can also be helpful. After defining the total sales, divide it by the number of stores or competitors in your geographical area. This would yield your equal share of the total market. If you run a new business, you can easily anticipate your share to be somewhat below this equal share, unless you have specific promotional or marketing plans to offset your newness. You can also anticipate that, due to industrial growth and/or inflation, your share of the market would even be higher than the current market.

Therefore, for a piano and organ store in an Eastern city with total sales for the city last year of $1.5 million and four competitors, the sales forecast can be computed as follows:

$$\text{Sales} \div \text{Number of stores} = \$1,500,000 \div 5 = \$300,000 \text{ per store}$$

The sales forecast for the piano and organ store would be equal to the market share ($300,000), times the strength (image, drawing power, and so on) of the store (0.1 to 2 or above), times economic conditions (0.1 to 10). Therefore, the sales forecast, assuming a new store with a large promotional package, would be equal to:

$$\begin{aligned}\text{Sales forecast} &= \text{Market share} \times \text{Business strength} \times \text{Environmental conditions} \\ &= \$300,000 \times 0.8 \times 1.2 \\ &= \$288,000.\end{aligned}$$

This is a simple method by which the owner of a new business or an existing business can project sales for a one-year period of time. It assumes and requires information about the strength of one's own business in relation to the competitors; it also assumes one is able to acquire one's fair total market share. In addition, it assumes that one knows about inflation factors or promotional packages and their ability to influence consumer behavior. The numerical values for "strength of the store" and "economic conditions" are estimates or subjective evaluations of those business factors.

An advanced sales forecast may also be figured upon: (1) long-range goals and objectives, (2) current and recent sales results, (3) current business outlook, and (4) outside influences. (See Table 18–4.)

Table 18-4. Advanced Sales Forecast

$$R' = aR + R(1+b) + cR + x$$

where: R' = Sales forecast
R = Sales revenue—$300,000
a = Long-range goals (percentage of sales)—10%
b = Recent sales growth rate as a percentage of sales in the past 5 years—6%
c = Percent based on current business outlook—+10%
x = Includes sales commission and special promotional items—$12,000

$R' = .10 \times (\$300,000) + \$300,000 \times (1 + .06) + .10 \times \$300,000 + \$12,000$
$R' = = \$390,000$

An advanced sales forecast provides a somewhat inflated, though realistic, dream goal for the small business owner. Factors are often influenced by inflation, recent sales growth or decline, and an optimistic sales manager who is interested in increasing profits. Other methods of sale forecasting may include (1) the owner's opinion, (2) an executive composite, (3) a sales force composite, (4) a trend analysis, and (5) an analysis of market and growth potential.

Owner's opinion. The owner or manager is faced with the problem of deciding which method of sales forecasting to use. Almost everyone is willing to make an estimate and these estimates will vary widely, but it is valuable to ascertain these estimates in order to get a better perspective on the sales for the immediate future. These methods may finally be comprised into a whole and used to develop a composite analysis including all the forecasting methods.

The owner's estimate is the oldest and most commonly used forecast. This method tends to be highly biased, although it does contain information important to the final sales estimate. Most owners are aware of historical and current sales trends, which will greatly influence the sales level of the business in the future. This is often the quickest and easiest sales forecast to obtain.

Executive composite. The owner may obtain information from employees or executives, and have them help to develop the sales forecast. This is very similar to the jury technique of establishing a consensus opinion from the jury members. They will deliberate only after they have obtained all the information important to establishing their forecast.

Sales force composite. A separate forecast may be made by the sales force. This will allow those directly related to the sales to estimate their own increases, and to compile them into a sales-force composite. This forecast is a composite forecast and is generally very accurate. It does allow the sales people to develop their own goals and objectives for the upcoming sales period. However, many sales people may undercut their projected sales in order to "look good" at the end of the sales forecast period.

Trend analysis. A projection of marketing trends requires that a mathematical trend model be applied to the historical sales figures. Both business conditions and the opinions (goals and desires) of individuals are excluded from this sales forecast. The future business activity of the organization will be estimated based upon the activity of the organization over its historical past.

Potential growth analysis. Yet another method of sales forecasting is to analyze those market factors that would affect future sales. This is based upon the assumption that the immediate prior sales level may be obtained, unless it is unduly changed by environmental conditions. The environmental, business, and economic conditions of a community will alter or influence a sales forecast. This method may be one of the more scientific approaches to developing a sales forecast. It allows one to investigate factors that may in any way influence the sales market.

It is probably best to simplify the sales forecast and the techniques for forming it; sound logic should be the basis of any forecast. If possible, more than one method should be used, and developing two or three of them into one final sales forecast figure. High and low forecasts should also be developed in addition to the basic sales forecast. These high and low forecasts may be estimated by viewing the economic and business conditions surrounding the business and future demand or increase in business level.

Sales Force Compensation Plans

A very important aspect of business is developing a sound compensation program for employees. Employees directly related to sales will have a tremendous impact on the sales volume of the business. It is important, therefore, to develop a compensation plan that will (1) attract and keep competent sales people, (2) ensure proper respect for customers, (3) provide some control and direction for sales, and (4) allow rewards for efforts and results. The method of compensation is also important in that it can ensure the motivation and retention of the sales force. The chosen method should allow the employees to reach a reasonable level of income while providing motivation and increasing work levels. The most common methods are by way of: (1) salaries, (2) commissions, (3) combination salaries and commissions, (4) bonuses, (5) drawing accounts, (6) expense accounts, (7) profit sharing, and (8) other monetary benefits.

salaries

Salaries are the most traditional of all payment plans and they are a direct monetary reward paid to employees for the performance of their duties. The amount of a salary is primarily based on competitive factors, (such as what other companies may be paying or the value of the employees to sales force). A salary is a fixed amount that is paid for a specific period of time. Salaries are paid on a regular basis (usually monthly, biweekly, or weekly) with the expectation that employees will work for a minimum number of hours a week (usually 40) or even more. The salary method to be used should be chosen when creating or starting a new sales territory or creating a new product. This compensation plan provides loyalty, and often well satisfied employees. The salary plan does not provide motivational or incentive programs. Salaries are generally based on minimum performance levels rather than encouraging maximum effort.

commissions

The commission plan provides a regular payment for the performance of a specific work unit. The commission is a percentage of the sales volume. The major advantage of a commission plan is the tremendous motivation and incentive it can provide the employees. If no ceilings are established, a commission sales representative will often receive a higher income than a salaried employee—perhaps even a higher income than the owner or manager. The major disadvantage of the commission plan is lack of control over the sales force. Due to the high incentive to increase sales, a sales representative may use questionable practices to make a sale, which can threaten future business. A combination of salary and commission is the most common of all compensation programs.

bonuses

Another method of compensation is a bonus, which is an extra, lump-sum payment that is given to an employee, generally at the end of a specific time period. Most businesses that provide bonuses do so as a profit-sharing technique with their employees. That is, at the end of the year in which the business has realized an increase in profits of $10,000 over the previous year, the owner may give a lump-sum bonus of $500 to each of ten employees as a bonus for the increased sales. Bonuses are generally not attached to specific units of work and no obligation to pay a bonus is ever established by a company. However, many companies have historically given bonuses and therefore one is often expected by the employees. Even then, the amount of the bonus is generally not known ahead of time. One of the most common methods of providing a bonus is based on total sales or individual sales.

drawing accounts

Another method of sales compensation is the establishment of drawing accounts. A drawing account is a fixed sum that is advanced to an employee for a particular time period (generally the salary period of a month). The employee can then draw against a limited amount of money; $600 a month, for example. At the end of that time period, the amount drawn is paid back to the company from the earnings, commissions, or salary of the employee.

Most drawing accounts are established to offset the uncertainty and drawbacks of a straight commission program. Due to sales fluctuations and the seasonal nature of many businesses, a drawing account may be carried over from one period to another. That is, if an employee drew out $600 one month but his or her sales commissions were only valued at $450, the remaining $150 would be carried over to the following month. Drawing accounts are primarily a convenience for the employees and provide little, if any, motivation or control by management.

335
SALES AND SALES
FORECASTING

Many employees receive additional compensation through profit sharing or expense accounts. Reimbursement for travel and other sales or business expenses that have been incurred by employees are often kept separate from the regular compensation. The expenses may also include such items as gas money for automobiles, country club visits, and business lunches. Expense account payments may result in a net addition or reduction of a person's earnings.

profit sharing

The profit-sharing compensation program is not a widely used form of compensation. The sales force does not usually have enough control over the profits of a business in order to make a profit-sharing program worthwhile. Problems—over which the salesperson has no control—may arise in the purchasing, production, service, or the quality of goods, which may drastically affect the profit picture of the business.

CASE STUDY: The Everett 3 Movie Theater

The Everett 3 movie theater, which is really three cinemas in one, is located in the downtown area of a metropolitan community with a population of 180,000. The theater has been in existence for seven years. It is located two blocks away from a major state university of 25,000 students.

The theater has been averaging an 87 percent capacity for Fridays, Saturdays, and Sundays, including the Saturday and Sunday matinees. The theater has only been drawing a 42 percent capacity on Monday through Thursday evenings. There are no matinees during the week.

The Everett 3 only shows first-run feature movies. Almost all of its movies are rated as either PG or R, with the majority in the PG classification. Approximately 20 percent of its movies have a G rating, and only about 4 percent of the movies shown during the year will have an X rating.

Feature movies are generally distributed on a competitive basis to the highest bidder in a city. The average feature movie will require a payment of $25,000 to $50,000, plus 95 percent of all gross receipts (ticket sales) of the first three-day week. After the initial prime run, the percentage take is reduced in increments of 5 percent for a two-to-four week period, until 80 percent or 75 percent of the gross receipts is obtained. These monies are paid directly by the movie theater to the distributor of the film. For example, the film "Superman: The Movie" cost $50,000 plus 95 percent of gross receipts or gross ticket receipts for the first ten weeks. For each succeeding four weeks, the percentage rate was reduced by 5 percent until it reached 75 percent. The Everett 3's managers are interested in knowing what their potential sales volume would be. The total sales potential, if 67 percent capacity was obtained the year round, would be a little less than $500,000. Two years ago, sales were at $416,000, and last year sales were $448,000.

The managers of the movie theater would also appreciate ideas on how to attract new customers. What type of personal selling or sales promotion should be undertaken? How can they also attract additional customers at the concession stand, which provides the bulk of the theater's profits? Due to the high cost of the films, it is extremely difficult to make money on the price of admission. Nearly all of the admissions paid will end up going back to the distributor of the film. To pay for the staff and still make a profit in the business, it is important that the concessions provide an adequate income.

The show times at the Everett 3 are usually at 7 and 9 P.M. during the week, and at 2, 4, 7, and 9 P.M. on weekends. The theater has sponsored contests on radio with limited success. They have also sponsored dances at local discos and have provided free tickets to local bars and dining places for customers. The advertising policy is generally limited to the Friday, Saturday, and Sunday editions of the local morning and evening papers. During the rest of the week, only a listing of a show and its times appear in the local papers. No advertising is currently done over television.

Another promotional idea that has been raised is to set aside one night per year when the Everett 3 would sponsor a charitable organization. On this particular night, all proceeds would go to this organization.

The Everett 3 was originally built at a cost of $700,000, with an interest rate of 9 percent over a period of twenty years. Monthly installments are approximately $6,400. The building was built close to the industrial average, which is $650 per seat for 900 seats.

The major films have a cost base of 95 percent of the gross receipts from the door. Other minor films may have a cost base of only $15,000 to $40,000 with a percentage rate of 80–90%. The Everett 3 usually shows two major films and one minor film at the same time. The average length of a major film showing is seven weeks, while the minor films are kept for only four weeks, on the average.

Questions

1. How do you increase profits?
2. What kind of films would be best?
3. What forms of advertising should be used?
4. How would you use the concession stands to improve business?
5. Does a "superstar" movie mean profit for the movie theater?

Chapter Questions:

1. Discuss the value of selling.
2. Discuss the four major classifications of selling activities.
3. Discuss the importance of the sales base.
4. Develop a sales plan for the product of your choice.
5. Discuss different prospecting and pre-approach activities.
6. Discuss different methods of overcoming objectives.

7. Discuss the use of sales forecast.
8. Develop a sales forecast for a ladies' clothing store, if the following is true:
   a. Prior years' sales: $210,000; $203,000; $190,000; $196,000, and $178,000.
   b. Similar stores in community: six.
   c. Total of ladies clothing sales in community: $1,600,000.
   d. Current business outlook: bright.
9. Discuss the advantages and disadvantages of different sales force compensation plans.
10. Discuss incentives and sales force promotional packages.

19

Photo courtesy of Irene Springer, Prentice-Hall, Inc.

LEADERSHIP AND MANAGEMENT

Chapter Objectives:

1. To learn about the factors involved in good leadership.
2. To understand the different sources of leadership and their degrees of influence.
3. To understand the role of goals in a business.
4. To appreciate the development and use of leadership.
5. To learn about different leadership styles and their effective use.
6. To learn about the current leadership theories.

Somebody said that it couldn't be done,
But he with a chuckle replied
That "maybe it couldn't," but he would be one,
Who wouldn't say so till he'd tried.
So he buckled right in with the trace of a grin
On his face. If he worried he hid it.
He started to sing as he tackled the thing
That couldn't be done, and he did it.

Edgar A. Guest [1]

INCIDENT:

Mike has just finished his college work, and has received a degree in business. He has been hired to be an assistant manager of the Pier Six Restaurant. The owner-manager at Pier Six is a close personal friend of Mike's father and Mike has been looking forward to the opportunity to return to his hometown and work at the restaurant ever since he was in high school.

The Pier Six Restaurant primarily provides service for the middle- to upper-class clientele. They serve steak and fish dishes, with menu prices ranging from $7 to $15 for the entrees.

The restaurant employs 106 people, including three full-time assistant managers, sixteen full-time cooks, two full-time bartenders, and three full-time receptionists. Additional staff are used as necessary.

Mike's responsibility will be to run the entire restaurant in the absence of the owner-manager or any of the other assistant managers. He is very concerned about what type of leadership style he should use and how he will get along with the other employees—he would like to become friends with the people with whom he will work. He is also concerned about his lack of experience in the restaurant business, and is confused by the different styles of management he has seen the owner-manager use with different employees. Mike does not understand why he would speak harshly to one employee for doing something wrong; yet to another employee who did the same thing wrong, he would sit and give counsel during off hours. Mike is puzzled at the strict control that the owner keeps over all the cooks and the lack of freedom they have in developing the entrees or other dishes—they all have to conform to the specifications of the owner.

Mike does not really know if this is how one should actually manage a business, and he is concerned as to how he will work with the owner as his boss, as well as with the other employees.

Almost everyone wants to be a great leader. Leaders have caused the rise and fall of nations as well as of businesses, families, and associations. Leadership is a skill that may be developed and trained within all individuals. Great leadership requires great followers. But great leadership can and must be developed.

[1] Reprinted from *Collected Verse of Edgar A. Guest* by Edgar A. Guest, © 1934 with permission of Contemporary Books, Inc., Chicago.

Management is both an art and a science. It is mainly concerned with establishing an environment in which the goals and objectives of an organization may be efficiently and effectively realized. Although managerial styles may differ, management is a universal activity. The art of managing is found in homes, hospitals, businesses, schools, and organizations. The specifics of a managerial function will vary from one organization to another, but most of the basic functions of management—planning, organizing, directing, staffing, and controlling—are found in all the settings and organizations.

While the owner or manager of a small business is accountable for the efficient and effective use of all the resources within the organization, it should be noted that this is accomplished through the people who work in the organization. In businesses, *people make the difference*. People are the creators and developers of ideas and the success which most businesses find. Competent people are the difference between a successful and an unsuccessful business.

The manager is responsible for the performance of the business; for the performance and operations of the individuals in that business, and the functions of the business. Performance is often measured by efficiency (doing well and not wasting resources) and effectiveness (the effect people have on work, the usefulness of goals, and the values and ethics in the working environment).

The Individual

All individuals have values, beliefs, and attitudes that help form the personality. This personality, coupled with individual perceptions, learning, and motivation, come together to develop the behavior of an individual. To best influence an individual, it is probably best to understand the attitudes and motivation that cause him or her to act.

Nearly all behavior is based on motives and attitudes. The motives and attitudes of an individual are generally developed from his or her own knowledge (see Figure 19–1). Knowledge is information about a subject, object, or person. It does not have to be correct. For example, automobile companies have built cars

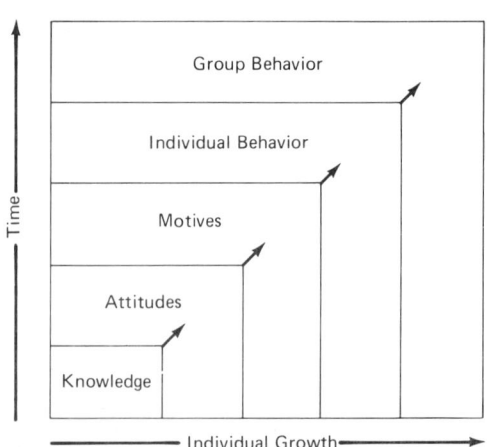

FIGURE 19–1. *Individual development*

based on the information that there was a strong and large market demand. Public officials have left office because of changes in the knowledge of the populace.

The primary sources of information come from parents and family, peer groups, friends, and associates. The news media are a very good source of information. If sufficient information is provided, the populace may be persuaded that a war effort is initially good; later, with new information, that populace may come to the decision that a war effort is bad. Have you ever wondered how the vast majority of politicians are elected? Do the people spend hours reading and studying and debating the issues or do millions of individuals vote based on very simple but perhaps persuasive visual images or news stories?

The advertising industry is built upon the foundation of providing information to individuals. It is reported that many people watch television at least six hours a day. If this is true, it is no wonder that many people buy a particular detergent or brand of toothpaste.

One's knowledge base may be limited by rejecting informational sources, by modifying or screening the information, or by rejecting the information provided. However, if the information is repeated several times, the likelihood of retention is greatly increased. This will help to further develop the attitudes and behaviors of individuals. Many businesses and government agencies will print newspapers or flyers proclaiming the benefits and opportunities available for working at that location. The individual, personality, and actions are made up of three major factors: (1) attitude, (2) motive, and (3) behavior.

Attitude is generally defined as a predisposition to behave. Attitudes are comprised of feelings, emotions, cognitions, values, and beliefs. Attitudes have a value dimension. People do tend to imitate the attitudes of others they admire and respect. If others feel it is "right" to wear Adidas running shoes, you are likely to hold that attitude, too. If your friends oppose smoking and busing, then you will probably hold similar attitudes. Advertisements are designed to alter your attitude in favor of their product or service. For example, Ford wants you to have a positive attitude about their products which may result in your buying (behavior) one of their cars.

In businesses, it is to the advantage of the owner or manager if the employees have positive and favorable attitudes toward the organization. If the employees have an attitude of work, loyalty, and diligence, the organization has a greater possibility for success. Many companies, including Ralston Purina, have gift catalogues from which employees or the public may purchase goods carrying the company logo (Ralston Purina's red and white checker-board square). The gifts improve the public and employee exposure to the company and enhance the company's image.

Motives are those functions within an individual that activate, direct, sustain, and channel behavior toward goals. Motives vary from one individual to another. The athlete may be motivated by a desire to excel. Jack Nicklaus may have a desire to be recognized as the greatest golf player ever; Mohammed Ali claims to be the greatest heavyweight champion ever. Businesspeople may have desires for fame or status within their communities. Others may want wealth or material positions. Many individuals wish to help others.

It is difficult to recognize the specific motives of individuals. Motives are also influenced by the expectancy a person has that a particular behavior will result in a particular outcome. For instance, does the student who studies hard expect to perform extremely well on the exam, or get only an average grade on it? Motives are also influenced by the valences that an individual has, *valences* being the attractiveness or intensity an individual has for an expected result. Valences are a person's strong desire for recognition, achievement, or a pay raise. If both the valences and the expectancy are high, the behavior of the individual will quite often be extremely productive, resulting in high performance.

Behavior is any action or performance that an individual displays. Behavior is the result of the knowledge, attitudes, and motives of an individual. Since most individuals would like to have their attitudes and behavior be consistent, most behaviors will be the result of the attitudes and motives of the individual. No behaviors are alike.

Most business owners will ask their employees to have positive and energetic attitudes, which will result in positive and energetic behaviors.

One of the easiest ways to change an individual's behavior is to provide him or her with different information or knowledge, which would result in a change in attitude and motives.

A store manager will do well to praise his or her employees when they do well, and to reprimand them when they do poorly. This provides them with a knowledge base (feedback) specific to their behavior in the business. Business training is a way of providing information about the proper performance or functions that individuals should follow in carrying out their assignments.

SUCCESS STORY: Jeno F. Paulucci

"I'm a maverick," Jeno Paulucci says. "I believe that's probably the main reason why I've succeeded. I've done things that everybody said couldn't be done and I've done them in what everybody said was a crazy way. If any young man comes to me and asks how he's to make his fortune, I tell him to do the same. Get off the beaten track. Be a little mad."[2]

Jeno believes what he says. In the late 1960s he wrote a book entitled *How It Was To Make $100,000,000 In A Hurry* to explain his maverick philosophy in depth.

Certainly it took a certain amount of audacity for an Italian to launch a Chinese food business in Minnesota. But selling food seemed to come naturally to him. At 14, he began working in a supermarket in Duluth as a stock boy, moving crates around, mopping the floor, and in general sweating for his pay. When customers asked him questions, he found that he was actively selling the food rather than giving the curt replies normally given by the muscle boys in the market.

The manager of the store noted his talent, and set him to hawk fruit outside the store. One day he received a shipment of 18 crates of damaged bananas. They were still edible but had turned speckled brown by a refrigeration accident. Bananas were selling at 4 pounds for 25 cents, and his boss suggested that he offer them at 4 pounds for 19 cents to get rid of them. Paulucci began shouting, "Argentine bananas!" Although there is no such thing as an Argentine banana, the cus-

[2] Max Gunther, ed., *The Very, Very Rich and How They Got That Way,* (New York: Playboy Press) 1972.

tomers flocked to him to see these exotic fruits. In no time at all, he had sold the entire quantity at the bargain prices of 10 cents per pound.

Paulucci sold fruit to put himself through college, and enrolled in law school. After three semesters, he decided to return to his first love, and got a job as a traveling salesman for a wholesale food company. He worked on straight commission, and was soon making more money than the company president. When the company told him to go on straight salary or leave, he left.

He returned to Minnesota and began to sell oriental bean sprouts under the label "Foo Young," although there was not a single Oriental working for the company. In the mid 1940s he changed the name to the more exotic sounding "Chun King." He convinced companies that Chun King was a solid company when it was little more than Paulucci himself with the products produced in a surplus quonset hut.

In 1966, Paulucci sold Chun King to R. J. Reynolds, for $63 million cash. Since then, he has concentrated on building his new company, Jeno's, to a similar stature.

Note: Jeno's, Inc., is the world's leading packer of pizza products, surpassing the sales volume of Chun King in just five years.

Leadership

It is a generally accepted idea that good leadership and management are essential to the success of a business. Businesses that do succeed can often attribute their growth and success to the leadership capabilities of the owner or manager. Those businesses that fail can often attribute their failure to a lack of expertise and leadership ability of management.

a definition of leadership

Leadership may be defined as the ability to influence individuals and groups toward the accomplishment of the goals or objectives. Leaders may receive their sources of influence from either formal or informal settings. Formal leaders are generally appointed or are established by the business or organization with which they work. Formal leaders use the positions they are given through legitimate authority, reward authority, or coercive authority, and they utilize these resources to bring to pass the goals of the organization.

Informal leaders usually emerge from within groups. They tend to rely on their (1) referent or charismatic power, or (2) their expert power to lead and direct the fellow members of their group. While a formal leader may have all the rights of leadership, these rights will not guarantee his or her success to effectively lead or motivate individuals to accomplish goals. The informal leader has a much greater chance of accomplishing his or her desired goals or objectives. (See Figure 19–2).

the history of leadership

The historical study of leadership centers on three major approaches: (1) traits theory, (2) behavioral approaches, and (3) contingency models.

traits theory

When describing an individual or discussing the characteristics of a great leader, one generally refers to that person's traits. Traits are the relatively stable and consistent behavior of individuals. The historical approach to leadership was to try

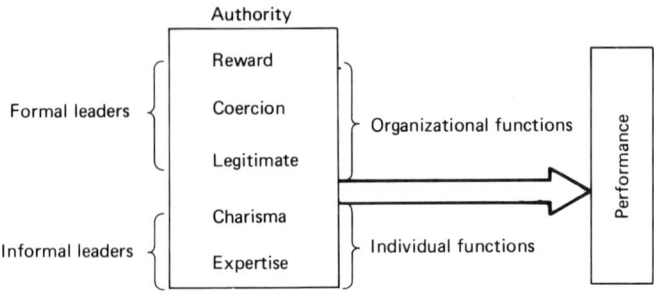

FIGURE 19-2. *Formal and informal leadership*

to identify traits common to all great leaders. However, it is difficult to isolate all the various traits that enabled Alexander the Great, Napoleon, Joan of Arc, Martin Luther King, Jr., Mahatma Gandhi, John F. Kennedy, or Mohammed Ali to become great leaders. Although these people may have some characteristics (traits) in common, their behaviors were/are widely different.

By the 1950s, most leaders and researchers had concluded that traits were unable to provide any substantial base which could explain leadership. Traits theory tended to ignore the situation and the environment. They also tended to take for granted the followers of each leader, and the individual personalities of the leaders. Traits theory also lead to the conclusion that some people were "born leaders," while others may never become leaders because they did not inherit certain traits.

Although it is interesting to discuss the personality traits of great leaders, it is difficult to effectively identify leaders by traits. It has been shown that successful leaders in business have varying traits, with no one definite trait absolutely required to be a leader.

behavioral approaches

Due to the inability of the traits theory to correctly identify and select definite traits of leaders, researchers turned toward investigation of leadership behavior. Researchers were interested in finding if successful leaders were more dictatorial or democratic in their leadership style.

While the traits approach was primarily concerned with selecting the "right" individuals for leadership positions, the behavioral approaches were concerned with training people and developing their leadership behaviors. The traits theorists assumed that one either did or did not already have leadership ability. The behavioral approaches, on the other hand, attempted to identify definite leadership behavior and then train these behavioral patterns into other individuals, feeling that successful leaders could be trained.

The Ohio State University studies. In the late 1940s, research from Ohio State University identified two major, independent dimensions of successful leader behavior. These two categories resulted from an original list of over a thousand dimensions, and accounted for most of the leadership behavior found in managers. These two dimensions were (1) initiating structure and (2) consideration.

Initiating structure is concerned with the extent to which a leader is likely to define and develop the role structure of the subordinates in the work situation. This structuring would also involve separation of work, organization of work, and categorizing tasks.

Consideration is primarily involved with the human side of the leader. The level of consideration referred to how much a person was likely to develop job relationships characterized by trust, respect for others, and sensitivity of personal feelings. A leader with a high level of consideration was viewed as being friendly, understanding, and willing to work with subordinates to overcome any personal problems. (See Figure 19–3.)

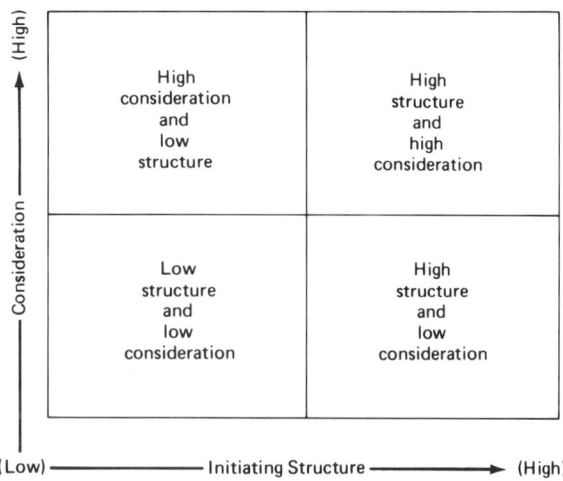

FIGURE 19–3. *The Ohio State University studies: leadership quadrants*

The University of Michigan studies. At about the same time as the Ohio State University studies in the late 1940s, the University of Michigan's Survey Research Center developed two measures of leadership performance effectiveness. These measures were called (1) employee orientation and (2) production orientation. Employee-oriented leaders generally emphasized interpersonal relations, concern for others, and acceptance of individual differences between employees. Production-oriented leaders, however, generally emphasized the task or technical aspects of the job and were concerned with satisfying the group's goals and the structuring of work.

These attempts to explain the behavior of leaders are valuable and important even today. However, it is very difficult to identify consistent behaviors across situations and business environment. Behavioral approaches do allow the training of individuals to improve their leadership behaviors. It is difficult, though, to defend the position that one kind of leadership behavior would be appropriate in all cases. Therefore, additional research was needed to more properly ascertain the proper functions and behaviors of successful leaders. Perhaps the "right" leadership style is dependent upon still other factors.

contingency models

It has become more and more important to understand that effective leadership is more than just certain traits or behaviors. The failure to obtain consistent results from either the traits theory or the behavioral approaches has forced researchers to look at the different situations surrounding leadership. This new focus has led to the study of situational variables. Researchers have tried to isolate the variables that may influence a situation and result in effective leadership. These attempts have developed into several contingency models. We shall consider three of these important contingency models: (1) Fiedler's model, (2) the path-goal model, and (3) the Vroom-Yetton decision-making model.

Fiedler's model. Fred E. Fiedler developed a model that assumes that effective performance is a result of the proper interaction between the leader's style and the situation at hand. Fiedler developed a "least preferred co-worker" (LPC) questionnaire as an instrument to measure the task or relationship orientation of a person. This basic instrument allows a worker to describe the leader with whom he or she has previously worked least well in a positive way.

This contingency model isolated three variables that make up the "favorableness of the situation": (1) leader–member relations, (2) task structure, and (3) position power. The *leader–member relations* variable focuses on the extent to which group members like and trust the leader and accept the leader's influence. The *task structure* variable is concerned with the level in which a leader clearly defines task requirements and the job assignments are highly procedurized (that is, structured). The *position power* variable refers to the formal influenceability or control a leader has over his subordinates.

The contingency approach focuses on two basic leadership styles as described by the LPC: (1) the task-motivated style and (2) the relationship-oriented style. The end result is that the most effective leadership style will depend upon the situational favorableness. That situational favorableness is determined by the three major situational variables: (1) leader–member relations, (2) task structure and (3) position power.

Fiedler's model argues that a task-motivated leader is more effective in situations that are favorable and unfavorable. The relationship-oriented leader is most effective in moderately favorable situations.

This contingency model emphasized the importance of interaction between leader, followers, and situation. Fiedler has cautioned against the idea that there is a one best style of leadership for all situations. A leader who is task-motivated in a brand-new position will probably be quite successful. But as the favorableness of the situation improves, that same leader's effectiveness will probably be decreasing and a new leader-manager should be brought in as a replacement. However, if the situation becomes quite favorable, it would be appropriate to bring back the initial leader, because the task-motivated leader is often more effective in favorable situations.

The path-goal model. The path-goal model is based on the assumption that an employee's performance level will be quite high if that employee can consider his or her work to be a means to achievement of a personal goal. This model also assumes the converse; that is, that an employee's performance level will be quite low if that employee cannot see his or her work as leading to any goal satisfaction.

The focus of the path-goal model is on the interaction of the leader with the personal characteristics of the employees, and on improving the environmental variables. The leader can work with employees to help them realize that their work accomplishments will provide them with some form of goal achievement. This will then allow the workers to perceive that their jobs are on the path to accomplishing personal objectives as well as business objectives.

The path-goal model applies the expectancy theory—which states that the successful completion of a job will lead to some reward or outcome—to help managers better understand the needs and desires of the employees. The intrinsic valences are associated with the internal rewards which an individual receives for the work he or she is accomplishing (goal-directed behavior) and for the actual accomplishment or finishing of work project (work–goal accomplishment). This is similar to the student who makes the basketball team where he or she feels inwardly rewarded for his or her accomplishment (goal-directed behavior) and also the internal reward or positive feeling for accomplishing an outstanding season in winning the league championship (work–goal accomplishment). The extrinsic valences that a worker has are primarily concerned with the actual material rewards or outcomes associated with accomplishing the task (work–goal accomplishment). This is similar to the trophies or cash awards the basketball player receives for his or her accomplishments.

There are two probabilities that an employee makes (1) the estimation that the job performance will lead to the accomplishment of some work goal or objective (work–goal attainment), and (2) the estimate of the actual accomplishment will lead toward desired outcomes or rewards (extrinsic valences). The probability of path instrumentality may be enhanced by proper training, lessening red tape or paperwork, improving the work environment, obtaining salary increases for employees, or providing improved benefits for the personnel.

Although this may be perceived as a rather complex approach to leadership, it is easily broken down into two contingency variables: (1) personal characteristics or desires of subordinates and (2) the work environment. By improving the work environment, the leader is able to improve the path instrumentalities and by strengthening the characteristics of the employees, he or she is able to increase the intrinsic and extrinsic valences of the workers. This, therefore, should lead to improved performances and productivity.

Vroom-Yetton decision-making model. The main focus of the Vroom-Yetton decision-making model is concerned with the decision requirements that a leader faces in terms of quality acceptance and time variables. This model is concerned with quality and decision acceptance in relation to various time constraints; it develops decision rules that can help leaders determine which approach is most feasible for a given decision problem.

This model identifies five different approaches that leaders may use in their decision-making processes. These five approaches (AI, AII, CI, CII, and GII) represent three different degrees: (1) autocratic (AI and AII), (2) consultative (CI and CII), and (3) group processes (GII). These five major approaches and the seven problem factors (questions) are shown in Figure 19–4.

The Vroom-Yetton decision-making model allows that any of five leadership approaches may be feasible in a specific situation:

> **AI.** You would solve the problem yourself, using the available information at the time.

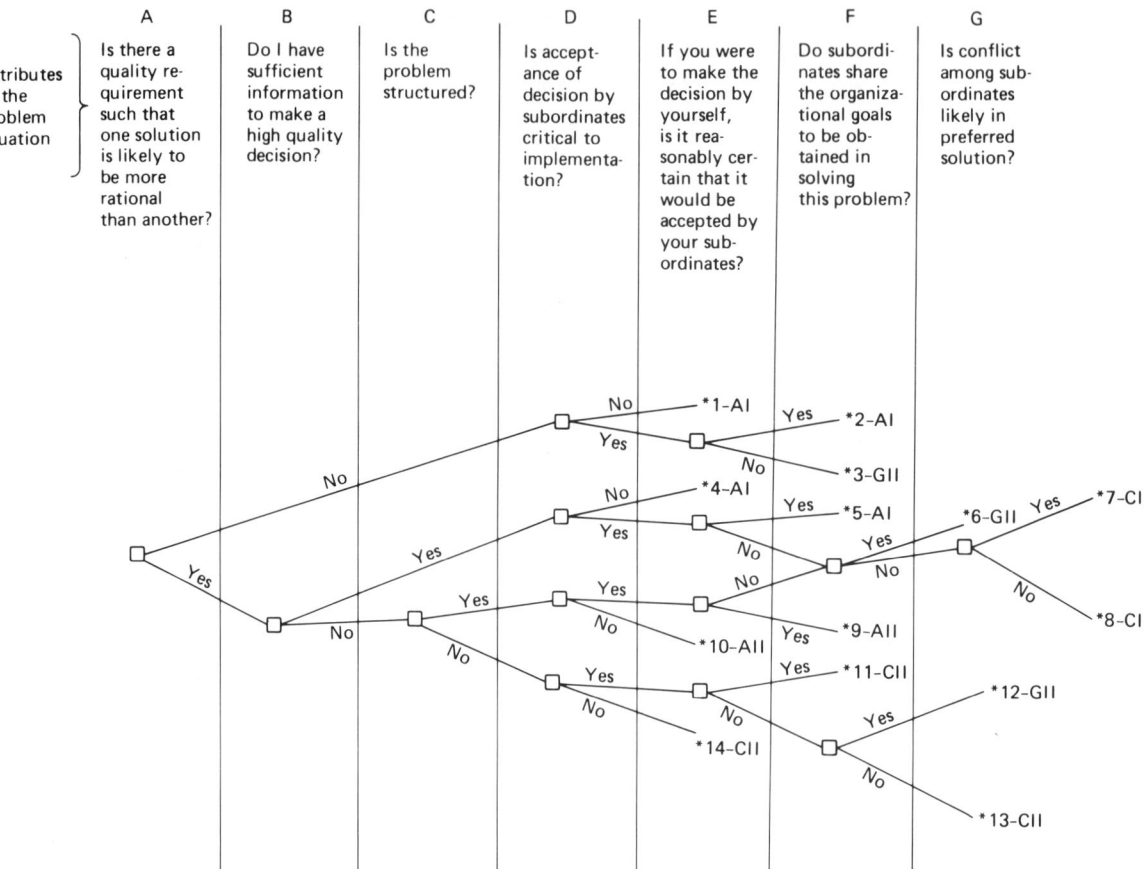

FIGURE 19-4. *The Vroom-Yetton decision-making model*

SOURCE: "A New Look at Managerial Decision Making" by Victor H. Vroom, *Organizational Dynamics*, Spring 1973, © 1973 by AMACOM, a division of American Management Associations, p. 70. All rights reserved. Reprinted by permission of the publisher.

    AII. You would solve the problem yourself, after seeking and obtaining additional sufficient information from subordinates.
    CI. You would share the problem with other subordinates, and make the decision yourself after obtaining ideas and suggestions.
    CII. You would share the problem with subordinates as a group, and make the decision after getting sufficient ideas and suggestions.
    GII. You would share the problem with the subordinates as a group, and together develop and accept any solution for implementation that is supported by the group.

    This model makes more sense in reference to participative and autocratic *situations* rather than autocratic and participative *leaders*. This is a major deviation from Fiedler's model, which emphasized changing the situation to match the given characteristics of the leader; the leader's style was assumed to be inflexible. Vroom and Yetton argue that leaders are not rigid, but are flexible and may adjust their styles and decision-making abilities to different situations.

Goals

Goals are the desired results of a business. A business may have a goal to reach a specific profit level, to obtain certain job performance levels, or to develop new and improved skills. A stated goal is an objective of the business. These organizational goals or objectives are derived from the individuals who are affiliated with the business. Only a person can have a goal. The individual is the only one who can engage in the directed behavior necessary to satisfy or accomplish the goal.

MBO

An approach that is used by many businesses and organizations for goal setting by management is called *management by objectives (MBO)*. MBO is a comprehensive organizational philosophy that is used to establish goals within an organization and to direct the behavior of individuals affiliated with the organization. It may be used in the organization, business, family, or group.

MBO may be described as a process where a superior and a subordinate discuss and jointly identify common goals, define individual responsibilities, and develop measures to be used as guides in assessing the performance of each individual within the organization. There are three basic components of an MBO program:

1. Joint goal setting.
2. Individual action and implementation.
3. Performance appraisal.

Figure 19–5 illustrates the relationship between these three components.

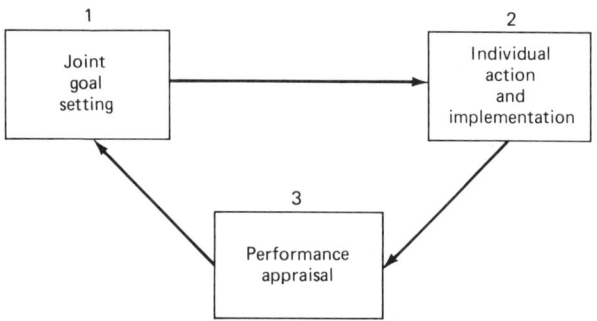

FIGURE 19–5. *Management by objectives (MBO)*

Joint goal setting. The strength of the MBO Program revolves around the give and take in which the superior and subordinate engage while developing their joint goals. The importance of this interaction is that it allows the subordinate as well as the superior to influence the final objectives and goals toward which the organization (and the subordinate) will move. These goals should contain three major elements; they should be: (1) definable, (2) measurable, and (3) accomplished within a specific time period. It is important that they be clearly defined, so that all individuals within the business may completely and fully understand what is to be accomplished. For instance, for a shoe salesperson to plan to increase sales during this coming year would be an incomplete goal. For the shoe salesperson to plan to increase the sales by 15 percent for all men's shoes, by 11 percent for all women's shoes, and by 26 percent for all athletic or running shoes within the next one-year period of time is a complete and specific goal. Definite goals will provide objectives toward which employees may work, while also allowing management to understand and forecast the future.

The goal-setting session should not be one in which the superior gives the subordinates a list of items and says, "Here are your goals for the year." This session should allow the subordinates to develop their own goal-selection processes, and to work them out so that they are fair to both the business and to themselves. Before any goals are established, it is important for both the employer and the employees to be able to explain the many goals or conditions that are important to the final result.

Individual action and implementation. The actual implementation of an MBO program within any business does not occur overnight; it will require time and patience. It is important that five major factors be allowed in any MBO program: (1) approval from the owner-manager to all employees, (2) a periodic re-evaluation, perhaps every three or six months, (3) sufficient time to implement and fully utilize the MBO program, (4) the realization of the different politics and personalities that may alter or affect the successful development of the program, and (5) the actual performance of the employees to take place without hindrance or obstacles.

It is important, in order to establish a successful MBO program, for the owner or manager to fully support and cooperate with all aspects of the MBO program. Time should be allotted for the superiors and subordinates to meet and to jointly develop their goals. Resources and supplies should be made available to all employees to allow them to successfully accomplish the objectives that have been established. It is also appropriate, because of economic conditions and changes in consumers' wants and needs, to call for a re-evaluation of the original goals established. These goals may be established upward or downward. It usually requires at least a one-year period of time for employees to successfully accomplish the established goals and objectives. This time must be allotted to employees without being a hindrance to other programs or projects.

It is also important to be sensitive to the personalities and politics existing within an organization, which may curtail or hinder an MBO program. The MBO program may occasionally redistribute the power sources within an organization, and may reduce the influence of certain supervisors over their subordinates. Such changes may cause resistance or conflict to the program. It is important, then, to allow the employees opportunity to successfully complete their goals and objectives. It may be necessary to rearrange supervising responsibilities or to change organizational structures.

Performance appraisal. The third major factor of an MBO program is performance appraisal. This is management's evaluation of the employees' performance in relation to the goals and objectives previously established. The performance appraisal should serve to: (1) provide constructive feedback to the employees relative to their actual job performances, (2) identify more effective and efficient ways of successfully accomplishing tasks, and (3) provide the basis for future goal-setting sessions. Most job or performance appraisals fall far short of accomplishing these desirable outcomes.

Quite often a performance appraisal situation allows the superior to utilize his or her power and control resources in "playing the big shot." Unfortunately, rather than being appraised as to their job performances, many subordinates are evaluated according to their friendliness toward the boss, their loyalty, their looks, or their ability to make the superior "look good."

The performance appraisal should allow the superior to work with the subordinate in analyzing and overcoming job-related problems. The subordinates should be praised for their accomplishments. Subordinates should also receive constructive criticisms or suggestions for improvement in areas where they are weak or lack required skills. The performance appraisal can also be a situation in which future training needs may be discovered and in which employees may be placed on the "right track" toward overcoming personal and professional obstacles.

MBO may not be applicable in all business organizations. For the majority of small businesses, however, the MBO approach is beneficial, logical, and a strong managerial tool. It provides for growth and expansion of all employees, and creates positive interactions between the owner or manager and the personnel. MBO programs throughout the world have shown large benefits to their businesses, and MBO has achieved widespread popularity.

CASE STUDY: The Inn

Roy Zimmerman started The Inn twelve years ago on a solid financial basis. His initial capital of $135,000 made him the sole proprietor of a four-star steak and lobster restaurant that has current gross assets of $722,000. Total sales this past year reached $2,226,300.

Roy Zimmerman operates in an industry that is increasing at the rate of 11 to 13 percent a year. For every two meals consumed at home, the average American eats one meal out; in the very near future, it is predicted that half of the meals consumed in America will be eaten away from home. Approximately $46 billion dollars is spent annually at restaurants and other commercial eating places. There is one restaurant for nearly every 575 people in America. Food chains account for approximately 38 percent of all restaurant sales. Roy Zimmerman also knows that the average restaurant does not survive the first two years of operation.

The dinner price at The Inn ranges from $6 to $10. Roy bought the land for The Inn twelve years ago and put up a $250,000 building that houses the restaurant and bar area. The Inn is on one of the business streets in town and is located toward the outskirts of town only two minutes away from the four-lane interstate highway that circles almost the entire town. The business has a license for on-site general public eating establishment as well as a license allowing the sale of liquor. The 22-foot bar area has a seating capacity for 64 and is located close to the main entrance. Past the bar area is the main dining room; it is divided into three equal size areas, each of which seats approximately 66 people. There is a large salad bar located in the corridor that connects all three dining areas.

Roy has come to appreciate the fact that the greatest asset he has is the people who work for him. He feels that his next greatest advantage is the high quality of food that he orders and maintains. He has a large staff, which numbers over eighty for any particular day. There are fifteen cooks, plus one executive cook who oversees the kitchen area; there are four maitre d's. In addition, there are three bartenders and twelve cocktail waiters and waitresses. There are also 32 to 36 waiters and waitresses who help serve between the hours of 11:00 A.M. to 1:00 A.M. There are also six full-time dishwashers and twelve full-time busboys.

Roy Zimmerman is the president and head of The Inn. His two sons serve as assistant managers; there is a third assistant manager who also serves as executive chef. In addition, there are four people who carry the title of receptionist and are responsible for all the cash that goes in and out of the cash register. Roy has been wondering how to organize this growing number of employees. Up until now, he has managed to direct and coordinate all their duties, but in doing so he finds that less and less of his time is being spent in controlling the quality of food and maintaining the restaurant itself. Roy wants to organize The Inn so that it will function smoothly without him, allowing him greater opportunity for expansion and innovation.

Receipts must be recorded each day in a daily register. Deposits are made to the bank each day either by Roy or by one of his sons. Roy does not feel that it is appropriate for the business to be open without one of the four "managers" present. He wonders what is the best way to control the cash register area and how to prevent employees from stealing.

The Inn
Income Statement
for year ending December 31, 1980

Sales:		
Food	$1,691,930	
Beverages	534,320	
Total sales		$2,226,250
Cost of goods sold		912,780
Gross profit		$1,313,470
Expenses:		
Administration	$180,600	
Wages and salaries	645,630	
Mortgage	89,050	
Laundry, uniforms	33,390	
Advertising	44,500	
Supplies	28,230	
Utilities and telephone	46,370	
Insurance	12,030	
Depreciation	42,360	
Miscellaneous	26,760	
Total expenses		$1,148,920
Net profit (before taxes)		$164,550

Questions

1. What kind of leadership practices should Roy employ?
2. What kind of policies or procedures should he use for the employees?
3. Should he change the organizational hierarchy?
4. Do you feel that Roy is understaffed or overstaffed?
5. What kind of control procedures should Roy implement to ensure against theft of money and food?
6. How should he allocate tips left at the tables?
7. Does Roy need additional managerial help and support?

Chapter Questions:

1. What influences affect an individual's performance?
2. Why are attitudes important to a leader?
3. What style of leadership is best suited for you? Why?
4. How should you use goals in leadership activity?
5. Discuss the value of the Vroom-Yetton decision-making model.
6. Discuss the value of performance appraisals.
7. Discuss the uses of management by objectives (MBO).
8. Evaluate the effectiveness of formal and informal authority.

20

Photo courtesy of The Record, Hackensack, NJ

RISK AND INSURANCE

Chapter Objectives:

1. To identify some common business risks.
2. To list the four basic types of risk management.
3. To list and define different types of insurance.
4. To understand the uses of life insurance in a small business.
5. To know the various options for employee group insurance.
6. To understand government-operated insurance programs.

Where profit is, loss is hidden nearby.

Japanese Proverb

We all covet wealth, but not its perils.

Jean De La Bruyere

INCIDENT:

Bob is looking around, surveying the damage to his store. The fire engines have just left, and water is still dripping through the holes chopped in the roof. The Greek restaurant next door had been totally destroyed and the fire fighters had contained the actual fire to just the one location.

Bob runs a speed printing franchise in a neighborhood strip shopping center. He shares his west wall with the Greek restaurant. The fire fighters had broken down his back door to see if the fire had come through. Although there is no actual fire damage in the store, Bob has noted there is a lot of smoke and water damage.

It looks to Bob as though his inventory of paper and other printing supplies will be a total loss. He leases the printing machinery from the franchiser, but if it is damaged, it might be several days before it will be repaired. It will probably take about that long to get a new supply of paper, anyway.

The jobs that Bob had finished yesterday are wet and totally unusable. The originals for those jobs, provided by his customers, have also been destroyed. Fortunately, Bob keeps the originals for work he has not yet started in a cabinet that had not been damaged. Still, he cannot possibly do those jobs now, so he will have to decide whether to call his customers and return the jobs or to farm out the work to a competitor. If Bob decides to farm out the work, he will probably lose money on it.

There are other problems facing Bob as well. He will have to give his employees a couple of days off while he cleans up the mess and gets set up to do business again. There is a payday coming up on Friday. Bob's business records have gotten wet, and some of them might not be usable.

Bob feels that his insurance will probably cover most of the inventory loss, but he is not sure about the rest. Will it be worthwhile for him to have his work done elsewhere? Will he lose any customers as a result of this crisis? Bob realizes that he has bills to pay, despite the fact that he is temporarily out of business.

There is an element of risk in everything. Birth, marriage, and death all have uncertainties associated with them. We live in a world of uncertainty; businesses operate in a world full of it, and individuals gamble on it.

Business has tried, as have individuals, to reduce the uncertainties in life. The introduction of social security, pension plans, and the welfare system are all developed to reduce the uncertainties in life. Humans generally desire to reduce uncertainties and thereby reduce their risks.

Risk in a business sense generally refers to the uncertainty of profit or loss. Risk is therefore a psychological (mental) block based on human emotions and reactions. Risk may also be viewed as an objective or concrete phenomenon that is based on probability and statistics. When dealing with business, it is important to reduce risk or uncertainty as far as possible. One would like to know for sure that the contract has been signed and the sale has been made, rather than just knowing that one has a 50-50 chance of that being the case.

Handling Risk

It is important to know how to handle risk. It is likewise important to know how much insurance to buy and what kind of insurance to carry. There are five general guidelines that are important in handling risks: (1) review all potential losses, (2) review the amount of money involved with potential losses, (3) determine how much of a loss can be sustained, (4) determine the probability of loss, and (5) identify those potential losses that should be transferred to another party (insurance).[1]

No business can ever eliminate all potential losses. (See Figure 20-1.) Therefore, some major risk must be assumed. This is important in determining whether a particular risk should be assumed (by the business firm) or transferred (to an insurance firm). If that total potential loss would force the business to close or to go into bankruptcy, it is probably advisable to purchase insurance (that is, to transfer the risk) to help save the business.

It is important to determine the probability of that loss occurring. If the probability is very high, then insurance should not be purchased. Rather than

---

SHOPLIFTING

The Good News:
   Retail sales in the United States are about $77.2 billion annually.

The Bad News:
   Shoplifters will steal about 4 percent of that, or $3.1 billion. Consumers will pay for this loss through higher prices.
   Shoplifting is the biggest and most widespread crime committed against retail businesses today. Small retailers are usually the most vulnerable and hardest hit. They cannot afford the loss, and often go bankrupt. The Commerce Department has reported that four million shoplifters are caught each year, yet they estimate that only one out of every thirty shoplifters is stopped.

Figure 20-1. *Consumers pay for shoplifting*

[1]Robert L. Mehr and Bob H. Hedges, *Risk Management In The Business Enterprise*, (New York; Richard D. Irwin, 1963), pp. 16—19.

transferring the risk, steps should be taken to either handle the risk, avoid the risk, or stay out of that business. Generally speaking, the higher the probability of loss, the greater the probability of control. For example, losses due to bad checks from customers may be eliminated by not accepting checks. If the probability is low and the resulting loss is high—such as in fire, theft, or casualty losses—then it is generally advisable to buy insurance to cover the risk.

It is also important to determine a reasonable relationship between insurance costs and loss amounts. If the insurance cost is small relative to a large possible loss in the business, then insurance should be purchased. It is important to not risk a lot (loss of business) for a little (insurance premium). The basic rules of risk management may be listed as:

- Know the possibilities of all losses.
- Do not personally risk more than you can personally afford to lose.
- Try to cover all possible losses.
- Do not become insurance poor (in other words, do not pay for more insurance than you can afford).

Business Risks

Business risks may be classified in many different ways. However, it is common to classify them in four different categories: (1) speculative risks, (2) pure risks, (3) fundamental risks, and (4) particular risks.

speculative risks

Speculative risks are the most common risks in business. They hold the possibility of gain *or* loss. A speculative risk occurs when a business owner opens for business. Small businesses may produce either a profit or a loss and are, therefore, speculative risks. Any increase in the price level may bring a large profit, or a reduction or sale of inventory, or this increase may be so large that potential customers will not be able to buy the product. Interestingly, with speculative risk a business owner has the opportunity of assuming as much or as little risk as he or she desires. The owner may even decide to not enter business, which would reduce all speculative risk concerning that business to zero.

Generally, the only form of risk that is not covered by insurance is speculative risk. The business person has his own choice of deciding how much risk he will assume when running his business and no insurance firm, therefore, is willing to insure him against the loss of his business or the loss of capital. Speculative risk is like gambling, and no one wants to insure the gambler.

pure risks

Pure risks occur when there is only an either-or possibility: loss or no loss. For example, a building may be destroyed by fire, thereby creating a loss, or if nothing was destroyed and the fire was quickly put out, no loss would occur. There is no possibility of gain or profit in either occurrence, but there is a possibility of loss. This type of risk is frequently handled by insurance.

fundamental risks   Fundamental risks primarily arise from losses that are due to impersonal environmental or situational happenings. Fundamental risks are not caused by one individual, and their impact is generally felt by all within the society. War, unemployment, and inflation are all examples of fundamental risks arising from the social environment. Floods, windstorms, hail, and earthquakes are fundamental risks arising from physical conditions. These risks may sometimes be handled by insurance.

particular risks   Particular (or individual) risk is where losses occur from individual events. These risks occur because of individual cause and effect. Bank robbery and automobile accidents are examples of particular risk.

There is basically no clear-cut line between fundamental and particular risk. An automobile accident (when two or more are involved), although it may have been caused by one particular individual, is being more and more considered to be a fundamental risk rather than a particular risk. Perhaps the automobile accident was caused by a combination of problems, and was not just the fault of any particular person.

Risk Management

The main purpose of dealing with risk is to reduce uncertainties, reduce losses, and increase profits. This does not demand elimination of the possibility of loss; rather, it just tries to reduce the likelihood of loss and improve the probabilities of success.

In general, four major methods of dealing with risk are recognized: (1) risk avoidance, (2) risk prevention, (3) risk absorption, and (4) risk transfer.

risk avoidance   It is generally impossible to buy insurance or coverage for all possible risks in a business firm. Risk avoidance assumes that you will never have to face the loss. The business person will find that there are some risks, speculative as well as pure, that must be avoided if at all possible.

Avoidance is basically a poor method. In order to avoid all possible risks, you would probably never start a business nor even own a home.

risk prevention   Risk prevention is probably the best and least expensive method of managing risk. If a business owner deposits all the cash receipts at the end of the day, then a night-time burglary will not result in a loss of cash. This common business practice reduces and prevents losses from ever occurring. A sprinkler system provides similar protection in that, if a fire breaks out, the system will come on, spraying water over the fire and putting the fire out. The use of burglary and/or fire alarms are additional examples of risk prevention. Both loss prevention and loss reduction are generally included in the risk prevention classification.

risk absorption   Risk absorption occurs when the risk is recognized but no action is taken to either prevent it or transfer it to another. For example, if you do not insure your business location against fire, you are absorbing or retaining that loss for yourself. That is, if a fire breaks out, you will pay for the damages yourself. When an automobile or truck becomes old, it is often the practice not to insure its $250 value for collision (although one would usually have a large liability insurance coverage).

A business owner will often absorb the risk when the potential loss is small or insignificant. You retain all risks of a business by doing nothing. If an unfortunate accident or event occurs, you will have to absorb all losses for that experience.

risk transfer

The final managerial technique used for dealing with risk is risk transfer—that is, assigning the risk to others. The most common type of risk transfer is the insurance policy. Business insurance is concerned with the transfer of risk from one party (business) to another (insurance company) by use of a contract (insurance policy).

The insurance policy brings in a second party—the insurance company—who now assumes the risk. Risk transfer generally occurs through the purchase of an insurance policy or some form of bond.

Types of Loss

The types of loss to an individual or a business may be classified in the following ways: (1) personal losses, (2) commercial losses, (3) property losses, (4) business record losses, and (5) liability losses.

personal losses

Personal losses relate directly to an individual. These are the losses that a person may encounter through his or her lifetime. The theft of an automobile, a personal accident or illness; unemployment, or a home destroyed by fire are all personal losses that greatly affect an individual.

commercial losses

Commercial losses are those relating to a business. The destruction of the business by fire, theft, or embezzlement of business funds are all examples of commercial losses. The commercial loss is a loss to the business, and generally results in decreasing profits and increasing costs to that business.

property losses

Property losses occur when the property of an individual or of a business, has been damaged or destroyed. If the clothing inventory of a store is damaged by smoke or water resulting from a fire, then property damage has occurred.

business record losses

Business records or financial statements (income statements, balance sheets, or cash flow statements) often provide an additional method of classifying a type of loss. Business record losses may be classified in terms of (1) a decrease in revenue or income, (2) an increase in expenses, (3) a decrease in assets, (4) an increase in owner's liabilities, or (5) a decrease in owner's equity (net worth).

liability losses

Liability is the result of a legal action against an individual's property. Liability loss may also occur as a result of an individual voluntarily giving up some property, due to a threat of legal action or because of a breach of contract or a legal wrong (tort).

The most common form of liability is if someone fell down on one's property and was hurt. The business owner is usually held liable for a person's health while that person is in his or her business establishment. Additionally, a manufacturer or retailer may be held liable for a poorly manufactured good, such as a toy that can cause harm to children.

SUCCESS STORY: W. Clement Stone

As W. Clement Stone has himself observed, he speaks from experience when he insists that any man can become wealthy, "no matter how poor his start in life." He was born in Chicago, Illinois, on May 4, 1902, to Louis and Anna M. (Gunn) Stone. Before the boy was three years old, his father died. At the age of six he began selling the *Examiner* newspaper on Chicago's streets, while his mother worked as a dressmaker, and at thirteen he ran a newsstand of his own. He devoured all the Horatio Alger stories available and was particularly inspired by Robert Cloverdale's Struggle.

When Stone was sixteen his mother moved to Detroit to open an insurance agency, representing the United States Casualty Company. Joining her in the summer, he began his career as an insurance salesman by calling office to office at the Dime Bank Building in Detroit and before long he was earning $100 a week. More important, although timid at first in his approach, by reflection and experience he soon began to develop the sales technique and the rationale of optimism to which he attributes his great fortune.

When he was twenty he used his savings of $100 to set up his own insurance agency in Chicago. He advertised for salesmen in newspapers, first in Illinois and then in other states, and by 1930 about a thousand agents throughout much of the country were selling insurance for him as the representative for large casualty companies.

"What's very important in making a fortune is how to use OPM—other people's money." Stone wrote in an article for *Nation's Business* (July, 1968). He then went on to explain how he purchased the Pennsylvania Casualty Company with the seller's money, by borrowing from the Commercial Credit Company of Baltimore, which owned the Philadelphia insurance firm. On December 23, 1946, three days after he had acquired Pennsylvania Casualty, he was elected its president. The following year he changed its name to the Combined Insurance Company of America, into which he merged his Combined Mutual Casualty Company of Chicago in late 1947.

Stone once estimated that every $10,000 invested in Combined Insurance Company of America in 1951, had earned several million dollars by 1968, when the company's assets exceeded $150,000,000. In early 1969, according to *Time* (February 7, 1969), the Combined Insurance Company had 23,000 stockholders, 3,500 salesmen and 1,200 employees.

The salesmen of Combined Insurance Company of America are trained in methods of merchandising based on inspiration to action, know-how and activity knowledge, and primarily, on what Stone calls PMA or Positive Mental Attitude. Their training exposes them to such self-motivation spurs to action as "What the mind can conceive and believe, the mind can achieve" and "Do it now." They are said to be instructed to renew or declare their PMA by chanting every morning, "I feel health, I feel happy, I feel terrific." Their training course includes learning how "to keep a smile in the voice" and when to make "eye contact" with a prospective customer. "Combined Insurance isn't the least bit worried about sounding corny," David Garino wrote in the *Wall Street Journal* (February 27, 1969). "When recruiting new salesmen, the company puts enthusiasm and energy ahead of academic attainment." Answering questions by members of the Investment Analysts Society of Chicago in March, 1974, Stone said: "In 1974 we are hiring more people, training more people and keeping more people. When times are difficult it's easier to sell insurance. I can speak with authority because I learned the art during the Depression years."

Because of the heartiness of his greeting, meeting him is said to be a "breathtaking experience," but his manner puts people quickly at ease. Ballroom dancing, horseback riding, and swimming are his recreations, and what he calls his "only luxury" is smoking pre-Castro Cuban cigars.[2]

Insurance

Insurance is a method of handling risk. Technically, insurance may be defined as a method of transferring risk from one party to another by use of a contract. Insurance gives the business owner the opportunity to trade a large but uncertain loss (fire, liability, for example) for a small and certain loss (such as expense). This "loss" (expense) is technically referred to as a premium. The main strength of insurance is that it provides risk reduction. Associated with insurance is a reduction of worry, an increase of ability, and a sense of security.

Insurance is provided to cover a large variety of pure risks. There are thousands of insurance agencies, providing over one hundred different kinds of policies to help cover risk. Insurance companies will try to sell you the idea that the probability of a harmful event occurring in the future is based upon similar incidents in recorded past. In other words, the probability of something happening is based upon how often it has happened in the past. The major idea for the insurance company, then, is to collect a large number of small premiums from policy holders, with a sufficient amount collected (1) to cover the actual losses occurring, (2) to pay the expenses of the insuring business, and (3) to provide a fair profit for investment from the insurance company stockholders (policyholders of a mutual insurance company).

There are basically four major types of insurance companies in the United

[2]*Current Biography* Yearbook, 1972.

States: (1) stock companies, (2) mutual companies, (3) reciprocals, and (4) Lloyds groups.

Stock companies are profit-making corporations that are chartered in the various states of the union. They account for approximately 73 percent of all property and liability insurance and 30 percent of all life insurance.

Mutual companies are chartered as nonprofit organizations under the various laws of the several states. They account for approximately 23 percent of all insurance coverage in the United States, including 70 percent of all life insurance.

Reciprocals—often referred to as *interinsurance exchanges*—are made up of individuals in associations that exchange contracts and insurance, generally covering one another's risks. Reciprocals are very few in number and only account for about 3 percent of insurance coverage in the United States.

Lloyds groups are made up of groups of individual insurance underwriters. They collect less than 1 percent of all premiums dealing with property insurance.

The small business owner generally buys insurance through either an independent agency or a direct underwriter. The independent agency is the traditional marketing system employed by most property and liability insurance companies. This independent, small-business insurance salesperson receives a commission for the various lines of insurance coverage sold. The independent agent often represents several different insurance companies. This agent has the right to solicit and renew insurance policies for the various companies that he or she represents to the business community at large.

A direct underwriter is considered to be a commissioned employee of the particular insurance company being represented. This person is not an independent businessperson, as is the independent agent. The direct underwriter has been the mainstay for the life insurance business and is increasingly becoming used for the property and liability insurance area. The direct agent can usually offer lower premiums as a result of his or her direct contact with the insurance company. However, comparison shopping should be done by any business owner when obtaining insurance.

what is insurable?

A basic legal requirement of nearly all insurance contracts is that the person buying the insurance must have an interest in what is being insured. For example, it is not legal to buy insurance on any building in town and then hope for a fire to occur so that you can collect insurance. This would be no more than another form of gambling, and it could strongly increase the possibility of criminal acts being committed in order to obtain insurance monies.

indemnity

Indemnity comes from the principle of insurable interest. Indemnity allows one to collect only the actual cash-value loss and not the amount named in the insurance policy. For example, suppose Jack's T-Shirt Shop has a $30,000 fire insurance policy but the business is only worth $10,000. If the shop were to be destroyed by fire, Jack could only collect $10,000 and not the $30,000, even though the business was totally destroyed by fire.

subrogation   The practice of subrogation is very important in the field of business insurance. Subrogation allows the insured business owner to give the insurance company the right of recovery against third parties causing harm. For example, if the delivery truck's brakes did not work and the back of your business was rammed, causing $6,000 damage, your property insurance would probably restore the $6,000 loss. The insurance company, with the right of subrogation, may seek recovery of its loss from the truck driver or owner for negligence. (The truck driver's or owner's insurance company may bear that loss through liability insurance coverage.)

Life insurance policies are not considered to be contracts covered by indemnity. That is, it is not possible to determine a set cash value for an individual's life. Therefore, the insurance company must pay the entire face value amount of a life insurance policy, and the principles of subrogation and indemnity will not apply. Our legal system allows for an individual to place any value on life that he or she chooses for reasons of insurance. A life is irreplaceable.

co-insurance   The term *co-insurance* generally implies that the business owner is willing to assume part of the loss himself or herself. That is, the owner does not buy insurance to fully cover all possible hazards, but takes a lower coverage with smaller premiums. For example, owners Miles and McCarty each had stores next to each other. Miles bought a fire insurance policy valued at $50,000, while McCarty purchased a fire insurance policy for $100,000. McCarty's premiums were approximately double that of Miles even though their businesses were almost identical in value.

However, most states now allow co-insurance clauses that require a building or business to be insured from 70 percent to 80 percent of a fair market value. Using the co-insurance clause, a business owner agrees to purchase insurance coverage for a specific percentage of the business's value (70 percent, 85 percent or even 100 percent); in return, he or she will receive a lower rate from the insurance agency.

Payment of co-insurance policies are generally provided according to the following formula:

$$\frac{\text{Amount of insurance carried}}{\text{Amount required by percentage}} \times \text{loss amount} = \text{amount received}$$

McCarty owns a building with an actual cash value of $125,000 and has insured it with an 80 percent co-insurance provision (or the amount required by percentage) that gives him a $100,000 coverage on his $125,000 business. If a fire resulted in a $20,000 loss immediately after the policy was enforced, then the value payable to McCarty would equal:

$$\frac{\text{Amount of insurance carried}}{\text{Amount required by percentage}} \times \text{loss amount} = \frac{\$100,000}{\$100,000} \times \$20,000 = \$20,000$$

However, if the loss occurred three years later and the business values were now $150,000, the amount payable would be determined by the following:

$$\frac{\text{Amount of insurance carried}}{\text{Amount required by percentage}} \times \text{loss amount} = \frac{\$100,000}{\$120,000} \times \$20,000 = \$16,667$$

The McCarty example illustrates an important point about co-insurance requirements; that is, the amount of payment is based on the ratio of insurance carried to the percentage that would be required at the time of loss. For example, McCarty needed $120,000 to fulfill his 80 percent agreement of the new value of his business which was set at $150,000 (80 percent of the $150,000 is $120,000—this was increased from 80 percent of the $120,000 which was $100,000).

Most insurance companies require co-insurance provisions with insurance policies to help cover major as well as minor losses common in the business industry.

Types of Insurance Coverages

There are many kinds of insurance coverages. For this reason, it is difficult at times for small business owners to plan their business insurance packages and to completely understand what programs or insurance policies they may need. The types of insurance policies that are most common to the small business are:

1. casualty insurance
2. liability insurance
3. worker's compensation
4. fire insurance
5. fidelity bonds
6. surety bonds
7. automobile insurance
8. business interruption insurance
9. FAIR insurance plans
10. life insurance
11. key-man coverage
12. group health insurance

casualty insurance

A casualty is often referred to as an "unfortunate, possibly fatal, accident." This is a very broad definition that is quite appropriate. There are two major areas of protection with casualty insurance: two-party insurance, and three-party insurance.

Two-party casualty insurance is designed by the policy holder and the insurance company and allows the policy holder, as an individual, to receive payment for any financial loss that may occur because of destruction of owned property, or injury to the policy holder or any member of his or her family.

Third-party casualty insurance includes the policy holder, the insurance company, and a claimant. This form of insurance is designed to protect the policy holder from any financial loss if he or she is held responsible (liable) for an injury to a third person (the claimant) or for damage to a third person's property.

Casualty insurance is designed to cover specific liabilities in a variety of personal and professional actions. In addition, specific kinds of casualty insurance (such as worker's compensation and even health risks) are also made available through special insurance policies. Generally, one may add riders and endorsements to insurance policies to cover whatever needs or requirements one may have with regard to casualty insurance.

liability insurance

Liability insurance is made to cover the policy holder for negligence occurring at his or her business with regard to customers, employees, or any other individual with whom he or she does business. A single liability judgment against one's business can easily wipe out the entire organization. The legal system has continued to increase rewards granted to individuals who have been harmed. Liability insurance will usually cover judgments against the policyholder brought by other individuals, such as medical and legal expenses arising from accidents, expenses involved in the investigation or settlement of a negligent accident, and often court costs accumulated during the suit.

worker's compensation

Employers must provide employees with (1) a safe working place, (2) safe materials and tools, (3) competent fellow employees, and (4) warnings of any existing dangers. Employers who do not meet these conditions are subject to common law liability suits and worker's compensation laws.

State laws will determine the rates, levels, and benefits of worker's compensation policies. Most state laws provide for medical care, lump sums for dismemberments and income payments for disabled employees. Premiums for worker's compensation are developed based on the record of the business. Audits are generally taken at the end of the policy year, and rates are then determined by the "safeness" of the business occupation. Rates may vary from 0.1 percent to about 25 percent to 30 percent of the payroll, based on the relative safety or hazard of the business.

fire insurance

Fire insurance is one of the most common forms of property insurance available. It usually includes the perils of fire, lightning, and losses of goods removed from the business because of the fire. Each state regulates the fire insurance rates by developing rating bureaus, which inspect business properties and establish ratings for different buildings and businesses. Fire insurance policies are made for three-, five-, or ten-year periods of time.

Most small business owners will find it necessary to extend their fire insurance coverage through additional endorsements. Extended coverages may include hail, windstorm, explosion, riot, vehicle damage, smoke damage, and even falling aircraft damage. Such extensions are also specified as to amount and coverage. For example, a loss due to smoke would only be allowed if caused by a sudden fire or a faulty heating unit. The extension would probably exclude smoke damage from industrial apparatus, automobiles, or fireplaces.

fidelity bonds   Fidelity bonds are employed by small business owners to protect against employee theft. Fidelity bonds are different from general insurance policies in that the fidelity bond is a three-party policy that involves an employee who becomes bonded (the principal), the business firm protected (the obligee), and the insurance or license-bonding corporation (the surety). If any employee theft occurs, the surety or insurance agency is obliged to pay the business or obligee, although the insurance company or surety does have the right to regain its losses from the employee or principal.

There are three basic types of fidelity bonds: (1) individual bonds, which name a specific individual, (2) scheduled bonds, which list the names or positions of all employees to be covered, and (3) blanket bonds, which cover all employees of a business but do not identify them by name or position title. Fidelity bonds are generally continuous until they are cancelled by either party; rarely is an expiration date attached to the bond. All bonds have limits of liability that are referred to as the *penalty*. The penalty is the maximum amount payable if a loss or theft occurs.

surety bonds   Surety bonds are found with businesses that do construction, plumbing, electrical, or other contractual business. The surety bond guarantees that the worker (the principal) will perform and carry out all work assigned and developed by the employer (the obligee). The insurance company or license-bonding corporation (the surety) is providing a statement to an employer that the principal is honest, has the necessary ability, financial capacity, and technical skills required to carry out the work for which he or she is bonded. The insurance company is backing the credit and honesty of the worker, and is vouching for his or her professional competence.

Surety bonds allow small business firms to compete equally with large corporations or better-known firms. For example, suppose that a church wishes to add a $180,000 addition to their building. Specifications were delivered to all local contractors, and any contractor providing a surety bond could bid for the project. Hurtz Construction Company, a very small contractor, was finally awarded the contract due to their low bid and the surety bond they could give the church.

automobile insurance   A small business owner will often choose to insure the automobiles, vans, trucks, and any other vehicles of the business in case of physical injury, theft, or damage to others. Most firms are held liable for the use of trucks or automobiles used in their business, even if they do not own them. It is advisable that the small business owner purchase commercial vehicle coverage (including collision insurance), thereby insuring against fire, theft, liability, and physical damage.

Rates on automobile insurance vary widely according to (1) the territory, (2) the age of the vehicle, (3) the type of vehicle, (4) the distance traveled, and occasionally (5) the age of the driver. Companies using a fleet of cars will often be able to gain "experience" rates, which are established on safe driving plans or merit rates available in most states. An insurance policy with a deductible-amount clause ($100) will provide a considerable savings in collision coverage.

business interruption insurance Business interruption insurance provides compensation for a business while its activities are interrupted due to fire or peril. The business interruption policy will generally pay the same approximate amount of fixed expenses and profits that the business would otherwise have earned. These policies generally have co-insurance requirements ranging from 60 percent to 100 percent of the business's insurable value. Payroll may also be insured for certain periods of time.

fair insurance plans There are many high-risk areas in our communities that are uninsurable due to a high possibility of theft, vandalism, or riots. Small businesses in these communities are often unable to obtain normal insurance plans. However, the FAIR (Fair Access to Insurance Requirements) Plan was developed in the U.S. Housing and Urban Development Act of 1968, ensuring riot and vandalism insurance programs for high-risk areas. Within the states using this plan, insurance is made possible through cooperative efforts from the insurance agencies, the federal government, and the state government, who together provide cooperative property insurance for problem areas at moderate rates.

life insurance Life insurance is primarily concerned with the economic value of an individual's life. Although it is not possible to place an economic value on the work of an individual, it is possible and often necessary to place an economic value upon the earning capacity and the financial dependence that the family and others have upon an individual's life. The foundations of life insurance rest upon an economic value placed on an individual's life. There are two approaches for determining the amount of life insurance an individual should have: (1) the value-of-human-life approach and (2) the needs approach. The value-of-human-life approach is primarily concerned with the earning capacity of the individual. It is concerned with the earnings of an individual that are used to support family members. The needs approach is developed around the needs that would be experienced by the family in case the head of the family dies. These expenses may include such things as funeral expenses, illnesses, personal loans, household payments and bills, taxes, and future life expectancies.

There are three basic forms of life insurance policies: (1) whole life, (2) term, and (3) endowment.

Whole life insurance. A whole life insurance policy is established to run for the entire life of an individual. If the individual dies before age 100, the face amount of the insurance policy will be paid to the family or beneficiary (whoever is designated to receive it). The cash value of a whole life policy is equal to the face amount of that policy. This form of life insurance also provides loan opportunities for the insured.

Term life insurance. Term insurance provides payment of the value amount of insurance to a designated beneficiary if the person named in the policy dies within a specified number of years that are stated in the original policy. For example, if a person has a twenty-year policy and dies after eighteen years, that person's beneficiary will receive the face value of the insurance. If the insured individual has not died at the end of twenty years, the insurance policy expires without value. Term insurance generally has a low premium and provides only temporary protection, unless it is converted to a whole life or endowment insurance policy. Most group life insurance policies are based on term insurance policies for periods of one to ten years. Group life insurance is generally issued on a term plan for one year, without a medical examination; it will have no accumulative cash values. Such plans are generally started for firms with ten or more employees and may allow for employee contribution (up to a 50–50 employer–employee split).

Endowment life insurance. Endowment insurance policies provide payment to a designated beneficiary if the insured person dies within a specific period of time (endowment period of time). However, if the insured person lives to the completion of the endowment period of time, the insurance value (maturity value) will be paid to the owner of the policy. For example, a woman might have taken out a $100,000 endowment insurance policy on her husband, when he is at the age of 35, for a twenty-year endowment period. Her husband lived to age 55, so she would then be entitled to receive the maturity value of that policy. Because of this promise to pay at the end of the endowment period, the premiums on an endowment policy are the highest of the three different forms of insurance. An endowment plan allows the policy owner to get large sums of money quicker than under a whole life policy. However, the amount of money (premium) applied to purchase an endowment plan would, in a whole life plan, allow for a larger death benefit and would still obtain a substantial savings goal for the policy owner.

key-man coverage

Another use of life insurance is referred to as *key-man coverage*. This is the purchase of a life insurance policy for key personnel in a business. Banks, financial lending agencies, or even government agencies often require key-man insurance on people borrowing money. The bank would often be named as the beneficiary of the life insurance policy for a borrower of $100,000. For example, the bank may require that an additional $100,000 life insurance policy be taken out by the business owner, with the bank as the beneficiary as an addition to the endowment policy. In case of accidental death of the insured, the bank would receive the face value of that insurance policy and could pay off any bank loans which that person had taken.

Another form of key-man insurance is referred to as a *cross-purchase plan*. In this kind of plan, partners who are stockholders in a business agree to purchase sufficient insurance on each other's lives, in order to buy out one partner at the time of his or her death. This will allow the surviving owners to buy their proportionate interest in the business in case of death to one of the owners.

For example, if three partners (Smith, Jones, and Lee) all have an equal interest in a business valued at $120,000, each will buy a $20,000 life insurance policy on the other two individuals. If Smith dies, then Jones and Lee will each receive $20,000, and their total of $40,000 can be used to purchase Smith's share of the business. This would allow Jones and Lee to maintain their equal interest in the business.

group health insurance

The major forms of group health insurance vary throughout the United States. There are four major types of group health insurance: (1) basic medical and hospitalization insurance, (2) major medical insurance, (3) disability insurance, and (4) health maintenance organizations.

Basic medical and hospitalization insurance. A basic medical and hospitalization insurance plan will pay for the medical, hospital, medication, and doctor fees based on a need basis. These insurance plans pay the employee a particular number of dollars for different medical treatments, and a certain amount for each day of hospitalization. The physician or medical services are often paid on a service or indemnity basis through various medical care programs.

Major medical insurance. Major medical insurance plans cover catastrophic illnesses of or injuries to employees. Such plans are generally added onto basic medical and hospitalization plans and often provide a large maximum benefit, such as $100,000.

Disability insurance. A disability plan provides for an employee to receive a specific portion of his or her annual salary, should the employee suffer physical disability or illness which prevents him or her from working. This sort of plan is often added as a rider, or employees are given an option of buying such a plan for themselves.

Health maintenance organizations. Health maintenance organizations (HMOs) are uniquely structured to provide comprehensive health care at reduced costs. HMOs provide a personal family physician for each member. The personal physician provides the member's health care and coordinates any additional medical or hospitalization needs. Standards for HMOs are established by the U.S. Department of Health and Human Services. Membership is opened to anyone with most members being the employees (and their families) of the employers who offer this alternative to traditional health insurance.

CASE STUDY: Campbell's

Steve Campbell has been the owner-manager of a men's clothing store in the mall since it opened about seven years ago. Prior to that time, he had worked in his father's clothing store in the downtown area. After Steve had been working with his father for approximately two years, he heard of a new mall opening in the southwest section of town in a couple of years. He immediately asked his father about the opportunities of opening a branch in the mall.

The Campbell's clothing store carries traditional men's clothing (as opposed to fashionable dress clothing). This implies a conservative clothing line that is classic in styling, traditional in fabric and texture (that is, natural fibers such as wool and cotton as opposed to synthetics), and features old-world tailoring and durability. This durability exists both in the quality of the merchandise and in style (style that has lasted through the seasons and through the years). This store carries dress shirts, sport shirts, sweaters, sport slacks, dress slacks, sport coats, suits, ties, belts, socks, jackets, coats, and a very limited selection of billfolds, tie pins, clasps, and shoes. Campbell purchases these clothes himself on buying trips in the spring and fall to New York, Chicago, San Francisco, and Dallas.

Two years after his contact with his father, a second Campbell's men's clothing store was opened in the mall, with its front door accessible to the most foot traffic in the entire mall. The clothing store is located right in the center part of the mall, right next to the water fountain.

The mall location is very favorable. The business traffic has been extremely profitable and during the fifth year of operation, the mall store outsold the downtown store by $7,100. A very exclusive men's clothing store, Campbell's primarily caters to the upper-middle to higher-class clientele. Campbell's is one of only two stores in the entire state approved to sell the Oxford line of very expensive, high-quality men's suits.

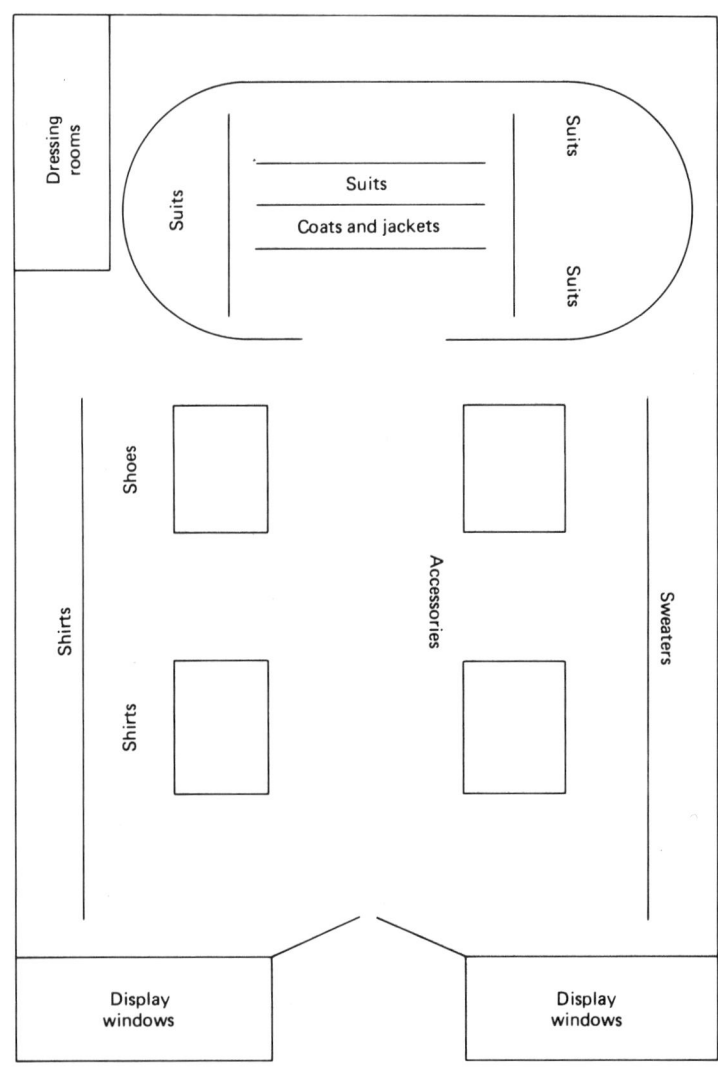

371
RISK AND INSURANCE

Last year was the first time that Campbell's ever had to use their insurance to cover for any damage. There was a fire that erupted about four stores down in the mall area, and smoke damage caused some loss to Campbell's clothing store. Their basic insurance policies cover general fire but they did not have a written policy for smoke. Their liability went up to $300,000, but that was only for those people immediately in the mall area surrounding their store. Inside the clothing store their liability coverage was only for $100,000 per accident.

Steve Campbell is now seriously discussing insurance problems with his father, because he recently slipped twice inside their own store because of a new wax compound that the maintenance people were putting down at night. Their mall store has never suffered any kind of vandalism; however, several other stores have sustained considerable loss due to shoplifting as well as to broken picture windows and general mischief. A fast-food and drink chain store located next door is involved in a court case—a $1.3 million damage suit brought by a customer who fell in the store and broke his back.

Campbell's Income Statement
198X

Net sales		$464,236
Cost of goods sold		273,435
Gross Profit		190,801
Expenses:		
Wages and salaries (including owners')	$126,000	
Lease	18,000	
Advertising and promotion	8,000	
Utilities	3,660	
Accounting and legal	1,500	
Insurance	XX,XXX	
Other	2,000	
Total expenses		159,160
Profits Before Taxes		$ 31,641

Questions

1. What kind of insurance policy (policies) should the Campbells have on their mall store?
2. What kinds of risks should the Campbells cover, and what kinds should they transfer to insurance?
3. What kind(s) of insurance policies should the mall's owners require each store to have for the common areas in the mall?

Chapter Questions:

1. What are the various methods of handling or managing risk?
2. What is risk management about?
3. Develop a list of the risks you would face upon entering a service business as a business owner. Which of these risks are speculative and which are transferable?

4. What is insurance?
5. Why are indemnity and subrogation policies important to the insurance industry?
6. List the types of insurance policies and the amounts of coverage that you would need for a business of your choice.
7. List the advantages and disadvantages of life and health insurance policies for the business owner.

APPENDIX

Essential Insurance Coverages

Four kinds of insurance are essential: (1) fire insurance, (2) liability insurance, (3) automobile insurance, and (4) worker's compensation insurance. In some areas and in some kinds of businesses, crime insurance, which is discussed under "Desirable Coverages," is also essential.

Are you certain that all the following points have been given full consideration in your insurance program?

	No action needed	Look into this

fire insurance

1. Other perils—such as windstorm, hail, smoke, explosion, vandalism, and malicious mischief—can be added to your basic fire insurance at a relatively small additional cost. _____ _____
2. If you need comprehensive coverage, your best buy may be one of the all-risk contracts that offer the broadest available protection for the money. _____ _____
3. The insurance company may indemnify you—that is, compensate you for your losses—in any one of several ways: (1) It may pay actual cash value of the property at the time of loss, (2) it may repair or replace the property with material of like kind and quality, or (3) it may take all the property at the agreed or appraised value and reimburse you for your loss. _____ _____
4. You can insure property you do not own. You must have an insurable interest—that is, a financial interest—in the property when a loss occurs but not necessarily at the time the insurance contract is made. For instance, a repair shop or a dry-cleaning plant may carry insurance on customers' property in the shop, or a person holding a mortgage on a building may insure the building although he or she does not own it. _____ _____
5. When you sell property, you cannot assign the insurance policy along with the property unless you have permission from the insurance company. _____ _____

	No action needed	Look into this

6. Even if you have several policies on your property, you can still collect only the amount of your actual cash loss. All the insurers share the payment proportionately. For example, suppose that you are carrying two policies—one for $20,000 and one for $30,000—on a $40,000 building, and a fire causes damage to the building amounting to $12,000.

   The $20,000 policy will pay $4,800; that is:

   $$\frac{20{,}000}{50{,}000}, \text{ or } \frac{2}{5}, \text{ of } \$12{,}000 = \$4{,}800$$

   The $30,000 policy will pay $7,200; which is:

   $$\frac{30{,}000}{50{,}000}, \text{ or } \frac{3}{5}, \text{ of } \$12{,}000 = \$7{,}200$$

7. Special protection other than the standard fire policy is needed to cover the loss by fire of accounts, bills, currency, deeds, evidences of debt, and money and securities.

8. If an insured building is vacant or unoccupied for more than sixty consecutive days, coverage is suspended unless you have a special endorsement to your policy canceling this provision.

9. If, either before or after a loss, you conceal or misrepresent to the insurer any material fact or circumstance concerning your insurance or the interest of the insured, the policy may be voided.

10. If you increase the hazard of fire, the insurance company may suspend your coverage even for losses not originating from the increased hazard. (An example of such a hazard might be renting part of your building to a dry-cleaning plant.)

11. After a loss, you must use all reasonable means to protect the property from further loss, or run the risk of having your coverage canceled.

12. To recover your loss, you must furnish—within sixty days (unless an extension is granted by the insurance company)—a complete inventory of the damaged, destroyed, and undamaged property showing in detail quantities, costs, actual cash value, and amount of loss claimed.

13. If you and the insurer disagree on the amount of loss, the question may be resolved through special appraisal procedures provided for in the insurance policy.

14. You may cancel your policy without notice at any time and get part of the premium returned. The insurance company also may cancel at any time but it must give you a five-day written notice.

	No action needed	Look into this

15. By accepting a co-insurance clause in your policy, you can get a substantial reduction in premiums. A co-insurance clause states that you must carry insurance equal to 80 percent or 90 percent of the value of the insured property. If you carry less than this, you cannot collect the full amount of your loss, even if the loss is small. The percent of your loss that you can collect will depend on the percent of the full value of the property you have had insured. _____ _____
16. If your loss is caused by someone else's negligence, the insurer has the right to sue this negligent third party for the amount it has paid you under the policy. This is known as the insurer's right of subrogation. However, the insurer will usually waive this right upon request. For example, if you have leased your insured building to someone and have waived your right to recover from the tenant for any insured damages to your property, you should have your agent request the insurer to waive the subrogation clause in the fire policy on your leased building. _____ _____
17. A building under construction can be insured for fire, lightning, extended coverage, vandalism, and malicious mischief. _____ _____

	No action needed	Look into this

liability insurance

1. Legal liability limits of $1 million are no longer considered high or unreasonable, even for a small business. _____ _____
2. Most liability policies require you to notify the insurer immediately after any incident on your property that might cause a future claim. This holds true no matter how unimportant the incident may seem at the time it happens. _____ _____
3. Most liability policies, in addition to bodily injuries, may now cover personal injuries (libel, slander, and so on) if these are specifically stated in the policy. _____ _____
4. Under certain conditions, your business may be subject to damage claims, even from trespassers. _____ _____
5. You may be legally liable for damages, even in cases where you used "reasonable care." _____ _____
6. Even if the suit against you is false or fraudulent, the liability insurer pays court costs, legal fees, and interest on judgments in addition to the liability judgments themselves. _____ _____
7. You can be liable for the acts of others under contracts you have signed with them. This liability is insurable. _____ _____

375
RISK AND
INSURANCE

| | *No action needed* | *Look into this* |

8. In some cases you may be held liable for fire loss to property of others in your care. Yet, this property would normally not be covered by your fire or general liability insurance. This risk can be covered by fire legal liability insurance or through requesting subrogation waivers from insurers of owners of the property. _____ _____

| | *No action needed* | *Look into this* |

automobile insurance

1. When an employee or a subcontractor uses his or her own car on your behalf, you can be legally liable even if you do not own a car or truck yourself. _____ _____
2. Five or more automobiles or motorcycles under one ownership that are operated as a fleet for business purposes can generally be insured under a low-cost fleet policy against both material damage to the vehicles and liability to others for property damage or personal injury. _____ _____
3. You can often get deductibles of almost any amount—say $250 or $500—and thereby reduce your premiums. _____ _____
4. Automobile medical-payments insurance pays for medical claims, including your own, arising from automobile accidents, regardless of the question of negligence. _____ _____
5. In most states, you must carry liability insurance or be prepared to provide other proof (such as a surety bond) of financial responsibility when you are involved in an accident. _____ _____
6. You can purchase uninsured motorist protection to cover your own bodily-injury claims from someone who has no insurance. _____ _____
7. Personal property stored that is in an automobile and is not attached to it (for example, merchandise being delivered) is not covered under an automobile policy. _____ _____

| | *No action needed* | *Look into this* |

worker's compensation insurance

1. Common law requires that an employer: (1) provide his or her employees a safe place to work, (2) hire competent fellow employees, (3) provide safe tools, and (4) warn employees of any existing dangers. _____ _____
2. If an employer fails to provide the above, under both common law and worker's compensation laws, he or she is liable for damage suits brought by an employee. _____ _____

	No action needed	*Look into this*

3. State law determines the level or type of benefits payable under worker's compensation policies. _____ _____
4. Not all employees are covered by worker's compensation laws. The exceptions are determined by state law, and therefore vary from state to state. _____ _____
5. In nearly all states, an employer is now legally required to cover his or her workers under worker's compensation. _____ _____
6. You can save money on worker's compensation insurance by seeing that your employees are properly classified. _____ _____
7. Rates for worker's compensation insurance vary from 0.1 percent of the payroll for "safe" occupations to about 25 percent or more of the payroll for very hazardous occupations. _____ _____
8. Most employers in most states can reduce their worker's compensation premium costs by reducing their accident rates below the average. They do this by using safety and loss prevention measures. _____ _____

Desirable Insurance Coverages

Some types of insurance coverages, although not absolutely essential, will add greatly to the security of your business. These coverages include: (1) business interruption insurance, (2) crime insurance, (3) glass insurance, and (4) rent insurance.

	No action needed	*Look into this*

business interruption insurance

1. Insurance can be purchased to cover fixed expenses that would continue if a fire shut down your business—such as salaries to key employees, taxes, interest, depreciation, and utilities—as well as the profits you would lose. _____ _____
2. Under properly written contingent business interruption insurance, you can also collect if fire or other peril closes down the business of a supplier or customer, which interrupts your business. _____ _____
3. The business interruption policy provides payments for amounts you spend to hasten the reopening of your business after a fire or other insured peril. _____ _____
4. You can get coverage for the extra expenses you suffer if an insured peril, while not actually closing your business down, seriously disrupts it. _____ _____

	No action needed	Look into this

5. When the policy is properly endorsed, you can get business interruption insurance to indemnify you if your operations are suspended because of failure or interruption of the supply of power, light, heat, gas, or water furnished by a public utility company. _____ _____

	No action needed	Look into this

crime insurance

1. Burglary insurance excludes such property as accounts, articles in showcase windows, and manuscripts. _____ _____
2. Coverage is granted under burglary insurance only if there are visible marks of the burglar's forced entry. _____ _____
3. Burglary insurance can be written to cover (in addition to money in a safe) inventoried merchandise and damage incurred in the course of a burglary. _____ _____
4. Robbery insurance protects you from loss of property, money, and securities by force, trickery, or threat of violence on or off your premises. _____ _____
5. A comprehensive crime policy, written just for small business owners, is available. In addition to burglary and robbery, it covers other types of loss by theft, destruction, and disappearance of money and securities. It also covers thefts committed by your employees. _____ _____
6. If you are in high-risk area and cannot get insurance through normal channels without paying excessive rates, you may be able to get help through the federal crime insurance plan. Your agent or State Insurance Commissioner can tell you where to get information about these plans. _____ _____

	No action needed	Look into this

glass insurance

1. You can purchase a special glass insurance policy that covers all risk to plate-glass windows, glass signs, motion-picture screens, glass brick, glass doors, showcases, countertops, and insulated glass panels. _____ _____
2. The glass insurance policy covers not only the glass itself, but also its lettering and ornamentation, if these are specifically insured, and the costs of temporary plates or boarding up when necessary. _____ _____
3. After the glass has been replaced, full coverage is continued without any additional premium for the period covered. _____ _____

		No action needed	Look into this

rent insurance

1. You can buy rent insurance that will pay your rent if the property you lease becomes unusable due to fire or other insured perils and if your lease calls for continued payments in such a situation. _____ _____
2. If you own property and lease it to others, you can insure against loss if the lease is canceled due to fire and you have to rent the property again at a reduced rental. _____ _____

Employee Benefit Coverages

Insurance coverages that can be used to provide employee benefits include (1) group life insurance, (2) group health insurance, (3) disability insurance, and (4) retirement income. Key-man coverage (5) protects the company against financial loss caused by the death of a valuable employee or partner.

		No action needed	Look into this

group life insurance

1. If you pay group insurance premiums and cover all employees up to $50,000, the cost to you is deductible for federal income tax purposes; yet the value of the benefit is not taxable income to your employees. _____ _____
2. Most insurers will provide group coverages at low rates, even if there are ten or fewer employees in your group. _____ _____
3. If the employees pay part of the cost of the group insurance, state laws require that 75 percent of them must elect coverage for the plan to qualify as group insurance. _____ _____
4. Group plans permit an employee leaving the company to convert his or her group insurance coverage to a private plan, at the rate for his or her age, without a medical exam if that person does so within thirty days after leaving the job. _____ _____

		No action needed	Look into this

group health insurance

1. Group health insurance costs much less than would individual contracts, and it provides more generous benefits for the worker. _____ _____
2. If you pay the entire cost, individual employees cannot be dropped from a group plan unless the entire group policy is canceled. _____ _____
3. Generous programs of employee benefits, such as group health insurance, tend to reduce labor turnover. _____ _____

	No action needed	*Look into this*

disability insurance

1. Worker's compensation insurance pays an employee only for time lost due to work-related injuries and illnesses—not for time lost due to disabilities incurred off the job. But you can purchase, at a low premium, insurance to replace the lost income of workers who suffer short-term or long-term disability that is not related to their work. _____ _____
2. You can get coverage that provides employees with an income for life in case of permanent disability resulting from work-related accident or illness. _____ _____

	No action needed	*Look into this*

retirement income

1. If you are self-employed, you can get an income tax deduction for funds used for retirement for you and your employees through plans of insurance or annuities approved for use under the Employees Retirement Income Security Act of 1974 (ERISA). _____ _____
2. Annuity contracts may provide for variable payments in the hope of giving the annuitants some protection against the effects of inflation. Whether fixed or variable, an annuity can provide retirement income that is guaranteed for life. _____ _____

	No action needed	*Look into this*

key-man coverage

1. One of the most serious setbacks that can come to a small company is the loss of a key person. But this person can be insured with life insurance and disability insurance owned by and payable to your company. _____ _____
2. Proceeds of a key-man coverage insurance policy, which accumulates as an asset of the business, can be borrowed against and the interest and dividends are not subject to income tax as long as the policy remains in force. _____ _____
3. The cash value of key-man coverage insurance, which accumulates as an asset of the business, can be borrowed against—and the interest and dividends are not subject to income tax as long as the policy remains in force. _____ _____

SOURCE: Mark R. Greene, *Insurance Checklist for Small Business*, Small Marketers Aid No. 148, Small Business Administration.

21

Photo courtesy of Irene Springer, Prentice-Hall, Inc.

THE LAW AND TAXES

Chapter Objectives:

1. To develop an understanding of the legal structures of businesses.
2. To learn about the regulations to which small businesses are subject.
3. To know about the laws which govern and regulate small businesses including contracts, sales and warranties.
4. To understand the legal aspects of property and negotiable instruments.
5. To understand the tax structure faced by small business persons.
6. To understand those taxes and schedules necessary to comply with state and federal regulations.

Confirm thy soul in self-control, thy liberty in law.

Katherine Lee Bates

The world no longer has a choice between force and law. If civilization is to survive it must choose the rule of law.

Dwight D. Eisenhower

INCIDENT: John Jones had just finished getting his hair cut in Steve Smith's Barber Shop. He had just paid for his haircut and was leaving the shop when he slipped on some loose hair and fell to the floor. His fall resulted in injury to his head and back. Several weeks later, after Mr. Jones had recovered and left the hospital, he went back to see Mr. Smith and asked to be reimbursed for all hospital expenses and back wages. Mr. Smith explained that he was sorry the accident had occurred but that he did not see any reason why he should pay for Mr. Jones's hospital expenses or inconvenience. He explain to him that, "Accidents will happen. I'm sorry if you've been inconvenienced or hurt."

Mr. Jones then saw his lawyer, who drew up a petition and filed it with the proper court, seeking damages and monies for John Jones's accident. When Mr. Smith received his summons to appear in court as the defendant, he realized the seriousness of the situation.

Mr. Smith was worried about his legal obligations and limitations. He did not know if he could be personally sued or if only his business and business assets were liable in this case. Was Mr. Smith negligent in the general care and running of his business? Might the courts and jury system rule against him and his business practices? Will he have to pay for Mr. Jones's lost wages and/or hospital expenses, or for any other damages or costs?

When playing Scrabble, tennis, or any game, it is important to follow the rules. Most people who develop skills with games have a keen insight into the rules and regulations that govern those games. People generally know when it is their turn and the different choices that they have as their turn approaches. Games require skill, strategy, planning and a basic knowledge of all rules. The master games player is very similar to a successful business owner.

To become a successful business owner, it is necessary to acquire the skills (a knowledge of the business, service, or trade) and to develop the necessary planning and strategy. The successful business owner must also be very knowledgeable as to the rules (or laws) that govern the conduct of the business. The plans and actions of the business owner must conform to the federal, state, or local laws and tax regulations that govern the operation of his or her business. Before entering the legal and tax constraints of the business arena, it is important to first choose that legal structure that would help most in the business. The proper legal structure will both free and protect a business owner to conduct a business and be successful. The legal structures—sole proprietorships, partnerships, and corporations—were discussed in Chapter 2.

The Law

Even when the settlers of the new frontier were crossing the plains, laws were being formulated to help society. In early America, the craftspeople, the merchants, and the early business owners helped establish the first commercial American enterprises. Businesses have formulated this nation's industrial and economical strength. Since the early parts of American history, laws have been established to help regulate and govern human beings and businesses concerning their relationships with one another. These laws are designed to govern our society. As the society has grown more complex and as individuals have tended to live closer and closer together in greater numbers, the laws governing our society have also become more complex.

Agencies of the federal government are found throughout the federal bureaucracy (see Table 21–1). Most of their authority or power comes from federal statutes and some of it from provisions in the federal constitution. These agencies have established a vast amount of business controls and paperwork. They conduct hearings and inquiries (rather than trials) to determine proper business practices and provide case verdicts or levy fines. These agencies have the power to collect evidence and testimonies before issuing legally binding decisions. Governmental agencies are established through all levels of government, the Federal Trade Commission (FTC), the Food and Drug Administration (FDA), and the Federal Communications Commission (FCC) are among the most powerful at the federal level. Public utility commissions and licensing boards are important agencies at the state level. Zoning boards, planning councils, and appeal boards are important city or county agencies.

The study of business law can be a very complex and time-demanding occupation. However, it is important for a business owner to be versed in some of the fundamentals of law that concern business activities. Therefore, the following legal topics will be covered: (1) contracts, (2) sales, (3) warranties, (4) agencies, (5) property, (6) negotiable instruments, and (7) pricing.

contracts

A contract is an agreement between two or more individuals that the law will uphold and enforce. In order for this agreement to be a valid and lawful contract, it must contain: (1) a mutual agreement, involving an offer and an acceptance, that is free of fraud, mistake, duress, or unlawful purpose; (2) competency, in that both parties must be competent and capable of entering into the agreement; and (3) consideration, in that the agreement must be supported by consideration—usually money, goods, or services—from both sides. The contract may be written or oral. However, it is strongly preferable that the agreement be written—in detail. The Uniform Commercial Code (UCC), which has been adopted by all states except

Table 21-1. Major Federal Regulators

REGULATOR	SCOPE OF AUTHORITY
Interstate Commerce Commission (ICC) Founded in 1887	Eleven Commissioners set rates, routes and practices for interstate railroads, truckers, bus companies, and pipelines.
Federal Reserve Board (FRB) Founded in 1913	Seven-member Board of Governors sets monetary and credit policy and regulates commercial banks belonging to the Federal Reserve System.
Federal Trade Commission (FTC) Founded in 1914	Five Commissioners enforce some anti-trust laws, protect businesses from unfair competition and enforce truth-in-lending and truth-in-labeling laws.
Federal Power Commission (FPC) Founded in 1920	Five Commissioners set wholesale rates for the interstate transportation and sale of natural gas and for interstate transmission of electricity.
Food and Drug Administration (FDA) Founded in 1931	A Commissioner in the Department of Health and Human Services sets standards for certain foods and drugs and issues licenses for the manufacturing and distribution of drugs.
Federal Communications Commission (FCC) Founded in 1934	Seven Commissioners license radio and television stations and oversee interstate and international telephone and telegraph operations.
Securities and Exchange Commission (SEC) Founded in 1934	Five Commissioners regulate securities issues, supervise stock exchanges and regulate holding and investment companies.
Civil Aeronautics Board (CAB) Founded in 1938	Five Commissioners determine interstate airline routes, passenger fares, and freight rates.
Federal Aviation Administration (FAA) Founded in 1948	An Administrator in the Department of Transportation certifies airworthiness of aircraft, licenses pilots, and sets safety standards for airports.
Equal Employment Opportunity Commission (EEOC) Founded in 1964	Five Commissioners investigate and rule on charges of racial and other discrimination by employers and labor unions.
Environmental Protection Agency (EPA) Founded in 1970	An Administrator develops and enforces environmental quality standards for air, water, and noise pollution and for toxic substances and pesticides.
Consumer Product Safety Commission (CPSC) Founded in 1972	Five Commissioners set product-safety standards and initiate recall notices for defective products.
Federal Energy Administration (FEA) Founded in 1974	An Administrator regulates price and allocation controls of petroleum products.
Nuclear Regulatory Commission (NRC) Founded in 1975	Five Commissioners issue licenses for the design, construction and operation of nuclear power plants.

SOURCE: Adapted from "Federal Regulators: Impact on Every American," Special Section: The ABC's of How Your Government Works, *U.S. News and World Report,* May 9, 1977, p. 62.

Louisiana, requires that any contract over $500 be written to be valid. There are several different forms of contracts, broken down into the following classifications: (1) expressed or implied contracts, (2) quasicontracts, (3) bilateral and unilateral contracts, (4) void and voidable contracts, or (5) joint and several contracts.

Expressed or implied contracts. An expressed contract is one that has been either written or spoken and has been formally developed by both parties. An implied contract is developed without any written or spoken actions but is developed through simple actions or indications from the different parties. For example, on the commodity or stock exchanges, several contracts are developed through actions. An action may be a valid implied contract, such as when the movement of an individual at an auction creates a contract with an auctioneer.

Quasicontracts. Another classification of contracts exists when contracts are created without voluntary actions or consent of the parties. Quasicontracts are obligations created by law. For example, if the law declares that one businessperson has defrauded another, the law might declare a quasicontract, which would require that the businessperson who was defrauded be reimbursed.

Bilateral and unilateral contracts. A bilateral contract is a valid contract that is an exchange of one promise for another promise. For example, Jane promises to buy from Richard a pocket calculator for $48 and Richard promises to sell Jane the pocket calculator for the given amount. A unilateral contract is a valid contract in which a promise is given for the performance of an act. If Jane lost her watch and offered a $20 reward for its return, Bob could enforce that unilateral contract by demanding the $20 reward when he returned the watch to her.

Void and voidable contracts. A void contract is not valid or legal. For example, if Mr. Black agreed to set prices on his television sets at a given level in his store, and if Mr. White agreed to set a reasonably high price on his television sets in his store, this would be illegal and the contract would be void. A voidable contract is a valid contract that contains promises that, if not fulfilled, may allow the contract to be cancelled. For example, if Ron paid $100 down to buy a used car that had reportedly been driven only 10,000 miles, and if this was a false representation, then Ron would have the option of either enforcing that contract and/or denying or cancelling that contract and getting back his $100. This contract was a voidable contract due to misrepresentation, failure to fulfill promises, or fraud.

Joint and several contracts. Joint and several contracts are agreements between three or more parties. A several contract would require that Bob and Dick be individually responsible for payment of the car to the car dealer. A joint contract would require that Bob and Dick be only responsible for a pro rata share of the actual contract. Most multiparty contracts are assumed to be either several or joint, unless otherwise stipulated or stated.

Any contract is designed to ease and help in conducting business, and bring two or more parties to a mutual agreement. A contract is a meeting of minds. It permits the offer of work, goods, or services by one business person and the acceptance of such work, goods, or services by a second party. Many contracts will have a duration period for the contractual offer. For example, most newspaper advertisements for grocery or department store sales only apply to a given week or time period.

Contracts may not be developed or used to restrain trade. The Sherman Antitrust Act, the Clayton Act, the Robinson-Patman Act, and the Federal Trade Commission Act enforce criminal penalties for contracts that restrain trade or develop monopolistic business practices.

sales

The Uniform Sales Act states: "A sale of goods is an agreement whereby the seller transfers the property (title) in the goods to the buyer for a consideration called the price." The purpose of the Uniform Sales Act is to provide rules and regulations that will help develop common practices in selling goods or services. The legal restraint on sales is an attempt to establish fair and common sales practices.

There is a distinction made between a contract of sale and a contract to sell. As defined by the Uniform Sales Act, "A contract to sell goods is a contract whereby the seller agrees to transfer the property title in the goods to the buyer for a consideration called the price." The act further states: "A sale of goods is an agreement whereby the seller transfers the property title in the goods to the buyer for a consideration called the price." Time is the principle difference between these two contracts. When the title passes immediately to the buyer, it is a *contract of sale*. However, if the title passes at a future time, the transaction or contract is called a *contract to sell*. For example, if Marv is out of stock of hot-air popcorn poppers, he may enter into a contract to sell by providing rain checks so that customers who want to buy one can do so when additional stock is received. If Marv already had hot-air popcorn poppers in stock, and people came into the store and purchased them, a contract of sale would occur and the transfer of title would take place when the hot-air popcorn popper was purchased.

Bailment. A bailment is a temporary transfer of property from one individual to another for a definite purpose. For example, leaving a car in the garage for repairs, borrowing a book from the library, renting a television, or having your clothes cleaned at the cleaner's are instances in which a bailment has been created. When you take your car in for repairs, you become the bailor and the garage becomes the bailee. The bailment is a transfer of possession only, not of title, to the bailee. The title will at all times remain with the bailor. Because there is a possibility of losing your car due to fire or natural catastrophe, it is important to determine whether your action was a sale or bailment. Such a risk of loss remains with the owner (bailor) rather than with the garage (bailee) in case of natural catastrophe. When a business person takes goods on consignment it is a bailment. The consignment sale occurs when the buyer is given possession of goods to sell them and to accept money for their sale. The original seller would retain the title to the goods. The consignee would return any unsold goods back to the seller.

The title to goods is very important. Free on board (FOB) from the seller's place of business means that the seller will take the goods to a carrier (truck, plane, or train) and that the buyer would then pay all freight charges to the final destination. The title to the goods would pass when the seller delivers the goods to the carrier. A CIF (cost, insurance, and freight) sale indicates that freight charges are included in the selling price and that the title will transfer to the buyer upon delivery to the buyer.

warranties

A warranty is an insurance that a seller gives a buyer with respect to quality of the goods purchased. A warranty allows the seller to assume responsibility for the goods being as represented by the seller. The Uniform Sales Act states: "Any affirmation of fact or any promise by the seller relating to the goods is an expressed warranty if the natural tendency of such affirmation or promise is to induce the buyer to purchase the goods and if the buyer purchases the goods relying thereon."

A warranty does require an affirmation of fact. It is not necessary to state, "I guarantee" or "I warrant"—a bare statement of fact is sufficient for a warranty to exist. This statement is not opinion. For example, "smells like heaven" or "looks like a million" are statements of opinion and do not constitute warranties. "These tires will last 30,000 miles with normal usage," or "This is a three karat diamond" are both warranties, facts.

Warranties are designed to protect buyers from defective or malfunctioning goods. Sellers must honor an expressed or an implied warranty for their products. Warranties allow purchasers a replacement, refund, or repair to a faulty purchased item. Warranties must express which parts are actually warranted, who is responsible, and any terms or limitations that are placed upon the warranty. A warranty provides specific legal rights to a buyer for the character and usefulness of the product.

agencies

The law of agency is an important part of most businesses today. A corporation can act only through its agency, and many sole proprietorships and partnerships also work with third-party agents to conduct their business. The relationship of agency is developed by either a written or an oral contract by a principal and an agent. The agent has the right to act for the business employer (principal) to contract with third persons. An agent works for the principal and not for himself or herself; therefore, any contracts that an agent develops or signs is between his or her principal and the third party, not between the third party and himself or herself. It is reasonable to assume that a person may be both an agent and an employee for the same employer. For example, a salesperson would be an employee when selling merchandise to customers and an agent when purchasing merchandise from a wholesaler for later resale.

The principal–agent relationship exists when an agent agrees to work for a principal for a given fee or commission. There is a mutuality of consent between the principal and the agent, with the agent agreeing to follow the rules and regulations of the principal. The agent may be classified either as a general agent, with broad powers and authority to act for the principal, or as a special agent, with limited powers and many restrictions. A general agent (often the president of a company) usually acts with very broad powers and authority for the principal. A special agent is generally hired to perform a specific act or task, such as negotiating a sales contract or developing accounting figures. Accountants, real estate brokers, and often lawyers serve as special agents to businesses.

A principal is legally responsible for all contracts made by his or her agent, but not for any contracts made by employees or independent contractors. (Independent contractors are not told how to accomplish a task or what to do on a job—they are only told the desired results.) A principal, though, is liable for all torts (wrongs) of employees and agents, but is not responsible for those of independent contractors.

Many small business owners will employ agents to purchase goods or materials to be sold in their businesses. The business owner is responsible for all contracts signed and developed by that agent. A good agent may provide the materials and necessities that are important to the success of the business. A dishonest agent can ruin a business.

property

The law of used property relates to either real property (real estate being buildings, land, and the like) or personal property (such as inventory, investments, money, automobiles, and so on). Generally speaking, that which is not real property is viewed as personal property. The ownership of property—real and personal—provides certain rights that include the right of possession, enjoyment, use, and disposal of that property according to the desire of the owner. There are a number of different ways to own property.

Real property may be owned by individuals, groups, or corporations. Two of the most common forms of joint ownership are tenancy in common and joint tenancy.

Tenancy in common, the first of the two common forms of joint ownership, is a valid and useful way of property being owned by two or more people; each individual retains complete control of his or her property. For example, if Winn and Bill buy some land as an investment, they can split the purchase on a 50–50 basis. They would then become tenants in common, and each would hold a separate, half interest in the property. The law would then view the ownership of these interests as being separate, as with any other property that is fully owned by an individual. Each piece of property owned by tenants in common is a separate part of each owner's personal estate, and upon either owner's death, it would pass to his or her heirs.

Joint tenancy, the second of the two common forms of joint ownership, is a favorite means of holding property. For example, if a married couple buys a house, they will generally take ownership as joint tenants with a right of survivorship. Joint tenancy means that if either owner dies, ownership of the entire property is transferred to the survivor. Joint tenancy is by far the most widely used method of ownership.

The rights of property owners may also be divided. If you own property "fee simple," you have possession of all rights to that property. However, if you become a landlord (lessor) and create a leasehold on that business property, the renter (lessee) has the right of possession and enjoyment of that property for the specified time period described in the lease.

Leases are contracts, and are a matter for bargaining and negotiation. A lease is usually a lengthy and complex legal document. It generally contains all terms and conditions necessary to rent a business property. Most leases are prepared beforehand by the landlord, and are developed in favor of the landlord rather than of the renter. A lease will generally contain provisions for rent, length or term of the lease, renewable options, additional fees (such as water fees, real estate costs, taxes, insurance clauses, renovations, and repairs), use of the space, assignment or subleasing, security, the tenant's rights, and the cost or use of common areas.

Although most leases contain a fixed, flat rental fee for a given year, many landlords also require a so-called percentage lease. Percentage leases are very common with retail and shopping center establishments. Such a lease usually contains a provision for the payment of a fixed lease fee or of a percentage of sales based on a monthly sales figure of the business. For example, a percentage lease may charge $300 per month or 6 percent of the average monthly gross receipts, whichever is higher. Thus, if a movie theater has to pay 6 percent of its monthly gross receipts, and if it averages $10,000 worth of business a month, then for each month the movie theater will pay $600 (6 percent of $10,000 gross) rather than a $300-a-month fixed rental figure. Most retail establishments that have percentage clauses in their leases will pay the percentage amount during their most profitable months of business.

negotiable instruments

In the thirteenth century, Italian traders developed a convenient commercial device called a "bill of exchange." This device was used throughout Europe and later in England. In 1882, England codified a law of negotiable instruments in what is known as the Bills of Exchange Act. In 1896, the United States drafted the Uniform Negotiable Instrument Law, which applies to negotiable instruments. *Negotiable instruments* may be defined as contracts that are transferable from one party to another. Negotiable instruments are similar to cash in that they may be transferred to another person with full rights and without any defenses. They are transferred by negotiation. The holder in due course takes the instrument, free from any defenses that may have been asserted against the original payee. A negotiable instrument, by law, should be free to be transferred from person to person, as is money. Negotiable instruments include promissory notes, drafts, checks, and certificates of deposit. Quasi-negotiable instruments would include warehouse receipts, bills of lading, and stocks certificates.

Promissory notes. A negotiable promissory note is described as being an unconditional promise, in writing, made by one person (maker) to another person (payee) that is signed by the maker and that requires payment, on demand or at a fixed time, of a certain sum of money to bearer. Promissory notes are generally credit instruments that may or may not specify interest. (See Figure 21–1.)

Drafts. A draft (bill of exchange) is an unconditional order written by one person (drawer) to another (drawee) requiring the drawee to pay on demand or at a fixed time a sum of money to bearer. The person receiving the money is known as the payee. This is generally a three party action and occurs when the drawee owes money or is in debt to the drawer.

Checks. When the drawee is a bank, the instrument is called a check. A check may be defined as a bill of exchange that is drawn on a bank and that is payable to a payee on demand.

Certificate of deposit. A certificate of deposit (CD) is a receipt made by a bank

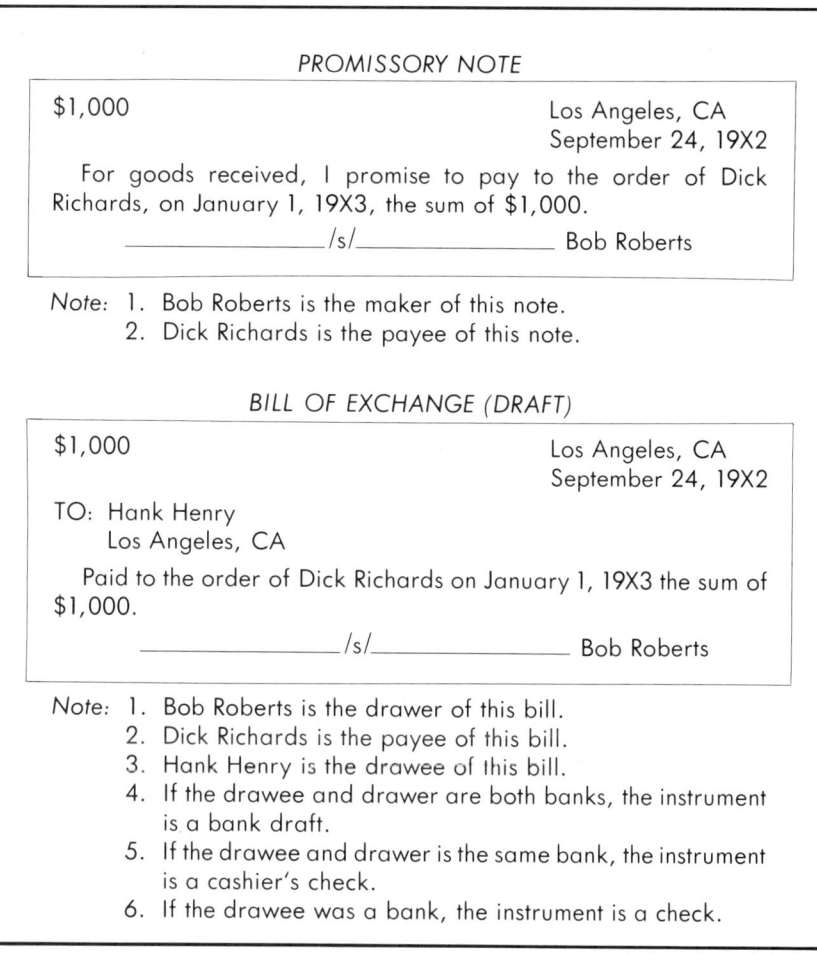

Figure 21-1. *Illustrations of negotiable instruments*

or financial institution that recognizes a deposit of money and that promises to repay that money on a specific date at a specified rate of interest.

The Uniform Negotiable Instrument Law explains the tests or provisions that are necessary in order for an instrument to be considered negotiable. These requirements state that in order for something to be considered a legal negotiable instrument it must:

1. Be a written instrument signed by the maker or drawer.
2. Contain an unconditional promise or order.
3. Specify a certain sum of money.
4. Be payable on demand or within a given time period.
5. Be marked "payable to order or repayable to bearer."
6. Name the drawee with reasonable certainty.
7. Not require an act in addition to payment of money.

When all of these conditions have been met, the instrument may be negotiated and transferred from one person to another (the latter becomes the holder). The holder of a negotiable instrument is:

1. The person for whom the instrument is drawn.
2. The person to whom the instrument is issued.
3. The person who endorses (or will endorse) the instrument.
4. The bearer of the instrument.
5. The person to whose order the instrument is designated.

This instrument may be paid when it has been properly endorsed. A negotiable instrument is endorsed when the holder signs it. The signing of a check is the endorsement of a negotiable instrument.

pricing

A business owner usually has the right to determine what prices he or she will charge for merchandise. Our economic system provides a competitive market, and prices in a competitive market act as regulators of supply and demand. Manipulation of prices in various ways may be illegal.

Price cutting. Ordinarily, price cutting is a fair competitive practice. However, when price cutting is done for the purpose of inflicting harm or in an effort to eliminate competition, it is then a deceptive sales practice, and is unlawful by the Fair Trade Law and the Uniform Consumer Credit Code. A successful price cutting technique that eliminates competition is often followed by a high "monopoly price" set by the remaining large business. Most states now have established laws prohibiting below-cost prices that restrain competitive practices.

Price fixing. Price fixing is what occurs when competitors engage in setting prices relative to one another. Price fixing is usually considered illegal under federal antitrust laws when businesses practice or engage in interstate commerce.

Price discrimination. The Clayton Act, as amended by the Robinson-Patman Act, declares it unlawful for a person engaged in commerce to discriminate prices between different purchasers for goods. Any differences in the price of goods of similar grade and quality to different buyers is an illegal practice unless justified by a cost difference in manufacturing, selling, or handling. However, a seller may be permitted to discriminate in prices between buyers only in order to meet competitors' lower prices in regional markets.

Fair trade statutes. Most states have now enacted fair trade statutes which permit manufacturers to make contracts that fix resale prices for trademark or trade name commodities. This identifies the price at which an item may be sold, or a minimal price below which it cannot be sold.

Consumers had long been opposed to fair trade practices and were often willing to overlook them. Finally, in state after state, the courts began to rule against individual state trade laws, and manufacturers finally became convinced that high fair trade prices were actually working against them (retailers could not lower prices and gain a competitive advantage). There is little security in fair trade laws or other legal devices used to establish pricing. It is difficult to prove that any wrong or illegal activity has occurred such as: (a) monopolistic agreements, (b) conspiracies in restraint of trade, (c) price discrimination, or (d) any unfair or deceptive practices (false advertising). Generally consumer demand will help determine the best price.

SUCCESS STORY: Kemmons Wilson

Kemmons Wilson was born January 5, 1913, at Osceola, Arkansas. When he was but nine months old, his father passed away and left his mother without income or resources. She decided to journey north to Memphis, Tennessee, and there found work.

While still a young man, Kemmons learned the value of work. When he was fourteen years old, he was fortunate to obtain a job at a drugstore as a delivery boy. By the time he was seventeen, he had purchased a popcorn machine on credit and sold his popcorn at a local movie theatre. Selling the popcorn machine, he used the $50 sales price to purchase five used pinball machines. With these five machines he started a very successful coin machine route.

By scrimping and saving, he finally managed to gather together $1,700, which he used to build a home for his mother. This activity led him into his life-long occupation of building homes and motor inns. Working eighteen hours a day plus, he was able to build a highly successful home building company. Through this company, he was able to save $250,000 by 1941. During the war, he participated in the aviation service, but after World War II, he returned to his building construction trade.

In 1952, he founded Holiday Inn. One year later, he and Wallace E. Johnson developed a partnership to build and sell franchises for Holiday Inns. By 1966, they had built the largest motor inn chain in the world. Holiday Inn franchises have helped to develop many highly successful small business ventures.

Taxes

Nearly all small business owners are required to collect and pay taxes. Every business is affected by federal tax laws; in addition most small business is affected by local and state tax laws.

Any business activity that results in profit develops a tax liability. If a business owner is a sole proprietor or a partner, there is a liability for self-employment tax. Small business corporations have a whole other set of tax laws to deal with. Some of the most vexing tax problems involving corporations relate to distributions to shareholders.

In addition business owners must address themselves to withholding taxes—Federal Insurance Contribution Act (FICA); unemployment taxes, property taxes, sales taxes, manufacturers and/or retailers' excise taxes, highway-use taxes, craft-use taxes, and so on.

In order to keep informed and current about tax laws, the small business owner should consult with an accountant. There is such a variety of taxes, some of which are applicable to specific businesses, that professional help for dealing with taxes is appropriate for most businesses.

employer-employee taxes

If the business has employees, the business owner is required to deduct taxes from the employee's salary and to pay these plus the employer's share of taxes to the appropriate levying body. For instance, the Federal Insurance Contribution Act (FICA) provides for a system of social security, disability and hospital insurance payments; these monies are provided from payroll deductions and employers' contributions and it is the employer who is responsible for the bookkeeping in this area. The state in which the small business operates may also require that the employer withhold tax monies from employees. In fact, one of the first forms an employer may fill out when a business opens is likely to be the Application for Employer Identification Number (IRS form SS-4, see Figure 21–2). Along with the IRS employer identification number the business owner receives an Employers Quarterly Federal Tax Return Form (IRS form #941) and several copies of the Federal Tax Deposit Form (IRS form #501) for each quarter.

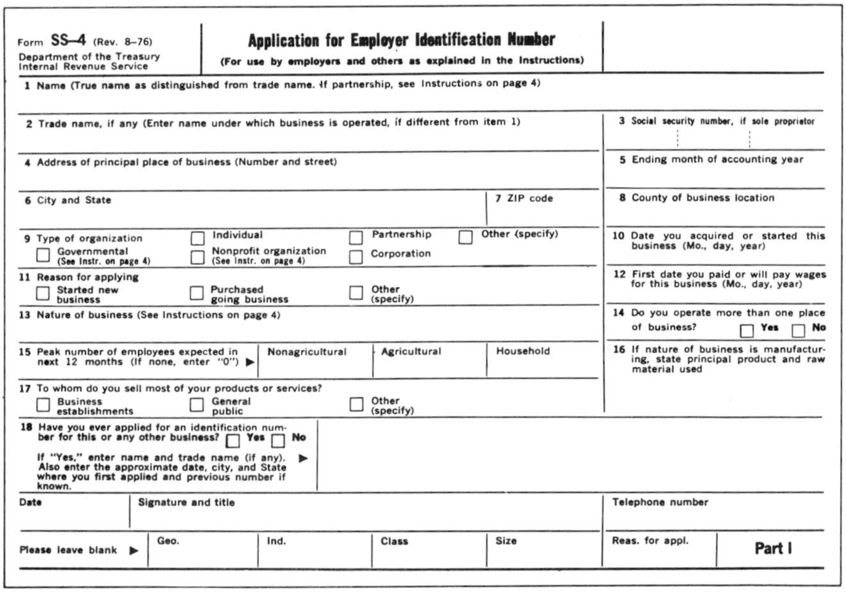
Form SS-4 (Rev. 8-76)
Department of the Treasury
Internal Revenue Service

Application for Employer Identification Number
(For use by employers and others as explained in the Instructions)

1 Name (True name as distinguished from trade name. If partnership, see Instructions on page 4)

2 Trade name, if any (Enter name under which business is operated, if different from item 1)

3 Social security number, if sole proprietor

4 Address of principal place of business (Number and street)

5 Ending month of accounting year

6 City and State

7 ZIP code

8 County of business location

9 Type of organization ☐ Governmental (See Instr. on page 4) ☐ Individual ☐ Nonprofit organization (See Instr. on page 4) ☐ Partnership ☐ Corporation ☐ Other (specify)

10 Date you acquired or started this business (Mo., day, year)

11 Reason for applying ☐ Started new business ☐ Purchased going business ☐ Other (specify)

12 First date you paid or will pay wages for this business (Mo., day, year)

13 Nature of business (See Instructions on page 4)

14 Do you operate more than one place of business? ☐ Yes ☐ No

15 Peak number of employees expected in next 12 months (If none, enter "0") ▶ Nonagricultural | Agricultural | Household

16 If nature of business is manufacturing, state principal product and raw material used

17 To whom do you sell most of your products or services? ☐ Business establishments ☐ General public ☐ Other (specify)

18 Have you ever applied for an identification number for this or any other business? ☐ Yes ☐ No

If "Yes," enter name and trade name (if any). Also enter the approximate date, city, and State where you first applied and previous number if known. ▶

Date | Signature and title | Telephone number

Please leave blank ▶ Geo. | Ind. | Class | Size | Reas. for appl. | **Part I**

FIGURE 21–2.

When a person is hired the business must require the employee to complete a W-4 form which shows the number of allowances he or she is entitled to. (See Figure 21–3.) This form tells the employer how much is to be deducted from the employee's pay, and should be completed when a person is hired or before December 1 of the coming year.

Before January 31, or no later than one month following the close of the business's tax year, the employer must provide to the employee a W-2 form which

Form **W-4**
(Rev. December 1978)
Department of the Treasury
Internal Revenue Service

Employee's Withholding Allowance Certificate
(Use for Wages Paid After December 31, 1978)
This certificate is for income tax withholding purposes only. It will remain in effect until you change it. If you claim exemption from withholding, you will have to file a new certificate on or before April 30 of next year.

Type or print your full name | Your social security number

Home address (number and street or rural route)

City or town, State, and ZIP code

Marital Status
☐ Single ☐ Married
☐ Married, but withhold at higher Single rate
Note: *If married, but legally separated, or spouse is a nonresident alien, check the single block.*

1 Total number of allowances you are claiming . . . .
2 Additional amount, if any, you want deducted from each pay (if your employer agrees) . . . . $
3 I claim exemption from withholding (see instructions). Enter "Exempt" . . . .

Under the penalties of perjury, I certify that the number of withholding allowances claimed on this certificate does not exceed the number to which I am entitled. If claiming exemption from withholding, I certify that I incurred no liability for Federal income tax for last year and I anticipate that I will incur no liability for Federal income tax for this year.

Signature ▶.. Date ▶.., 19..........

.... Detach along this line ....

▲ *Give the top part of this form to your employer; keep the lower part for your records and information* ▲

Instructions

The explanatory material below will help you determine your correct number of withholding allowances, and will assist you in completing the Form W–4 at the top of this page.

See **Publication 505** for more information on withholding.

Avoid Overwithholding or Underwithholding

By claiming the number of withholding allowances you are entitled to, you can fit the amount of tax withheld from your wages to your tax liability. In addition to the allowances for personal exemptions to be claimed in item (a), be sure to claim any additional allowances you are entitled to in item (b), "Special withholding allowance," and item (c), "Allowance(s) for credit(s) and/or deduction(s)." While you may claim these allowances on Form W–4 for withholding purposes, you may not claim them under "Exemptions" on your tax return Form 1040 or Form 1040A.

You may claim the special withholding allowance if you are single with only one employer, or married with only one employer and your spouse is not employed. If you have unusually large itemized deductions, make alimony payments, or credit(s) for child care expenses, earned income, credit for the elderly, or residential energy credits, you may claim additional allowances to avoid having too much income tax withheld from your wages.

If you and your spouse are both employed or you have more than one employer, you should make sure that enough has been withheld. If you find that you need more withholding, claim fewer allowances or ask for additional withholding or request to be withheld at the higher "Single" status. If you are currently claiming additional withholding allowances based on itemized deductions, check the worksheet on the back to see that you are claiming the proper number of allowances.

How Many Withholding Allowances May You Claim?

Use the schedule below to determine the number of allowances you may claim for tax withholding purposes. In determining the number, keep in mind these points: if you are single and hold more than one job, you may not claim the same allowances with more than one employer at the same time; or, if you are married and both you and your spouse are employed, you may not both claim the same allowances with your employers at the same time. A nonresident alien, other than a resident of Canada, Mexico, or Puerto Rico, may claim only one personal allowance.

Completing Form W–4

If you find you are entitled to one or more allowances in addition to those you are now claiming, increase your number of allowances by completing the form above and filing it with your employer. If the number of allowances you previously claimed decreases, you must file a new Form W–4 within 10 days. (If you expect to owe more tax than will be withheld, you may increase your withholding by claiming fewer or "0" allowances on line 1, or by asking for additional withholding on line 2, or both.)

You may claim exemption from withholding of Federal income tax if you had no liability for income tax for last year, and you anticipate that you will incur no liability for income tax for this year. You may not claim exemption if your joint or separate return shows tax liability before the allowance of any credit for income tax withheld. If you are exempt, your employer will not withhold Federal income tax from your wages. However, social security tax will be withheld if you are covered by the Federal Insurance Contributions Act.

You must revoke this exemption (1) within 10 days from the time you anticipate you will incur income tax liability for the year or (2) on or before December 1 if you anticipate you will incur Federal income tax liability for the next year. If you want to stop or are required to revoke this exemption, you must file a new Form W–4 with your employer showing the number of withholding allowances you are entitled to claim. This certificate for exemption from withholding will expire on April 30 of next year unless a new Form W–4 is filed on or before that date.

The Following Information is Provided in Accordance with the Privacy Act of 1974

The Internal Revenue Code requires every employee to furnish his or her employer with a signed withholding allowance certificate showing the number of withholding allowances that the employee claims (section 3402(f)(2)(A) and the Regulations thereto). Individuals are required to provide their Social Security Number for proper identification and processing (section 6109 and the Regulations thereto).

The principal purpose for soliciting withholding allowance certificate information is to administer the Internal Revenue laws of the United States.

If an employee does not furnish a signed withholding allowance certificate, the employee is considered as claiming no withholding allowances (section 3401(e)) and shall be treated as a single person (section 3402(l)).

The routine uses of the withholding allowance certificate information include disclosure to the Department of Justice for actual or potential criminal prosecution or civil litigation.

Figure Your Total Withholding Allowances Below

(a) Allowance(s) for exemption(s)—Enter 1 for each personal exemption you can claim on your Federal income tax return* . . . . ______
(b) Special withholding allowance—Enter 1 if single with 1 employer, or married with 1 employer and spouse not employed** . . . ______
(c) Allowance(s) for credit(s) and/or deduction(s)—Enter number from tables on page 2 . . . . ______
(d) Total (add lines (a) through (c) above)—Enter here and on line 1, Form W–4, above . . . . ______

*If you are in doubt as to whom you may claim as a dependent, see the instructions that came with your last Federal income tax return or call your local Internal Revenue Service office.
**This allowance is used solely for purposes of figuring your withholding tax, and cannot be claimed when you file your tax return.

FIGURE 21–3.

Form W-4 (Rev. 12-78) Page 2

TABLE A.—Table for Determining Number of Withholding Allowances Based on Tax Credits

Figure the number of additional withholding allowances for the amount of tax credits for child care expenses, earned income credit, credit for the elderly, or residential energy credits, from the appropriate column (see line (c) on other side). For an explanation of these credits, see the Instructions for Form 1040.

Note: Watch for announcements that could affect the number of withholding allowances you may claim.

Allowances ▶	0		1		2		3		4		5		6
Estimated salaries and wages from all sources:	\multicolumn{13}{l}{If the amount of estimated tax credits is:}
	Under	At least	But less than	At least	But less than	At least	But less than	At least	But less than	At least	But less than	At least	But less than

Part I — Single Employees

Under $5,000	No additional allowances												
5,000–15,000		250	250	500	500	700	700	900	900 or more				
15,001–25,000		350	350	700	700	1,000	1,000 or more						
25,001–35,000		580	580	950	950 or more								

Part II — Head of Household Employees

Under $5,000	No additional allowances												
5,000–20,000		150	150	400	400	650	650	900	900 or more				
20,001–35,000		1	1	200	300	650	650	1,000	1,000 or more				
35,001–45,000		450	450	650 or more									

Part III — Married Employees (When Spouse is Not Employed)

Under $8,000	No additional allowances												
8,000–15,000		200	200	350	350	500	500	700	700	800	800 or more		
15,001–25,000		250	250	500	500	700	700	950	950 or more				
25,001–35,000		300	300	650	650	950	950 or more						
35,001–45,000		650	650	1,050	1,050 or more								

Part IV — Married Employees (When Both Spouses are Employed)

Under $8,000	No additional allowances												
8,000–15,000		250	250	400	400	450	450 or more						
15,001–25,000		550	550	800	800	950	950 or more						

How to Use Table A

1. Find your filing status under Part I, II, III, or IV.
2. Using your filing status, find your estimated salaries and wages in the left column.
3. Read the shaded amounts to the right until you get to the amount of your estimated tax credits.
4. Look to the top of the column to find the number of allowances you may take for your estimated tax credits.
5. Enter this number on page 1, line (c), together with the number of allowances from Table B for itemized deductions, and alimony payments.

Example: A taxpayer who expects to file a Federal income tax return as a single person estimates annual wages of $12,000 and tax credits of $650. The taxpayer uses Part I for single employees. The $12,000 falls in the wage bracket of $5,000 to 15,000 in the left column. Reading in the shaded area to the right, $650 falls within the estimated tax credits bracket of At least 500 But less than 700. Looking to the top of the column, the taxpayer finds that 2 allowances are permitted. The taxpayer adds "2" to the number of any allowances from Table B below and enters the total on page 1, line (c).

TABLE B.—Table for Determining Number of Withholding Allowances Based on Itemized Deductions and Alimony Payments, if Any*

Estimated salaries and wages from all sources:	Column (A) Single Employees (only one job)	Column (B) Married Employees (one spouse working and one job only)	Column (C) Married Employees (both spouses working or employees with more than one job)
Under $10,000	$2,800	$3,900	$4,000
10,000–30,000	2,800	3,900	5,800
30,001–40,000	3,500	3,900	8,000
Over $40,000	15% of estimated salaries and wages	13% of estimated salaries and wages	23% of estimated salaries and wages

*If you are paying alimony but will not itemize deductions, figure the number of withholding allowances by dividing the estimated alimony payments by $1,000 (round off fractions to the nearest whole number) and enter on page 1, line (c).

How to Use Table B

1. Enter the amount of your estimated itemized deductions, including alimony payments, for the year.
2. Find your total estimated salary and wage amount in the left column. Read to the right and enter the amount from column (A), (B), or (C) for your filing status.
3. Subtract line 2 from line 1.
4. Divide the amount on line 3 by $1,000. Enter here and on page 1, line (c) together with the number of any allowances for tax credits from Table A, above. (Round off fractions to the nearest whole number.)

*U.S. GOVERNMENT PRINTING OFFICE:1978-0-263-298-E.I.#56-2890346

Figure 21–3. *(Continued)*

shows the employee his or her earnings for the past year. (See Figure 21–4.) (This is the form used by the employee to develop his or her personal income liabilities.)

Both federal and state governments collect and use unemployment taxes. Each state has its own form, rate, and collection procedures. The amount that is paid to the federal government is dependent upon what the statement requires to be paid and payments to the state depend upon federal requirements. Unemployment taxes vary greatly from state to state.

1 Control number	22222	

2 Employer's name, address, and ZIP code	3 Employer's identification number	4 Employer's State number
	5 Stat. employee ☐ Deceased ☐ Pension plan ☐ Legal rep. ☐ 942 emp. ☐ Subtotal ☐ Correction ☐ Void ☐	
	6	7 Advance EIC payment
8 Employee's social security number / 9 Federal income tax withheld	10 Wages, tips, other compensation	11 FICA tax withheld
12 Employee's name, address, and ZIP code	13 FICA wages	14 FICA tips
	16 Employer's use	
	17 State income tax / 18 State wages, tips, etc.	19 Name of State
	20 Local income tax / 21 Local wages, tips, etc.	22 Name of locality

Form **W-2 Wage and Tax Statement 1980** — Copy D For employer — Department of the Treasury Internal Revenue Service

Instructions for Preparing Form W–2

The 6-part wage and tax statement is acceptable in most States. If you are in doubt, ask your appropriate State or local official.

Prepare Form W–2 for each of your employees to whom any of the following items applied during 1980.

(a) You withheld income tax or FICA (social security) tax

(b) You would have withheld income tax if the employee had not claimed more than one withholding allowance.

(c) You paid $600 or more.

(d) You paid for services any amount, if you are in a trade or business. Include the cash value of any payment you made that was not in cash.

By January 31, 1981, give Copies B, C, and 2 to each person who was your employee during 1980. For anyone who stopped working for you before the end of 1980, you may give copies any time after employment ends. If the employee asks for Form W–2, give him or her the completed copies within 30 days of the request or the final wage payment, whichever is later. Send Copy A to the Social Security Administration by February 28, 1981. (For more information, please see Forms 941, 942, W–3, or Circular E. Farmers, see Circular A.)

See separate **Instructions for Forms W–2 and W–2P** for more information on how to complete Form W–2.

☆ U.S. GOVERNMENT PRINTING OFFICE : 1980—283-030 EI-36-2441915

Figure 21–4. *W-2 form front and back*

property taxes

Property taxes are collected by most local taxing authorities based on some value of the business value. Generally the local government will establish a taxing base and fix a percentage of assessed values for property in the government community. The actual assessed value is a percentage of the appraised value or real value of the property. The final tax charged, then, is the assessed value times the tax rate. For example, if your current business property is valued at $50,000 with an assessment rate of 60 percent and a tax rate of 5 percent then your tax liability will equal $600:

$$\text{Assessed Value} = 60\% \times \$50{,}000 = \$30{,}000$$
$$\text{Tax Liability} = 5\% \times \$30{,}000 = \$600$$

personal property taxes

Many state or federal taxing authorities also collect personal property taxes levied against business equipment and inventory. The value of the equipment and inventory is generally based on the first or last day of calendar or physical year. There-

Nebraska and City Sales and Use Tax Return

FORM 10

nebraska department of revenue

- Returns must be filed every tax period even though there have been no sales
- Read instructions on reverse side and complete enclosed worksheet

Nebraska Identification Number
City Code
Tax Period

☐ Check this box if you are discontinuing your business and this is your final return

NAME AND LOCATION ADDRESS

NAME AND MAILING ADDRESS

1 Gross sales and services (line 14 of worksheet)......................... 1 $ | 00
2 Net taxable sales (line 26 of worksheet)................................ 2 | 00
3 Nebraska sales tax (line 2 multiplied by   )................... 3
4 Nebraska consumer's use tax (line 32 of worksheet)................... 4
5 City Tax...

City Name	Line Number From Worksheet	City Code	Column A City Consumer's Use Tax	Column B City Sales Tax
1 Omaha	33	365		
2 Lincoln	34	285		
3 Bellevue	35	046		
4 North Platte	36	355		
5				
6				
7				
8				
9				

6 Total city tax (total of lines 5 [1] through 5 [9])........... 6a | 6b
7 Total Nebraska and city sales tax (line 3 plus line 6b)................. 7
8 Sales tax collection fee (line 7 multiplied by .03)..................... 8
9 Sales tax due (line 7 minus line 8).................................... 9
10 Total Nebraska and city **consumer's use tax** (line 4 plus line 6a)..... 10
11 Total Nebraska and city sales and use tax due (line 9 plus line 10)..... 11
12 Previous balance due or credit calculated through   12
13 BALANCE DUE (line 11 plus line 12). Pay in full with return............ 13 $

Under penalties of perjury, I declare that I have examined this return, including accompanying schedules and statements, and to the best of my knowledge and belief, it is correct and complete.

sign here Authorized Signature ▶ Signature of Preparer Other Than Taxpayer

Title   Date   Address   Date

THIS RETURN IS DUE ON OR BEFORE THE LAST DAY OF THE MONTH FOLLOWING THE TAX PERIOD INDICATED ABOVE.
Mail this return and payment to: NEBRASKA DEPARTMENT OF REVENUE, BOX 94841, LINCOLN, NE 68509

FIGURE 21–5.

fore, most business owners desire to reduce their inventory to the lowest possible extent for that day.

sales tax

The vast majority of states has sales taxes. A retailer, manufacturer, or business owner collects these sales taxes and makes a quarterly report and payment to the

INSTRUCTIONS

WHO MUST FILE. Every person collecting Nebraska sales and use tax must file a Nebraska and City Sales and Use Tax Return, Form 10, on or before the due date. The person is required to hold a sales and use tax permit issued by the Nebraska Department of Revenue. Out-of-state retailers shall report only Nebraska sales on this return.

WHEN AND WHERE TO FILE. This return, properly signed and accompanied by a check or money order payable to the Nebraska Department of Revenue, will be considered timely filed if postmarked on or before the last day of the month following the tax period covered by the return. A return is required even though there have been no taxable sales. Mail to the Nebraska Department of Revenue, Box 94841, Lincoln, Nebraska 68509.

PREIDENTIFIED RETURN. This return is to be used only by the retailer whose name is printed on it. If you have not received a preidentified return for the reporting period, request a duplicate from the Nebraska Department of Revenue. Do not file returns which are photocopies, returns for another tax period or returns which have not been preidentified. If the business name, location or mailing address is not correct, mark through the incorrect information and plainly print the correct information.

This return provides for the reporting of both sales and use tax. The entries for each tax remain separate. If the retailer intends to file a return for both taxes, a word, statement, number or figure must be entered on the appropriate lines of the return. Failure to do so will extend the statute of limitations for audit and collection purposes to five years.

CONSUMER'S USE TAX LIABILITY. Nebraska consumer's use tax is to be paid on items consumed within a business that were originally purchased tax free for resale, nonexempt purchases delivered in Nebraska from a retailer who has not collected sales tax on the purchase and purchases from Federal government agencies and instrumentalities. These transactions are to be reported on this return if the permitholder is the consumer.

REQUEST FOR TERMINATION OF PERMIT. If the permitholder has ceased making sales or providing services subject to the Nebraska sales tax and wishes the sales and use tax permit to be terminated, the permitholder must check the block above the Name and Location Address. The sales and use tax permit must be attached to this final return. The permit may be reinstated upon the permitholder's request without charge by filing a Nebraska Change Request, Form 22.

SALES TAX COLLECTION FEE. The permitholder is allowed to deduct three percent of the total Nebraska and city sales tax collected as a reimbursement for collecting the tax.

PENALTY AND INTEREST. In the event that the return is not filed by the prescribed due date, a penalty will be assessed in the amount of $5.00 or forfeiture of the collection fee, whichever is greater. Interest will be assessed at the rate of one half of one percent for each month or fraction thereof for which the tax is delinquent.

WORKSHEET. A Form 10 Worksheet is supplied with each preidentified tax return. The worksheet provides space to compute the net taxable sales, consumer's use tax and city sales and use tax. The worksheet is to be completed and retained with the business records.

VERIFICATION AND AUDIT. Records to substantiate this return shall be retained and be available for a period of at least three years following the date of filing the return.

SPECIFIC INSTRUCTIONS

LINE 1. Enter the gross revenue from services, sales, leases and rentals. Record both taxable and exempt gross revenue rounded to the nearest whole dollar.

LINE 2. Enter the net taxable sales from line 26 of the Form 10 Worksheet rounded to the nearest whole dollar. Refer to the worksheet instructions for allowable deductions.

LINE 4. Enter the Nebraska consumer's use tax due for the period from line 32 of the worksheet.

LINE 5, Column A. Enter for each city the corresponding use tax due for the period from column A, beginning with line 33 of the worksheet.

LINE 5, Column B. Enter for each city the corresponding sales tax due for the period from column B, beginning with line 33 of the worksheet.

LINE 6. Enter the total city consumer's use tax in column A and the total city sales tax in column B.

LINE 12. A previous balance due or credit resulting from mathematical or clerical errors or penalty or interest relating to prior returns may be entered in this space by the Nebraska Department of Revenue. If the balance due has been settled by a previous remittance, it should be disregarded in computing the amount to remit on line 13.

If a credit is shown, it may be applied to current tax liability. If the credit can not be exhausted in a reasonable amount of time a Nebraska and City Refund Claim for Sales and Use Tax, Form 7, may be filed.

LINE 13. Attach a check or money order payable to the Nebraska Department of Revenue for the amount reported on line 13.

SIGNATURES. This return must be signed by the taxpayer, partner or corporate officer. If the taxpayer authorizes another person to sign this return, there must be a power of attorney on file with the Nebraska Department of Revenue.

Any person who is paid for preparing a taxpayer's return must also sign the return as prepared.

Figure 21-5. *(Continued)*

state. Most states provide a small allowance or discount for collecting taxes. Sales taxes are generally controlled by the state's controller's (comptroller's) office.

Sales tax rates vary from state to state. A copy of the Nebraska (state) and Omaha (city) sales tax form is shown in Figure 21-5.

excise taxes   Federal excise taxes are collected on sales of certain articles, transactions, or occupations and also on the use of specific items. Excise taxes are not imposed on profits of the business or profession. Excise taxes are generally collected on fuels, diesel fuel, aviation fuels, gasoline, tires, fishing equipment, bows and arrows, pistols and revolvers, firearms and cartridges, telephone and tele-typewriter services, gaming devices, and wagering taxes. Many state and local government agencies also collect excise taxes for tobacco, alcohol, automotive and gasoline use. These excise taxes vary from state to state and state or local agencies should be consulted.

Tax Calendar

	Form	Due Dates [1]
US Individual Income Tax Return	1040	April 15
Declaration of Estimated Tax for Individuals	1040–ES	April 15
Estimated Tax Declaration-Voucher for Individuals	1040–ES	4th voucher Jan. 15 / 1st voucher April 15 / 2d voucher June 15 / 3d voucher Sept. 15
U.S. Corporation Income Tax Return	1120	March 15 for calendar year taxpayers. Return for fiscal year taxpayers is due on the 15th day of the third month following the close of the fiscal year.
U.S. Small Business Corporation Income Tax Return	1120S	March 15 for calendar year-electing small business corporations. Fiscal year returns are due on the 15th day of the third month following the close of the fiscal year.
U.S. Partnership Return of Income	1065	April 15 for partnerships operating on a calendar year. Return for fiscal year partnerships is due on the 15th day of the fourth month following the close of the fiscal year.
Employer's Annual Federal Unemployment Tax Return	940	January 31
Federal Tax Deposit, Unemployment Taxes	508	4th quarter Jan. 31 / 1st quarter April 30 / 2d quarter July 31 / 3d quarter Oct. 31
Employer's Quarterly Federal Tax Return	941	4th quarter Jan. 31 / 1st quarter April 30 / 2d quarter July 31 / 3d quarter Oct. 31
Employer's Quarterly Tax Return for Household Employees	942	4th quarter Jan. 31 / 1st quarter April 30 / 2d quarter July 31 / 3d quarter Oct. 31
Federal Tax Deposit, Withheld Income and FICA Taxes	501	If your liability for the quarter is less than $200,[2] make your payment with Form 941 on the dates shown above.
Quarterly Federal Excise Tax Return	720	4th quarter Jan. 31 / 1st quarter April 30 / 2d quarter July 31 / 3d quarter[3] Oct. 31
Federal Tax Deposit, Excise Taxes	504	If you are liable for more than $100 of excise taxes in any calendar quarter,[2] you are required to make semi-monthly, monthly, or quarterly deposits on Form 504 in accordance with instructions in Form 720, Quarterly Federal Excise Tax Return.
Wage and Tax Statement	W–2	You must complete and give this form to the employee on or before January 31; or, if his employment ended before December 31, within 30 days after his last wage payment.
Statement for Recipients of Income	1099 (Series)	Generally, these statements should be given to recipients on or before January 31.

[1] Due dates that fall on a Saturday, Sunday, or legal holiday are postponed until the next day that is not a Saturday, Sunday, or legal holiday.

[2] For special deposit rules that apply to large liabilities for employment and excise taxes see Publication 509, Tax Calendar and Check List for 1974.

[3] The due dates for filing Form 720 to report excise taxes for transportation and communications are:
4th quarter Feb. 28 / 1st quarter May 31 / 2d quarter Aug. 31 / 3d quarter Nov. 30

Note—This list is not all-inclusive. Due dates for returns filed less frequently, such as Forms 11, 2290, and 4638, are covered in Publication 509.

☆ U. S. GOVERNMENT PRINTING OFFICE : 1974 O - 540-434

FIGURE 21–6.

CASE STUDY: Barb's Clothing Manufacturer

Barb is setting up her women's apparel manufacturing plant on the eastern sea coast. She has worked as a designer for another women's clothing manufacturer for the past sixteen years. She has had experience as a seamstress, designer, and manager.

Barb belongs to an industry that manufactures clothes for current "in" fashions. Over the years, clothing manufacturers have learned to change fashions in a way that will generate sales. Barb is proud that her industry reflects the changes in American life style. Barb has learned to move with the changes. Most clothing manufacturers are small businesses; the four largest dress manufacturers in the United States account for less than 8 percent of the total volume sold.

Barb is going to manufacture women's sports clothes. Women's apparel business is generally operated on a five-season basis: fall-line merchandise offered for retail store buyers in June, holiday selections in September, resort sportswear for early spring in November, spring sports and summer clothes in January, and summer and early-fall collections in March and April. The women's wear industry is divided into five basic economic areas: haute couture, better dresses, moderate dresses, less expensive or item houses, and budget line manufacturers. Barb is seeking the moderate to less expensive fashion design. Her clothes will be medium-priced, made for fashionable young women and career women as well as for impulse buyers who are buying for the season or for special sporting occasions.

Barb has found a good downtown location for approximately 10¢ a square foot. She has located the equipment necessary, including cutting tables, machines, sewing machines, pressing equipment, and space for inventory handling. She will maintain her office at the factory and have sufficient furniture and supplies for her needs.

She has checked on the insurance requirements and finds that she will probably need to consider fire and property insurance, liability and product liability insurance, worker's compensation, and vehicle insurance.

However, Barb is quite concerned about the legal and tax situation that she must face. Barb knows that she must apply to the Federal Trade Commission for a registered number. The Textile Fabric Fibers Act requires that this registered number or the manufacturer's name, appear on every label or identifying tag placed on a garment. She is also required to provide a general description of the fiber content for each garment.

Questions

1. What requirements and laws will Barb face from federal, state and local levels?
2. What taxes will she need to pay?
3. How often will she need to report federal income taxes?
4. Will Barb need an Employer's Identification Number from the IRS?
5. What other types of laws or regulations should she look for?
6. Which agencies would be the major federal regulators to which she should apply for additional legal and tax information?

Chapter Questions:

1. Discuss the basic legal requirements of a business.
2. What are some of the major regulatory agencies in the United States? Why are they so powerful?
3. What are the basic components of a contract?
4. When and why should warranties be used?
5. Discuss the legal aspects of negotiable instruments.
6. Discuss the tax requirements of most businesses.

4
managing the future

22

Photo courtesy of Irene Springer, Prentice-Hall, Inc.

GROWTH PLANNING AND ASSISTANCE

Chapter Objectives:

1. To understand business growth cycles.
2. To learn about a product's life cycle.
3. To learn about business employment and employment outlook.
4. To improve an understanding of industry growth.
5. To know about professional managerial assistance.

There is always room at the top, but the elevator is not running. He must walk up the stairs on his own feet.

David Starr Jordan

People do not lack strength, they lack will.

Victor Hugo

INCIDENT: Joyce has operated her high-fashion dress shop for about six years now. The first two years were very tight and it was difficult to show a profit, but during this last year the shop has shown a sizable increase in profit and Joyce is thinking about expansion.

Joyce sells designer clothes: women's dresses and suits. Her price range is from a low of about $50 to a high of over $3,000. She also sells imported special dresses from designers for over $10,000. She has three excellent salespeople who work with her, and a seamstress who is probably the best in the state.

The store owner next door to Joyce's shop is moving and selling out. He has about 2,000 square feet in his store, which would approximately double Joyce's floor space. Two of Joyce's salespeople have mentioned that, by expanding the store, they could sell other lines of women's clothing, including sweathers, skirts, and tops.

Is Joyce ready for expansion? What kind of plans does she need for the next five years? Where can she go to get some advice and counseling?

Every year almost 400,000 new businesses are started in the United States. Each new business is founded on the hopes, dreams and ideas of the owner. Each business will find difficulties, problems and uncertainties. The business will go through (a) different growth or life cycles, (b) different planning requirements, and (c) changing needs for professional assistance.

Businesses, like people, pass through a series of stages from birth to death. A business may start out in the garage and grow to become a giant corporation, as did the Ford Motor Company, or a business may start in a small shopping center next to the local grocery store and stay there for years and years. Businesses may be started by anyone at any time. Some succeed and some fail.

The Business Life Cycle

Most businesses will follow a business life cycle, which cycle consists of: (1) an introduction stage, (2) a growth stage, (3) a maturity (or professional) stage, and (4) a decline stage. (See Figure 22–1.)

One businessman left school at the end of the sixth grade after they tried to

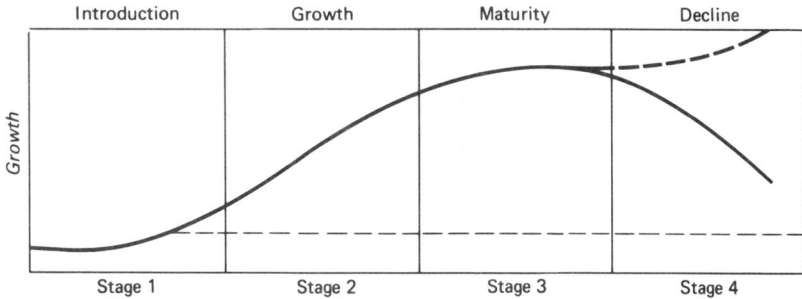

Figure 22-1. *Business life*

teach him that X equals an unknown. He started his own business at the age of 65 (when most people quit), which today is one of the largest food service companies. He established a little plant in Shelbyville, Kentucky; managed his own warehousing; did his own bookkeeping; established his own contracts; and controlled his own business. He built the very sound and solid business that has become Kentucky Fried Chicken. That man is "Colonel" Harland Sanders.

introduction stage The first stage of the business life cycle is the *introduction stage*. The vast majority of small businesses in the United States and throughout the developing nations are in this first stage of the business life cycle, and most will never move beyond it. Over 95 percent of the business firms in the United States today have less than twenty employees. New businesses have a tendency to start, and then level off at a given volume of sales. Most businesses will maintain this level of sales volume (with slight increases due to inflation) for the remainder of their business lives. The business life cycle is shown in Figure 22-1.

Barber shops, shoe stores, and beauty salons are examples of this form of small business. Automotive mechanics will generally remain in this introduction stage of business. Success in the introduction stage is related to the personal objectives of the owner-manager, which is generally measured by the survival of the firm and an adequate profit to maintain a comfortable living. The owner is in control, manages the business, and maintains his or her control through legitimate sources of power.

The operations of this form of business are dependent upon the owner of the business. If the owner is skilled in a trade or craft, then the business will grow based on the degree of professional skill of that individual. Employees in these stores will generally consider their jobs to be secure and fixed. There is little internal demand for growth or expansion, and there is generally a genuine respect for the owner-manager.

Once established, such a firm is not usually viewed as a major competitor in the market place. This type of firm builds a steady clientele, upon which it will rest for most of its business activity and success. This business will not try to "rock the boat" or to force competition out of business. It will seek its own fair share of the market and be satisfied by its own small success and profits.

growth stage The second stage is the take-off or *growth stage* of a small business, which is involved with new products, new management, or new innovations in the business. This is the stage when a business owner decides to expand or franchise his or her business opportunities. Ray Kroc entered this stage early in his business experience, when he franchised the first McDonald's restaurant.

The growth stage is the take-off point for most businesses that will some day become large business concerns or corporations. This stage generally requires a new product, a new market, a new service, a new manufacturing system, a new distribution system, or even new raw materials. The entrepreneur, with a desire for growth and competition, and a desire to make things happen, has the qualities required of a manager in this situation. This growth period also requires additional money or capital investment. Most young entrepreneurs and young business owners will seek to borrow money to enter this growth stage (debt financing) rather than to give up ownership in the business by using equity financing (ownership). Financing is difficult for most young small business owners who want to go through the growth stage. The entrepreneur often seeks a growth and increased size of the organization rather than an increase in personal earnings. The owner also tends to display personal qualities that often show signs of charismatic leadership, faith in one's own ability, and centralized direction.

Many small businesses going through the growth stage have not yet developed an internal planning or centralized control system for the business. The business owner is working in a rapidly changing marketplace and is exploring new opportunities, rather than spending time in planning and controlling operations. Profit requirements are high, while cash and investment capital are often low—all funds are used in the expansion effort.

The growth rate begins to decline toward the end of this second stage of the business life cycle, due to the development of the business along the traditional functional lines of finance, production (buying), or selling. Due to the success of the growth period, the owner is now faced with many more problems and individuals within the business. At the beginning of the growth stage, the owner only had to deal with three or four employees or managers, but he or she must now deal with twelve to twenty new managers or employees. This "management overload" requires additional managers and an organizational structure.

the maturity (or professional) stage

The business enters the *maturity (or professional) stage* of its life cycle due to its large size and complexity. The growth stage requires that the business establish a more formal and central administration and management. The loan owner or entrepreneur is now faced with a body of executives who perform the administrative processes of planning, organizing, staffing, directing, and controlling. Managers now seek to accomplish organizational goals and to maintain current levels of output. The entrepreneur's desire for growth is replaced by more conservative and demanding nature of the business. Profits now reflect internal efficiencies rather than new product or new market developments.

The policies and procedures of the business are generally formalized and written. Committees, boards of directors, and managerial groups meet and spend time developing short- and long-range planning for the business. The maturity (or professional) stage is run by the professional manager, and it requires managers to maintain production efficiencies and reach the goals and objectives of the business.

the decline stage

The fourth and last stage of the business life cycle is called the *decline stage*. This occurs after the business has matured and has reached most of its clients. The typical example would be the slide-rule industry or the manufacture of black-and-white television sets.

The decline stage occurs after the marketplace has been filled, the market demand changes, the product becomes obsolete, or the business can no longer make a profit by selling the good or service. Many businesses will try to offset the decline stage by introducing new products, such as color television sets or pocket calculators. The crisis in the automotive industry is caused by a declining market without an introduction of new automobiles to meet the new market demand.

summary

The business life cycle allows small businesses to go through different stages of business life. Most small businesses will remain in the introduction stage or at the level of success which they found at that point. Anywhere from 1 percent to 5 percent of successful small businesses will enter and go through the growth stage of the business cycle. This requires innovation and creative thought. After the business grows so large, it will enter the maturity or professional stage and require professional managers who specialize in different areas, such as marketing, sales, advertising, personnel, finance, accounting and production. If the market place becomes filled with the product or the demand changes then the business will often decline and possibly even go through bankruptcy. A creative and enterprising owner will always strive to maintain a viable business for himself and his employees.

SUCCESS STORY: William Petersen

William Petersen came to America from Denmark in 1901, at the age of 19. A blacksmith by trade, he settled in Nebraska, where his expert skills and unusually strong wrists and arms were a matter of interest and conversation. Yet Bill Petersen had more than mere strength, he had a head full of ideas—including one for a new kind of tool. This tool would lock and hold workpieces securely in place, leaving hands free for other tasks.

In 1924 he patented his idea calling it a "locking wrench," and for it he coined the now-famous trademark VISE-GRIP®. Initially, forgings were purchased from another hand tool manufacturer in New York and assembled in his DeWitt, Nebraska, blacksmith shop. In time, these forgings proved too cumbersome, and in the early 1930s Bill Petersen and his sons set out to manufacture an improved version of the tool, completely "in house."

Though early sales were small, the sale of each tool provided the cash to construct a second one. The Petersens designed and built much of the equipment they used, some of which is still in service today. The VISE-GRIP locking wrench was first successful among farmers, who soon discovered that having one they needed yet another. By 1937 the company had outgrown the original shop, and a factory building was acquired. As users discovered the remarkable utility of VISE-GRIP tools, retailers and distributors took an increasing interest, and sales went up rapidly. From the beginning, Bill Peterson had thought of his employees as a sort of enlarged family, an attitude that prevails today, and the company's employee benefit programs are considered exceptional by most standards.

The basic patent for the original VISE-GRIP tool expired in 1941, and many other companies soon began to produce imitations of the product. Peterson countered with additional models, with the quality construction that still remains an integral characteristic of the product. The trademark VISE-GRIP, however, did not expire and it is one of the company's most valuable assets, having been registered in most countries of the world.

When Bill Petersen died in 1962 his children continued to run the family business. How? According to Allen Petersen, current chairman and grandson of the founder, "the company was managed by consensus, first by Bill Petersen and his children as partners; later by the children alone. There was no formal planning, as such, no grand design for growth. The company grew like Topsy."

Yet despite the lack of planning, Petersen Manufacturing Co., Inc. flourished. Today it is one of the largest hand tool manufacturers in America, and one of the best known. Many millions of VISE-GRIP locking hand tools are sold annually, about a third of them outside the United States. More than 600 people are employed in the small town where the company was founded. Still owned by the Petersen family, the company is a family business in yet another sense: over 90 husband and wife teams are in the VISE-GRIP work force!

The Product Life Cycle

There is a product life cycle, very similar to the business life cycle, that goes through the same four stages: (1) the introduction stage, (2) the growth stage, (3) the maturity stage, and (4) the decline stage. These stages of the product life cycle explain the introduction, development, growth, and decline in demand for a particular product. (See Figure 22–2.) It is easy to historically follow the introduc-

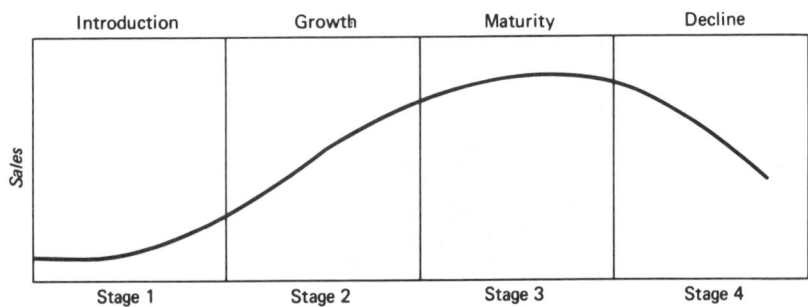

Figure 22–2. *The product life cycle*

tion, growth, maturity and decline stages of black-and-white television sets. Although currently in the decline stage, their manufacturers have been able to replace them through the introduction of color television sets, which are now in the growth and maturity stage, and that will soon be replaced by video tape recorders (VTR), which are now in the introduction stage.

the introduction stage

The introduction stage of any product or service is concerned with obtaining a market for that product or service. Information supplied by small businesses should be aimed at making people aware of the product's availability and value. For example, how many people owned pocket calculators ten years ago? Yet today, most business people, as well as students, own personal pocket calculators. The computer field is just now beginning to introduce computers for personal and home use. Advertisements of this type of product concentrate on making the people aware of the product, its uses, and services.

One of the reasons for failure in the introductory stage is lack of proper management. Also, the expenses necessary to properly introduce a new product or service are not always available. It is during the introduction stage that, hopefully, the "opinion leaders" will buy the product, use it, and recommend the product to others.

the growth stage

After the product or service has been introduced, sales will generally be on the increase during the growth stage. During the growth stage, the "early majority" will purchase and use the product. Many people find that color television sets, dishwashers, and pocket calculators are in this exciting growth stage.

Word-of-mouth and person-to-person referrals tend to increase sales and demand for the product in this stage. Advertising continues to inform, and now begins to persuade individuals to buy or purchase the product. It is generally during this stage that profits are realized on the product.

the maturity stage

The third stage of the product life cycle, the maturity stage, finds the product reaching the heights of sales. At the maturity level, the product reaches the height of its demand and the vast majority of the market have bought or are now buying the product. Refrigerators, automobiles, and shoes are generally considered to be in the maturity stage of product life cycle. This stage is characterized by saturation of the market, intense competition, availability of product, and intensive price competition for product sales. Advertisement is concerned with persuading individuals to buy the product. Any comparative advantage that one product has over another is stressed.

the decline stage

The decline stage often occurs with a shift in customer demand, which is often caused by a change in a product's relative value (pocket calculators are preferred more than slide rules). Sales fall in the decline stage. Profits also fall, as price cutting and competition forces the product out of the market. The decline stage in one business, though, is often the growth stage for another. For example, as football season ends, basketball season begins.

Products do tend to follow a product life cycle. Many of the products that our grandparents used are no longer manufactured. Most of the clothes we wear today were not being made twenty years ago. Pocket calculators, color television sets, and home computers were little more than dreams when we were born. Many products will always be in demand, such as food, clothing and shoes. However, because of technological and engineering improvements, many new businesses will come into existence within the next few short years and cause revolutionary changes in buying and selling practices.

Employment Growth

Historically, people have often followed their parents into the business or occupation of their choice. Young men quickly became farmers, traders, or craftsmen. Young women generally became housewives and mothers, with few paid occupations. Today, there are thousands of jobs and occupations available for men and women. As our socioeconomic environment changes, so do the opportunities for growth in the business community.

The demand for businesspeople in any occupation depends upon the desires of consumers. There is a large increase expected in the demand for businesspeople in our economy for the next several years (see Figure 22–3). Ever since 1960, there has been a sharp increase in the labor force due to the introduction of larger numbers of women in the labor market. It is expected that in 1985, there will be 104.3 million people holding civilian jobs, which would be a 19 percent increase over the 1976 level of 87.5 million. These expected changes will be primarily due to technological innovations and an increase in new products and product development.

A good portion of this increase in the civilian labor force will be due to an increase in the percentage of women entering the labor market (see Figure 22–4).

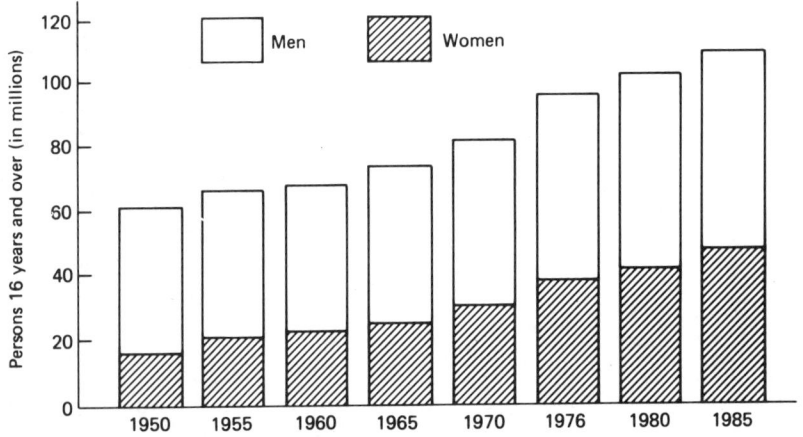

Figure 22–3. *Civilian labor force growth, 1950–1976 and projected 1980 and 1985*

SOURCE: Bureau of Census, U.S. Department of Commerce, *Occupational Outlook Handbook*, 1979, (Washington, D.C.: Department of Commerce, 1979).

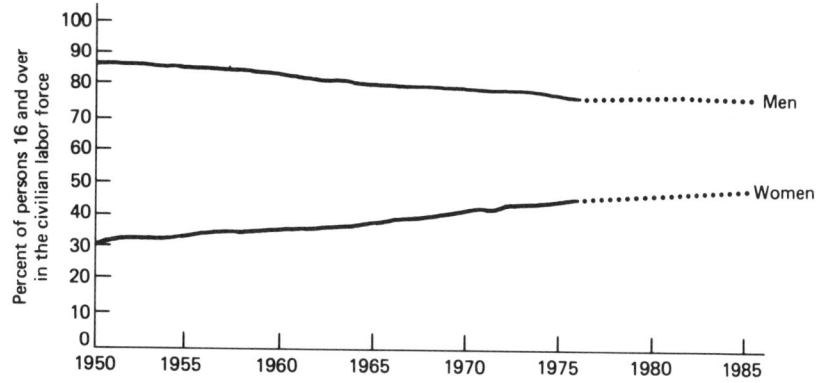

Figure 22-4. *Percent of women and men in the labor force, 1950–1985*

SOURCE: Bureau of Census, U.S. Department of Commerce, *Occupational Outlook Handbook*, 1979, (Washington, D.C.: Department of Commerce, 1979).

There is expected to be a steady increase in women in the business community, with a small decline in the number of men involved in the business community.

Industrial Growth

It is easy to divide business activity into two major groups: (1) goods producing and (2) services producing. Approximately two-thirds of our nation's workers are involved in services-producing activity, such as education, trade, maintenance, government, transportation, health care, banking, and insurance. The goods-producing side of our economy employs about one-third of the country's work force through farming, construction, mining, and manufacturing. As illustrated in Figure 22-5, employment levels in the goods-producing industries have remained

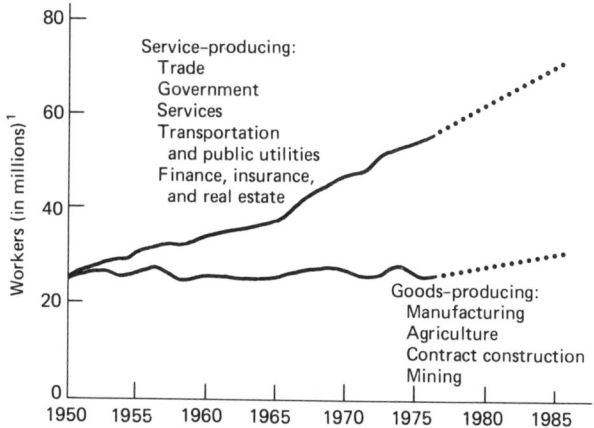

Figure 22-5. *Industries providing services offer more jobs than those providing goods*

SOURCE: Bureau of Census, U.S. Department of Commerce, *Occupational Outlook Handbook*, 1979, (Washington, D.C.: Department of Commerce, 1979).

fairly constant since the 1950s. The rapid growth has been found in the service-producing industries, and has occurred not only due to technological developments but also due to migration from rural suburban areas to the urban metropolitan areas. Due to increased living standards, rising incomes, and greater demands for local government services, the services-producing areas are expected to continue to grow at a larger rate than the demand for goods.

People in the services-producing businesses are expected to increase from 56.1 million workers in 1976 to 71 million employees in 1985, causing an increase of 26 percent. (See Figure 22-6.) Although other businesses and trade classifications will continue to grow, only the agricultural section expects a decrease in employment levels through 1985. The health-care, maintenance and repair, advertising, and commercial-cleaning services are expected to be the primary causes for growth in the services industry during the next decade.

Industries are expected to grow during the next decade. New businesses will be created by logical developments, which will require a larger work force and the introduction of new products and services. Larger numbers of women will be obtaining employment in these businesses.

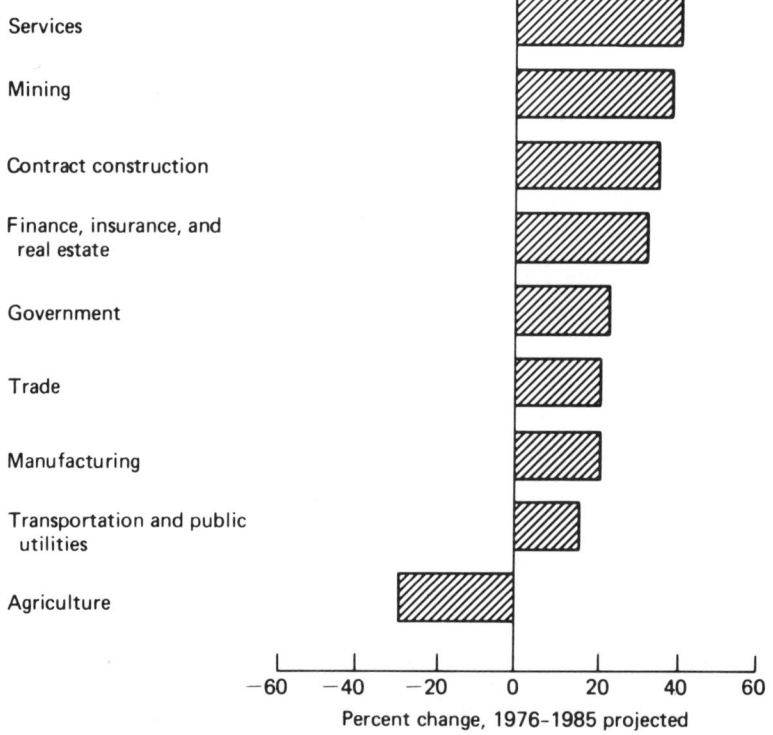

Figure 22-6. *Mid-1980s employment growth*

SOURCE: Bureau of Census, U.S. Department of Commerce, *Occupational Outlook Handbook,* 1979, (Washington, D.C.: Department of Commerce, 1979).

Planning

Planning for the future is developing a framework or course of action that must be taken in order to achieve company objectives. Business owners need to plan for the future. It is very difficult, though, for them to get out of the current planning or operational planning stages. Most small business owners are faced with the need of maintaining daily surveillance over the operations of their company. It is difficult for them to find time to plan months, one year, or several years in advance.

Long-range planning is concerned with establishing a course of action which would lead to increased sales and business profits. Planning involves three major fundamental characteristics: (1) the future, (2) the action to be taken, and (3) personal responsibility.

The small business owner needs to expand his or her time horizon for long-range planning up to and including five years. The owner should look into the future to establish the goals, objectives, and policies that would be appropriate for the business to follow. The business owner also needs to look at the action steps that must be taken in order to accomplish the long-range goals. Will the future involve expansion, or new products or services? Will the action be able to accomplish the goals and organizations of the business? Long-range planning should also identify a person or group of persons who will be responsible for carrying out the long-range actions. (See Figure 22–7.) A sales manager may want to increase sales by 15 percent each year with an increase in profits of 10 percent over the next five years. Would this require an increase in the product line or additional expenses for new employees?

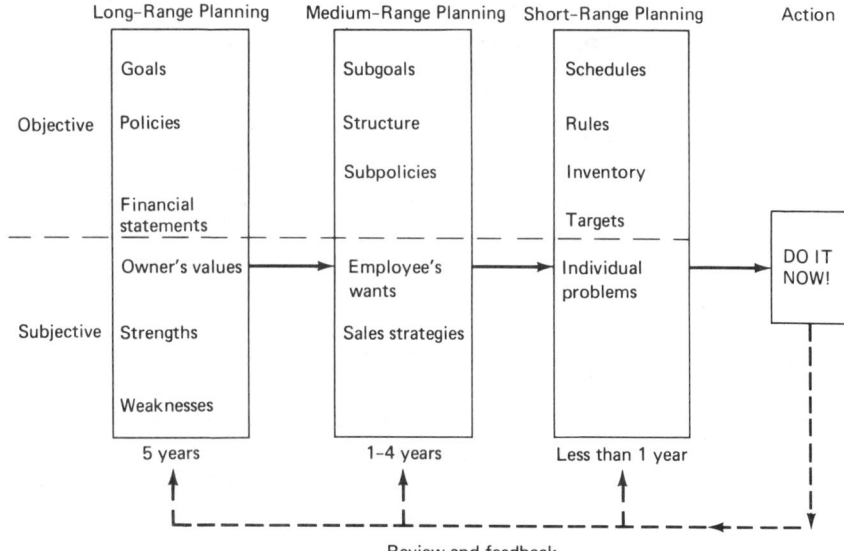

Figure 22–7. *Planning*

One of the easiest ways to develop long-range goals is to (1) develop the needs of the business, (2) establish the goals of the business, (3) identify the problems that hinder goal achievement, (4) identify problem-solving actions, and (5) establish and perform the actions.

A small business owner should view the needs of the business from both the personal as well as the professional viewpoint. Does the business need to expand or introduce a new product or service in order to keep it viable and alive during the next five years?

In the second step, the needs of the business are directly coupled with the goals of the business. The goals are primarily established by the needs and wants of the business owner. Goals may be for growth. Any business goals should be both *definable* and *measurable*. A statement to "increase sales" is not really a goal. However, a statement to increase sales by 15 percent during the next twelve months *is* a goal, because it defines the activity (a sales increase) in a measurable term (15 percent over one year). The goals of a business should fulfill and satisfy the needs of the business and of the business owner.

The third step in developing a long-range planning program is to identify any problems that hinder goal achievement. Is the current sales force inadequate? Is there a need for additional inventory? Does management lack the experience and ability necessary to run the business successfully? Is there sufficient capital and cash flow to maintain a business in a good financial posture? Any problem that hinders the achievement of the business goals should be identified and overcome.

The fourth step of the goal-planning system is to identify the problem-solving actions. Once hindering problems are identified, it is important to develop action steps that will eliminate the problem. If there is a problem in sales, it may be necessary to fire one of the current salespeople and hire a new salesperson. However, the problem-solving action must be realistic, and it should be accomplished within the management's abilities and with a concern for the financial position or statements of the business. For example, it may be necessary to hire a new salesperson to increase sales at a toy store. However, the income statement and cash flow statement indicate that it is not feasible to hire a new employee at this time. Therefore, other actions should be taken. Perhaps some employees would be willing to work longer or on days that they are not currently working.

The fifth step is to make the actions, or to lay out the five-year plan. This requires the execution and implementation of the problem-solving actions that have been identified. These actions should also satisfy and accomplish the goals of the business and meet the needs of the owner. After the actions have been taken, a review-and-feedback process should occur in all parts of the planning process.

Planning for growth is very important in any business. Long-range planning is an important and continual process. "Change may be the only constant" in business today. Business does continually change. Business owners must continually review their plans and develop new plans to ensure their success and profitability. A successful business is unlikely without proper and solid long-range planning.

Managerial Assistance

Small business owners are typically independent people. They have a tendency to think for themselves and to act on their own insights and ideas. Most of them have been successful through their own diligence, work, and effort. They have been able to develop their businesses from an idea, with the help from some loyal employees and their own guts and determination.

This independent attitude is praiseworthy in most instances. However, at times it can become detrimental to the business. When an individual lacks the understanding of when to bring in outside professional help, an independent spirit is bad for business.

Traditionally, most small business owners do not know what advice is available or where to go to seek professional consultant help. Some business owners are so independent that they would rather fail than be forced to rely on "outside help."

The use of outside consultants or advisors can provide small businesses with the managerial expertise and tools that are used by large corporate firms. The professional consultant brings objectivity, knowledge, experience, and know-how to a small business that is in need of understanding and development. The art of management, whether for growth, long-range planning, or running current operations includes the use of professional consultants. There are many types of professional assistance that are available to the small business owner. Major professional consultants are: accountants, attorneys, bankers, insurance agents, and managerial or marketing consultants.

accountants One of the most valuable and often-used advisors to small business are the private accountants. A good accountant can help establish a workable bookkeeping system that is easy to operate and follow. An accountant will also provide and develop statements for tax purposes. Many small business owner-managers will use accountants to establish cash-flow and fund-handling systems, as well as to gain advice on expansion and growth possibilities.

An accountant is especially equipped to provide advice to small business owner-managers on how to use financial statements. A manager needs to use the financial statements to establish sales budget and income projections. An accountant can provide this advice, and can point out the danger signals that the income statements may readily indicate. An accountant may readily provide financial advice for the day-to-day managerial decisions as well as the long-term considerations. He or she may also be knowledgeable about cash registers, sales forms, handling checks, and working with banks.

A small business owner should talk to several accountants before choosing one. The accounting fee structure will generally be based on a daily, monthly, or annual rate, whichever best serves the business owner. An accountant may handle all or only a small portion of the bookkeeping and record-keeping functions of the business. It is always advisable to use an accountant for tax and consulting purposes.

attorneys   An attorney is a valuable resource of which any business owner should be aware. Attorneys may easily help in the formation of the business, even a sole proprietorship.

An attorney can check on all licensing and contract requirements for a business, and can take care of the proper filing of government papers. An attorney is indispensable when developing contracts or signing a lease. Most small business owners who sign leases need legal interpretation to protect them. An attorney should be contacted in case of any legal disputes against the business for negligence or liability. A small business owner should contact an attorney at any time when the owner is unsure of his or her legal rights or obligations.

There are many attorneys who specialize in business or corporate law. These attorneys are the ones who should be contacted concerning legal business advice. Fees may be established on a per-visit or an annual retainer basis. Certain legal fees (such as incorporation or partnership agreements) are often predetermined by the attorney's office (such as a $500 fee for incorporating a new business).

bankers   A banker has a vast reservoir of financial knowledge, and also has a fairly well established and commercial business that is heavily involved in your financial community. A banker may advise you on financial matters, and provide you with industrial financial averages for your business.

A banker may also provide you with certain banking services, such as Visa or Master Card or payroll services. A banker can also provide loans for both short- and long-term periods. A banker is available to provide checking services for your business and personal funds.

Your banker should be kept well informed of the financial condition of your business. This is especially true when there is a loan outstanding to your business from that bank. The banker is interested in seeing that you succeed, so that he or she will be able to get the bank's money back. But the banker is also interested in your success so that he or she can have your business for future growth and loan needs.

insurance agents   An insurance agent or broker will help you to set up insurance packages to cover the needs of your business. The agent may provide comprehensive coverage or simple health insurance for the principal owner.

Insurance agents may be used to help develop entire insurance policies for the business. This may include such areas as liability, fire, theft, life, health, casualty, and many more. These insurance programs may also be a major fringe benefit for your employees, such as family health insurance.

managerial or marketing consultants   One of the most useful forms of professional assistance comes from managerial or marketing consultants. A managerial consultant may help the small business owner to understand the needs, goals, and problems of the business. He or she will allow the small business owner an outside, objective approach to the decision-making process.

The managerial consultant can help the owner stay away from procrastination or "acting like an ostrich." The consultant may easily show where a business owner is behind in his or her billing collections or confused with financial statements.

Inventory problems, such as stocking too much or too little of an item, may be easily pointed out by a professional consultant. A managerial consultant may easily point out the lack of planning and organizing that exists within a business. The consultant also brings in outside experience and expertise that may point out shortages in working capital, sales, excessive costs, or below-average profits. Stock-outs, poor inventory turnover and lack of balance in inventory handling are often easily detected by the managerial consultant.

The professional advisor may also provide information about work levels, improper scheduling, backlog of paperwork, or rushed work conditions in the business.

A marketing consultant is an invaluable professional in developing sales, promotion, advertising, and marketing programs. The marketing advisor may help eliminate the guess work in pricing decisions. This individual will also help in location analysis for expansion location or in analyzing new products or services.

A good marketing consultant can also provide information through marketing research about the desires and opinions of customers. The marketing researcher can explain the probability of success that different products or services will have. They will also be able to explain the preferences individuals have for food items or hard goods.

The marketing consultant may help you to better define your own target market. This person may also better define the age groups and socioeconomic conditions of the marketplace.

Marketing and managerial consultants have vast expertise and connections that most small business owners will never be able to develop. They are often aware of many hidden details, resources, and advertising that are often not readily seen by the small business owner.

While the small business owner may be involved in the daily management of the business, moving from crisis to crisis, the professional consultant may provide the insights and advice necessary to ensure the success of that business. The consultant may help provide the planning, organizing, staffing, directing, controlling, and even analyzing the growth potentials of that business, which are vital to a small business owner. A good consultant may usually be the "right arm" or "vice-president" of the business.

CASE STUDY: Mary's Secretarial Service

Mary has owned her own secretarial service for ten years now. She has developed a fantastic business, which has a net profit (before taxes) of over $50,000. Over the years, she has learned to charge a regular hourly rate rather than to charge by the page, which is a bad business practice that is only employed by beginners. She generally charges from $10 to $15 per hour for standardized work, with technical work going as high as $25 an hour.

418
GROWTH PLANNING AND ASSISTANCE

Mary's business offers the typical typing services of letters, manuscripts, proofreading, reports, editing, correspondence, financial statements, dictation, transcription, and statistical typing. She also provides special resume typing and legal typing. Two years ago, she started the word-processing service, a computerized system that is able to handle repetitive typing chores. This allows her to do fifty personalized letters per hour. She has been able to charge up to $50 an hour for this service.

Mary has a very convenient location in the downtown business area. She also has four full-time workers, one of whom is trained as a legal secretary. She has 500 square feet at her business location. One of the typists also serves as the receptionist, handling most of the phone calls coming into the business.

Mary has been considering growth and expansion. She is interested in finding out if she can provide notary-public work. Many customers have stated this need to her. She is also wondering about providing personal services, such as going to the client's office for dictation or correspondence. She has had several requests for medical typing as well as bookkeeping, file organizing, file preparation, record keeping and even translation services. She believes that she could take one additional person, possibly two, into her existing business. However, any more than that would require additional office space and a new location.

If Mary does expand, she has thought about providing a copying service, which would require a fairly expensive Xerox copying machine. She has also thought about a telephone-transcription service, using a tape recorder with a telephone pick-up system. This would allow her to develop correspondence from the businessperson before that person came to the office.

She would like to hire a part-time person for delivery and pick-up service. She has recently been doing this for some of her larger contract clients.

Mary's Secretarial Service
Income Statement 198X

			Percent of Sales
Sales		$150,000	100.0
Expenses:			
Payroll (4 full-time workers)	$60,000		40.0
Owner's salary	18,000		12.0
Supplies	3,600		2.4
Rent	7,200		4.8
Telephone	2,500		1.7
Utilities	2,400		1.6
Legal and accounting	1,600		1.1
Promotion and advertising	2,600		1.8
Other	1,000		0.6
Total Expenses		$ 98,900	66.0
Profit before taxes		$ 51,100	34.0

Questions

1. Should Mary expand?
2. Where should she go to seek the information she needs to make her decision?
3. What planning must be done before the idea of expansion can become a reality?

Chapter Questions:

1. Discuss the stages of the business life cycle.
2. Discuss the stages of the product life cycle. At what stages are: color televisions; automobiles; dishwashers; calculators; and microwave ovens?
3. Discuss the labor force and its influence on business.
4. What are the advantages of long-range planning to a small business owner?
5. Discuss the steps of planning.
6. Discuss uses of professional managerial assistance.

23

Photo courtesy of Irene Springer, Prentice-Hall, Inc.

SUCCESSION OF MANAGEMENT

Chapter Objectives:

1. To learn how to prepare for a change in management.
2. To understand the process of managerial succession.
3. To learn what a buy/sell agreement achieves.
4. To be able to develop an inventory of financial facts.
5. To know about managerial development and successor profiles.
6. To understand how to develop an inventory of business and operations.
7. To learn about retirement procedures.

We must preserve the incentive to succeed and the right to fail.

Richard L. Evans

INCIDENT: Don Barber has worked for over forty years developing and expanding his farm. He took over his father's farm about twenty-two years ago, and was able to buy out an adjoining farmer's land so that he now owns 580 acres of choice cotton farmland.

Twelve years ago, Barber and his wife Ann opened a farm implement and machine business in the adjacent town. The sales of this small business were $32,000 during the first year and grew to last year's sales of $212,000.

The Barbers have six children. Two of their sons, Bill and Jackie, are both in their mid-twenties and they have decided to stay on the farm and work the business. Both sons are graduates of the state university's agricultural college, and they have worked at developing the farm all their lives. Bill loves the physical demands that the farm requires, and enjoys working at the business and in dealing with customers. However, he does not really like to manage the business, and stays away from its financial operations as much as possible. Jackie is the scholar of the two, and enjoys the managerial side of the business and farm. However, Don is skeptical of Jackie's abilities as a manager: Jackie had lost a sizable sales order to a weaker competitive firm this past year.

Ann and Don Barber want more time off from their business and farm duties. They have worked all their lives raising their six children (three girls and three boys), and they are now interested in spending time by themselves to relax from the very demanding day-to-day requirements of their farm and business.

Don is wondering how he can semiretire and still maintain an adequate income, while at the same time making sure that the farm and the business remain profitable. A friend of his, who lives in a neighboring county, also owned a farm implement and equipment business. This friend had formed a corporation and made his son and daughter partners in that corporation. But once this man's son and daughter had acquired controlling interest (51 percent of the stock) in the business, they voted the father out of the business without pay, and they have not declared a dividend since doing so. Don trusts his sons, but...

The center goes up for the basketball as four players crash the boards for the rebound. The guard turns and breaks down court, the forward quickly moves over to the side and waits for the outlet pass. Elbows fly and legs criss-cross as the mayhem underneath the basket continues for a split second. The center crashes to the floor and writhes in pain. He grasps his leg and rolls over in agony. The ball slides out of bounds, the whistle blows, the play is stopped. The coach and trainer come running off the bench. The center needs to be replaced. How do you replace the leader? How do you replace the star? How do you replace an owner or manager?

The star, the leader, the focal person of any small business is the owner or manager. This person is generally the most valuable and also the most vulnerable asset of any business. The replacement value of this person is often immeasurable. The importance of this person is unquestionable. However, the replacement protection or insurance of the owner or manager is often neglected or completely overlooked. Too often the owner or manager does not have the time to seek or train a replacement. Too often the owner or manager does not protect his or her business interest, or family interest, by ensuring the continuation of the business or the succession of the firm's management. If a business is successful for an individual and his or her family, it is important to ensure the succession and continuity of that business should the owner become ill or the business be interrupted.

When reviewing or contemplating succession of management, it is important to develop five major factors: (1) plans of succession, (2) a successor profile, (3) an inventory of business and operations, (4) an inventory of managerial development, and (5) an inventory of retirement. The investigation and development of these five areas will ensure a successful and continuous operation in the business due to a succession of management or a change of owners in a business.

Plans of Succession

The sudden loss of an owner or manager or a key executive in any business calls for drastic moves and changes within the organization. Plans should be developed along two lines. One set of plans should provide for immediate transfer of the business from one owner to another upon the death or disability of the current owner or manager. Another set of plans should provide long-range guidance for the gradual transfer of business management and ownership to a trained successor. Without such detailed plans, a business may be placed under court jurisdiction or receivership, or it may be sold outright to cover creditors' claims. In other words, without some form of future planning, a business may die with its owner. Legal costs and estate settlement may likewise require the liquidation of a business, due to the death of an owner. Forced liquidations will generally result in a loss for the survivors because the inventory and assets will often be sold below the market value. The dissolving of a business may mean that the family, without a business to support it, would be left without income.

Surviving stockholders of closely held corporations (family corporations, or small joint corporations with few stockholders) may bring problems to the corporation. Such survivors can often create havoc in a small corporation. Controlling interest of the corporation may even pass to incompetent or unworthy persons who are incapable of leading the corporation successfully. Unless otherwise stipulated, deceased stockholder's heirs may choose to sell their interest to outside parties. Thus, there are several major considerations involved in planning for a smooth succession of the business.

two plans   First, succession plans should be developed for two different contingencies: (1) succession in times of death of the owner or other emergency, and (2) succession for retirement or sale of the business. Both types of plans will become highly technical and involve many legal and financial considerations. Professional advice and consultation should be sought to ensure the continued success of the business. An attorney who is familiar with business successions and estate problems should be used when developing comprehensive plans to ensure the continuity of business upon the death of the owner. There is a need to develop an agreement among the business owners or corporate stockholders that would direct what becomes of the owner's equity when one or more owners dies, quits, or leaves the business. This agreement, generally referred to as the buy/sell agreement, provides safeguards for a business from being destroyed or severely altered when an owner leaves. (The buy/sell agreement will be discussed in more detail in the next section.) Therefore, the attorney may also develop buy/sell agreements, lease agreements, comprehensive agreements, wills, stock transfers, and deal with tax considerations needed to ensure the legality of staying in business.

financial considerations   Second, succession plans should include financial considerations and tax implications in case of the death or transfer of business ownership from one party to another. An accountant who is familiar with tax and estate planning should clarify the situation to the family or other parties involved in the business.

managerial transfer   Third, the business successor plan should contain information about managerial transfer from one owner to another. This would include an inventory of the business's financial, administrative, and operational information, as well as an inventory of the training and development of management.

retirement objectives   The fourth major area in the plan should explain, in detail, the retirement objectives and conditions that the owner desires. This may include an adequate insurance program, the outright selling of the business, or the possibility of financing a new buyer-owner over a long period of time.

Once completed, the succession plan should allow for the smooth and continuous operation of a business as it is transferred from one owner to another. The succession plan should explain and indicate how the business will continue to be operated—or be closed or liquidated—at the time of the death or retirement of the business owner or manager. Whether the business is to stay in the hands of one particular family, or it is to be sold to other relatives or to people outside of the family is a matter that should be handled in a buy/sell agreement.

The Buy/Sell Agreement

The buy/sell agreement is often overlooked by most small businesses. However, it is of vital importance in helping stave off misery for the owner's family or relatives in case of a death. The major reasons for the adoption of a buy/sell agreement occur in conjunction with several conditions:

1. When a principal partner (or stockholder) wants to pass control to his or her family upon his death, but high state or inheritance taxes force the family to sell all interest in the business.

2. When a partner wants to cash in his or her share (stock) of the business when he or she retires at a "fair" price.

3. When a partner (or stockholder) wants his or her family's interest in the business to be sold for cash so that the other partners will be allowed to carry on the business without undue influence but the remaining partners may not have sufficient funds to buy out their partner. What would be even worse is if the family would have to sell the controlling interest to outside individuals.

4. When the remaining partners (or stockholders) in a business want to keep all profits in the business for expansion and development but the widow(er) who has inherited a sizable portion of the business decides to use all monies as dividends.

The buy/sell agreement safeguards the business so that the remaining partners (or stockholders) have the right and opportunity to buy out their former partner. The purpose of the buy/sell agreement may be to save the business, or to aid the partner who is leaving or the family of the deceased partner.

four options

Generally, the following methods are used to accomplish such an agreement:

1. **Choice of the remaining owners:** The buy/sell agreement may provide those partners who are remaining with the option to buy out the departed owner's interests. If this option is exercised by the remaining owners, the estate of the deceased is obligated to sell.

2. **The required transfer:** A buy/sell agreement may require the estate of a deceased to sell its interest in the business to the remaining owners at a fair market price.

3. **Choice of the owner's estate:** The buy/sell agreement may grant the estate the right to retain ownership or to offer its interest in the business to the remaining partners or owners. If the estate chooses to sell, the remaining owners are obliged to buy out the estate's share of the business.

4. **Right of first refusal:** The buy/sell agreement may provide the remaining owners with the right of first buy or first refusal. This means that the owners who remain will have the first opportunity to buy the departed owner's interest before it can be sold to any outside parties. This does not require the remaining owners to buy out the departed partner, but it does provide them with the right of first refusal.

It is important to remember that of the four methods only the third—choice of the owner's estate—provides ensurance to an owner or an owner's family that control over his or her share of the business will be retained. This option allows the owner's estate to maintain control of its interest in the business, or requires the remaining owners to buy out the deceased's share.

availability of money

Quite often buy/sell agreements assume that money will be available to the other partner, or corporation, to buy out the interest of the former owner. This is not always so. It is very difficult to accumulate a sufficient amount of money to buy out a partner in a thriving business. In this day and age, it is also difficult to save sufficient funds to buy a sizable interest in any successful business. The major form of cash accumulation present in small business, to buy out previous partners, is life insurance. Insurance policies can be purchased on the life of each of the major partners (or stockholders) in the business; the premium is paid by the business. If sufficiently large, life insurance can and usually does provide enough capital to buy out a former partner.

summary

In conclusion, a buy/sell agreement is a legal document that carefully stipulates who is to purchase an owner's share of a business. It generally requires that: (1) the remaining owners buy out the departing owner (a cross-purchase agreement), or (2) that the corporation buys out the interest of the stockholder (a stock-redemption agreement), or (3) that the owner's estate retains control of the owner's interest in the business. In order to be complete a buy/sell agreement should:

1. List the names of the individuals or corporation involved in the buy/sell agreement.
2. Indicate the method of purchase, such as cross-purchase, stock-redemption, or a combination of the two.
3. State whether the buy/sell agreement will have a required transfer of interest, a choice of remaining owners, a choice of owner's estate, or a right-of-first-refusal inclusion.
4. Indicate if the buy/sell agreement will be contractual or optional.
5. List each partner as a particular portion of the business, with a stipulation that no liens or incumbrances are or will be placed on his or her part of the business.
6. State the price and how to evaluate the price of the business.
7. Explain from where the money will come to purchase the departing owners portion of the business: business funds, insurance, notes, loans, or corporate funds.
8. Explain how to modify or terminate the buy/sell agreement, indicating the laws under which the buy/sell agreement is being made.
9. State whether for tax consideration, some thought should be given to using an installment purchase plan.
10. Name a trustee, if any.
11. State what items will be sold or transferred to the remaining partners or stockholders.

As part of the succession plan, the buy/sell agreement is an aid in the smooth and continuous operation of the business while it is being transferred from one owner to another.

SUCCESS STORY: Aristotle Socrates Onassis

Greek-Argentine businessman Aristotle Socrates Onassis amassed a multimillion dollar fortune in shipping and other enterprises and was known for his lavish style of living.

He was born in Smryna (now Izmir), Turkey, on January 15, 1906, the son of a prosperous Greek tobacco merchant. In 1922, during the Anatolian War between Greece and Turkey, the family fled from Smyrna to Greece leaving behind their entire fortune. At the age of 17, he was sent to Argentina to recoup the family fortune. He arrived in Buenos Aires with only sixty dollars. Working nights as a switchboard operator, he launched a tobacco importing business and then expanded into grains, hides and whale oil. By the time he was 25, he was a self-made millionaire. In this same year, he invested $120,000 in six old freighters, the beginning of his enormous shipping fleet.

During the depression of the early 1930s, Onassis went into the shipping business in a big way, buying up freighters and later tankers. He made his largest profits from his shipping fleet during World War II. Beside owning one of the world's largest merchant fleets, Onassis owned Olympic Airways, the world's largest privately held airline, a Swiss bank and large holdings in gold and tin mines in South Africa.

Onassis followed three basic business principles in running his empire: (1) to reinvest at least 50 percent of earnings into the business; (2) to merge with another company, unless he could buy control of it first, and (3) to sell no ship that could still possibly turn a profit.

Onassis died in France on March 15, 1975, with an estate estimated by some people at one billion dollars.

Successor Profile

The personality and managerial characteristics of a successor will not necessarily be the same as those of the owner, nor those of an appropriate assistant manager or vice-president. Often successors who have strengths where the current owner has weaknesses are sought. However, the successor should be able to lead, manage, and be responsible for the profitability of the business.

A list of desirable traits or qualities that the successor should bring to the business should be developed. The following are major items that must be included in such a successor profile:

1. Important personality factors.
2. Important managerial skill requirements.
3. Formal education requirements.
4. Technical skill requirements.
5. Ethical standards.
6. Age or family relationship.
7. Leadership skills.
8. Human-interaction skill requirements.
9. Outside training or experience requirements.

This profile will help in choosing a suitable successor for the position. Of course, these factors are only general guidelines, and should be developed in detail for any specific job or business.

But where will you find the successor needed when it really counts? Generally speaking, there will be no one immediately available. The ideal place to look for potential new management is within the organization. This should be done only after reviewing all contractual obligations, buy/sell agreements, relatives, and partners. It may be the intent of a business owner to leave the business in the hands of a spouse or to another relative. In-house candidates are usually either family members, or people in the company's employ. An in-house inventory may locate managers who have done extremely well and who have the potential for growth. Nonmanagerial employees, given the opportunity and training, may also prove to be excellent candidates for managerial positions.

Other important candidates to consider are outside recruits. These recruits may come on recommendations from suppliers, business associates, trade associations, or universities, or they may be walk-ins.

Whoever the final choice is, he or she will need an opportunity to work within the company in the various positions available. In this way, the successor-to-be will acquire experience in different departments and varied areas of the small business. The successor-to-be should also be invited to managerial meetings, and asked to participate in the decision making and in managerial team work. He or she should also be sent on buying trips and to special sales conferences. This successor should take part in business contracts with bankers, accountants, lawyers, and other trade people. One way to evaluate possible successors is to provide them with special assignments to complete.

The Inventory of Business and Operations

One of the most difficult tasks for any manager is to write in detail the functions and operations of his or her business. Although the vast majority of information concerning daily operations, accounts, and practices of any business is in the head of its owner, it is important that a successor know as much as possible about the business. To accomplish this, it is important that the owner commit to paper (1) an inventory of the financial affairs of the business, (2) the administrative organization and history of the business, and (3) operations and technical information relating to the business.[1] (See Tables 23-1, 23-2, and 23-3.)

Table 23-1. Inventory of Financial Facts

For the successful operation or succession of any business, it is important to include the following information in an inventory of financial facts:

1. Financial statements for the past five years.
    a. Balance sheets.
    b. Income statements.
2. Copies of budgets for the last three years, and a projected budget for the next year.
3. Description of the company as working capital, return on investment, operating ratios, and so on.
4. List of current bank accounts and other financial accounts from financial institutions.
5. Indication of line of credit, banking connections, and banking officers.
6. List of paid tax bills: federal, state, and local.
7. List of insurance policies: coverage and premiums, name of agent, broker, or representatives.
8. Copies of financial and control reports.

[1]Frederick E. Halstead, *Preparing for New Management,* Management Aids for Small Manufacturers, No. 183, Small Business Administration, 1972.

Table 23-2. Inventory of Administration

Any successor in a business transfer will require information about the administration and the decision-making policies of the business. In order to accomplish this vital task and to ensure successful continuation of any business, it will be important to include the following information in an inventory of administration:

History of Industry
1. Historical development of industry.
2. Size and number of businesses in general industry including SIC numbers and any Dun & Bradstreet figures.
3. Names and addresses of any related industrial or trade associations and publications.

Company History
1. Date organized, founders, major events (such as expansions or moving from a rented building to a new plant).
2. Newspaper clippings or stories or other articles of publication about the company.
3. Brochures issued by the company about new products, processes, sales personnel, and so on.

Organization
1. Organizational chart indicating key positions and persons.
2. Job description for all key officers, including owner-manager.
3. Description of key employees, concerning demographic data as well as history of company, education, training, and potential.
4. Any reports from consultants, suppliers, or creditors that are relevant to the organization.

Policy
1. Policy file of information on vacation, employee loans, retirement plans, credit and selling terms, advances, and so on.
2. Policy announcements; letters or memos relating to policies.

Legal Matters
1. Patents, licenses, royalty agreements, trademarks, or copyrights.
2. List employment and labor agreements, including changes made in past years.
3. List all leases and conditions.
4. List contracts with suppliers or customers.
5. List any legal action or lawsuits pending.

Outside Services
List and describe outside professional people who work with the company, including:
  a. Accountants.
  b. Bankers.
  c. Brokers.
  d. Representatives.
  e. Insurance agents.
  f. Advertising agencies.
  g. Public relations agencies.
  h. Managerial consultants.

The Inventory of Managerial Development

It is critical that any new owner or manager receive training in his or her new managerial role. The prime purpose of the manager is to ensure that the organization will move toward optimizing revenues while minimizing costs in an efficient and effective fashion. The new manager will need to be able to organize and control the stability of the operation. The new manager will need to be able to serve (1) the customers, (2) the employees, and (3) those individuals who own the business. The small firm needs to provide the opportunity for the new owner or manager to develop the skills necessary to ensure the success of the business.

Table 23-3. Inventory of Operations and Information

How any business organization operates and performs its major functional areas is vital information for a successor to have him or her to understand. This would require that information about marketing, purchasing (finance), production, and other areas be included in an inventory of operations and information:

Marketing with company products or services, and related customer acceptance, profitability, and product future.
1. List customers' geographical areas, and five or ten of the largest customers.
2. List distribution channels.
3. Describe training for salespeople.
4. Develop an outline of advertising programs and objectives.
5. Describe how prices are set for current and future products.
6. List descriptions of competitors, including size, product, share of the market, policies, pricing determination, and method of distribution.

Purchasing
1. List major materials, where purchased, and how often.
2. List suppliers and years of doing business with each.
3. List current contracts and agreements with suppliers and creditors.
4. List procedures for buying and any required approval for various types or sizes of purchases made.

Production
1. List major pieces of equipment, their ages and histories.
2. List each product, and its manufacturing specifications, and process procedures.
3. List studies showing layout, production flow, and quality control.
4. List how each product is scheduled and controlled.
5. Describe quality control and the standards for measuring performance.

Other Areas
If available, it would be valuable to have information about inventory control, research and development, engineering, traffic, and energy usage.

A thorough and comprehensive program must be established for any individual taking over the business. This may be primarily on-the-job training (that is, learning by doing the day-to-day operation) or it may be a preprogrammed training situation, lasting from one week to several months, that fully prepares the new owner. Most franchise organizations provide in-depth training at a central location (such as McDonald's Hamburger University or Holiday Inn University) and/or on the site. Programs may also be designed to allow the former owner to stay on and provide transfer assistance (managerial training) for the new owner for a period of from one week to one or two months.

This training should cover four major areas of concern:

1. Business operations (including the areas of finance, administration, and operations previously mentioned).
2. Interpersonal relations and skills.
3. Informational roles.
4. Technical roles.

business operations

A new manager needs to be aware of all the managerial processes and functions of the organization. The new manager should be able to understand the financial limitations as well as the profits that the organization may produce. He or she should be able to understand the financial statements, banking, and insurance connections with which the business is involved. He or she should also appreciate the history and administration of the organization, including the policies, legal matters, and services that the business renders and receives. The manager should be aware of the different operating systems involved in production, purchasing, marketing, sales, advertising, research, engineering, and quality control.

interpersonal relationships

The role of the owner or manager requires that the manager be led into interpersonal relationships, which means that he or she is not only a leader and motivator, but is also a figurehead and a liaison agent of the business. The new owner or manager, due to his or her formal authority and newly acquired status, must successfully fulfill these roles to increase the probability of success for the business.

informational roles

In fulfilling the informational role of the manager, the new owner must supervise, monitor, and disseminate information throughout the organization. The manager must be able to assume, correlate, and use all the information developed within as well as outside the business. He or she must be able to utilize marketing research reports as well as quality control, inventory control, and scheduling information. The owner or manager should be the focal person for all information flowing in and out of the organization.

technical roles

The new manager fills a technical role as the chief decision maker, the common negotiator, the entrepreneur, and the resource allocator. This role requires the manager to be able to decide between alternative suppliers or channels of distribution. It also requires the manager to be the major handler of disturbances from within the organization and in dealing with customers or government agencies. Furthermore, the technical role requires that certain actions and services be performed successfully, that the manager develop the organization, and that he or she chart its course through (1) planning, (2) adaptive strategy, or (3) inspired visionary programs. The entrepreneur tends to follow the visionary track, while the professional manager tends to follow the planning program.

The new manager, because of his or her recently acquired authority, status, and prestige, has tremendous power in causing the success or failure of the business. This is primarily determined by the policies or strategies that he or she makes. The more knowledgeable and understanding the new manager is, the greater his or her possibility of success will be.

Inventory of Retirement

In order to be successful, a succession plan must include some program for the owner's retirement. The company will benefit by planning the succession of management for a specific time and period so that it will not be forced into receivership or be forced to close down for a period of time due to probate or state laws. The owner or manager may step down gracefully at a particular time to help in the smooth transition of new ownership. He or she may even be retained as a professional consultant for a short period of time.

SUCCESSION OF MANAGEMENT

When planning for retirement, the business owner should investigate: (1) life insurance and social security, (2) financing the sale of the business, (3) the state laws and regulations, and (4) taxation. All these areas are of vital concern to the retiring individual, and planning ahead may provide greater income to the retiree.

life insurance and social security

Life insurance and social security are probably the most common means of providing income for retired people. Life insurance may be handled through any number of reputable agencies and firms. The insurance may be varied in size and longevity. This determination should be up to the owner and his or her family.

financing the sale of the business

One of the most technical aspects of retirement is selling the business. The business may be sold for large sums of money and the owner or manager may easily and quickly retire. This method, however, provides no income after the initial period, and leaves nothing after it has been spent, although this money may be spent or invested in other financial opportunities.

A method often more desirable than direct sale is selling the business on terms, or for financial considerations, over a period of time, and allows the buyer greater flexibility in purchasing the business.

state laws and regulations

Other areas of concern would be the establishment of an estate for the transfer of the business upon the retirement or death of the owner or manager. It is important for the original owner or manager to develop a will covering the disposition of the business. Included in this will may be a standard buy/sell agreement, limiting other partners or shareholders to contractual obligations regarding the disposition of the business. This buy/sell agreement may also develop a specific plan for the disposal or the proper continuation of the business.

In a closely held corporation or family-owned business, stockholders may continue the business upon death of one of the major stockholders, but only when proper preparations will ensure the continuance. Some legal plans need to be developed so the surviving owners may continue to control and operate the business while providing financial security to the heirs of the deceased. The buy/sell agreement made by all stockholders prior to retirement or death may ensure that the surviving stockholders will have adequate protection for the survival of the business.

taxation

Inheritance and state taxes make it important for any business owner to review the laws with a competent attorney. Such a review may allow the owner or manager to plan ahead and transfer part of a business to heirs, prior to his death or retirement.

CASE STUDY: Egbert's Home Furnishings

Bob Egbert is approaching his late 50s. He had developed his own home furnishing store from nothing during the past twenty-two years. Bob has enjoyed raising his family of seven children in his community of 280,000 people. He enjoys his community and church work and is actively engaged as an elder in his church and serves on the board of directors for the local Rotary Club.

Bob is part of a $40-billion annual furniture industry. He discovered that people of all ages are in the home furnishing business or want to have home furnishing businesses. Families with an average disposable income of $8,000 to $12,080 will spend up to 12 percent of their income on home furnishings.

Bob's general-line furnishing store caters to the broad middle segment of the market, and is in direct competition with chain stores, department stores, discount outlets, and warehouse showrooms. He has 1,600 square feet of space in his store, with an average inventory valued at $80,000 in cost. He guarantees delivery of all merchandise within the county within a one-week period of time, free of charge. Bob's attached warehouse has a floor space of 120,000 square feet, and it contains inventory valued at almost $400,000.

Bob has three sons and four daughters. The three eldest daughters are all married and all living out of town. His youngest daughter is a senior in high school. The two oldest sons are now working in the business on a straight commission. They had originally started on a straight monthly salary, which was the pay most commonly given to new employees selling accessories and housewares (as opposed to the "big ticket" items such as carpets, furniture, and appliances). Salespeople on commission receive a straight 7 percent commission on furniture and appliance sales, and a 6 percent commission on carpet sales. The store decorator receives an 11 percent commission for all decorative sales. The youngest son is just graduating from college and is already married. He also wants to go into the family business.

To help ease the tax burden, Bob had given 10 percent of the business to each child at his or her one-year-old birthday party. The parents, therefore, own 30 percent of the business.

The two older sons have been on buying trips to the National Furniture Market in North Carolina, and between them they had been to the Regional Markets in New York, San Francisco, Chicago, Dallas, Los Angeles, Atlanta, and Tacoma.

The outlook for the business is encouraging. The home furnishing industry

Egbert's Home Furnishings
Income Statement

Sales	$568,700	
Cost of goods sold	329,850	
Gross profit		$238,850
Expenses:		
Administrative	$ 51,180	
Salaries and wages	62,550	
Mortgage	31,280	
Advertising	22,700	
Delivery	17,060	
Bad debts	4,550	
Miscellaneous	11,370	
Total expenses		$200,690
Net income (before taxes)		$ 38,160

is expected to jump ahead in the next two decades, and no decline is anticipated.

Bob would like to withdraw from the business to spend more time with his wife and to travel. He would also like to visit with his children and grandchildren, and allow his sons more time to run the business.

Questions

1. What should Bob do to plan for management succession?
2. How should Bob prepare for retirement?
3. What should the children do, if anything, to ease their father out of business?
4. Should Bob retain 30 percent control of the business?
5. How might a buy/sell agreement be used by Bob?
6. What type of management development is needed to ensure the continuity and success of the business?

Chapter Questions:

1. Discuss the advantages and disadvantages of management succession.
2. Discuss the importance of preparing for management change.
3. Discuss the necessity of a buy/sell agreement.
4. Discuss the importance of personnel management that is required of a successor.
5. Discuss the ingredients of inventory in business.
6. Discuss the importance of retirement and preparing for retirement.
7. Using material from the Incident at the beginning of this chapter, discuss:
    a. How Don should go about giving more control to his sons.
    b. What the family should do now about the outstanding shares of stock that control the company.
    c. What additional information Don Barber should have before deciding on how to turn the store over to his sons.
    d. How the children easily could take the store away from their father.
    e. What you would do if you were the eldest son of Don Barber.

24

Photo courtesy of Irene Springer, Prentice-Hall, Inc.

SMALL BUSINESS CONSULTING

Chapter Objectives:

1. To learn more about the consulting process.
2. To understand the steps involved in consulting.
3. To realize the importance of interpersonal communication in the consulting process.
4. To understand the different levels of managers and their expertise.
5. To learn how to develop a written report.
6. To be able to analyze a small business consulting case.

Begin to be now which you will be hereafter.

St. Jerome

INCIDENT:

Jeri was both happy and perplexed. She had spent the last fifteen years in the printing industry. The first seven years, spent printing business forms, were followed by three years as a printer for a book publisher. The last five years she has owned her own commercial printing business. The only major sector of the printing industry with which Jeri is unfamiliar is newspaper printing.

Jeri has twelve employees and is one of over 23,000 commercial printing shops in the United States (where 80 percent employ less than twenty people). Jeri's profits during the past year were in excess of $42,000 on sales of $372,000. She has been quite successful and looks forward to continuous growth and prosperity.

However, Jeri is currently faced with several major problems: (1) technological advances including computerized typesetting equipment, (2) shortages of raw materials, (3) rising labor costs, and (4) increasing governmental regulations. New typesetting equipment would cost close to $36,000.

Jeri is perplexed. She may need to increase sales to obtain new equipment and meet rising labor costs. She has thought about spending more time as a sales person and less as a printing manager. What should she do?

"The only constant is change." People in business change. Businesses, markets, and consumers change. Change may occur slowly or abruptly. The important factor is *controlling* the change. Planned change is a fundamental principle of business.

People plan their vacations and their own entertainment. They establish goals so that they can broaden their horizons, increase their skills, and expand their talents. However, it is difficult to always control change and its direction.

Traditionally, changes have occurred in business through the desires of the owners or managers. However, in the past decade, new individuals and professionals have emerged as consultants; they are also known as change agents, trainers, facilitators, or organizational development (OD) specialists. This breed of individual has brought along a design for diagnosing human systems as well as business systems. Consultants help a business to change in the desired direction, based on investigation, analysis, and business know-how.

The small business consultant—whether he or she is a student, an owner, or a professional—needs to follow the correct steps in order to ensure success. It is not appropriate to change ballerinas unless the new one is as good if not better than the current one. The advice of the consultant should improve the business situation and not hinder it.

The Consultant

The professional consulting experience generally consists of six steps that allow a consultant to investigate, analyze, plan, and help the small business owner. These steps, shown in Figure 24–1, are:

1. The first contact.
2. The definition of needs, objectives, and goals.
3. The collection of information.
4. The development of a plan.
5. The follow-up.
6. The termination.

the first contact   First impressions are generally lasting ones. The first contact that any consultant makes with the business owner should be friendly, warm, and supportive. The first contact is not the time to make destructive or constructive criticisms, as there has been no time in which to gather sufficient information.

During the first contact, the consultant should meet with the business owner and discuss the owner's wants or objectives. The consultant should not be forceful, but should gather information and develop a friendly relationship with the owner. The consultant should listen. Consultants should not find faults, but should show concern and interest. Consultants may take a tour of the business.

The first contact is also the time to ask yourself the question, "Will I be able to help this owner?" The consultant should also try to determine preliminarily what resources and knowledge will be necessary to handle each business situation. Will accounting expertise or financial knowledge be required to help the business owner?

A consultant needs to learn how to listen. Ears are one of the most important tools that a successful consultant uses. It is easier to talk than to listen. Most of us have been trained in oral communication but few of us have been trained to listen.

The consultant's ability to listen can provide confidence to the owner. It also provides an opportunity of gaining information and collecting data. A good listener will be a valuable asset in the consulting process. Listening is a good discipline, and it is also a good learning tool, because the consultant might learn something while listening.

the definition of needs, objectives, and goals   The second step in any professional consulting experience would be to define the needs, objectives, and goals of the business owner. The business owner may seek status, recognition, and/or achievement for his or her efforts. Many small business owners have as a major objective to obtain a "comfortable" living. Few small business owners have great wealth as their major goal.

When determining the goals or objectives of a business owner, it is important to realize that these need to be both definable (understandable) and measurable. After talking with the owner and/or manager, the consultant should formally write down these goals or objectives, and come to an agreement with the owner about whether or not the consultant can supply the help or resources necessary to fulfill their needs. The consultant should formally agree with the owner concerning the major activities that the consultant will perform. All available resources, knowledge, and techniques should be listed.

No formal advice or suggestions have yet been given the business owner. The consultant is still developing a professional relationship with that person. By listening to the owner the consultant will build trust, communication, and acceptance with the owner. The consultant will become a "sensitive manipulator."

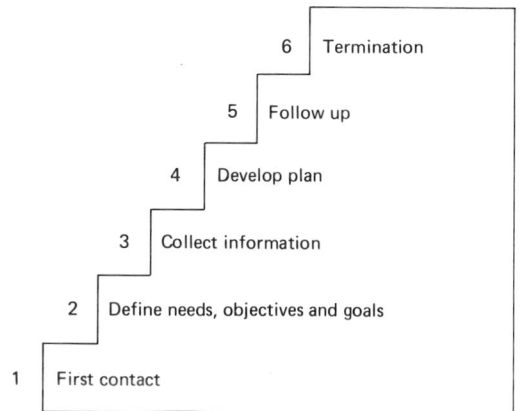

Figure 24-1. *Consulting steps.*

the collection of information

The consultant should next collect all available information. This should include financial statements, managerial reports, inventory levels, and personal interviews. This information should be as objective as possible.

It may be necessary at this time to consult with outside agencies, such as Internal Revenue Service, Federal Trade Commission, the local zoning commission, accountants, or trade associations. Information should be gathered about all aspects of the business. Whatever information is available concerning that business or industry should be collected for further reference and use. Industrial information is valuable in comparing one business with the industrial averages.

Many consultants find it useful to consult with state and national trade associations. They utilize the Robert Morris Associates' *Annual Statement Studies,* Dun & Bradstreet's *Business Ratio,* or NCR's *Expense Statements.* A good deal of information can be obtained by comparing one business with another business in the same industry.

At this point in the consulting process, the consultant needs to develop trust and confidence with the owners. Strengths and weaknesses of the business should be investigated. Employees may be asked what they believe the greatest strengths and/or weaknesses of the business to be. The consultant may also ask employees what is necessary to help the business become better. Many consultants find it necessary to visit the business five or six times during this period.

By the end of this step, it is important that the consultant have an understanding of how the organization operates, its programs, policies, procedures, and operations.

Table 24-1. Business Plan Study

I. Introduction
   a. History
   b. Description of the business

II. Marketing
   a. Product or service description
   b. Market demand/competition definition
   c. Marketing area description
   d. Market segmentation
   e. Location
   f. Advertising and promotion
   g. Price determination (optional)
   h. Distribution (optional)

III. Management
   a. Managerial skills requirements
   b. Personnel-Management Policies
   c. Organizational hierarchy (chart)/committees
   d. Customer relations policies
   e. Inventory control

IV. Accounting and Finance
   a. Balance sheet (current and/or projected)
   b. Income statement (current and/or projected)
   c. Cash flow analysis (current and/or projected)
   d. Break-even analysis (current and/or projected)
   e. Ratio analysis (explain differences compared with Robert Morris Associates' *Annual Statement Studies*)
   f. Profitability

V. Conclusion
   a. Individual and overall impression of the study by the consultant
   b. Benefits gained by the owner(s)
   c. Additional references for business owner(s) on the subject matter (list numbers on back with references)

VI. Appendix
   a. Maps
   b. Layouts
   c. Flyers
   d. Trade association material

the development of a plan

The consultant should put together a business plan that will help the owner to satisfy his or her needs, objectives, and goals. (See Table 24–1.) This plan should utilize the resources available and provide help and support to the business. The plan may provide technical expertise, in the way of handling inventory, an improved accounting system, or even new managerial procedures.

The decision to use or not to use the development plan is the owner's. The owner should examine the plan and its usefulness to the business. The consultant may try to persuade or present the plan in its most favorable light, but the final decision still rests with the owner.

The plan should be simple, understandable, and useful. It should be as inexpensive and beneficial as possible.

the follow-up

After presenting the plan to the business owner, the consultant must follow up. This follow-up should seek information about the usefulness of the plan, as well as its implementation.

If problems have arisen, the consultant should know of them. Changes may be necessary to improve the plan.

The strengths and weaknesses of the plan should be discussed between the owner and the consultant. Feedback should be provided to the consultant from the owner as to the parts of the plan that have been used and implemented. Additional consulting work may be determined feasible and advisable at this time.

the termination

It is important that, at the conclusion of the consulting program, the client contact be terminated in the same professional manner as the initial contact was developed. This termination may occur because of a lack of time to continue the consulting process. It may also be terminated at that time when the business owner has determined that he or she is self-sufficient and no longer in need of consulting help.

The consulting process, however, should not be terminated until everyone understands the plan and/or the needs, and the objectives and goals of the business have been satisfied. A formal termination session between the client and the consultant is recommended. An evaluation may be conducted at this time. (See Figure 24–2.)

CONSULTING EVALUATION FORM

	Poor	Fair	Average	Good	Excellent
I. Introduction					
a. History	[ ]	[ ]	[ ]	[ ]	[ ]
b. Description of the business	[ ]	[ ]	[ ]	[ ]	[ ]
II. Marketing	[ ]	[ ]	[ ]	[ ]	[ ]
a. Product or service description	[ ]	[ ]	[ ]	[ ]	[ ]
b. Market demand/competition definition	[ ]	[ ]	[ ]	[ ]	[ ]
c. Marketing area description	[ ]	[ ]	[ ]	[ ]	[ ]
d. Market segmentation	[ ]	[ ]	[ ]	[ ]	[ ]
e. Location	[ ]	[ ]	[ ]	[ ]	[ ]
f. Advertising and promotion	[ ]	[ ]	[ ]	[ ]	[ ]
g. Price determination (optional)	[ ]	[ ]	[ ]	[ ]	[ ]
h. Distribution (optional)	[ ]	[ ]	[ ]	[ ]	[ ]
III. Management	[ ]	[ ]	[ ]	[ ]	[ ]
a. Managerial skills requirements	[ ]	[ ]	[ ]	[ ]	[ ]
b. Personnel–management policies	[ ]	[ ]	[ ]	[ ]	[ ]
c. Organizational hierarchy (chart)/committees	[ ]	[ ]	[ ]	[ ]	[ ]
d. Customer relations policies	[ ]	[ ]	[ ]	[ ]	[ ]
e. Inventory control	[ ]	[ ]	[ ]	[ ]	[ ]
IV. Accounting and Finance	[ ]	[ ]	[ ]	[ ]	[ ]
a. Balance sheet (current and/or projected)	[ ]	[ ]	[ ]	[ ]	[ ]
b. Income statement (current and/or projected)	[ ]	[ ]	[ ]	[ ]	[ ]

CONSULTING EVALUATION FORM (continued)	Poor	Fair	Average	Good	Excellent
c. Cash flow analysis (current and/or projected)	[ ]	[ ]	[ ]	[ ]	[ ]
d. Break-even analysis (current and/or projected)	[ ]	[ ]	[ ]	[ ]	[ ]
e. Ratio analysis (explain differences compared with Robert Morris Associates, *Annual Statement Studies*)	[ ]	[ ]	[ ]	[ ]	[ ]
f. Profitability	[ ]	[ ]	[ ]	[ ]	[ ]
V. Problems	[ ]	[ ]	[ ]	[ ]	[ ]
a. Identified	[ ]	[ ]	[ ]	[ ]	[ ]
b. Handled	[ ]	[ ]	[ ]	[ ]	[ ]
VI. Conclusion	[ ]	[ ]	[ ]	[ ]	[ ]
a. Individual and overall impression of the study by the consultant	[ ]	[ ]	[ ]	[ ]	[ ]
b. Benefits gained by the owner(s)	[ ]	[ ]	[ ]	[ ]	[ ]
c. Additional references for business owner(s) on subject matter (list numbers on back with references)	[ ]	[ ]	[ ]	[ ]	[ ]
VII. Appendix	[ ]	[ ]	[ ]	[ ]	[ ]
a. Maps	[ ]	[ ]	[ ]	[ ]	[ ]
b. Layouts	[ ]	[ ]	[ ]	[ ]	[ ]
c. Flyers	[ ]	[ ]	[ ]	[ ]	[ ]
d. Trade association material	[ ]	[ ]	[ ]	[ ]	[ ]

Figure 24–2. *The consulting process may terminate with an evaluation*

The Client

The success or failure of any small business is highly dependent upon the owner or manager. Two different owners using the same resources, money, and materials will produce surprisingly different results. One may often fail, while the other will achieve fantastic success.

The consultant should recognize the differences between clients, and should realize that different managers are at different levels of expertise and have different knowledge bases. Different managers have different skills and competencies. What a business needs today may be entirely different from what it needed five years ago or what it will need five years from now. A consultant can easily recognize three different stages of managers: (1) entrepreneurs-operators, (2) managers, and (3) executives. (See Table 24–2.)

Table 24-2 The Client

ENTREPRENEUR-OPERATOR	MANAGER	EXECUTIVE
Single Owner: generally only one manager	*Multiple Managers:* striving to reach goals of business	*One Executive:* multiple managers, seeking new goals
Time Perspective: short-range, crisis orientation	*Time Perspective:* medium-range, planning and organizing	*Time Perspective:* long-range, development, innovations
Technical: highly skilled in one area	*Planning:* determines goals and objectives, follows plans	*Innovative:* encourages new plans and ideas
Commercial: involved with buying, selling, promoting, pricing	*Organizing:* establishes formal working relationships	*Creative:* rewards new thoughts, motivates employees
Supervisory: oversees all personnel and day-to-day activities	*Staffing:* manages hiring, training and development	*Development:* initiates new products or services
Business: manages business money, forecasts sales, uses accountant	*Directing/Controlling:* provides supervision and controls	*Leadership:* develops respect and status for business

entrepreneurs-operators

Most small businesses operate entirely under the direction of one individual, the owner-manager. The success of that business depends upon that owner. This individual, although highly technically skilled, often lacks managerial competency, experience, or skill. This person works with a very short time perspective, usually handling all crisis situations himself or herself. It is difficult for the entrepreneur-owner to find time to plan and organize the business.

The entrepreneur-operator is usually skilled in the technical or commercial areas of business. The operator has the technical competence to manufacture rubber hoses or to sell electronic calculators. He or she has an accounting system sufficient to manage, operate, and control the money required for the business. The operator uses supervisory skills to direct the work of employees on a face-to-face basis. Few, if any, administrative skills are demonstrated by this person except for forecasting sales and expenses.

The entrepreneur-operator is the most common form of manager a consultant in the small business field will encounter. They have a limited knowledge base of business principles and practices. They have developed their expertise through technical training or business experience.

managers

As a company grows larger, it is necessary that a professional manager be used. A manager must be able to handle the paperwork and administrative problems associated with the business. The owner no longer has time to supervise all the activities of the business alone. Managers become specialized: they may be responsible for sales, servicing, or production.

The business is sufficiently large now so that managers are employed to perform the basic managerial functions of any business: planning, organizing, staffing, directing, and controlling. The manager must be able to use and follow the plan of the business. Managers often divide the business into different departments or functions, such as advertising, sales, accounting or purchasing.

One manager may be entirely responsible for the staffing or hiring of new employees. Managers are also responsible for directing or motivating their employees to fill sales quotas or achieve company objectives. They are responsible for controlling or checking on the performance of employees. Personnel review and evaluation should also be conducted by the managers.

executives

After a great deal of experience and growth, a business may require an executive. This is the person whose responsibility it is to oversee and be held accountable for all the many facets of a business organization. In addition to the basic managerial functions of a manager, the executive must also provide insight and direction to the company. The executive is responsible for innovation, decision making, motivation, and leadership.

The executive needs to encourage research, development, and growth. He or she may find it necessary to change the business operations or policies to improve business growth and profit. The executive needs to be responsible for the final major decisions. He or she is responsible for committing the firm to long-range plans and projects.

The executive will also spend a considerable amount of time in building team work, morale, and pride in the business. Although not directly involved with everyday operations, as the operator or manager are, the executive will provide leadership and develop public interest in the business. The executive will also encourage managers to work hard and to achieve company goals and objectives. Through effective leadership, the executive will cause the company to grow and improve.

The professional consultant should realize that many owners are at the beginning or mechanistic stages. They often have limited managerial skills or business knowledge. Some owners have progressed to a manager's stage, and are involved in basic managerial functions. Very few, however, will ever reach the executive stage, or a stage of planning and development. Most owners will generally stay at the operator level, will be responsible for day-to-day operations, and will be concerned directly with the commercial, technical, and monetary activities of the business.

The Written Report

One of the major activities of any consultant is to provide a formal written report to the business owner-manager. The consultant report should be as simple and comprehensive as possible. Most consultant reports are descriptive, objective, or a combination of the two, known as an executive report.

The descriptive report includes a summary of the information gathered, a description of any results, and an interpretation or suggestions for improvement. Many reports may include statistical procedures, and as such would be prepared as descriptive reports. Additionally, many studies may just recommend different plans of action and would also be descriptive reports. Most descriptive reports do include recommendations for subsequent action, with the recommendations coming from the area of study. The descriptive report is the most commonly used consulting report. This kind of report will include representation of all information, plus a summary and an interpretation of any data with suggested plans of action.

The objective report presents factual information to the owner. This kind of report generally consists of research data and statistical findings. Any conclusions or suggestions are left to the owner, who will interpret the results.

Another form of reporting is referred to as executive reports. These reports are generally one to five pages long, and they provide a summary of data for the business owner. These reports emphasize recommendations, and key results of any research may be included in the report, but the major goal of the report is to provide plans or recommendations for the business owner.

Many consultants will utilize a descriptive report as well as an executive summary at the front of the report. This allows the business owner to read the first two pages and to understand the basics, which are discussed later and are further developed in the remainder of the report.

The use of any consultant's report is to provide guidance in developing and improving the business. The successful report should provide information which may be used to improve his business and market. The report will generally serve three major functions: (1) data collection, (2) conclusions or recommendations, and (3) quality of work performed. All consultant's reports contain a great amount of information which reflect the actual data or interviews collected during the consulting process. The report will also include those recommendations or plans which the owner should undertake to improve his business. The report will also indicate the quality of work which the consultant did. The report will reflect the work of those who consulted the client and the ability of the consultants to work together in developing recommendations and policies for the owner.

content of the report

The final preparation of a consultant's report is for the image of the consultant as well as properly identifying and developing the suggestions and information provided. Most business persons seek a straightforward and concise reporting of factual information. Business people are interested in obtaining all possible information and data with appropriate summaries and analysis. To develop this consultant report the following outline is presented:

1. Title page.
2. Table of contents.
3. Executive summary (1 to 3 pages).
4. Introduction and history.
5. Problem definition and study objectives.
6. Findings.
    a. Management.
    b. Marketing.
    c. Finance.
    d. Accounting.
    e. Legal.

7. Methodology (if appropriate).
8. Conclusions and recommendations.
9. Appendix and bibliography (if appropriate).

It is important for the report to be easy to understand and follow. An important guideline to follow is the "kiss" principle—keep it simply simple. The report should be clear and concise and free of difficult language.

Above all, the consultant's report should be brief. The executive summary may include all the vital important information for the business owner. However, it is also important that the remainder of the report be straightforward and short. Although some people may feel that they have accomplished a great task by providing a sixty-page report, a business owner will probably not read past the first ten pages unless he or she knows precisely where something of value is found.

SUCCESS STORY: Samuel G. Rautbord

A chance personal contact gave Sam Rautbord, 38, the opportunity of a lifetime.[1] Then a moderately successful lawyer, he was asked to draw up a will for one of his neighbors, who was part owner of a small duplicating machine firm. By 1944, the small company was in such dire straits that one of the partners wanted out. Rautbord, serving as part-time legal counsel for the company, put up $120,000, half of it his own money, and bought out that partner's interest.

A few months later, the company, American Photocopy Equipment Company, or APECO, was on the verge of bankruptcy. The company owed more than $100,000 and had under $4,000 in the bank. Rautbord was convinced that improper management was the main issue, and made a deal to take control of the company. He assumed the presidency of APECO and put the company on a pay-as-you-go basis.

Within a year, all of APECO's debts had been paid, and the company was operating in the black. In 1950, the company came across a Belgian photocopy machine that was a great improvement over its competitors. APECO set out to purchase the rights to sell the machine, but ran into trouble with the U.S. Alien Property Custodian, which had seized rights to the machine during World War II. APECO began selling the machine, eventually, and it was a great success. The Belgian firm filed a patent infringement suit, but APECO resolved the dispute with a licensing agreement. Over the years, the "small royalty" agreed upon with the Belgian firm added up to well over $5 million.

Rautbord maintained the rigid control he established at APECO until his retirement, at which time the company was turned over to his son. This is one story, however, that does not have a happy ending. In 1975, Sam Rautbord reassumed the presidency of APECO for a brief period while he sought a new president. The company had made several unprofitable investments, most notably in data processing, and had lost a considerable sum of money. Moreover, the photocopy equipment field changed and APECO did not keep up with it. APECO filed for Chapter 11 bankruptcy in 1977, and has been forced to discontinue or sell many parts of its business.

[1] William R. Klabby, "The New Millionaires and How They Made Their Fortunes," 1960.

CASE STUDY: The Racquet Place

The Racquet Place is a racquetball and health club facility located on the outskirts of a large midwestern town. Warren Evans has been the owner of the place for the past seven years, and he has been able to increase his profits from $13,000 the first year to over $64,000 last year.

The Racquet Place is comprised of ten lighted regulation handball courts, with a separate sauna for men and women, a combined whirlpool, separate weight-lifting facilities, a small pro shop, and a snack bar with limited refreshments. Warren's staff consists of himself as the owner-manager, an assistant manager, a racquet pro, a program coordinator, and a part-time bookkeeper. In addition, there are six part-time employees and one full-time court manager. The full-time court manager substitutes as a secretary and receptionist for the business. The staff has organized two racquetball tournaments and one handball tournament for each of the last four years. They have thought about developing leagues and other special court activities, but as of yet these ideas have not been developed.

There are four other racquetball clubs in the city. The Racquet Place charges $75 for an individual membership, $100 for a family membership, and $200 for a corporate membership, with monthly fees of $25. There is also a court rental charge of $7 during prime time, and $5.50 during nonprime time.

During the last year, a new racquetball court was opened in town, with twenty-four courts. This new competition has had an adverse effect upon the current level of business. Warren is seriously concerned about the competition and about the lack of people currently involved in the racquetball sport. Jogging, golf, and other outdoor activities tend to take away from the racquetball enthusiasts. The Racquet Place is currently open seven days a week, with the following hours of operation:

	Nonprime	Prime
Monday–Friday	6:00 A.M.–11:30 A.M.	11:30 A.M.–1:50 P.M.
	(Note: Club opens at 7:00 A.M. instead of 6:00 on Mon.)	
	1:30 P.M.– 4:00 P.M.	4:00 P.M.–9:30 P.M.
	9:30 P.M.–12:00	
Saturday	7:00 A.M.– 8:30 A.M.	8:30 A.M.–6:00 P.M.
	6:00 P.M.–12:00	
Sunday	7:00 A.M.– 8:30 A.M.	8:30 A.M.–6:00 P.M.
	6:00 P.M.–10:30 P.M.	

Warren is considering changing his business operation. He has thought about extending business hours; he has also thought about an extension of league play or other speciality activities for his courts. Warren is undecided about the direction that he should currently take, and he is interested in finding out how he might continue to be profitable and even increase his business.

The Racquet Place
Balance Sheet
December 31, 198X

Assets		Liabilities	
Cash	$ 4,000	Accounts payable	$ 5,000
Accounts receivable	10,000	Accrued liabilities	6,000
Inventory	2,400		
Current assets	$ 16,400	Current liabilities	$ 11,000
Furniture	$ 6,000	Mortgages	$420,000
Equipment	12,000	Bank loan	20,000
Autos (2)	14,600	Noncurrent liability	$440,000
Building	550,000	Total liabilities	$451,000
Land	120,000	Owner's equity	$240,000
Fixed assets	$702,600	Retained Earnings	28,000
Total assets	$719,000	Total liability & equity	$719,000

The Racquet Place
Income Statement
December 31, 198X

Sales (Revenue)	$267,800
Cost of sales	40,000
Gross margin (profit)	$227,800
Expenses:	
Wages and salaries	$146,000
Utilities	2,800
Supplies	1,200
Maintenance	6,800
Accounting and legal	600
Advertising and promotion	2,600
Insurance	2,200
Miscellaneous	1,600
Operating expenses	$163,800
Net income	$ 64,000

Questions

1. Discuss any management recommendations a consultant should offer.
2. What should be done to improve profits?
3. Discuss the financial situation of the Racquet Place.
4. What changes should be made to the layout design?
5. Discuss the marketing situation.
6. Should changes be made with the membership fees?

Chapter Questions:

1. Discuss the basic steps in a consultation.
2. Why is the first contact so important in a consulting relationship?
3. Why are objectives important to a business?
4. What value is a business plan to a business?
5. Why are clients different? Is this difference important?
6. What should be contained in a written report? Why?

GLOSSARY

Amortize. To repay a debt or allocate acquisition costs through scheduled periodic payments.

Annual Percentage Rate. Equals interest on a loan divided by the average amount of loan. The Truth In Lending Act established by Congress requires lenders to specify the annual percentage rate in loan contracts.

Appreciation. Increase in economic worth generally created by rising market prices or value of an asset.

Assets. Those resources expected to benefit future business activities.

Automobile Insurance. Protection on automobiles, trucks, and vehicles against possible physical damage, theft or bodily injury to self or others.

Balloon Payment. The last and large payment that retires a loan obligation that had received minimal payments previously.

Bond. A debt instrument usually secured through real estate fixtures or equipment.

Business Interruption Insurance. Compensation for expenses (generally fixed) that need to be paid while business was interrupted by serious loss.

Capital. The owner's equity in a business. This is generally the owner's personal net worth of the business: assets minus liabilities.

GLOSSARY

Cash Flow. The cash revenue minus expenses for a given period.

Co-insurance. Allows lower insurance premium rates to those insuring property more fully (states may establish laws regulating minimum insurability at 70 percent to 85 percent).

Collateral. Assets or possessions that a borrower pledges to a lender for debt repayment. If repayment is not made, then the lender assumes ownership of collateral.

Cross-purchase Plan. Owners buy sufficient insurance on each other's lives to buy each other's business interest in case of death.

Current Debt. The amount owed that must be paid within a year including interest on long-term debt or taxes.

Debenture. An unsecured bond.

Depreciation. The cost of writing off, or allocating, the cost of an asset to expenses over the useful life of a depreciable item or asset.

Equity. The ownership of the assets, the net worth of the business, or the money that shows ownership of a business.

Expenses. Costs that are deducted from revenue for a given period of time.

Factor. A firm that buys accounts receivable, generally at a discount, and then collects them.

Fidelity Bond. Protects business against loss due to theft or dishonesty on the part of employees.

Fire Insurance. Protection against damage caused by fire. May also include lightning; windstorm, hail, explosion, smoke, riot, and even vandalism and malicious mischief.

Fundamental Risk. Losses that are not caused by individual and affect entire groups, such as inflation and war.

Indemnity. Individual can collect only actual loss.

Insurance. Transference of pure risk from one party to a second party by means of a contract.

Key-man Coverage. Insurance purchased by company to compensate for the loss of an important executive due to death.

Leverage. The extent that a business is financed through debt, or the ability to produce business funds by the injection of debt.

Liability. The business's obligation to creditors or suppliers.

Liability Insurance. Protection against legal actions brought for negligence to customers, employees or other business contacts.

Liquidity. The level at which business assets are in cash or can be quickly converted into cash.

Loan Principle. The original amount of money borrowed from the lender or the unpaid loan balance still owed, not including interest payments.

Net Worth. Assets minus liabilities or the result of subtracting what is owed from what is owned.

Obligee. A protected employer of a bonded employee.

Particular Risk. Losses from events that are personal in both cause and effect, such as bank robbery and house burning.

Prime Rate. An interest rate offered by banks to its low-risk customers, usually short-term credit to large corporations or wealthy individuals.

Principal. An employee who is bonded.

Pure Risk. Event with only loss or no loss possible.

Risk. Uncertainty of loss or profit.

Speculative Risk. Event where gain or loss are possible.

Subrogation. Individual gives an insurance company the right of recovery against liable third parties.

Surety. An insurance company or licensed bonding corporation contracting for fidelity bonds.

Surety Bond. Guarantees performance by contractors to other businesses or employers.

Term Loan. A loan repayable over a number of periodic payments; may terminate in a balloon payment.

Usury Law. A ceiling set by state legislatures on loan interest rates that commercial lenders may charge, often developed to protect the consumer.

Working Capital. Current assets minus current liabilities, or those funds available to operate normal business procedures.

BIBLIOGRAPHY

Avoiding Management Pitfalls. Small Business Reporter Series. San Francisco: Bank of America, 1980.

BRESSLER, RAYMOND G., JR. and RICHARD A. KING. *Markets, Prices, and Interregional Trade*. New York: John Wiley & Sons, 1970.

Business Management: Advice From Consultants. Small Business Reporter Series. San Francisco: Bank of America, 1980.

Business Plan for Retailers. (Small Marketers Aid No. 150.) Washington, D.C.: Small Business Administration, 1979.

Business Plan for Small Construction Firms. (Management Aid for Small Manufacturers No. 221.) Washington, D.C.: Small Business Administration, 1974.

Business Plan for Small Manufacturers. (Management Aid for Small Manufacturers No. 218.) Washington, D.C.: Small Business Administration, 1980.

Business Plan for Small Service Firms. (Small Marketers Aid No. 153.) Washington, D.C.: Small Business Administration, 1980.

DIBLE, DONALD M. *Up Your Own Organization*. Santa Clara, Calif.: Entrepreneur Press, 1971.

ENIS, BEN M. *Marketing Principles*. 2d ed. Santa Monica, Calif.: Goodyear Publishing, 1977. Chapters 7 and 12.

KOTLER, PHILLIP. *Marketing Management*. 3d ed. Englewood Cliffs, N.J.: Prentice-Hall, 1976. Chapters 7, 11, 12, and 21.

MANSFIELD, EDWIN. *Microeconomics*. 2d ed. New York: W. W. Norton, 1970.

McConnell, Campbell R. *Economics*. 7th ed. New York: McGraw-Hill, 1978. Chapters 4 and 5.

Rimler, G. W. and N. J. Humphreys. "Successful Delegation—A Must for Small Business," *Journal of Small Business Management* 14, No. 1 (1976). pp 42–44.

Stegall, Donald P., Lawrence L. Steinmetz, and John B. Kline. *Managing The Small Business*. rev. ed. Irwin, 1976.

Steps to Starting a Business. Small Business Reporter Series. San Francisco: Bank of America, 1980.

Vesper, Karl H. *New Venture Strategies*. Englewood Cliffs, N.J.: Prentice-Hall, 1980.

Webster, F. A., and J. Ellis. "The Very First Business Plan,": *Journal of Small Business Management* 14, No. 1 (1976). pp 46–50.

Weston, J. Fred and Eugene F. Brigham. *Managerial Finance*. 5th ed. Hinsdale, Ill.: The Dryden Press, 1975. Chapter 3.

Woodward, H. N. "Management Strategies for Small Companies," *Harvard Business Review* 54, No. 1 (1976). pp 113–121.

Index

A

ABC method of inventory control, 272–73
Accountants, 415
Accounting:
    Balance sheet *(figure)*, 88–89
    Cash flow statement, 91–92
    Double-entry bookkeeping system, 202–4
    Profit and loss statement *(figure)*, 88–91
    Single-entry bookkeeping system, 201–2
    Uses and purposes, 210–11
Accounts payable, 208
Advantages of owning a small business, 10–12, 58–59
Advertising:
    Budget, 313–14
    Direct mail, 312–13
    Magazines, 312
    Newspaper, 311–12
    Outdoor, 313
    Point-of-purchase displays, 313
    Professional services, 28
    Radio, 312
    Specialty, 313
    Television, 312
    Trade shows, 313
Agents, 386–87
Agriculture, 29

Allen, Woody, 270
Almanac of Business and Industrial Financial Ratios, 224–25
Application for employment form, 169
Ash, Mary Kay, 130
Assets:
    Book value, 127
    Current, 208
    Fixed, 208
    Liquidation value, 127
    Replacement value, 127–28
Attitudes:
    Towards business, 24
    Towards customers, 24
    Towards employees, 24
Attorneys, 416
Automobile insurance, 366, 375

B

Bailment, 385–86
Balance sheet, 88–89, 206–9
    Comparative common-sized *(table)*, 233
Balancing a checkbook *(figure)*, 203
Bankers, 416
Bank of America, 118
Banks, 151–53, 156
    Loan guidelines 153

Bank statement *(figure)*, 202
Barrow, Charles, 63–64
Basic financial needs:
    Expansion, 142
    Improving cash flow (working capital), 143
    Inventory, 142
    Remodeling, 143
Behavior, 340–42
    Attitude, 341
    Motives, 341–42
Better Business Bureau (BBB), 23
Blue collar occupations, 67
Bombeck, Erma, 41
Bonding, 100
Bonuses, 334
Book value, 127
Break-even analysis, 94, 288–90
Budgets:
    Balance sheet, 239
    Cash, 236–38
    Cost of goods, 238
    Direct labor, 238–39
    Income statement, 238
    Objectives, 234
    Periods, 234–35
    Preparation, 235
    Production, 238
    Sales, 235–36
    Selling and administrative, 236
Bureau of Business Research, 114
Bureau of Census, 248–49
    Census of Retail Trade, 254
    Standard Metropolitan Statistical Area (SMSA), 248
Business:
    Attitudes towards, 24
    Choosing an existing, 125–59, 181–92
        Assets, 126–28
        Earnings or profit evaluation, 126
        Image and other areas, 128–29
            Capital return, 129
            Debt repayment, 129
            Dividends, 128
            Fringe benefits, 128–29
            Salary and interest, 128
         Liabilities, 128
        Reason for sale, 125–26
    Considerations, 248–50
    Description, 117–18
    Environment, 117–18
    Interruption insurance, 367, 376–77
    Life Cycle, 404–7
        Decline stage, 407
        Growth stage, 405–6
        Introduction stage, 405
        Maturity (or professional) stage, 406

Business *(con't)*
    Organization (sole proprietor, partnership, or corporation), 29–33
    Records loss, 359
    Risks, 357–58
    Stages, 109–13
        Business stage, 110–11
        Growth stage, 111–12
        Pre-businesss stage, 109–10
        Termination, 112–13
Businesses:
    Finance, 28
    Service, 28
Buying a business *(See also* Business, choosing an existing), 181–92
    Decision to buy or not, 186–88
    Determining available resources, 181–82
    Determining kind of business, 181
    Evaluate opportunities, 182–86
        Determine what is being bought, 185–86
        History, 183
        Other areas of concern, 186
        Profit, sales and expense figures, 184
        Reason for sale, 184–85
    Find opportunities, 182
    Negotiating the selling price, 190–91
    Pricing the business, 188–91
    Purchasing a business, 192–93
    Tax free reorganizations, 193–94
Buy/Sell agreement, 423–25

C

Capacity, 153–54
Capital, 153–54
    Expenditures, 151
    Initial, 63
    Return, 129
    Working, 63, 143, 151
Capital stock, 209
Cash flow:
    Cycle, 217–18
    Projection *(figure)*, 219
    Statement, 91–92, 218–20
Casualty insurance, 364–65
Certificate of deposit, 388–89
Chamber of Commerce, 114, 252
Character, 153–54
Checkbook, balancing *(figure)*, 203
Checks, 388
CIF (cost, insurance freight), 386
Classroom training, 171
Clayton Act, 385
Client *(table)*, 441
    Entrepreneurs-operators, 441
    Executives, 442

Client *(table) (con't)*
    Managers, 441–42
Co-insurance, 363–64
Collateral, 144, 153–54
    Summary of collateral *(figure)*, 146
Commercial loss, 359
Commissions, 334
Common-sized forms, 223–24
    Balance sheet *(table)*, 223
    Income statement *(table)*, 223
Common stock, 148
Community involvement, 23
Community location, 248–52
Comparative businesses, 253
Comparative-size forms, 222
Compensating balance, 151
Competition (in pricing), 292–93
Competitive businesses, 253
Computers, 275–79
    Do for small business, 279
    Hardware, 276–77
    Living with, 278–79
    Preparations for a new computer, 277–78
    Small Business Computer System (SBCS), 276
    Software, 277
    System components, 275–77
Consultants:
    Business plan study *(table)*, 438
    Characteristics of *(table)*, 39
    Collection of information, 439
    Definition of needs, objectives, and goals, 436–37
    Development of a plan, 438
    Evaluation form *(table)*, 439–40
    First contact, 436
    Follow-up, 438–39
    Managerial, 416–17
    Marketing, 416–17
    Role requirements *(table)*, 39
    Services of *(table)*, 51
    Termination, 439
    Where to find *(table)*, 51
    Written report, 442–44
        Content of the report, 443–44
Contracts, 97, 382–85
    Bilateral and unilateral, 384
    Contract of sale, 385
    Contract to sell, 385
    Expressed or implied, 384
    Joint and several, 384–85
    Quasicontracts, 384
    Void and voidable, 384
Control (management function), 176–77
Convertible debentures, 148
Corporations, 29, 32–33,
    Privately held, 147

Corporations *(con't)*
    Publicly held, 147
    Stockholders in, 147
    Subchapter S (section 1244 stock), 98
Cost centers, 239
Cost-plus analysis, 287–88
    Absorption approach, 287
    Contribution approach, 287
    Traditional approach, 287
Coverage ratios, 228
Credit:
    Collections, 242–43
    4 C's of credit, 153–55
    Policy, 242
    Short term, 151–53
        Bank, 151
        Trade credit, 153
Credit unions, 156
Crime insurance, 377
Current assets, 208
Current liabilities, 208
    Accounts payable, 208
    Income taxes, 208
    Notes payable, 208
Current ratio, 226
Customers, 24, 156
    Attitude towards, 24
Customer traffic, 260–61

D

Daily summary of cash receipts, 201
Death of owner, 423
Debt:
    Repayment, 129
    Warranties, 148
Debt-to-equity ratios, 144–46, 158–61
    How to determine, 158–61
Debt financing, 146–47, 150–55
    Capital expenditures, 151
    Working capital, 151
Debt-to-worth ratios, 229
Delegation, 71
Demand, 283
Department of Economic Development, 114, 252
Direction (management function), 174–76
    Cognition, consistency, clarity, 175
    Drive, 174
    Incentives and expectations, 174–75
    Reinforcement, 175–76
Disability insurance, 369, 379
Disadvantages of owning a small business, 12–13, 59
Dividends, 128
Double-entry bookkeeping system, 202–4
Drafts, 388

Drawing accounts, 334–35
Drive, 174
Dun & Bradstreet, 126, 211
Dun & Bradstreet's Business Ratios, 79

E

Earnings before interest and taxes-to-interest ratio, 228
Earnings evaluation, 126
Economic considerations, 252
Economic environment, 114–15
Economic order quantity, 273–74
Education, 69
   and income, 69
Elasticity, 283
Employee benefit insurance coverages, 378–79
   Disability, 379
   Group health, 378
   Group life, 378
   Key-man coverage, 379
   Retirement income, 379
Employees:
   Acquisition, 168–71
   Attitudes toward, 24
   Characteristics *(table)*, 39
   Financial resource, 156
   Hiring, 168–70
   Insurance benefits, 100
   Interviewing, 170–71
   Involvement, 23
   Motivation, 171–72
   Retention, 172
   Role requirements *(table)*, 39
   Taxes, 392–94
   Training, 171
Employment growth *(figure)*, 410–11
Endowment life insurance, 368
Entrepreneur, 38–44, 441
   Characteristics, 39–40
   Role requirements *(table)*, 39
Entrepreneur, 118
Environment, 114–18
   Business, 117–18
   Economic, 114
   Industrial, 115
   Marketing, 115–16
Equipment manufacturers, 156
Equity, 209
Equity financing, 146–50
   Common stock, 148
   Convertible debentures, 148
   Debt warranties, 148
   Preferred stock, 148
Equity, return on, 225
Excise taxes, 397–98
Expansion, 142
Expectations, 174–75
Expenses of Retail Businesses, 224–25

F

Factoring companies, 156
Failure of small business, 12, 14–16
Fair Credit Billing Act of 1975, 241
FAIR insurance plans, 367
Fair Trade Law, 390
Family:
   Considerations, 251
   Investment firms, 156
   Involvement, 23, 50–52
Farm workers, 67
Feasibility study, 63, 77–103
   Accounting finances, and taxes, 89–96
      Accounting, 87–91
         Balance sheet, 88–89
         Cash flow statement, 91–92
         Profit and loss statement, 88–91
      Finances, 91–95
         Break-even analysis, 94
         Provisions for taxation, collateral, credit references, loan requests and terms, 95
         Ratio analysis, 94–95
         Start-up or turnkey costs, 93–94
      Taxes, 95–96
         Federal, 96
         Local, 96
         State, 96
   Appendix, 101–3
   Checklist *(figure)*, 78–79
   Introduction, preface, or general overview, 79–80
   Legal aspects, 96–101
      Business structure, 97–98
      Contracts, licenses, and other legal documents, 97
      Insurance: type and costs, 98–100
         Liability, 100
         Personal, 100
         Property, 99
      Provisions for business termination and/or succession, 101
   Management, 84–87
      Inventory control, 87
      Organizational structure, 85
      Personal expertise, 85
      Personnel management, 86
      Policies and procedures, 86–87
      Production and operations, 87
   Marketing, 80–84

Marketing *(con't)*
    Identification of target market, 82
    Objective and supporting strategies, 81
    Place: location, size, traffic counts, channels and distribution, 83
    Price determination, 83–84
    Product description, 81
    Promotion, 84
Federal Insurance Contribution Act, 392
Federal regulators *(table)*, 383
Federal taxes, 96
Federal Trade Commission Act, 385
Feedback, 43
Feedback (marketing), 315
FICA, 392
Fidelity bonds, 366
Fiedler's model, 346
Finance companies, 156
Finances, 91–95
    Break-even analysis, 94
    Provisions for taxation, collateral, credit references, and loan requests and terms, 95
    Ratio analysis, 94–95
    Start-up or turnkey costs, 93–94
Financial:
    Businesses, 28
    Consultants, 156
    Needs, 141–42
      Basic, 142
      Planning, 141
    Planning, 234–39
      Balance sheet, 239
      Budget objectives, 234–35
      Budget preparation, 235
      Budgeting periods, 234–35
      Cash budget, 236–38
      Cost of goods budget, 238
      Direct labor budget, 238–39
      Income statement, 238
      Production budget, 238
      Sales budget, 235–36
      Selling and administrative budget, 236
    Records, 143–46
    Statement form, 152
    Statements, 204–9, 222–24
      Balance sheet, 204–6
      Income statement, 204–6
Financing, 146–55, 187
    Debt, 146–47, 150–55
    Equity, 146–50
    New business *(figure)*, 187
Fire insurance, 365, 372–74
Fisher, Helen, 240–41
Fixed assets, 208

Fixed-to-worth ratios, 228–29
Flitter, Gerald, 173
FOB, 299, 385–86
Foreign markets, pricing, 298
Form 1040, 30
Form 1065 (United States Partnership Return of Income), 31
Foundations:
    Charitable, 156
    Tax exempt, 156
Founders and industrial banks, 156
Franchising, 131–35
    Checklist for evaluating a franchise, 137
    Controls, 134
    Duration and termination, 134
    Franchise agreement, 132
    Franchisee, 131–32
    Franchisor, 131
    Government restrictions and the future, 134
    Initial cost, 132
    Location and territorial rights, 133
    Product service method, 132–33
    Royalties, 133
    Summary, 134–35
Freight charges, 299
Friends, 156
Fringe benefits, 128–29

G

General partnership, 30
Gestalt, 42
Glass insurance, 377
Goals, 349–51, 413–14
    MBO (Management by objectives), 349–51
Government regulations, 13
Government restrictions, 134
Group health insurance, 369, 378
    Basic medical and hospitalization, 369
    Disability, 369
    Health Maintenance Organizations, 369
    Major medical, 369
Group life insurance, 378

H

Hardware (computer), 376
Health Maintenance Organizations (HMO), 369
Hiring, 168–70
Holding company, 98
How to Get Control of Time and Your Life, 70

I

Image, 128–29
Incentives, 174–75

Income statement, (See also Profit and loss statement), 204–6, 238
   Budgeted, 238
   Comparative common-sized *(table)*, 223
Income taxes, 208
Indemnity, 362
Individual development *(figure)*, 340
   Attitude, 341
   Behavior, 342
   Motives, 341–42
Industrial environment, 115
Industrial groups, 113–14
   Manufacturing, 113
   Retailing, 114
   Services, 114
   Wholesaling, 113–14
Industrial growth, 411–12
Inelastic prices, 283
Initial capital, 63
Insurance:
   Agents, 416
   Co-insurance, 363–64
   Companies, 156, 362
      Lloyds groups, 362
      Mutual companies, 362
      Reciprocals, 362
      Stock companies, 362
   Coverages:
      Automobile, 366–75
      Business interruption, 367, 376–77
      Casualty, 364–65
      Crime, 377
      Disability, 379
      FAIR insurance plans, 367,
      Fidelity bonds, 366
      Fire, 365, 372–74
      Glass, 377
      Group health insurance, 369, 378
      Group life, 378
      Key-man coverage, 368, 379
      Liability, 365, 374–75
      Life, 367
      Rent, 378
      Retirement income, 379
      Surety bonds, 366
      Worker's compensation, 365, 375–76
   Indemnity, 362
   Liability, 100
   Personal, 100
   Property, 99
   Subrogation, 363
   What is insurable, 362
Integration:
   Backward, 309
   Forward, 309

Integration *(con't)*
   Horizontal, 309
Interest rate:
   On loans, 155
   Prime, 155
Internal Revenue Service, 148
Interviewing job applications, 170–71
Inventor, 48
   Characteristics *(table)*, 39
   Role requirements *(table)*, 39
Inventory, 87, 142, 271–75, 427–30,
   Business and operations, 427–29
      Administration (table), 428
      Financial facts (table), 427
      Operations and information, 429
   Control, 271–75
      ABC method of inventory control, 272–73
      Economic order quantity, 273–74
      Holding costs, 271
      Out-of-stock problems, 275
      Systems, 274–75
         Periodic inventory method, 274–75
         Perpetual inventory method, 274
         Two-bin method, 275
   Managerial development, 428–30
      Business operations, 429–30
      Informational roles, 429
      Interpersonal relationships, 429
      Technical roles, 429
   Retirement *(See* Retirement)
Investment:
   Bankers, 156
   Clubs, 156
   Companies, 149
      Minority Enterprise Small Business Investment Companies (MESBIC), 149
      Small Business Investment Companies (SBIC), 149
      State Business and Industrial Development Corporations (SBIDC), 149
Investors:
   Equity, 147–48
   Professional, 147, 149
IRS, 148

J

Joint tenancy, 387

K

Kaiser, Henry J., 209–10
Key Business Ratios, 244–45
Key-man coverage, 368, 379
Kroc, Ray A., 13–14, 406

L

Lakein, Alan, 70
Law, 382–91
   Agencies, 386–87
   Contracts, 382–85
   Negotiable instruments, 388–90
      Certificate of deposit, 388
      Checks, 388
      Drafts, 388
      Promissory notes, 388
   Pricing, 390–91
      Fair trade statutes, 390–91
      Price cutting, 390
      Price discrimination, 390
      Price fixing, 390
   Property, 387–88
   Sales, 385–86
      Bailment, 385–86
      Warranties, 386
Lawyers, (*See* Attorneys)
Layout, 258–62
   Manufacturers and warehouses, 259
   Retail stores, 259
Leadership, 339, 343–48
   Definition, 343
   History, 344–45
      Behavioral approaches, 344
         Ohio State University studies, 344–45
         University of Michigan studies, 345
      Contingency models, 345–48
         Fiedler's model, 346
         Path-goal model, 346–47
         Vroom-Yetton decision making model (*figure*), 347–48
      Traits theory, 344
Leases, 387–88
Leasing companies, 156
Legal (*See* Law)
Leverage ratios, 228–29
Liabilities, 128, 208–9
   Current, 208
   Long-term, 208–9
Liability insurance, 100, 365, 374–75
   Automobile, 100
   General, 100
   Product, 100
Liability loss, 359–60
Licenses, 97
Life insurance, 367–68
   Endowment, 368
   Term, 367
   Whole, 367
Limited partners, 147
Limited partnership, 30
Liquidation value, 127
Lloyds groups, 362
Loan guidelines, 153
Local taxes, 96
Location, 83, 133, 247–58
   Community, 248–52
Long-term liabilities, 208–9
Loss, types of, 359–60
   Business record, 359
   Commercial, 359
   Liability, 359–60
   Personal, 359
   Property, 359

M

Macy, Rowland, 329–30
Major medical, 369
Management:
   By objectives, 349–51
   Functions, 164–77
      Control, 176–77
      Direction, 174–76
      Organization, 165–67
      Planning, 164–65
      Staffing, 167–73
   Succession of, 421–31
Manager, 42, 45–47, 441–42
   Characteristics (*tables*), 39, 42
   Role requirements, (*table*), 39
Managerial assistance:
   Accountants, 415
   Attorneys, 416
   Bankers, 416
   Insurance agents, 416
   Managerial or marketing consultants, 416–17
Managerial consultants 416–17
Managerial Development (inventory of), 428–30
Managerial transfer, 423
Manufacturers, 27, 113
Markdowns, 286
Market development, 309
Marketing, 80–84
   Consultants, 416–17
   Definition of markets, 307
   Development of marketing concept, 306–7
      Marketing concept, 306–7
      Production concept, 306
      Selling concept, 306
   Environment, 115–16
   Factors (in pricing), 291–94
   Research, 316–19
      Analysis and forecast, 319
      Collection and tabulation of data, 319
      Questionnaire development, 317

Marketing *(con't)*
   Sample design, 319
   Strategy, 308–15
      Analyzing opportunities and alternatives, 309
         Integration, 309
         Market development, 309
         Market penetration, 309
         Product development, 309
      Carrying out implementation, 315
      Defining objectives, 308–9
      Developing marketing strategy for implementation, 309–15
         Market entry, 310
         Marketing mix, 310
            Place, 310
            Price, 311
            Product, 310
            Promotion, 311
         Market timing, 315
      Feedback and control, 315
Market penetration, 309
Market share, 254–56
Markups, 285–86
   Relationship between markup on cost and markup on retail *(table)*, 286
MBO, 349–51
   Individual action and implementation, 350
   Joint goal setting, 349–50
   Performance appraisal, 350–51
Medical and hospitalization insurance, 369
Merchandise classifications for small retail stores *(table)*, 118
MESBIC, 149, 156
Meyer, Paul J., 31–32
Minorities in small business *(table)*, 7, 9
Minority Enterprise Small Business Investment Companies (MESBIC), 149, 156
Mitsui, Hachirobei, 150
Monthly disbursement record, 201
Monthly summary of cash receipts, 201
Motivation, 171–72
Mr. Businessman's Kit, 95
Mutual companies, 362
Mutual funds, 156
Mutual savings banks, 156

N

National Cash Register, 126
National Cash Register (NCR) expense statement, 79
National Economic Forecast, 114
Negotiable instruments, 388–90
  Certificate of deposit, 388
  Checks, 388
  Drafts, 388
  Promissory notes, 388

Net profit margin, 225
Net worth, 209
Notes payable, 208

O

Occupations:
   Blue collar, 67
   Farm workers, 67
   Projections *(figure)*, 67
   service, 67
   white collar, 67
Ohio State University studies, 344–45
   Consideration, 344–45
   Initiating structure, 344
Onassis, Aristotle Socrates, 425–26
On-the-job training, 171
Operating ratios, 229–30
Organization *(figure)*, 166–67
Out-of-stock problems, 275

P

Partner, 48–49
   Characteristics *(table)*, 39
   General, 48
   Limited, 48, 147
   Role requirements *(table)*, 39
Partnership, 30–31, 98, 156
   General, 30
   Limited, 30
   Private investment, 156
Path-goal model, 346–47
Paulucci, Jeno F., 342–43
Penetration pricing, 294
Penney, J.C. 221
Pension funds, 156
Percent of profits before taxes to tangible net worth, 229–30
Periodic inventory control, 274–75
Perpetual inventory method, 274
Personal appraisal, 58–59
   Checklist for going into business *(figure)*, 60–61
Personal financial statement *(figure)*, 144–45
Personal involvement, 22
Personal loss, 359
Personal property taxes, 395
Personal selling, 314
Personnel:
   Acquisition, 168–71
   Application for employment form *(figure)*, 169
   Management, 86
Petersen, William, 407–8
Planning, 164–65, 413–14
   Financial needs, 141, 234–39
   Succession, 422–23

Preferred stock, 148
Pricing, 390–91
   A business, 188–91
   Economic factors, 283
      Demand, 283
      Elasticity, 283
   Making the pricing decision, 299–300
      Choose reasonable range of prices, 300
      Identify pricing characteristics, 300
      Monitor results, 300
      Select a final price, 300
      Market segments, 291–92
         Combined outlet, 292
         Discount outlet, 292
         Exclusive outlet, 291
         Regular outlet, 292
         Specialty outlet, 292
   Marketing factors, 291–94
      Competition, 292–93
         Alternative goods, 293
         Distant competitors, 293
         Nearby competitors, 292–93
         Substitute goods, 293
      Pricing and product's life cycle, 293–94
         Declining products, 294
         Matured products, 294
         Maturing products, 294
         New products, 293
   Markdowns, 286
   Markups, 285
   Mathematical factors, 285–90
      Break-even analysis, 288–90
      Cost-plus analysis, 287–88
         Absorption approach, 287
         Contribution approach, 287
         Traditional approach, 287
      Relationship between markup on cost and markup on retail *(table)*, 286
Pricing in Actual Practice, 294–99
   Discriminatory prices, 297
   Geographical prices and freight charges, 299
   Introduction of new product, 294–95
      Penetration pricing, 294
      Skimming the cream, 295
   Odd pricing, 295–96
   Pre-defined prices, 296
   Price controls, 296–97
   Price lining, 296
   Price tags, 297
   Pricing and inflation, 299
   Pricing in foreign markets, 298
      Discrimination, 298
      Market characteristics, 298
      Risk, 298
      Time lags, 298
   Relationships between cost and volume, 290–91

Prime interest rate, 155
Private individual investors, 156
Private investment partnerships, 156
Privately held corporations, 147
Problems of small business, 16
Product development, 309
Product life cycle, 293–94, 408–10
   Decline, 409–10
   Growth, 409
   Introduction stage, 409
   Maturity, 409
Profit:
   Evaluation, 126
   Net margin, 225
   Sharing, 335
Profit and loss statement, 88–91
Promissory notes, 388
Promoter, 47
   Characteristics *(table)*, 39
   Role requirements *(table)*, 39
Promotion, 311–15
   Advertising, 311
   Personal selling, 314
   Publicity, 314
   Sales promotion, 314–15
Property, 359, 387–88, 395
   Loss, 359
   Personal, 387–88
   Real, 387
   Taxes, 395
Publicity, 314
Publicly held corporations, 147
Purchasing, 266–70
   Agent, 268–69
   Control, 268–69
   Discount, 268
   Ethics, 269–70
   Manufacturing environment, 269
   Stages, 266–68
      Follow-up, 268
      Selection of supplier, 267–28
      Specifications, 267
Purchasing a business (*See also* Buying a business, and Business, choosing an existing), 192–93

Q

Questionnaires, 317–19
Quick ratio, 226

R

Ratio analysis, 94–95, 222–24
Ratios, 224–30
   Coverage, 228
      Earnings before taxes and interest ratio, 228
   Debt-to-equity, 144–46, 158–61

Ratios *(con't)*
   Leverage, 228–29
      Debt-to-worth, 229
      Fixed-to-worth, 228–29
   Liquidity, 226–28
      Cost of sales to inventory, 227–28
      Current, 226
      Day's inventory, 228
      Day's receivables, 227
      Quick, 226
      Sales to receivables, 227
      Sales to working capital, 228
   Operating, 229–30
      Percent of profits before taxes-to-tangible net worth, 229–30
      Sales-to-total assets, 230
   Profitability, 225
      Net profit margin, 225
      Return on equity, 225
Rautbord, Samuel G., 444
Reciprocals, 362
Reinforcement, 175–76
Relatives, 156
Remodeling, 143
Rent insurance, 378
Replacement value, 127–28
Researching a venture checklist, 121–22
Retailers, 114
Retail Sales, 26, 324–25
Retained earnings, 209
Retention of employees, 172–73
Retirement:
   Financing the sale of the business, 431
   Income, 379
   Life insurance and social security, 431
   State laws and regulations, 431
   Taxation, 431
Revenue centers, 240
Risk:
   Assumption, 99
   Avoidance, 99, 358
   Business, 357–58
      Fundamental, 358
      Particular, 358
      Pure, 357–58
      Speculative, 357
   Handling, 356–57
   Liability, 99
   Management, 358–59
      Absorption, 358–59
      Prevention, 358
      Transfer, 358–59
   Personal, 99
   Property, 99
   Reduction, 99
   Shift, 99
   Transfer, 99, 358–59

Robert Morris Associates, 126
Robert Morris Associates' *Annual Statements Studies,* 79, 158–61, 211, 224–25
Robinson–Patman Act, 385
Rockefeller, John D., Sr., 284–85
Royalties, 133
Roylance, H. H. (Bill), 191–92

S

Salary, 128, 333–34
Sale of business:
   Buy/sell agreement, 423–25
   Financing, 431
   Reasons for, 125–26, 183–85
Sales (*See also* Selling):
   Base, 325–26
      Display, 326
      Image, 326
      Need fulfillment, 326
      Product, 325
      Product knowledge, 325–26
   Force Compensation Plans, 333–35
      Bonuses, 334
      Commissions, 334
      Drawing accounts, 334
      Profit sharing, 335
      Salaries, 333–34
   Forecasting, 330–35
      Advanced sales forecast *(table)*, 332
      Other methods:
         Executive composite, 332
         Owner's opinion, 332
         Potential growth analysis, 333
         Sales force composite, 332–33
         Trend analysis, 333
      Simplified method, 331–32
   Plan, 326–29
      Approach stage, 327
      Closing stage *(table)*, 329
      Meeting objections stage *(table)*, 328
      Pre-approach stage, 327
      Presentation stage, 328
   Promotion, 314–15
   Retail, 26, 324
   Tax, 396–97
   Wholesale, 26, 324–25
Sales and Marketing Management, 249–52
   "Survey of Buying Power," 254
Sales-to-total assets ratio, 230
Sanders, "Colonel" Harland, 405
Savings and loan associations, 156
SBA, 149, 156
SBCS, 276–77
SBIC 149–56
SBIDC, 149–50, 156
Scalar chain, 166

Schedule C, 30
Schedule K (Partner's Shares of Income, Credits, Deductions, Etc.), 31
Selling, 323–30
   Distribution and wholesale, 324
   Industrial, 324
   Manufacturing, 324
   Retail, 324–25
Selling process *(table)*, 325
Service businesses, 28
Service occupations, 67
Sherman Antitrust Act, 385
Shopping centers, 256–57
   Community, 257
   Neighborhood, 256–57
   Regional, 257
Short-term credit:
   Banks, 151
   Trade credit, 153
Sims, Bob and Priscilla, 82–83
Single-entry bookkeeping system, 201–2
   Daily summary of cash receipts, 201
   Monthly disbursements record, 201
   Monthly summary of cash receipts, 201
Skimming the cream, 295
Small business:
   Minorities in, 7
   Trends, 5
   What is, 5
   Women in, 7
Small Business Administration, 149, 156
Small Business Computer Systems, (SBCS), 276–77
Small Business Investment Companies (SBIC), 149, 156
SMSA (Standard Metropolitan Statistical Area), 248
Software (computer), 277
Sole proprietorship, 29–30, 98
Sources of funds, 156–57
Staffing, 167–73
   Acquisition, 168–71
   Motivation, 171–72
   Needs, 168
   Retention, 172–73
Stages of a business (*See* Business, stages of)
Standard Metropolitan Statistical Area (SMSA), 248
State Businesses and Industrial Development Corporation (SBIDC), 149–50, 156
State Department of Economic Development, 79
Statement of financial position (*See* Balance Sheet)
State taxes, 96
Stock:
   Common, 148
   Preferred, 148

Stock *(con't)*
   Subchapter S, 148
Stock companies, 362
Stockholders, 147
Stone, W. Clement, 360–61
Subchapter S, 96, 98, 148
Subrogation, 363
   Succession, 422–25
      Buy/sell agreement, 423–25
      Death of owner, 423
      Financial considerations, 423
      Inventory of business and operations, 427–29
      Inventory of managerial development, 428–30
      Inventory of retirement, 430–31
      Management transfer, 423
      Retirement objectives, 423
      Retirement or sale of business, 423
      Sale of business, 423
      Successor profile, 426–27
Successor profile, 426–27
Suppliers, 49, 156
   Characteristics *(table)*, 39
   Role requirements *(table)*, 39
Surety bonds, 366
"Survey of Buying Power," 254

T

Tax calendar, 398
Tax forms:
   Application for Employer Identification Number, 392
   Employees Withholding Allowance Certificate (W-4), 393–94
   Employers' Quarterly Federal Tax Return Form #941, 392
   Federal Tax Deposit Form (#501), 392
   Form 1040, 30
   Form 1065 (United States Partnership Return of Income), 31
   Nebraska and City Sales and Use Tax Return *(figure)*, 396–97
   Schedule C, 30
   Schedule K (Partner's Shares of Income, Credits, Deductions, Etc.), 31
   Wage and Tax Statement (W-2), 395
Taxes, 391–98
   Employee-employer taxes, 292–94
      Application for Employer Identification Number *(figure)*, 392
      Employers' Quarterly Federal Tax Return Form (#941), 392
      Federal Tax Deposit Form (#501), 392
      W-4—Employees Withholding Allowance Certificate, 393
      W-2—Wage and Tax Statement, 395

Taxes *(con't)*
    Excise, 397–98
    Federal, 96
    Local, 96
    Personal property taxes, 395
    Property, 395
    Retirement, 431
    Sales, 396–97
    State, 96
Tax free reorganizations, 193–94
Tenancy in common, 387
Term life insurance, 367
3–2–1 rule, 261
Time management, 70–71
Trade credit, 153
Traffic counts, 83
Training:
    Classroom, 171
    On-the-job, 171
    Personnel, 171
Trust companies, 156
Turnkey costs, 93–94
20/80 rule, 272
Two bin method of inventory control, 275
Types of Business:
    Comparative, 253
    Competitive, 253
    Unique, 253

U

Underwriter, 362

Uniform Consumer Credit Code, 390
Uniform Negotiable Instruments Law, 388–89
Unique business, 253
United States Department of Commerce, 114
University of Michigan studies, 345
    Employee orientation, 345
    Production orientation, 345

V

Venture capitalists, 147, 149–50, 156
Veterans Administration, 156
Vroom-Yetton decision making model, 347–78

W

Wallace, DeWitt, 116–17
Wanamaker, John, 307
Warranties, 386
White collar occupations, 67
Whole life insurance, 367
Wholesale sales, 26, 324
Wholesalers, 113–14
Wilson, Kemmons, 391
Wizer, Phil G., Jr., 258
Women in small business *(table)*, 7–8
Worker's compensation, 100, 365, 375–76
Working capital, 63, 143, 151, 209

Y

Yellow pages, 313